THE CENTURY PSYCHOLOGY SERIES

Richard M. Elliott, *Editor*

Kenneth MacCorquodale and Gardner Lindzey, *Assistant Editors*

HILGARD AND MARQUIS'

Conditioning and Learning

HILGARD AND MARQUIS'
Conditioning and Learning

REVISED BY

Gregory A. Kimble
DUKE UNIVERSITY

Second Edition

New  York

APPLETON-CENTURY-CROFTS
Division of Meredith Corporation

PREFACE

SINCE THE PUBLICATION of the first edition of this book much has happened in the fields of conditioning and learning. New theories have appeared and old ones have been given up or modified. There have been important advances in experimental design and statistics. Knowledge of the philosophy of science, considered esoteric in the 1930's, is now commonplace. Experimental technology has seen a vast improvement. And the amount of research which has been done is enormous.

Naturally these developments have had an influence upon this revision. Most important has been a restriction of the range of materials covered. A comparison of tables of contents will show that four of the original chapters have been omitted—those on serial learning, problem solving, voluntary action, and neurophysiological mechanisms. It has been possible to include some of the content of these chapters elsewhere in the revision; but with the exception of the physiological materials, the amount of space devoted to these topics is significantly reduced. In place of the four omitted chapters there are four new ones. Two of these resulted from the subdivision of the original chapters on the nature of reinforcement and on generalization and discrimination. The two other additional chapters, on secondary reinforcement and motivation, are almost totally new to this edition.

In spite of these, and other, modifications, this revision retains the essential characteristic of the parent edition, that of being basically empirical rather than theoretical in approach. To paraphrase the statement of Hilgard and Marquis, in their preface written in 1940: This book makes no effort to present a finished theory of learning. The attempt, instead, has been to place the facts and alternative conceptions of the nature of learning in some sort of order. It may be that such ordering will prove to be a small step in the direction of the formulation of a better theory than is now available.

There are many people to whom I owe a considerable debt of gratitude for help in the preparation of this revision. In the first place, there are the hundreds of individuals who generously contributed reprints, un-

v

published manuscripts, and, frequently, sound advice on particular topics. Then there are those who assisted in the tedious details: Mrs. Margaret S. King, who did most of the job of assembling a bibliography of some 3,000 titles, half of which found their way into the book; Mrs. Ann Boneau, who served as copy editor, as well as typist; my wife, Lucille L. Kimble, who prepared most of the figures; and my two children, Jeffrey and Judith, who kept my card file more or less in order. I am especially grateful to R. M. Elliott, Kenneth MacCorquodale, and Harold Schlosberg, who read much or all of the manuscript and made suggestions which were invaluable. Finally, I should like to thank the following publishers for permission to reproduce figures or quotations: The American Psychological Association, for its various journals, *The American Journal of Psychology*, Appleton-Century-Crofts, Cambridge University Press, Harcourt, Brace, Holt, Rinehart and Winston, The Humanities Press, McGraw-Hill, The New York Academy of Sciences, Prentice-Hall, *The Psychological Record* The Ronald Press, *Scientific American*, University of California Press, Williams and Wilkins, and Yale University Press. In each case, acknowledgment to the original source is given with the material reproduced.

G. A. K.

PREFACE TO THE FIRST EDITION

THEORIES OF LEARNING which make use of conditioning principles are not related in a simple manner to the facts from conditioning experiments. This book represents an effort to place the facts and theories into some sort of order through critical exposition. The net result is not a finished theory; in many instances we have found it necessary to point to several alternative conceptions. The examination of the relation of conditioning to other basic learning experiments has at other points revealed serious gaps in our knowledge which future experimentation must fill.

Although conditioning has sometimes been proposed as a basic concept for the fields of cerebral physiology, of mental hygiene and personality, and of the higher thought processes, we have found it desirable to place greatest emphasis upon the relation of conditioning to learning theory. In the later chapters we have surveyed the possibilities of applying conditioning concepts within some of the other fields.

Our own experimental work in conditioning was first undertaken in the laboratories of Professors Raymond Dodge, Harold S. Burr, and John F. Fulton of Yale University, and to these and other teachers, colleagues, and collaborators, we owe much. We have profited greatly from the reading and criticism of the entire manuscript by Professor R. M. Elliott, editor of this series. The manuscript was improved through suggestions following critical reading of different portions by R. L. French, V. E. Hall, G. L. Heathers, W. T. Heron, C. I. Hovland, C. L. Hull, J. L. Kennedy, A. A. Lumsdaine, T. L. McCulloch, N. E. Miller, Helen Peak, T. C. Ruch, R. R. Sears, B. F. Skinner, K. W. Spence, E. C. Tolman, and S. B. Williams. That their suggestions were all useful to us does not mean that they have approved the use which we made of them. The kindness of Dr. G. H. S. Razran in furnishing us an advance copy of his bibliography is gratefully acknowledged. He and several other authors kindly placed in our hands manuscripts prior to publication. Material has been drawn upon from personal communications received from the following: W. H. Burnham, W. H. Gantt, K. S. Lashley, R. B. Loucks, Florence Mateer, J. J. B. Morgan, Richard Parmenter, J. B. Watson, and R. M. Yerkes.

Acknowledgment is made to D. Appleton-Century Co., The Macmillan Company, Oxford University Press, and Prentice-Hall, Inc., from whose publications figures or quotations are reproduced, and to the editors and publishers of the following journals for similar reproductions: *American Journal of Psychology, Archives of Psychology, Journal of Comparative Psychology, Journal of Experimental Psychology, Journal of General Psychology, Journal of Genetic Psychology, Proceedings of the National Academy of Sciences, Psychological Monographs, Psychological Review,* and *Psychosomatic Medicine.* Citation to the original source is given in each case.

E. R. H.
D. G. M.

CONTENTS

HILGARD AND MARQUIS'

Conditioning and Learning

·1·

The Definition of Learning

THE TERM *conditioning* as it is used in present-day psychology refers to two procedures, known as classical conditioning and instrumental conditioning. The first of these procedures derives from the early work of Pavlov; the latter stems from that of Bechterev and Thorndike. Together these two simple experiments, with their superstructures of theory, have had a profound effect upon the history of psychology and its related sciences.

The classical conditioning experiment is familiar to every student of physiology and psychology. When meat powder is placed in a dog's mouth, saliva flows in response to this *unconditioned stimulus* (UCS). This natural and relatively automatic behavior is called an *unconditioned reflex* or *unconditioned response* (UCR). An incidental stimulus, such as the sound of a ringing bell, does not at first result in the flow of saliva. If the bell sounds each time just before the food is presented, however, it soon comes to elicit salivation. The new response to the bell is called a *conditioned reflex* or *conditioned response* (CR), and the bell is called a *conditioned stimulus* (CS). A relationship (association) has been established between the bell and food, so that a response resembling the one originally made to the food is now made to the bell.

The instrumental conditioning experiment, perhaps less well-known outside of psychology, has been more popular within the field. In a typical experiment, a hungry rat is placed in a soundproof compartment into which a small bar or other manipulandum can be inserted. Whenever the animal presses the bar, food, in the form of a small pellet, is delivered into a tray for the rat to seize and consume. With practice, the response of pressing the bar, which the rat first discovered in exploring the apparatus, becomes the most salient feature of the rat's behavior. So long as the animal remains hungry and receives food for pressing the bar he concentrates on this response.

These two experimental procedures differ in important methodological ways and may also differ in terms of the principles which underlie them. For our present purposes, it is important only to note that they are relatively simple forms of learning.

1

The term *learning* is broader than the term *conditioning*, since it covers a range of processes from the classical conditioned reflex to human problem solving. Some writers believe that conditioning is a prototypical form of learning. This may or may not be true. Different views of the relationship between conditioning and learning are treated in Chapter 2. Chapter 1 discusses the more general concept in order to introduce a number of important ideas which reappear at later points in the book. Among these are the most important theoretical issues in the field of learning and the most fundamental questions of fact.

Factual Definitions

Definitions of learning are of two different general sorts which we will refer to as factual and theoretical definitions. The factual definitions are all alike in that they relate the phenomenon of learning to observable events in the physical world. The theoretical definitions describe the essential conditions or the basic processes which the writer believes to be necessary for learning to occur.

As regards the factual definitions, there has always been general agreement among authorities on the subject that *learning refers to a more or less permanent change in behavior which occurs as a result of practice.* In such a statement, both the dependent variable (changes in behavior) and the independent variable (practice) are reasonably objective. The term *learning* itself has the status of an intervening, unobserved variable linking these two sets of observables. Several expressions of this general point of view selected from the writings of psychologists of very different theoretical opinions are the following:

We consider any systematic change in behavior to be learning whether or not the change is adaptive, desirable for certain purposes, or in accordance with any other such criteria. (Bush and Mosteller, 1955)

These changes in behavior which follow behavior we shall call learning. (Guthrie, 1952)

. . . we may say that learning is taking place whenever behavior shows a *pro_ gressive change* or *trend* with a repetition of the same stimulating situation and when the change cannot be accounted for on the basis of fatigue or of receptor and effector changes. (W. S. Hunter, 1934)

Learning, as we measure it, is a change in performance which occurs under conditions of practice. (McGeoch and Irion, 1952)

Learning is a more or less permanent incremental modification of behavior which results from activity, special training, or observation. (Munn, 1955)

We can define learning as that process which manifests itself by adaptive changes in individual behavior as a result of experience. (Thorpe, 1956)

Any more than transient modification of behavior which presumably results from past experience and not from known organic change. (Wenger, Jones, and Jones, 1956)

Such definitions accomplish several things. *First,* by limiting learning to relatively permanent changes, they exclude modifications of behavior due to motivational factors, to sensory adaptation, or to fatigue. *Second,* by identifying practice, training, or experience as the essential condition for learning, they exclude behavioral changes resulting from maturation, senescence, or physiological variables. *Third,* by implication they establish the status of the concept learning as an intervening variable (Bergmann and Spence, 1941, 1944; MacCorquodale and Meehl, 1948). The diagram below presents the essentials of the various definitions in a way which makes this last point.

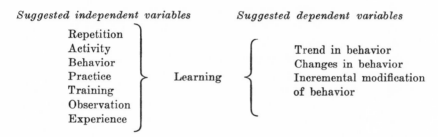

The right-hand side of this schema contains a series of obviously parallel alternatives expressing the idea that learning produces progressive changes in behavior. The left-hand terms are all expressions to describe the successive exposure of the organism to the same situation. Even the term *experience* seems to be meant in this sense by those who use it in such definitions. Maier and Schneirla, who are most explicit on this point, say that "the term *experience* as used here . . . refers to the effect of stimulation on the organism" (1935, p. 337), a statement which makes *experience* as objective as *practice* or *training.* At the same time, the particular expressions used in a factual definition are often predictive of the theoretical view espoused by a given author. The connotations of the term *experience,* for example, are such as to leave no one surprised when, later on, Maier and Schneirla adopt a cognitive theory for certain forms of learning. This last observation should not be permitted, however, to obscure the fact that, at the factual level, there is good agreement as to the meaning of the term *learning.*

Another point worth making with respect to the factual definitions of learning is that they are *operational definitions* (Pratt, 1948) in that they reduce the concept to observations which can be made on the physical world. As we have seen, both the independent variables (e.g., practice) and the dependent variables (changes in behavior) are open to public inspection. This is the essential feature of operational definitions: "To call them definitions is to say that they are concerned with concepts and not with laws. And, to call them operational is to eliminate everything but the reduction bases and mathematical manipulations" (Gustav Bergmann, personal communication). The factual definitions so far considered have typically said little or nothing about the mathematical relationship of learning to its independent variables, being content merely to suggest that learning "occurs" or "increases" with practice. More exact definition, however, is desirable; and the form such a factual definition might take may be illustrated by Hull's (1943) basic definition of learning or habit ($_sH_R$):

$$_sH_R = M - Me^{-iN}$$

in which M is the theoretical limit of habit growth, e and i are mathematical constants, and N is the number of reinforcements. This definition, thus, is like the other factual definitions in relating learning to practice and differs from them only in making a precise assumption about the form of the mathematical relationship involved.

Redefinition

There are three points about the factual definitions of learning which deserve further discussion, especially since they underlie certain basic conceptions. These three points involve (1) the learning-performance distinction, (2) the empirical fact of reinforcement, and (3) the nature of practice. We shall treat each of them in turn.

1. *The Learning-Performance Distinction.* Although, as the typical factual definition implies, learning often does consist in changes in behavior which occur concomitantly with practice, there are may cases in which it does not. Suppose, for instance, that one examines a map for a while and then drives directly to another city on the basis of this study. If we assume that the act of driving to the city would have been impossible without consulting the map, it clearly depends upon such practice and qualifies as an example of a learned response. On the other hand, it is equally clear that learning in some sense occurred prior to the change in behavior, and that the trip might have been postponed for a considerable period of time without altering the fact that learning had occurred. More technically this means that learning is not, as is so often said, a change in behavior. Rather it is a change in behavior *potentiality*. Or to put it another way, through learning the organism acquires the capability to perform certain acts, although sometimes this capability may remain *latent* and its appearance in behavioral change may not be immediate.

Such reasoning leads rather naturally to the distinction between *learn-*

ing and *performance* which has figured in most of the influential systematic accounts of learning.[1] The distinction is chiefly in terms of temporal considerations. *Learning* refers to long-term changes of the organism produced by practice. As we have just seen, the products of learning are carried with the organism on a fairly permanent basis and are available as a basis for action as the occasion demands. *Performance,* on the other hand, refers to just this translation of learning into behavior. The level of performance depends upon relatively short-term factors such as motivation, the existence of appropriate environmental circumstances, and fatigue. The implicit assumption made by most writers and the explicit one made by Hull (1943) is that learning sets an upper limit to performance. Depending upon temporary conditions, therefore, performance may provide a relatively accurate or inaccurate index of learning. This last point raises a difficult question for the psychologist interested in learning. As we have seen, learning is an intervening variable, an unobservable. As such we recognize it and gauge its strength through its symptoms in performance. But, as we have also seen, performance may be a good indicator of learning or a poor one, depending upon other factors. Thus, to arrive at a detailed and quantitative knowledge of *learning* it is necessary to study its progress under conditions where these other factors are optimal, or where their effect is exactly known. Recent years have seen a considerable advance toward the realization of both of these possibilities.

2. *The Empirical Law of Effect.* Turning now to the second problem associated with the factual definitions of learning, a careful rereading of our sample definitions will reveal that none of them distinguishes adequately between learning and the loss of learning, or extinction,[2] which also depends on practice. The point is that practice *alone* does not produce learning, but only fatigue or extinction. In order to insure the occurrence of learning, it is necessary to employ, in addition, the operation of *reinforcement.* To paraphrase Skinner (1938), reinforcement refers to the occurrence of one of a certain class of events called reinforcers, in the proper relation to the to-be-learned response; the proper relation being that which tends to increase the probability that the response so reinforced will recur with representation of the situation. The failure to reinforce a response decreases the probability of occurrence of the response. Some events possess reinforcing power; others do not. The ques-

---

[1] Tolman, who was chiefly responsible for promoting this distinction, gave it its clearest expression from his theoretical point of view in his paper on ''performance vectors'' (1955). In Hull's theory $_sH_R$ (*habit*) is the learning concept; $_sE_R$ (*excitatory potential*) is the major performance concept. Skinner (1938), at one time at least, made a similar distinction, with *reflex reserve* representing a learning construct and *reflex strength* a performance construct.

[2] Technical terms presented without definition in the text are defined in the glossary at the end of the book.

tion of which events do have it is an empirical one, to be answered by a series of defining experiments designed to identify the conditions which are effective in producing learning.

The usage of the term *reinforcement* in the preceding treatment is an empirical one. The statement that such events, placed appropriately with respect to some response, lead to an increase in the probability that the response will recur in the situation is a statement of the empirical law of reinforcement (effect), sometimes called the ''weak'' law of effect. Its acceptance does not commit the user to any stronger version of the law of effect such as Hull's drive-reduction hypothesis. For this reason, the term *reinforcement* in the empirical or weak sense is available for use in a revised definition of learning which takes the two points so far made into account: *Learning is a relatively permanent change in behavior* potentiality *which occurs as a result of* reinforced *practice.*

3. *The Problem of the Nature of Practice.* With learning thus redefined, it will be possible to consider the third problem referred to at the outset of this section, although in this case it will not be possible to solve it. This problem concerns the term *practice.* What does it consist of? Evidently it does not require the complete rehearsal of the response ultimately to be performed. Otherwise it would be impossible to learn anything from maps, demonstrations, books, or lectures (May, 1946). The question of just what does have to occur has been a problem of interest to workers in the field of learning almost from the beginning. Attempts to answer this question have often taken the form of a search for the neuroanatomical locus of conditioning. If it were possible to find such a locus, the nature of practice would probably be considerably easier to describe. Using the salivary conditioning experiment described at the beginning of this chapter as an example, and without specifying exact neurological levels, we might imagine the critical event in practice to be any or all of the following neurological mechanisms: (*a*) the pathways activated by the CS (bell), (*b*) the pathways activated by the UCS (food), (*c*) the motor pathway of the UCR (salivation), or (*d*) an association pathway connecting certain of the previous three. Consideration of each of these possibilities suggests that the neurological effects of practice are essentially central and associative.

a. The pathway of the conditioned stimulus. Complete interruption of the afferent pathway of the conditioned stimulus prevents the formation or performance of the conditioned response to exteroceptive stimuli. Sense organ stimulation, however, is not necessary, and may be replaced by stimulation of a central projection of the afferent pathway. To demonstrate this fact, Loucks (1934) developed a method for stimulation of the nervous system in intact unanesthetized animals. A paraffin-covered coil of wire was embedded under the skin of the animal, and insulated wires were led from it to the particular point to be stimulated. No wires penetrated the skin, and the animal remained in normal health for long periods of times. The buried coil could be activated by induction from a primary coil external to the animal. With this and similar methods, successful conditioning has been obtained by substituting for the CS, electrical stimulation of the spinal cord, cerebellum, (Gantt, 1937), and a variety of cortical areas (Loucks, 1938b; Doty, Rutledge, and Larsen, 1956).

b. The pathway of the unconditioned stimulus. The sense organ and afferent pathway of the unconditioned stimulus are not essential in the establishment of the conditioned response as long as excitation reaches some central point and evokes an unconditioned response. Successful conditioning has been produced by substituting for the unconditioned stimulus, electrical excitation of lumbar posterior roots or dorsal columns of the spinal cord (Loucks and Gantt, 1938) and of the lateral cerebellar lobe (Brogden and Gantt, 1937).

The evidence regarding the importance of stimulation by the UCS for the performance of an *established* response is less straightforward. In an early experiment by Lang and Olmsted (1923) leg withdrawal in dogs was conditioned to a buzzer using shock to the leg as a UCS. Hemisection of the spinal cord on the side opposite the trained leg, interrupting the ascending pathway of pain fibers, abolished the foot withdrawal response to the buzzer although the respiratory response remained. Similarly, Martino (1939) reported that the conditioned blink response in dogs is abolished by anesthetization of the skin around the eye—the receptive field of the unconditioned response. He concluded that a constant stream of neural impulses from the unconditioned receptor must be present to summate with the excitation from the conditioned stimulus in evoking the conditioned response. More recently, Whatmore and Kleitman (1946) have performed a series of experiments to test the effect of hemidecortication on the performance of conditioned motor responses based on shock. They discovered that the removal of the cortical projections of the UCS, together with the motor cortex for the responding muscles, completely abolished an avoidance response, and concluded that it is the projection of the UCS to the central nervous system which is important, because other responses involving the same muscles survived the cortical ablation. Other investigators (Raeva and Rappoport, 1934; Yushchenko, Rolle, and Pupko, 1934; Settlage and Harlow, 1936) failed to find any disruption of the conditioned response resulting from interruption of the pathway of the unconditioned stimulus. The divergent results remain unexplained.

c. The unconditioned response. Conditioning does not occur if the unconditioned response is directly elicited by stimulation of the motor pathway, but only if the excitation is initiated by way of the central nervous system. If a conditioned stimulus is repeatedly followed by electrical stimulation of a motor nerve evoking muscular movement, conditioning is unsuccessful (Tracy, 1927; Hilgard and M. K. Allen, 1938). Similarly, a UCR elicited by direct stimulation of the motor cortex in dogs fails to appear to the CS, even after hundreds of pairings (Loucks, 1935). In much the same vein, if the UCR is produced by drugs which act directly on the response mechanism, conditioning is impossible. The injection of pilocarpine causes salivation, by a peripheral effect upon the glands themselves; but no amount of pairing with a neutral stimulus will lead to conditioned salivation (Kleitman, 1937; Finch, 1938b). On the other hand, salivation produced through the activation of neural centers, by morphine injection, is readily conditionable. Such evidence indicates quite clearly that the peripheral pathway of the UCR is not essential to conditioning.

Similar conclusions may be drawn from experiments in which the UCR is prevented during conditioning. Conditioned salivary responses may be established using morphine or acid as the UCS, even if the salivary glands are paralyzed by an injection of atropine (Crisler, 1930; Finch, 1938c). In addition, it now appears that conditioning occurs under complete motor paralysis produced by curare (R. L. Solomon, personal communication; see also Black, 1958). This is the strongest evidence favoring the assumption that the UCR need not occur for conditioning to be established.

d. An association pathway. The effect of the evidence cited in the previous three sections is to push the effects of practice to some central region of the nervous system. We have seen, in brief, that (*a*) peripheral stimulation by a CS is unnecessary, (*b*) the response need not occur overtly, and (*c*) the peripheral pathway of the UCS is not a critical element for conditioning, although its central representation may be. Although such evidence suggests that conditioning involves a central association process, there is no implication of an anatomically isolable "association center." In fact, available evidence suggests that conditioning is accompanied by widespread modifications throughout the central nervous system (Galambos, Sheatz, and Vernier, 1956).

As regards the definition of learning, the results of the search for the neural locus of conditioning simply point up the fact that our definitions must contain a measure of ambiguity. The term *practice* will mean different things in different experiments; and clarity will come only with a more exact knowledge of the effects of practice.

Theoretical Definitions

The factual definitions of learning, so long as they remain factual, are pure abstractions which do nothing to relate learning to events in any other universe. In and of themselves, they make no effort to describe underlying mechanisms or to identify the "true nature" of learning.

Definitions which do attempt to accomplish such objectives are of a different type, which we have chosen to call theoretical definitions.

Many of the theoretical definitions of learning are physiological. It is well known that Hull thought of learning in terms of "receptor-effector" connections. And Hunter (1934), having defined learning operationally in terms of progressive changes in behavior with repetition, goes on to add that "such changes are presumably due to changes in the nervous system and are possible because of the plasticity and retentivity of this system." Other examples of physiological theoretical definitions are the following:

... if one afferent (i.e. sensory) path already has a connection with a motor path, then another afferent path if stimulated simultaneously, or nearly simultaneously, with the first will tend to acquire the same motor path of discharge. (Holt, 1931)

Learning is the process of the formation of relatively permanent neural circuits through the simultaneous activity of the elements of the circuits-to-be; such activity is of the nature of change in cell structures through growth in such a manner as to facilitate the arousal of the entire circuit when a component element is aroused or activated. (Bugelski, 1956, p. 120)

Another, different, idea which occurs quite frequently in theoretical definitions of learning treats the phenomenon as one closely related to perception and defines it in terms of a reorganization of the perceptual, psychological, or behavioral world of the learner. The theories of learning deriving from such definitions are often called cognitive theories.

. . . learning consists in the reorganization of a field determined by an obstructed need. (Adams, 1931)

Learning is a reorganization of the cognitive field. (Krech and Crutchfield, 1948, p. 112n.)

A third conception apparent in several definitions is such as to make learning a modification of behavior already in the organism's repertoire of activity.

All learning involves, and in reality consists in a modification of instinctive or reflex responses. (Franz, 1939)

Learning turns out upon analysis to be either a case of differential strengthening of one from a number of responses evoked by a situation of need, or the formation of receptor-effector connections *de novo;* the first occurs typically in simple selective learning and the second in conditioned reflex learning. (Hull, 1943)

Then there is the contiguity proposition adhered to by several theorists, that learning is a matter of developing associations between events occurring closely together in time. Guthrie (1938) is, perhaps, most explicit on the point: "Stimulus patterns which are active at the time of a response tend, on being repeated, to elicit that response."

Finally, the idea of reinforcement in the strong sense of the word is often a part of the definition of learning. Statements of this sort include Thorndike's classical expression of the law of effect.

The Law of Effect is that: Of several responses made to the same situation, those which are accompanied or closely followed by satisfaction to the animal will, other things being equal, be more firmly connected with the situation, so that, when it recurs, they will be more likely to recur; those which are accompanied or closely followed by discomfort to the animal will, other things being equal, have their connections with that situation weakened, so that, when it recurs, they will be less likely to occur. The greater the satisfaction or discomfort, the greater the strengthening or weakening of the bond. (Thorndike, 1911)

Obviously the diversity among these theoretical definitions is very great. Most of the important systematic issues in the field of learning are implicit in them. The conflicts foreshadowed by differences among these definitions include those between the proponents of physiological and non-physiological conceptions of learning, between cognitive (reorganization of the field) and S-R (modification of behavior) views, and between law-of-effect and non-law-of-effect positions. Such issues, along with one or two others, have provided the impetus for much experimental work in the psychology of learning. They are topics which we will meet again.

The Field of Learning

Changes of behavior of the sort we call learning range from the simplest modifications of the simplest organisms, to the most impressive contributions of human intelligence. Learning is basic to the development of athletic prowess, of tastes in food and dress, and of the appreciation of art and music. It contributes to ethnic prejudice, to drug addiction, to fear, and to pathological maladjustment. It produces the miser and the philanthropist, the bigot and the patriot, the coward and the hero. In short, it influences our lives at every turn, accounting in part for the best and worst of human beings and for the best and worst in each of us. Can such a range of influence be encompassed by a single concept such as learning? As of the present time psychologists are divided on this question. Some say that all learning is basically the same thing; some say that there are two fundamental processes; still others say that there are many.

At the level of operations, it is clear that there are many different learning procedures, which have been used to identify research clusters such as instrumental conditioning, classical conditioning, maze learning, motor learning, verbal learning, and problem solving. But differences in procedure may or may not necessitate different theoretical treatments to account for the effects they produce. It is at this level that psychologists disagree. Some hold that a single principle, such as the law of effect or contiguity, is involved in all learning. Others maintain that different principles are required to account for learning under different procedures. The most common position in this latter multiprocess category holds that instrumental conditioning is the simplest representative of one form of learning, and that classical conditioning typifies the other. The single-process theorists, on the other hand, hold that one of these forms of conditioning, because of its simplicity, is, in some sense, basic. These views of the importance of conditioning set our immediate task for us. We shall want to look first at the various conceptions of the place of conditioning in psychology.

SUMMARY

In order to provide a general orientation to materials to be covered later, it has seemed wise to begin our discussion of conditioning and learning with a consideration of the meaning of these two basic terms. Traditionally, learning has been regarded as a more general conception than conditioning. Conditioning, which includes two subvarieties called classical and instrumental conditioning, is a form of learning which occurs in carefully controlled laboratory situations. Some theorists believe that all learning obeys the laws discoverable in these simple conditioning experiments. Others feel that additional principles will be required to explain the more complex forms of learning.

The more general term *learning* has been defined in two generally different ways. Most of the content of this chapter has involved the implications of these two kinds of definition. Definitions of the first sort describe learning as any relatively permanent change in behavior which occurs as a result of practice. There are four points at which such definitions require comment or clarification.

First, it must be recognized that changes in behavior, which are basic to the definition, are performance phenomena, whereas learning is a hypothetical process which underlies these changes. Depending upon other circumstances, performance may reflect the level of learning relatively accurately or inaccurately.

Second, unless some reference is made to the process of reinforcement, definitions of this sort fail to distinguish learning from extinction. Reinforcement, in one sense, refers to any of a set of conditions which, appropriately employed, favor learning. In the same sense, reinforcement is essential to learning. Unreinforced practice produces only fatigue or extinction. For purposes of definition, it is unfortunate that the conditions which qualify as reinforcers are quite varied and appear to fit no recognizable category beyond their ability to produce learning. This leads to an inevitable element of ambiguity in the definition of learning.

Third, another inescapable source of ambiguity lies in the term *practice.* Efforts to make this term mean anything exact lead to questions about the precise events which go to make up a practice occasion. Attempted answers to these questions lead to matters of physiology. In the simplest form of learning, classical conditioning, it has been discovered that learning can take place when stimulation of the central nervous system is substituted for the usual external stimuli, and also that learning can occur in the absence of an overt motor response. The effect of such evidence is to suggest that the critical event in practice is some unknown process in the central nervous system, so that, again, it is impossible to define learning as precisely as might be desired.

Fourth, definitions of learning in terms of behavioral changes occurring with practice are very close to the level of direct empirical observation. Therefore, we have referred to them as operational, or factual, definitions to distinguish them from the theoretical definitions also considered in this chapter.

Theoretical definitions of learning either offer some hypothesis regarding the "true" nature of learning or propose some general condition as theoretically essential for learning. These definitions tend to be less closely tied to empirical observation than the factual definitions. The theoretical definitions are of special interest, however, because differences among them implicitly represent many of the issues on which theorists of learning are divided.

First of all we find that some of these theoretical definitions describe learning in the language of neurophysiology, suggesting that learning must be understood in such terms. Other definitions are completely without neurophysiological reference. Proponents of these theories often hold that such speculation is neither necessary nor desirable.

Second, some theoretical definitions of learning describe the process in perceptual terms as a reorganization of the world of the learner. As a result of learning according to these definitions, the learner sees among events (stimuli) relationships which had not previously existed for him. For this reason, these definitions present what has come to be called a stimulus-stimulus (S-S) or cognitive conception of learning. As such they are opposed to S-R definitions, and to related S-R theories, in which learning consists in the establishment of new associations between stimuli and responses.

Third, theoretical definitions differ with respect to their interpretation of the nature of reinforcement. Some hold that learning occurs only when the response to be learned is followed by the satisfaction of some motive. Others maintain, by contrast, that all that is necessary for learning to occur is for some response to be elicited in a particular situation, or for the situation to be perceived in a new way. Nothing more.

The differences of opinion reflected in these divergent definitions constitute foci of dispute about which experiment and argument have centered for several decades. Many of the experiments to be reviewed in subsequent chapters bear directly or indirectly upon these issues. These research studies in the field of learning have approached the problems of learning in many different ways. But there is at least one point of agreement among all students of the learning process, namely, that learning is a very pervasive phenomenon, occurring in all of the important aspects of human life.

·2·

Conditioning in Historical Perspective

ONE OF THE paradoxical facts in the history of psychology is that the concepts of conditioning were accepted with enthusiasm, particularly by American psychologists, in spite of the fact that many of these concepts rested on infirm empirical foundations (Loucks, 1933). Similarly the methods of conditioning seemed to many persons to promise a completely objective technique for the study of psychological problems, although the validity of the conditioning procedure was never compared with that of the established methods. In a sense this evaluation seems to persist today. It will, therefore, be instructive to examine the reasons for this uncritical acceptance of conditioning for the light such examination will throw on the considerations which still govern this judgment.

PREPARATION WITHIN PSYCHOLOGY FOR THE ACCEPTANCE OF CONDITIONING

When new concepts are incorporated into a scientific system prior to a sufficient demonstration of their adequacy, it is apparent that there existed within the system some kind of preparation or readiness for their assimilation. When such preparation is lacking, important discoveries and new methods are often refused admittance. There must have been some natural affinity between psychology and the conditioned-reflex method. Otherwise conditioning would not have been proposed as a technique for measuring sensory thresholds until it had been compared with the highly refined psychophysical methods already available, nor as a basis for learning theory before some effort had been made to compare what it accomplished with well-established findings from other types of experiments using problem boxes, mazes, skilled tasks, and nonsense syllables. It was accepted, however, without such tests.

The reason for this easy acceptance seems partly a matter of preparation within the immediate field of psychology, but possibly more basically

14

a matter of the suitability of classical conditioning to a more general pattern of thought which had been developing for three centuries or more prior to the Pavlovian demonstration. The origins of psychology, as of science in general, are in philosophy. Although the history of psychology may be traced to pre-Aristotelian times, the influences most important to the understanding of contemporary psychology are clearest in the work of the British Empiricists: Locke, Hobbes, Berkeley, Hume, Hartley, and the Mills. Their thought set psychology its initial problems, dictated its method and, most importantly, determined its rationale. Emphasis upon the experiential basis of knowledge naturally led to psychology's initial interest in the senses and in perception. The rationalistic approach foreshadowed the introspective method. But, more important for the later acceptance of conditioning than either of these were the principle of association and the conception of an analytic approach to the problems of science.

Association

Beginning with the assumption that the mind, or consciousness, was composed of ideas, the British Empiricists had been led to formulate laws of association to account for the relations between ideas. The set of laws as conventionally stated included three primary ones (contiguity, similarity, and contrast) and numerous secondary or quantitative laws which regulated the effectiveness of the primary ones. These laws, especially the secondary ones, were the antecedents of laws of learning formulated by Thorndike and others. The laws of association underwent many changes, and no one list was ever officially canonized. There was a noticeable tendency, however, to subjugate the laws of similarity and contrast to the law of contiguity, which states that associations are most easily formed between experiences that occur close together in space or in time. It is the one law which was found in all the lists; and it has survived as one of the basic principles of conditioning.

In an effort to find a physiological basis for association, the principle of contiguous excitation had been proposed, prior to the appearance of conditioning on the psychological scene. As expressed by William James, the principle stated: "When two elementary brain-processes have been active together or in immediate succession, one of them, on reoccurring, tends to propagate its excitement into the other." (W. James, 1890, p. 566). This idea, too, has persisted in the thinking of psychologists who seek to define learning in physiological terms. With association reduced to contiguous events and stated as a relation between brain states, the transition to a physiological doctrine of conditioning is straightforward and does no violence to established modes of thought.

Analysis

To understand the easy acceptance gained by conditioning, the idea of analysis as a way of approaching scientific materials is at least as important as the concept of association. The problem of understanding the mind, as the British Empiricists conceived it, was the dual one of analyzing the content of consciousness into its elements, after the manner of chemistry, and finding the principle by which these elements could be synthesized to reconstruct mental life. The elements which emerged from their analysis of mental processes were ideas described in sensory terms, and the principle of synthesis was association.

Psychology in its earliest versions followed this pattern of thought very closely. Consciousness was accepted as the subject matter of the new science, and the introspective method was used to discover the sensory elements of the mind. These elements were just noticeable differences (*j.n.d.'s*) in sensations, measured by the various psychophysical methods. It was suggested that the laws of association were the principles which accounted for the combination of these elementary processes into complex conscious experience.

The notable degree to which the concepts of conditioning could be made to conform to this pattern is no doubt a large part of the reason that psychology in the second decade of this century found them so appealing. Although, in their writing, the behaviorists stressed the contrasts between conditioning and the older methods, it has since become clear that early behaviorism had much in common with the structuralism it sought to displace. Pratt (1948) has presented the important parallels in a way which is reproduced in the table below. It is obvious that, in spite of a

	CLASSICAL PSYCHOLOGY	BEHAVIORISM
Subject matter of psychology	Consciousness	Behavior
Method of psychology	Experimental observation and analysis	Experimental observation and analysis
Results of analysis (elements)	Sensations	Reflexes
Principle of synthesis	Association	Conditioning

difference in opinion as to the appropriate subject matter for psychology, there was a basic agreement between classical psychology and behaviorism on matters of general strategy. In a very important sense, it was, again, because conditioning followed a traditional pattern of thought that it was so readily accepted.

This is not to say that there have been no objectors to the concept of association or to the analytic approach to psychology. From the time of the Scottish philosophers to the present-day phenomenologists, there have been those to argue that this approach is wrong because it fails to capture the substance of human life in anything like our firsthand experience of it. Of such objectors, Koffka was one of the strongest. Concerning the early form of behaviorism he wrote:

Learning could not be reduced to more mechanical terms. Even the questions how the selection among different ways of response is to become effective, and what factor gradually determines the elimination of useless movements, have been answered by [the behaviorists] in the simplest, but also in the crudest, and, as regards a natural feeling for living creatures, in the most unsympathetic manner. (Koffka, 1931, p. 174. By permission of Humanities Press Inc.)

The answer which the behaviorists had to this criticism was that there is nothing in scientific methodology which requires psychology to concern itself with "natural feelings for living creatures," and that, beyond this, psychology is not required to return from its analysis of behavior with an account which matches our naive experience of it, any more than atomic physics needs to reproduce our awareness of the physical world (Spence, 1948). Whatever the merits of the two arguments, this latter sort of reasoning won the day, and the method of analysis of which conditioning theory is a representative continues to be the more widely accepted.

Physiological Orientation

Although most of psychology recognizes the importance of environmental influences and has certain ties with the social sciences, the older and more basic branches of the field have always remained closer to the biological sciences than to any other broad division of knowledge. This fact, too, contributed to the early acceptance of conditioning. Biology and physiology had made great strides by 1915 in the study of simple reflex activity, but they had been unable to use the same methods in the investigation of the complex functions of the brain. Since psychologists were certain that the physiology most relevant to their problems was brain physiology, this constituted a serious failure. The methods of conditioning offered a possible way of unravelling the mystery of the brain. Indeed Pavlov's avowed purpose in studying conditioning was to investigate the activity of the cerebral hemispheres. Psychologists accepted both his purpose and his method. Conditioning, it was now declared, provided a method of investigating the higher brain functions which was just as physiological as the methods for studying the spinal reflexes. Thus, because of its pertinence to the physiology of greatest concern to psychology, the conditioned reflex method had very wide appeal.

The Adaptive Character of Behavior

Although psychology was, by its tradition, prepared for the elementarism of the conditioned response and for its brain physiology, classical psychology had placed no emphasis upon habit and learning as important psychological concepts. Titchener, writing in 1909, preferred not to use the word *learning* in his chapter on association, excusing himself on the grounds that learning was such a complex affair. In the following chapter, on memory and imagination, he devoted two pages to a discussion of slow and rapid learners and to cramming. The word *habit* was mentioned once in relation to the habit of introspection, and again in the chapter on attention. That is all. Although Titchener was in some sense an associationist, it is evident from his writings that affiliation with association is not enough to force habit and learning into the foreground of a psychological system.

It was another development, Darwinian biology,[1] which brought learning into focus as a psychological process. An organism's struggle to adapt to its environment introduced problems with which introspective psychology was poorly equipped to deal. Whereas classical psychology had emphasized the rational, cognitive, intellectual functions of the mind, adaptive behavior as described by Darwin appeared unreasoned and emotional. Such characteristics of behavior resist description in purely conscious terms. Thus the fact that behavior is adaptive required the development of concepts which extend beyond the boundaries of an association theory limited to conscious processes.

As a result of this need, the concept of habit came to the fore as a way of combining psychology's interest in the products of past experience with the adaptive function of behavior stressed by the Darwinists. The concept of habit was specifically conceived in the Darwinian pattern. Just as instincts were regarded as modes of behavior that had been found advantageous in the history of the species, habits were considered modes of behavior that had proved advantageous in the history of the individual (Hunter, 1928). William James gave prominence to habit in his *Principles,* not only by writing an important and readable chapter, but by placing it early in his book (Volume I, Chapter 4) among other chapters dealing with the fundamental characteristics of psychological and brain

---

[1] Darwin's influence on psychology in general has been great, but indirect. Darwin, himself, was probably unfamiliar with the works of the important figures in the history of psychology, having read neither Fechner nor Mill. Thus he was uninfluenced by the developing psychology of his time. Among Darwin's contributions we may count the following: (1) the conception of mind as a product of evolution, a view which favored a natural-science study of mental processes, (2) the view of natural selection as partly sexual (therefore, psychological) selection, (3) the thesis that the emotions are vestigial reactions, (4) a psychological biography of an infant son, and (5) the notion of continuous variation which is basic to the normal-curve concept (Thorndike, 1909).

processes. Indeed he interpreted the organism's capacity to learn in biological terms, explaining it as a result of the plasticity of protoplasmic material. The usual introductory discussions of sensation and perception he postponed for later chapters. James R. Angell at the University of Chicago gave habit a central place in his systematic psychology which came to be known as functionalism. Although consciousness remained the primary subject matter of psychology, it was argued that the investigation of adaptive behavior could not always be carried out with introspective studies, and that mentalistic concepts did not always apply. Animals had come to be used increasingly in studies of habit where introspection was obviously impossible. Yet the experiments were undeniably producing significant information about the learning process—information which seemed out of place in the framework provided by the concepts of mind and consciousness.

The conditioned reflex method was admirably suited to appeal to this new trend, for the subjects were animals, the procedures simple and straightforward, the results impressive. The conditioned response was called the unit of habit by psychologists to whom habit was the most important concept in psychology; the conditioning method was proclaimed as a substitute for introspection, once the chief method of psychology; and the conditioning process, said a distinguished psychologist-philosopher, brings the mind into being. (Holt, 1931, p. 28).

Objectivity

The study of habit contributed to a general trend in psychology away from the so-called subjective methods to more objective types of observation. This trend, begun with the establishment of psychological laboratories, with their emphasis on measurement and control, was fostered by developments outside of psychology. From biology came the voices of the mechanists calling for an objective study of life sciences, without recourse to mentalistic concepts. The famous paper by Beer, Bethe, and V. Uexkull (1899) suggested new terms for the usual psychological ones, substituting, for example, *reception* for *sensation*. Jacques Loeb, the leader of the movement, who resided in America from 1891 until his death, taught for some years at the University of Chicago, where the influence of biology on psychology was strong. Not without influence was a movement among certain philosophers to dispense with the mind-body dichotomy and to give a more objective account of mind. James entertained doubts about the need for a concept of consciousness in psychology, and Holt (1914) attempted a physiological account of the phenomena associated with the term. At Pennsylvania, Singer (1911) lectured on *Mind as an Observable Object*. And Tolman, influenced by the Vienna philosophers, as early as 1922, began a series of articles in which he proposed a behavioristic formula for the treatment of such mentalistic concepts as consciousness and purpose. Such emphasis upon physical objectivity was a symptom of the readiness of psychology to receive a method in which the mind was reduced to a reflex of the brain.

THE ENTRANCE OF CONDITIONING INTO PSYCHOLOGY

In spite of the anticipations of conditioning in the writings of the Greek philosophers, in Locke, James, and others, the history of conditioning, as such, is dominated by the figures of Pavlov and Bekhterev. Its tradition is directly traceable to the nineteenth century Russian physiologist Sechenov.

Ivan Mikhailovich Sechenov (1829-1905) is properly counted as the father of modern Russian physiology; and, to this day, Russian conditioning articles frequently begin with a tribute to him and to Pavlov. Trained in the days when Russian scientists did their postgraduate work in Western Europe, Sechenov studied first in the laboratory of Johannes Müller in Berlin, and was especially influenced by Muller's assistant, Emil DuBois-Reymond who was, at the time, obtaining evidence for the electrical character of nerve conduction. Subsequently Sechenov worked with Ludwig, Helmholtz, Bunsen, and Bernard. In Bernard's laboratory he performed experiments which provided the basis for his hypothesis of the reflex action of the brain (cf. Sechenov, 1935). This hypothesis, which set the tradition within which the work of Pavlov and Bekhterev finds its meaning, looked upon the function of the brain as a physical reflex, consisting of three components: sensory input, a central process, and efferent outflow. All behavior was to be understood in terms of these material processes plus an interaction of excitation and inhibition operating at the central link of the reflex arc. This last conception is remarkably close to Pavlov's later theory of cortical function.

Ivan Petrovich Pavlov (1849-1936) encountered the phenomenon of conditioning in the course of his studies of the digestive glands, for which he was awarded the Nobel Prize. Briefly, as early as 1880, Pavlov observed that sham feeding (in which food eaten by a dog fails to reach the stomach, being lost through an esophageal fistula) produces gastric secretion, just as real feeding does. This suggested that the stimulation provided by the taste of food and the act of swallowing it influences the stomach, leading to a "psychic secretion." Unfortunately the methods employed by Pavlov in this first demonstration were exceedingly tedious and required a degree of surgical skill which Pavlov, but few others, possessed. Probably for this reason, Pavlov turned in his later work to salivary secretion, which is easier to measure.

The first Pavlovian conditioning experiments were very crude. They consisted simply in showing a dog a piece of bread which it was later allowed to eat. The evidence for conditioning was that salivation occurred at the sight of the food, prior to eating. In these early experiments Pavlov also demonstrated the phenomenon of conditioned discrimination, by showing that animals could be trained not to salivate at the sight of bread dyed some particular color, which it had not been allowed to eat, although the response persisted to the undyed bread (Brazier, 1959a). Presumably in this case, the discrimination was actually on the basis of brightness, since dogs are color blind.

Although Pavlov's experimental findings were limited to the salivary responses of dogs, the concepts which he used in dealing with his data were extended by others to discussions of all types of learning. Conditioned and unconditioned stimuli, reinforcement, extinction, irradiation, discrimination, and so on, were later employed in analyzing a range of topics extending from normal individual behavior to psychopathologic and social action. In spite of the broad uses made of his work, Pavlov continued to think of it as belonging to physiology, and he made no attempt to formulate a system of psychology. In fact, he distinguished between his work and that of the American animal psychologists because he was always interested in the physiology of the nervous system, whereas they appeared to him to be concerned with essentially human problems, even when they worked with data from animals.

As early as 1886 Vladimir M. Bekhterev (1857-1927) had studied the localized representation in the dog's cortex of learned movements such as giving the paw, but his systematic study of *association-reflexes* began in the winter of 1906-1907. In his experimental investigations, which used first dogs and later human subjects, he studied the withdrawal and respiratory responses evoked by electrical shock stimulation. Unlike Pavlov, Bekhterev was very much interested in creating a new psychology. As early as 1904, before his work on association-reflexes began, he delivered a lecture on "Objective psychology and its subject-matter." He had studied for a time in Wundt's laboratory, and his writings reflect his familiarity with the problems of psychology. It is probably to him more than to Pavlov that we owe the bold acceptance of conditioning by psychologists, although the details of conditioning studies which came to be known were Pavlov's. Bekhterev's *Objective Psychology* appeared serially from 1907 to 1912 and was translated into both French and German in 1913. The German translation carried the subtitle *Psycho-Reflexologie*, and Bekhterev's position gradually became known as reflexology. In 1932 the translators of a later book were able to declare: "Reflexology is the dominant note in Russian psychology today, and the late Bekhterev is the guiding light of humanistic science in the U.S.S.R." The range of Bekhterev's interests was enormous. He wrote widely (600 titles) on neurology, psychiatry, infancy, education, social psychology, judicial psychology, and aesthetics, and he founded a number of institutes for the study of problems in various areas of neuropsychiatry and child study. Among his contributions to the subject matter of psychology which found at least temporary acceptance, were (1) methods of conditioning leg and finger flexion and cardiac and respiratory responses, (2) the concept of thinking as subvocal speech, (3) the idea of using conditioning for testing sensory thresholds, (4) the interpretation of concept formation in terms of generalization, (5) a fairly clear statement of a stimulus-substitution theory of conditioning, and (6) a denial of introspection as a fundamental psychological method (Bekhterev, 1928).

The 1913 translations of Bekhterev's book were very important in arousing the interest of American psychologists, and most of the American experimenters preferred to use his motor conditioning methods rather than the salivary method of Pavlov. Nevertheless, both Pavlov's terminology and his conceptual system were more widely adopted than Bekhterev's. It may be that Bekhterev's term *association-reflex* carried with it too much of the flavor of the association of ideas, and thus seemed to continue a tradition against which behaviorism was reacting. This might be one reason why Pavlov's term *conditioned reflex* was more acceptable. Moreover, Pavlov's careful working out of one variety of experiment with great precision gave his results greater usefulness to laboratory workers than Bekhterev's more general applications.

Early Interest in Conditioning in America

Pavlov's 1906 Huxley lecture, delivered at Charing Cross Hospital, on "The scientific investigation of the psychical faculties or processes in the higher animals" appeared in *Science* and was thus made available to the American public. Details of the experiments from his laboratory were summarized for presentation to psychologists in a thorough review by Yerkes and Morgulis in 1909. The review, however, did not lead to any immediate repetitions of Pavlov's work in America, so far as published records reveal.

Krasnogorski, a student of Pavlov, performed some conditioning experiments on children, reported in German in 1909 and in 1913. These came to the attention of W. H. Burnham at Clark University, who incorporated the material into the lectures in his course on the mental hygiene of the school child. Among his students in 1913-1914 was Florence Mateer, who became interested in repeating Krasnogorski's work. She devoted the next two years to work in this field which was incorporated into a doctoral dissertation in 1916 and published in book form in 1918. Mateer's experiments constitute the pioneer study of conditioning in this country. She used the ingenious method of placing a bandage over the eyes of the child just before food was placed in his mouth. The bandage came to serve as the conditioned stimulus, eventually evoking chewing and swallowing movements before the food was presented. The movements were recorded kymographically from tambours fastened under the chin and on the throat. The use of the bandage as a conditioned stimulus was discovered more or less accidentally. Mateer writes:

The great significance of the method came to me all at once about the fourth or fifth day of my first experiments with Phil, in 1914. I learned that even acceptance of a test posture, or entrance into the experimental laboratory, was a conditioning factor and that these and other casual environmental factors had to be unconditioned through disuse before any arbitrary conditioning factor might be used as predetermined in a planned procedure. Even with babies who could not sit up, the bandage was a conditioning factor, as valuable as other stimuli in evoking response. Neither Bekhterev or Krasnogorski prepared me for this, and, though I had read Pavlov, it took personal experience to show how significant the minutiae of an experimental setting must be.

Mateer's successful conditioning of children furthered the case which Burnham made for the place of the conditioned reflex in mental hygiene (1917, 1921, 1924).

The appearance of the translations of Bekhterev's *Objective Psychology* brought conditioning strongly to the attention of psychologists, and references to it began to appear in 1916. H. C. Brown (1916) pointed out a possible connection between language and the conditioned reflex, and F. L. Wells (1916) suggested that conditioning could supply a convenient account of affective transference.

Watson's Influence[2]

As we have seen, the preparation within psychology for the acceptance of conditioning extends hundreds of years into its history. The most important elements in this development had been (1) associationism, (2) the analytic approach to science, (3) a physiological orientation, (4) the habit concept, and (5) objectivity. The convergence of these five historical influences gave rise in America to Behaviorism, launched by John B. Watson in 1913. Watson's theory was related to all five trends: It was an objective association psychology, with an emphasis upon habit, biological in viewpoint and analytic in approach. Initially it did *not*, however, place great importance upon the concept of conditioning. Prior to his presidential address entitled "The place of the conditioned reflex in psychology" (1916a), which was delivered in 1915 before the American Psychological Association, the conditioned-reflex concept had little influence on American psychology. After this date, it occupied an increasingly promi-

[2] For a thoughtful analysis of Watson's place in the history of psychology, see Bergmann (1956).

nent place in the textbooks, if not, for a time, in the research laboratory. In recounting his relation to Pavlov, Watson writes:

I had worked the thing out in terms of *Habit* formation. It was only later, when I began to dig into the vague word *Habit* that I saw the enormous contribution Pavlov had made, and how easily the conditioned response could be looked upon as the unit of what we had been calling *Habit*. I certainly, from that point on, gave the master his due credit. (Personal communication)

During the winter of 1914-1915, while Mateer was working independently at Clark University, Watson's seminar at The Johns Hopkins University was devoted to the translation and discussion of the French edition of Bekhterev's book. In the spring of 1915 a number of Bekhterev's experiments were repeated, chiefly by Lashley who was then working with Watson; and experiments on finger withdrawal, respiration, and heart rate provided the factual substance of Watson's presidential address. In this presentation Watson exploited conditioning primarily as a substitute for introspection. He sensed its importance, however, in relation to emotion, mental disease, language, and habit, and wrote about these matters within the next year.

The conditioned response was prominent in Watson's textbook (1919), although it had not yet completely displaced other concepts, such as instinct. But the way had already been paved for the extension of conditioning concepts into mental hygiene (Heilbronner, 1912; Watson, 1916b; Wells, 1916; Watson and J. J. B. Morgan, 1917; Burnham, 1917), and Watson's last experiment (with Rosalie Rayner) in 1920 was soon to suggest important applications to child psychology. This experiment, with the boy Albert, whose fear of a loud sound was conditioned to a white rat and then to other furry objects, probably provides the most famous single case in the conditioning literature. In Watson's later book, *Behaviorism* (1925), conditioning was the central theoretical concept. There he espoused a radical environmentalism and discarded instincts and other forms of inherited tendencies. The remaining unit of native behavior was the unconditioned reflex; the unit of habit was the conditioned reflex.

Conditioning, 1916-1929

During the first ten years after Watson's presidential address, the concept of the conditioned reflex gained great systematic importance, but there were very few psychologists performing experiments on conditioning. Mateer's experiments, completed in 1916, were published in 1918, and Cason (1922a, 1922b) reported some success in conditioning the pupillary and blink reflexes. But, on the positive side, that was nearly all. Lashley (1916a, 1916b) gave up as unsuccessful his attempts to condition the salivary response in man. Hamel (1919) concluded from his studies of finger withdrawal that conditioning in man was confused by voluntary processes, but neither his monograph nor the paucity of new experimental data could stem the rising tide of popularity of the conditioned reflex as the basic idea employed by a number of psychological theorists. The first general textbook to use a conditioning concept throughout was that of S. Smith and Guthrie (1921). They adopted the term conditioned *response* instead of conditioned *reflex,* broadening the conditioning concept to include all that had formerly been treated as associative learning. Allport (1924) first gave prominence to the conditioned reflex in a textbook of social psychology at a time when social psychology was seeking desperately for a substitute for instincts. Burnham's *Normal Mind* (1924) presented an extended review of conditioning literature in a textbook on mental hygiene. In the later twenties, textbook writers in psychology, sociology, and education allotted increasing space and prominence to the subject.

In 1927, the Anrep translation of Pavlov's *Conditioned Reflexes* appeared, making a comprehensive treatment of Pavlov's work available in English for the first time and leading to a strengthened interest in experimentation on the conditioned reflex. This volume made available in rich detail the facts discovered by Pavlov and his co-workers during more than a quarter of a century devoted to the study of conditioned salivation in dogs. Pavlov's experiments and theories called for repetition and confirmation, using other organisms and other responses. Many laboratories now followed the example of the pioneering few and initiated programs of conditioned-reflex experimentation. In 1926, Liddell began a series of conditioning experiments on several different animals. Kleitman and Crisler's important study of conditioned salivation to morphine injection appeared in 1927; Schlosberg's study of the conditioned knee jerk was published in 1928; and Upton's study of hearing in the guinea pig (1929) was followed by a series of investigations by others on the sensory capacities of animals. In the next few years, experimental reports on conditioned responses appeared in rapidly increasing numbers, and the usefulness of the method for the study of learning, sensory acuity, and related problems was clearly demonstrated.

Although the laboratory importance of conditioning was on the increase during the late 1920's, the textbook treatment of the topic had begun to decrease. This was because of a waning confidence in the narrowly formulated behaviorism of earlier years and the emergence during this period of several strong competitors for the theoretical allegiances of psychology. Köhler's *The Mentality of Apes,* appearing in English in 1925, brought the concept of insight dramatically before animal experimenters. Yerkes had already been promoting similar concepts, and had never accepted behaviorism. In spite of his great respect for Pavlov, he had always thought of the conditioned reflex as one among many methods of experimentation and had never, strictly speaking, used the method himself. With animal psychology, the stronghold of behaviorism, becoming more skeptical of this system, it was natural for the other fields in which behaviorism had been strong, such as child psychology, to become more eclectic. Koffka's *The Growth of the Mind* (1924) emphasized maturation, which, as a kind of substitute for certain aspects of growth formerly included in instinct, now became a formidable competitor to conditioning as a factor in the development of the child's behavior.

Conditioning, 1929 to the Present

Perhaps the most significant development in the decade following the appearance of Anrep's translation of *Conditioned Reflexes* was the emergence in America of a number of theories of learning. In this development the conditioned reflex experiment assumed a new role. Whereas it had been the object of study in its own right, it now provided the concepts which Guthrie, Hull, and others applied to more complicated learning. The part played by conditioned-reflex work was central in some of these theories and secondary in others.

In 1929, Clark L. Hull, at Yale, began a highly provocative series of articles in the *Psychological Review* making use of the findings of Pavlov and of other workers with the conditioned response in a manner not previously attempted. His presidential address before the American Psychological Association in 1936 (Hull, 1937), two decades after Watson's, shows the changes in the use of the conditioning experiment. Hull, like Watson, stressed the conditioning process but, in the light of the new detailed knowledge of conditioned responses, he presented a system of definitions, postulates, and theorems, by which to bridge the gap from conditioning to more complex forms of learning.

Hull's original article, entitled "A functional interpretation of the conditioned reflex," bore the stamp of Darwinism and set a general theme which characterized Hull's work to the end of his life. One of the first questions Hull tended to ask about any behavioral phenomenon concerned its biological utility or survival value. Later articles dealt with such complex phenomena as trial-and-error learning (1930a), knowledge and purpose (1930b), problem-solving (1935c), and serial rote learning (1935a). These systematic formulations led to numerous experiments by Hull's own students and by others. They also led to efforts to work out theoretical systems to handle still other learning phenomena using conditioned-response concepts.

In all of his efforts at system building, Hull attempted formal rigor and patterned his theorizing after the model of Newtonian mechanics. He referred to his method, somewhat inaccurately, as "hypothetico-deductive'' and set for himself the following four criteria as necessary for adequate theorizing in psychology: [3]

I. The definitions and postulates of a scientific system should be stated in a clear and unambiguous manner, they should be consistent with one another, and they should be of such a nature as to permit rigorous deductions.

II. The labor of deducing the potential implications of the postulates of the system should be performed with meticulous care and exhibited, preferably step by step and in full detail. It is these deductions which constitute the substance of a system.

III. The significant theorems of a truly scientific system must take the form of specific statements of the outcome of concrete experiments or observations. The experiments in question may be those which have already been performed, but of particular significance are those which have not previously been carried out or even planned. It is among these latter, especially, that the crucial tests of a theoretical system will be found.

IV. The theorems so deduced which concern phenomena not already known must be submitted to carefully controlled experiments. The outcome of these critical experiments, as well as of all previous ones, must agree with the corresponding theorems making up the system. (Hull, 1935a, p. 495-496)

The high point in Hull's series of efforts at system building appeared in 1943 with the publication of his *Principles of Behavior*. In this book, he returned to a consideration of simple learning and presented a deductive system to account for the major phenomena of classical and instrumental conditioning. One of the outstanding characteristics of this theory was a heavy reliance upon Thorndike's law of effect, interpreted as drive reduction. This feature of Hull's theory had played a very small role in the earlier miniature systems, but now assumed a position of central importance. The other major distinguishing feature of Hull's system was the hypothesis that learning is a gradual process rather than a sudden or insightful one.

Principles of Behavior was hailed by some (Koch, 1944) as providing evidence that psychology had finally reached a stage of maturity where rigorous system building was at least worth trying. By others (Leeper, 1944), it was criticized as the culmination of a series of unfortunate trends in psychology. The first of these evaluations won out, and Hull's theory directly or indirectly dominated research in the field of learning for the next decade. In a lesser degree it continues to do so. After *Principles of Behavior*, Hull published two more books (1951, 1952) in which he described major revisions in his thinking. Some of these revisions have been accepted by Hull's followers and worked into still further revisions of the system (Spence, 1956). Others have not met with general accept-

[3] The formal aspects of Hull's theory have been subjected to analysis by Adams (1937), Kattsoff (1939), J. G. Miller (1939), Woodger (1938), Koch (1954), and Dunham (1957).

ance and, as a strictly Hullian system, the 1943 version remains the most influential theory.

The decade of the thirties saw, in addition to the development of Hullian theory, the appearance of three important rival positions. In 1935 Guthrie published the first edition of his *Psychology of Learning,* which proposed what has come to be called a non-reinforcement view of learning. In this book Guthrie developed the thesis that all that is necessary for learning to occur is for a response to occur in a given situation and for that situation, then, to change. The response, in one such occurrence, becomes conditioned to the stimuli in the situation and can be eliminated only by the conditioning of some new response to the same cues. This position differs from that of Hull in two important respects: (1) learning is regarded by Guthrie as a sudden rather than a gradual process and (2) the mechanism of reinforcement is stimulus-change rather than drive reduction. On the other hand, there are certain points of agreement between Hull's theory and Guthrie's on matters of strategy: (1) both theories assume that learning consists in the development of stimulus-response associations or connections and (2) both imply an approach in which the consequences of certain basic premises are arrived at by a process of deduction. Experimental tests of these consequences then may be taken as support for or argument against the theory.

Another important psychologist who presented the first detailed statement of his systematic position in this period was B. F. Skinner. Skinner agreed with the S-R approach but rejected many of the other features of prevailing theorizing. In his book, *The Behavior of Organisms,* published in 1938, Skinner described the results of a series of experimental studies of the bar-pressing behavior of rats, begun in 1930,[4] and offered a general approach to psychological investigation which differed sharply from that of Hull and Guthrie. For one thing, Skinner made a distinction between classical (respondent) and instrumental (operant) conditioning and held that the laws of one were not the same as the laws of the other. For another thing, Skinner objected to the conception that the essential procedure in the development of scientific understanding is deduction. He was particularly opposed to the hypothetico-deductive method advocated by Hull:

A quite different emphasis is to be found in the preceding chapters. Deduction and testing of hypotheses are actually subordinate to the quantitative determination of the properties of behavior and through induction to the establishment of laws. The difficulty seems to lie in the model Hull has chosen. A science of behavior cannot be patterned after geometry or Newtonian physics because its problems are not necessarily of the same sort. . . . If Hull had chosen experimental physics or chemistry as a model, the place of deduction in his system would have been much less important. (Skinner, 1938, p. 437)

[4] For example, Skinner, 1930, 1934, 1935a, 1935b, 1936a, 1936b, 1936c, 1936d, 1936e.

In place of a hypothetico-deductive explanation, Skinner proposed a purely behavioral system and argued against the use of neural hypotheses to account for behavior. He put his position strongly:

The gain to the science of behavior from neurological hypotheses in the past is, I believe, quite certainly outweighed by all the misdirected experimentation and bootless theorizing that have arisen from the same source. (Skinner, 1938, p. 426)

Beyond this, Skinner studied behavior in a free-responding situation whereas almost all psychologists in the field of learning employed trial-by-trial procedures; he was most interested in a problem (intermittent reinforcement) which had not yet caught the imagination of American psychologists; and he presented his data unorthodoxly in the form of kymograph records produced by the rats pressing the lever in the Skinner apparatus. For all of these reasons, Skinner's view gained few adherents until relatively recently. Now, nearly twenty-five years after the publication of *The Behavior of Organisms,* the full impact of Skinner theory is finally being felt.

A final influential figure contributing to the psychology of learning in the 1930's was E. C. Tolman, whose major statement appeared in his book, *Purposive Behavior in Animals and Men* (1932). Tolman's influence upon psychology was partly through the development of a theory and party through his treatment of methodological matters. Tolman's theory differed from that of the other theorists discussed here in that he was a cognitive theorist. Learning, for Tolman, consisted in the acquisition of bits of knowledge, which he called sign-gestalts, about the environment:

Sign-gestalts are to be conceived as having three parts: a *sign,* a *significate,* and a *behavior-route leading from sign to significate.* A sign-gestalt is equivalent to an "expectation" by the animal that "this," (that is, the sign) "if behaved to in such and such a way" (that is, the behavior-route), will lead to "that" (that is, the significate). A sign-gestalt sets the animal to "expect" that when he actually behaves, "this field-feature will lead, "by such and such a behavior route" to "that" field-feature. And learning, according to the theory, will consist in the making or the remaking of such expectation-sets. . . . (E. C. Tolman, in F. A. Moss, Ed., *Comparative Psychology,* 1934a. Prentice-Hall, Inc., Englewood Cliffs, N. J.)

This passage marks Tolman as one who believes in learning as the acquisition of expectancies, or knowledge about "what leads to what," in the environment. The position is one which has been called the stimulus-stimulus (S-S) view of learning. Although there is nothing in the S-S position which demands it, Tolman's theory is also a non-reinforcement theory.

Tolman also influenced the psychology of learning very profoundly in basic, methodological ways. He was responsible for the first clear statement of the learning-performance distinction. He was one of the first to hold that conditioning was a limited form of learning. And, in a series of articles begun in 1922, he brought the concept of the intervening variable to American psychology. In these articles Tolman (1922a, 1922b, 1922c, 1923, 1926, 1927) made clear a fact which his anthropomorphic terminology tends to obscure, that his position was a behavioristic one, a position which he, himself, called an operational behaviorism (Tolman, 1936b).

Current Trends

Although emergence of major systematic positions was the most important single development in the field of learning during the decade following the appearance of Anrep's translation of Pavlov's *Conditioned Reflexes,* there were several other trends worth mentioning. With the appearance of relatively definitive systematic positions there occurred differences of theoretical opinion which led to crucial experiments, polemic, and more crucial experiments, concerned most often with the principle of reinforcement, the question whether learning is gradual or insightful, and the controversy implicit in the S-S versus S-R interpretations of learning. Neither polemic nor experiment, however, dissuaded the major theorists, and it gradually became clear that the theories were so complex, so ambiguously formulated, or both, that none of them could possibly be disposed of by a single empirical or dialectic *coup de grace.* This led to a lessening of interest in such attempts.

Instead, more recent efforts have been made to explore the range of applicability of certain of the theories. Hull's theory was made the basis for accounts of verbal learning (Hull and others, 1940), social behavior (Miller and Dollard, 1941), motor learning (Ammons, 1947; Kimble, 1949), and psychotherapy (Dollard and Miller, 1950). Toman's theory was extended to certain aspects of social behavior (Tolman, 1941, 1942), and Guthrie's theory was applied to neurotic behavior (Guthrie, 1938). Skinner's theory found important applicability in practical problems of animal training (Breland and Breland, 1951), in the evaluation of drugs, and in a theory of verbal behavior; it even provided the basis for a utopian novel (Skinner, 1948).

These developments now appear to be part of a major change of direction in the psychology of learning. The chief theoretical activity on the current scene is a systematic stock-taking (Koch, 1959), in which the theorists are attempting to consolidate such gains as were made from research instigated by the theories of the 1930's and to incorporate, where possible, new facts and interpretations which have come from a number of sources. Although it is always risky to attempt to point out the very most recent trends in a field, the following few seem to be among the most important:

1. With the realization that the great theories developed in the 1930's are inadequate both on systematic and factual grounds, the process of deduction is playing a smaller role than it once did in the psychology of learning. In its place there has appeared an increased emphasis on fact-finding, parametric studies. Where the learning psychologist once had a "theory," he now has only a "point of view."

2. There has been a great strengthening of interest in the biological aspects of psychology. New and exciting discoveries relating behavior to neural and endocrine functioning are leading to important modifications in our conceptions of motivation and reward. And the research of the ethologists has brought a revival of interest in instinct and other forms of inborn behavior.

3. The phenomenon of attention no longer seems one which can be omitted in the description of even the simplest behavior. Work on the reticular formation by the neurologists and physiological psychologists has provided a physiological basis for arousal and attention. Behaviorally there is a greater interest than formerly in observing responses (Wyckoff, 1952, 1954).

4. The concept of behavior as always, in some measure, mediated has taken on increased significance (Osgood, 1953). It now seems clear that the S-R formula, however powerful in the hands of a Hull or Skinner, is, at best, incomplete. There must be a recognition that a great deal goes on between S and R.

5. The great complexity of human behavior is currently a matter of stress. Accumulating evidence shows clearly that even the simplest conditioned response is controlled by a great many variables. Furthermore, these variables interact in ways which mean that a condition which has one effect under a certain set of circumstances, may have a different, even opposite effect under another.

6. Conditioning procedures, both classical and instrumental, are more popular today than at any time in the past. Two main factors seem to be contributing to this: (1) Improved apparatus makes excellent stimulus control, automatic scheduling of trials, and detailed recording of responses possible, and (2) closer contact with Russian research, mainly in physiology, has brought the fruitfulness of conditioning methods again to the attention of psychology.

THE PLACE OF CONDITIONING IN PSYCHOLOGY

Different writers have made a variety of interpretations of the place of conditioning in psychology. Pavlov, himself, believed that his methods were purely physiological, and his aim in conducting his conditioning studies was entirely that of gaining an understanding of the functioning of the central nervous system. Similarly, his theories were expressed in

the terms familiar to the neurophysiologist. The extension of Pavlov's
work in America more typically consisted of attempts to formulate a
theory of learning in conditioning terms. Naturally such applications
sometimes reflected opinions which were very much at odds with those
of Pavlov.

Pavlov's Theory of Cortical Function

The fundamental conceptions in Pavlov's physiological theory were
those of excitation and inhibition, conceived as cortical processes.[5] According to the theory, afferent stimulation produces an excitatory process
at a definite point on the cortex from which it gradually "irradiates" or
spreads over the entire sensory area or "analyser," diminishing in intensity with distance from the primary point.

The mechanism of the formation of simple conditioned responses was
explained by Pavlov as follows. The excitation initiated by a neutral
stimulus at point A irradiates over the cortex, and will be concentrated
at any other focus of excitation such as that aroused by an unconditioned
stimulus. After a number of repetitions of the two stimuli, the excitation
aroused by the neutral stimulus is drawn to the locus of the unconditioned stimulus in sufficient intensity to elicit the conditioned response.
The direction of drainage of excitation is from the weaker to the stronger
or more dominant focus of excitation. The phenomenon of generalization
(p. 87) [6] was predicted from the assumption that excitation at point B,
aroused by a stimulus similar to the conditioned stimulus, will likewise
irradiate widely and be drawn into the excitable focus of the unconditioned response, either directly or by way of point A. If point B is extinguished (p. 82) by presenting its stimulus without reinforcement, the
process at this point is changed from excitation to inhibition, which also
irradiates over the surrounding region of the cortex. This mechanism
provides a means whereby nonreinforcement may reduce the strength of
a response to stimuli other than the training stimulus, yielding the generalization of extinction (p. 92). The phase of irradiation was assumed by
Pavlov to be followed by a recession or "concentration" of the process
to its point of initiation, the entire sequence of irradiation and concentration requiring from a few seconds to twenty minutes to occur.

In actual experimental situations the progress of irradiation and excitation was detected by conditioning a response to a certain stimulus, or
alternatively extinguishing an already conditioned response, and then

[5] Pavlov's theory is described in several available sources (Pavlov, 1902, 1927,
1928, 1930, 1941, 1955; Konorski, 1948).

[6] In order to present Pavlov's theory at this point, it has been necessary to refer to
certain familiar conditioning phenomena in anticipation of more extensive coverage.
The reader who is unacquainted with these processes will find very brief descriptions
on the pages listed in parentheses.

observing the effect of this treatment upon the response to neighboring stimuli which were assumed to be projected to nearby cortical areas in rough geometric correspondence to their physical similarity. The following example of Pavlov's (1927, p. 165-166) method of tracing the spread and recession of cortical effects involves the inhibitory mechanism. Separate and equally strong conditioned responses were first established to three different tones and a hissing sound. Then the response to one tone was extinguished and tests were made with the other stimuli at times up to fifteen minutes later. Figure 2.1 shows the results obtained when the

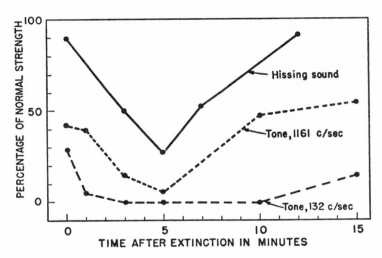

FIGURE 2.1. Pavlov's evidence for the irradiation and concentration of inhibition. Following the conditioning of a salivary response to three tones and a hissing sound, the response to the tone of lowest pitch was extinguished. Tests were, then, performed with the other stimuli. Note that the extent to which the CR is inhibited is greatest for the most similar stimulus and that the effect increases and then decreases in time. Data from Pavlov (1927).

extinguished tone was of 123 cycles per second and the test stimuli were tones of 132 or 1161 cycles per second or the hissing sound. Two points of importance appear in Figure 2.1: (1) The extinction carried out with the low tone produces a diminution of response strength to the other tones by an amount which depends upon the similarity of the stimuli. This is the familiar process of the generalization of extinction. (2) The amount of inhibition increases at first and then decreases. This is Pavlov's evidence for the initial irradiation and subsequent concentration of the inhibitory process.

Pavlov assumed that the production of excitation or inhibition in any cortical center automatically produced the opposite process in surrounding areas, and that as the cortical process subsided, it might be succeeded by the opposite process. Pavlov called these effects positive and negative induction, and referred to their behavioral consequences (p. 93) in the same terms. Thus negative induction referred to the intensification of inhibition under the influence of excitation; and positive induction referred to the intensification of excitation under the influence of inhibition.

The chief environmental variable thought to determine the intensity of the cortical process, and therefore the degree of irradiation, was the intensity of stimulation. This hypothesis was based upon the fact that, as a general thing, Pavlov obtained a marked positive correlation between the intensity of the conditioned stimulus and the magnitude of the conditioned response (Pavlov, 1930). Eventually, however, it became necessary to postulate two different physiological variables to account for the fact that certain other conditions also affected the magnitude of the response.

One of these additional variables was the *excitability* of the cortical cells. It was necessary to assume different levels of excitability to account for the facts that mild hunger and small doses of certain drugs such as caffeine tended to increase the magnitude of the conditioned response and certain other conditions such as satiation and old age tended to decrease it. Other evidence gave rise to the second new concept, that of the "limit" or *top capability* of the cells (Konorski, 1948, p. 27). Specifically, exceedingly strong stimuli sometimes led to a destruction of the normal relationship between CS strength and reflex magnitude and produced responses considerably smaller than those elicited by a CS of moderate strength. To account for this, Pavlov assumed that the cortical cells respond to increasing CS intensities with increasing excitation only up to their top capability. Beyond this point, the CS produces a *protecting inhibition* which reduces reflex magnitude and prevents damage to the cortical cells from overstimulation.

The top capability of the cells was assumed to vary from animal to animal; such factors as old age, neurosis, and fatigue were believed to lower it. Lowering the top capability of the cells theoretically could have any of a number of effects, depending upon the degree to which the top capability was lowered. For instance, a strong CS which had previously evoked a very strong response might, with a modest lowering of the top capability of the cells, now produce the response typical of a weak stimulus. This was Pavlov's *phase of equalization*. Still further lowering of top capability produced a *paradoxical phase*, or even an *ultra-paradoxical* phase. In the first of these, only weak conditioned stimuli can evoke a response. Strong stimuli either evoke no response at all or have a barely noticeable effect. The ultra-paradoxical phase, indicative of a still further lowering of the top capability of the cortical cells, is one in which only inhibitory stimuli have a positive effect. The explanation for this is that the completely inhibited cell, receiving the inhibitory impulse, is made to respond with excitation through induction.

Evaluation of Pavlov's Theory

The outline of Pavlov's theory sketched above shows that it contained a sufficient number of concepts to produce an elaborate theory to explain the operation of the cortex. This was Pavlov's aim, and he and his colleagues tried very hard to construct such a theory. Moreover, Pavlov was fully aware of the complexities inevitably to be encountered in brain function. He regarded the cortex as capable of responding to sensory stimulation from all parts of the body and believed that the irradiation of the cortical representations of these effects and their inductive interactions with the CS would have to be taken into account in order to explain the functioning of the cerebral cortex.

Toward the end of his life, Pavlov also began to develop his theory in directions which suggested the possibility of dealing with important psychological problems in conditioning terms. Sleep was considered the result of extreme irradiation of the inhibitory process over the entire cortex and into the lower brain regions. Hypnosis was a form of partial sleep, or less extensive irradiation of inhibition. Neurosis was regarded as a functional pathology of the cortex in which, as a result of an unusually acute clashing of the excitatory and inhibitory processes or of the influence of strong and extraordinary stimuli, there is an exaggerated predominance in the animal of either excitation or inhibition, analagous respectively to the hysteria or neurasthenia observed in human patients. Language was treated in terms of higher-order conditioning as a *second signalling system* in which words bore the same relationship to conditioned stimuli as conditioned stimuli do to the UCS.

In spite of the elaborate nature of Pavlovian theory, its fruitfulness in yielding experimental ideas, and its apparent relevance to important issues, severe criticism was directed at the theory for a number of reasons. In summary, some of these are the following:

1. Concepts of cortical physiology should be based upon more direct measures of cortical function. Pavlov's inhibition and excitation are purely inferential concepts derived from measures of overt movements or of amount of saliva secreted. Likewise irradiation, concentration, and induction are derived solely from the behavioral observations of generalization, discrimination, and after-effect. The concept of drainage is merely a figure of speech without any accepted neurophysiological basis. Inferential concepts are of course necessary in the systematization of the experimental data, but little is gained by asserting that such concepts denote cortical processes unless specific verification can be obtained through more direct observation of the cortex.

2. The temporal characteristic of irradiation, one of the most fundamental points in Pavlov's systematization, does not rest upon adequate experimental verification. A careful analysis by Loucks of the original data of the experiments on irradiation indicates that there is no "significant evidence for a sluggish spreading of an inhibitory disturbance from one restricted region to surrounding areas" (1933, p. 44). The general validity of any simple statement of irradiation for all regions of the cortex must be seriously doubted in view of findings by Dusser de Barenne and W. S. McCulloch (1938) that neural activity induced by application of strychnine to certain points on the cortex shows almost no spread of activity to surrounding cortex, although in other areas there is irradiation to widely distant regions. This irradiation, moreover, is not symmetrical. Stimulation of a point in one area activates a second area, whereas the second area may not activate the first. A given point may augment the spontaneous activity of one area and depress that of a second.

3. Assuming that Pavlov's cortical mosaic is a matter of the extent to which different portions of the body are represented on the brain, the results of certain studies of generalization call this interpretation into serious question. Grant and Dittmer (1940a), for example, compared the generalization gradients for Galvanic Skin Responses conditioned to tactile CS's on the back (small area of cortical representation) and on the hand (large area of cortical representation) and found the gradients to be essentially equal in slope. The irradiation hypothesis requires a steeper generalization gradient for the latter stimuli. Moreover, as Grant and Dittmer point out, Bass and Hull (1934) had obtained a gradient without inversions from shoulder to back to thigh to foot in spite of the fact that, in cortical representation, thigh, calf and foot are interpolated between the waist and the buttocks.

4. The spatial character of Pavlov's conception of cortical irradiation limits its general application. The assumption of a geometric projection of stimulus attributes onto the cortex does not seem applicable to generalization among stimuli differing in intensity or quality. In these cases the distance of cortical irradiation cannot determine the degree of generalization. The difficulty becomes clear in considering generalization in the intensity dimension, where the neural excitation may be mediated by identical fibers but at different frequency. All discrimination may perhaps depend on some sort of dynamic separation of areas of excitation, as suggested in the Gestalt concept of isomorphism (Köhler, 1929), but this remains to be empirically demonstrated. Even the theory of isomorphism does not imply simple areal representation as proposed by Pavlov.

5. Pavlov's theory of irradiation proposes a form of neural transmission which is acceptable to very few neurophysiologists, because it assumes

that there is a propagation of neural impulses by means other than those of synaptic transmission. Such a possibility remains to be demonstrated.

6. Pavlov's physiological conceptions are explicitly based upon the premise that conditioning is exclusively a cortical function. Experimentation demonstrates, however, that conditioning is possible at a subcortical level. Although the importance of the cortex in learning by higher mammals is unquestionable, any theory that neglects the functioning of lower levels of the nervous system must be inadequate. Pavlov's judgment, that conditioning is impossible in the absence of the cerebral cortex, was based upon the failure of Zeliony (1929) in 1912 to establish conditioned responses in dogs after surgical removal of the cerebral hemispheres. Later, Poltyrev and Zeliony (1930) were able to establish motor conditioned responses to visual and auditory stimuli in three decorticate dogs, and Lebedinskaia and Rosenthal (1935) were successful in conditioning a salivary response to a metronome. In all of the animals the operations left a small remnant of cortex at the base of the brain, and so great was the influence of Pavlov's opinion that, in both studies, the conditioning was attributed to the residual cortical tissue. Clear evidence of subcortical conditioning, however, has been presented by Ten Cate (1934c), who established a conditioned response to a bell in a totalling decorticate cat, and by Culler and Mettler (1934), Girden, Mettler, Finch, and Culler (1936), Poltyrev (1936), Zeliony, and Kadykov (1938), who trained decorticate dogs in conditioned responses to optic, cutaneous, and auditory stimuli based on unconditioned electric shock to the foreleg. In some of these studies and in one by Bromiley (1948) the decorticate animal has shown to be capable of forming simple discriminations.[7]

Alternative Conceptions of the Place of Conditioning in Psychology

These criticisms of Pavlov's theory of cortical functioning seem to indicate that the conditioned response probably does not represent a *direct*

---

[7] Although conditioning in decorticate animals seems well-established, there is still controversy as to whether conditioning is possible in the *spinal* animal. The possibility of establishing CR's in the isolated spinal cord was first suggested by the work of Culler (1937) and Shurrager and Culler (1938) on flexion responses in spinal dogs. A pressure stimulus at the tip of the tail was followed repeatedly by shock to the paw of one hind leg. No CR involving movement of the limb developed, but when the semitendinous muscle was exposed, a small twitch of one end of the muscle was apparent, in response to the pressure stimulation. Subsequent investigators using similar techniques have sometimes obtained positive results (Dykman and Shurrager, 1956; Shurrager and Culler, 1940, 1941; Shurrager and Dykman, 1951; Shurrager and Shurrager, 1941, 1946, 1950) and sometimes negative results (Deese and Kellogg, 1949; Kellogg, 1947; Kellogg, Deese, Pronko, and Feinberg, 1947; Kellogg, Pronko, and Deese, 1946; Pinto and Bromiley, 1950). Investigators obtaining negative results have usually attributed the positive results to operative procedures and have concluded that the spinal ''CR'' is actually some variety of UCR or at least a response which is different from the conventional flexion CR (Pronko and Kellogg, 1942, p. 237n).

reflection of brain mechanisms. For this reason the importance of classical conditioning is to be sought in other connections. Psychological theorists have offered a variety of interpretations of this sort. As has been stressed before, conditioning won its acceptance in psychology by appealing to a set of influences which had dominated the field for centuries. For this reason it is not surprising that the first evaluation of conditioning was in terms of this background.

1. *Conditioning as a Substitute for Association.* One such view was that *conditioning* was a substitute for *association.* S. Smith and Guthrie gave the initial impetus to this usage in their textbook (1921). They used the term *conditioning* for a case in which the association occurs between stimuli and movements rather than between ideas. They extended the language of conditioning to the whole range of psychological phenomena. Conditioning, in their hands, became a general formula which provided a single principle of learning, analogous in importance to the primary law of association, contiguity. Guthrie's theory still retains its heavy reliance upon the principle of contiguity. The connection to classical associationistic psychology has, however, largely been lost, probably because psychology, generally, is presently not much interested in the problems central to classical psychology.

2. *The Conditioned Response as the Unit of Habit.* Another early view of the conditioned response was that it is the unit of all learned activity or that complex habits are simply compounds of conditioned reflexes. Thus Pavlov states: "It is obvious that the different kinds of habits based on training, education, and discipline of any sort are nothing but a long chain of conditioned reflexes." (Pavlov, 1927, p. 395). This is the position which Watson promulgated, and it enjoyed a great vogue in America for some years. From the beginning, however, attacks on Watson's statement of conditioning theory were numerous and vigorous. It is now clear on both theoretical and experimental grounds that simple chaining of conditioned responses will not predict the characteristics of complex habits. The component responses are greatly altered by virtue of their combination with other responses, and the influence of combination must be experimentally determined. Watson's simple conception of the conditioned response as the unit of habit is no longer held by anyone in the field of learning, although it occasionally is resurrected by critics of behaviorism, as Bergmann (1956) says, "to scare little children in the existentialist dark."

Thus the early interpretations of the place of conditioning have disappeared, and in their place there have appeared two others which stand out today. One of these holds that the conditioned response is, in some sense, representative of all learning. The other maintains that conditioning is a limited or special form of learning.

3. *Conditioning Experiments as Representative of Other Forms of Learning.* If the conditioning experiment proves to exhibit in sharp focus all the essential characteristics of other learning, it should be a useful area in which to search for laws of learning. It is obviously under better control than many of the practical learning situations in education and everyday life, and to the extent that it is a "pure case" of learning, it should be a good source for the determination of the principles which hold true for all learning. Symonds (1927) presented an early exposition of this possibility. He listed 23 laws of conditioning and showed the analogies between them and learning in practical situations. Such reasoning, however, shares the weakness of much argument by analogy, in that it calls attention to what may be merely superficial similarities, and it oversimplifies the relationship between conditioning and more complex learning.

A sounder view, which is a somewhat different version of this position, regards the conditioning situation as a source of deductive principles. This is the position most prominently advocated by Hull, who used conditioning principles to deduce such facts as the backward order of the elimination of blind alleys in maze learning and the excess of errors in the middle of a memorized series of nonsense syllables. In these applications, the deduced behavior is very unlike the simple conditioned response used in the deduction. In the hands of Hull and others, the conditioning experiment has become the tool for harmonizing many facts already known about learning, and for predicting a variety of new facts.

This use of conditioning does not carry the implication that all habits are compounded of simple conditioned responses or that the principles discovered in conditioning experiments are *directly* applicable to complex habit situations. The conditioning experiment, because of its simple and well-controlled structure, is a fruitful source of postulates from which deductions can be made concerning complex learning. The following statement from Hull is a straightforward expression of this point of view. It also presents a major issue on which Hull's position differed from that of Watson.

In order to correct a frequent misunderstanding, due presumably to the wide dissemination of the views of J. B. Watson, the writer wishes to make it quite clear that neither here nor in any previous publication has he assumed that the more complex forms of behavior are synthesized from reflexes which play the role of building blocks. This may or may not be true. His working hypothesis is, rather, that the *principles of action* discovered in conditioned reaction experiments are also operative in the higher behavioral processes. The compound adjective in the expression, "conditioned-reflex principles," accordingly refers to the locus of *discovery* of the principles rather than to their locus of *operation*. (Hull, 1935c, p. 227n)

4. *Conditioning as a Subordinate and Restricted Form of Learning.*
Psychologists who object to the foregoing point of view do so for one
of two reasons: Either they are opposed to all association or conditioning
theories of learning, or they believe that the conditioned response represents a limited form of learning. The Gestalt psychologists belong to the
former group. They see conditioning as epitomizing the atomistic-mech-
anistic approach to science and they object to it on that ground.

The argument of the other group is that there is more than one kind of
learning (Tolman, 1949) and that conditioning is only one of these forms.
Moreover, the common further assumption is that *different laws* govern
the progress of the different forms of learning. The most common statement of this idea maintains that (*a*) it is useful to discriminate between
classical and instrumental conditioning, and that (*b*) classical conditioning is contiguity learning and instrumental conditioning is governed by
the law of effect. Whether this view is correct or not is a theoretical question upon which agreement has not been reached in psychology. The next
two chapters will present some of the basic facts associated with classical
and instrumental conditioning, and these hopefully, will provide a basis
for adopting one point of view or the other on this question.

SUMMARY

The immediate reaction of psychology to Pavlov's demonstration of
the conditionability of the salivary reflex was one of enthusiastic acceptance. The conditioning method was hailed as providing psychology with
a method as scientific and objective as the methods of physiology. And
the concepts of conditioning were offered as explanatory devices of wide
applicability. It was proposed that conditioning theory would improve
our understanding in such diverse fields as social behavior, psychopathology, and the learning of school subjects. From our present vantage
point such enthusiasm seems unwarranted. Much of what we have attempted to do in this chapter has been to try to explain this uncritical
initial reaction to the facts and theories of conditioning.

Philosophical Background

To a very important extent, it is possible to understand the easy acceptance of conditioning principles in terms of psychology's historical
background. The general approach which dominated psychological
thought at the time the conditioning experiment was introduced was a
direct continuation of a pattern of thinking established by the British
empirical philosophers. Two aspects of this tradition were of particular
importance. One was the idea of analysis as a way of approaching scientific subject matter. It was assumed that complex phenomena are synthe-

sized of simpler components and that the way to scientific understanding is to isolate these elements so as to reveal the true nature of the events in question. The conditioned reflex was accepted as the probable simplest element of learning.

A second direct contribution of the British Empiricists was the concept of association. On the basis of their analyses of the mind these philosophers had proposed that mental phenomena are composed of simple ideas, bound together by associations. The early structural psychologists had accepted this interpretation and had set out to discover the elements of human experience by the method of introspection. The elements they discovered were unanalyzable sensory units welded together to produce consciousness, they claimed, by the laws of association. Although Pavlovian theory differed considerably from this interpretation at the level of factual content, the basic idea was the same. In the case of the conditioned reflex, the bond between conditioned stimulus and conditioned response was very similar to the familiar idea of association.

Scientific Background

While psychology's philosophical history had prepared it to accept the style of thought which was implicit in the concept of the conditioned reflex, other developments had prepared it even more directly to accept the subject matter. For one thing, psychology had always maintained a close tie with biological science. Early research on the sensory processes had led to an interest in physiology and to a tendency to place great faith in physiological explanation. Conditioning was introduced by a world-famous physiologist and described as a physiological method. This account of the conditioning method made it a part of a respected approach to psychological problems, and did so at a time when traditional psychology was in serious trouble.

With the increasing use of lower animals in psychological research, the older introspective psychology, which mainly dealt with sensory attributes and the association of ideas, was finding itself poorly equipped to deal with certain experimental observations. Among the most difficult for a psychology designed to handle the rational characteristics of the mind was the fact that the behavior of lower animals was often irrational, emotional, and almost reflexly automatic. Faced with the problem of describing such actions, some psychologists had already turned away from the older conceptions and had begun to develop new ones suggested by the work of Darwin. There was an emphasis upon the adjustive character of behavior, epitomized by the concept of habit. The translation of habitual behavior into the concepts of conditioned reflexes was an easy matter to accomplish.

Finally, in all biological science as well as in psychology there was a powerful trend in the direction of objectivity. This trend constituted a serious threat against contemporary introspectionism, which seemed overly subjective. Conditioning was accepted, in part, because it seemed entirely free of such subjectivism.

Russian Background

The Russian physiologist Pavlov first encountered the phenomena of conditioned reflexes incidentally in his studies of the gastric secretions associated with digestion. Recognizing the importance of what he had observed, he turned his considerable scientific talents to the direct investigation of these "psychic secretions." After initial crude and relatively uncontrolled experiments, Pavlov developed his now famous conditioning methods and carried them out under conditions of rigid control. With these methods Pavlov discovered all of the basic phenomena of conditioning and developed an elaborate quasi-neurological theory to account for them.

Pavlov's theory of conditioning treated behavioral phenomena in the purely materialistic tradition of physiology begun by Sechenov. The basic concepts were those of excitation and inhibition, conceived as cortical events. The interactions of these two processes provided an explanation for the various facts of conditioning. In spite of this strength, Pavlov's theory is objectionable for a number of reasons, of which the most important are these: (1) We now know that conditioning is possible in the absence of the cerebral cortex; so more than cortical function must be involved. (2) Certain facts of conditioning do not fit the theory. Many of these facts involved the phenomenon of stimulus generalization. (3) What passes for physiology in Pavlov's theory is nothing more than the translation of behavioral facts into neurophysiological language.

The History of Conditioning in America

A contemporary of Pavlov's, Bechterev, was mainly responsible for bringing the details of the conditioning experiment to the attention of the Western world, because his books were translated into known languages much earlier than Pavlov's. By about 1915, the conditioning experiment was reasonably familiar to American psychology, and there had been a few pioneer experiments. From the beginning, however, it was not the facts, but the concepts of conditioning, which had the important impact upon American psychology.

The most important application of conditioned-reflex concepts has always been in the effort to develop a general theory of learning. Initial efforts of this sort, adopting the mode of thought set down by the early sensory psychologists, assumed that all habits are synthesized of unitary conditioned-reflex elements. This view is no longer popular. Contemporary theorists who hypothesize that the conditioned reflex is basic to learning hold that, although the *laws* of conditioning may apply to all learning, this does not mean that every learned act is made up of a chain of reflexes. These theorists have attempted to show that the laws of conditioning may be used as a set of postulates from which the phenomena of more complex learning may be deduced.

Other theorists disagree with this approach, either because they think that conditioning and other forms of learning are quite separate processes, or because they regard this heavy stress on deduction as inappropriate at psychology's present stage of development. Theorists who take either of these positions are apt to agree on the point that we need much more factual information than we now have before attempting theoretical organization of the psychology of learning.

·3·

Classical and Instrumental Conditioning Experiments

THE BASIC DISTINCTION between classical and instrumental conditioning procedures is in terms of the consequences of the conditioned response. In classical conditioning, the sequence of events is independent of the subjects' behavior. In instrumental conditioning, by contrast, rewards and punishments are made to occur as a consequence of the learner's response or failure to respond. The difference between these two procedures did not seem important to the earliest investigators of conditioning, and the two procedures were used quite indiscriminately. In some experiments with shock, for example, the shock was unavoidable and occurred on every trial; in others the occurrence of the correct response prevented the onset of the shock. More recently, the distinction between these two methods has become a matter of very great interest. Before considering the possible importance of the difference, however, it will be necessary to consider more fully the nature of the methods.

CLASSICAL CONDITIONING

The reference experiment for classical conditioning is the study of conditioned salivation in dogs. The essential features of the procedure may be presented by describing a typical experiment in Pavlov's laboratory (Anrep, 1920): In order to permit the recording of the magnitude of the salivary response, the dog was first subjected to a minor operation in which the duct of the parotid gland was diverted so that the saliva flowed through an opening on the outside of the cheek. A small glass funnel was firmly cemented over the opening to collect the saliva, which could be measured with an accuracy of one-tenth drop by suitable devices. The dog was trained to stand quietly in a loose harness on a table in a room which was insulated against any distracting noises or vibrations (Figure 3.1). The experimenter occupied an adjoining room, observing the dog through a small window and presenting the stimuli by means of automatic devices. A tuning fork was sounded, and 7 or 8 seconds after the begin-

FIGURE 3.1. Pavlov's arrangement for the study of salivary conditioning. From Yerkes and Morgulis (1909).

ning of this stimulus, a plate containing a small measured quantity of dry powdered food was moved within reach of the dog's mouth. No salivation was evoked by the tone, but during the eating there was a copious flow of saliva. Combinations of the tone and food were presented three times during a daily session, separated by intervals of from 5 to 35 minutes. The strength of the conditioned response was determined by presenting the tone alone for 30 seconds and measuring the amount of salivation. After ten double stimulations there was a slight conditioned salivation, and after thirty combinations the tone evoked a salivation of sixty drops. On the early tests the conditioned salivation did not occur until the tone had sounded for 18 seconds; on later tests the salivation began after only 1 or 2 seconds. Both measures indicate an increase in the strength of the conditioned response with training.

Another example of classical conditioning, which employs a motor rather than a secretory response, may be selected from Liddell's (1934) studies on sheep. A metronome was set beating once per second for 5 seconds and then a shock was delivered from an inductorium through electrodes attached to the left foreleg of the animal. The metronome had no apparent effect upon the sheep's behavior, whereas the shock evoked a definite brief flexion of the limb, accompanied by changes in respiration and in electrical resistance of the skin (The Galvanic Skin Response, GSR). After four presentations of the metronome and shock in combination, the conditioned stimulus caused a definite change in breathing and skin resistance, and on the sixth trial there was a slight movement of the leg. By the eleventh trial the conditioned leg flexion was fully established and with further training was quite constant and stable. The reactions of the eleventh trial are illustrated in Figure 3.2. Since the conditioned response occurred at a latency of 3 or 4 seconds following the onset of the metronome, it was possible to detect the conditioned response on the basis of its anticipatory character.

A final example, again involving a motor response, is the eyelid condi-

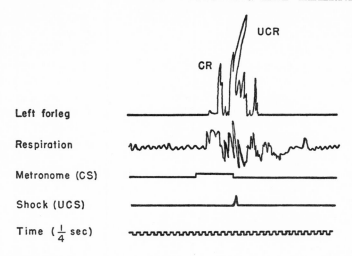

Left forleg

Respiration

Metronome (CS)

Shock (UCS)

Time ($\frac{1}{4}$ sec)

FIGURE 3.2. Conditioned responses in the sheep. The diagram represents a tracing from a kymograph record of the eleventh presentation of a metronome (conditioned stimulus, CS) combined with a shock (unconditioned stimulus, UCS) delivered to the left foreleg. The metronome beat once a second for 5 seconds prior to the shock. Both the conditioned leg movements and respiratory changes began while the metronome was sounding, anticipating the shock. These conditioned responses (CR) may be distinguished from the unconditioned responses (UCR) following shock. After Liddell (1934, p. 268).

tioning experiment. Such studies, most often with human subjects, usually employ an airpuff as a UCS to elicit a reflex blink, although loud noises, mild shocks, and taps on the cheek have been used for this purpose. The response has sometimes been recorded photographically (Dodge, 1926). More recently, electronic devices have been used to record the blink. The CS may be any detectable stimulation. Mild visual and auditory stimuli have been most commonly used.

Basic Concepts

The essential features of the conditioning experiment are the following:

1. *Unconditioned stimulus* (UCS)—a stimulus which, at the outset of an experiment, evokes a regular and measurable response.

2. *Unconditioned response* (UCR)—the regular and measurable response to the unconditioned stimulus just referred to. It is worth mentioning specifically that the unconditioned response is not necessarily an unlearned or reflex response to the UCS. In many cases, such as salivation to food placed in the mouth, it is; but in other cases, such as salivation at

the sight and smell of food in the distance, which Pavlov also used as a UCS, it is not.

3. *Conditioned stimulus* (CS)—a stimulus which (*a*) does not evoke the UCR, in this respect being neutral, and (*b*) is paired with the UCS for experimental purposes. Again one point is worth mentioning: often the CS does evoke an observable response, if only the reaction involved in "paying attention" to the CS, which Pavlov called an *orientation reflex, what-is-it reflex,* or *investigatory reflex.* In some experiments, such as eyelid conditioning with a visual CS, the response to the CS may even be of the same general kind as that to the UCS, in this example, a blink. In neither case, however, is the response to the CS *exactly* like that to the UCS. The investigatory reflex is always qualitatively different, and responses of the other kind differ from the UCR quantitatively, being of different latency and magnitude. More of this later.

4. *Conditioned response* (CR)—sometimes, as a result of the pairing of CS and UCS, a response resembling the UCR follows the CS, either on *test trials* with the UCS omitted or in anticipation of the UCS. Such a response is the conditioned response. Note especially that the CR merely resembles the UCR. This is another point to which we shall return later.

Classical Conditioning Procedures

The ordering and temporal spacing of stimuli in the classical conditioning experiment have given rise to a number of terms which describe different forms of the experiment. In the typical conditioning experiment, the CS begins a brief time before the onset of the UCS. It may either overlap the UCS in time or terminate before the appearance of the UCS. The time between CS and UCS may be short or long, and so on. The technical terminology of conditioning describes such relationships.

Figure 3.3 is a schematic representation of some of the possible relationships of CS to the UCS. In this figure, time is represented on the top line. The lower lines in the figure indicate stimulus onset and cessation, respectively, by upward and downward jogs. The second line represents the occurrence of the UCS which is the same for all of the following examples. The third line shows the arrangement for a simultaneous conditioning procedure in which the CS and UCS come on together. The next four lines illustrate *delayed conditioning* procedures in which the CS appears prior to the UCS and lasts at least until the latter stimulus appears. It, then, may go off as the UCS comes on (line 4), go off when the UCS does (line 5), or persist beyond the cessation of the UCS (line 6). As line 7 shows, the CS may be either stimulus onset or cessation. This is true of the other forms of conditioning, too, although no examples are presented in Figure 3.3. Line 8 shows a *trace conditioning* procedure in which the CS comes on briefly and goes off again before the UCS. Line 9

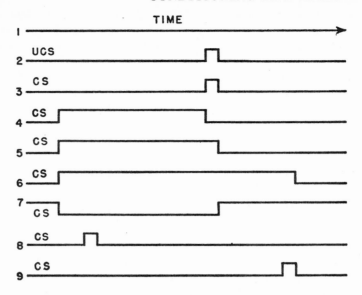

FIGURE 3.3. Some possible relations between CS and UCS in classical conditioning. Lines 1 and 2 represent, respectively, the passage of time and the onset (upward excursion of the line) and cessation (downward excursion) of the UCS. Line 3 illustrates the placement of the CS for strictly simultaneous conditioning. Lines 4, 5, 6, and 7 are examples of delayed conditioning procedures. Line 8 presents the procedure for trace conditioning. Line 9 illustrates backward conditioning.

illustrates *backward conditioning* in which the CS follows the UCS. Conditioning is difficult and perhaps impossible to obtain with this method.

One final conditioning procedure, not illustrated in Figure 3.3, is *temporal conditioning* in which a time interval functions as a CS. An unconditioned stimulus, such as food, is presented at regular intervals of time. If it is now omitted, a conditioned response may occur at approximately the usual interval. Pavlov obtained conditioning in dogs, using intervals as long as 30 minutes.

Organisms Which Have Been Conditioned

One of the earliest questions to arise in the history of classical conditioning concerned the generality of the process. This question breaks down into several more specific ones involving (1) the range of responses which can be conditioned, (2) the stimuli to which conditioning is possible, (3) the phylogenetic limits within which conditioning occurs, and (4) within a given species, the effect of age upon ease of conditioning. This section is concerned with the last two of these questions.

The planarian (flatworm), which has bilateral symmetry and a cerebral ganglion, seems to be the simplest organism which is certainly capable of forming *classical* conditioned responses, although its performance is not impressive. Thompson and McConnell (1955) conditioned planaria in a light-shock situation. The CS was provided by turning on two 100-watt lights. The UCS was a 28-milliampere shock passed through the water in a plastic trough used for the apparatus. Two different conditioned responses were observed, a turning of the head to one side or the other and a longitudinal contraction of the entire body. In 150 trials the probability of occurrence of one or the other of these responses increased from just under 30 per cent to just over 40 per cent. For this, and all higher phylogenetic levels, there seems to be no doubt that conditioning can occur.

There have been far fewer investigations of the ontogeny of conditionability than there have been of the phylogenetic range within which conditioning can occur. Such studies as have been done, however, show that conditioning is possible at a very early age, almost certainly prior to birth. E. L. Hunt (1949), employing chick embryos as subjects, paired a bell with electric shock and obtained conditioning of a gross bodily movement on the fifteenth day of incubation. In some cases the response was retained until after hatching. Spelt (1938, 1948) apparently obtained conditioned responses from human fetuses 6 1/2 to 8 1/2 months of age. He used a very loud noise, which produced an unconditioned startle-like response, as the UCS and a tactile vibration of the mother's abdomen as the CS. Movement of the fetus was measured by tambours attached to the mother's abdomen. After pairings of CS and UCS, movement responses occurred to the CS alone.

Dorothy Marquis (1931) conditioned the sucking reactions of newborn infants to the sound of a buzzer.[1] She also showed that it is possible to alter the feeding schedule of the neonate to a degree by manipulating the amount of time between nursings. Morgan and Morgan (1944) suggest the conditioned eyeblink as a possibly useful developmental index. They gave 42 infants of different ages 100 conditioning trials. Their procedure consisted of bringing the hand with a baby syringe (CS) near the eye of the infant and squeezing it to produce a puff of air (UCS) which made the baby blink. To test for the existence of conditioning, the experimenter brought the syringe near the baby's eye, but did not squeeze it. A blink to the syringe under these circumstances is a CR. In tests of children from 15 to 124 days of age, Morgan and Morgan found that no child 53 days of age or younger conditioned, whereas only one infant 66 days of age or older failed to condition.

[1] Other studies of conditioning in young infants are those of Kantrow (1937), Wenger (1936b), and Wickens and Wickens (1940). Razran (1933) and Irwin (1939) have developed theories of conditioning involving ontogenetic considerations.

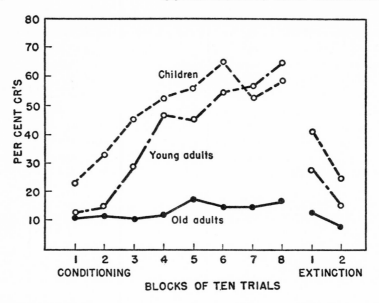

FIGURE 3.4. The effect of age upon the conditioning and extinction of the eyelid reflex. From Braun and Geiselhart (1959).

At the other end of the age scale, the evidence is quite good that conditionability is impaired. Braun and Geiselhart (1959) conditioned the eyelid reflexes of children, young adults, and old adults, obtaining the results appearing in Figure 3.4. It is obvious that, with increasing age, the level of conditioning diminishes. Pavlovian investigators interpret this in terms of a lowered excitability of the cortical cells (Gakkel and Zinina, 1953; see also p. 34, this book). Braun and Geiselhart prefer an explanation in terms of the adaptation with experience of the reflex mechanism.

Responses Used as Unconditioned Responses

Over the years, conditioning studies have been carried out with a variety of responses. Table 1 lists some of the responses which have been used, together with the unconditioned stimuli which have been used to elicit them. At least in terms of procedure, the classical conditioning method has been employed with responses of almost every type the organism can make. Whether the learning obtained in all of these cases is the same is one of the most basic questions to be asked in the field of conditioning. It is a point which will be dealt with in the next chapter.

Extreme difficulty or failure has been encountered in attempts to condition certain responces. These failures appear to fall into two categories.

(1) Conditioning is unsuccessful in vertebrates if the unconditioned response is evoked otherwise than by way of the central nervous system. Passive flexion of a limb, or direct electrical or chemical stimulation of a muscle or its motor nerve are ineffective as unconditioned stimuli. Similarly the conditioning of spinal animals is difficult, and perhaps impossible. (2) Certain simple reflexes are extremely difficult to condition. The abdominal, patellar, plantar, and pupillary reflexes fall in this category. When conditioning does occur is may be that voluntary facilitation is an important factor (Schlosberg, 1928). The reason for the difficulty encountered in conditioning may relate to the fact that these reflexes are very slightly involved in the processes of motivation and reward.[2]

TABLE 1

UNCONDITIONED RESPONSES AND THE STIMULI USED TO ELICIT THEM

Responses	*Stimuli*
Salivation	Dry food, acid
Blocking of EEG Alpha Rhythm	Light
Change in skin resistance (GSR)	Electric shock
Pupillary reflex	Change in illumination, shock
Gastro-intestinal secretions	Food
Vasomotor reactions	Shock, thermal stimuli
Nausea, vomiting, and so on	Morphine
Immunity reactions	Injection of toxin and antigen
Diuresis	Increased water intake
Flexion reflex	Electric shock
Knee jerk	Patellar blow
Eyelid reflex	Shock, sound, air-puff
Eye movements	Rotation
Change in respiration	Electric shock
Change in pitch of voice	Electric shock
Withdrawal movements	Electric shock
Mouth opening, swallowing	Food
Locomotion	Shock
Instructed responses	Various
Previously conditioned (higher-order) responses	Various

Conditioned Stimuli

Although unconditioned stimuli are chosen in reference to the response to be elicited, any environmental change to which the organism is sensi-

[2] In the laboratory, the pupillary reflex is readily elicited either with a change in illumination or by administration of an electric shock. Although the division of studies on this basis is not perfect, success in conditioning the pupillary reflex has been notably better in experiments employing electric shock. It seems likely that the emotional accompaniments of the shock may have been important. Successful conditioning of the pupillary reflex has been reported by Baker (1938), Cason (1922a), Gerall, Sampson, and Boslov (1957), Girden (1942), Harlow (1940), Harlow and Stagner (1933), Hudgins (1933), Kotliarevsky (1935), Metzner and Baker (1939), Ten Cate (1934b), and Watson (1916). Unsuccessful attempts have been carried out by Crasilneck and McCrannie (1956), Hilgard, Dutton, and Helmick (1949), Hilgard, Miller, and Ohlson (1941), Steckle (1936), Steckle and Renshaw (1934), Wedell, Taylor, and Skolnick (1940), and Young (1954, 1958). See also Hudgins (1935).

tive may serve as a conditioned stimulus. Visual stimuli have included lights of various colors, papers, geometrical forms, rotating objects. Auditory stimuli have included pure tones, horns, buzzers, bubbling water, metronomes. Various thermal, tactual, olfactory, and proprioceptive stimuli have been used. Pavlov tended to prefer continuing stimuli, such as metronomes, electric fans, rotating disks. Experimenters using reflexes in striate muscles have tended to prefer stimuli with sharp onset, such as flashes of light, clicks, contact stimuli. The effectiveness of some stimuli may depend on their sudden onset, and others may depend for their effectiveness on summation. It is known that a change in the intensity of a stimulus or the termination of a stimulus may serve as well as the appearance of a stimulus.

Internal stimuli are not as frequently employed in conditioning experiments as external stimuli because they are not so susceptible to precise control and measurement. As we have seen, however, there have been studies in which the CS was direct stimulation of the brain (p. 6), and the Russians have done some experiments using as CS's stimulation of the internal organs (Bykov, 1957). The following illustrative example is described by Razran in his unpublished book *Interoceptive Conditioning*: Intestinal loops were isolated surgically, in two dogs, and tubes were provided for the introduction of liquids (to serve as CS's) into the intestine. For one dog the CS was a .2 per cent solution of hydrochloric acid; for the other it was a 5.5 per cent solution of glucose. In each case the UCS was a shock administered to the left hind paw 10 to 15 seconds later. The animal receiving the hydrochloric acid CS formed a stable motor CR in just sixteen trials. The animal receiving glucose required thirty. The fact that the CS was the specific chemical solution was demonstrated by the ability of the subjects to form a discrimination between the liquid used for a CS and a saline solution of the same volume and temperature.

The Relationship between Conditioned and Unconditioned Responses

At one time it was believed that the conditioned response was simply the response originally elicited by the UCS, evoked by the CS as a consequence of learning. This assumption demands that the dog which formerly salivated only to food should salivate in exactly the same way to the metronome; and the human subject's conditioned GSR should be precisely like that previously elicited by a shock. It is now recognized that this assumption is incorrect, that the CR and UCR are never strictly the same, and that the conditioned response is not simply a duplicate of the unconditioned one. In experiments where the conditioned response does appear to be an exact replica of the unconditioned response, the reason always seems to lie in imprecise measurement or incomplete recording of the details of the reaction. Thus, it is reported that in the early stages of conditioned leg withdrawal, dogs act in the presence of the conditioned stimulus as though they were being shocked (Culler, Finch, Girden and Brogden, 1935; Kellogg, 1938a); but it seems quite certain that detailed, quantitative records would reveal differences. Similarly Pavlov's records of salivation seldom provide an indication of the temporal patter of salivation. When such records have been provided (Konorski, 1948) differences between CR and UCR are easily detectable. This evidence that the CR and UCR are different suggests the importance of attempting to determine the precise nature of the relationship between them. The views held most commonly have been that the CR is either a fractional component of the UCR, or that it is a preparation for the occurrence of the UCS.

The CR Viewed as a Fractional Component Response

In many experiments, the conditioned response appears to be weaker than the unconditioned response or to represent only a component part of it. The conditioned salivary response, for example, is often of smaller magnitude than the unconditioned response. Moreover, where the unconditioned response to food consists of salivation, chewing, and swallowing, the conditioned response may involve only one or two of these components. A dog which has received shock on the leg together with a buzzer may give a conditioned withdrawal response without the vocalization that was a part of the reaction to shock.

Although it is doubtful that the description of the CR as a fractional component of the UCR provides a complete explanation of the former response, one point about such responses is very important, namely, that the fractional component can occur in the absence of the unconditioned stimulus and at points remote from it in time or space. Hull made considerable use of this characteristic of the CR in a series of papers dealing with complex behavior, and many of the same explanations appeared in his last book (Hull, 1952). In these treatments Hull referred to the complete unconditioned response as a *goal response* (R_G) and to the component as a *fractional anticipatory goal response* (r_G). We shall meet the concept of r_G, its proprioceptive stimulus, s_G, and the combination, $r_G \longrightarrow s_G$, at a number of later points in the book. Among the phenomena to which it has been applied are latent learning, frustration, place learning, delay of reinforcement, problem-solving and conflict behavior (Hull, 1952). In each of these cases the fractional anticipatory goal responses has been made to serve much the same function as the idea of expectancy does in the cognitive theories. Probably no single development in either camp has done quite so much to reconcile differences between the two theories (Behan, 1953; Seward, 1956a).

The CR Viewed as a Preparatory Response

Other writers have taken the position that the function of the conditioned response is to prepare the organism for the occurrence of the unconditioned stimulus. In such discussions it is often noted that the CR may not resemble the UCR at all. It is as if the subject "expects" the forthcoming stimulation and prepares to receive it. The preparatory character of some conditioned behavior in the Pavlovian situation has been described by Zener (1937). Salivary responses were conditioned to a bell which preceded feeding in the usual manner. The total behavior was recorded by motion pictures, and the differences between conditioned and unconditioned behavior were summarized as follows:

Except for the component of salivary secretion the conditioned and unconditioned behavior is not identical. (a) During most of the time in which the bell is reinforced by the presence of food, chewing generally occurs with the head raised out of the foodpan but not directed either at the bell or into the foodpan, or at any definite environmental object. Yet this posture practically never, even chewing only occasionally, occurs to the conditioned stimulus alone. Despite Pavlov's assertions, the dog does not appear to be eating an imaginary food. (b) Nor is the behavior that does appear an arrested or partial unconditioned reaction consisting of those response elements not conflicting with other actions. It is a different reaction, anthropomorphically describable as a looking for, expecting, the fall of food with a readiness to perform the eating behavior which will occur when the food falls. The effector pattern is not identical with the unconditioned. (c) Movements frequently occur which do not appear as part of the unconditioned response to food: all the restless behavior of stamping, yawning, panting. (Zener, 1937, p. 393.)

When the restraining straps were removed, so that the range of the dog's activity was increased, the preparatory character of the behavior became even more evident. At the conditioned signal for food, the dog would approach the food pan; at another signal which had been associated with the release of acid into the mouth, the dog would either do nothing (since the acid-delivering tube was not attached), or it would walk away from the neighborhood of the stimulating devices. Furthermore, when the dog was satiated with food, the reactions to the conditioned stimulus were not only decreased in amount but qualitatively altered.

One of the chief virtues of Zener's detailed description is that it exhibits the complexity of the behavior which occurs in the conditioning situation. Obviously the common expression, "*the* conditioned response," is misleading, and probably in important ways. At the same time it should be recognized that the behavior described by Zener was almost certainly instrumentally, rather than classically, conditioned. This may be true of all responses of readiness acquired in classical conditioning situations.

The Specification of the Conditioned Response

Some of the differences between conditioned and unconditioned responses appear very clearly in Figure 3.5, which presents pairs of records taken from an eyelid-conditioning experiment, showing conditioned and unconditioned responses on adjacent trials of the same subjects. It is quite clear that the CR is very different from the UCR, having a longer

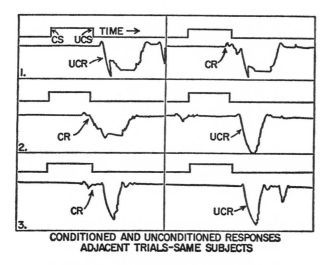

CONDITIONED AND UNCONDITIONED RESPONSES
ADJACENT TRIALS–SAME SUBJECTS

FIGURE 3.5.   Conditioned and unconditioned responses in the same subjects on adjacent trials. The upper line in each panel represents the onset of the light employed as a CS (upward jog) and the UCS which was an airpuff (downward jog) half a second later. The CR is distinguishable from the UCR in terms of latency. The CR anticipates the onset of the UCS. Unpublished records of the writer.

latency and characteristically different form. In the actual conditioning situation, the conditioned eyeblink is recognized as such because it appears in anticipation of the UCS. This criterion alone, however, is not sufficient to identify the CR because there are several other responses which may also occur in the interval between CS and UCS and be confused with a true CR. These other responses include reflex blinks to the CS (*alpha responses*), *beta responses* (see below), voluntary responses, and random blinks. With the possible exception of the random blink, these responses differ from CR's in latency, form, or both. Table 2 presents typical latency ranges from various responses which may occur in an eyelid conditioning situation. Figure 3.6 illustrates some of the ones which do not appear in Figure 3.5 The latency figures in Table 2 assume an interval between CS and UCS of about .5 second.

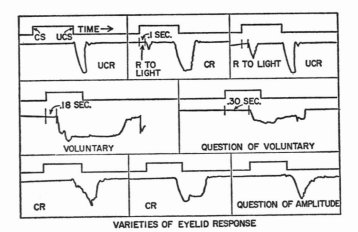

VARIETIES OF EYELID RESPONSE

FIGURE 3.6. Varieties of response which occur in the eyelid conditioning situation. Note the short latency and distinctive form of the typical voluntary response presented in the left-hand panel in the middle row. The right-hand response in the same row has the form of a voluntary response but the latency of a true CR. Experimenters must decide whether to count these as CR's or as voluntary responses. The record in the lower right-hand panel illustrates the problem encountered when anticipatory responses of small amplitude appear. Whether or not this is a CR depends upon the experimenter's criteria. Unpublished records of the writer.

The latency characteristics of both CR's and voluntary responses change with changes in the interstimulus interval.

The beta response mentioned in Table 2 was discovered by Grant and his co-workers (Grant, 1945; Grant and Norris, 1947). It is a reflex blink to light which is sensitized by dark adaptation. Figure 3.7 presents the results of one study in the form of a frequency distribution, which shows the latency characteristics of the alpha, beta, and conditioned responses. With subjects run in the light (lower graph) the responses in the beta

TABLE 2

VARIETIES OF RESPONSES IN EYELID CONDITIONING EXPERIMENTS AND CHARACTERISTIC LATENCIES

Response	Latency Range in Milliseconds	
Reflex blink to light (Alpha response)	50—110	See Fig. 3.6
Beta response	120—240	See Figs. 3.6, 3.7
Conditioned response	250—500	See Figs. 3.5, 3.6, 3.7
Voluntary response	200—500	See Fig. 3.6
Random blink	———	See Fig. 3.6
Unconditioned response	50—100 msec. after UCS	See Figs. 3.5, 3.6

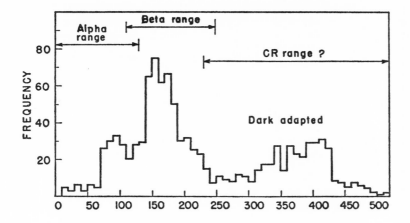

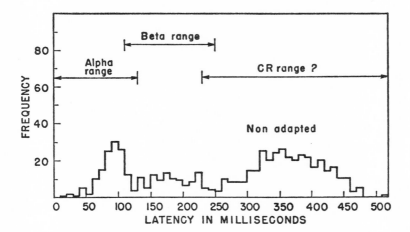

FIGURE 3.7. Latency distributions of reactions evoked by the CS in an eyelid conditioning experiment under conditions of dark adaptation and light adaptation. The Beta responses are unconditioned reflexes to light which are easily confused with the true CR. The small distribution of responses with latencies in the range from about 60 to about 120 milliseconds are unconditioned reflexes to light (Alpha responses). In order to eliminate the contaminating effects of Beta responses experimenters usually run their subjects under conditions of light adaptation and count as CR's only those responses with latencies greater than some specified minimal value. Data from Grant and Norris (1947).

range tend to disappear. Those remaining are probably mainly random blinks.

The importance of an exact specification of the nature of the CR may be illustrated by considering the effect which a failure to distinguish among voluntary, beta, conditioned, and unconditioned responses has probably had upon the history of eyelid conditioning. Early studies were almost always run with the subjects in the dark, a procedure necessitated by the photographic method of recording responses. This means that many of the responses counted as CR's in these studies were beta responses and that the progress of conditioning was not accurately represented. Voluntary responses have introduced a somewhat different set of complications, which may be illustrated by the early eyelid conditioning studies on rats (Hughes and Schlosberg, 1938), dogs (Hilgard and Marquis, 1935), monkeys (Hilgard and Marquis, 1935, 1936), and infants (Morgan and Morgan, 1944). In each of these studies, the unconditioned response was lid closure to a puff of air directed at the eye. Records from dog, monkey, and man are reproduced in Figure 3.8. The gross similarity

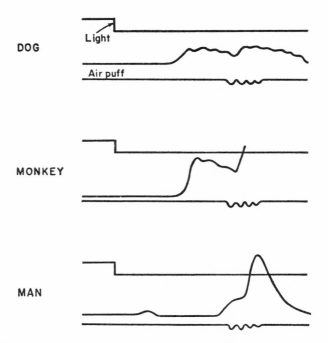

FIGURE 3.8.   Tracings of records obtained from dog, monkey, and man in the eyelid conditioning situation. The original records were photographs obtained with Dodge's photochronographic procedure. In such records, eyelid closures appear as upward excursions of the response line. Note especially that the amount by which the airpuff is anticipated is much less for man than for the dog or monkey. This suggests that the responses in the upper two records are voluntary. Records from top to bottom were obtained by Hilgard and D. G. Marquis (1935), Hilgard and D. G. Marquis (1936), and Hilgard and A. A. Campbell (1936).

of the results in the different studies must not be permitted to obscure the differences. A careful examination of the conditioning records shows that the form of the response is different for the different species, and that the latency is somewhat shorter in the lower species than in man. Indeed the responses for dog and monkey are like the voluntary responses of human subjects, and probably are voluntary. Informal and unpublished observation of the conditioned eyelid response in infants (Kimble) leaves no doubt at all that what they develop is a voluntary conditioned response rather than the automatic reflex-like CR.

A final example in the same general connection concerns the value of requiring the subject to make a "mediating" response, such as a key press, to the CS. Studies of this sort (Miller and Cole, 1936; Beck, 1939) have routinely demonstrated much better conditioning and greater resistance to extinction with than without the added response. Careful studies of records obtained with this procedure, however, show that the act of pressing the key produces a strong tendency to blink simultaneously, and that these unconditioned blinks are indistinguishable from low-amplitude CR's (Ost, 1960). Thus, the reasonable hypothesis that a mediating motor act aids eyelid conditioning remains to be validated.

Further Complexities

As we have just seen, the conditioning process presents many problems, even at the relatively simple level of the identification of the conditioned reflex. Further consideration of the behavioral changes which occur in conditioning reveals that this is only the beginning of the matter. The conditioning procedure sometimes leads to other modifications which require separate specification and treatment; these include adaptation, a conditioned suppression of the UCR, pseudoconditioning, and reflex sensitization.

1. *Adaptation.* Presentation of a noxious UCS alone, prior to a conditioning procedure, sometimes leads to a diminution of response strength known as adaptation. Systematic studies of this phenomenon have not been numerous, but the results have been quite consistent. MacDonald (1946) conditioned the eyelid reflex and finger retraction in human subjects with and without a series of 50 prior adaptation trials with the UCS, air-puff, or shock for the two different procedures. By comparison with control groups which received no adaptation trials, she found that the effect of the adaptation trials was to reduce the number of conditioned responses from 27.7 to 6.0 in the case of the eyeblink, and from 27.1 to 10.0 in the finger retraction experiment. Taylor (1956) studied the effectiveness of different levels of UCS, using three adaptation groups and a control group in an eyelid conditioning experiment. Expressed in terms of millimeters of mercury (a measure of the pressure behind the puff)

the UCS intensities during 50 adaptation trials were 80, 30, 15, and 0 (control group). For these groups respectively the percentages of CR's in 50 conditioning trials were 9.14, 12.20, 16.36, and 22.22. Kimble and Dufort (1956) present data from a similar study in a form which shows the effect during the course of conditioning. They gave 20 adaptation trials with the UCS to their experimental group and none to a control group in an eyelid conditioning experiment. The results appear in Figure 3.9. Presumably the relatively small amount of adaptation is a function

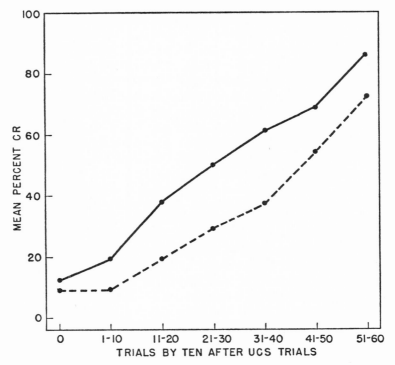

FIGURE 3.9. **Conditioning curves obtained with (lower curve) and without (upper curve) previous adaptation trials with the UCS. The CS in this experiment was a light, the UCS an airpuff (Kimble and Dufort, 1956).**

of the limited number of adaptation trials. The effect of different numbers of such trials seems not to have been investigated.[3]

2. *Pseudoconditioning.* Curiously, the procedures for producing adaptation sometimes have exactly the opposite effect: Instead of a decrease

[3] The studies cited in this section have all concerned adaptation of the response to the UCS, which has been the matter of greatest interest in this area. Adaptation does occur to the CS, however. McAllister (1953) found nearly complete adaptation of a blink response to a tone used as a CS in eyelid conditioning over a period of one hundred trials.

in ease of conditioning, they produce responses like conditioned responses on the very first presentation of the conditioned stimulus. Such reactions are called pseudoconditioning, because they resemble true CR's but do not depend upon double stimulation. After a reflex to light had been adapted out in fish, so that the light no longer evoked a response, the fish were shocked repeatedly, no illumination change accompanying the shock. Following this treatment, both light and a vibratory stimulus produced reactions which might have been interpreted as conditioned if the light and vibration had been combined with the shock (R. R. Sears, 1934). Similarly, monkeys were frightened several times by a powder flash (or a "snake" blowout). Following this series of experiences, a bell was sounded, and fright responses were evoked which the bell had not previously elicited (Grether, 1938). Grant (1943a, 1943b) has demonstrated pseudoconditioning of the eyelid reflex. Harlow (1939) used a carefully determined threshold shock as a CS and a strong shock as a UCS in a study with goldfish, in which he compared forward conditioning, backward conditioning, and pseudoconditioning. Trials with the strong shock alone produced stable pseudoconditioning very quickly. Similarly 10, 20, or 30 shock trials produced increasing amounts of psuedoconditioning in cats, with the function essentially asymptotic after 20 trials (Harlow and Toltzien, 1940). In this latter study, tests were postponed for 5 minutes, 3 hours, or 24 hours after the shock trials. Pseudoconditioning occurred to about the same degree in each of these conditions. The importance of this fact is that it seems to indicate that an explanation in terms of generalized excitement is unsatisfactory. Such excitement (fear, anxiety) would presumably subside in 24 hours. An alternative possibility seems more likely: that conditioning of responses to shock to the general situation mediates the pseudoconditioned response.

The most extensive study involving pseudoconditioning was that of Harris (1941) with finger withdrawal. He compared forward conditioning, backward conditioning, and pseudoconditioning with a random conditioning procedure in which CS and UCS were presented alone. The CS was a loud tone which lasted 4.75 seconds; the UCS was a .25-second shock. In the forward-conditioning situation, the shock followed the tone by 4.75 seconds. All groups received a total of 80 shocks. The measure of the effectiveness of the different procedures was percentage of conditioned responses on a series of 10 trials without shock. The results on this measure appear in Table 3. These results actually show a higher proportion of "CR's" after the pseudoconditioning procedure than any other. Harris points out that the responses to tone in all conditions except the forward conditioning one are probably pseudoconditioned responses.

Kimble and his associates (Kimble, Mann, and Dufort, 1955; Kimble and Dufort, 1956; Dufort and Kimble, 1958) gave human subjects a series of conditioning trials and then omitted the CS on a series of trials

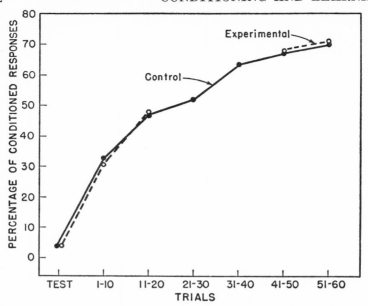

FIGURE 3.10. Graph showing the effect of interpolated trials with the UCS upon performance. Data from Kimble, Mann, and Dufort (1955).

in eyelid conditioning. The procedure of omitting the CS is, of course, a pseudoconditioning one. Figure 3.10 presents a set of typical results. Quite clearly, the trials with the UCS alone facilitated conditioning as would be expected from other evidence on pseudoconditioning. These

TABLE 3

PERCENTAGE OF RESPONSES TO TONE FOLLOWING
VARIOUS TRAINING PROCEDURES
(From Harris, 1941)

Condition	Extinction Trials					
	1	2	3-4	5-6	7-8	9-10
Forward conditioning	90.0	70.0	60.0	35.0	30.0	35.0
Backward conditioning	84.6	46.1	30.7	23.0	26.8	23.0
Random presentation	44.4	33.3	22.2	16.6	22.2	22.2
Pseudoconditioning	100.0	80.0	30.0	10.0	20.0	10.0

studies make the additional point, however, that the effect of the UCS trials may be exactly the same as those in which CS and UCS are paired. *The implication of this is that pseudoconditioning may be a part of all conditioning in which a noxious stimulus is employed.*[4]

[4] Recently this finding has been questioned. Experiments attempting to replicate the results in Figure 3.10 have been unsuccessful (Goodrich, Ross, and Wagner, 1957). No satisfactory explanation for this disparity has yet been advanced.

A further application of the pseudoconditioning procedure is to be found in the restoration of extinguished responses. With the omission of the UCS, the conditioned reaction gradually subsides or extinguishes. Following such extinction the conditioned response is completely restored (reconditioned) by a few pairings of the CS and UCS. It may also be restored in another way, by presenting the UCS alone, without the CS, for several times. In this case, again, unpaired applications of the UCS have the effect of producing an increment in the strength of the response, after the manner of pseudoconditioning.

The mechanism by which pseudoconditioning and related phenomena occur (if, indeed, there is only one mechanism) is not known. Sears (1934) and Harlow (1939) have employed a variant of Ukhtomski's (1926) concept of *dominance* for this purpose. According to this principle, any reaction which has been repeatedly elicited by a strong stimulus may become dominant over reactions, so that it is elicitable by a much wider range of stimuli than is normally the case. Grether (1938) and Harlow and Toltzien (1940) have suggested that pseudoconditioning occurs because of the development of an attitude of expectancy. It is characteristic of all of these explanations that they are performance, or nonassociative, interpretations. No learning process is involved.

Wickens and Wickens (1942), on the other hand, have interpreted pseudoconditioning as a case of true conditioning. They believe that, during training with the noxious stimulus, the organism acquires a response which is transferred to the neutral stimulus on test trials because the two stimuli are, in some sense, similar. Both, for example, may come on suddenly. To test this hypothesis, Wickens and Wickens trained two different groups of rats to escape from a shock which came on suddenly for one group and gradually for the other. Subsequently, each group was subdivided and tested with a light which came on suddenly or gradually. Ultimately the four groups consisted of two in which the onsets of shock and light were similar (both sudden or both gradual) and two groups in which the onsets were different (one being sudden, the other gradual). On the tests with the light, 15 of 19 animals in the two groups where the stimuli were similar showed pseudoconditioning by performing the response originally learned to escape the shock. In the case of the animals tested with dissimilar stimuli, however, only 3 of 18 produced a pseudoconditioned response. These results support the idea that pseudoconditioning may actually be a form of ordinary learning.[5]

Unfortunately the amount of experimentation on pseudoconditioning is very small. It seems quite likely that paucity of evidence is directly traceable to the connotations of the prefix *pseudo*, and that research on

---

[5] The experiments of Grant and Dittmer (1940) showing generalization of the pseudoconditioned reflex and Switzer (1933) demonstrating disinhibition suggest a similar interpretation.

an important problem has been inhibited on grounds that are merely semantic.

3. *Inhibition of the UCR by Double Stimulation.* Although the normal effect of pairing the CS and UCS is to produce conditioning, the procedure is known to have two others: 1) a suppression of the response to the UCS and 2) sensitization of the response to the CS. This section is concerned with the first of these influences; the next section is concerned with the second. Figure 3.11 presents a set of records from an eyelid

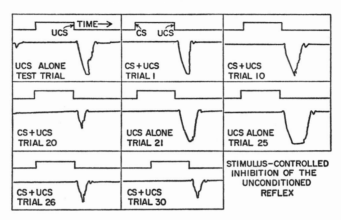

FIGURE 3.11. A selection of response records showing the inhibition of the unconditioned reflex on trials with the CS and recovery on trials without the CS. Note that no CR's occur on these trials (Kimble and Ost, 1961).

conditioning study which show this phenomenon quite clearly. In this study the CS was a light, followed in .5 second by the UCS, an air puff. During paired presentations of the two stimuli there is what appears to be an adaptation of the UCR. Removing the CS, however, restores the full magnitude of the UCR, indicating that the response diminution resulted, not from adaptation, in the sense of reflex fatigue, but from an inhibitory process under the control of the CS. The nature of this inhibition is not completely understood, having, when observed, been attributed to the interaction of reflexes (Hilgard, 1933b), personality factors (Pfaffman and Schlosberg, 1936), and Pavlovian inhibition of delay (Kimble and Ost, 1961).

Sensitization

The augmentation of the response to the conditioned stimulus through a conditioning procedure is called *sensitization* or *alpha conditioning* (Hull, 1934) because the so-called alpha response is the one involved.

Such conditioning was detected in conditioning the knee jerk by Wendt (1930), in conditioning the eyelid reflex by Hilgard (1931) and Bernstein (1934), and in conditioning a startle response in rats by Prosser and Hunter (1936). In the Prosser and Hunter experiment, auditory stimuli just too weak to elicit startle responses were paired with an electric shock. This procedure increased excitability to the point where the startle reaction was elicited by the previously ineffective sound. It seems unlikely that this was a true conditioned response because its latency was the same as the latency exhibited with more intense sounds. In a later experiment, Hunter (1937) showed that true conditioned startle reactions differed in latency and other characteristics from the unconditioned reaction.

Subsequent work on sensitization has most often involved the conditioned eyelid reflex. Hilgard and Biel (1937) reported that they were unable to obtain the effect. However, two later studies were successful. In one of these, Weber and Wendt (1942) obtained alpha conditioning as an incidental result in a study concerned with a comparison of different unconditioned stimuli. More substantial evidence for the reality of the process comes from a study of Grant and J. K. Adams (1944) designed specifically to demonstrate the phenomenon. In this study the percentages of alpha responses were compared under two different conditions. One was a regular conditioning procedure in which a CS (light) and UCS (air puff) were paired for 50 trials. The other was an adaptation procedure consisting of 50 presentations of the CS alone. In the conditioning procedure, alpha responses occurred on about 45 per cent of the trials. The comparable percentage under the adaptation procedure was about 16 per cent. The frequency of the occurrence of the alpha response increased rapidly during the first few reinforced trials and then showed a slight tendency to decline.

INSTRUMENTAL CONDITIONED RESPONSES

The classical Pavlovian training procedures described in the previous section do not exhaust the methods of establishing simple learned responses. We turn now to a presentation of several other methods which have also come to be called conditioning. These training methods, derived from the work of Bekhterev and Thorndike, differ from the classical Pavlovian procedures in that the subject's behavior is instrumental to the production of reward or avoidance of punishment. Hence the name *instrumental conditioning.*

Twofold classifications of learning corresponding roughly to the distinction between classical and instrumental conditioning have been proposed by other writers. Table 4 presents the terminology suggested by several of them.

These classifications are purely operational ones and describe training methods rather than underlying processes. Where the distinction is made, however, the reason for it often lies in a belief that the two kinds of learning obey different laws. Of these the two commonest are: (1) that classical conditioning is basically a process of association by contiguity, whereas instrumental conditioning is under the control of the law of effect, and/or (2) that classical conditioning operates mainly on responses of the auto-

TABLE 4

TWOFOLD CLASSIFICATIONS OF LEARNING PROPOSED BY DIFFERENT AUTHORS

Author(s)	Term for Classical Conditioning	Term for Instrumental Conditioning
Thorndike (1911)	Associative shifting	Trial-and-error learning
Miller and Konorski (1928); Konorski and Miller (1937a, 1937b)	Type I	Type II
Skinner (1937)	Type S, or Respondent	Type R, or Operant
Schlosberg (1937)	Conditioning	Success learning
Hilgard and Marquis (1940)	Classical conditioning	Instrumental conditioning
Mowrer (1947)	Conditioning	Problem solving

nomic nervous system, whereas instrumental conditioning is limited to nonautonomic reactions. A detailed discussion of such interpretations is reserved for the next chapter.

Procedural Variations

Distinctions among a variety of instrumental conditioning procedures to be presented in this section turn upon what is basically Thorndike's distinction between satisfiers and annoyers, or in contemporary terminology, *positive and negative reinforcers*: "By a satisfying state of affairs [positive reinforcer] is meant one which the animal does nothing to avoid, often doing such things as attain and preserve it. By a discomforting or annoying state of affairs [negative reinforcer] is meant one which the animal commonly avoids and abandons." (Thorndike, 1911, p. 245). This statement shows that the term *reinforcement* and its various derivatives may have a purely operational and essentially factual meaning. It also leads to the identification, on logical grounds, of four possible instrumental conditioning procedures, in which the response under observation produces or avoids a positive or negative reinforcer. This classification of instrumental training procedures was proposed by Konorski (1948) and overlaps in some degree that of Hilgard and Marquis (1940).

Reward Training

Instrumental reward training has been studied extensively for many years in many different animals and with various responses. It is the same as that described by Lloyd-Morgan in 1894 and designated a few years later by Thorndike (1898) as "trial, error, and accidental success." Thorndike carried out a series of experiments in which cats were trained to escape from problem boxes to secure food outside. The boxes were constructed with sides of vertical slats so that the food was visible to the cat. A door in the box opened as soon as the cat performed a certain movement, such as pulling a string hanging from the top, or pressing a latch. A hungry cat when first placed in such a box shows a continued but variable activity, reaching between the slats toward the food, scratching at the sides, moving all about the box. In the course of this activity the cat eventually hits the release mechanism and immediately secures the food. The first successful response appears to be largely a matter of chance. On successive trials the cat's activity becomes concentrated in the region of the release mechanism and other activities gradually drop out until eventually the animal performs the correct act as soon as it is placed in the box.

In more recent years, psychologists have introduced reward-training procedures designed to further the investigation of less complicated behavior. The most common of these have been the T-maze, the straight runway (Graham and Gagné, 1940), and the Skinner box (Figure 3.12), in

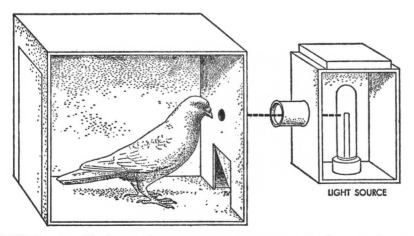

FIGURE 3.12.   The key-pecking apparatus for pigeons. In the typical experiment the pigeon is reinforced for pecking the key when it is illuminated. Placing filters or a monochromator between the light source and the key makes it possible to vary the intensity and hue of the light falling upon the translucent key. The sketch is adapted from one published by Guttman and Kalish (1958).

which an animal, usually a rat or a pigeon, learns to operate a device of some sort to obtain food. In each of them the subject receives food for performing the correct response.

The conception of instrumental act must not be understood too narrowly. In the illustrations which have been given, the subject produces the reward in some mechanical fashion, either by bringing itself into the presence of the reward through its own movements, or by bringing the reward to itself through some release mechanism. However, the act which precedes the reward need not be mechanically related to the delivery of the reward, but instead may be purely arbitrary. For example, in one experiment Thorndike taught the cat to lick itself in order to be released from the cage. Training the dog to "shake hands" by rewarding is another illustration of an arbitrary act of this sort. The only essential aspect of instrumental training is that the reward follows the response in some systematic fashion.

Most reward-training experiments proceed in a series of discrete trials, with a signal, such as raising the door in a runway, marking the beginning of a trial. Skinner's procedures, however, do not employ trials, but rather a free-responding situation. When the rat or pigeon makes the appropriate response it is immediately free to make the same response again. Because of this training method, the progress of learning is measured in terms of *rate* of responding, that is, the number of responses per unit of time.

Avoidance Training

In the usual form of the avoidance-training experiment, the subject, by responding to a signal, prevents the appearance of a noxious stimulus. The reference experiment is the classical one by Bekhterev on conditioned-withdrawal responses of hand or foot, in which the responding member rested on the electrode, and electric shock could be avoided by the performance of the conditioned response. If the electrodes are attached to the subject and the shock is delivered on every trial, the experiment is changed to a classical conditioning one. The majority of recent avoidance-learning experiments have been with lower animals. Some of the common responses investigated in such procedures are lever pressing, wheel turning, and hurdle jumping.

As is true of reward training, most of the studies of avoidance training use trial-by-trial procedures. Sidman, however, has carried out a series of investigations of avoidance training in a free-responding situation (Sidman, 1953a, 1953b). In Sidman's work, rats are used as subjects in a modified Skinner situation. At a fixed interval, such as every 20 seconds, the rat is shocked unless it presses a bar in the interval. If it does, the shock is postponed and, therefore, avoided for a certain amount of time, say 10 seconds. Under these conditions rats develop high rates of responding. Note especially that no discrete exteroceptive warning signal is used in this method.

Another procedure, employing no definite warning signal, closely related to avoidance training, and seemingly a subvariety of it, is *escape training*. In this method the instrumental response turns off a noxious stimulus. This type of training procedure has not been widely used in laboratory conditioning experiments, although numerous examples are found in the learning of animals in their natural environments. An experiment reported by Mowrer (1940) may serve as the paradigm of instrumental escape training. A rat was placed in a box with a metal grille floor through which an electric shock could be administered. The shock was gradually increased during 2.25 minutes from zero to a stable intense value. At one end of the box was a pedal arrangement which would turn off the shock whenever pushed. The shock remained off as long as the pedal was depressed, but when the pedal was released the shock would automatically start to build up again.

Rats in this situation began to show agitated behavior about 60 seconds after the beginning of the shock. As the shock became more intense they engaged in vigorous undirected activity characterized by jumping, running, squealing, biting at the grille, and random thrashing about. In the course of this activity the rat always chanced to hit the pedal and thus terminated the shock. The pedal response on the first trial occurred only after from 3 to 6 minutes of activity, but by the tenth trial the rats pressed the pedal as soon as they began to feel the shock. The obvious difference between this and the more usual avoidance-training situation is that the warning signal and the unconditioned noxious stimulus are in the same modality. In this example, weak values of shock serve as the signal to which the rat can respond and avoid the stronger shocks to come. In other escape-training procedures, the shock is turned on full-force at the beginning of a trial, and the subject must learn to respond quickly to it (Sheffield and Temmer, 1950).

Omission Training [6]

Reward and avoidance training are the forms of instrumental conditioning most frequently used in the laboratory. Probably this is because they represent a parallel to the majority of real-life learning situations in which the organism performs in order to receive some positive reinforcement or to escape from or avoid some negative reinforcement. At the same time, somewhat less frequent everyday situations, and logic, both suggest two other instrumental training procedures. In the first of these

[6] F. D. Sheffield (personal communication) suggested this name for the procedure.

a specified response would lead to the nonoccurrence of a positive reinforcer; in the second, it would lead to the occurrence of a negative reinforcer. The first of these situations is roughly the same as that in which the parent withholds privileges for undesirable behavior. We have decided to call it *omission training*. The second procedure is essentially the punishment situation, and we have called it punishment training. The only extended discussion of these methods available in English seems to be that of Konorski (1948, Chap. 12).

Omission training is a procedure in which a positive reinforcer occurs if the organism *fails* to make some particular response; that is, if the specified response occurs, reinforcement is omitted. In this respect it differs from the extinction procedure in which reinforcement never occurs. Konorski (1948) describes this method and its outcome in a series of experiments carried out on dogs. A given stimulus, such as a metronome, is first paired with food and a classical CR formed to it. Then, occasionally, the metronome is set in motion, and at the same time, the dog's leg is passively flexed. On such trials food is *omitted;* on other trials

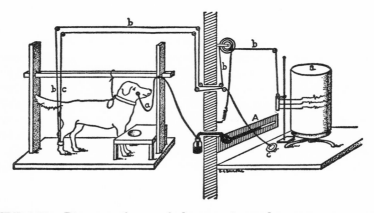

FIGURE 3.13. Diagram of one of the experimental arrangements used by Konorski and S. Miller in Pavlov's laboratory. *a*—system to measure salivation; *b*—system to measure flexion of the dog's leg; *c*—system to produce passive flexion. From Razran (1939d).

the metronome continues to be reinforced with food. Under this training procedure (see Figure 3.13) Konorski reports that:

We shall soon find that the raising of the leg becomes a conditioned inhibitor, i.e., when applied concurrently with the metronome it inhibits the secretion of saliva to this stimulus. But in addition, more or less at the same time, the animal begins to resist the passive flexion of the leg by actively extending it. After a time the animal performs an active movement of extension to the metronome itself. . . . Finally the movement of extension becomes so strong that we are almost able to raise the animal into the air by its extended limb. . . . (Konorski, 1948, p. 226-227).

The important thing about this observation is that it shows that nonreinforcement does not lead merely to a failure of the CR to develop but rather to the strengthening of an antagonistic response.

In passing, it should be mentioned that Konorski's work represents one of the very few research programs in which an investigator has studied classical and instrumental responses established simultaneously in the same situation. The importance of this is that it provides a way of studying the possibility, held by many theorists, that classical conditioning provides the basis upon which instrumentally conditioned responses are developed. If this were the case one would expect the two forms of conditioning to respond to various experimental treatments in roughly parallel ways. Such results as can be gleaned from Konorski's report support such a view.

Punishment Training

This procedure consists in making the occurrence of some noxious stimulus, such as electric shock or the introduction of a mild acid solution into the mouth, contingent upon the occurrence of a specified response. It should be noted carefully that this procedure is different from (and essentially the opposite of) avoidance training, in which the painful stimulus occurs only if the to-be-learned response fails to occur. Moreover, in the avoidance-training situation, the noxious stimulus, if it occurs at all, is administered *before* the response. In punishment training the noxious stimulus occurs after it. Konorski reports one such method, in which the procedure parallels that described above as omission training. In these experiments, mechanical flexion of a limb, in the presence of a CS, is reinforced (punished) with acid. Under these circumstances, the dog again learns an antagonistic extensor response. It is a matter of some interest that responses leading to the production of a negative reinforcer are influenced in exactly the same way as those which lead to the omission of a positive one; and, conversely, responses leading to the avoidance of a negative reinforcer behave like those leading to the production of a positive one.

The more common experiments on punishment differ from Konorski's in the behavior investigated. The usual experiment is concerned with the use of punishment as an adjunct to an extinction procedure. The main interest is in the speed with which some response is abandoned, rather than in the development of antagonistic behavior. For this reason the American literature contains very few, if any, experimental demonstrations which parallel Konorski's.

Organisms Which Have Been Conditioned

As with classical conditioning, a question of great interest in the early history of instrumental conditioning involved the phylogenetic range over which the process occurs. Efforts to condition one-celled organisms have usually employed instrumental conditioning procedures and have produced contradictory results. Beatrice Gelber[7] attempted to obtain conditioning in the paramecium in the following manner: She dipped a platinum wire, which had been swabbed with a fluid containing bacteria upon which the paramecia feed, into a culture of paramecia for a series of 40 trials. She found that the number of paramecia congregating near the wire increased steadily as a result of such training, and attributed this outcome to conditioning. The CS, in such an interpretation, is the stimulation provided by the wire; the UCS is food, and both the CR and UCR are instrumental responses which bring the animals near to the wire. The evidence for conditioning is the increasing number of subjects collecting in the region of the platinum wire. Both Jensen (1957) and Katz and Deterline (1958), however, have argued that Gelber's procedure may have increased the bacterial concentration in the vicinity of the wire and that the paramecia may only have been gathering in bacteria-rich areas. These investigators have also presented data to show that such an interpretation is possible. Control colonies into which food was introduced without the training series behaved in ways indistinguishable from those subjected to the conditioning procedure. Such evidence leads to a rejection of Gelber's conclusion that her procedure produces conditioning. It is possible, of course, that some other method might.

There is, in fact, some evidence that even paramecia can learn; but rather than consisting of the formation of new association, it involves the inhibition of unnecessary responses. French (1940), for example, observed the behavior of paramecia in learning to escape from a glass tube .6 mm. in diameter to get to a culture medium. Half of his subjects showed a significant improvement in performance in terms of time required to reach the culture medium. Moreover, French noted specifically that this improvement resulted from the elimination of extraneous responses which occurred early in the test series.

Most if not all of the successful experiments employing one-celled animals have produced this form of learning, rather than the formation of a new association (Warden, Jenkins, and Warner, 1940). Even at slightly higher phylogenetic levels learning seems to be of the same sort. Fleure and Walton (1907) reported an experiment on the sea-anemone in which pieces of filter paper were placed on certain tentacles at 24-hour intervals. At first the tentacles grasped the filter paper and carried it to the mouth where it was swallowed and, later, rejected. After two to five

[7] Gelber (1952, 1954, 1956a, 1956b), Gelber and Rasch (1956).

trials, however, the paper was rejected by the animals and the tentacles so trained failed to grasp the paper at all. Again note that the response is an inhibitory one and that the conditioning procedure is instrumental.

As with classical conditioning, studies employing animals phylogenetically higher than the very simplest have usually been successful. Description of instrumental learning in a great range of species may be found in any book on comparative psychology.

The Nature of Conditioned Instrumental Responses

Instrumentally conditioned reactions are usually specified in terms of their consequences. All reactions which depress the bar in the Skinner box, turn the wheel a certain distance in the wheel-turning apparatus, or close the electrical contact in the key-pecking situation qualify as responses, no matter how much they may differ in detail. At least up to the present time, the researcher in instrumental conditioning has not been forced to concern himself with the description of the exact form of the CR in the way which has been found to be necessary in eyelid conditioning.

Since in all types of instrumental learning the response which is learned must occur before it can be reinforced, the response is obviously already in the behavior repertory of the subject; and the learning process consists only in strengthening the response so that it occurs promptly and with dependable frequency in the presence of the conditioned stimulus. One concept appropriate to the description of instrumental conditioning in such terms is Hull's (1934a) concept of *habit-family hierarchy*. The organism, at the outset of training in the instrumental-conditioning situation, has at its disposal a variety of responses (*habit-family*) which vary in strength, or form a *hierarchy*. Since it is a learning situation, the dominant response is, by definition, incorrect, and instrumental conditioning consists of a reordering of the strengths of the various responses in the habit-family hierarchy.

An obvious question concerns the origin of the responses in the habit-family hierarchy, since they are released independently of identifiable external stimuli. For this reason Skinner (1938) refers to them as *emitted* acts, or as *operants,* to distinguish them from *elicited* reactions or *respondents,* evoked by recognized stimuli. They are not, however, entirely random as the trial-and-error theorists have sometimes implied. The cats in Thorndike's puzzle box spent much time on the first trial reaching through the slats toward the food, and the rats in Skinner's situation explored the corners and projecting portions of the box. In some cases, these reactions seem to be native responses to stimulation. In others they are reactions to drive or result from previous training.

Responses Determined by the Drive

Often the problem situation is characterized by the presence of a drive which increases the restless behavior. Since drives have been associated in the animal's past with certain acts leading to reward, the responses likely to appear in a new experimental situation may include those which have occurred previously while the particular drive was active. Several experiments have demonstrated that animals can discriminate among their own drives, that a drive may be a conditioned stimulus evoking specific behavior (Hull, 1933; Leeper, 1935).

Generalized Responses to External Stimuli

When an organism is in a novel situation, it reacts to features of the environment bearing some marks of familiarity. In conditioning terms this is an example of stimulus generalization; that is, previously conditioned responses are evoked by stimuli similar to the original learning situation. A rat which has secured food by digging in one box with a sawdust floor is more likely to begin digging when in a new box with a sawdust floor than is an animal without this previous experience.

Special Training

The appropriate response in instrumental learning may be encouraged in many artificial ways, depending upon the ingenuity of the experimenter or animal trainer. The response may be suggested by passive movement. This is common practice in animal training, as in teaching a dog to "shake hands." Or the leg movement which is rewarded may be originally produced by shock to the foot. Lever pressing is sometimes enhanced by placing a bit of food on the lever to direct the animal's exploratory activity to that region. String-pulling behavior is facilitated by smearing food on the string, jiggling the string, and so on (T. L. McCulloch, 1934). The experiment proper consists in the strengthening of the response after it has once appeared. This is an important difference from Pavlov's experiment. The difference is illustrated by the question: How many trials are needed before the first conditioned response appears? This may be asked with respect to Pavlov's experiment, but is meaningless with respect to instrumental training in which the conditioned response must always occur before the first trial is completed.

SUMMARY

It is possible to distinguish between two forms of conditioning experiment, called classical and instrumental conditioning, by considering whether reinforcement is contingent upon the occurrence of the conditioned response. In classical conditioning the unconditioned stimulus occurs whether or not a conditioned response occurs. In instrumental conditioning, by contrast, the conditioned response must occur if reward is to be obtained or punishment avoided.

Classical Conditioning

The reference experiment in classical conditioning is the one with dogs, in which a neutral stimulus, such as the sound of a tuning fork, was presented a few seconds before food. After several such pairings, the dog began to salivate to the sound of the tuning fork. In such experiments, the neutral stimulus (tuning fork) is the conditioned stimulus (CS). The originally effective stimulus (food) is the unconditioned stimulus (UCS). The original response (salivation) to the UCS is the unconditioned response (UCR). And the new response (also salivation) to the CS is the conditioned response (CR).

Varieties of classical conditioning procedure are defined in terms of the relationship between CS and UCS. Those in which the CS precedes the UCS are called forward-conditioning procedures. If the UCS precedes the CS, the experiment involves backward conditioning, a method which is very ineffective in the production of conditioned responses. Thus most experiments employ the forward-conditioning arrangement. Within the category, forward conditioning, there are two subvarieties, delayed conditioning and trace conditioning. In delayed conditioning the CS comes on before the UCS and continues at least until the onset of the UCS. In trace conditioning the CS comes on, only momentarily, some time prior to the UCS. Conditioned responses, in trace conditioning, occur in the absence of the CS, perhaps to a "memory" trace of it. A final classical conditioning procedure, temporal conditioning, involves the presentation of the UCS on a fixed time schedule, such as every 30 seconds. In these experiments there is no CS, unless the time interval is considered to be one.

The variety of responses, organisms, and stimuli successfully used in classical conditioning studies has been very great. Such learning apparently can occur prior to birth and in a range of organisms extending from at least the level of the flatworm to man. Stimuli employed have included exteroceptive stimulation in most, if not all, modalities, as well as interoceptive stimuli applied to the internal organs and directly to the nervous system. The variety of responses studied in what have been called classical conditioning experiments is also very great. We should reserve judgment, however, as to whether the procedures in these experiments have all been truly classical conditioning.

Although the conditioned and unconditioned response are usually similar in classical conditioning, it is a mistake to think of them as exactly the same, or to imagine that the conditioned response is simply the UCR transferred to the CS. There are always differences in at least the quantitative characteristics of the reaction. Because of this fact various views of the nature of the conditioned response have been set forth. These include the proposals that the CR is (a) a fractional component of the UCR and (b) a preparation for the occurrence of the UCR.

Particularly in eyelid conditioning, in which the blink reflex is conditioned, much work has been done on the form of the responses which occur in the conditioning experiment and on the ways in which the response can be altered through means which are not essentially conditioning. Among the different responses observed in such an experiment there are, in addition to the UCR and CR, unconditioned reflexes elicited by the CS, ''beta'' responses to light sensitized by dark adaptation, random blinks, and voluntary responses. These must be identified and excluded from the conditioning measure. Other processes which take place in the course of conditioning also complicate things. These include (a) adaptation of the response to the UCS, a phenomenon occurring at the receptor or reflex level, (b) a stimulus-controlled inhibition which resembles adaptation but is not, (c) pseudoconditioning, in which applications of the UCS alone produce responses like conditioned responses, and (d) sensitization, or alpha conditioning, which results in an augmentation of the unconditioned response to the CS. It is quite apparent that the seemingly simple conditioned reflex experiment actually contains features of great complexity.

Instrumental Conditioning

The instrumental conditioning procedure has been known to animal trainers for centuries and has been used in the laboratory since the 1890's. In this procedure what the animal does in the situation determines what happens to it; technically, there is a response-reward contingency. In general, the arrangement is that some specific response leads to the presentation or omission of reward or punishment. Instrumental conditioning comprises four different procedures which we have called reward training, avoidance training, omission training, and punishment training. Of these the first two are most commonly used in the laboratory.

1. *Reward Training.* In this procedure, the performance of some response leads to a goal object for which the subject is motivated. With lower animals the responses required have involved running mazes, pressing panels and levers, (in the case of birds) pecking at illuminated disks, pulling strings, and jumping across gaps in a runway.

2. *Avoidance Training.* In this procedure the correct response, if performed promptly after a warning signal, prevents the occurrence of some noxious stimulus such as electric shock, so that the subject avoids it. In a

subvariety of avoidance training, called *escape training,* the warning signal is omitted and the subject must respond quickly to the presentation of the painful stimulus to avoid its continuation.

3. *Omission Training.* In a few experiments, the procedure has been to omit reward when a particular response occurs. Under these conditions the subject develops a tendency which is antagonistic to the response leading to the omission of reward. Unfortunately there have been very few experiments on this kind of learning.

4. *Punishment Training.* In another form of experiment which has not been studied much, the occurrence of some specified response leads to the application of some unpleasant stimulus. As in omission training the subject develops an active antagonism to making the response in question.

As with classical conditioning, instrumental learning occurs in a wide range of species. In fact, one-celled animals seem to be capable of a form of instrumental learning by which they acquire an inhibition of unnecessary movements. The range of responses and stimuli employed in studies of instrumental learning is also at least as great in classical conditioning.

In instrumental learning the response to be conditioned must occur before it can be rewarded or punished. Therefore this response must have been in the animals' behavioral repertory prior to the experiment. The source of such responses has not been a matter of primary interest to students of instrumental conditioning, but several possibilities have been suggested. These have included (*a*) innate or previously learned responses to drive, and (*b*) responses generalized from previous learning because of similarities between the two situations. In many experimental studies special training has been used to evoke the first few responses.

·4·

Classical and Instrumental Conditioning Compared

THE ORIGINAL DISTINCTION between instrumental and classical conditioning is made on purely operational grounds. The two designations refer respectively to training procedures in which the response of the subject does and does not determine whether the UCS appears. With this distinction established, the question naturally arises as to whether the two procedures also lead to different forms of learning. An adequate answer to this question requires that classical and instrumental conditioning be separately examined to determine basic differences and similarities. This is a research program which is simple in conception, but extraordinarily difficult to carry out. Some of the problems are these:

1. It is impossible, on logical grounds, to perform an instrumental conditioning experiment without also arranging the conditions for a classical conditioning one. To obtain instrumental conditioning it is essential to reinforce a subject for performing some act. Obviously this reinforcement must occur in some situation. Thus the situational cues are conditioned stimuli regularly associated with reinforcement, after the manner of classical conditioning. The importance of the classical conditioning accompaniments of instrumental learning has been clearly recognized by learning theorists and given formal status in such conceptions as secondary reinforcement, secondary drive, and incentive motivation. But it should be recognized that these processes complicate the problem of separating classical and instrumental conditioning in order to compare their properties.

2. It is also difficult, if not impossible, to perform a completely pure classical conditioning experiment, with the result that the classically conditioned CR may contain instrumental components. For one thing, in an entirely quantitative way, the appearance of an anticipatory CR often has an effect upon the UCS. In the Pavlovian experiment, the anticipatory salivary response no doubt changes the taste of the food when it is used as a UCS and dilutes the acid when it is the reinforcement. Similarly, in

eyelid conditioning, an anticipatory blink partially avoids the air puff and diminishes its intensity. A rather different complication is depicted by Zener's description (p. 54) of the "expectant" behavior of the dogs in his salivary conditioning study and by Pavlov's account of the investigatory, orienting behavior commonly evoked by the CS. Such behavior, quite clearly, is of an instrumental sort and is probably modified instrumentally during the course of conditioning. This, again, means that the CR obtained in the classical conditioning situation may be modified by a concomitant instrumental response.

3. It is difficult to insure the occurrence of the same responses under the two procedures when experimental attempts are made to compare classical and instrumental conditioning. A series of such comparisons has appeared in the literature, using an unavoidable noxious stimulus as the reinforcement in the classical situation and an avoidable one in the instrumental parallel. In some cases, the results have been very similar, whether or not the conditioned response prevents the shock (Schlosberg, 1934, 1936; Hilden, 1937; Munn, 1939). In other cases there has been a distinct difference, most often in favor of the instrumental procedure (W. S. Hunter, 1935a; Whatmore, Morgan, and Kleitman, 1946). The best-known study in this latter category is that of Brogden, Lipman, and Culler (1938). A guinea pig was placed in a revolving cage and, after a conditioned stimulus (buzzer), it was given a shock designed to evoke running behavior. One group of animals, trained according to the classical procedure, were shocked whether they ran or not. Another group, subjected to the method of instrumental avoidance training, were not shocked if they ran. Learning began similarly in both groups, but it reached a much higher level of performance in the second group. The results are plotted in Figure 4.1. Guinea pigs which were shocked whether or not they ran *continued to show anticipatory agitation at the sound of the buzzer,* but after the first few trials the tendency to run did not increase; those shocked only if they did not run developed the habit of running promptly at the sound of the buzzer. This study, superficially considered, seems to show that avoidance conditioning is superior to its classical counterpart. Sheffield (1948), however, was quick to point out that such an interpretation is unwarranted, for the onset of shock in the classical situation might occur while the animal was running, thus punishing the animal for the response to be learned. Under these conditions, the subject might perform and learn responses other than running in the nonavoidable-shock situation. Sheffield repeated the Brogden, Lipman, and Culler experiment, keeping detailed records of what the animal was doing when the shock came on. His general results were essentially the same as those of the original experiment, but detailed analysis of the records showed that the animals in the nonavoidable-shock condition sometimes ran and sometimes stopped running when the shock came on. Moreover, the be-

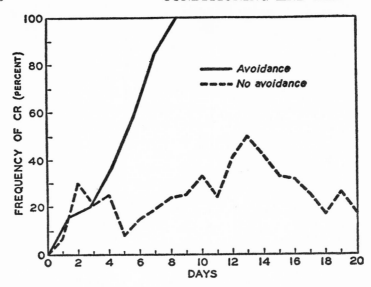

FIGURE 4.1. Comparison of performance under classical (no avoidance) and instrumental (avoidance) conditions. The solid line represents the frequency of conditioned responses (running) of 4 guinea pigs during the two seconds that a buzzer sounds, when running prevents the appearance of a shock which occurs on those trials in which the animal does not run. The broken line represents the corresponding values for another group of 4 animals when the buzzer is invariably followed by shock whether or not the animal runs. Data from Brogden, Lipman, and Culler (1938).

havior incompatible with running tended to be repeated on succeeding trials. The animals in the avoidable-shock condition more uniformly learned to run in response to shock. Thus the animals under the two conditions learned different things, and comparison with a measure which reflects only one of the possible responses cannot reveal the relative effectivenesses of the classical and instrumental training procedures. Brogden, Lipman, and Culler's observation that subjects conditioned by the classical procedure continued to show agitated behavior in the presence of the CS, whereas those in the instrumental procedure did not, is important in the same connection. It sounds very much as if an emotional response were actually *better* conditioned under the classical procedure than under the instrumental one.

That classical conditioning may lead to better conditioning of at least some responses is supported by the results of two studies of the conditioned eyelid reflex (Logan, 1951; Kimble, Mann, and Dufort, 1955). In both of these experiments classical eyelid conditioning was compared with an instrumental procedure in which a blink in the CS-UCS interval avoided the UCS (shock or air puff). The results were exactly the same in the two studies. The classical procedure was very much superior to the instrumental one. The results of one comparison appear in Figure 4.2.

SOME SIMILARITIES BETWEEN CLASSICAL AND INSTRUMENTAL CONDITIONING

An extreme position never actually held, [although Mowrer's (1960) new theory comes close to it], might be that classical and instrumental conditioning are basically so different that it is a mistake to use the same term *conditioning* to describe them. Presumably the reason that

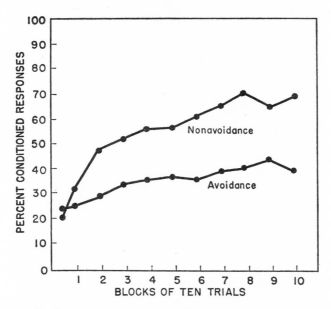

FIGURE 4.2. Performance in eyelid conditioning under conditions where the CR does and does not prevent the occurrence of the UCS (Logan, 1951).

no theorist has proposed so bold a view is that, whatever their differences, classical and instrumental conditioning have many properties in common. These similarities are to be found in the fact that both forms of learning display certain common basic phenomena. These will be described briefly in this section.

Actually this section is intended to serve two rather different purposes. *First,* it will present for the first time a set of fundamental learning processes which will be discussed in detail later. The advantage of this procedure is that many of these processes must be discussed incidentally, in other connections, prior to a detailed treatment. The following presentation will make it possible to assume an acquaintance with these topics in such later discussion. *Second,* this presentation will provide a documentation of the point that classical and instrumental conditioning are similar in many ways. The plan of the section is to present, wherever necessary and possible, two examples of each phenomenon discussed, one from classical conditioning and one from instrumental.

1. *Acquisition.* The first two phenomena to be described require no specific experimental examples, since they will be familiar to everyone. Acquisition is the basic process assumed to operate in learning studies. It is reflected in changes in several different response measures, the most common of which are the following: (*a*) *probability of occurrence,* expressed as the percentage of trials on which a given subject produces a CR, or the percentage of subjects giving a CR on a given trial; (*b*) *latency,* the time between the presentation of a signal and the occurrence of a CR; (*c*) *response speed,* the reciprocal of some time measure such as latency; (*d*) *rate of responding,* the number of CR's produced in some standard period of time; (*e*) *response magnitude;* some measure which reflects the vigor of a response on trials when it occurs, and (*f*) *resistance to extinction.* Occasional investigators have given different groups of subjects different numbers of acquisition trials and then have employed the number of unreinforced responses which occurred before the attainment of some criterion of extinction in each group as a measure of the strength of conditioning. Almost any of these measures will reflect the process of acquisition, at least under certain circumstances.

2. *Extinction.* Experimental extinction, as Pavlov called it, or more briefly, extinction, refers to the decrease of response strength with nonreinforcement. Again no specific experimental documentation seems necessary. It is a process with which everyone is familiar, in both classical conditioning and experimental conditioning. A longer discussion of the topic appears in Chapter 10.

3. *Spontaneous Recovery.* A response which has been extinguished recovers some of its strength with rest. Pavlov (1927), for example, describes an experiment in which a series of 7 extinction trials reduced the number of drops of saliva secreted to the CS from 10 to 3. As another measure of extinction, the latency of the response increased from 3 to 13 seconds. Twenty-three minutes later the salivary secretion on the first test with the CS was 6 drops; the latency was 5 seconds. Both measures show a spontaneous recovery of response strength during the 23-minute rest.

In the instrumental conditioning situation, Ellson's (1938) investigation will serve as a reference experiment. He trained rats to press the bar in a Skinner box for a food reward, extinguished this response, and after various periods of time tested the rats for spontaneous recovery, obtaining the results shown in Figure 4.3. Apparently the process of spontaneous recovery follows a time course. On the basis of statements of

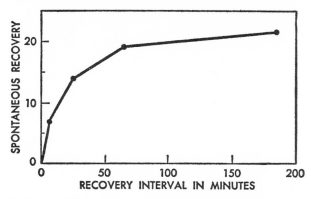

FIGURE 4.3. Spontaneous recovery of the bar-pressing reaction as a function of time since the end of the extinction series (Ellson, 1938).

Pavlov, it seems very likely that the precise nature of this function depends upon the original strength of the CR, the number of extinction trials, and the number of times the response has been extinguished and reconditioned. Again a more extensive discussion appears in Chapter 10.

4. *External Inhibition.* During the process of acquisition, a conditioned response is easily influenced by any alteration of the conditioning procedure. Any new stimulus presented along with the CS, for example, tends to reduce the strength of the CR. Pavlov referred to this reduction as external inhibition and to the new stimulus as an *external inhibitor.* Evans (1925) describes an experiment in which the CS was a visual one and the external inhibitor was the playing of a gramaphone "for a few seconds." The results are expressed in terms which assign the uninhibited CR a value of 100 per cent. They appear in Table 5. This table also shows that the subject may adapt to the external inhibitor with repeated presentation.

TABLE 5

EXTERNAL INHIBITION BY AN EXTRA STIMULUS

Strength of visual CR	—	—	—	—	—	—	—	—	100%
Strength of CR to visual CS plus gramophone 1st application									10%
"	" " "	"	" "	"	2nd "				50%
"	" " "	"	" "	"	3rd "				65%
"	" " "	"	" "	"	4th "				85%
"	" " "	"	" "	"	5th "				90%
"	" " "	"	" "	"	6th "				94%
"	" " "	"	" "	"	7th "				100%

Winnick and Hunt (1951) report a study of external inhibition in the Graham-Gagné runway. Different groups of rats received the sound

of a buzzer as an external inhibitor just before raising the door (CS) to
begin Trial 4, 8, 12, or 14. Table 6 presents a comparison of the latencies
on these trials together with the latency on the immediately preceding
trial without a buzzer. These results show that the effect of an external
inhibitor decreases with increasing strength of the learned response. This
also happens in Pavlovian conditioning.

TABLE 6

Mean Latent Period in Seconds on Buzzer and No-Buzzer Trials

Buzzer Trial	Latency	No-Buzzer Trial	Latency	Difference
2	31.40	1	9.12	22.18
8	17.40	7	8.13	9.27
12	6.90	11	4.27	2.63
14	3.89	13	2.30	1.59

5. *Disinhibition*. In the experiment just described, Winnick and Hunt
also studied the effect of the buzzer during extinction. The four groups
which had had the buzzer presented on Trials 2, 8, 12, and 14 during
conditioning received it respectively on Trials 2, 4, 5, and 6 of extinction.
Presentation of the buzzer on Trial 2 produced a signficant *decrease* in
latency; that is, a *strengthening* of the response. On the other trials, the
extra stimulus had no discernible effect.

When Pavlov observed such a phenomenon in classical conditioning he
called it *disinhibition* or *inhibition of inhibition*. In several studies of
this phenomenon reported in the 1927 English translation, Pavlov used
natural reflexes to the sight of food. In one example, the meat powder
presented at a distance produced 11, 4, and 0 drops of saliva on 3 successive trials. In short, the salivary CR to the sight of food extinguished.
On the fourth and fifth trials, meat powder was presented again, but, on
these occasions, tactile stimulation of the skin or an auditory stimulus was
presented simultaneously. The response strength on these trials increased
to 2 drops of saliva on one trial and to 3 on another. In short, the extra
stimulus had the same effect in this experiment as the buzzer did in the
Winnick and Hunt study. Pavlov reported that applications of the unconditioned stimulus were particularly effective in disinhibiting an extinguished response, as were other stimuli capable of eliciting the UCR.
The fact that various methods could be demonstrated for restoring an
extinguished CR, without pairings of CS and UCS, led Pavlov to the
position that extinction did not consist of an "irreparable destruction
of the conditioned reflex," but that it was inhibited or, somehow, held
in check. It was for this reason that Pavlov sometimes referred to disinhibition as *inhibition of inhibition*.

6. *Inhibition of Delay*. In Pavlov's long-trace and long-delay experi-

ments the interval between the onset of the CS and the administration of the UCS was sometimes several minutes. In such cases the conditioned response, when well established, displayed a characteristic pattern. No response occurred until the CS had been on for a while, and the amount of salivation became greater as the time of presentation of the UCS came nearer. In one study the CS was a whistle of 3-minutes duration. The UCS was acid. After considerable training the number of drops of saliva occurring in each of the 30-second periods between onset of CS and the presentation of the UCS were: 0, 0, 2, 2, 3, 6.

The instrumental parallel to this pattern is to be found in the performance of subjects conditioned on a fixed-interval (periodic) schedule. In such a schedule, the subject is rewarded for the first response (for example, a bar-press or a key peck) after a specified period of time. An example of the sort of response pattern obtained under such schedules appears in Figure 4.4. This pattern has come to be called a periodic-reinforcement or fixed-interval "scallop." The similarity of this to the salivary data mentioned above is obvious.

Whether this is more than a superficial similarity depends upon whether the two processes respond in the same way to the same experimental operations. In at least one respect, they do. The extent of the period of inactivity in the fixed-interval scallop depends upon the duration of the interval. The same is true in the classically conditioned salivary response. A more important test of whether the two functions are basically the same is potentially provided in the fact that the salivary response can be disinhibited during the early parts of the period of delay. An example of this comes from an experiment in which the CS is a tactile stimulus of 3-minute duration. A representative response pattern to it for successive 30-second intervals is 0, 0, 0, 8, 10, and 11 drops of saliva. The same CS presented together with a metronome elicited 3, 2, 1, 5, 6, and 5 drops on the next trial. The effect of the metronome was to disinhibit the response during the first 1.5 minutes on this trial and to externally inhibit the CR for the last 1.5 minutes. Pavlov found that the precise effect of an extra stimulus presented this way depended upon the intensity of the added stimulus. Very weak stimuli had no effect at all. Moderately weak stimuli disinhibited the salivary response in the first part of the period of the CS. Moderately strong stimuli disinhibited salivation during the initial phase of the CS and inhibited it later, as in the example above.[1] Very strong stimuli had no effect in the initial portion of the period and produced only the later inhibitory effect. Tests for similar effects during responding on a fixed-interval schedule have not been made. This lack suggests an important area for future experimentation.

[1] Wenger (1936a) obtained a similar result with the conditioned GSR.

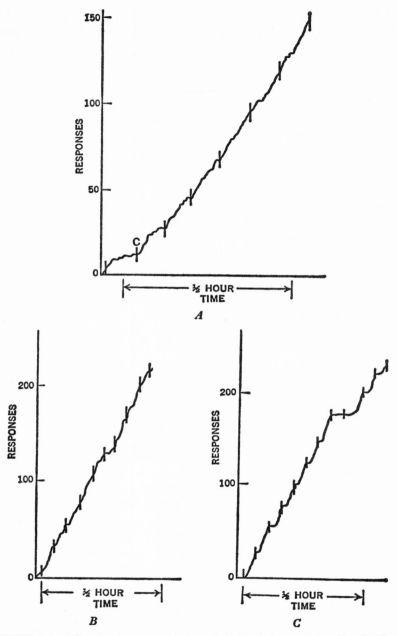

FIGURE 4.4. The development of a typical fixed interval "scallop." The interval employed was three minutes. That is, the first response to occur three minutes or more following the previous reinforcemnt was reinforced. Early in training (as in A) the actual interval between reinforcements is typically more than three minutes because the animal does not respond rapidly enough to obtain reward as soon as it is available. With increased rates of responding (as in B) rewards occur oftener, and the typical behavior is a fairly steady rate of responding, although "scalloping" occasionally occurs. Still later (as in C) a pronounced scallop may appear. (After Skinner, 1938; as presented by Keller and Schoenfeld, 1950).

7. *Summation*. When two stimuli to which the same response has been separately conditioned are presented together, the strength of the response is often greater than it is to either stimulus alone. This is called summation. The following Pavlovian example illustrates the process. One CS was the odor of oil of camphor. Presented alone it ordinarily evoked 60 drops of saliva. The other stimulus, a mild shock, ordinarily produced about 30 drops. Presented together they evoked 90 drops. Such linearity in the summation effect is not the rule. Most often the effect of the combined stimuli is less than would be predicted from simple addition of the individual response strengths.

An experiment of summation, using an instrumental procedure, was performed by Eninger (1952). He trained rats to run a T-maze for food, requiring them to take a right or a left turn at the choice point on different trials, in response to different signals. For one group the signal was visual: the subject was required to make a right turn after passing through a black maze stem and a left turn after passing through a white maze stem. For another group the right turn was correct when a tone was present, and the left turn was correct when it was not. A third (summation) group received both the visual and the auditory cues. The number of trials required for each group to attain a criterion of 90 per cent correct choices were: For the visual group, 148; for the auditory group, 234; for the summation group, 55. The marked superiority of this last group illustrates the operation of a summation effect.

8. *Stimulus Generalization*. A response conditioned to a certain stimulus tends to appear to similar stimuli to a degree which diminishes with increasing differences between the conditioned stimulus and the test stimulus. The study of Bass and Hull (1934) will provide an illustrative example using classical conditioning procedures. These investigators conditioned the GSR's of 16 college students using a vibrotactile stimulus as a CS and a brief shock as the UCS. In conditioning, the CS was applied to the shoulder or to the calf for different groups of subjects. After such conditioning all subjects received tests with the CS applied to the shoulder, back, thigh, and calf. In order to combine data for the two groups, responses when the CS was applied to the shoulder for one group were averaged with those obtained when the CS was applied to the calf for the other, these being the points of application of the CS for the two groups respectively. Similarly responses to the CS applied to the back for first group were combined with those to the CS applied to the thigh for the second group, these being one step away from the CS point for the two groups. This combining procedure makes it possible to present all of the data for the experiment in a single graph such as that in Figure 4.5. The horizontal axis represents the four test stimuli; the vertical axis is a scale of response strength in terms of average deflections of the galvanometer needle. The term *stimulus generalization* refers to the fact that the

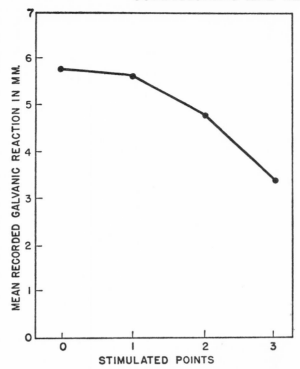

FIGURE 4.5. Stimulus-generalization gradient which shows the spread of the GSR conditioned to tactile stimulation of one point on the body to others. See text for fuller description of the experiment and manner of plotting data (M. J. Bass and Hull, 1934).

response spreads from the CS to adjacent stimuli. The function represented in the graph is often called a *generalization gradient*.

The procedures described by Guttman and Kalish (1956) will provide an illustration of generalization in an instrumental situation. In this method pigeons are trained to peck at a round key on the wall to receive food. The key is illuminated with light of a certain color. After training the birds are tested with other colors on the key, the rate of pecking providing the measure of response strength. A typical set of results appears in Figure 4.6. Obviously the results show all of the general features of similar data obtained by classical conditioning procedures.

9. *Response Generalization*. The response acquired in any conditioning experiment has a modal value determined by the exact conditions of the experiment and the capabilities of the organism. It has been pointed out, however, that an organism which has learned to respond in a certain way to stimulus A, has thereby learned also to respond in a similar way to an almost equivalent stimulus A'. The counterpart on the response side

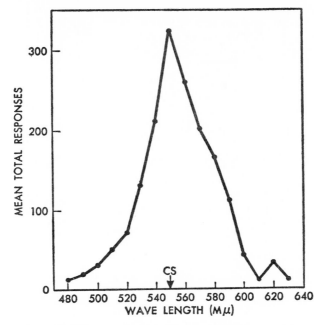

FIGURE 4.6. Generalization of response strength along a dimension of hue in the pigeon. The birds were trained to peck at a key illuminated with a light of 550 mu and tested with other lights in extinction. (Guttman and Kalish, unpublished).

is as follows: if an organism has learned to react with response B to a stimulus A, it has also learned thereby to react with a response B', which is unlike B, but in some respects equivalent to it. One illustration comes from Bekhterev (1932, p. 216) who found that a dog lifted another foot to the conditioned stimulus when the one which normally responded was fastened down. Another instance is furnished by Lashley's (1924) monkey, which quickly solved a problem of manipulation with the other hand after the hand which had always been employed previously was paralyzed due to a brain operation. Further observations of the kind suggested by Bekhterev have been reported by Kellogg (1939). Following buzzer-shock conditioning in which the shock was applied only to the right hind foot of a dog, it was found that each of the four legs occasionally responded to the buzzer. Responses in the more remote legs were less frequent than those in the shocked leg, the relative frequencies of conditioned responses being in the order right hind leg (the one shocked), left hind leg, right foreleg, left foreleg. This represents a crude gradient of response strength, corresponding somewhat to the sensory gradients previously described.

A more detailed picture of the response-generalization process requires closer inspection of the exact characteristics of the response. Such inspection always reveals quantitative variation in response strength. Figure 4.7 shows two examples of this for the Skinner box situation. The data

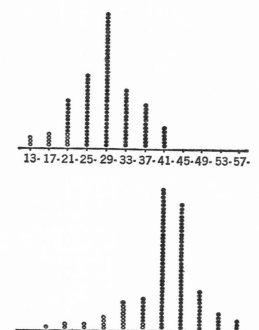

13- 17-21-25- 29- 33- 37- 41- 45-49- 53-57-

13- 17-21- 25- 29- 33- 37- 41- 45-49- 53-57-

INTENSITY OF PRESSURES IN GRAMS

FIGURE 4.7. The distribution of bar-pressures under conditions where 21 gm. of pressure (upper figure) or 38 gm. of pressure (lower figure) were required to obtain food. Note the variability in pressures (response generalization) and also the fact that the modal pressure is such as to certainly secure reinforcement (response differentiation). Data from Ruth Hays and C. B. Woodbury, presented in this form by Hull (1943).

are simply the pressures with which individual rats pressed the bar on a series of 100 responses. In one case a pressure of 21 grams was required to secure food reinforcement; in the other it was 38 grams. This difference accounts for the differences in the functions.

Figure 4.8 shows a set of similar data for the classical eyelid-conditioning situation presented by Boneau (1958). The data are distributions of CR latencies in blocks of 30 trials. Obviously the classically conditioned reaction shows the same sort of distribution on a quantitative dimension as did the instrumental response.

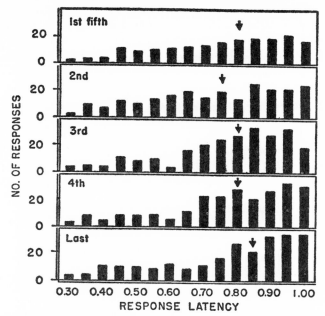

FIGURE 4.8. The distribution of response latencies in eyelid conditioning. The interval between the CS (light) and UCS (airpuff) was 1.0 second. The several panels in the graph, from upper to lower, are for fifths of the conditioning session. Note that there is considerable variability in the latencies of the various responses (response generalization). Also note the tendency for the median, indicated by the arrow, to move to the right (response differentiation) so that the blink is timed to just anticipate the onset of the UCS (Boneau, 1958).

<u>10. *Response Differentiation.*</u> In each of the previous examples the main interest was in the spread of responses or in their generalization along these quantitative dimensions. Each example, however, shows another characteristic of the responses obtained in conditioning experiments; namely, that they come to form a distribution whose central tendency is dictated by the requirements of the situation. Note that the distributions of pressures in Figure 4.7 are such as to insure that the subject receives reinforcement on most trials. Similarly, the median latency of the blink changes with practice so that it just anticipates the onset of the air puff. Pavlov reports a similar phenomenon for long-trace salivary conditioning. This phenomenon is sometimes referred to as *response differentiation.*

The most extensive discussions of response differentiation have been those of Skinner and his associates (Skinner, 1938; Ferster and Skinner, 1957) who report studies in which restricted values of intensity, duration, and rates were reinforced. These investigators find that rats and pigeons are capable of learning to modify these quantitative features of their behavior in order to maximize the probability of receiving reinforcement.

11. *Generalization of Extinction.* In the Bass and Hull study previously described to illustrate stimulus generalization, a second procedure was employed to show the operation of a different phenomenon. The conditioned response was first established at all of the four reinforcement points (shoulder, back, thigh, and calf) so that the magnitude of the response was approximately the same at all points. Then one of the extreme points (shoulder for one group, thigh for another) was subjected to extinction. Following this all points were retested. The results appear in Figure 4.9, in the form of a generalization gradient. Clearly

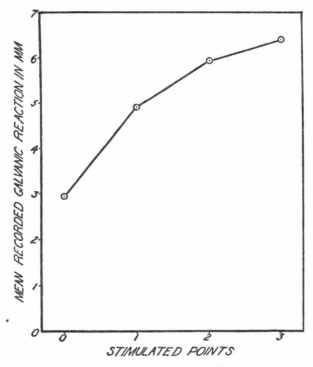

FIGURE 4.9. The generalization of extinction. Responses were first conditioned to all stimulated points. Then extinction was carried out at point zero and tests were made at the others (M. J. Bass and Hull, 1934).

the effect of extinction at point 0 spread or generalized to the adjacent points in a manner exactly analogous to the generalization of excitation. Pavlov referred to the process, in cortical terms, as the *irradiation of inhibition.* He referred to the empirical fact as *secondary extinction.*

Youtz (1939) performed a study with rats which showed that extinction also generalizes in instrumental conditioning. Nineteen rats were trained to press two bars in the Skinner box, one a vertical bar and one a horizontal bar. After the rats had learned to operate both bars, he extinguished the two responses one after the other. The average number of trials required to produce extinction was 43 for the response extinguished first and 16 for the response extinguished second. This reduction of 63 per cent shows that the effect of the first extinction generalized and aided in the extinction of the second.

12. *Discrimination.* If a subject is reinforced for responding to one stimulus and not to another, a discrimination between the two gradually develops. The end result of this process is that the subject comes to respond consistently to the reinforced stimulus and not at all to the nonreinforced one. Pavlov reports numerous examples of this for salivary conditioning. There are also many illustrations available in the literature on instrumental conditioning. Examples appear in the section on induction below.

13. *Conditioned Inhibition.* A special form of discrimination in which studied by Pavlov was what he referred to as *conditioned inhibition.* In such studies the positive CS was a single stimulus, such as a tone. The negative CS was the same stimulus in combination with another stimulus, perhaps a tactile one. After training the dog came to respond to the single stimulus, but not to the combination. Because the added stimulus, through conditioning, came to interfere with salivation, Pavlov called it a *conditioned inhibitor.*

Woodbury (1943) has performed a similar study in an instrumental situation. Dogs were placed in a wooden stock and trained to lift a bar with the nose to obtain food. After this initial training, they were prevented from performing this response until after the presentation of a signal, which on different trials might be a high-pitched buzzer, a low-pitched buzzer, or a combination of the two stimuli. In the portion of the study most nearly resembling the Pavlovian prototype, the dog learned to respond to either tone in isolation, but not to the combination. The course of this learning is presented graphically in Figure 4.10. The very slow learning probably depends upon two factors: (1) all of the stimuli were in the same modality, creating a problem in sensory discrimination; (2) since three stimuli were used the problem was more difficult than the Pavlovian demonstration involving only two.

14. *Induction.* The growth of a discrimination is accompanied by the simultaneous development of a set of complicating phenomena referred to by Pavlov as *positive* and *negative induction.* Positive induction refers to the augmentation of an excitatory process by a preceding inhibitory one; negative induction refers to the intensification of an inhibitory effect by a preceding excitatory one. In this usage, the excitatory and

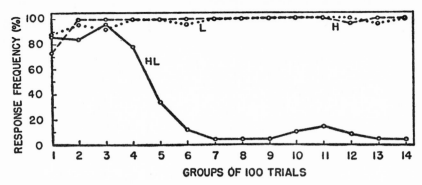

FIGURE 4.10. Graph showing the progress of learning in a single dog to respond positively to either a high- or a low-pitched buzzer, but not to the combination. Data from Woodbury (1943).

inhibitory processes are those associated with the reinforced and non-reinforced stimuli in a discrimination experiment.

The example summarized in Table 7 provides an illustration of positive induction. The positive CS was a tactile stimulation of the front paw; the negative CS was tactile stimulation of the hind paw. Both were of 30-seconds duration. The inductive effect occurs on the fourth trial in the table. It consists of an increase of approximately 50 per cent in the strength of the salivary response and a decrease in latency. This example also illustrates certain other typical features of positive induction: (a) To obtain it, it is necessary to test with the positive CS immediately after the application of the negative stimulus. (b) Following the response augmented by positive induction, the next trials tend to elicit reactions of lesser magnitude and of longer latency. This was taken by Pavlov as evidence for the existence of a slower acting *inhibitory after-effect.* Positive induction seems to occur with greatest intensity in newly established discriminations and with discriminations involving somewhat similar stimuli. It may completely disappear after protracted discrimination training and may fail to develop when the positive and negative stimuli are very different.

Demonstrations of induction in instrumental conditioning experiments are difficult to find. There is one study, however, (Hanson, 1959) which demonstrates what may be an instrumental parallel to the process of positive induction. This investigation was concerned with the form of the stimulus generalization gradient following discrimination training. The procedure consisted of training pigeons to make a hue discrimination, pecking the key in a Skinner apparatus when it was illuminated with one color and not when it was illuminated with another. After this discrimination was established, the pigeons were tested on a range of colors. Among other things, Hanson found that response strength, measured in these tests, was considerably raised to stimuli other than the negative CS or those like it, by comparison with control groups tested without discrimination training. See Figure 4.11.

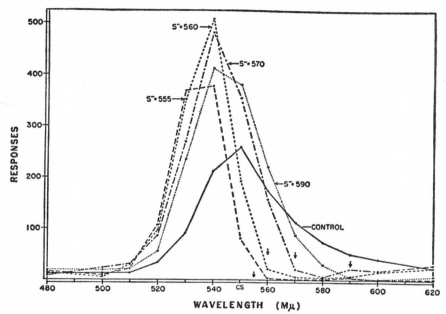

FIGURE 4.11. The effect of discrimination training upon stimulus generalization in the pigeon. The birds were trained to peck at a key illuminated with a light of 550 mu, and not to respond when the light (for different groups) had a hue corresponding to 555, 560, 570, or 590 mu. The control group was trained to peck at the key illuminated with a light of 550 mu, but it received no discrimination training. Generalization tests were conducted in extinction. Observe the greatly increased strength of response to stimuli to the left of the CS on the hue dimension. This may be an instrumental parallel to the phenomenon of induction described by Pavlov for classical conditioning. Data from Hanson (1959).

TABLE 7

DEMONSTRATION OF POSITIVE INDUCTION

Time	CS	Salivation in 30 seconds	Latency
4:20	Front paw	8	3
4:36	Front paw	7.5	3
4:45	Hind paw	0	—
4:45½	Front paw	12	2
4:58	Front paw	5	8
5:10	Front paw	6.5	5

Pavlov also described a process of negative induction and seemed to regard it as exactly opposed to positive induction. This conception, however, has been criticized (Konorski, 1948) on the grounds that the two kinds of demonstration were very different. The original evidence for negative induction involved an attempt to extinguish a *conditioned inhibition*. In this experiment (Pavlov, 1927, pp. 196-198), the positive CS was a tone and the negative CS was the same tone in combination with a tactile cutaneous stimulus. Previous to the portion of the study to be described here, a perfect discrimination between the two had been established: the dog always salivated to the tone alone, never to the combination of tone and tactile stimulation. The attempt to extinguish the conditioned inhibition consisted simply in reinforcing the combination with acid in the same way as the single tone was reinforced. In a series of 23 trials, carried out in three sessions, with tone trials and combination trials *alternated,* the conditioned inhibition failed to extinguish. That is, the dog continued to salivate to the single tone but did not begin to salivate to the combination. It was as if the reinforced trials with the tone alone deepened the inhibition already associated with the combination of stimuli. When the experimental procedure was changed and the previously negative combination of stimuli was reinforced on *successive trials,* the discrimination broke down on the second trial and the dog salivated to the combination of tones. No instrumental analogue to negative induction appears to have been demonstrated.

15. *Higher-Order Conditioning.* Under certain conditions, Pavlov found it possible to use the conditioned stimulus from one phase of an experiment as the unconditioned stimulus for a further conditioning of the salivary response.[2] In one demonstration the original CS was an auditory stimulus. When the CR to this stimulus had been very firmly established, a black square was presented briefly before it. On the tenth pairing of the black square and the auditory stimulus a salivary response, about half as strong as the response to the auditory stimulus, occurred to the square. This is an example of higher-order conditioning, specifically a *conditioned reflex of the second order.* Pavlov found third-order conditioning possible, but only with defense reflexes such as those in response to shock. Fourth order reflexes could not be established in dogs.

Typically the higher-order CR's were small in amplitude, long in latency, and had only a short life span. This last fact follows from the consideration that the higher-order conditioning procedure is the same as that for establishing conditioned inhibition. In short, a singly-presented stimulus is reinforced; the same stimulus in combination with the higher-order CS never is. Because of this, trials with the paired stimuli lead,

[2] See also Brogden (1939), J. V. Murphy and Miller (1957), Razran (1955d).

following an early establishment of the secondary reflex, to its gradual disappearance.

The fact that the secondary conditioned reflex is a somewhat evanescent phenomenon does nothing to diminish its theoretical importance, which is that the reinforcement (UCS) in the higher-order conditioning procedure obtains its reinforcing power as a result of learning. The secondary conditioned reflex, in modern terminology, is established on the basis of a *secondary reinforcement* (or secondary reward, or acquired reward). The process of secondary reinforcement has been of much greater interest in the field of instrumental learning than classical conditioning.

The basic procedure for providing a neutral stimulus with secondary reinforcing power is to pair such a stimulus with another stimulus which already is a reinforcer. Stimuli regularly associated with food or water, for example, become secondary reinforcers. The evidence that these, originally neutral, stimuli now have reinforcing properties most often consists of a demonstration that the secondary reinforcer will function as a reward in the learning of a new response. Wolfe's (1936) study of token incentives in the behavior of chimpanzees illustrates this type of demonstration. The tokens were small disks similar to poker chips to which the animals were originally quite indifferent. Preliminary training consisted of teaching the chimpanzees to insert tokens in the slot of a vending apparatus which automatically released a grape to the animal. After having learned the reward value of tokens, the chimpanzees were trained to perform simple instrumental responses to secure the tokens. One task required the lifting of a lever; another involved pulling in a small sliding tray by means of a cord. The animals would continue to work at these tasks for a number of tokens which could not be exchanged for food until later. In an extension of these experiments, Cowles (1937) found that token rewards were effective as rewards for the acquisition of simple position habits and visual discriminations. A position habit requiring as many as 20 trials could be completely learned in one session with tokens as the sole reinforcing agent and, therefore, prior to any reception of food reward.

Secondary rewards such as approval, money, prestige, and so forth are of unquestioned importance in directing most learning by adult human individuals. In the typical learning experiment with college students the only reward provided is the knowledge of which responses are correct and which incorrect. The mechanism of secondary reward training is difficult to analyze in the case of human learning because of the long and complicated history of learning through which such reinforcement develops. The essential features of the procedure have, however, been successfully demonstrated with animals such as rats, cats, and dogs, as well as with chimpanzees. The results in general indicate that a secondary reward is somewhat less effective in the establishment of new learned responses than the primary reward with which it has been associated. Moreover, the secondary reward loses its reinforcing value (extinguishes) if it is not itself repeatedly followed by the primary reward. In the chimpanzee experiments it was found that a token which was immediately exchangeable for food was more effective as an incentive than tokens which were exchangeable only at the end of a series of trials.

DIFFERENCES BETWEEN CLASSICAL AND INSTRUMENTAL CONDITIONING

The materials in the foregoing section amply testify to the fact that the similarities between classical and instrumental conditioning are sufficiently impressive to make the assumption that the two processes are basically the same at least tenable. There is, however, an alternative possibility which should not be overlooked. As we have seen, it is impossible to perform an experiment involving instrumental conditioning without at the same time arranging the circumstances under which classical conditioning occurs. Thus, the similarities just catalogued may occur because of a classically conditioned component common to all learning. Generalization, according to such an argument, might actually be a phenomenon of classical conditioning exclusively. But, because of the inevitable element of classical conditioning in all learning, generalization seems to occur in instrumental learning, too.[3] Although the details of such an explanation have not been worked out, the possibility that one could be developed means that the existence of parallel phenomena does not *prove* that classical and instrumental conditioning are different varieties of the same basic process. To be completely clear on this point, the bulk of the evidence suggests that classical and instrumental conditioning *are* different forms of learning; but a different view is more than barely possible.

Various investigators taking a less extreme position have held that classical and instrumental conditioning are both forms of learning, but that they differ in one or more important detail. The most important points of difference which have been proposed are the following:[4]

[3] Among the individuals whose writings suggest a development of this sort are Spence (for example, 1956) whose use of the incentive concept represents the introduction of a classical conditioning component in instrumental learning, Tolman (1949) whose separation of expectancies (classically conditioned) and motor patterns (instrumentally conditioned) does not at all deny the concept of these processes' going on together, Solomon and Brush (1956), Mowrer (1947), Reese (1953), Welch (1955), and Collier and Siskel (1959).

[4] Discussions of the differences between classical and instrumental conditioning which distinguish between the two in terms of these or related categories are to be found in the references cited in Table 4, p. 66. See also Skinner (1935b, 1937), Keller and Schoenfeld (1950), and Konorski (1948).

1. Some investigators have suggested that classical conditioning is S - S →C
stimulus-stimulus learning and that instrumental learning is stimulus- S - R →I
response learning. Schlosberg has maintained this view since 1937. The
following description of his position is a slight paraphrase of a recent
personal communication in which he puts his position very plainly:

> I prefer to think of classical conditioning as peculiarly appropriate to setting up
> preparatory responses. This leads to a theory of stimulus substitution in the sense
> that Pavlov meant it; that is, signalizing, which is fundamentally S-S learning.
> Thus, I am arguing for S-S learning, but sophisticated to the extent that, in
> avoidance conditioning for example, the conditional stimulus stands for "shock-
> about-to-come," so that the animal makes all sorts of responses which are more
> or less appropriate in Nature for shock-about-to-come. Instrumental condition-
> ing fixates the response which is effective in avoiding the shock. I would have no
> objection to speaking of some kind of cortical activity as set up by classical
> conditioning, but I certainly would not want to call it a response.

The last sentence in this passage is basic. Other two-process theorists,
such as R. L. Solomon, have held a similar position, with the exception
that the classically conditioned process was assumed to be a fear *response*
having drive properties capable of evoking what correspond to Schlosberg's "all sorts of responses which are more or less capable of shock-
about-to-come in Nature." Otherwise these other theories and Schlosberg's tend to be much the same.

2. As a part of the two-process theory it has very often been proposed
that different basic laws of learning apply to classical and to instrumental
conditioning. Specifically the usual position is that the primary law of
classical conditioning is the law of *contiguity;* whereas instrumental
conditioning involves, in addition, a law of *effect.* Thus, classical conditioning is thought by such theorists to occur as a result of the mere pairing of the conditioned stimulus and either the unconditioned stimulus or
the unconditioned response. A detailed discussion of the validity of his
position will have to be postponed (see pp. 267 to 277) for three reasons:
(*a*) An adequate treatment of the question cannot very well be presented
without a more extensive discussion of the law of effect than is feasible
here. (*b*) The data relevant to the two-process theory are also better
considered in connection with the general problem of reinforcement. In
anticipation of a lengthier discussion, it may be said that the bulk of
the evidence supports the two-factor theory. (*c*) It seems possible to
establish the fact that the two forms of learning differ in one basic respect
on other grounds to be considered later.

3. It has sometimes been suggested that an important difference between classical and instrumental conditioning is in the similarity or dissimilarity of the conditioned and unconditioned responses (Hilgard and
Marquis, 1940). More specifically this proposition is that, in classical

conditioning, the conditioned and unconditioned responses are always the same, whereas in instrumental conditioning they are always different. Although this observation is approximately correct, it is not exactly so in either of its two particulars. For (*a*) in classical conditioning the CR and UCR are only grossly similar. They involve the same effectors, but as we have previously seen, the responses are found to differ when subjected to close inspection. And (*b*) although the conditioned and unconditioned responses can be very different in instrumental conditioning (for example, bar pressing as opposed to eating in the Skinner situation) they can also be very similar. The typical shock-avoiding conditioned flexion responses are good examples of this.

4. One aspect of certain of the two-process theories has been the proposal that the organism's responses are of two basic sorts, which differ in the learning processes by which they can be modified. The clearest statement of this position appears in Skinner's (1938) distinction between elicited and emitted behavior and in his hypothesis that these two forms of behavior are subject, respectively, to respondent (classical) and operant (instrumental) conditioning. In addition to this, two-factor positions have often held that the classically conditionable responses are "involuntary" responses of the autonomic nervous system and that instrumentally conditionable responses are "voluntary" responses of the central nervous system. The evidence, although generally favorable to such a dichotomization, raises certain difficulties, specifically: (*a*) there are some nonautonomic responses which can be conditioned classically and (*b*) the voluntary-involuntary dichotomy is difficult to support on objective grounds.

One fact which supports the division of responses into dichotomous categories is the following. Although autonomically mediated reactions such as the GSR and vasoconstriction are readily conditioned classically, they seem to be impossible to condition by instrumental methods. The Pavlovians simply state (without documentation available in English) that glandular responses cannot be conditioned instrumentally. Mowrer (1938) was unsuccessful in an attempt at instrumental conditioning of the GSR, and Skinner (1938) reports that he and Delabarre could not condition vasoconstriction by making reinforcement contingent upon the response. Thus, for autonomically mediated behavior, the evidence points unequivocally to the conclusion that such responses can be modified by classical, but not instrumental, training methods.

Such evidence does not, however, establish the fact that classical conditioning succeeds only with autonomic responses. There are, in fact, several nonautonomic reactions which can be conditioned classically. These include the knee jerk, various flexion responses, and the eye-blink. These responses are of special interest because they seem, at first, to violate the rule that responses which are classically conditionable cannot be modified instrumentally. It is obvious that, outside the laboratory, these reactions often do serve an instrumental purpose, as in kicking a football, avoiding a painful object, or winking at a member of the opposite sex. This seems to indicate that they can also be modified by instrumental conditioning.

Careful consideration of the evidence, however, suggests an alternative explanation: that the classically and instrumentally modified forms of these responses are different reactions. Data in support of this contention are most complete for the conditioned eyelid reflex. Detailed investigations of the form of the response have yielded the following significant facts: (a) the instrumental ("voluntary") response which might be employed in winking at another person or in deliberate response to an approaching object is quite different in form and latency from the conditioned blink based on a puff of air blown into the eye (Spence and Ross, 1959) and (b) the innervation of the eyelid is quite complex enough to mediate more than one variety of eyelid response.

Both Marquis and Porter (1939) and H. E. King and Landis (1943) have compared the progress of eyelid conditioning with procedures in which the UCR was elicited by an air puff for one group of subjects and an instructed voluntary response to a click for another. The CS in each of these experiments was a light. Although conditioning occurred using the voluntary response as a UCR, there were significant differences between the response conditioned in this way and that obtained using a reflex blink. Conditioned voluntary responses were found to be brisk, complete lid closures; conditioned involuntary responses were smaller and developed more slowly with practice.[5] This adds to the evidence that voluntary and involuntary blinks are probably different reactions.

A more critical test of this conception would be provided if a way could be found to limit the eyelid response by some procedure to just the voluntary or just the involuntary variety. Under such conditions it should be possible to show that only one kind of learning is possible. Although precisely this experiment has not been done, those of Logan (1951) and of Kimble, Mann, and Dufort (1955) (p. 81), in which instructions were employed to eliminate most voluntary blinks, come close to meeting the initial requirement. The subjects in these experiments did show some acquisition (Figure 4.2) under the instrumental conditioning procedure, but the amount of conditioning was small and may have resulted from the classical conditioning trials on which a CR failed to occur.

[5] Similar characteristics have been found for conditioned finger responses established with a voluntary reaction as the UCR (Yacorzinski and Guthrie, 1937; Wickens, 1939a). In general such "conditioned responses" tend to be identical with the voluntary response, and there is no gradual increase in amplitude with training.

Voluntary Control over Involuntary Behavior

One line of evidence which offers a potential threat to the hypothesis that involuntary responses can be conditioned only classically and voluntary responses only instrumentally comes from the well-known, and experimentally demonstrated, fact that involuntary responses can sometimes be brought under voluntary control. This again implies that these responses can be modified instrumentally. The range of involuntary responses for which there is sound evidence of voluntary control is quite wide, including an "invisibly small thumb twitch" (Hefferline, 1959), ear movements (Bair, 1901), the GSR (Noble, 1950), pulse retardation (Kotliarevsky, 1936), vasoconstriction (Menzies, 1937; Roessler and Brogden, 1943), and perhaps pupillary responses (Cason, 1922a; Hudgins, 1933). As Skinner points out, however, it is important to determine whether these cases are ones in which the response involves a mediating step. Many responses, as we have already seen, are producible in two or more physiological ways, one of which is involuntary, the other voluntary. Descriptions of the Yoga procedures which provide the most impressive examples of voluntary control over involuntary responses suggest that the method makes use of this fact, and that the involuntary responses are controlled indirectly through skeletal mechanisms. In the experimental examples mentioned above, the possible nature of the mediating step is usually fairly obvious. Voluntary control of vasomotor responses, the GSR, and pulse retardation might require only that the subject become a little tense to acquire voluntary control over the involuntary process. According to Skinner (1938) controlling breathing can also mediate voluntary control over these responses. Corresponding intermediaries may be found for the pupillary response, since the pupil is activated, not only by the amount of light falling on the retina, but by emotional changes and accomodation and convergence as well. These latter changes being under a measure of voluntary control may mediate the control of the involuntary response. It thus appears that there is no evidence which clearly violates the rule that the organism is capable of two forms of learning and that they are differentiated in terms of the responses to which they apply.[6]

[6] A related point of importance which this discussion has not touched upon involves the extensive literature on "learning without awareness" (for example, Postman and Phillips, 1954; Postman, Adams, and Phillips, 1955; Postman and Adams, 1954, 1956a, 1956b; Postman, Adams, and Bohm, 1956) and "verbal conditioning" (for example, Greenspoon, 1955; Taffel, 1955; Cohen, Kalish, Thurston, and Cohen, 1954; Verplanck, 1955a, 1955b, 1956). Both of these procedures involve instrumental, rather than classical, conditioning methodology. Particularly in the verbal conditioning experiments, much is often made of the subject's lack of awareness, either of what he is learning or of the response-reinforcement contingency. Although the position taken above would survive a demonstration of the validity of this phenomenon, it would lead one to expect that such learning would not occur, because of the fact that volun-

Effects of Partial Reinforcement upon the Two Forms of Conditioning

Where comparisons are possible, most of the usual conditioning variables seem to influence classical and instrumental conditioning in the same ways. The factors for which evidence to this effect is available include the temporal spacing of conditioning trials, the amount of a positive reinforcer such as food, the intensity of a negative reinforcer such as electric shock or corneal air puff, and the intensity of the CS. The most important exception to this rule is to be found in the case of *partial reinforcement*, in which the reinforcer occurs on only some fraction of the trials. Other trials are unreinforced presentations of the CS in classical conditioning, or unreinforced responses in instrumental conditioning. In the instrumental situation, very large ratios of unreinforced to reinforced trials (for example, 192 reinforced trials to 1 reinforced trial, Skinner, 1938) are possible. Such procedures may produce a slight diminution in rate of learning, but they create a very great resistance to extinction. In classical conditioning, by contrast, partial reinforcement seriously interferes with learning (Razran, 1955a, 1956). Pavlov (1927) found that giving food less frequently than every second or third trial made conditioning impossible. Similarly, in eyelid conditioning, a 50 per cent reinforcement schedule produces a significant response decrement (W. F. Reynolds, 1958). Moreover, it has been shown that a shift from continuous to partial reinforcement in eyelid conditioning produces an immediate response decrement (Ross, 1959). This is in contradistinction to instrumental conditioning, where a very common procedure is to develop the response under continuous reinforcement and then to switch to a partial schedule, under which the response strength is typically maintained intact.

A closely related difference in the effect of a particular variable upon classical and instrumental conditioning involves the influence of regular, as opposed to irregular, alternation of reinforced and nonreinforced trials. In instrumental conditioning the organism usually shows that it detects the pattern by responding appropriately, tending to respond on the reinforced and not on the nonreinforced trials. Nothing of this sort occurs in classical conditioning. Regular patterns of reinforced and nonreinforced trials are a particularly destructive form of partial reinforcement schedule, in spite of the fact that human subjects are perfectly aware of the properties of the sequence (Grant, Riopelle, and Hake, 1950). The importance of this difference in response to partial reinforce-

---

tary responses are usually also ones of which the performer is aware. Evidence is accumulating, however, (for example, Levin, 1959) that such learning actually does not occur. Close questioning indicates that awareness of the condition of reinforcement was necessary for learning to occur.

ment and to patterns of reinforcement is not known. One good possibility appears to be that acquisition and, especially, extinction may be more rapid in classical than in instrumental conditioning. If so, this would mean that extinction occurring in a small number of nonreinforced trials would lower the level of responding on the reinforced trials.

The Effect of Voluntary Factors on Conditioned Responses

The suggestion that the classical conditioning process applies only to involuntary responses does not mean that voluntary processes are of no importance in the control of such learning. Just as the unconditioned reflex can be influenced by ongoing voluntary acts, the conditioned reflex is similarly affected. Indeed such variables are probably much more important in the control of conditioned behavior than in the control of unconditioned responses.

Razran (1955b) has routinely found that conditioning is better in subjects who have no knowledge of conditioning than it is in subjects who understand the process. Several studies of the conditioned eye-blink have shown that the set of the subject may have a marked effect upon the level of conditioning attainable. The effect of various types of instructions on the rate of acquisition and extinction of the conditioned lid response has been studied systematically by J. Miller (1939). Some of his results under different instructions are summarized in Table 8. Efforts to inhibit response (Groups 1 and 2) reduce the frequency very little

TABLE 8

Effect of Supplementary Instructions on Frequency
of Conditioned Responses

Conditioned stimulus, light; unconditioned stimulus, air puff to one eye; interval 400 msec. The groups are arranged in order of increasing success of conditioning. (Modified from J. Miller, 1939)

Group	Instructions	Per Cent of Trials on Which Conditioned Responses Appeared
(1) Inhibitory	"Be sure that you do not wink or start to wink before you have felt the puff" (n = 20)	26
(2) Voluntary antagonism	"Open your eyes each time the air puff strikes your eye" (n = 20)	28
(3) Noncommittal	Only minimum instructions necessary for photographic recording (n = 25)	38
(4) Informed	Told that light would be followed by air puff (n = 20)	44
(5) Facilitatory	"In case you feel your eyes closing or starting to close, do nothing to prevent it" (n = 20)	71

below that of the control groups uninstructed with respect to response (Groups 3 and 4). This suggests that the subjects in Groups 3 and 4 may have adopted an inhibitory set without specific instructions. Instructions not to prevent responses (Group 5) resulted in a greatly increased frequency of response, and in slow extinction. The form of the responses showed clearly that they were not voluntary reactions. The results confirm the conjecture that conditioned eyelid responses normally develop against opposed inhibitory sets (Hilgard, 1938).

The conclusion that inhibitory instructions do not reduce the level of conditioning much has been questioned by Norris and Grant (1948) who believed that the responses counted as CR's in this study were actually beta responses. They repeated the study using conditions essentially like those of Groups 1 and 3 of Miller's study. Their results shown in Figure 4.12 indicate that there is a very large difference between the levels of

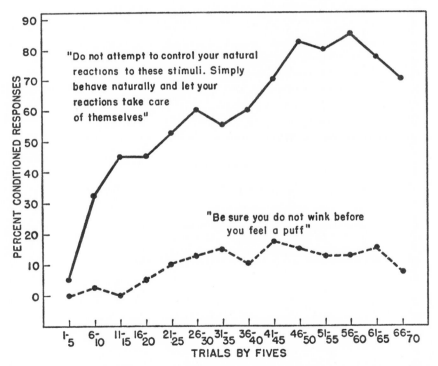

FIGURE 4.12. The effect of instructions upon the level of conditioning. The emphases of the two different sets of instructions are suggested by the quotations appearing within the body of the figure (Norris and Grant, 1948).

conditioning obtained under inhibitory and noncommittal instructions. In any event, it is evident that the nature of the instructions can determine the degree of conditioning, even though the response is not completely under voluntary control.

The degree to which specific instructions can influence the conditioned eyelid response has been further studied in the discrimination experiment. In a study of the effect of instructions, all subjects were conditioned on the first day to the positive stimulus, all trials being reinforced. On the following two days, during which the negative stimulus was introduced without reinforcement, the groups differed in the instructions given. The resulting characteristics of responses to the positive stimulus are summarized in Table 9.

TABLE 9

EFFECT OF INSTRUCTIONS ON CHARACTERISTICS OF CONDITIONED EYELID
RESPONSES TO POSITIVE STIMULUS WITHIN A DISCRIMINATION EXPERIMENT

(After Hilgard and Humphreys, 1938a, p. 301)

Groups in Order of Amount of Voluntary Supplementation of Response 10 subjects in each group	Characteristics of Responses to Positive Stimulus		
	FREQUENCY —PER CENT	AMPLITUDE —MM.	LATENCY —MSEC.
Instructed to refrain from responding to either stimulus	55	13	448
Instructed to refrain from responding to positive stimulus but instructed to respond to the negative stimulus .	71	16	404
Without instructions with respect to response	74	19	401
Instructed to respond to positive stimulus, not to negative stimulus . . .	90	35	319

Responses are found to show increasing frequency, increasing amplitude, and decreasing latency when they are arranged in order from voluntary restraint through no instructions to voluntary facilitation. This is evidence that instructions make some control over the process possible. On the other hand, voluntary restraint does not succeed completely in overcoming the positive conditioning tendencies. Corresponding results were found for responses to the negative stimulus. Except under direct instructions to respond, the negative stimulus always elicited responses at lower frequency and with smaller amplitude than the positive stimulus, but the same trends were found. Conditioned responses persisted in spite of voluntary effort to restrain them, and they increased when voluntary restraint was reduced as well as when there was added voluntary effort to respond.

SUMMARY

The distinction between classical and instrumental conditioning on operational grounds naturally leads to the question whether there are other differences between these two forms of learning and, for that matter, whether they are even forms of the same basic process. One conceivable way of attempting to obtain an answer to this question would be to condition the same response instrumentally and classically, and to compare the progress of learning under these different circumstances. Such experiments have not been successfully carried out, however, for several reasons: (1) It is impossible to perform a purely instrumental conditioning experiment, because such learning requires reinforcement (in the weaker sense in which that term is used). Since reinforcement must occur in some situation, there is always a chance for classical conditioning to occur, and for the responses to reinforcement to be conditioned to these situational cues. (2) It is also very difficult to perform a strictly classical conditioning experiment, because the classical CR usually has some effect upon the stimulational consequences of the UCS. (3) When the two forms of conditioning have been compared, the actual responses occurring under the two procedures seem always to have been somewhat different. This effect may be unavoidable. (4) There is good evidence that most (we think *all*) responses which can be conditioned classically cannot be conditioned instrumentally, and vice versa.

On the other hand, classical conditioning and instrumental conditioning possess many features in common. They seem to respond similarly to manipulations of many experimental variables. The only important exception is intermittent reinforcement which is more detrimental to classical than to instrumental conditioning. In this chapter we have described fifteen basic phenomena of conditioning which classical and instrumental conditioning both display. The fact that the two forms of learning are similar in so many respects means one of two things: Either the inescapable classical conditioning component of all learning is responsible for these effects, or classical and instrumental conditioning really are different forms of the same basic process. There is, to our knowledge, no psychologist who has taken the first of these positions.

If classical and instrumental conditioning are, indeed, two different forms of learning process, the next question to arise is whether they should be considered as separate at all. Some psychologists, such as Hull and Guthrie, have maintained that distinction cannot be made at other than the operational level, but the majority have adopted two-process theories of one sort or another, maintaining that a distinction is necessary. At this level, distinctions between classical and instrumental conditioning have involved two general ideas. It has been held (1) that the laws of learning which apply to the two procedures are somewhat different, and (2) that the responses which can be manipulated by these two mechanisms are different. As a general thing, the two-process theorists have held both of these hypotheses at the same time. It has seemed desirable to postpone discussion of the first of these propositions to a later chapter. It has been noted, however, that the most common form of the two-process view holds that classical conditioning is learning by contiguity and that instrumental learning is governed by the law of effect. Anticipating later discussion, we may say that the evidence with regard to this theory is more strongly positive than negative.

When we turn to the second idea, we find that it is possible to identify two separate positions regarding the responses which have been considered to be manipulable by classical and instrumental conditioning. One view is that classical conditioning is stimulus-stimulus learning, which serves to establish preparatory reactions, whereas instrumental conditioning is stimulus-response learning. The alternative position is that both forms of learning can be conceptualized within the S-R framework, but that some *responses* can be conditioned classically, and other *responses* can be conditioned only instrumentally.

The evidence favoring the last of these points is of the following sort: There seem to be no established demonstrations that *exactly* the same responses can be conditioned both classically and instrumentally: (1) Autonomic responses apparently cannot be instrumentally conditioned at all. (2) Responses, such as the eyeblink, which seem to be modifiable both classically and instrumentally, turn out upon close inspection to be different responses in the two cases. And (3) the voluntary control over autonomic reaction which suggests that instrumental conditioning of these responses might be possible probably always requires a mediating response involving the central nervous system.

Although such evidence leads quite directly to the conclusion that classically and instrumentally conditionable responses correspond to what we know in personal experience as involuntary and voluntary responses, this does not mean that voluntary factors have no influence over classical conditioning. There is good evidence that they do, and it seems quite likely that, in the actual case, the conditioned response is a combination of voluntary and involuntary processes. The same state of affairs probably also exists in the case of instrumental conditioning. One of the most difficult tasks in the psychology of learning is to unravel these components so that they can be dealt with separately.

·5·

Practice and the Strength of Conditioning

ONE OF THE most basic questions in the fields of conditioning and learning concerns the form of the function which relates these processes to practice. This question has been a matter of discussion almost from the beginning of the study of learning. It has been proposed by some that learning is a sudden, insightful process, by others that it occurs gradually, and by still others that it occurs suddenly in some situations and gradually in others. In spite of extensive argument, the issue has not yet been resolved. The reasons for this are to be found in a set of difficult methodological problems which must be considered before turning to a presentation of the main theoretical positions regarding the relationship between learning and practice.

METHODOLOGICAL PROBLEMS

In the final analysis the major methodological difficulties confronting the psychology of learning stem from this fact: the psychologist who sets out to discover the laws of learning must rely in his search upon indirect manifestations of the process in which he is interested. What is involved here is the learning-performance distinction developed earlier (p. 4). Although the psychologists' interest is in *learning,* all of the data available for analysis are *performance* data. The problem of assessing the value of the former from measures reflecting the latter is a very difficult one.

The Problem of Response Specification

The difficulties begin at the basic level of response specification. Most students of learning, following Skinner (1938), define a response in terms of its consequences, as any act on the part of the organism which has some particular effect upon the environment. Such definitions are in terms of the requirements of the experiment only. There is no specific concern for the details of the movements which press the bar, lift the limb in response to a buzzer, or transport the rat through the maze. Yet, it is known that the exact form of these movements changes with practice. This creates a question of the legitimacy of combining the various forms of a reaction to produce a learning curve. Is it justifiable, for example, to average amplitudes or latencies of responses as if they represented the dimensions of some single reaction when it is known that the precise response changes with practice?

However indefensible this procedure may appear, the alternative has seemed even less appealing to the majority of psychologists interested in learning. This alternative is to regard quantitatively different reactions as if they were qualitatively different; that is, to treat an eyeblink with a latency of 300 msec. as different from one with a latency of 450 msec. in somewhat the same sense as either of them is different from a patellar reflex or a salivary response. Although this view of the response is obviously cumbersome, there is some evidence to recommend it. This evidence consists in a variety of demonstrations that the organism can be taught to give responses which have certain quantitative values, in much the same way that it can be taught responses with specified topographic characteristics. Ferster and Skinner (1957), for example, show that pigeons can learn to respond slowly or rapidly if reinforcement is made contingent upon these aspects of behavior. Logan (1956) has attempted to develop a theory of learning which starts with the assumption that different response values qualify as different responses. He calls it a *micromolar theory* of learning. The choice between this position and the more obvious conventional one depends, finally, upon which is more successful in expressing lawful regularities in the field.

Psychometric Problems

The traditional viewpoint, that variations in the different measures reveal differences in the strength of a single response entity, is not without problems of its own. Specifically, it raises a series of questions about the value of the various indices as measuring instruments. Of such questions, the first to be mentioned concerns reliability. Probably because of the relative simplicity of the conditioning situation, the reliability coefficients have tended to be satisfactory. Thus, Schlosberg (1932) reports a reliability coefficient of +.66 for the amplitude of the conditioned knee jerk, and Grant and Schneider (1949) report one of +.92 for the GSR.

A second problem of this general sort, associated with measures of conditioning, involves their ability to reflect changes in conditioning at all levels. Probability measures suffer from the fact that they have a ceiling. Two groups conditioned under different conditions may both reach 100 per cent, although other measures (such as resistance to extinction) will reflect differences. Similarly, measures of speed and vigor are restricted in range by the capacities of the subject and cannot reflect increases in learning beyond this physiological limit.

A more difficult problem concerns the extent to which different measures reflect the same thing. There is a heterogeneous body of evidence to indicate that there are important differences among them, and that some measures are influenced more than others by various experimental procedures. (1) Studies of the effect of motivation on learning (Hillman, Hunter, and Kimble, 1953) have shown that *running speed* in the maze changes markedly with changes in drive level but that *number of errors* does not. (2) Estes (1944) reports that punishment during extinction slows down the rat's *rate of responding* in the Skinner box but has no effect upon *resistance to extinction.* (3) The reliabilities of *frequency* and *amplitude* measures have been found to be appreciably higher than those of *latency* measures. (4) Reinforcements beyond the first in the Skinner box sometimes produce no change in *rate of responding* but do increase *numbers of responses to extinction* (Skinner, 1938). (5) Partial reinforcement scheduling has a more profound effect upon *resistance to extinction* than it does upon *percentage of conditioned responses* during training. (6) When they have been compared, the correlations among various measures have usually been too low to support a common-process view. Table 10 presents some of the relevant data. It will be seen that the majority of the correlations indicate relatively poor correspondence among the various measures. Indeed, when the correlation is at all substantial, it sometimes turns out that the measures being correlated are

TABLE 10

Correlations Among Various Response Measures Obtained in Conditioning Experiments

Investigator(s) and Response	Measures Correlated	Correlation
Kellogg and E. L. Walker (1938b) Flexion (dog)	Frequency and amplitude Latency and amplitude Latency and frequency	+.94 —.22 —.18
A. A. Campbell and Hilgard (1936) Eyeblink (man)	Frequency and amplitude Latency and amplitude Latency and frequency	+.63 —.15 —.54
A. A. Campbell (1938) Knee jerk (man)	Frequency and amplitude Latency and amplitude Latency and frequency Frequency and resistance to extinction	+.63 —.27 —.27 —.60
Hunter (1935a) Running response based on shock (rats)	Trials to learn and trials to extinction	—.36

not separate measures at all. The typically moderate correlations between percentage of conditioned responses and amplitude, for example, often occur because the amplitude measure includes instances of zero amplitude, cases in which no response occurred. Thus the two measures are not independent, because amplitude is, in part, a frequency measure. When only amplitude of conditioned responses is counted, the correlations are markedly reduced.

The suggestion that the different measures reflect different processes carries with it the implication that some measures may be better than others as indicators of learning, and this raises the question of which indicator is best. At the present time no definite or final answer to this question seems possible. Different measures are appropriate in different situations, and a variety of practical considerations helps to determine which to choose in connection with a given experimental problem. For example, resistance to extinction is not used as a measure of learning very often, because it is so costly in terms of experimental time and subjects, especially where one's purpose is to trace the acquisition function. Other measures provide an index of the strength of conditioning on every trial; but to obtain comparable information using resistance to extinction as the measure, it would be necessary to condition and extinguish a separate group of subjects for each trial point. Along the same practical lines, rate of responding is an easy measure to obtain in free-responding situation, time scores and error measures lend themselves to studies of maze learning, and percentages of correct responses are convenient to use in experiments involving blocks of trials.

Another set of considerations, also largely practical, which determines the choice of a measure, is statistical in nature. Response speed, for example, is often a better measure than response latency for such reasons. Latency measures tend to be badly skewed in the positive direction, since very long latencies are possible and negative ones are not. As a result, the means of latency measures are difficult to compare by conventional statistical methods. Converting to a speed measure (reciprocal latency), however, tends to normalize the distribution. Other transformations, such as the logarithmic one for time scores and the arcsin transformation of percentages, are also used for the purpose of normalizing distributions and making them amenable to statistical treatment (Mueller, 1950).

Finally, at a more abstract level, there are certain implicit initial assumptions made by all learning theorists which suggest the selection of one measure rather than another in a given situation. Of such assumptions, the commonest is that learning increases uniformly with practice and that, for purposes of depicting the acquisition process, a measure which changes monotonically with practice is better than one which changes in a nonmonotonic manner. Thus, although latency and other time-based measures are useful for plotting learning curves in many instrumental situations (Graham and Gagné, 1940), they are less often employed in classical conditioning situations where they may decrease at first and then increase (Boneau, 1958). Similarly, response magnitudes were the standard measures in Pavlovian conditioning, but are less often used in instrumental conditioning because they either change very little in the course of conditioning or tend to come to match the minimal value required to obtain reinforcement. Thus, if it takes 20 gm. of pressure on the bar to get food, the rat may press with increasing force for a time, but gradually the pressure will come to approximate 20 gm. (Hull, 1943, pp. 305-306). It should be recognized that even monotonically increasing measures probably do not reveal the underlying processes directly. Attempts to develop rational measures which truly reflect learning have not met with much success.[1]

Typical Learning Curves

The different measures of learning behave in different ways with practice. Amplitude, probability of occurrence, speed of responding, and rate curves show an increase; latencies and other time measures decrease. Probability and percentage of response curves often show a double inflection. Since conditioned responses sometimes do not appear until after several reinforcements, the first portion of the curve may be flat. This portion is followed by a positively accelerated increase, which is soon replaced by a negatively accelerated one, as a maximum is approached. The exact course of conditioning revealed by this measure varies considerably depending upon the level at which the function begins. Curves which start at a low level show a more protracted period of positive acceleration than those with a higher starting point.

Resistance to extinction has been used so rarely as a measure of conditioning as to make firm statements of the function by which it reflects learning somewhat risky. There is, however, unanimity among the data available. For eyelid conditioning (Kimble and Dufort, 1956; Prokasy, 1958) and for bar-pressing (Williams, 1938; Perin, 1942; Miles, 1956) the functions have been negatively accelerated and increasing.

Skinner and his associates (Skinner, 1938; Ferster and Skinner, 1957) have reported the results of their studies almost exclusively in terms of a cumulative response measure. A set of typical conditioning functions of this sort appears in Figure 5.1. This curve differs from the ones in the

[1] See, for example, the series of papers on the quantification of reaction potential by Hull and his students (Felsinger, Gladstone, Yamaguchi, and Hull, 1947; Gladstone, Yamaguchi, Hull, and Felsinger, 1947; Hull, Felsinger, Gladstone, and Yamaguchi, 1947) and the comment by Koch (1954). Spence has sometimes used what amounts to a Z-score transformation to obtain reaction potential from response probabilities, but he has also claimed that this procedure is, at best, a poor first approximation (Spence, 1958b).

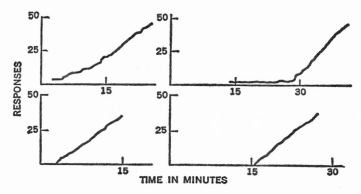

FIGURE 5.1. Some typical response curves obtained from a bar-pressing experiment with rats. The curves are tracings from bar-pressing records of
individual rats. After Skinner (1938) as presented by Keller and Schoenfeld
(1950).

preceding examples in that the base line is time rather than trials and the
ordinate is cumulative. Because of this latter feature such functions do
not flatten with protracted practice, and it is difficult to tell the degree to
which such learning functions reflect the same process as the more common ones. Youtz (1938a) has plotted data obtained by Skinner's method
in somewhat more conventional units. He finds that the time required for
10 successive responses in the lever situation gradually decreases in a
curve roughly resembling that of Thorndike's time-reduction curves for
trial-and-error learning. The curve cannot be carried beyond the first 30
or 40 reinforcements in this manner, because the ingestion of food changes
the drive, and the "learning curve" becomes more nearly a "satiation
curve."

The Problem of Averaging

Most learning curves are for groups of subjects, rather than individuals. For many purposes this creates a problem, especially in experiments
where subjects are run to some criterion such as 100 per cent conditioning in a block of trials. Different subjects will take different numbers of
trials to reach the criterion, and it becomes difficult to find a base line
against which to plot the response measures to represent the course of
acquisition. One solution to this problem is in the use of the *Vincent curve*
(Vincent, 1912; Kjerstad, 1919). The total number of trials required for
each subject to reach the criterion is divided into fractional parts such as
tenths, and measures are plotted for these portions. (For a subject requiring 35 trials the units would be 3.5 trials long; for a subject requiring 40 trials, they would be 4.0 trials long, and so on.) This method makes

it possible to combine data for subjects whose performances are widely different. Figure 5.2 presents acquisition and extinction as functions of this sort for the conditioned avoidance response in dogs. In this presentation the acquisition data were divided into elevenths of the total series. Extinction data were plotted in fourths (Brogden, 1949).

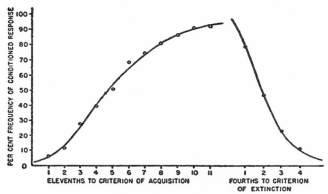

FIGURE 5.2.   Vincent curves of acquisition and extinction of an instrumental avoidance response in dogs. Adapted from Brogden (1949).

Unfortunately this and other procedures for combining data may distort the picture of acquisition presented by the learning curve. For one thing, the typical performance of individual subjects in a learning experiment is irregular, showing chance upward and downward excursions. To select the first point at which a subject reaches some arbitrary level as the criterion of learning is very often to stop the learning session at a point which is accidentally high. This fact accounts for at least some of the *end spurts* obtained in Vincentized data. These appear as rather sudden increases in the final segment of practice. At one time these were thought to be the result of motivational factors deriving from the subject's knowledge that the end of the session was near. Although they may sometimes reflect such a process, it now seems that they often occur as *criterion artifacts;* that is, as the result of the fact that the experiment is terminated after a series of unusually good performances.[2]

Another difficulty with any averaging procedure is that it can be shown mathematically that the group curve will often differ somewhat from those for the individual subjects (Merrell, 1931; Sidman, 1952; Bakan, 1954; Estes, 1956). For the theorist interested in the exact details of the learning process this is a serious matter, because the curves to which this applies include the functions (such as the exponential) most often proposed as representing the learning process. An even more severe distor-

[2] For a more extensive discussion of the Vincent method see Hilgard (1938).

tion is possible, though not common, in the averaging of stepwise curves which go from 0 to 100 per cent in a single trial. Figure 5.3 illustrates what can theoretically happen under these circumstances. In actual ex-

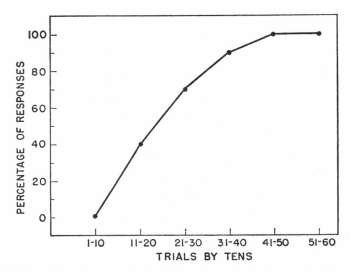

FIGURE 5.3.   Smooth curve derived from hypothetical stepwise data. Assume that 10 subjects given six blocks of ten conditioning trials each produce the following percentage of CR's:

		Blocks of Trials				
Subject	1-10	11-20	21-30	31-40	41-50	51-60
1	0	100	100	100	100	100
2	0	100	100	100	100	100
3	0	100	100	100	100	100
4	0	100	100	100	100	100
5	0	0	100	100	100	100
6	0	0	100	100	100	100
7	0	0	100	100	100	100
8	0	0	0	100	100	100
9	0	0	0	100	100	100
10	0	0	0	0	100	100
Mean	0	40	70	90	100	100

The means, when plotted, produce a regularly increasing, negatively acceler- ated function.

periments, the differences between individual curves and group curves are probably never as great as this, but the problem, nevertheless, exists.

Several methods of plotting learning functions to circumvent these difficulties have been proposed. Hayes (1953) described a "backward learning curve" which is particularly adapted to the situation where a criterion is employed and some subjects reach it suddenly. Hilgard and

Campbell (1936) and Spence (1956) have presented data for homogeneous subgroups of subjects. Skinner relies almost exclusively upon the curves of single subjects to illustrate various influences upon the progress of learning.

The Learning-Performance Problem

Most theorists either assert or imply that the level of learning, itself, provides a hypothetical upper limit which performance would reflect directly under absolutely ideal conditions. Unfortunately, however, conditions never are completely optimal; and performance, therefore, always underestimates the level of learning to a degree which varies directly with the extent to which the training conditions depart from the ideal. To mention just one specific example, the mere act of responding is known to create an inhibitory state which interferes with performance. For reasons of which this example is typical, it is very difficult to isolate the learning process and to study it alone in any given situation.

In a general way the nature of the solution to this problem is obvious. It is necessary, first, to discover the variables which influence performance, to determine the laws by which they lower performance, and then, by the extrapolation of such functions, to determine the level of performance which would be obtained with all performance variables set at their optimal values. Such levels plotted as a function of practice would reveal the progress of learning in a given situation and would constitute the learning curve for that situation. In actual practice, this general program is very difficult to implement for a variety of reasons: (1) It is probably overly optimistic to hope that the factors involved will divide themselves co-operatively into learning and performance variables. Many will, no doubt, turn out to be both. The amount of reward given a rat for running a maze, for example, may very well turn out to have an influence directly upon habit structures, as well as to have a performance effect through a motivational (incentive) mechanism. (2) Different performance variables will probably be of different degrees of importance in different learning situations. Again, to be specific, the temporal spacing of practice trials is quite important in human motor learning where large amounts of work are involved and relatively less important in human verbal learning or eyelid conditioning which require relatively effortless responses. Such considerations mean that it is impossible to generalize the function obtained in one situation to other, different, situations with any degree of confidence. (3) Different response measures seem to respond differently to different variables. There will be numerous occasions in what follows to call attention to one of the important applications of this point: Motivation has a marked effect upon speed and vigor measures, little or none upon measures reflecting only the accuracy of performance.

(4) The methodological techniques for separating the learning and performance variables have not been worked out. Analysis-of-variance (factorial design) methods (see below) which are most often used are of limited applicability; they are completely satisfactory only in cases where the evidence points unequivocally to the conclusion that the variable under investigation is a performance variable.

Separation of Learning and Performance by Factorially Designed Experiments

Practically speaking, a major difficulty encountered in separating the learning and performance variables is that of establishing criteria by which they may be distinguished. The criterion most commonly accepted for this purpose derives directly from the definition of learning as a relatively permanent change in behavior which occurs *as a result of practice*. Thus changes which occur without practice (as a result of deprivation, feeding, or rest) are taken to be performance changes. In many cases, however, it is impossible to change the value of the variable in which we are interested without also giving the subject training. If we want to study the effect of a change from immediate to delayed reinforcement, from continuous to partial reinforcement, or from massed to distributed practice, it is necessary to provide training in order to allow the changes to produce their effects. For problems of this sort, the factorially designed experiment is commonly accepted as a method of separating learning effects from performance effects.

In experiments of this sort, two or more groups of subjects are first trained under different conditions, known to produce different levels of performance. Then, each of the original groups is subdivided. One subgroup continues under the original condition; the other is switched to the alternative condition. The decision as to whether a variable influences learning or performance depends upon what happens in the second phase of the experiment, after the shift. If the change in conditions alters the subject's performance appropriately, leaving no indication of an effect of the previous training condition, the variable is assumed to be a performance variable. If the previous training has a residual effect, even after the training conditions are altered, the variable is assumed to be a learning variable, at least in part. Examples of the application of this method to testing the effect of CS intensity, motivation, and amount of reinforcement will help to make the method clear.

1. *Conditioned Stimulus Intensity.* Razran (1957a) cites a considerable amount of Russian literature to show that conditioned stimulus intensity has a marked effect upon response strength. As is usual with such evidence, this leaves open the question whether the influence of CS intensity is on learning or performance, since no special procedures were imple-

mented for separating the two processes. The factorial method of determining whether the effect of CS intensity is on learning or on performance is nicely illustrated by the studies of this problem by Grant and Schneider (1948, 1949). In one of their studies, these investigators conditioned the GSR's of four groups of human subjects to tones of four different intensities. Then, for extinction, they subdivided these groups into four smaller groups, making sixteen groups in all. In the extinction procedure, each subgroup was tested with one of the original tones. The logic of the analysis used to evaluate the results of factorial experiments can be made clear by reference to the results of this experiment in Table 11. In this table, the rows represent the four conditioning intensities, from greatest to least. The columns represent extinction intensities, from least to greatest. The whole table illustrates the experimental design, in which subjects were conditioned under one procedure and then subdivided for extinction.

It is essential, in interpreting these data, to remember that the entries in the table are GSR magnitudes *during extinction*. Differences among the row means (165.8, 275.8, and so on) reveal the effects, if any, of the intensity of the CS *during conditioning,* since these means are based on subjects originally trained under varying conditions, with CS intensity equated during extinction. The column means, on the other hand, reveal the effects of the intensity of the CS during extinction, since as a group the subjects whose performances these means reflect have had identical histories. In learning-performance terms the row means are learning measures; the column means are performance measures.

Looking first at the row means, it is clear that the differences among them present no consistent pattern. The lowest GSR magnitude occurs to the strongest stimulus and the greatest GSR magnitude is in response to the next-to-the-strongest stimulus. Appropriate statistical analysis supports this impression: there is no significant effect of CS intensity upon

TABLE 11

GSR Magnitude Scores During Extinction

CS Intensity During Conditioning in Decibels	CS Intensity in Extinction in Decibels				Row Means Differences Attributed to Learning
	76	86	96	106	
106	199.2	77.6	155.8	230.8	165.8
96	119.8	297.4	258.6	427.4	275.8
86	119.0	155.6	331.4	270.8	219.2
76	265.1	213.0	180.2	244.2	225.7
Column Means Differences Attributed to Performance	175.8	185.9	231.5	293.3	221.64 (General Mean)

learning. The column means do show a trend in the expected direction, but it is not of sufficient magnitude to satisfy the statistical requirements for significance. Thus we come to the conclusion that CS intensity has no effect upon learning and that its effect upon performance, described by Razran, has not been verified. Studies by Carter (1941) using eyelid conditioning procedures and by Hovland (1937b, 1937c, 1937d) again with the GSR lead to the same conclusion.

One possible complication in all of these studies is that they have used human subjects, whereas the positive results from the Russian laboratories were obtained with animal subjects. It may be that this accounts for the differences in results. Specifically, the conditioned responses of human subjects may be mediated by subvocal verbal processes which, in a sense, equate the CS intensities for all groups. That is, when the CS comes on, the subject may respond implicitly with some reaction such as, "there it is," or "the tone," which would tend to make the situation similar for all subjects regardless of the intensity of the CS. On the

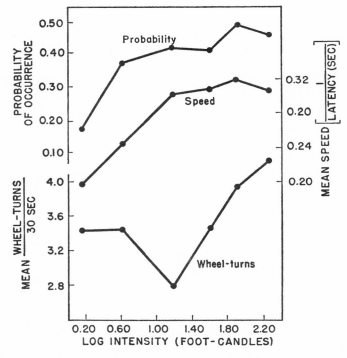

FIGURE 5.4. Three measures of response strength plotted as a function of the logarithm of CS-intensity. The subjects were rats performing in a wheel-turning, avoidance conditioning situation. All animals were tested at all intensities (Kessen, 1953).

common-sense assumption that lower animals are less able to make mediating reactions, it is to be expected that they might show a more marked CS intensity effect than human subjects.

Kessen (1953) obtained such results in an experiment where rats learned to avoid a shock by rotating a wheel in response to lights of different intensities. In one experiment, the subjects were all tested with different lights. In another he used a factorial design similar to that of Grant and Schneider. The results of the study appear in Figures 5.4 and 5.5. Both of them show an influence of CS intensity during training. The

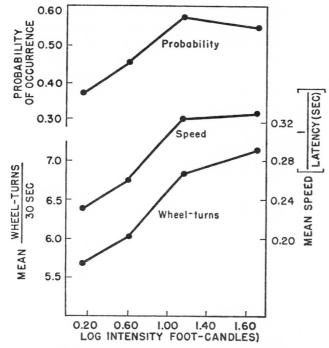

FIGURE 5.5. Three measures of response strength as a function of CS-intensity. Individual groups of rats were tested at each point (Kessen, 1953).

interpretation of this as a purely performance effect derives from two lines of evidence. First, the experiment in which all subjects were tested with the various lights shows that different CS intensities elicit different response strengths when the amount of learning is known to be the same. Second, in the factorial study, the differences in response strength disappeared in extinction as was the case in the experiments with human subjects described above.[3]

[3] Other relevant studies have been done by Barnes (1956), Kupalov and Gantt (1927), Kupalov, Lyman, and Lukov (1931) and Passey and Passenti (1956).

Recently Perkins (1953) has argued that the effect of CS intensity is to be explained in terms of a contrast phenomenon. His point is that learning to respond to any stimulus, whatever its intensity, always involves the making of a discrimination, between the situation with the CS present, and the situation with the CS absent. Specifically, what the animal must learn is to respond to the former condition and not to the latter. Now, if the animal is tested with a series of stimuli of varying intensities, it is to be noted that the presentation of a weak stimulus resembles the stimulus-absent condition, under which the subject has learned not to respond. Conceivably the failure to respond would generalize to this condition, since it is known that extinction effects do generalize. At least up to a point, stimuli of increasing strength would resemble the positive training situation more and more, with the result that there would be an increasing tendency for the CR to occur. This hypothesis, thus, explains the stimulus intensity phenomenon in what are essentially learning terms. Experiments performed to test the theory, by and large, have been positive (Perkins, 1953; Bragiel and Perkins, 1954; Johnsgard, 1957). Whether the entire stimulus-intensity effect can be so explained remains to be seen.

   2. *Motivation.* The effect of motivation upon performance has been the subject of a large amount of research which will be described in more detail in Chapter 13. For our present purposes, it provides a particularly clear example of the method of separating learning from performance variables by the factorial experiment. The study of Hillman, Hunter, and Kimble (1953) is typical. Two groups of rats were trained on a complex maze for a water reward, initially under 2 and 22 hours of water deprivation. After 15 initial training trials, the groups were subdivided. Half of the animals in each group continued under the original deprivation condition; the other half were switched to the alternative condition. The results in terms of running time appear in Figure 5.6. The important point is that the switch in deprivation produced a rapid shift in performance, to the level characteristic of the group which had been on the same drive from the beginning.

   3. *Amount of Reinforcement.* Several experiments, employing both classical and instrumental conditioning procedures, have shown that the amount of reinforcement influences performance in the learning situation. Passey (1948) conditioned the eyelid responses of human subjects using air puffs of four different pressures as the unconditioned stimuli and obtained better conditioning with the stronger puffs. Spence (1956) reports several other demonstrations of the same effect. Crespi (1944) and Zeaman (1949a, 1949b) have both reported studies which show that rats traverse a straight runway more rapidly for a large amount of food than for a small amount of food. Guttman (1953) manipulated the quality of

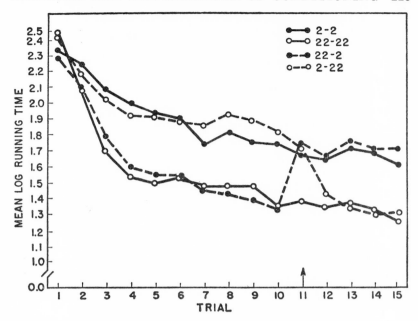

FIGURE 5.6. The results of a factorially designed experiment to determine the effect of drive and drive-shift upon the speed with which rats run a maze. For 10 trials two groups were run under 2 or 22 hours of food deprivation. From Trial 11 on, the original groups were subdivided. Two groups (2-2; 22-22) continued under the original motivational condition. Two others (22-2; 2-22) were switched to the alternate condition. The important point is that performance on Trials 11-15 seems to depend only upon motivational level during these trials; that is, drive affects only performance (Hillman, Hunter, and Kimble, 1953).

reinforcement for rats in a Skinner box in a different way, by using liquid reinforcements of different sweetnesses. He showed that both performance under a periodic reinforcement schedule (p. 160) and resistance to extinction varied with sweetness. These data leave no doubt that performance in the learning situation depends upon the amount of reinforcement. There is now rather good evidence that the effect is upon performance. The evidence comes from studies in which the amount of reinforcement was increased or decreased during the course of the experiment. Crespi and Zeaman included this feature as a part of their studies, and both obtained rather abrupt changes in speed of running. Zeaman's data presented graphically in Figure 5.7 show that changes in amount of reinforcement produce a sudden increase or decrease in response latency in a way which parallels that produced by changes in motivation. This is the sort of result to be expected with a performance variable.

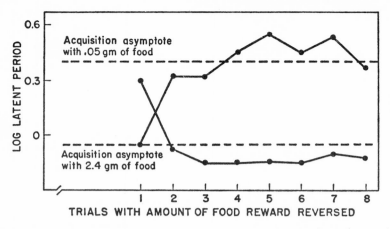

FIGURE 5.7. The effect of a change in food reward upon the latency of the response in the Graham-Gagne runway. The acquisition asymptote is estimated from latencies on the last several trials before the shift in amount of reward. Note that the change in amount of food employed as a reinforcer produces an immediate shift on trial 2 after one trial with the new amount. Adapted from Zeaman (1949).

Evaluation of the Factorial Procedure

From the evidence just cited it is clear that the factorial method can be a powerful tool in determining the place at which a particular variable has its effect. This is true whenever the results of an experiment are clearly of the sort to be expected when the influence is entirely upon performance. In other cases, the data may be much more difficult to interpret. To illustrate the point, suppose that the curves in Figure 5.8 represent the outcome of a factorially designed experiment intended to determine whether a certain variable influences learning or performance. With the change in conditions, performance also changes, but only gradually, and it is several trials before the curves for the groups subjected to the change reach the levels of the groups which had not been switched. Do these results show an effect upon learning, performance, or both? In the statistical procedure employed in the factorial experiment, the answer depends upon the portion of the performance function selected for evaluation. If the section of the function immediately after the shift is selected, the result will be one which seems to indicate that the variable influences both learning and performance. Spence's (1953) assignment of both roles to the UCS intensity variable apparently was on the basis of data of this sort. If the last portion is selected for analysis the effect will be on performance. It, thus, becomes clear that the value of the factorial method is more limited than is sometimes believed; it finds a straightforward application only in the case where changes in experimental procedure

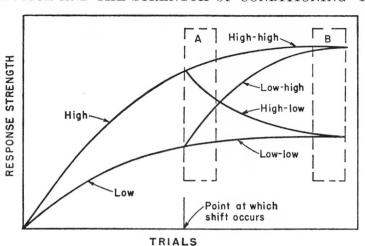

FIGURE 5.8. Graph showing the outcome of a hypothetical factorially designed experiment which would be difficult to interpret. The terms high and
low refer to the magnitudes of the variable manipulated. If statistical analyses
are carried out on data in section A of the post-shift graph, the effect will
appear to be upon learning and performance. If the data in section B are
evaluated, the effect will appear to be only upon performance.

produce immediate shifts to the level of performance typical of subjects
trained from the beginning under the new condition.

Other Performance Variables

The set of performance variables considered above does not exhaust the
list of conditions which apparently affect behavior at the performance
level. Two other sets of performance variables should be mentioned. Of
these the temporal distribution of practice trials is the most important.

The typical effect of the crowding of practice trials in time (massed
practice) is to diminish performance to a degree which depends upon the
degree of massing (Calvin, 1939; Reynolds, 1945; Vandermeer and
Amsel, 1952; Spence and Norris, 1950). The results of the last-mentioned
study appear in Figure 5.9. Theoretically this diminution has been attributed by the Pavlovians to *inhibition with reinforcement,* by Razran
(e.g., 1930, 1955c) to *overreinforcement,* and by Hovland (1936) to *inhibition of reinforcement.* The evidence that what is involved is a performance factor comes from a variety of demonstrations that the effect of
massed practice is temporary and that the decremental process dissipates
spontaneously with rest. Reminiscence in verbal and motor learning and
spontaneous recovery following extinction have both been interpreted in
this way. In conditioning experiments similar evidence sometimes is ob-

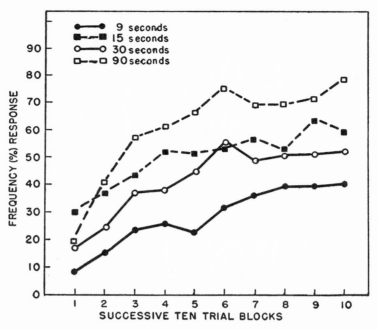

FIGURE 5.9. The effect of the time between trials upon the acquisition function for eyelid conditioning (Spence and Norris, 1950).

tained in a distortion of the form of the extinction curve. These functions
tend to be decelerated, response reduction being rapid at first and then
gradually tapering off as the base line is approached. Following massed
practice, however, extinction curves occasionally show an initial rise, as
if they had previously been depressed by some inhibitory mechanism.
Hovland (1936) conjectured that the inhibitory process was an "inhibition of reinforcement" and that the omission of reinforcement at the beginning of extinction changed the stimulus situation enough to produce
disinhibition. On these assumptions he predicted that the usual extinction
curve would occur after spaced practice, the rising type with massed
practice. Accordingly he conditioned the GSR's of human subjects under
massed and distributed practice and then extinguished them. His results
as shown in Figures 5.10 and 5.11 agreed with his prediction. It is important to note that the rising type of curve could be obtained only if
training were under conditions of massing *and* if extinction began immediately. Postponing extinction would produce the monotonic decreasing
type of function even if conditioning occurred under conditions of massing. This suggests that the lapse of time allowed the inhibition to dissipate
and that no initial rise was possible.

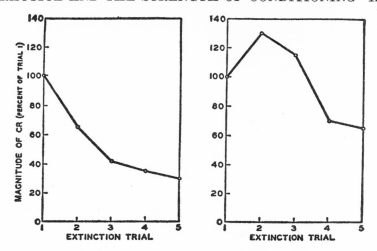

FIGURE 5.10.   Extinction of galvanic skin response immediately following 24 distributed reinforcements. Mean, 20 adult human subjects. (Hovland, 1936).

FIGURE 5.11.   Extinction of galvanic skin response immediately following 24 massed reinforcements. Mean, 20 subjects. Note the initial rise. If reinforcements were fewer or if time elapsed before extinction began, this initial rise was lacking. (Hovland, 1936).

The other additional set of performance factors derives from the consideration that most learning is complex and requires the simultaneous learning of several components. Possibly the clearest illustration of this is in the appearance during learning of *plateaus* (Bryan and Harter, 1897) during which practice does not lead to improvement. In complex learning, plateaus often seem to be temporary periods devoted to the organization of component habits into larger units or to the learning of particularly difficult portions of a problem (Hunter, 1934). In code-sending, for example, plateaus may occur when the learner is making the transition from a letter habit to a word habit. Although this transition depends upon learning, there is no concurrent improvement. Even at simpler levels of learning similar complexities arise. For example, the rat in the Skinner box learns to press the bar only as competing reactions are extinguished (Estes, 1950b). It also seems quite likely that the more positive components of what the animal learns comprise at least two habits. One of them involves conditioning to elements in the experimental situation of responses to food, so that animal learns that food is available. The other consists in the acquisition of the bar-pressing habit. It seems unlikely that these two processes would develop as exactly the same function of practice, or that they would be reflected equally well by any given measure of performance.

THE NATURE OF THE ACQUISITION FUNCTION

If we had a complete understanding of the influence of all of the performance variables upon the progress of behavioral change in the learning situation, it would be much easier to determine whether a single acquisition function applies to all learning, and if so, the nature of that function. We do not have this information, however, with the result that alternative theories about the nature of the acquisition function have been offered. Two hypotheses have been advanced: (1) Some theorists have held that learning is a gradual process, as the learning curves suggest. (2) Others believe that learning occurs in a single training trial, but that factors in the performance situation somehow obscure it. The first of these theories is called a *continuity* view of learning. The second, one-trial position is a *noncontinuity* view. In the disputes which have arisen over the issue implicit in this difference of opinion, the burden of proof seems to rest with the theorist accepting the one-trial view, because the performance functions obtained in almost all learning experiments show a gradual course of acquisition. Clearly the easiest assumption to make is that the underlying process is also gradual. This view has been most vigorously supported by Hull (1943) and Spence (1945).

Opposed to the continuity position are two discriminable variations of the noncontinuity view. One of these was originally Guthrie's (1935) position. Its more recent champions have been Estes (1950), Sheffield (1949), and Voeks (1950). The other position derives from the writings of Lashley (1929) and Krechevsky (1932a, 1932b, 1933a, 1933b). The basic difference between these two versions of noncontinuity theory has to do with the question of what is learned. The followers of Guthrie hold that it is S-R connections; those in the Lashley tradition view learning from the S-S point of view, as a matter of developing cognitions or acquiring bits of knowledge about the world. This difference has led to rather different experimental efforts to substantiate the two views.

The S-R noncontinuity position maintains that conditioning is complete in a single trial; that is, that the connection between a response and the stimuli in whose presence it occurs is fully established in just one such pairing. It is possible within such a theory to account for the gradual course of most performance functions on the further assumption that the stimulus situation varies from trial to trial.

The essential nature of these theories is as follows: the stimulus side of learning is regarded as a large, but finite, collection of stimulus elements, comprising a *stimulus population*. On any given trial only a *sample* of the stimuli in the population is assumed to be present. Those which are present are conditioned to the response on that trial. After the first trial, the stimulus sample will consist of some stimuli which have been previously conditioned to the response and some which have not. With continued practice the number of stimulus elements not conditioned to the response will diminish, and the number which have been conditioned will increase, until the entire population of stimuli has been conditioned to the response. Assuming that the proportion of previously conditioned, stimuli present in the sample on any trial directly represents the prob ability that a conditioned response will occur on that trial leads to the prediction of a gradual increase in response probability with practice. The exact form of the function will depend upon the trial-to-trial variability in the stimulus situation. If the situation is perfectly controlled so that the sample of stimuli is exactly the same from trial to trial, one-trial learning should occur. In a general way, this prediction is that learning will be more rapid in a very constant situation than it will be in a highly variable one. There is considerable reason to accept this idea as a valid one. We have previously seen that extraneous stimuli disturb the course of acquisition through external inhibition. In order to guard against the effects of uncontrolled disturbances of this sort, Pavlov eventually had to build a laboratory carefully shielded from outside stimulation.

Voeks (1954, 1955) has made a direct test of the effect of variability in the stimulus situation upon eyelid conditioning, attempting to control internal, proprioceptive stimuli as well as external stimuli. To provide a condition of maximum control, she had the subjects (1) close their eyes between trials, opening them at a signal as the trial began, (2) inhale and hold their breath during the trial, and (3) press down on two keys which turned on the CS, a buzz. The UCS, an airpuff, was delivered .45 sec. later. Under these conditions about half of the subjects showed step-wise acquisition functions which rose from 0 to 100 per cent on a single trial. Voeks interprets these results as representing an instance of one-trial learning. Before such an explanation can be accepted, however, several alternatives will have to be ruled out. One of these is that the subjects may have responded voluntarily. Another is that the responses counted as conditioned responses were unconditioned responses related to the key press. This possibility was developed earlier (p. 59) in connection with the problems of specifying the conditioned response. Still another explanation has been offered by Spence (1956, pp. 108-109) and will be presented here because of its potential applicability to a variety of problems.

This explanation makes use of a version of Hull's (1943) continuity theory of learning. Hull assumed that learning is a gradual process in which habit strength accumulates as a simple positive growth function of the number of reinforced trials. Before habit reveals itself in performance, however, it is transformed into *reaction potential* through its interaction with such variables as generalization and motivation. Then, in order to predict whether or not a response will occur on a given trial (to obtain a probability of occurrence measure), it is necessary to consider the effects of two additional intervening variables, *threshold* ($_sL_R$) and *oscillation* ($_sO_R$). Very briefly, a response occurs if reaction potential is suprathreshold, but on a given trial whether it is above or below threshold depends in part upon the oscillation function.

The essential elements of this position appear in Figure 5.12. Reaction potential, it will be seen, increases steadily with practice, rising above

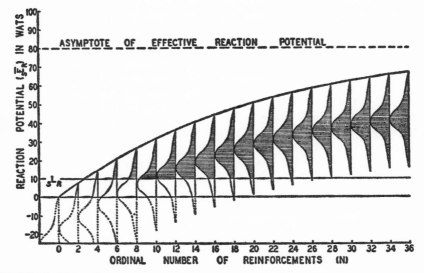

FIGURE 5.12. Diagrammatic representation of Hull's theory of response-evocation. Note that the curve of reaction potential moves above the reaction threshold ($_sL_R$) at about Trial 3. The up-ended bell-shaped functions depict the function of oscillation which reduces reaction potential randomly from moment to moment. The area of the oscillation function lying above the reaction threshold corresponds to the probability that a CR will occur. Observe that the zone of supra-threshold reaction potential becomes increasingly greater with practice. The discussion in the text assumes that the range of the oscillation functions varies inversely with the degree of control of experimental condition. Figure is from Hull (1943, p. 327).

threshold at about the third reinforcement. The bell-shaped oscillation functions, operating randomly downward from the reaction-potential curve, decrease the value of reaction potential by an amount which varies in a chance manner from moment to moment, sometimes allowing it to fall below threshold. As this last statement implies, the oscillation concept represents Hull's introduction into his theory of a random process, corresponding in a sense to Estes' stimulus variability hypothesis. On this assumption it is rather natural to proceed (although Hull, himself, did

not) to the further assumption that the breadth of the oscillation function varies directly with the number of uncontrolled conditions of the
experiment. In terms of Figure 5.12, this is to say that the area of the
bell-shaped curves would vary *inversely* with the amount of control in
the conditioning situation. With perfect control the oscillation function
would disappear completely; with less and less trial-to-trial stability, its
area would progressively increase.

Such reasoning makes it possible to explain stepwise conditioning
curves within the framework of a continuity theory. The case is clearest
for the situation of perfect control. Under such circumstances, conditioning would reach 100 per cent on the trial on which the reaction potential
function first rose above the reaction threshold, as on Trial 3 in the conditioning situation depicted schematically in Figure 5.12. Such control, of
course, cannot easily be obtained in conditioning experiments. Even those
in which the greatest pains have been taken to insure stimulational stability can do no more than reduce the variations in the situation from
trial to trial to a practical minimum. Because of this, not all subjects
would be expected to show step-wise acquisition, and there would be occasional failures following the first successful response. It thus develops
that extensions of Hull's and Guthrie's theories make similar assumptions
of the operation of a random process and that sudden learning is predictable from either type of theory. It is perhaps important to note that,
in the accomplishment of this goal, the two theories become surprisingly
similar, considering the fact that they began with opposite initial
assumptions.

The other, S-S, noncontinuity view represents an extension of Lashley's
(1929) opinion that: "[The form of the learning curve] suggests that the
actual association is formed very quickly and that both the practice preceding and the errors following are irrelevant to the actual formation of
the association." Its more familiar form was developed by Krechevsky
(1932a, 1932b). According to this theory, learning consists in the acquisition of knowledge about the learning situation, or of *expectancies* developed through experience with the environment. The process is one in
which the learner theoretically tests and rejects a series of *hypotheses*
until the correct one is hit upon: "Learning consists of changing from
one systematic, generalized, purposive way of behaving to another and
another until the problem is solved." (Krechevsky, 1932a, p. 532). Obviously such a description of learning is more applicable to complex situations where alternative ways of responding are possible than it is to the
conditioning situation where response possibilities are limited. The discrimination-learning experiment provides the situation in which the
majority of tests of the cognitive view have been made.

Krechevsky's analysis of discrimination learning breaks the process down into two stages or periods, a *presolution period,* in which erroneous hypotheses are tried out, and a *solution period,* in which the subject adopts, and perhaps strengthens, the correct hypothesis:

Once the animal is immersed in a given problem-situation, the animal selects out of the welter of possible stimuli certain sets of discriminanda to which he reacts. Each time (while "paying attention to" this particular set of discriminanda) he makes what proves to be a "correct response," he learns (wrongly perhaps) something about the significance *of this particular stimulus;* each time he makes a "wrong" response he learns something else, but he *does not learn anything about the "correctness" or "wrongness" of the* to-be-finally-learned *set of discriminanda.* Eventually he gives up responding to his first set of discriminanda and responds to another set, and another set, etc. (Krechevsky, 1938, p. 111)

Two features of this description are worthy of special note. The first is that Krechevsky regards the behavior of the subject during the presolution period as systematic, although wrong. There is considerable evidence that this opinion is a sound one, in that animals show consistent position preferences, brightness preferences, or tendencies to alternate during the early stages of discrimination learning. Krechevsky used such evidence to provide an operational definition of hypotheses as any response tendency which appeared with a greater than chance expectancy (Krechevsky, 1932a, 1932b). The other point to note is that incorrect hypotheses (responses while the animal is paying attention to the incorrect stimuli) have no effect upon the later mastery of the correct (finally-to-be-learned) response. That is, they are "irrelevant to the actual formation of the association." It is this feature of Krechevsky's position which makes it a noncontinuity one. A continuity view employing the concept of hypothesis is entirely feasible although no one seems to have espoused one.

The continuity theory (Spence, 1936) differs from that of Krechevsky, specifically in regard to what happens during the presolution period. It holds that while the animal is responding incorrectly, but systematically, the tendency to respond to the reinforced stimulus is increasing and other tendencies are being extinguished. To illustrate, suppose that the learning situation requires a black-white discrimination and that black is positive. Suppose further, that a certain subject has a strong left position preference and responds to the stimulus on the left on every trial for the first 40. Since the black and white stimuli are randomly shifted from side to side the subject will be reinforced in the presence of the black 20 times and, according to the continuity position, there will develop an increasingly strong tendency for the subject to respond to the black stimulus. Eventually this tendency will be greater than the left-going tendency and will appear, perhaps suddenly. This differs from the view of Krechevsky, who would hold that the black stimulus would acquire no strength until the animal began to pay attention to it.

This specific difference has led to a number of studies which have employed a discrimination reversal procedure to determine whether the reinforced stimulus has acquired a degree of strength during the pre-solution period. Suppose, in the hypothetical example above, that the reinforcement contingency were switched and the animal now rewarded for responding to the white stimulus rather than the black one. Krechevsky's noncontinuity position leads to the prediction that this alteration would have no effect upon the development of the discrimination. Continuity theory, on the other hand, leads to the prediction that this reversal would interfere with discrimination learning through the mechanism of negative transfer.

Many experiments of the general design just described have been performed. The first was that of McCulloch and Pratt (1934) which obtained results consistent with Spence's position. Krechevsky (1938) performed two experiments; one supported his view, the other did not. Subsequent investigations by various authors have most frequently supported the continuity position.[4]

Recently a new dimension of complexity has been added to the continuity-noncontinuity issue as a result of the work of Harlow (pp. 385-391) and others on *learning sets* or *learning to learn*. Specifically, it has been demonstrated that animals given 200 to 300 discrimination problems to solve, over a long series of sessions, gradually acquire the ability to solve them suddenly. Somewhat analogous results have been obtained for other species, using other procedures. Dufort, Guttman, and Kimble (1954) ran an experiment in which rats were required to learn a position-discrimination, for example, to choose the right-hand goal in a discrimination apparatus. When this had been mastered, reinforcement was switched to the other goal box and the subjects learned to choose this new goal box. When the subjects had learned this, the problem was reversed again and so on through a series of 10 discrimination reversals. On the last three discriminations, the rats all responded correctly after the first nonreinforced choice of the previously correct goal box. Results of this same sort have also been reported by Buytendijk (1930), Krechevsky (1932c), and North (1950a, 1950b).

Studies of repeated conditioning and extinction also provide evidence of an improved ability to learn as a result of experience in the learning situation. Following extinction, reconditioning is very rapid, even though time for spontaneous recovery has not intervened. As specimen findings,

[4] Blum and Blum (1949) have published an excellent and constructive review of the problem which covers most of the important literature up to 1946. In addition see: Ehrenfreud (1948), Grice (1948), Krechevsky (1932a, 1932b, 1938), Lashley (1942), McCulloch (1939a, 1939b), McCulloch and Pratt (1934), Ritchie, Ebeling, and Roth (1950), and Spence (1937a, 1937b, 1938, 1939, 1940, 1942, 1945).

involving just one reconditioning series, the results of two experiments with dogs may be cited. Finch and Culler (1935) report for flexion responses a reconditioning after extinction in from 20 to 25 per cent of the original trials, whereas Hilgard and D. G. Marquis (1935) report for eyelid responses relearning in from 20 to 40 per cent of the original trials. This effect becomes more marked when additional series of extinctions and conditionings are used. Brogden, Lipman, and Culler (1938) report that one dog required the following numbers of reconditioning trials to reinstate the CR: After a first extinction, 18 reinforcements; after a second, 11; after a third, 5; after a fifth, 1; after a seventh, 2. Bullock and Smith (1953) performed a similar instrumental conditioning experiment in which they conditioned and extinguished rats in the Skinner situation. Rates of responding for 10 successive conditioning sessions were 1.0, 4.6, 6.5, 7.3, 7.8, 7.2, 7.5, 7.1, and 7.8 responses per minute. All of these data thus show that practice at learning a given kind of task increases the probability that it will be learned suddenly. In summary, this suggests that the naïve subject learns gradually and that sudden learning, when it occurs, is the result of learning to learn.

SUMMARY

The general question with which this chapter has been concerned involves the form of the learning curve. From the beginning of the study of learning this question has been a matter of special interest because it touches one of the basic properties of the learning process. For much the same reason it has been a matter of theoretical controversy. In spite of a great deal of experimentation and debate, however, there is as yet no agreement on an answer.

The Problem of Measures

It will be possible to determine the form of the acquisition function (if there is just one) only when we have available satisfactory measures. The need is for indices which are (1) psychometrically adequate and which also (2) accurately reflect the underlying process. The question of psychometric adequacy leads to investigations of the reliability of the various measures of learning. Such studies indicate that these measures can attain satisfactory degrees of consistency. Similarly, judiciously selected measures are capable of reflecting differences in the amount of learning at all levels.

The second consideration, which requires our measures to reflect the process of learning accurately, poses questions which are harder to answer. Since the available measures are always measures of performance, these questions all involve the problems of transforming such measures into units appropriate to describing the degree of learning. At the present time such units have not been developed. In fact there is not even complete agreement as to exactly what constitutes a measurable response in the learning situation. For example, given the fact that with practice an organism can learn to respond rapidly, vigorously, or persistently, is it appropriate to use speed, vigor, and persistence as if they were quantitative reflections of the strength of some underlying process? Or is it eventually going to be necessary to adopt a more molecular approach in which responses with different quantitative characteristics will be treated as different responses? Similarly, since the various available measures do not respond in the same ways to manipulations of such variables as drive strength and numbers of reinforcements, is it proper to consider all measures as revealing the degree of learning in the same way? Along the same lines, correlational studies have found so little correspondence among response measures that it seems improbable that they can be regarded as all reflecting the same thing. When one asks which of the possible measures is best, it turns out that the answer is different for different situations, and that it depends in part upon practical considerations.

Learning vs. Performance

A large part of the difficulty of studying the course of learning stems, as we have seen, from the fact that learning and performance are difficult to separate. Attempts to untangle their individual contributions have often taken the form of factorially designed experiments. In these experiments, different groups of subjects are first trained under different experimental conditions. Later on, these main groups are divided into subgroups, some continuing under their original conditions, others switching to the alternative conditions. Appropriate statistical treatment makes it possible, under certain circumstances, to determine whether a variable influences learning or merely performance. In effect, these statistical techniques ask whether a variable produces a relatively permanent effect upon behavior, as the definition of learning requires. If such an influence can be detected, a particular variable is said to influence learning. If it cannot, the variable is said to affect performance.

Variables which presently seem to be performance variables, on the basis of such studies, include (1) the intensity of the conditioned stimulus, (2) motivation, (3) the amount of reinforcement, and (4) distribution of practice. We should recognize, however, that the factorial method is completely satisfactory only under limited conditions, where the outcome of the experiment provides a clear indication that the variable is a performance variable. Moreover, the concept that these variables have their effect exclusively upon performance is subject to revision on the basis of later experimental evidence.

Continuity vs. Noncontinuity Theory

There are two general theories of the form of the "true" learning function. One of these (continuity theory) takes the typical learning curve at face value and holds that learning is a gradual process. The other (noncontinuity theory) maintains that learning is sudden and insightful. Noncontinuity theories of two rather different sorts have been developed within the more general framework of S-R and S-S learning theories. The S-R noncontinuity position accounts for the gradual nature of most acquisition functions by the assumption that the stimulus situation changes from trial to trial, together with the further assumption that the strength of a learned response depends upon the proportion of these stimuli which have previously been conditioned to the response in question. Quantitative statements of this theory turn out to have much in common with certain versions of S-R continuity theory.

The S-S noncontinuity position explains the gradual form of the typical learning curve on the assumption that learning requires the testing and discarding of successive hypotheses until the subject hits upon the correct one. Although there is no doubt that hypothesis testing, as operationally defined in the S-S theory, occurs, tests of deductions from this theory for discrimination-reversal experiments have favored continuity theory rather than the S-S noncontinuity position.

Some of the disagreements between the continuity and noncontinuity positions may ultimately be resolved on the basis of experiments on learning sets. These studies have demonstrated that practice improves discrimination learning to the point where even lower animlas can solve a discrimination problem in one trial, if they have had considerable experience with problems of the same sort. Similar demonstrations have been made for other forms of learning as well. This suggests that insightful learning occurs as a result of abilities developed with practice.

·6·

The Parameters of Reinforcement

THE TERM *reinforcement* has two different meanings. As with the term *learning*, it is important to distinguish between its theoretical and its factual, or empirical, meanings. In its factual sense, reinforcement refers to any of a wide variety of conditions which may be introduced into the learning situation to increase the probability that a given response will reappear in the same situation. The theoretical meaning of reinforcement varies considerably from one systematist to another: Hull (1943) equates it with drive reduction; Skinner (1938) and Tolman (1932) deal with it in stimulus terms; for Thorndike (1911) it is a satisfier or annoyer; Guthrie (1935) regards it as something which alters a situation; Sheffield (1948) and Denny and Adelman (1955) view it as an elicitor of behavior.

These different views of the nature of reinforcement raise a number of basic problems to which we will turn in later chapters. In this chapter we will discuss a set of studies which require no theoretical commitment, being concerned most directly with an empirical description of the operation of reinforcement. Such researches have had as their aim the delineation of a set of functions describing the manner in which certain parameters of reinforcement control performance in the learning situation. The four main clusters of such parametric studies involve: (1) amount (quantity and quality) of reinforcement; (2) delay of reinforcement, (3) the interstimulus interval in classical conditioning, and (4) schedules of reinforcement. We will deal with each of them in some detail.

AMOUNT OF REINFORCEMENT

The phrase *amount of reinforcement* covers two rather different properties of reinforcers, which have sometimes been referred to as the quantity and quality of reinforcement. The quantity of reinforcement is easily specifiable in terms of some physical measure such as weight or volume. Quality of reinforcement, on the other hand, is usually specified in terms of the organism's preference. A reinforcer high in quality is one which the organism chooses in preference to others. P. T. Young (1945, 1947) has carried out a very extensive series of researches investigating the food preferences on one species, the rat.

In the previous chapter several of the studies of the effects of the amount of reinforcement were reviewed, chiefly for the purpose of setting forth the view that this variable seems to function as a performance variable. We are concerned here with the nature of the function which relates performance to the amount of reinforcement. In general, these studies have yielded results in agreement on the point that performance increases as a negatively accelerated function with increases in the amount of reinforcement. Among the investigations leading to this conclusion are those of Gantt, described by Hull (1943), Crespi (1942), Hutt (1954), and Zeaman (1949a) for quantity of reinforcement and those of Guttman (1953) and Hutt (1954) for quality of reinforcement.[1]

Hutt's investigation is of special interest because it is one in which amount of reinforcement was varied in two ways, by manipulating quantity and quality of reinforcement in a factorially designed experiment. Hutt used a semiliquid mixture of milk, flour, and water as a basic reinforcer. To produce three variations in quality of this basic mixture, Hutt added citric acid to it to make it sour and less acceptable for one group of rats; for another variation he added saccharin, producing a mixture which the rats preferred. The unadulterated basic mixture provided the third, intermediate, variation in quality. Different groups of rats were trained to press the bar in the Skinner box for each of these mixtures. Beyond this, three different subgroups within each quality group received different quantities of the mixture. The three quantities were: small, 3 mg.; medium, 12 mg.; and large, 50 mg.

The results of the experiment appear in Table 12, where mean response rate appears for each of the 9 subgroups in the experiment on the fifth day of training. The mean rates entered in the table show that both variables had an effect, that of quantity being somewhat greater than that of quality. This, however, may only mean that a wider effective range of quantities than qualities was sampled. Close examination of the entries in the table will show that there were no inversions. Increasing quantity led to an increasing response rate for each value on the quality dimension; similarly the order of the quality groups is citric, basic, saccharin for all quantity conditions.

The number of experiments concerned with variations in the intensity of a negative reinforcer is fewer than the number concerned with positive reinforcement, probably for several reasons: (1) It is more

---

[1] See also: Collier and Marx (1959), Crespi (1944), Denny and King (1955), Dufort and Kimble (1956), W. O. Jenkins and Clayton (1949), Maher and Wickens (1954), Nissen and Elder (1935).

TABLE 12

MEAN RATES OF BAR-PRESSING UNDER DIFFERENT COMBINATIONS OF AMOUNT AND QUALITY OF REINFORCEMENT (Hutt, 1954)

Quantity	Citric	Basic	Saccharin	Mean
Small	3.0	3.9	5.0	3.9
Medium	4.2	6.9	8.0	6.4
Large	8.2	11.1	13.8	11.0
Mean	5.1	7.3	8.9	

difficult to specify and control the intensity of most negative reinforcers. (2) There is a natural reluctance on the part of experimenters to employ strong negative reinforcers. (3) In an important theoretical way, the psychological significance of variations in the strength of a negative reinforcer is ambiguous. This is because the noxious stimuli employed in escape, defense, and avoidance learning seem to serve both as motivators and as reinforcers.

Such evidence as is available on the effects of the amount of negative reinforcement is quite consistent with data from studies employing positive reinforcement. Increasing intensities yield increasing amounts of conditioning (Boren, Sidman, and Herrnstein, 1959; Passey, 1948; Prokasy, Grant, and Myers, 1958); and there is some evidence that the

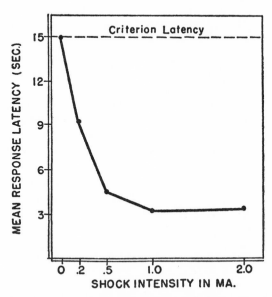

FIGURE 6.1. The latency of the instrumental wheel-turning avoidance reaction as a function of shock intensity (Kimble, 1955).

typical function is asymptotic beyond a certain intensity value. Kimble (1955) conditioned rats to rotate a wheel to avoid shock, using different shock intensities as the unconditioned stimuli for different groups of rats. The effect of these different shock intensities upon reaction latency appear in Figure 6.1.

DELAY OF REINFORCEMENT

Several independent lines of evidence suggest that responses spatially or temporally near reinforcement are learned more quickly than responses remote from reinforcement: (1) Tolman (1934b) showed that rats, running a maze which required two black-white discriminations, one after the other, learned the second of two discriminations more easily than the first. (2) It is well known that blinds in a complex maze tend to be mastered in a backward order (Montpellier, 1933). (3) Rats tend to take a short path to a goal rather than a long one (Yoshioka, 1929; Grice, 1942). (4) If, during the extinction of a running response in a straight alley, rats are blocked at various distances from the goal, extinction is more rapid if the block is placed near the starting box than if it is near to the goal box. (Lambert and Solomon, 1952). (5) There is a clear-cut speed of locomotion gradient in the behavior of a rat in a straight runway. The animal runs faster as it nears the goal (Hull, 1934c). All of these suggest that learning (or, perhaps, performance) varies directly with the immediacy with which reward follows the response to be learned. This *goal gradient,* or *delay-of-reinforcement gradient,* represents one of the most important applications of conditioning principles to more complex behavioral situations. The goal-gradient hypothesis as Hull originally formulated it is as follows:

The mechanism . . . depended upon as an explanatory and integrating principle is that the goal reaction gets conditioned the most strongly to the stimuli preceding it, and the other reactions of the behavior sequence get conditioned to their stimuli progressively weaker as they are more remote (in time or space) from the goal reaction. (Hull, 1932, pp. 25-26)

Two ideas are important in this statement. The first is the delay-of-reinforcement principle itself. The other is the implied analysis of a serial chain of behavior into smaller stimulus-response elements. This latter conception is basic to many of Hull's earlier theoretical treatments and represents an interest to which he returned later (Hull, 1952).

In many experiments the learned activity is more than a single response such as an eyelid closure or a finger withdrawal. This is particularly true of instrumental conditioning, in which the response involves a series of movements. The rat in the Skinner apparatus secures food by taking successive steps to approach the region of the lever, lifting its forelegs from the floor, pressing downward on the lever, lowering its body to the food cup, lowering its head, and opening its mouth to seize the food. In a straight alley, the locomotion of the rat from one end to the other may be considered a series of responses by analyzing the speed of running separately for the successive segments of the total path.

When an instrumental act is considered as a single response, it is possible to apply the principles of conditioning directly. For example, the maze habit, considered as a unit, will be acquired more rapidly if the reward is large and the animal is hungry. Gradual disappearance of the reaction will occur with trials on which the reward is omitted, and spontaneous recovery from this extinction will take place after an interval of no training. There are many facts about maze learning, however, which cannot be encompassed by this direct application of conditioning principles to the reaction as a unit. There is no possibility of explaining why the rat takes a shorter rather than a longer route through the maze, why some blind alleys are eliminated sooner than others, why mazes of different pattern vary in difficulty. The answers to such questions can be obtained only if the total maze reaction is analyzed in terms of its component parts and the stimuli to which these part-reactions occur.

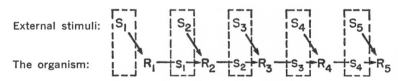

FIGURE 6.2. Stimuli and responses involved in a serial act. The reactions R_1, R_2, R_3, R_4, R_5 to the external stimuli S_1, S_2, S_3, S_4, S_5 become integrated as a series by the proprioceptive stimuli s_1, s_2, s_3, s_4 from the muscles used in the reactions. Original responses are represented by solid arrows, learned responses by broken ones. According to the goal-gradient hypothesis the strength of the connection $S_5\text{-}R_5 > S_4\text{-}R_4 > S_3\text{-}R_3$, and so on and similarly $s_4\text{-}R_5 > s_3\text{-}R_4$, and so on. After Hull (1930a).

Such an analysis, that of Hull (1930), in conditioning terms appears in Figure 6.2. S_1, S_2, and so on, represent the successive external stimuli provided by the environment, each evoking in the organism a separate response, R_1, R_2, and so on. Each of these responses produces a characteristic proprioceptive stimulus, such as s_1, s_2. Thus, in the chain of responses, a given reaction occurs in fairly close temporal proximity to a complex of stimuli which is partly external and partly internal. Learning consists in a strengthening of the tendency for these environmental and proprioceptive stimuli to evoke the appropriate response. The arrows in Figure 6.2 represent the stimulus-response connections in question.

Restated, the goal-gradient hypothesis is that these connections are more readily established for stimuli and responses near the goal than they are for stimuli and responses early in the sequence.

Learning the Shorter Path to a Goal

A common conception of maze learning is that it is a complex case of learning of the shortest of several possible routes to reward. Errors, such as entries into blind alleys, retracings, are actually reinforced, but a correct run results in reward sooner. According to the goal-gradient principle, the responses involved in a correct run should, therefore, be learned better (see Figure 6.3). More generally, animals should learn to take the shortest of several alternative paths to a goal.

Yoshioka (1929) performed a test of this deduction. Rats in his experi-

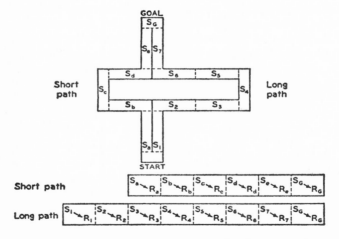

FIGURE 6.3. Explanation of the preference for the shorter of alternative paths according to Hull's goal-gradient hypothesis. In the upper diagram a maze is shown in which the short path consists of 5 units of length from start to goal, the long path, of 7 units. The stimuli associated with each unit are simplified as a series S_a to S_G and S_1 to S_G for the two paths. The goal-gradient hypothesis assumes that sequences of stimuli and responses as represented in the lower portion of the figure will be strengthened in proportion to their distance from the goal. If, then, there have been equal runs by way of the two paths in the past, when the animal is now confronted with the two stimuli S_a and S_1, the choice will be made on the basis of the tendency of S_a to evoke R_a as compared with the tendency of S_1 to evoke R_1. It is evident that the sequence S_a-R_a will be the more strongly conditioned because it lies nearer the goal. Therefore the short path will be entered. Stimulus components furnished by the drive and the movements of the organism have been omitted for purposes of simplicity in exposition. They have been included by Hull (1932).

ment ran a maze in which there were two alternative paths to food. The longer path was 211 inches from start to goal; for another maze of the same pattern, the longer path was twice as long, 422 inches. In either maze, the other path could be shortened to any desired length. Yoshioka tested rats in these two mazes, using ratios of long to short paths of 1.07, 1.14, 1.23, 1.33, and 1.44. He found (1) that rats did learn to take the short path, (2) that the rats took more trials to learn the short path when the ratios were small than when they were large, and (3) that equal ratios were equally difficult to learn in the short and in the long mazes. This led him to propose that it was the *relative* response strength, produced by differing delays of reinforcement, that determined the ease or difficulty of acquiring the short-path habit, and that the ease of learning to take the short path is independent of the lengths of the paths. According to this hypothesis learning to take the short path would be just as easy in a very small maze as in a very large one, as long as the ratios of short to long paths were equal. More recent evidence (Anderson, 1933; Grice, 1942) suggests that this specific interpretation is wrong and that the ratio and the absolute length of paths combine to determine the number of trials required to learn to take the shorter path.

The Form of the Delay-of-Reinforcement Gradient

Such evidence, together with the results of temporal delay-of-reinforcement studies to be considered presently, led Hull (1943) to propose the following equation as relating the limit of habit growth (M') to delay of reinforcement:

$$M' = M \times 10^{-KT}$$

where M is the maximum habit strength possible (in arbitrary units called *habs*), given the other conditions of the experiment (amount of reinforcement, and so on), T is delay of reinforcement, and K is an empirically determined constant. The form of this equation is that shown in Figure 6.4 for the case where $M = 80$ and $K = .00672$.

One application of this function explains the tendency of an animal to take the shorter of two alternative paths to a goal in a maze. To illustrate this application, let us consider a hypothetical experiment in which five different groups of subjects learn to take the short path in five different mazes which differ in absolute size while the ratio of delays of reinforcement remains constant at 2 to 1. To be specific, let us suppose that choosing the long path means that reinforcement is delayed by 10, 40, 160, 240, and 360 seconds. Choosing the short path leads to delays of 5, 20, 80, 120, and 180 seconds, and the ratios of delays in the five mazes are 10/5, 40/20, 160/80, 240/120, and 360/180. A glance at Figure 6.4 will show that the animals should eventually come to prefer

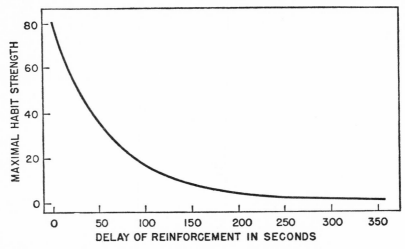

FIGURE 6.4. The exponential delay-of-reinforcement gradient proposed by Hull (1943). For purposes of dealing with problems in the text, values of maximal habit strength may be estimated by reading from a given delay value to the curve and from the curve to the vertical axis of the graph.

the shorter path in each of these cases because the limit of habit growth is greater with the shorter delay of reinforcement. The more specific question of the degree of this preference depends upon the manner in which the conflict between the tendency to take the short path and that to take the long path is resolved. In order to maintain consistency with other aspects of his theory, Hull assumed that it is the *difference* between the two habit strengths, not their ratio, which determines the degree of preference. For the five mazes in our hypothetical experiment the differences between the maximal habit strengths for the short and long paths are 5.51, 15.63, 16.47, 10.54, and 4.63 for the five mazes. The reader may verify this fact by reading in Figure 6.4 the maximal habit strengths associated with each delay and subtracting the smaller (long delay) from the larger (short delay) for each maze. The pattern of these values means that the discrimination between the two paths will be easiest when they are of intermediate length and more difficult when they are very short or very long. This prediction has never been tested in detail. Grice's (1942) data fit the prediction remarkably well, however, and Anderson's (1933) results show the predicted bow-shaped function for two ratios. It is of particular interest that the Yoshioka's original data are also in line with this interpretation, assuming that his maze lengths were within the fairly wide range of intermediate distances where equal ratios are nearly equally easy to discriminate.

The Order of Elimination of Blinds

A similar application of the goal-gradient principle predicts the backward order of elimination of blinds in maze learning. To illustrate, suppose that entering a blind alley adds 5 seconds to the time required to run the maze, and therefore, 5 seconds of delay of reinforcement. In short a correct response is always rewarded 5 seconds sooner than an error. Now let us consider the situation as it theoretically exists at choice points three different distances from the goal: a near, intermediate, and remote choice point. For illustrative purposes, assume that the correct response at the choice point near to the goal is rewarded after only 2 seconds; an error will be reinforced, therefore, after 7 seconds. Assume further that the intermediate and far choice points lead to reinforcement after 80 and 120 seconds for a correct response. This means that errors are reinforced after 85 and 125 seconds respectively. The delays of reinforcement associated with correct and incorrect choices at these three points in the maze are, thus, 2 and 7 seconds, 80 and 85 seconds, and 120 and 125 seconds. Reference to Figure 6.4 will show quite clearly that the difference in habit strength is greater in the case of the two shortest delays and becomes less and less for the pairs of longer delays. Therefore, the choice point near to the goal should be easiest to learn. The intermediate and far choice points should be progressively more difficult, because the maximal values of habit strength are more nearly the same.

Experimental tests of this deduction from the goal-gradient principle in complex mazes have yielded somewhat ambiguous results and have shown that many factors other than this principle enter to complicate the picture. For example, certain purely physical factors are important in controlling choice-point behavior. These include inertia, which favors a forward-going tendency, and *centrifugal swing* (Schneirla, 1929; Ballachey and Buel, 1934) which leads the animal to run off at a tangent after a turn and to take the opposite turn at the next choice point. Beyond this, animals tend to orient in the direction of the goal box, or sometimes their home cages, leading to errors into blinds pointing in that direction. Finally and most important, they tend to make *anticipatory responses,* that is, to make the response which is correct at the last choice point too soon. Because of such complexities, it is seldom that the blinds in a maze are eliminated in a perfect backward order, although a tendency toward such an order is usually obtained.

Detailed studies of the patterns of errors made by rats learning to traverse a maze have attempted to eliminate as many of these complicating factors as possible. But even under the best conditions, the functions obtained have been complicated. Depending upon the particular maze pattern, there are too many or too few errors in the middle of the maze. To account for such effects it has been necessary to assume the operation of additional theoretical mechanisms. The most thorough attempt to treat the order of elimination of maze blinds is that of Hull (1952) who combines the goal-gradient concept with that of the *fractional anticipatory goal response* (r_G) in order to make a series of deductions about the ease of learning different portions of the maze. From the goal-gradient principle Hull deduces, as we did above, that the response at the final choice point in a maze will be easiest to learn. Once it is learned,

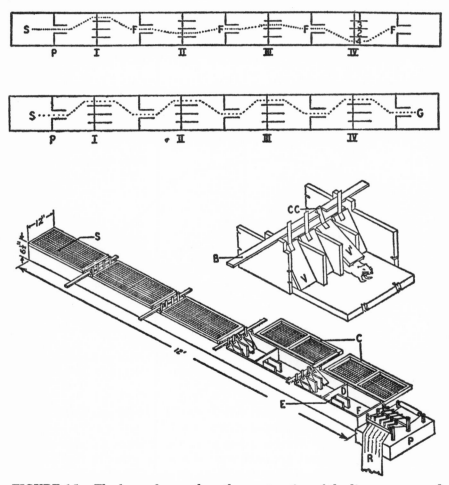

FIGURE 6.5. The lower figures show the construction of the linear maze used to study the order of elimination of blinds. The upper maze patterns illustrate, from top to bottom, a heterogeneous and homogeneous pattern. The figure is a composite constructed from figures published by Hull (1947a, 1948) and Sprow (1947).

however, it will tend, on the basis of stimulus generalization, to appear at other choice points, that is, in anticipation of the final choice point. Whether such anticipatory response tendencies aid or interfere with learning the maze depends upon the maze pattern.

Figure 6.5 illustrates a maze used by Hill (1939), Hull (1947a), and Sprow (1947)[2] to study the order of elimination of errors in a linear maze. As the two schematic ground plans illustrate, the correct path through the maze may require either a series of identical responses (*homogeneous compound trial-and-error learning*) or a series of different responses (*heterogeneous compound trial-and-error learning*). In the homogeneous case, anticipatory responses are always correct and aid learning; in the heterogeneous case these responses are always anticipatory errors and interfere. Figure 6.6 illustrates this point by means of

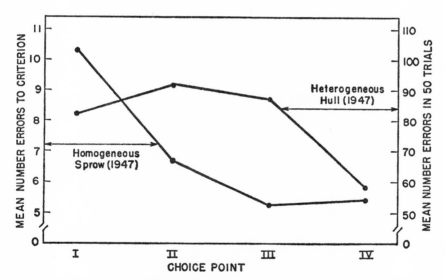

FIGURE 6.6. Comparison of the pattern of errors obtained in heterogeneous and homogeneous compound trial-and-error learning. Data from Hull (1947a) and Sprow (1947).

the data obtained by Hull (1947) and Sprow (1947) for the heterogeneous and homogeneous cases respectively.

The general shape of the functions plotted in Figure 6.6 shows that predictions from the goal gradient will be most in error in the middle portion of the maze. It predicts too many errors in this region for the homogeneous case and too few for the heterogeneous one. Hull (1952) theorizes that this reflects the fact previously mentioned, that anticipa-

[2] See also Arnold (1947a, 1947b, 1948, 1951), Herbert and Arnold (1947), and Gladstone (1948).

tory responses hinder learning in one case and benefit it in the other. The problem is to account for the fact that these aids and interferences are concentrated in the middle of the maze. Hull shows that the principles of stimulus generalization and stimulus intensity dynamism can be made to deal with this fact. In this derivation Hull stresses the control of the response by proprioceptive rather than exteroceptive stimuli, because the latter are nearly identical at all choice points and, by generalization, should tend to elicit the goal reaction equally. The proprioceptive stimulus situation, however, changes from choice point to choice point in important ways. Specifically Hull proposes that the intensity of the stimulus traces left by the responses involved in making previous choices will be greater in the middle of the maze than anywhere else. This is because the first choices occur in the absence of such traces and, by the time the last choice point is reached, the strength of the proprioceptive traces has already begun to deteriorate. It is for this reason that the final correct response shows the greatest tendency to be elicited anticipatorily in the middle of the maze, leading to an excess of errors in the case of heterogeneous compound trial-and-error learning and to a pre-

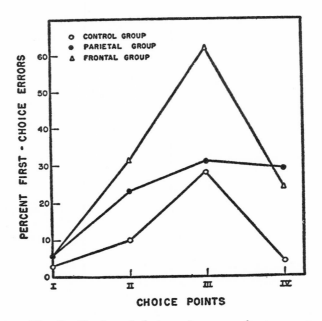

FIGURE 6.7.   The distribution of choice-point errors for two groups of brain-damaged rats and a normal control group. It will be observed that the group with damage in the frontal areas made a great many errors at the second and third choice-points. Since these were anticipatory errors, the inference is that one function of the frontal cortex is to inhibit such premature responses. Data from Carpenter (1952).

ponderance of correct responses in the homogeneous case. A basic assumption in this deduction is that the probability of occurrence of a proprioceptively controlled response depends upon the intensity of the proprioceptive stimulus trace. As we have seen, there is reason to accept such an assumption for exteroceptive stimuli (p. 120).

There is evidence from brain ablation studies that anticipatory errors are, to some extent, prevented in normal animals by functions of the frontal cerebral cortex. Carpenter (1952) trained rats in a four-choice linear maze in which the pattern of correct choices was right, right, right, left. The purpose of this order was to provide an optimal opportunity to study the appearance of the final left response at the other, preceding, choice points. Some of the animals in this study were normal and some had had extensive portions of the frontal or parietal cortex removed. Figure 6.7 is a presentation of the pattern of errors for these three groups. The brain-damaged animals made many more errors than the normal ones, but this difference was not statistically significant in comparisons of the behavior of normal and parietal animals. The animals with frontal ablations were, as the graph suggests, inferior to either of these groups. Similar evidence, that the frontal cortex inhibits the early appearance of the final correct response, has been obtained by Crawford, Fulton, Jacobsen, and Wolfe (1948), Harlow, Davis, Settlage, and Meyer (1952), and Jacobsen, Wolfe, and Jackson (1935).

The Speed-of-Locomotion Gradient

Exactly the same reasoning used in the prediction of the order of elimination of blinds applies to the speed with which an animal traverses a maze. The goal gradient alone leads us to expect ever-increasing speeds as the animal approaches the goal. Considerations involving an application of the principle of stimulus generalization, however, suggest that speed may be greater at some point prior to the final maze segment than it is in this segment itself. Such an argument, it will be seen, treats speed of running as a chaining of homogeneous responses.

Figure 6.8 presents data obtained by Hull on the time spent by rats in various segments of a 40-foot straight runway. As anticipated, the animals spent most time in the maze sections nearest the starting box and showed a progressive increase in speed as they approached the goal, slowing up slightly in the final segment. All of these features tended to be more marked early in training than late. The bottom line in Figure 6.8 shows that protracted training flattened the gradient. The effects were later confirmed by Drew (1939) who also showed that the gradient occurs in many situations and is more pronounced under conditions of massed than under conditions of distributed practice. The goal-gradient hypothesis, particularly the empirical representation of it in the speed-of-loco-

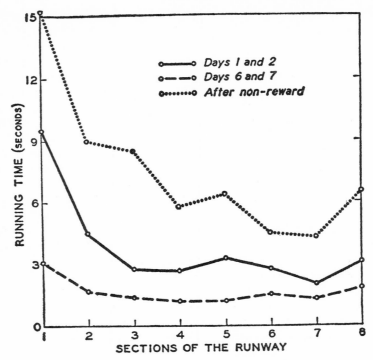

FIGURE 6.8. The speed-of-locomotion gradient of the rat in a 40-foot runway.
Composite graphs from 14 animals showing the time consumed in traversing
each of the eight 5-foot sections at the two extremes of training and a subsequent restoration of the gradient following non-reward (that is, absence of
food at the end of the alley). Although the gradient has virtually disappeared
by the end of training, non-reward restores it in its earlier form. (Hull,
1934b, p. 404.)

motion gradient, has been extended to an S-R analysis of conflict behavior
(Ch. 14).

The Temporal Delay-of-Reinforcement Gradient

In various ways the studies described up to this point suggest the
importance of the time between the occurrence of a response and its
reinforcement, and they imply the existence of a temporal gradient
according to which reactions followed by immediate reinforcement are
better learned than those more remote from reinforcement. Experiments
employing mazes and runways of different lengths, however, are poorly
suited to an uncomplicated investigation of the temporal delay gradient.
Increasing delay introduces an increasingly long chain of responses between a response and reinforcement, which probably simultaneously inter-

feres with performance through an inhibitory mechanism and facilitates it through a mediation process to be discussed later. Clearly there is a need for studies of delay of reinforcement in which the effects of these chains of responses are somehow nullified.

The general method employed in several studies of this sort has been to allow the animal to perform some response and then to restrain it in a delay chamber for a period of delay required by the plan of the experiment. The first such investigation seems to have been that of Watson (1917) who trained rats to dig through sawdust to get to a cup containing food. One group was allowed to eat the food immediately; the other was required to wait for 30 seconds before eating. Watson obtained no difference between the performance of the two groups. The delay group in this experiment remained in the vicinity of the food cup which gave off the odor of food. Moreover, the subjects were familiar with the food cup, having eaten from it in pretraining. Thus the sight of the food cup and the odor of food were present as powerful secondary reinforcers, which probably accounts for the fact that the rats in the delay condition learned as well as those given immediate primary reinforcement. Later studies have often attempted to eliminate the effects of secondary reinforcement, and a few have compared learning under delayed-reward conditions with and without secondary reinforcement.

In general these studies have obtained delay-of-reinforcement gradients, the durations of which depend upon the success with which secondary reinforcement has been eliminated. In some preliminary experiments, Skinner, (1938, pp. 72ff.) found delays of 1, 2, 3, and 4 seconds equally efficacious in the lever-pressing situation. The delay was introduced between the pressing of the lever and the delivery of the food, with a provision for starting the interval over again if a response occurred in the delay period. Although no gradient appeared under these conditions, Skinner did (1938, pp. 139ff.) find one in other forms of his experiment. In one study with a periodic, or fixed-interval, schedule delays of 2, 4, 6, and 8 seconds were introduced before the reinforcement. Rate of responding declined following the introduction of these delays. Intervals of 6 or 8 seconds produced reductions in rate of approximately 50 per cent. Perin (1943) also studied delay of reinforcement in a Skinner situation, employing a trial-by-trial procedure and delays of 0, 2, 5, 10, 20, and 30 seconds. Using the slope of the learning curve as an index of response strength, Perin's results are quite consistent with those of Skinner, slopes for the 5-second and 10-second delay groups being a little less than half those for the 0-second delay group (see Figure 6.10).[3]

Wolfe's (1934) experiment is representative of a number of studies of delayed reward carried out in other instrumental learning situations.

[3] For other studies of the effect of delay of reinforcement using Skinner-type procedures, see Harker (1956), Logan (1952), and Seward and Weldon (1953).

Wolfe found that delays as short as 5 seconds interfered with the learning of a single T-maze by rats. Longer delays, up to 20 minutes, produced progressive decreases in the efficiency with which the task was mastered, the greater part of the decrease occurring within the first minute. Later investigators have pointed out that even this relatively steep gradient is probably too extended. Perkins (1947) calls attention to the fact that, in such studies, any differences between the delay chambers preceding reward and those preceding nonreward can provide the basis for differential secondary reinforcement. In what amounts to a repetition of the Wolfe study, with this source of secondary reinforcement eliminated by interchanging delay chambers from trial to trial, he obtained a gradient which fell to a lower level with long delays than Wolfe's gradient had. This comparison appears in Figure 6.9. There was, however, a significant amount of learning with a delay of 2 minutes. Perkins attributes this to secondary reinforcement provided by the differential proprioceptive cues produced by making the correct or incorrect turn in the T-maze.

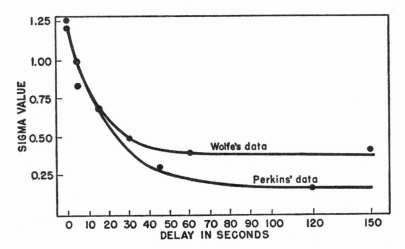

FIGURE 6.9. Delay-of-reinforcement gradients obtained by Wolfe (1934) and Perkins (1947) in the T-maze. The superior performance at long delays in Wolfe's experiment is attributed by Perkins to the operation of secondary reinforcement.

In an attempt to eliminate even these proprioceptive cues, Grice (1948) performed an experiment with a black-white discrimination problem, in which different delays of reinforcement followed the response. Since the positive and negative stimuli shift from side to side on different trials in discrimination learning, there can be no distinctive proprioceptive stimuli associated with the correct response. Under these conditions Grice obtained the delay of reinforcement function shown in Figure 6.10. It is

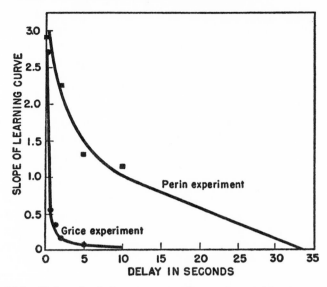

FIGURE 6.10. Delay-of-reinforcement gradients obtained by Perin (1943a) in the Skinner box and Grice (1948) in discrimination learning. Grice's procedure effectively eliminated secondary reinforcement with the result that there is little learning with delays of 5 seconds or longer.

clearly much steeper than any of the gradients previously obtained, a fact attributed to the complete elimination of secondary reinforcement.

Both Grice and Perkins ran additional groups of subjects in their experiments for the purpose of attempting to assess the importance of secondary reinforcement directly. Perkins, for example, ran one group of subjects using a 45-second delay and very different delay chambers following correct and incorrect turns. This group learned significantly better than the group in the main experiment in which the boxes were identical. Grice used two groups for which he introduced secondary reinforcement. For one of these groups, the correct and incorrect goal boxes were the same color (black or white) as the positive and negative stimuli. For the other group the responses required in traversing the two routes to the goal were very different. One route required a sharp turn, the other climbing an inclined plane. With a 5-second delay of reinforcement, both of these groups mastered the discrimination with greater ease than the group without such sources of secondary reinforcement.

Delay of Reinforcement in Aversive Conditioning

It is impossible to formulate a plan to study delay of reinforcement in escape and avoidance learning without making an initial commitment to some particular theory of the nature of reinforcement. If one holds that the reinforcing power of an aversive stimulus occurs with the onset of this stimulus, then one studies delay of reinforcement by manipulating the time between the presentation of a warning signal and the onset of the aversive stimulus. Experiments of this sort represent a version of the interstimulus-interval experiment to be discussed later.

If, on the other hand, one accepts a drive-reduction theory of reinforcement and regards escape from a noxious stimulus to be the critical reinforcing event, the appropriate experiment to use in the investigation of delay of reinforcement is one in which shock termination follows the response to be learned by varying periods of time. No experiments using exactly this procedure seem to have been done. Various studies manipulating the duration of a noxious UCS in classical conditioning have been done, however, (Mowrer and Solomon, 1954; Wegner and Zeaman, 1958). They have uniformly found UCS duration to have no effect upon conditioning. This seems to mean that the critical reinforcing event in classical conditioning occurs with UCS onset, and that the drive-reduction analysis does not apply.

Instrumental avoidance conditioning provides a somewhat different opportunity to investigate delay of reinforcement by manipulating the time at which the warning signal terminates. This procedure again as-

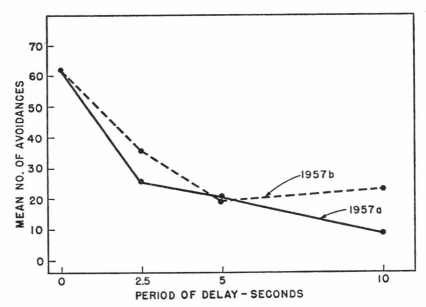

FIGURE 6.11   Delay-of-reinforcement gradient obtained when the delay period is the interval between the response and the cessation of a stimulus previously associated with pain (Kamin, 1957a, 1957b).

sumes a drive-reduction interpretation of reinforcement. Briefly the reasoning is as follows: the warning signal, through its association with punishment, becomes a noxious stimulus, itself. Thus the termination of this stimulus should be reinforcing, and postponing the time at which it terminates should be the same as delaying any other reinforcement. Kamin (1957a, 1957b) investigated this possibility in a series of studies with rats. In his experiments the CS was a buzzer, and the response required of the subjects to avoid a shock was that of running from one side of a shuttle box to the other. For different groups, the offset of the buzzer followed the execution of the correct response by 0.0, 2.5, 5.0, or 10.0 seconds. Learning was much better when the response terminated the buzzer immediately than it was under any of the other conditions. Figure 6.11 presents the results from two of Kamin's experiments in terms of mean number of avoidance reactions. The function is quite similar to those which have been obtained by other investigators using positive reinforcers.

The Delay-of-Punishment Gradient

Possibly because of the undependable effect of punishment upon behavior, the number of studies concerned with a possible delay-of-punishment gradient is small. The experiments of Bevan and Dukes (1955), Warden and Dymond (1931), and Kamin (1959) exhaust the list. In Kamin's study rats learned to go from one compartment to the other in a shuttlebox in order to avoid shock. Then, in extinction, five groups of animals were punished with electric shock for making the avoidant response and one group was not. For the different punishment groups the shock was delayed by 0, 10, 20, 30, or 40 seconds after the occurrence of the reaction. As an over-all effect, it was found that punishment markedly reduced the number of trials to extinction. Whereas the control group gave about 45 responses, the experimental group showing the greatest resistance to extinction gave only about 10. Median number of responses in extinction for the 0-, 10-, 20-, 30-, and 40-second delay groups were 3.0, 5.5, 10.5, 9.5, and 9.5 respectively. It thus appears that there is a delay-of-punishment gradient which has some of the same features as the more widely studied delay-of-reinforcement gradient. It would be interesting to know whether this gradient is approximately the same for the situation in which the punished response was established with a positive reinforcer.

INTERSTIMULUS INTERVAL

In classical conditioning experiments the time between conditioned and unconditioned stimuli is a variable which parallels delay of reinforcement in instrumental learning. In this case, however, the delay period is measured from the onset of the CS rather than from the occurrence of a response.

Pavlov regarded the "simultaneous" conditioned response as basic to other types and usually established it before proceeding to develop a trace or delayed CR. The ordinary procedure for producing a delayed conditioned reflex, for example, was to condition simultaneously and then to postpone the unconditioned stimulus for five seconds each day until the desired delay was reached. By a "simultaneous" CR Pavlov meant one in which the CS-UCS interval was 5 seconds or less. He apparently found no important differences in ease of conditioning with the CS-UCS intervals between 0 and 5 seconds. More recent American evidence, however, indicates that the optimal interval is much shorter than 5 seconds, probably being something more like a tenth of that value. Pavlov's success in obtaining conditioning with relatively long intervals raises a question to which we will return in the next chapter, when we will be in a position to consider the possible relevance of secondary reinforcement to this fact.

TABLE 13

RESULTS OF TYPICAL STUDIES OF THE INTERSTIMULUS-INTERVAL FUNCTION

Investigator(s)	Response	Intervals in seconds. Negative numbers refer to backward conditioning procedures.	Results
Bernstein (1934)	Eyeblink	—.90, —.50, .10, .25, .30, .50, 1.0, 1.5	Best conditioning at .30 sec. Little or none in backward procedure. No reliable difference between .30 interval and longer.
Boneau (1958)	Eyeblink	.50, shifted to 1.0 or 1.5	Level of conditioning and latency of CR altered appropriately by shift.
Cohen (1950)	Flexion in sheep	0, that is, CS and UCS strictly simultaneous	CR (perhaps pseudo-CR) appeared early in conditioning and extinguished with further practice.
Fitzwater and Riesman (1952)	Finger withdrawal	—.5, 0, .5	Confirmed Cohen (above) for 0-second group. Conditioning with forward procedure; not with backward.
Fitzwater and Thrush (1956)	Finger withdrawal	0, .1, .2, .3, .4, .6	Best conditioning at .4 seconds.

TABLE 13—*Continued*

Investigator(s)	Response	Intervals in seconds. Negative numbers refer to backward conditioning procedures.	Results
Kappauf and Schlosberg (1937)	Leg flexion & respiration	1/3, 2/3, 1, 2, 4	Flexion response showed little conditioning at any interval. Respiration conditioned best at 2/3 second.
Kimble (1947)	Eyeblink	.1, .2, .225, .250, .3, .4	Conditioning best at .4 seconds.
Kimble, Mann, and Dufort (1955)	Eyeblink	.5, 1.0, 2.0	Conditioning best at .5 seconds.
Kish (1955)	Wheel turning to light to avoid shock (rats)	.25, 1.0, 5.0	Resistance to extinction of avoidant response greatest after .25 sec. training interval.
McAllister (1953a)	Eyeblink	.1, .25, .45, .70, 2.0	Conditioning best and equally good at .25 and .45 sec. intervals.
McAllister (1953b)	Eyeblink	.45 shifted to .035 or 2.5	Level of response altered appropriately with shift.
Moeller (1954)	GSR	.25, .45, 1.0, 2.5 and backward conditioning control	Best conditioning at .45 sec. confirmed White and Schlosberg (below).
Nagaty (1951a)	Instrumental wheel turn to avoid shock. Nonshock control (rats)	Backward procedure. Shock presented 1 sec. before CS in extinction.	Backward conditioning produced response decrement.
Nagaty (1951b)	Bar press to obtain food (rats)	Food presented 2 sec. before CS (presentation of bar) in extinction	Confirmed experiment with shock (Nagaty, 1951a, above).
Spooner and Kellogg (1947)	Finger withdrawal	—.5, —.25, 15, 1.0, 1.5	Best conditioning at .5 sec. Confirmed Cohen, in that level of responding decreased with practice in backward conditions.
White and Schlosberg (1952)	GSR	0, .25, .50, 1.0, 2.0, 4.0 plus pseudoconditioning control	Best conditioning at .50 sec.

Studies of the interstimulus interval have most often been carried out on the conditioning of motor reflexes, although exceptions do occur.

Table 13 presents a sample of relevant investigations in very brief form, and Figure 6.12 presents the results of three of them graphically. As these materials indicate, the most typical finding has been that the optimal interval is in the quarter-second range on either side of .5 seconds. Exceptions to this rule (Kamin, 1954; F. R. Brush, E. L. Brush, and Solomon, 1954; Church, F. R. Brush, and Solomon, 1956) have almost always come from studies of avoidance learning where the interstimulus interval may play a different role than it does in classical conditioning. Moreover, these studies have usually failed to sample intervals shorter than about 5 seconds. Where such intervals have been employed (Kish, 1955), there is some suggestion that the optimal interval is less than one second.

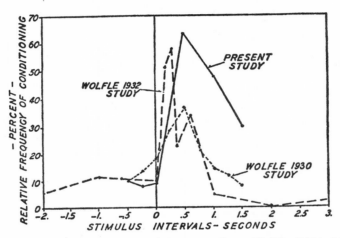

FIGURE 6.12.   Interstimulus-interval functions from Wolfle (1930, 1932) and Spooner and Kellogg (1947). Graph is from the paper by Spooner and Kellogg.

Other facts of importance appearing in the materials in Table 13 and Figure 6.12 are the following: (1) It is apparent that backward conditioning in which the UCS precedes the CS leads to little conditioning. With only one or two exceptions (Switzer, 1930) attempts at backward conditioning have met with little success (Cason, 1935; Porter, 1938b). The small amount which does occur is probably the result of pseudo-conditioning rather than the development of a true conditioned association between CS and UCS. Both Barlow (1956) and Konorski (1948, p. 136) have suggested that the backward conditioning procedure actually leads to the conditioning of a response antagonistic to the CR. (2) It is important to note that the shapes of these functions show that the absolutely optimal interval is difficult to determine. Since the curves increase in a negatively accelerated way from zero to their maxima, there will obviously be a range of nearly optimal intervals. (3) When the interstimulus interval has been changed in the course of conditioning, the result has been a gradual shift in the level of conditioning to a level appropriate to the new interval. (4) It is a matter of considerable interest that the interstimulus-interval function for GSR conditioning seems to be the same as that for skeletal responses such as finger retraction and the eyeblink. This is somewhat surprising because the temporal characteristics of the two types of response are very different, longer latencies and durations being typical of autonomically controlled reactions like the GSR. Two possibilities have been offered as explanations for this similarity of function. White and Schlosberg (1952) take such results to mean that the associations formed in classical conditioning are of a stimulus-stimulus sort rather than stimulus-response, so that the precise nature of the response would make no difference. Moeller (1954) and Smith (1954), on the other hand, adopt the position that the "conditioned" GSR is not a direct response to the CS, but is, rather, an unconditioned response which occurs as a by-product of unmeasured skeletal reactions which are the true CR's in these experiments. This latter position, thus, explains the unexpected similarity of the interstimulus interval functions for GSR and skeletal reflexes by the hypothesis that both involve motor responses. There is little evidential basis for choosing one of these explanations over the other. (5) It is to be noted that the delay-of-reinforcement function obtained in the absence of secondary reinforcement and the interstimulus-interval function appear to be quite similar. Both Duryea (1955) and Smith (1951) have noted this fact and have performed experiments designed to make a comparison of the two functions possible.

The reasoning behind these two studies is most easily presented in terms of the concrete learning situation (Figure 6.13) which both of them employed. This apparatus was a T-maze in which the color of one section of the stem could be changed from trial to trial in order to provide a distinctive cue. The procedure involved a form of successive discrimination (p. 362) in which the subjects were required to learn to go one way at the choice point if the distinctive section of the stem had been white and the other if it had been black. To study delay of reinforcement, the interval between response and reward, the subjects were confined for a fixed period of time in the section of the maze *following* the choice point. To study a process conceived to be analogous to the interstimulus interval, the subjects were delayed in the section *before* the choice point. In both studies delays of the latter sort were found to interfere with learning. The results obtained by Smith also suggested that the function relating the amount of such interference to time is similar to the delay-of-reinforcement gradient obtained by Grice, reach-

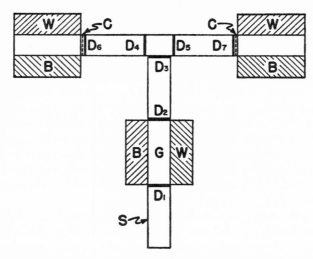

FIGURE 6.13. T-maze used by Duryea (1955) in his study to compare the effect of delay before and after the choice point in a maze. Symbols are to be read as follows: S = starting box; D = door; B, G, and W = black, gray, and white, respectively; C = curtain. Delay before the choice point was manipulated by closing doors D_2 and D_3 to confine the animals. Confinement following the choice-point was accomplished in the same way. Color of one section of the approach alley and the goal boxes could be changed so that they matched or did not match.

ing an asymptote in a matter of 5 or 10 seconds. Duryea's results also suggest that a delay of only a few seconds before the choice point produces a marked increase in the difficulty of learning. But in this experiment a similar delay of reinforcement following the choice failed to impede the progress of learning.

SCHEDULES OF REINFORCEMENT

In experimental practice, reinforcement may occur on every trial or after every correct response, or it may occur less often than this. The first procedure is that of *continuous reinforcement*; the second is *partial* (or *intermittent*) reinforcement. Partial reinforcement is administered according to some *schedule* in which reinforcement is given either on a time-contingent basis or for a certain proportion of correct responses.

In one of the earliest experiments on partial reinforcement, Pavlov (1927, pp. 384-386) found that conditioned responses developed rapidly if reinforcement was given only every second or third trial, but failed to develop if reinforcement was given only on every fourth trial. Later studies employing rats in the Skinner box and in the T-maze (Brunswick, 1939), eyelid conditioning (Grant and Schipper, 1952; Humphreys,

1939a; Kimble, Mann, and Dufort, 1955) and the GSR (Humphreys, 1939c) in human subjects, flexion responses in dogs with food and shock reinforcement (Brogden, 1939a), and an object-displacing response in monkey (Michels, 1955) have obtained results in general agreement with Pavlov's finding. In summary these investigations have shown that performance during conditioning is usually, but not always, somewhat poorer under partial reinforcement than under continuous reinforcement, and that a marked reduction in level of conditioning occurs when the proportion of reinforced trials is reduced to 20 or 25 per cent. Several of these investigations have also demonstrated that resistance to extinction is greater following partial reinforcement than following continuous reinforcement. This fact will be considered in more detail in Chapter 10.

The Michels study mentioned above investigated response latencies of monkeys under 11 different proportions of reinforcement ranging from zero to 100 per cent. On each trial the experimenter presented the subject with a single object in the Wisconsin General Test Apparatus

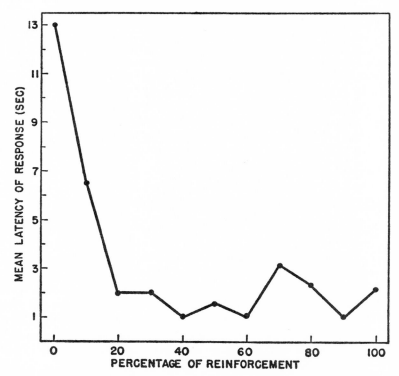

FIGURE 6.14.   Response latency as a function of percentage of reinforcement
(Michels, 1955).

(shown in Figure 12.11, p. 386). A food reward was placed under the object in the proportion of trials dictated by the experimental condition. The response measure obtained was the time between the presentation of the object and the monkey's response. Averages of these measures are presented in Figure 6.14, where is it quite apparent that an increase in response latency occurs in the neighborhood of 20 per cent reinforcement. Above 20 per cent reinforcement, increasing values seem to make little difference. It is a matter of some interest that this latter result seems to appear only in instrumental conditioning situations. Classically conditioned responses suffer more from low percentages of reinforcement.[4]

The most extensive work on schedules of reinforcement is that of Skinner and his associates (Skinner, 1938; Ferster and Skinner, 1957). These investigators have confined their research almost exclusively to the free-responding behavior of rats and pigeons and have amassed very large amounts of data on the instrumental, or operant, bar-pressing and key-pecking reactions of these organisms. The schedules studied by Skinner's group are of four basic varieties derived from the considerations (*a*) that reinforcement may be administered on a time- or response-determined basis, and (*b*) that the temporal or response contingency may be regular or irregular. Time-based schedules are *interval schedules*; response-based schedules are *ratio schedules*. Regular schedules are referred to as *fixed;* irregular schedules are *variable*. The four basic schedules, thus, are the following: (1) *Fixed Interval* (which Skinner, 1938, previously called *periodic*). In this schedule reinforcement follows the first response which occurs after some specified period of time measured from the last reinforcement. In a one-minute fixed-interval schedule, for example, reinforcement occurs for the first response to occur one minute or more following the previous reinforcement. (2) *Variable Interval* (previously called *aperiodic*). In this schedule, reinforcement occurs after a period of time which varies from reinforcement to reinforcement. A simple one-minute variable-interval schedule might consist of a haphazard sequence of reinforcements administered for the first responses to occur after 20, 40, 60, 80, or 100 seconds. It is called a one-minute schedule because the mean inter-reinforcement interval is 60 seconds. (3) *Fixed Ratio*. In this schedule, reinforcement occurs after every n^{th} response, such as every fifteenth. In this case the ratio of unreinforced

[4] Jenkins and Stanley (1950) and Lewis (1960) have surveyed the literature on partial reinforcement and provide a comprehensive summary up to the dates of their publications. Skinner's (1938) book presents a large amount of material on schedules of reinforcement in the white rat. As a treatise on general problems of learning, it is probably of greater interest today than when it was published. The Ferster and Skinner (1957) book provides a catalogue of response functions, chiefly for pigeons, under a variety of schedules. The paper of Long, Hammack, and Campbell (1959) is of particular interest in showing the extent to which children's performance under intermittent reinforcement resembles that of lower animals.

to reinforced responses is 15:1. (4) *Variable Ratio.* Reinforcement occurs after a number of responses which changes from one reinforcement to another. A 15:1 variable ratio schedule might be produced by randomly reinforcing every 5th, 10th, 15th, 20th, or 25th response.

These different schedules of reinforcement affect responding in characteristic ways. Performance on the fixed-interval schedule often consists of a pause followed by a positively accelerating rate of response until the moment of reinforcement. The pause is of greater duration for long fixed intervals than for short ones and may disappear with extended practice. Variable-interval schedules produce a pattern of performance characterized by constant rates of responding over long periods of time. Because of the great stability of behavior produced by the variable-interval schedule, animals are often trained on it as a preliminary to some other treatment such as a test for generalization (Guttman and Kalish, 1956) or the administration of a drug (Sidman, 1955c, 1956a).

By comparison with the interval schedules, fixed-ratio schedules tend to produce very high rates of responding. If the ratio is a small one, responding begins immediately after reinforcement. If the ratio is large, however, a pause occurs after reinforcement, and responding begins only after a delay which increases with increases in the size of the ratio (see Figure 6.15). The subject tends in this schedule to respond either at a maximal rate or not at all. The same general statement applies to per-

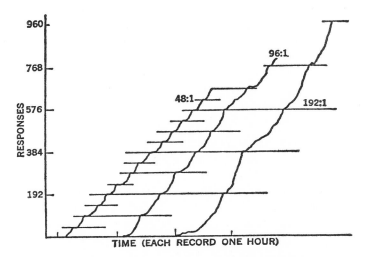

FIGURE 6:15. Cumulative response records obtained under three different fixed-ratio schedules. Reinforcement occurred at the points indicated by the horizontal lines. The pauses following reinforcement are particularly conspicuous in the 48:1 ratio. After Skinner (1938) as modified by Keller and Schoenfeld (1950).

formance under variable-ratio schedules. The pauses, however, tend to occur at times other than immediately following reinforcement. As with the fixed-ratio schedule, low variable-ratio schedules tend to produce high response rates without pauses.

Ferster and Skinner (1957) report the effects of several additional schedules such as the *tandem schedule,* in which a single reinforcement is programmed by two different schedules operating in succession; *rate-reinforcement schedules,* in which high or low rates of responding are reinforced; *multiple schedules,* in which a signal marks a change from one reinforcement contingency to another; *chained schedules,* in which responses in one schedule produce the stimulus which indicates that another schedule is now in operation, the new schedule being the one on which reinforcement occurs; and *concurrent schedules,* in which two or more schedules function at the same time, with reinforcement occurring according to both. These schedules have not been investigated so thoroughly as those described previously. The interested reader is referred to the Ferster and Skinner book.

SUMMARY

Without becoming deeply involved in the question of the theoretical meaning of the term, *reinforcement,* it is possible to consider a variety of empirical relationships between certain aspects of reinforcement and the rate of learning. The parameters which occupy the position of independent variables in these functions are: (1) the amount of reinforcement, (2) the delay of reinforcement, (3) the interstimulus interval, and (4) schedules of reinforcement. The most important points to be made about each of these are outlined in summary form below.

Amount of Reinforcement

The expression, *amount of reinforcement,* refers to two aspects of reinforcers, their quantity and quality. The quantity of reinforcement is specifiable in terms of physical measures of volume, concentration, weight, and so on; the quality of reinforcement is specifiable in terms of the organism's preferences for one reinforcer as opposed to another. Manipulation of these parameters of reinforcement in a variety of experiments leads to the conclusion that, with increasing amounts of reinforcement, performance in the learning situation increases according to a negatively accelerated function. This statement holds for negative reinforcers as well as for positive reinforcers. We have seen in the last chapter that the influence of the amount of reinforcement is mainly upon performance. We shall see in the next chapter that the effect involves the mechanism of secondary reinforcement.

Delay of Reinforcement

Evidence of many kinds indicates that responses which are followed by reward immediately are learned more rapidly than responses for which reward is delayed. On the basis of such evidence Hull was led in 1932 to formulate the *goal-gradient hypothesis,* in which he proposed: (*a*) that complex chains of behavior could be analyzed profitably into component elements; and (*b*) that the response elements occurring near the goal were learned more easily than those remote from the goal. Hull showed that applications of this principle could account for the major details of the speed of locomotion gradient, which is characteristic of the behavior of rats in a straight runway, and the ability of animals to learn to take the shorter of two paths to a goal. Some of the finer details of these same phenomena, however, can be understood only if the exact form of the delay-of-reinforcement gradient is taken into account.

For this reason Hull proposed, later, that the delay-of-reinforcement gradient is a decelerated negative function of time, when the level of learning is expressed in terms of theoretical units of habit strength. One of the predictions to which this reformulation leads is that the ease with which the short path to a goal can be learned (in cases where the ratio of the lengths of short to long paths remains constant) will vary with the absolute lengths of the paths. Specifically, such learning will be easier when the paths are of intermediate length than when they are either very long or very short. Incomplete evidence supports this prediction.

Other applications of the revised goal-gradient hypothesis require additional assumptions. For example, any version of this theory applied without modifying assumptions predicts a strict backward order of the elimination of blinds in a maze. That is, the final choices will be learned first and the initial choices will be learned last. Experimental data support this deduction only in a very general way. The failure of confirmation is due in part to a set of complications which are peculiar to the complex maze, and in part to the fact that it is necessary to take additional considerations into account to explain the order of elimination of errors. A combination of the principles of stimulus generalization and delay of reinforcement seems capable of predicting the pattern of errors in certain simple linear mazes with four choice points.

Experiments designed to determine the exact form of the delay-of-reinforcement gradient have led to successive revisions downward of the estimated amount of time by which reinforcement can be delayed if learning is to occur. At the present time it seems unlikely that learning can take place at all with delays of more than a few seconds. This statement applies to negative as well as to positive reinforcers. Instances of learning with protracted delays of reward are always cases where immediate secondary reinforcement occurs. This point will be discussed further in the next chapter.

The Interstimulus Interval

The interstimulus interval refers to the time between the onset of a conditioned stimulus and the onset of an unconditioned stimulus. Strictly speaking, this variable applies only to classical conditioning. Studies in which the interstimulus interval has been manipulated have shown that the optimal temporal separation of CS and UCS is about .5 seconds, with the CS appearing first. Either longer or shorter intervals lead to poorer learning. Backward conditioning, in which the UCS precedes the CS, probably leads to no learning at all, unless perhaps it produces the acquisition of a response which is antagonistic to the intended CR.

The optimal value, .5 seconds, seems to apply as well to long-latency, autonomically controlled responses, such as the GSR, as it does to short-latency skeletal reactions such as the eyeblink. This has been interpreted by some investigators as evidence in favor of the S-S interpretation of classical conditioning. Others have taken the same fact to mean that the GSR is not the true CR in these studies, but the unconditioned consequence of an unmeasured set of motor reactions.

Schedules of Reinforcement

Reinforcement may be administered consistently for each response or on every trial or it may occur only on some fraction of these occasions. The alternative arrangements thus described are, respectively, conditions of continuous and partial, or intermittent, reinforcement. Our interest at the moment is the latter arrangement.

Intermittent reinforcement is administered on some schedule, according to which reinforcement occurs either for the first response after a given period of time (interval schedules) or after a specified number of responses (ratio schedules). Moreover, the time interval or ratio may be either constant from reinforcement to reinforcement (fixed) or haphazardly changed (varied). There are, thus, four basic schedules of reinforcement to be considered: fixed interval, variable interval, fixed ratio, and variable ratio. Each of these has a characteristic effect upon the behavior of the animal.

One of the most important effects of intermittent reinforcement remains to be mentioned. This is its ability to produce great resistance to extinction. We will see in Chapter 10 that this, probably more than any other single fact, has had a profound influence upon the development of theories of extinction.

·7·

Secondary Reinforcement

THE FACT THAT some sources of reinforcement are learned is now well-established. In general, stimuli regularly associated with primary reinforcement take on some of the same characteristics as primary reinforcement and are referred to as secondary reinforcers. Saltzman's (1949) study will serve as a reference experiment in terms of which to present the methods employed in the study of secondary reinforcement. It illustrates a number of important procedural points and also anticipates many of the factual and theoretical issues with which numerous later investigations have dealt.

Saltzman, using the apparatus shown in Figure 7.1, began by training rats to run the straight alley to obtain food in a distinctive goal box. Two of these groups, a consecutive reinforcement group and a control group, were treated in exactly the same way during the training phase of the experiment. Over a five-day period they received 25 rewarded trials in which food was, therefore, paired with the distinctive stimuli in the goal box. A third group, an intermittent reinforcement group, also received 25 reinforced trials. But, in addition, they received 14 non-reinforced trials using the same goal box. These non-reinforced trials were placed haphazardly in the series but were always preceded and followed by a reinforced trial. A fourth group, a differential reinforcement group received the same treatment as the intermittent reinforcement group except that the goal box was discriminably different for rewarded and non-rewarded trials.

Following this training, all of the rats received 15 trials in the U-maze. For all groups except the control group the previously reinforced goal box was placed at the end of one arm of the U, and a different goal box was placed at the other. For the differential reinforcement group, this latter box was the box used on the non-reinforced trials in secondary reinforcement conditioning. For the control group, both boxes were identical but different from the one used in previous training. Thus all groups except the control group could receive secondary reinforcement by choosing one arm of the U. These groups were never fed in the U-maze. The control group was reinforced on one side of the U-maze, primarily, with food.

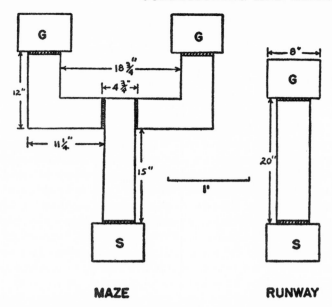

MAZE   **RUNWAY**

FIGURE 7.1. Typical apparatus employed in several studies of secondary reinforcement. Animals are trained in the straight maze first, and then tested in the U-maze. The areas designated by S are the starting boxes; those marked G are goal boxes. This particular maze was employed by Saltzman (1949).

The results of the experiment were as follows: Out of 15 trials, the rats in the control group, which received primary reinforcement, chose the side reinforced with food on an average of 10.0 trials. The consecutive, intermittent, and differential reinforcement groups chose the side leading to the previously reinforced (now empty) goal box on 8.3, 9.0, and 10.7 trials, respectively. Since there were 15 trials in all, and since the U-maze is a two-choice situation, a chance performance would consist of the selection of either goal box on 7.5 trials. All of the groups chose the previously reinforced box sufficiently often to lead to the conclusion, on statistical grounds, that the performance was not chance. This means that the animals showed at least some learning. For three of the groups the reinforcement for this learning was secondary rather than primary.

In addition to providing a reference experiment, Saltzman's study suggests a number of important points which will come up for later discussion: (1) The differential reinforcement group performed better than the intermittent reinforcement group, suggesting the importance of discrimination in the establishment of secondary reinforcement. (2) During the 15 test trials the number of correct responses of the continuous reinforcement group increased at first, and then decreased, suggesting that, for this group, the secondary reinforcement value of the goal box stimuli underwent extinction. (3) It is of some interest that secondary reinforcement seems to be at least as powerful as primary reinforcement when secondary reinforcement is established by the differential technique.

One feature of Saltzman's experiment which is not typical of secondary reinforcement studies in general is the use of the primary reinforcement control group; according to some authors (Myers, 1958), it has not been used often enough. Two more common procedures have been the following: (1) There are two groups of subjects in the experiment. One group, the experimental group, undergoes secondary reinforcement training in which some neutral stimulus, such as a light, a buzzer, or the stimulation provided by a goal box, is paired with a primary reinforcer such as food. Another group, the control group, does not receive such training. Then both groups of subjects are tested in some situation in which a given response is followed by the stimulus whose secondary reinforcement power is being tested. If the experimental group shows an increase in the frequency of the response in question, and the other group does not, this is taken as evidence that the neutral stimulus has acquired secondary reinforcing power for the experimental group. (2) Again there are two groups of subjects. In this design, both groups receive the training designed to establish a neutral stimulus as a secondary reinforcer. In the test, however, only one of the groups receives the secondary reinforcer for making the measured response. The difference in performance between the two groups provides the measure of secondary reinforcement.

A final point to be made is terminological. In the description of Saltzman's experiment, above, we have employed a distinction which seems worth maintaining in the discussion of secondary reinforcement. Specifically the term *secondary reinforcer* will be used when the reference is to the stimulus; the term *secondary reinforcement* will be used when the reference is to the effect of this stimulus upon the organism's behavior.

THE NATURE OF SECONDARY REINFORCEMENT

A primary reinforcer, such as food, has its effect, at least in part (pp. 242 to 248), because it reduces a related drive, hunger. This suggests the following question: Does a secondary reinforcer based on a primary food reward have its effect through a *conditioned* hunger-reduction? Experiments designed to test this hypothesis (Miles and Wickens, 1953; Calvin, Bicknell, and Sperling, 1953b) have produced negative results by showing that the presentation of stimuli associated with food and eating does not reduce the amount the animal eats. It is necessary, therefore, to look elsewhere for the answer to the question of the nature of secondary reinforcement.

In terms of *operations*, it is clear that the procedures required to provide a neutral stimulus with secondary reinforcing powers are those of classical conditioning. A neutral (conditioned) stimulus is paired with a primary reinforcer (unconditioned stimulus), and the former stimulus acquires certain of the properties of the latter. Figure 7.2 makes this

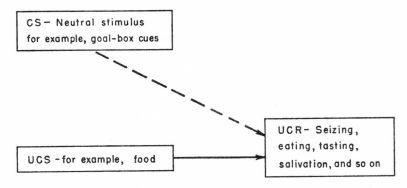

FIGURE 7.2. Secondary reinforcement conceived as a case of classical conditioning. It is to be noted that the establishment of secondary reinforcement always involves the pairing of a neutral stimulus (CS) with a primarily reinforcing stimulus. It should also be noted that the same conditions are required to produce incentive motivation (p. 170). Latent extinction may be conceived as the extinction of the CR suggested in the paradigm above.

point for the case in which previously neutral stimuli, such as those in a goal box situation, become secondary reinforcers through their association with food. The question, of course, is: Does this identity of operations mean that the basic *process* underlying the development of secondary reinforcement is the conditioning of some response to distinctive cues in the learning situation? At the present time, it is probably premature to answer this question with an unqualified affirmative. On the other hand, such an answer has much to recommend it and is implicit in a great deal of what follows. The main advantage of the assumption that secondary reinforcement can be reduced to a matter of classical conditioning is that it brings together several processes which are presently considered as separate, or at best, vaguely seen as similar. Some of these are considered in the sections which follow.

Incentive Motivation

In addition to their power to strengthen responses, it is clear that primary reinforcers have another function which is essentially motivational. The evidence for this statement is to be found in the results of studies of the amount of reinforcement, particularly those studies in which the amount of reinforcement is changed during the course of a learning experiment. Investigations of this sort have already been reviewed (pp.

122 to 124). In summary, they have shown that changes in the amount of reinforcement produce changes in performance which seem best considered as the result of motivational (incentive) influences.

There is also evidence, but of a somewhat different sort, that secondary reinforcers can function as incentives. One form of support for this belief comes from the repeatedly demonstrated fact that secondary reinforcers are capable of providing the instigation for a response. For example, Estes (1943) first conditioned the bar-pressing response of rats in a Skinner box on fixed-interval schedule. After this response was well established he gave the animals 30 trials of "discriminative training" in which a tone was presented for 60 seconds, followed by the delivery of food. In this part of the experiment the bar was absent. Observe that this is precisely the procedure used to provide a neutral stimulus (the tone) with secondary reinforcing power. A test of the effect of this training was obtained during extinction. For some of the animals (experimental group) the tone was presented for two ten-minute periods during a one-hour extinction session; for others (control group) it was not presented. The effect of the tone during extinction was to produce an elevation in rate of responding. Other studies have shown that the same effect can be obtained if the pairing of tone and food occurs prior to the establishment of the conditioned bar-press reaction (Estes, 1948) or in another situation (K. C. Walker, 1942). All of these studies show that the training ordinarily used to establish secondary reinforcement can provide a stimulus with what seem to be incentive properties.

Dinsmoor (1950) made a direct comparison of the incentive and secondary reinforcing properties of stimuli. After 10 initial reinforcements in the Skinner box, 36 rats received discrimination training in which light (for half of the subjects, darkness[1]) was made the occasion for a response. Such training appears to be essential to the establishment of incentives or secondary reinforcement (Ferster, 1951). Specifically, after 30 seconds without response in darkness, the light was turned on, and the next response, necessarily one which occurred to the light, was reinforced with food. After 200 reinforcements administered in this way, the rats were extinguished under one of three conditions: (1) For a control group, extinction occurred in the dark. (2) For a second group, extinction also occurred in the dark, but every response produced a light of 3 seconds duration. This was a secondary-reinforcement group. (3) For a third group, extinction occurred in the light, but every response turned the light off for 3 seconds. This was a condition, in which the onset of the light after its 3-second cessation provided the occasion or incentive for a

[1] For half of the subjects in the Dinsmoor experiment conditions were reversed and reinforcement occurred in darkness. Because of the similarity of results as regards the point under discussion, however, the procedure is described for the subjects reinforced in the light

response. The results of the experiment appear in Figure 7.3. Observe that the curves for the two experimental groups are virtually identical. In 3 extinction days, the number of responses produced by the secondary reinforcement group and incentive groups were 234.9 and 235.6, respectively. The control group emitted only 128.5 responses. Obviously the

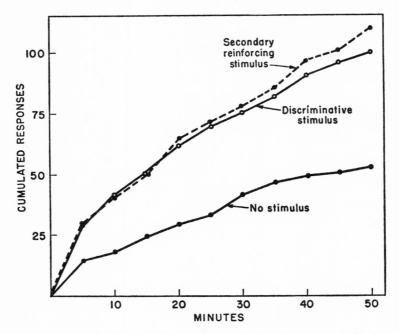

FIGURE 7.3. Graph showing the similarity of the effect upon behavior of a discriminative and secondarily reinforcing stimulus. During training rats received discrimination training, being reinforced for responses in the presence of a particular stimulus. During extinction the stimulus continued to function as a discriminative stimulus for one group. For a second group the response produced the stimulus, occupying the position of a secondary reinforcer. For a third group the stimulus was not employed. The discriminative and secondary reinforcing functions of the stimuli are approximately equal. After Dinsmoor (1950).

incentive and secondary reinforcing values of the light both exist and are of approximately equal value.

The fact that a reinforcing stimulus can also function in a motivational way creates problems: How are we to account for these double and essentially opposite functions of secondary reinforcing stimuli? How is experience with a reinforcer translated into a motive state? And how does experience which coincides with the *termination* of behavior (as at the end of a maze run) come to contribute to the *instigation* of the response in a different situation (as in the starting box of the maze)?

Faced with problems of this sort, both Seward (1950, 1951, 1952) and Spence (1956) have proposed that incentive motivation develops through the conditioning of a goal response, R_G, to the stimuli in the reinforcement situation, by what appears to be the same process as was outlined in the classical conditioning paradigm for secondary reinforcement in Figure 7.2. Thus these theories contain the proposition that the operations for producing incentive motivation are the same as those for producing secondary reinforcement. In order to account for the functioning of incentive motivation in places remote from the original conditioning situation, these theorists call upon the concept of stimulus generalization. To the extent that the stimuli in the starting situation are similar to those in the reinforcement situation, there is a tendency for the goal reaction (R_G) to be elicited. Since the primary reinforcer is absent, only a fractional component (r_G) of the complete goal response can occur. It is this fractional anticipatory goal reaction which is regarded as having motivational properties and energizing the organism's behavior. Why r_G should have motivational properties remains a question. Seward (1956b) proposes that incentives contribute to motivation by adding to the animal's excitement. Spence prefers to deal with the concept abstractedly, but also suggests two possible mechanisms: one involves the idea that evocation of r_G places the animal in conflict; the other employs Hull's (1949) concept of stimulus intensity dynamism (V) and proposes that the stimuli, s_G, produced by r_G add to the intensity of the stimulus complex controlling the animal's behavior and energize behavior in this way.

Secondary Reinforcement Based on Negative Primary Reinforcement

The implication in the previous discussion, that secondarily reinforcing stimuli have two functions, rewarding and motivating, finds a parallel in connection with the cues associated with negative reinforcers such as electric shock. In fact the situation may be even clearer in this context, because the motivational and rewarding aspects of pain stimuli are more sharply separable than they usually are in the case of positive reinforcers. The motive is aroused by the onset of the noxious stimulus; reward or satisfaction accompanies its offset. With this distinction made clear it is easy to see that: (1) stimuli associated with the onset of pain might be expected to acquire drive properties, and (2) stimuli associated with the cessation of pain might be expected to acquire positive reinforcing properties. Mowrer (1956) describes this possibility, referring to the two kinds of learning as leading, respectively, to the development of "fear" and "hope." [2]

The bulk of experimentation involving noxious stimuli has been concerned with the first of these relations. Since it represents a clear case of drive conditioning and has always been regarded as such, discussion of typical experiments has been postponed to Chapter 13 on motivation. In anticipation of more extended treatment, these studies show that neutral stimuli paired with painful stimuli do take on drive properties and that their elimination is reinforcing. That is, after such pairing, presenting the previously neutral stimulus will lead the organism to make responses which can be strengthened if they are followed by the removal of the same stimulus.

There are fewer experiments testing the other proposition, that stimuli signalling the termination of pain become positive secondary reinforcers. With occasional exceptions (Nefzger, 1957), however, such studies as

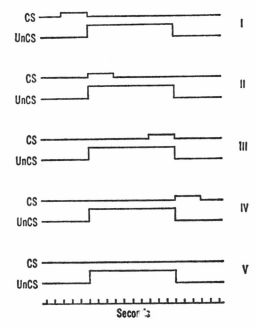

FIGURE 7.4. Relationships between CS and UCS for various groups in the experiment of Mowrer and Aiken (1954). See text for explanation.

[2] More recently Mowrer (1960) has made the observation that the failure to recognize this separability probably accounts for the failure of some experiments to demonstrate secondary reinforcement for stimuli associated with the cessation of pain. In these studies the noxious stimulus has been omitted, a procedure which effectively eliminates drive. In studies of secondary reinforcement based on positive reinforcement, by contrast, the animal is always tested with the drive (hunger) present.

there are have yielded positive results. Mowrer and Aiken (1954) taught rats to press a bar to obtain food in the first stage of an experiment. In a second stage they paired a three-second flickering light with a ten-second shock under the 5 arrangements shown in Figure 7.4 in which the CS (1) terminated as the UCS came on, (2) came on with the UCS, (3) came on 3 seconds before UCS termination and went off with the UCS, (4) came on as the UCS went off, and (5) came on 2 minutes after the offset of shock and, therefore, was not paired with it. The effect of these different procedures was tested later by turning on the CS when the rats were pressing the bar to obtain food. In general, the flickering light tended to depress the rate of bar-pressing. The extent of this effect, however, differed for the different groups, as is shown in Figure 7.5. It is especially

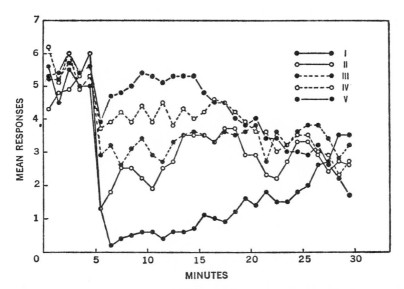

FIGURE 7.5. Effects of feared stimulus upon response strength. The neutral stimulus and shock were paired under the conditions depicted in Figure 7.4. Note that, in condition IV, where the CS followed the UCS and was associated with safety it had little effect upon response strength. Mowrer and Aiken (1954).

to be noted that the conditions in which the CS had been paired with the termination or absence of shock produced the least interference. Other results (Barlow, 1956; Goodson and Brownstein, 1955) show that a stimulus associated with shock termination will reinforce a new response. These two demonstrations, together, seem to indicate that stimuli associated with the cessation of a noxious stimulus function in exactly the same way as stimuli associated with a positive reinforcer.

Smith and Buchanan (1954) demonstrated the secondary reinforcement value of stimuli associated with shock termination with a somewhat different procedure. They trained rats to run a gray straight alley to reach a distinctive (black on some trials and white on others) goal alley and, eventually, food. On some trials, the straight alley floor was covered with sponge rubber and terminated in one goal alley. On other trials the floor was an electrically charged grid and led to the other goal alley. For half of the rats the white alley followed the grid; for the other half, the black alley followed the grid. After 36 trials of such training the rats were tested in a discrimination situation with black as the positive stimulus and food as reinforcement. This meant that the animals originally trained with the black alley following shock had, as the positive stimulus, the color previously associated with shock cessation. If such stimuli have secondary reinforcing value, these animals should learn the discrimination sooner than animals for which white is now positive. The results of the experiment confirmed this expectation. Averaging across different testing conditions, which are not important for this discussion, the mean numbers of trials required for the two groups to reach a criterion of 9 out of 10 correct choices were 15.1 and 19.7, and the group trained with the black alley following shock required fewer trials. Similarly the average numbers of errors made by the two groups were 3.0 and 5.5.

The evidence, though sparse, thus seems to indicate that stimuli associated with the cessation of shock are secondary reinforcers. Looked at another way, they take on a value seemingly the opposite of that acquired by stimuli which accompany shock onset. A more general question, therefore, arises: Do stimuli associated with the termination of any UCS (positive or negative) always acquire a tendency opposite to that produced when they are paired with UCS-onset? The evidence for positive reinforcers is even scantier than for negative reinforcers, but again it is affirmative. Konorski (1948, pp. 135-136) and Pavlov (1928, pp. 381-383) both describe the effect of presenting a CS while the animal is eating the food provided as the UCS in salivary conditioning, and both state that such a procedure provides the CS with very strong inhibitory properties.

VARIABLES CONTROLLING THE STRENGTH OF SECONDARY REINFORCEMENT

Since a secondary reinforcer acquires its power through a learning procedure, it is to be expected that the parameters which control the rate of learning will also determine the rate of acquisition of secondary reinforcement. In previous chapters we have discussed five of the most important of such variables: the number of reinforcements, schedules of reinforcement, amount of reinforcement, delay of reinforcement, and the interstimulus interval. The specific expectation is that each of these variables will control the intensity of secondary reinforcement in the same way as it controls the level of learning. Several studies have been performed to test each of these hypotheses.

Secondary Reinforcement and the Number of Primary Reinforcements

The most obvious learning variable controlling the amount of secondary reinforcement is the number of pairings of the originally neutral stimuli with primary reinforcement. On the assumption that the development of secondary reinforcement is influenced by the same factors as other learning, increasing numbers of such pairings should lead to increasing amounts of secondary reinforcement. There are three large-scale studies of this variable, each employing a somewhat different apparatus and introducing important procedural variations, yet the results have been in general agreement. In each experiment (Bersh, 1951; Hall, 1951; Miles, 1956) secondary reinforcement has been found to be an increasing function of the number of pairings of the secondary reinforcing stimulus with the primary reinforcer.

One of these studies, that of Hall (1951), employed a procedure which was almost exactly the same as that of Saltzman, described previously. Hall ran 72 rats, after 22 hours of water deprivation (22-hours thirsty), in a straight alley with water as a reinforcement. The animals received 8 trials a day. On 5 of these trials the goal box was a distinctive color (white for some subjects, black for others) and contained water. On the other three trials the goal box was the other color and was empty. Note that this is essentially Saltzman's differential reinforcement procedure.

There were three subgroups of animals in the experiment, differing in the number of secondary reinforcement trials they received in this phase of the experiment. One subgroup received 25 such reinforcements; another received 50; a third received 75. Following this training the rats received 15 test trials in a T-maze, with the previously reinforced goal box at the end of one arm of the T and the previously non-reinforced box at the other. The average numbers of responses leading to the positive goal box were 10.7, 11.5, and 12.3, respectively, for the groups receiving 25, 50, and 75 reinforcements in the training series, indicating that the strength of secondary reinforcement depends, as expected, upon the number of acquisition trials. It is reassuring to note that the measure for the 25-trial group is exactly the same as that obtained by Saltzman for his comparable group. Bersh's (1951) study was very unlike Hall's in that Bersh used a free-responding situation, the Skinner box, and a different method. In Bersh's study the secondary reinforcing stimulus was a light, produced by pressing the bar in the Skinner box, and, therefore, paired with food. There were six different groups of rats in the experiment, approximately equated for response rate without reinforcement (*operant level*). One group was a control group which received 120 reinforcements without the light. The other 5 groups received 10, 20, 40, 80, or 120 pairings of light and food. Specifically, the response of pressing the bar produced a light of three-seconds duration, with food delivered at the end of the first second. Thus, food followed the onset of the potential secondary reinforcer by one second, a condition which we will later see is a favorable one for the establishment of secondary reinforcement.

The plan of the experiment was to extinguish all groups with a procedure in which the bar press produced the light, and then to compare the number of responses to extinction of the various groups. It is clear, however, that the different numbers of prior primary reinforcements for bar pressing would produce different numbers of responses to extinction without involving the function of secondary reinforcement. For this reason the rats were first extinguished *without the secondary reinforcer* to bring them all to the same level. Following this there was a final testing phase of the experiment in which the response of pressing the bar produced a light of one-second duration. The median numbers of responses for each group, obtained in two 45-minute test sessions separated by one day, ap-

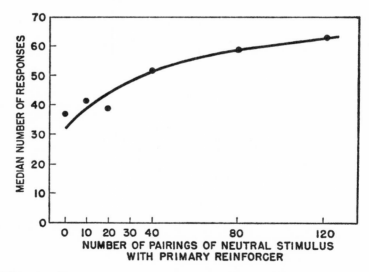

FIGURE 7.6. The effect of number of pairings of neutral stimulus with a primary reinforcer upon the strength of secondary reinforcement. Bersh (1951).

pear in Figure 7.6. Clearly the increasing numbers of secondary reinforcement trials produced an increasing rate of responding. Moreover, the extinction procedure seems to have been successful in erasing initial response strengths due to different absolute numbers of training trials. The control group, which has received 120 reinforcements without the light, produced the fewest responses in the test sessions with light as a reinforcement. The experimental group which had also received 120 primary reinforcements, by contrast, produced the most. This difference can only be attributable to the role of secondary reinforcement.

An alternative to Bersh's procedure of extinguishing the rats prior to the test for secondary reinforcement would have been to have a special control group for each experimental group, and then to extinguish some rats in each group with the secondary reinforcing stimulus and some without it. This is the procedure employed by Miles (1956a) in his investigation of secondary reinforcement. Miles conditioned 240 rats in the Skinner-box situation with 6 subgroups receiving 0, 10, 20, 40, 80, or 160 pellets of food as primary reinforcement. The secondary reinforcer was a click produced by the response of pressing the bar and a dim light which the experimenter added to the situation. Following this training the rats were extinguished. For half of them, a bar press during extinction produced the light-click combination; for the other half it did not. The general procedure is the same as that employed by Bugelski (1938) in his classical demonstration of secondary reinforcement. For all groups, the secondary reinforcer retarded extinction; that is, on the average, the rats extinguished with the light-click stimulation produced more responses than those extinguished without it. The magnitude of this effect, as is shown in Figure 7.7, increased as a function of the number of light-click-

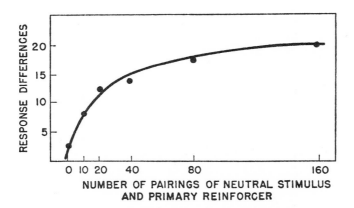

FIGURE 7.7. Secondary reinforcement as a function of the number of pairings of the neutral stimulus with food. The measures are differences in performance between subjects receiving and not receiving secondary reinforcement for the bar-pressing response (Miles, 1956a).

food pairings in a way which resembles a typical learning curve. The fact that secondary reinforcing stimulus retarded extinction, even in the zero-trial group, is possibly the result of the fact that dim lights are innately mildly reinforcing (Kish, 1955).

The Extinction of Secondary Reinforcement

As would be expected, when a secondary reinforcer is presented alone, without the primary reinforcer, it loses its secondary reinforcing power. Demonstrations of such extinction of secondary reinforcement are numerous. Pavlov encountered it as a difficulty in the establishment of higher-order conditioned responses. He also often deliberately extinguished the "natural" salivary reflex to the sight of food for experimental purposes. This demonstrates the interesting and important incidental point that the sight of food is a secondary, rather than a primary, reinforcer. Grindley, in an early investigation of the amount of reinforcement (1929), ran one group of chicks to food under a glass cover, which

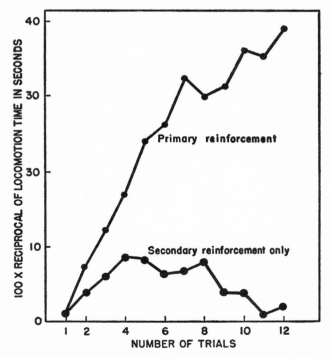

FIGURE 7.8   A comparison of the performance of chickens learning to traverse a four-foot runway for primary and secondary reinforcement. (After Grindley, 1929, as presented by Hull, 1943).

made it visible but unavailable. He found that, after a short acquisition period, the chickens ceased to run under this condition (see Figure 7.8). One possible interpretation is in terms of the extinction of secondary reinforcement. Saltzman, in the study already described, found that secondary reinforcement tended to extinguish after a few trials without the primary reinforcer, particularly if it had been established by continuous reinforcement. Grindley's results seem to reflect exactly the same sort of process.

Miles (1956b) has performed an experiment which provides a curve revealing, in a preliminary way, the course of extinction of secondary reinforcement. As in his previous (1956a) study, Miles trained rats to press the bar in the Skinner box to obtain food, the administration of which was accompanied by a combination of light and click. For extinction of the bar-pressing response the rats were divided into two groups, one of which was extinguished with, and one without, the secondary reinforcers. To balance out possible innate differences in rate of responding, the conditions were switched for the two groups from day to day. On one day the secondary reinforcers followed the response; on the next day they did not. Proceeding in this manner, Miles administered a series of hour-long extinction sessions. For each session, the difference between the numbers of responses in the two conditions provides a measure of the strength of secondary reinforcement. When these differences are plotted as a function of the extinction session, the resulting curve is a decreasing ogive shown in Figure 7.9 with very little extinction of secondary rein-

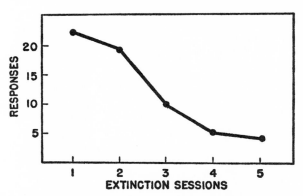

FIGURE 7.9. The extinction of spontaneous recovery (Miles, 1956b).

forcement in evidence for the first two sessions. Whether this function is typical of the extinction of secondary reinforcement remains to be seen. The rats in Miles' study had had a relatively large number of training trials (80) and the curve may be somewhat distorted by the procedure of alternating conditions from day to day.

Another demonstration of the extinction of secondary reinforcement, detailed discussion of which seems more appropriately postponed until we discuss extinction in general (Chap. 10), comes from studies of *latent extinction*. In these experiments all subjects (usually rats) learn some instrumental response, such as running a maze. Then, prior to extinction, an experimental group is placed in the goal box without primary reinforcement for a time. The control group is placed in some unfamiliar place, also without primary reinforcement. The test of the influence of this differential procedure is in a series of extinction trials. The demonstration of latent extinction consists in the more rapid loss of the instrumental response by the group previously confined to the goal box without reinforcement. Interpreted in secondary reinforcement terms, a possible explanation for latent extinction is that the experimental treatment was such as to extinguish secondary reinforcement which often supports behavior during extinction (Mote and Finger, 1942).

Secondary Reinforcement and the Interstimulus Interval

The line of investigation bearing most directly upon the assumption that secondary reinforcement develops as a result of classical conditioning is that concerned with the relationship between the strength of secondary reinforcement and the interval between neutral and primarily reinforcing stimuli in the establishment of secondary reinforcement. In the conventional classical conditioning experiment there is an optimal interval of approximately half a second, and either shorter or longer intervals lead to poorer conditioning. If secondary reinforcement results from what is basically a classical conditioning process, the same function should apply to it.

The probability that the interstimulus-interval function does apply seems to have been suggested first by the results of a study in which secondary reinforcement failed to appear (Schoenfeld, Antonitis, and Bersh, 1950). In this study, rats in a Skinner box learned to press the bar to obtain food, which was paired with an intended secondary reinforcer, a light, for some subjects and not for others. The assumption, of course, was that the light would be a secondary reinforcer for the first of these groups and not for the second. To test this assumption, the two groups were compared in a session where pressing the bar turned on the light but did not deliver food. If the assumption were correct, the group originally trained with the light should produce more responses under these conditions than the group trained without the light. No such difference occurred, however; the performances of the two groups were virtually identical.

In attempting to understand the reason for this failure, Schoenfeld and his associates were led to re-examine the details of the procedures they had used in their efforts to demonstrate secondary reinforcement, and to compare their procedure with other, successful ones. The one condition which was clearly different in their study was in the temporal relation of the light to the food. Specifically, their procedure had been to wait, after the rat pressed the bar, until it seized the food and began eating; then the light was turned on. This meant that the light came on after the food, and that the procedure could be looked upon as a case of backward conditioning, which produces little, if any, learning in the typical classical conditioning experiment. It will also be recalled that Pavlov and Konorski both claim that a stimulus presented during eating acquires strong inhibitory properties.

Pursuing this suggestion as a second part of the study already described in connection with the number of primary reinforcements, Bersh (1951) first paired a light with food in the Skinner situation, with the bar temporarily removed. For different groups of subjects, a pellet of food appeared 0.0, 0.5, 1.0, 2.0, 4.0, or 10.0 seconds after the onset of light, on a total of 160 trials. Following this procedure, the bar was made available and conditions were arranged so that a bar depression produced

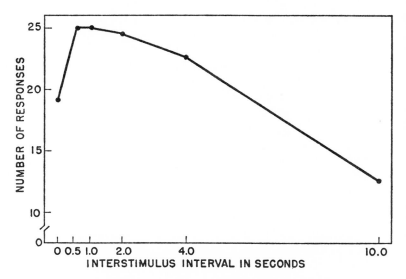

FIGURE 7.10. Strength of secondary reinforcement as a function of the interstimulus interval during training. The measures are the number of responses during the first 10 minutes of the test session (Bersh, 1951).

a light of one-second duration, but no food. The numbers of responses occurring in the first 10 minutes of this test are plotted as a function of the interstimulus interval in Figure 7.10. The overall resemblance to the functions obtained in classical conditioning is quite apparent. At the same time, substantial amounts of secondary reinforcement were obtained at intervals considerably longer than one would think possible from comparable studies of the interstimulus interval in regular classical conditioning.

Similar results were obtained in an experiment by Jenkins (1950). This study involved six groups of rats and a procedure much like that of Bersh. The secondary reinforcing stimulus, a buzzer sounding for three seconds, was presented to rats in a Skinner box on 100 trials to 5 of the 6 groups. Food followed the termination of the buzzer by 1, 3, 9, 27, or 81 seconds. The sixth group was a control group for which the buzzer was not sounded. For all groups the bar was absent during secondary reinforcement training. The test for the magnitude of secondary reinforcement was a 6-hour period in which the bar was continuously available, and in which pressing it produced the sound of the buzzer. The numbers of responses occurring in this period for each group are plotted as a function of the training interval in Figure 7.11. Again the amount of

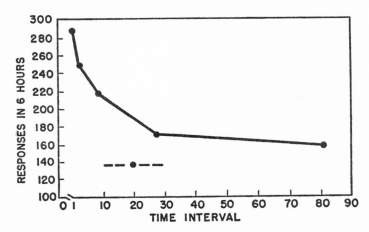

FIGURE 7.11. Strength of secondary reinforcement as a function of the inter-stimulus interval during training. Horizontal dashed line illustrates the level of response obtained in the absence of secondary reinforcement (W. O. Jenkins, 1950).

responding decreases as a function of the interval; but again, too, long intervals appear to have some effect. At the present time, the reasons for this difference between the usual interstimulus-interval function and this one are far from clear. Other evidence, to be discussed later, suggests that behavior going on in the interval would be important.

Secondary Reinforcement and the Amount
of Primary Reward

Studies of secondary reinforcement as it is related to the amount of primary reward employed in its development have been of two rather different sorts: Lawson (1957) refers to them as *absolute* and *differential* methods. In the absolute method, independent groups of subjects receive training designed to establish some neutral stimulus as a secondary reinforcer. The various groups differ in the amount of primary reinforcement paired with the neutral stimulus. In the differential method, each subject serves as his own control and is given training designed to establish two stimuli as secondary reinforcers. By varying the amount of primary reinforcement associated with each, an attempt is made to give the two stimuli different secondary reinforcing power. The differential method has tended to produce clearer results than the absolute method.

In a typical experiment employing the differential method, D'Amato (1955a) gave 20 rats 70 trials in a straight alley. On half of these trials the rats received 5 food pellets in one of two distinctive goal boxes. On the other half of the trials, they received one pellet in the other goal box. If the amount of primary reinforcement governs the strength of secondary reinforcement, this procedure should make the box associated with the 5 pellets a more powerful secondary reinforcer than the box associated with just one pellet. To test this hypothesis, D'Amato gave the rats 15 trials in a T-maze with the five-pellet box on one arm, and the one-pellet box on the other. Otherwise there was no reinforcement. As evidence of the greater secondary reinforcement value of the box associated with the greater amount of primary reinforcement, 18 of the 20 subjects in the experiment ran 8 or more times to this goal box, a result which is statistically highly reliable. See also Greene (1953).

A good example of the absolute method of investigating this problem is to be found in the Skinner-box study of Butter and Thomas (1958). As different primary reinforcers, these experimenters used two different concentrations of sucrose, 8 per cent and 24 per cent, which had previously been shown (Guttman, 1953) to possess different reinforcing value for rats in the Skinner box. The secondary reinforcer employed was the audible click of the mechanism which delivered the sugar solution. Each rat received 48 trials in which this sound was paired with a 0.1-ml. drop of the 8 per cent or 24 per cent solution, depending upon the group it was in. Following this training the bar was made available and each bar depression was reinforced with the click, but not with sucrose, for seven daily tests. The mean numbers of such secondarily reinforced responses obtained from the 8 per cent and 24 per cent groups, respectively, were 9.4 and 17.6, a statistically reliable difference.

A third investigation which shows that secondary reinforcement depends upon the amount of primary reinforcement approached the problem in a somewhat different way, by varying the amount of eating time allowed in different goal boxes (Powell and Perkins, 1957). In this study rats ran a straight alley to food reward in preliminary training designed to establish differential secondary reinforcing values for two distinctively different goal boxes. To this end the subjects were allowed to eat for 10 seconds or 150 seconds in the different goal boxes on different trials. Then they were tested in an E-maze with the two goal boxes at the ends of the two routes in the maze. All of the subjects soon began to choose the path which terminated in the goal box previously associated with 150 seconds of eating time, although they now were fed for 20 seconds whichever path they took. In a second part of the study rats were allowed different amounts of eating time (10 or 150 seconds) in the different goal boxes at the end of the E-maze. In this experiment, the rats received interspersed trials in the straight maze in which they were reinforced with a long eating period in the goal box associated with a short eating time in the E-maze, and vice versa. Under these circumstances the rats showed no reliable tendency to choose the 150-second goal box in the E-maze. This fact makes a point of considerable importance, namely that different eating times, and probably different amounts of primary reinforcement in general, have their effect indirectly, through the establishment of differential amounts of secondary reinforcement.

Although the fact that the amount of primary reinforcement does control the value of the secondary reinforcer associated with it seems reasonably well established, there have been several well-controlled studies (Hopkins, 1955; Lawson, 1953, 1957) which have obtained negative results. The reason for these occasional failures is not clear. Butter and Thomas suggest that some of these studies may have employed amounts of primary reinforcement which differed, but were both at the asymptote of the primary reward gradient. This explanation seems implausible, considering the great range of quantities of primary reinforcement used in some studies (for example, Hopkins, 1955) and the fact that the subjects in other experiments (for example, Lawson, 1953) were responding differentially to the different amounts of primary reinforcement during training. An interpretation of these negative results must probably await a better understanding of the nature of secondary reinforcement.

Secondary Reinforcement and Reinforcement Schedules

There is good evidence that partial reinforcement schedules tend to produce conditioned responses which are more resistant to extinction than those established by continuous reinforcement. On this ground it might be predicted that an intermittent pairing of neutral stimulus and primary reinforcer would lead to the establishment of secondary reinforcement that is especially durable. Although several experiments of this sort have been done, none of them has employed what seems to be the most appropriate procedure. Such an ideal experiment would begin by providing some neutral stimulus with secondary reinforcement power in a training situation uncontaminated by the presence of the response later to be used to test for the strength of secondary reinforcement. During this initial training, there would be two groups. For one group the primarily reinforcing stimulus would follow the neutral stimulus on every trial. For the other group, the primarily reinforcing stimulus would follow the presentations of the neutral stimulus only on some predetermined fraction of the training trials. Then both groups would be tested by putting them into a situation where a certain response produced the (now) secondary reinforcer. Under these conditions the group which had been trained with an intermittent schedule should learn better and continue responding longer than the group trained with a continuous schedule.

In the studies which have been done on this problem (Saltzman, 1949; Dinsmoor, 1952; Melching, 1954; Clayton, 1956) the response ultimately to be used in the test situation has also been required of the animal during initial secondary reinforcement training. Melching, for example, used rats in a Skinner box. Following habituation and routine pretraining, they were given 20 reinforcements for bar pressing. For two subgroups, every response produced the sound of a buzzer (secondary reinforcer); for two other subgroups, the buzzer appeared haphazardly following half of the bar presses; for a third pair of subgroups, the buzzer never sounded. Following this training the rats were extinguished. One subgroup from each main experimental condition was extinguished with the buzzer sounding after each response; the other subgroup was extinguished without it. There were no differences in resistance to extinction which could be attributed to the greater secondary reinforcing value of the buzzer for the two 50 per cent groups than for the two 100 per cent groups. In Dinsmoor's experiment, the comparison was between the reinforcing value of a light when it was used as the signal for the beginning of a three-minute fixed-interval schedule or as a signal that the next response would be rewarded. In later extinction tests for the effectiveness of the light as a secondary reinforcer, it was found that the light contributed more to resistance to extinction for the three-minute reinforcement group, an outcome which might mean that the strength of secondary reinforcement is increased if it is established by means of an intermittent schedule.

It should be noted, however, that in both of these experiments, the comparison is complicated by the primary reinforcement conditions during training. In Melching's experiment all of the animals were reinforced *primarily* on all trials. It seems quite likely that resistance to extinction would be similar for all groups and that the difference between a continuous and partial schedule of secondary reinforcement would have little effect. In Dinsmoor's experiment, the original schedules of primary reinforcement produce very different resistances to extinction in their own right and in the same direction as the differences attributed to the schedule on which the neutral stimulus and primary reinforcer were paired. This makes the secondary reinforcement values following the two schedules very difficult to assess.

In what is more a demonstration than an experiment, Zimmerman (1957) describes a way of developing very strong secondary reinforcement by gradually decreasing the probability that primary reinforcement will be associated with the operation of the magazine in the Skinner box until a situation is reached where the rat is on a variable ratio schedule of 10 to 1. From Zimmerman's description, it seems very likely that the strength of secondary reinforcement does, as expected, depend upon the schedule of reinforcement. Subsequently, Zimmerman (1959) again demonstrated that his procedure produces very durable secondary reinforcement. In neither case, however, is there a proper experimental comparison of continuous and intermittent schedules.

Secondary Reinforcement and Drive

In discussing the relation of drive to learning we shall see later (pp. 411) that the level of motivation exercises great control over performance, but little or none over learning. A parallel state of affairs appears to exist in the relation of drive to secondary reinforcement. We shall consider first the effect of drive level upon performance for a secondary reward. Miles (1956a), in a second part of the study described above, conditioned 240 rats to press the bar in the Skinner box using a combination of light and click as a secondary reinforcer. After 80 bar presses with this stimulus combination paired with food, the rats were extinguished, half with, and half without, the secondary reinforcing stimuli, under 0, 2.5, 5, 10, 20, or 40 hours of food deprivation. Figure 7.12 shows the results of the experiment in terms of the increase in number of extinction responses produced by the presence of the secondary reinforcer. The function is not unlike those relating the vigor of other learned responses to food deprivation.

A somewhat special problem concerns the question of the value of a secondary reinforcer for satiated organisms. From studies like that of Miles it is clear that the level of responding is reduced for low drive levels, but it is not certain that the reduction is to zero. Experimentally this general question has been asked in two more specific forms concerning the value of a secondary reinforcer: (1) when the relevant drive under which it was acquired is satiated, but some other important motive is

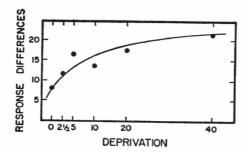

FIGURE 7.12. The strength of secondary reinforcement based upon primary food reward as a function of the number of hours of food deprivation (Miles, 1956a).

operating, and (2) when all motives under the control of the experimenter are minimized. The evidence on the first of these specific questions is consistent. As with other learning, secondarily reinforced behavior is maintained when the only drive is an irrelevant one. Estes (1949) studied the bar-pressing behavior of three groups of rats reinforced by the sound of a stimulus previously associated with the presentation of water for two of the groups. The third group was a control group which had had no secondary reinforcement training. In the test the rats were satiated for water but 6- or 23-hours hungry. The hungrier group produced more responses than either the six-hour group or the control group, indicating that a secondary reinforcer will exert its reinforcing influence upon behavior in the absence of the original drive. The six-hour hunger group, however, did not differ from the control group, suggesting that a fairly strong irrelevant drive is necessary for the effect to appear.

This last result raises the question in its other form: Does a secondary reinforcer exert its reinforcing influence upon behavior when all drives are minimally low? Estes' experiment suggests that they do not. Schlosberg and Pratt (1956) offer the same interpretation on the basis of the results of a T-maze experiment in which rats were secondarily reinforced by the sight and smell of inaccessible food. Satiated rats learned nothing, but hungry rats learned to take the path leading to the secondary reinforcer. Wike and Casey (1954b) have obtained data in support of the opposite conclusion in an experiment employing a straight alley apparatus. Having previously found, in agreement with Estes, that the sight of food is reinforcing for thirsty rats satiated for food (Wike and Casey, 1954a), they did another study with rats satiated for both food and water. Their results showed that such satiated animals ran faster if they were rewarded by reaching a goal box containing food than if they found an empty goal box at the end of the alley. Seward and Levy (1953) have also obtained data in support of the conclusion that a secondary reinforcer will support the behavior of satiated rats.

These discrepant results seem to require a methodological comment: the only evidence so far proposed to demonstrate the existence of a secondary reinforcer depends upon the ability of secondary reinforcement to maintain behavior or to provide the basis for learning a new response. In either case, the demonstration depends upon the occurrence of behavior; otherwise no secondary reinforcement effect is possible. The behaviors involved in every experiment on this problem, however, are ones which almost certainly would not occur in the complete absence of motivation. Inasmuch as some responding did occur in each experiment, it follows that the subjects were not completely satiated. The residual motives may not have been hunger or thirst; but such drives as the activity, exploratory, curiosity, and sexual ones are obvious possibilities to consider in attempting to understand why any behavior at all occurred. If such motives were present, the question under investigation takes a somewhat different turn, and new possibilities suggest themselves. Possibly the mechanism by which irrelevant drives enter the picture is that of generalization. It is, therefore, entirely thinkable that the particular irrelevant motive is important. Because of their history of frequent simultaneous occurrence, transfer between hunger and thirst may be much greater than transfer between hunger or thirst and (say), curiosity or sexual drives.

The investigations described up to this point are all concerned with the functioning of a secondary reinforcer as it depends upon drive level after the secondary reinforcer has been established. We turn next to the question of the effect of drive present at the time the secondary reinforcing value of a stimulus is acquired. Does drive level at the time of the acquisition of secondary reinforcement affect the power of the secondary reinforcer? Experimentally this question requires that different groups of subjects learn the secondary reinforcement under varying drive levels and demonstrate its magnitude with drives equated. Using the same procedure as in his previous study (Hall, 1951a), Hall (1951b) compared the effect of two intensities of thirst motivation, at the time of the establishment of secondary reinforcement, upon the value of the secondary reinforcer later. Rats, either 6- or 22-hours thirsty, ran a straight alley, on some trials to a distinctive goal box where they obtained water, and on other trials to a different goal box where they obtained none. As in the previous experiment, different subgroups received totals of 25, 50, and 75 reinforcements in this way. After this training the two goal boxes were placed at the ends of the two arms of a T-maze in which the rats received 15 trials to measure the value of the previously positive goal box as a secondary reinforcer. As in Hall's first study, the rats chose the previously positive goal box more often than the negative one. The results of the previous study were further confirmed in that this tendency increased as a function of the number of training trials used to establish the secondary reinforcing status of the goal box. There was, however, no difference between the groups which had been trained under 6 and 22 hours of deprivation. Averaged across all subgroups the number of choices of the positive goal box were: for the 6-hour group, 11.6; and for the 22-hour group, 11.5. These results again parallel those obtained with other forms of learning.

EFFECTS OF SECONDARY REINFORCEMENT ON BEHAVIOR

The general properties of secondary reinforcers, as outlined by Miller (1951), are the same as those of primary reinforcers: (1) a secondary reinforcer can be used to produce new learning; (2) it will support the performance of a learned response; (3) it provides the organism with a means of bridging gaps in time, and (4) it possesses an incentive function in that the sight of a secondary reinforcer will lead an organism to strive to obtain it, or, in the case of a secondary negative reinforcer, to avoid it. Some of the evidence for assigning secondary reinforcement these properties has been presented earlier in this chapter. In addition, the concept of secondary reinforcement has been used by S-R theorists to explain a wide variety of special behavioral phenomena. The sections which follow consider some of these applications.

Intermittent Reinforcement and Secondary Reinforcement

Several investigators have obtained data to show that secondary reinforcement makes an important contribution to performance in partial reinforcement learning experiments. In such experiments the non-reinforced trials are not really non-reinforced because the typical procedure is one in which the animal comes into the presence of cues previously associated with reward; that is, into the presence of secondary reinforcers. What would happen if such secondary reinforcers were minimized? Denny (1946) performed the first experiment directly aimed at answering this question. He ran rats in a T-maze to a food reinforcement given on either 50 per cent or 100 per cent of the correct trials. For one pair of groups the end-boxes were identical. The 50 per cent and 100 per cent groups learned the maze equally well under these circumstances. In a total of 11 trials, the mean numbers of correct choices were 8.4 and 9.2 for the two groups, respectively. The difference is not statistically significant. For another pair of groups the procedure in the partial reinforcement condition was different; the end-boxes were different on reinforced and non-reinforced trials. In theory, this technique should reduce or eliminate secondary reinforcement on the non-reinforced trials and retard learning for the partially reinforced subjects. The results confirmed this expectation. The 100 per cent group made 8.5 correct choices in 11 trials, whereas the 50 per cent group made only 6.0. The difference of 2.5 correct responses was highly reliable in statistical terms.

Other evidence that the so-called non-reinforced responses in a partial reinforcement schedule actually are reinforced comes from studies in which the number of primarily reinforced trials remains the same for several groups of subjects which differ in the number of non-reinforced (that is, secondarily reinforced) trials. These studies (Notterman, 1951; Denny and Dunham, 1951) have shown that the greater the number of non-reinforced trials, the better is the subject's performance.

Discrimination Learning and Secondary Reinforcement

In discrimination learning, the animal is required to choose between alternative stimuli and is rewarded if it chooses correctly. Within such an experiment, secondary reinforcement has two main opportunities to operate. In the first case, if the correct and incorrect responses lead to similar goal situations, differing only in the presence of a primary reinforcer in one and not in the other, the incorrect response is actually secondarily reinforced. This should make such a discrimination more difficult to master than one in which the two goal situations are different. Studies with the T-maze (Denny, 1948; Saltzman, 1950) and with a black-white discrimination problem (Ehrenfreund, 1949, 1954) have yielded results in support of such reasoning. Ehrenfreund, for example, called attention to the most obvious interfering secondary reinforcer introduced into many two-choice learning situations, the empty food dish in the goal box following an incorrect response. Since most studies of this general sort make the response which is correct for one subgroup incorrect for another, thus balancing out natural tendencies to respond predominantly in one way or the other, it is sometimes convenient to have food dishes in both goal boxes and to put food in the one which is correct for the animal being run. As Ehrenfreund points out, however, this means that a very strong secondary reinforcer is present to reward an incorrect response. To test the validity of such reasoning, Ehrenfreund performed a black-white discrimination experiment using two groups of rats. The only procedural difference was that, for Group 1 (a non-secondary reinforcement group) there was never a food cup in the negative goal box, whereas for Group 2 (a secondary reinforcement group) a food cup similar to the one in the positive goal box was always present in the negative goal box. The effect produced by this seemingly small variation is shown in Figure 7.13. Clearly the presence of the food cup made an important difference and led to a marked retardation in the speed with which the discrimination developed. For the non-secondary reinforcement group 24.4 trials and 7.2 errors were required to attain a criterion of 90 per cent correct responses. For the secondary reinforcement group the comparable values were 42.2 trials and 17.5 errors.

The second opportunity for secondary reinforcement to become involved in discrimination learning occurs if the cue identifying the correct

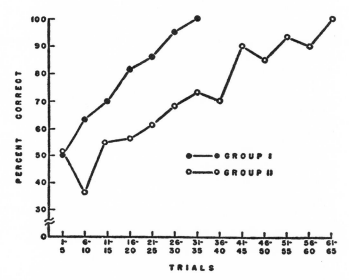

FIGURE 7.13. The effect of a secondary reinforcer upon the progress of discrimination learning. For group II a food cup like that used to contain reward on correct trials was present in the negative goal box. For group I there was never a food cup in the negative goal box. The relatively slower learning of group II is attributed to the fact that the incorrect responses received secondary reinforcement (Ehrenfreund, 1949).

choice in a discrimination situation has some of the same properties as the goal to which it leads. In such an event, the positive stimulus would be a secondary reinforcer and attract behavior through its incentive function. One of the most important kinds of evidence in favor of this interpretation has already been presented (p. 153) in connection with the delay-of-reinforcement gradient. This was Grice's (1948b) demonstration that making the correct and incorrect choice alleys the same color as the positive and negative goal boxes in a black-white discrimination enables the animal to learn for a delayed reward. This result has been confirmed by Bauer and Lawrence (1953) and by Webb and Nolan (1953). More recently, both Levy (1957) and Grice and Goldman (1955) have analyzed this effect further and have obtained good evidence that two kinds of secondary reinforcement are involved: positive secondary reinforcement generalizing from the reinforced trials in the distinctively colored positive goal situation, and negative secondary reinforcement generalizing from the non-reinforced trials in the other goal box.

To make this demonstration, Grice and Goldman ran four groups of rats in a black-white discrimination in which white was always positive and a two-second delay followed the choice. The four groups were run under the following conditions: For one group (WB, that is, White-Black) the two end boxes in the discrimination apparatus were painted white and black in correspondence with the correct and incorrect choices. For a second group (GG) both end boxes were gray. For the remaining two groups one of the end boxes matched the color of one of the choices and the other was gray. For Group WG, the positive goal box was white; and, for Group GB the negative goal box was black. Median numbers of errors required to master the black-white discrimination were: For Group GG, 128; for Group WB, 43; for Group WG, 58; and for Group GB, 40. There were important differences only between Group GG and the others. Grice and Goldman take this to mean that secondary reinforcement (positive or negative) established to the end box color generalizes to the choice situation and leads the animal to approach or avoid the cue in question. It is implicit in the magnitudes of the effects obtained that one process is about as beneficial as the other to the formation of the discrimination.

The Effects of Intermittent Schedules of Secondary Reinforcement

In all of the studies described so far, the test for the strength of secondary reinforcement has been one in which the secondary reinforcer has been present on every trial. From studies of other forms of reinforcement, it is to be expected that a partial reinforcement schedule would lead to the establishment of more persistent behavior than a continuous schedule of secondary reinforcement. Animal studies testing this expectation (Dinsmoor, Kish, and Keller, 1953; Clayton, 1956) have usually obtained negative results. There is, however, one successful demonstration with lower animals (Zimmerman, 1959), and a number of others on human guessing behavior. In these latter studies, the first of which was done by Humphreys (1939b), the experimental procedure provides a verbal analogue to classical conditioning. Two lights mounted on the two sides of a large board serve as "CS" and "UCS". When the CS light appears, the subject is required to guess whether or not the UCS light will come on also. By varying the probability that the UCS light will come on, it is possible to set up any desired schedule of reinforcement. A typical set of results obtained with this method appears in Figure 7.14. In this study (Grant, Hake, and Hornseth, 1951) the percentages of reinforcement (trials when the second light came on) were 0, 25, 50, 75,

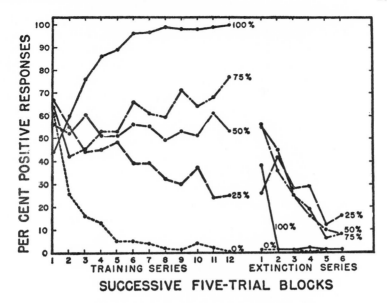

FIGURE 7.14.   The effect of percentage of reinforcement upon the acquisition
and extinction of a verbal guessing habit (Grant, Hake, and Hornseth, 1951).

and 100. Two important facts stand out: (1) The percentage of guesses
that the UCS light will come on begins at about 50 per cent and changes
gradually until it matches the actual probability fairly closely. This same
result has been obtained repeatedly (Estes and Straughan, 1954; Estes,
1957). (2) In extinction, the order of increasing resistance to extinction
is approximately the reverse of percentage of reinforcement in training.
The 25 per cent group is most resistant; the 100 per cent group is least
resistant. This result, too, has been obtained a number of times (Humphreys, 1939; Grant, Hornseth, and Hake, 1950). It, of course, corresponds very well to the result occurring in the typical animal experiment.

For our purposes, the important point is that the reinforcer employed
in this study is a secondary one. The subject has no innate capacity to be
reinforced by the appearance of a light. Any doubt on this point is dis-
pelled by the demonstration (Grant, Hake, and Hornseth, 1951) that,
with the instructions appropriately altered, the light's failure to come on
is just as good a reinforcement as its appearance. The fact that such a
reinforcer produces more persistent behavior when applied on a partial
schedule than when it is applied continuously shows that it shares this
characteristic with other reinforcers.

On the other hand the verbal conditioning situation differs from other
learning situations in a number of ways: (1) Other forms of learning do
not usually lead the subject to respond in proportion to the probability

of reinforcement. (2) The verbal conditioning situation is not influenced by distribution of practice as most forms of learning are (Humphreys, Miller, and Ellson, 1940; Grant, Hornseth, and Hake, 1950). For such reasons, interest seems gradually to have shifted away from this experiment as an analogue of simple learning. More and more it is being dealt with as something of interest in its own right as an elementary form of predictive or decision-making behavior (Estes, 1954, 1955).

The Generalization of Secondary Reinforcement across Drives

An important segment of the literature on secondary reinforcement has been concerned with the extent to which it generalizes from one drive to another. We have already seen in connection with the studies of Estes and Wike and Casey that such generalization apparently can occur. The results of a second study led Estes (1949) to the conclusion that such transfer from one drive to another may result in the loss of as little as 25 per cent in the value of a secondary reinforcer. In a complete and nicely controlled experiment on the transfer of secondary reinforcement from one drive to another, D'Amato (1955b) used a procedure very similar to Saltzman's intermittent reinforcement method to establish the goal box as a secondary reinforcer for two different groups of rats. In a straight alley, one group was run thirsty to water as a primary reinforcer. The other was run hungry to food. The reinforcement schedule was one according to which the rats received primary reinforcement on 24 of the 40 trials. Non-reinforced trials used the same goal box as the reinforced trials. After this training, drives were switched and the subjects were tested in a T-maze with the previous goal box at the end of one arm of the T; the previous starting box was at the other. The rats trained thirsty, and tested hungry, chose the previously reinforced goal box on 8.8 of 15 trials; those trained hungry and tested thirsty chose the same box on 8.7 trials. Although no control group run under the training drive was used, it will be recalled that Saltzman ran such a group in his experiment and this group chose the reinforced goal box on 9.0 trials, a value very similar to that reported by D'Amato. Thus, with an occasional exception (Reid and Slivinski, 1954), the evidence points quite clearly to the transferability of secondary reinforcement from one drive to another.

Secondary Reinforcement and the Mediation of Gaps in Time

It will be recalled that one of the properties assigned by Miller to secondary reinforcers was that of enabling the organism to bridge time spans which otherwise would be impossible. The best examples of this property of secondary reinforcement are to be found in the delay-of-reinforcement studies previously discussed (pp. 152) where it was demonstrated that the presence of a secondary reinforcer may enable the rat to learn for a reward which is postponed for several minutes. To say that secondary reinforcement is responsible for learning with long delays is to offer an abstract explanation which postulates no particular mechanism for the bridging the delay.

In this case, however, it is important to consider a possible mechanism, not only because it may lead to a better understanding of the time-spanning process, but also because it leads to important questions about (and, hopefully, therefore, a better understanding of) the nature of secondary reinforcement. The mechanism referred to is the following: Skinner (1938, pp. 52-55, 102-108) suggested that any response subsequent to another in a chain of behavior can reinforce the preceding response secondarily. This, in effect, reduces secondary reinforcement to a matter of response chaining, and implies that the mechanism through which secondary reinforcers acquire their time-bridging value is through the elicitation of chains of responses. The idea is that the animal in a delay chamber waiting for reinforcement learns to go through a series of responses and that the execution of these responses takes it through time, in the same way as its previous responses took it through space from start box to delay chamber. Skinner (1948) also demonstrated the behavioral phenomenon which is basic to this explanation. He showed that pigeons developed stereotyped routine behavior which he called *superstitious* in a situation where food was made available at fixed intervals no matter what the birds did. These superstitions consisted of complex chains of activity often including circling the experimental compartment and bowing. Ferster (1953) showed that such superstitious behavior made it possible for birds to bridge a delay of reinforcement of at least one minute. He trained pigeons to peck at an illuminated key to obtain food on a variable-interval schedule. Then he gradually lengthened the interval between the reinforced response and the reinforcment. Under these conditions three of four birds sustained normal rates of response with a 60-second delay. Observations of their behavior during the delay period reveal patterns of superstitious behavior which differed from subject to subject. In a somewhat different type of experiment, M. P. Wilson and Keller (1953) showed that rats could be trained to press a bar at a slow rate. As this response developed, there also occurred ''clearly defined collateral behavior during the intervals between successive responses.'' Kellogg has reported observing similar phenomena in a buzz-shock instrumental avoidance conditioning situation:

If the right-rear foot is the foot which is given the reinforcing shock, an animal which has received 100 or so conditioning trials may evolve a characteristically individual pattern of responding which includes the other three feet as well. As soon as the buzz spurs him to action on any trial he may, for example, (*a*) raise the right-front foot and immediately return it to its original position, (*b*) raise the left-rear foot and replace it at once also, (*c*) raise and replace the left-front foot, and finally (*d*) lift and hold up the right-rear (or shocked) member during the time when the shock would have occurred had he failed to respond. Almost any other reaction or combination of reactions . . . may come to be uniformly repeated as a preliminary to the flexing of the shocked limb itself. (Kellogg, 1949, p. 173)

Probably the behavior of the rat in the usual delay-of-reinforcement situation is somewhat different from this, consisting in the maintenance of a fixed orientation toward the goal; and the greatest delay of reinforcement with which the animal can learn is simply the length of time it can hold such a response. Carlton (1955) performed an experiment which produced results quite consistent with this interpretation. Rats learned to press a bar in the Skinner box to get food which was delivered either immediately or after 10 seconds for two main groups of subjects. Each of these main groups consisted of two subgroups for which the delay chambers differed. For one group, the confined group (C, in Figure 7.15), the delay chamber was small, 6 inches x 3 inches x 2 inches. For another group, the unconfined group (UC, in Figure 7.15), it was large, 6 inches

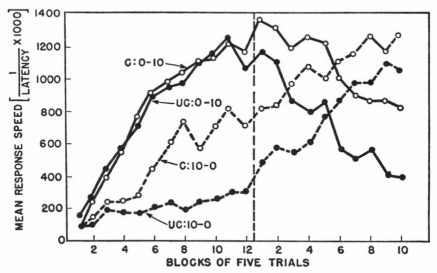

FIGURE 7.15. Bar-pressing performance as a joint function of delay of reward and restriction of movement. The functions to the left of the dashed line depict the performances of the confined (C) and unconfined (UC) groups with zero and ten seconds delay. On trials to the right of the dashed line, conditions were reversed. (After Carlton, 1955, as presented by Spence, 1956).

x 17 inches x 11½ inches. The purpose of introducing this difference was to test the hypothesis that the animals in the confined group, with less opportunity to produce interfering responses, would maintain their goal orientation during the delay period better than the unconfined group, and would learn better with the 10-second delay of reinforcement. To provide a more general test of the hypothesis, the delay conditions were reversed after 60 trials: those animals originally receiving food immediately were shifted to a 10-second delay and *vice versa*. The results of the experiment appearing in Figure 7.15 confirm the hypothesis in detail. Observe that, for subjects receiving immediate reinforcement, the confinement condition was unimportant and both groups learned better than the delay groups. For these latter groups the confinement condition makes the expected difference. The performance of the confined group was considerably better than that of the unconfined group.[3]

Related Phenomena in Classical Conditioning

In classical conditioning studies the long trace and long delay procedures create problems which are the same as those deriving from long delays of reinforcement in instrumental conditioning. In these experiments it is less likely, however, that overt motor responses are critical in mediating the delay. It may be that recent studies of the electroencephalographic correlates of conditioning provide an important lead in the direction of an explanation. Motokawa and his associates (Motokawa, 1949; Motokawa and Huzimori, 1949; Iwama, 1950; Iwama and Abe, 1952, 1953) have reported a series of interesting investigations in which autonomic and electroencephalographic responses were conditioned simultaneously, the main interest being in parallels between the two. The EEG response employed ("excitation potential" or "e. p.") is a complicated one consisting, in part, of the blocking of the alpha rhythm which had previously been shown to be conditionable (Jasper and Shagass, 1941a).[4]

[3] This interpretation of the effects of delay stresses just one of their aspects. It will be recognized, however, that delays have other effects such as those of producing "frustration" and "emotional upset." W. L. Brown and his associates have considered these influences in interpreting the effects of intramaze delay (Brown, Gentry, and Kaplan, 1948; Brown and Gentry, 1948; Gentry, Brown, and Kaplan, 1949; Brown, Gentry, and Bosworth, 1949; Brown and Sjoberg, 1950; Brown and Dalrymple, 1951). These concepts have also loomed large in discussions of extinction (pp. 309 to 317).

[4] The conditioning of the EEG and EEG correlates of other conditioning are becoming matters of increasing interest. General discussion of these topics are to be found in the transactions of the 1958 and 1959 Josiah Macy Jr. Foundation conferences on "The Central Nervous System and Behavior" (Brazier, 1959a, 1959b). These discussions include references to relevant literature. See also Ellingson (1956), Jasper and Shagass (1941a, 1941b), Knott and Henry (1941), Knott, Platt, and Hadley (1944), Morrell and Jasper (1956), Morrell, Roberts, and Jasper (1956), and Shagass and Johnson (1943).

In these studies, a conditioned excitation potential was shown to develop along with the conditioned GSR and seemed to be essential to the occurrence of the latter response. The evidence for this interpretation is fairly impressive: (1) The excitation potential occurs earlier in the interstimulus interval than the GSR. (2) It appears earlier in the course of conditioning than the GSR. (3) The excitation potential occasionally occurs in the absence of the GSR, but the reverse apparently never happens. (4) When a GSR reappears, as sometimes happens after it has been extinguished, the reappearance is always associated with the occurrence of an EEG reaction, which also extinguishes with non-reinforcement. The concept of the excitation potential as providing a mediating link which bridges long interstimulus intervals, thus, is at least tenable.

The possible value of the EEG as an indicator of events involved in spanning time gaps receives a degree of support from an additional set of facts. It is known that the latency of the conditioned alpha block provides a dependable index of time. For an interval of 9.4 seconds, Jasper and Shagass (1941b) found that the S.D. (standard deviation) of the latencies for this repsonse was only 0.7 seconds, and that this was a more accurate measure than voluntary judgments which had an S.D. of 2.5 seconds. Beyond this simple fact, the details of the underlying process become obscure. Iwama and Abe (1953) report that an interstimulus interval of 12 seconds produced two GSR's and two EEG reactions. In each case, one occurred early in the interval, the other later. With conditioning, the early reactions tended to disappear, leaving only the later ones. Moreover, with the disappearance of the early reaction, the alpha rhythm takes on a more regular than normal form (Motokawa and Huzimori, 1949) which may be a cortical reflection of Pavlov's inhibition of delay. Boneau (1958) reports a similar tendency for conditioned eyeblinks to occur early and late in a 2.5-second interval in eyelid conditioning. Hull (1952) predicts such a phenomenon from considerations involving the concept of stimulus trace.

SUMMARY

The fact that some forms of reinforcement are secondary, or learned, is well established. The early studies of Pavlov on higher-order conditioning, of Wolfe and Cowles on token rewards, and of Bugelski on sub-goal reinforcement are among the best-known early demonstrations of the process. More recent experiments on secondary reinforcement derive from the work of Skinner and of Saltzman. The latter of these two investigators first ran hungry rats to a distinctive goal box where they received food. Saltzman was able to show that, after such training, the animals learned to choose the side of a U-maze which terminated in an empty goal box which had previously contained food.

The Nature of Secondary Reinforcement

The conditions necessary to establish secondary reinforcement are the same as those employed in classical conditioning experiments: A neutral stimulus is paired with a primary reinforcer. As a result, this stimulus acquires the capacity to function much as the primary reinforcer originally did. Specifically, it is capable of reinforcing new learning and of retarding the extinction of previously established habits. Moreover, as with reinforcers in general, secondary reinforcers also possess an incentive property in that the presentation of a secondary reinforcer will lead the animal to strive to attain it.

One of the aspects of the operation of secondary reinforcers most difficult to explain is this last, incentive, function. Theorists who have addressed themselves to this problem sometimes have begun by noting, as we have above, that the operations required to provide a neutral stimulus with secondary reinforcing properties are those of classical conditioning, by which goal reactions could be conditioned to cues in the learning situation. Then it is assumed that these classically conditioned reactions, occurring in fractional form, add to the animal's tendency to perform the learned response by evoking an "expectant attitude," by increasing drive, or by adding to the intensity of the stimuli tending to elicit the reaction.

Careful analysis of secondary reinforcement in terms of conditioned association suggests that two processes may be involved. The nature of these two processes is somewhat clearer in the case of negative than in the case of positive secondary reinforcement. Experiments in which neutral stimuli have been paired with noxious stimuli indicate that (1) events associated with the onset of such stimuli acquire aversive properties and (2) although the evidence is less extensive than for (1), stimuli associated with the cessation of noxious stimulation become positive reinforcers. Very sparse data suggest that these relationships may be reversed when primary reinforcement is positive.

Variables which Determine the Strength of Secondary Reinforcement

Since secondary reinforcement is learned, it is to be expected that the variables which influence learning in general will also control the amount of secondary reinforcement. There is much experimental evidence in confirmation of this expectation. Among the variables which have been shown to exercise appropriate control over secondary reinforcement are the number of primary reinforcements, the number of unreinforced presentations (in extinction) of the secondary reinforcer, the interstimulus interval, and the amount of primary reinforcement. In the case of one variable, the schedule of primary reinforcement, the appropriate experiment remains to be done. An additional variable, which has *no* effect, is drive level at the time of the establishment of secondary reinforcement. This result is consistent with those obtained in experiments on ordinary learning.

Effects of Secondary Reinforcement on Behavior

The concept of secondary reinforcement has been employed by S-R theorists to explain a variety of experimental results. It has been shown, for example, that the effect of partial reinforcement in increasing resistance to extinction is partly a matter of secondary reinforcement which occurs on otherwise non-reinforced trials during training. Similarly, it has been demonstrated that discrimination learning benefits if the positive and negative stimuli to be discriminated somehow match the reinforced and non-reinforced goals. In related experimental tests it has been shown that secondary reinforcement generalizes across drives.

One of the most important influences of secondary reinforcement is in its ability to assist the organism in the mediation of gaps in time. There is good reason to believe that this influence occurs in some cases as a result of chains of "superstitious" behavior elicited by the secondary reinforcer. In other cases the responses may be implicit internal reactions, conceivably of the central nervous system.

·8·

General Theories of Reinforcement

THE PREVIOUS chapters have reviewed a considerable amount of material which shows that the empirical operation of reinforcement is essential to learning. In this empirical sense, a reinforcer is an event which, employed appropriately, increases the probability of occurrence of a response in a learning situation. Without exception these events are stimulus changes such as accompany presenting food or water, turning a shock on or turning it off, or presenting a stimulus that has a history of being correlated with such happenings. The statement that some such occurrence is necessary to learning is a statement of the empirical principle of reinforcement or the *empirical law of effect* (McGeoch and Irion, 1952). At this empirical level there is no important dispute about the validity of the principle of reinforcement, and there is no such thing as a non-reinforcement theorist. Even Guthrie, who is often described as holding a non-reinforcement position, maintains such a view only with respect to the so-called *theoretical law of effect,* specifically interpreted in terms of drive-reduction or satisfaction.

As this last statement implies, there are many different opinions at the theoretical level as to the mechanism through which reinforcement produces its effects. Moreover, these differences of opinion exist simultaneously on several dimensions. Conceivably the most basic question of all is whether the single concept, reinforcement, represents a single process. Is it possible that a response conditioned by the administration of an unavoidable noxious stimulus is reinforced in the same way as a response acquired because it avoids the same stimulus? And is reinforcement in either of these situations the same as that which occurs with the presentation of food or of a secondary reinforcer? We shall want to discuss this problem in some detail later. In the meantime, it is clear that, although all instances of reinforcement are abstractly similar in the sense of involving stimulus change, their variety is so great that many writers have been led to suspect that the underlying processes may not always be the same. Indirectly, this variation has led to the sketching of alternative theories of reinforcement: Different psychologists, drawing their empirical evidence from diverse experimental situations, have been impressed with various aspects of the reinforcement occasion and on this basis have proposed a variety of general theories of reinforcement.

THE HISTORY OF THE PROBLEM OF REINFORCEMENT

Classically there have been three influential views of reinforcement which have been termed *contiguity*, *effect*, and *expectancy* theories, respectively. In actuality these positions are better described as hypothetical principles of reinforcement and, as such, are merely parts of theories because each of them has always been assumed to operate in combination with other principles. On the other hand, different early theorists made one or another of the processes referred to in these terms bear the main explanatory burden in their theories. Hence, the designations *contiguity theory, effect theory,* and *expectancy theory* were appropriate, at least at one time. More recently the differences among theories have become blurred, chiefly because some of the expectancy theorists now accept effect theory for some forms of learning (Tolman, 1949), and the effect theorists have included expectancy-like conceptions in their newer formulations (Hull, 1952; Spence, 1956). As a result, we have now emerged from the era in which the dominant themes in the psychology of learning derived from these central assumptions. Even so, it is instructive to review the early history of reinforcement controversy in order to understand how it forced a change in the approach to, and even in the definition of, reinforcement. We shall therefore summarize the classical positions and illustrate the most important problems over which dispute has raged, describing, in the case of each, enough of the experimental work to illustrate some of the main lines of experimentation conceived within each tradition.

Contiguity Theory

The basic conception in contiguity theory is that the essential condition for learning is the simultaneous, or near simultaneous, occurrence of a neutral stimulus and the response with which it is to become associated. More explicitly, the contiguity position holds that a stimulus (such as a CS), present at the time another stimulus (such as a UCS) elicits a response, tends on subsequent occasions to evoke that response. It thus becomes clear that the mechanism of learning which the contiguity position implies is stimulus substitution: the CS comes to serve as a substitute for the UCS and to evoke the same response. For this reason contiguity theory was often referred to as substitution theory.

Clearly the contiguity or substitution interpretation is most directly applicable to classical conditioning. It was fundamental to Pavlov's theoretical formulations and, in one form or another, has been an integral part of many more recent treatments of classical conditioning. Even in this natural context of classical conditioning, however, contiguity theory encounters a major difficulty, that of explaining the form of the conditioned response. One of the most difficult problems confronting any theory of conditioning is to account for the observed differences between a conditioned response and the unconditioned response on which it is based. The principle of substitution is particularly embarrassed by these differences because it demands that the organism act in the presence of the conditioned stimulus as though it were in the presence of the unconditioned stimulus. Although something approximating this occasionally seems to happen, it does not occur often. Pavlov (1934) reports that his dogs, trained to salivate to a light preceding food, sometimes turned their heads toward the light and even licked the light globe; but this is an exception. The most common result of classical conditioning, as has been pointed out previously, is that the CR resembles but does not completely duplicate the UCR. The contiguity principle, simply formulated, cannot handle this fact.

Contiguity theory, in any form, is characterized by the fact that no additional motivational principle is introduced to account for learning. Motivation theoretically enters as a factor in determining the occurrence and magnitude of the original unconditioned response, but the substitution is dependent merely on the fact of response.

Effect Theory

Although somewhat similar statements appear in the writings of the earlier psychologists, the first clear expression of the law of effect is to be found in the writings of Thorndike (1911, p. 244. See also p. 10 of this book). Thorndike proposed that responses which have satisfying consequences are strengthened and those followed by discomfort or annoyance are weakened. More recent expressions of this principle differ from the original ones chiefly in that other terms (*reward, reinforcement, drive-reduction*) have been substituted for *satisfaction* and *annoyance*. These changes have been made, in part, to avoid certain philosophically grounded objections to the original statement.

Since the earlier forms of the law of effect were couched in the language of satisfaction and annoyance, they were related historically to the pleasure-pain theories of the various hedonisms and ran into trouble for this reason. Most of the hedonistic views localized the experience of pain and pleasure in consciousness and, therefore, made the law of effect subjective in a sense to which the temper of the times was opposed.

Because of this, there were numerous attempts to define the concepts of satisfaction and annoyance objectively. Thorndike, for example, proposed an essentially operational approach: "By satisfying state of affairs is meant one which the animal does nothing to avoid, often doing such things as to attain and preserve it. By a discomforting or annoying state of affairs is meant one which the animal commonly avoids and abandons" (1911, p. 245). Other definitions emphasized the tension-reducing character of reinforcement. It was pointed out that the animal in the problem-box or maze is aroused, restless, hypertensed, until the food is reached. After ingestion of food, the animal becomes relaxed and quiescent. S. Smith and Guthrie (1921) wrote of "maintaining stimuli" which are removed by the reinforcing act. In this they followed the conceptions of prepotent and consummatory response proposed earlier by Sherrington (1906) and Woodworth (1918). Raup (1925) described the end of goal activity to be the reaching of a state of "complacency" similar to that which Cannon (1932) has called "homeostasis." T. L. McCulloch (1939c) proposed that reinforcement may be effective because it causes the disappearance of restless, excited behavior. Hull's (1943) drive-reduction theory is similar.

Other attempts at objectification took a physiological direction and attributed the reinforcing effects of satisfiers and annoyers to changes in resistance to conduction along the appropriate nerve paths (Thorndike, 1911; Troland, 1928). The line of research barely hinted at in these proposals is perhaps the most important one today. As we shall see later, many psychologists are looking for the neurological and humoral loci of the operation of reinforcers and have made important advances in this direction.

Another methodological issue connected with the law of effect arises from its apparent circularity. If, as it seemed to some, the law of effect proposes that learning occurs whenever a response is followed by a satisfier, and if the identification of a satisfier reduces to a matter of its ability to strengthen a learned response, the circle is transparently obvious. Moreover, there is no doubt that there have been numerous studies carried out for the purpose of identifying reinforcers which fall into this logical trap. This is particularly the case in studies designed to illustrate the operation of unusual reinforcers such as light stimulation (Kish, 1955), saccharine (Sheffield and Roby, 1950), copulation without ejaculation (Sheffield, Wulff, and Backer, 1951), light termination (Keller, 1941), the opportunity for visual exploration (Butler, 1953), or activity (Kagan and Berkun, 1954). In every one of these cases, the reinforcing value of a stimulus change has been established by its ability to strengthen a learned response. In spite of the fact that the circle referred to above is involved here, no one worries about it anymore for two reasons: (1) A long history of research has revealed that a reinforcer in one situation will function as such in another. This transituational character of reinforcement (Meehl, 1950; Miller and Dollard, 1941) breaks the circle. (2) In a related way it is possible to demonstrate the reinforcing power of an event in a manner more remote from the learning situation, in a series of defining experiments designed, as Thorndike suggested, to determine the states of affairs which organisms tend to approach and to avoid.

Finally there is the methodological problem of *retroflex action* created by the law of effect. This problem is that Thorndike's statement seems to require a cause (reinforcement) to work backward in time and operate upon a consequence (S-R bond) preceding it. This violates the most elementary rules of the logic of science (Cason, 1932; Rexroad, 1932). Such criticism of the law of effect has been handled in three ways (Postman, 1947): (1) Various neurophysiological speculations, including retroflex circuits in the brain (Troland, 1928), were offered to provide a continuing mechanism to bridge the time gap between a response to a stimulus and the occurrence of a reinforcer designed to strengthen the connection thus established, making it possible for the two events to exist concurrently. Hull's (1943) concept of stimulus trace or afferent neural impulse was the most highly developed of such speculations. (2) Other theorists shifted to an argument which stressed the importance of the stimulus, rather than the response, in discussing the problem. ''The burned child shuns the fire not because pain did anything to his movements, but because, since that pain, the stimulus has changed; it is now flame plus fear, no longer flame plus curiosity'' (Hollingworth, 1928). Almost exactly the same position was taken somewhat later (Mowrer, 1939) by theorists concerned with the problem of avoidance conditioning. (3) It was pointed out that, operationally, the influence of reinforcers is measured on the trial following that on which it is administered and that, in this sense, its action is in a forward direction (Hilgard, 1956). Moreover, the basic terms in the law of effect (*satisfier, connection,* and so on) are hypothetical constructs. To give them physiological reality and then to deny on *a priori* grounds the possibility of their functioning as the law of effects proposes is logically unwarranted.

Comparison of the Principles of Effect and Contiguity

The basic difference between effect and contiguity theory turns on the question whether one or two principles are necessary to account for learning. Both theories hold that contiguity is an essential condition; and, in their typical forms, both include a stimulus substitution principle. That is, for both theories learning consists of a change in the organism such that a stimulus, which once would not do so, now evokes a response originally elicited by another stimulus. Effect theorists hold *in addition* that learning occurs because of the action of some outside agent (effect). Thus the most conspicuous difference between contiguity and effect accounts of learning is that the latter contain references to some consequence of a response, such as "satisfaction," "drive reduction," "relaxation," or "return to homeostasis," which the latter do not. Comparisons of the two positions have consisted in attempts to determine whether these hypothetical aftereffects are, in fact, necessary for learning to occur.

The difference between the contiguity and effect interpretations of learning may be illustrated by the concrete, but hypothetical, example in Figure 8.1. In this example it is assumed that a dog is presented with

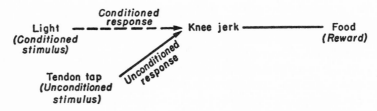

FIGURE 8.1. Comparison of the principle of contiguity with the law of effect. According to the principle of contiguity the conditioned response depends upon the occurrence of the unconditioned knee jerk. According to the law of effect, the conditioned leg extension depends upon the food reward. For further discussion, see text.

a conditioned stimulus (light), followed by a stimulus which elicits a knee jerk, which in turn is followed by a reward (food). According to the principle of substitution, the strength of the conditioned response (leg extension to light) depends upon the occurrence and the intensity of the unconditioned knee jerk response. The principle of effect states that the strength of the conditioned response is a function of the occurrence and amount of food reward.

Expectancy Theory

Tolman's theory of sign-learning is the most systematic formulation of the expectancy position. According to Tolman (1932), in learning a sequence of acts leading to a goal, the subject follows the "signs" which mark out the "behavior route" leading to the "significate," or goal. The expectancy interpretation involves the perceptual or cognitive capacities of the animal. In the presence of the "signs" the subject "expects" the goal to appear if it follows the "behavior route." The inference is made that the animal behaves in the ways which appear to it to be consonant with anticipated consequences. If the goal materializes, the expectation is confirmed; when the situation is repeated, similar expectancies and, therefore, similar behavior sequences will again be evoked. If the expected consequences do not materialize, the expectancy is weakened and behavior on the next trial may be different. Such tentative behavior, entered upon in accordance with expected consequences which are probable but not certain, will be immediately recognized by the reader as familiar in his own experience.

Expectancy theory, as developed by Tolman, is often referred to as a non-reinforcement theory. As in the case of Guthrie's theory, however, this designation is somewhat misleading. The position is a non-reinforcement position only in the sense of being a non-law-of-effect position. The terms *significate* and *goal* are the terms referring to reinforcement in expectancy theory. Learning is assumed to occur whenever a sign is followed in time or space (that is, reinforced) by some other signified object. It should be noted that learning, in expectancy theory, is of a "stimulus-stimulus" sort in that the learning organism acquires a knowledge of what (stimulus-one, or sign) leads to what (stimulus-two, or significate) in the environment.

In expectancy theory, there are two steps in explanation of any bit of learned behavior. The first involves the assumption of a sign-significate relationship, so that the situation has a new meaning for the organism, based on its prior experience in it. Thus the guinea pigs in the revolving cage of Brogden, Lipman, and Culler (1938) must learn that at the sound of the buzzer the cage is potentially dangerous (a shock is likely to occur) and that the shock is less likely to occur if they start running when the buzzer sounds. Wolfe's chimpanzees must know that tokens signify potential food. Very often this step is couched in terms of the reorganization of the perceptual field (Adams, 1931; Lewin, 1942). The second step in explaining a learned act requires a statement of the manner in which the aroused expectation or signification leads to appropriate conduct. It was originally assumed by Tolman that if a rat knew the behavior-route to a desired goal, it would follow the route. He was criticized by Guthrie (1935, p. 172) for not coming to grips with the problem of how the rat is led from its expectations to appropriate action. The expectancy theorists are not unaware of this problem, and, faced with such criticism, Tolman (1955) has developed the performance aspect of his theory in more detail. Specifically, he has proposed that the performance level of the learner varies with the value of a performance vector, an intervening variable which depends upon the organism's needs, upon the incentives available, and upon the amount of effort anticipated in acquiring a positive reward or escaping from punishment.

As is true of most theories, Tolman's expectancy position does not propose to predict the details of conduct. An expectancy can mediate the most varied behavior, as long as that behavior is consonant with anticipated consequences. A rat expecting punishment at the end of the maze may refuse to enter, may climb over the wall, or may simply crouch in the path and shudder. According to expectancy theory, it shows in its behavior that it anticipates an unpleasant consequence of running through the maze, but the details of the behavior cannot be accounted for by the mere acquisition of an expectation. Widely different performances may serve the purpose of keeping the animal away from the place where it expects to be punished.

DIFFERENCES AMONG THEORIES AND PROBLEMS RAISED

The foregoing descriptions of the classical opinions of the nature of reinforcement will suffice to illustrate the main differences among them. To summarize: (1) The contiguity view holds that reinforcement consists in the strengthening of an S-R connection through the contiguous occurrence of stimulus and response. (2) The effect theory proposes that S-R connections are strengthened as a result of subsequent satisfaction. (3) The expectancy position maintains that expectancies or cognitions are strengthened through the contiguous experience by the organism of signs and signified objects, both stimulus events. Now obviously each of these statements contains two basic elements: one refers to the process which a reinforcer hypothetically strengthens; the other refers to the nature of the reinforcer itself. The two components identify the main foci of theoretical disagreement about the nature of reinforcement. One subproblem concerns the nature of the process strengthened; another involves the nature of the mechanism which does the strengthening.

Spence (1942b, 1951a, 1951b) made what amounts to this same distinction and presented the various learning theories in a double classification scheme such as is represented in Figure 8.2. As that table shows, Spence discriminated two views of the nature of learning, (1) cognitive, signsignificate, or S-S theories, and (2) stimulus-response or S-R theories. Then he differentiated between theories which accepted the law of effect and those which did not. He referred to the effect theories as reinforcement theories and said of the others that they felt no need to appeal to a principle of reinforcement (Spence, 1942; p. 307). For this reason the non-law-of-effect theories are often called non-reinforcement theories, although in actuality they are simply alternative theories of the nature of reinforcement. It will be noted that certain theorists have held different theories for different forms of learning.

The table in Figure 8.2 provides a convenient means of introducing the most persistent theoretical questions which have divided theorists in the field of learning. They are:

	S–S (expectancy, cognition, hypothesis) theories	S–R (substitution) theories
Law-of-effect theories		Hull (1943)
	Tolman (1949) (for cathexis and equivalence beliefs)	Schlosberg (1937) Success learning Skinner (type R) Thorndike (trial and error learning) Tolman (1942) for instrumental learning, "social" techniques Spence (1956) for classical Mowrer (1947) for instrumental
Non-law–of effect theories	Tolman (1932)	Guthrie (1935, 1938)
	Tolman (1949) for expectancies Schlosberg (1937) for conditioning	Thorndike (associative shifting) Tolman (1949) for motor patterns Spence (1956) for instrumental Skinner (1938) for classical Mowrer (1947) for classical

FIGURE 8.2. Double classification of theories in terms of (a) what is learned and (b) position on the law of effect. Theories in the upper part of each box are single-process theories. Multiprocess theories are at the bottom.

1. Is learning a matter of establishing S-R connections or of building S-S cognitions? This has been termed the problem of what is learned.
2. Is reinforcement a matter of mere response elicitation, or is some additional consequence of behavior necessary? This is the effect-contiguity (reinforcement-nonreinforcement) issue.
3. Do the answers to the preceding two questions apply generally or only to certain forms of learning? This defines the single process-multiprocess issue.

The first two questions above are the ones which were the subject of controversy in early disputes over the nature of reinforcement. The third became more important in the light of accumulated evidence on the specific mechanisms of reward. Accordingly, experiments related to questions (1) and (2) are reviewed in this chapter. Material relevant to question (3) is covered in the next chapter.

HABIT OR EXPECTANCY?

In the disputes which have arisen over the nature of the associations formed in learning and the role of reinforcement, the concepts of habit and expectancy have played a central role. It will be well to begin our discussion with a consideration of the meanings of these terms. Hull defines his concept, habit, as follows:

> Whenever an effector activity ($r \longrightarrow R$) and a receptor activity ($S \longrightarrow s$) occur in close temporal contiguity ($_sC_r$), and this $_sC_r$ is closely associated with the diminution of a need ... there will result an increment to a tendency ($\Delta\ _sH_R$) for that afferent impulse on later occasions to evoke that reaction. The increments from successive reinforcements summate in a manner which yields a combined habit strength ($_sH_R$) which is a simple positive growth function of the number of reinforcements (N). The upper limit (m) of this curve of learning is the product of ... the magnitude of need reduction ... the delay (t) in reinforcement; and ... the degree of asynchronism (t') of S and R. ... (Hull, 1943, p. 178)

A definition of expectancy at exactly this level does not appear in Tolman's writings, although it is clear (Tolman, 1938) that many of the independent variables controlling the strength of an expectancy are the same as those postulated by Hull to govern the process of habit growth. These include the number of practice occasions, the amount of reinforcement, and the physical characteristics of the learning situation. This suggests that the two constructs, habit and expectancy, are really very much alike. Recognizing the essential similarity of the concepts, MacCorquodale and Meehl have proposed a formalization of Tolman's theory which includes a definition of expectancy which is roughly parallel to Hull's definition of habit. With S_1 referring to a sign, S_2 to a significate, and R to a response class, they define an expectancy as follows:

> The occurrence of the sequence $S_1 \longrightarrow R \longrightarrow S_2$ (the adjacent members being in close temporal contiguity) results in an increment in the strength of an expectancy (S_1RS_2). The strength increases as a decelerated function of the number of occurences of the sequence. The growth rate is an increasing function of the absolute value of the valence of S_2. (MacCorquodale and Meehl, 1954, p. 237-238)

The similarities between this statement and Hull's definition are at a basic level: Habit and expectancy emerge as (1) intervening variables which (2) depend in the same way upon the number of learning occasions and (3) vary with certain aspects of the reinforcing stimulus (S_2). Moreover, (4) there is *no* description of habit as an S-R connection or of expectancy as a mentalistic concept, nor (5) is there any specified link in these definitions of the concept to its supposed behavioral consequences. But there are differences: (1) The definition of expectancy contains no mention of anything analogous to the law of effect, whereas Hull refers to it directly, holding that the diminution of a need is essential to learning. (2) There are also trivial differences in the exact variables specified as responsible for the growth of learning and as to the locus (rate or limit) of their operation.

From this analysis, it is clear that the only important difference between the two types of construct, as presently formulated, is in terms of their positions on the law of effect. The other difference (S-S versus S R) which has been so important in the history of controversy between habit and expectancy theorists takes on diminished importance when it becomes clear that these two basic concepts *are*, after all, concepts. It is on this basis that Kendler has labeled the problem of what is learned (S-S versus S-R connections) a pseudoproblem and a theoretical blind alley (Kendler, 1950, 1952).[1] In the absence of a clear conception of the nature of scientific concepts, supposedly critical lines of experimentation were initiated in an attempt to decide once and for all which view was correct. In the main, the attempt was by the S-S theorists to discredit the S-R position, rather than vice versa. Strangely, the effect of the numerous experiments carried out in this tradition has been to strengthen rather than to weaken S-R theorizing, in spite of the fact that at least half of the studies have produced results which were negative to the S-R position. This is because the S-R theorists had to formulate more sophisticated theories which could explain the negative evidence. Such formulations have now eliminated many of the differences which once distinguished the two rival theories. Such concepts as mediation, r_G, and incentive motivation, presently stressed by the S-R theorists, have a distinctly cognitive ring. The effect on the S-S theories, on the other hand, was to weaken them to the point where Kendler (1959) was forced to write: "Cognitive learning theory of the sort espoused by Tolman . . . is either sleeping or dying, [in part because] the negative attitude toward S-R psychology dominated their activities to such an extent that they ignored the development of their own theory." (Kendler, 1959, p. 73).

The most common forms of experimental attack upon the main issues separating the major theories were the following: (1) attempts to condition subjects without employing one of the usual reinforcers at any point in the experiment, (2) sensory preconditioning, (3) perceptual learning, (4) place learning, (5) nonresponse conditioning, and (6) latent learning. It should be recognized at the outset that most of these experiments

---

[1] But see Rozeboom (1958).

have been conceived with a double purpose in mind. The first has been to evaluate the S-S as opposed to S-R hypotheses. The second has been to investigate the validity of the law of effect.

Conditioning without Reward

The ideal experiment for distinguishing between effect and contiguity theory would be one in which the response was simply elicited a number of times in the presence of some stimulus, to determine whether learning occurred in the absence of reward. Contiguity theory would predict that learning would occur. Effect theory would predict that it would not. Although such experiments are simple and straightforward in conception, not many of them have been done, because of the difficulties involved in evoking a response in a way which certainly involves no reward. There have, however, been a few. Loucks (1935), for example, attempted to condition the leg flexion of a dog to a buzzer when the response was elicited by electrical stimulation of the dog's motor cortex. He was unable to do so. When food was given following leg flexion, conditioning did occur. Along the same lines, Loucks and Gantt (1938) found that flexion elicited by electrical stimulation could be conditioned to a buzzer if the shock evoking the response were applied to the posterior root ganglion and stimulated pain fibers, but that it could not be conditioned if elicited in a way which involved only kinesthesis. It could thus be argued that the pain associated with the response was essential to learning, either as a part of the elicitation process or because its subsequent cessation was drive-reducing. For this reason, these experiments favor an interpretation in terms of the law of effect (Spence, 1950).

Studies providing evidence in partial support of a contiguity interpretation have been conceived within the context of Guthrie's theory which holds that the mere elicitation of a response in a given situation will lead to learning if the response is the last one to occur in that situation (Seward, 1942; Guthrie and Horton, 1946). Seward, for example, showed that rats learned to press the bar in a Skinner box simply to be lifted out of the apparatus, although they did not learn as well as rats rewarded with food. As with other, similar, demonstrations, however, the question arises as to whether being lifted from the apparatus was not secondarily reinforcing. A more effective way of taking the subject out of the situation with the occurrence of some response might be to render it immediately unconscious. Duncan (1945, 1949) performed such an experiment using electroshock through rats' heads to produce the state of unconsciousness. When the shock was applied immediately after the occurrence of an escape reaction, the animals learned nothing. It, thus, turns out that attempts to condition animals without reward have most often produced results in favor of the law of effect.

Sensory Preconditioning

In their reformulation of Tolman's cognitive theory of learning, Mac-Corquodale and Meehl referred to the concept expectancy as depending upon a sequence of events ($S_1 \longrightarrow R \longrightarrow S_2$) which included a response. Earlier expectancy formulae had either ignored or belittled the importance of the occurrence of a response, partly because it was assumed that learning could occur without it. One line of evidence favoring this conclusion was the existence of a phenomenon called *sensory preconditioning*, in which an association apparently was established by the mere simultaneous occurrence of two sensory events, whether or not a response occurred.

The basic paradigm for the sensory preconditioning experiment involves three stages of training: (1) two neutral stimuli, S_1 and S_2 (for example, a light and a tone) are presented together, usually for a large number of trials; (2) a response is conditioned to one of these stimuli, say, S_1; (3) the other stimulus, S_2, is presented to determine whether the response transfers automatically to it. If it does, the implication is that some association was formed in the first (preconditioning) phase of the experiment which facilitated the transfer of the response from one stimulus to the other. This effect, when it occurs, is termed *sensory preconditioning*. Brogden (1939c) is credited with the first clear demonstration of the phenomenon and for the name.

Early attempts (Prokofiev and Zeliony, 1926; Kelly, 1934; Cason, 1936; Bogoslavski, 1937) to produce "sensory conditioning" as it was called prior to Brogden's study, met with varying degrees of success. By and large, however, they were either negative or inconclusive because of a failure to employ control groups to evaluate the effects of stimulus generalization and familiarity with the test stimulus (Seidel, 1959).

The necessity for the control for stimulus generalization comes about because a response conditioned to a particular stimulus is known to be elicitable by other stimuli, even if these stimuli are in another modality. In the example above, the response conditioned to the light might be given to the tone for this reason, rather than because of any association which had been formed between light and tone during the preconditioning phase of the experiment. This phenomenon, known as *cross-modal* generalization, could easily occur in a sensory preconditioning experiment and produce apparently positive results on an artifactual basis. In order to control for this effect it is necessary to employ a control group in which S_1 and S_2 have not been paired. The evidence for sensory preconditioning, then, is in any superiority in response to S_2 on the part of the group for which the stimuli had been paired. Experiments which contain the control for stimulus familiarity make some provision for equating experience with S_1 and S_2, such as presenting them to the control group as often as to the experimental group, but unpaired.

In Brogden's classical study of sensory preconditioning eight dogs received 200 pairings of a buzzer and light presented simultaneously. Then a flexion response to shock was conditioned to one of these stimuli, the bell for half the dogs and the light for the other half, to a criterion of 20 CR's in 20 trials. Finally the animals were tested in extinction with the other stimulus. A control group of eight dogs were treated in exactly the same way, except that the preconditioning sessions were omitted. The animals in the control group produced an aggregate of only 4 conditioned responses to the test stimulus. Those in the two experimental groups produced 78. Clearly the preconditioning procedure had had an effect which somehow led to the transfer of the CR from the CS to the novel test stimulus.

Other studies have shown that sensory preconditioning is not the result of differential familiarity with the test CS, as might have been the case in Brogden's experiment (Bahrick, 1952; Brogden, 1947; Chernikoff and Brogden, 1949; Seidel, 1958). It has also been demonstrated that sensory preconditioning can be obtained when the conditioning procedure is instrumental rather than classical (Bahrick, 1952; Karn, 1947; Seidel, 1958) and with voluntary responses (Brogden, 1947; Chernikoff and Brogden, 1949). When the appropriate controls have been employed and when the importance of stimulus generalization has been adequately taken into account, the magnitude of the sensory preconditioning effect is usually small and subject to extreme modification by instructional factors. The unimpressive quantitative dimensions of the phenomenon should not, however, be allowed to detract from its theoretical importance. At face value, sensory preconditioning seems more easily interpretable in terms of sensory integration than in terms of S-R connections (Birch and Bitterman, 1949) and poses a real problem for theorists of the latter persuasion.

In their attempts to deal with sensory preconditioning, the S-R theorists have relied upon a version of the $r_G \longrightarrow s_G$ mechanism which they often call upon in the face of facts which apparently demand a cognitive interpretation. In brief, they hold: (1) that phase one of the sensory preconditioning study is an ordinary classical conditioning procedure but the responses involved are never measured, (2) that these responses (r_G) have proprioceptive consequences (s_G) which get conditioned to the measured CR during phase two of the typical procedure, and (3) that these conditioned proprioceptive stimuli provide a mediating link between the preconditioning stage of the experiment and the elicitation of the response in phase three. Diagrammatic representations of this explanation appear in a number of articles (Bitterman, Reed, and Kubala, 1953; Coppock, 1958; Seidel, 1958, 1959). A somewhat modified version appears in Figure 8.3. This explanation, following Osgood (1953, p. 460ff.), is often spoken of as invoking a process of mediation and of being closely related to mediated stimulus generalization (pp. 355 to 358).

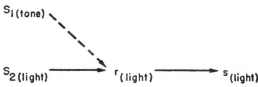

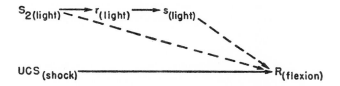

FIGURE 8.3.   S-R explanation of sensory preconditioning. Solid lines are un-conditioned connections. Dashed lines are conditioned connections. In Stage 1 an unmeasured response to light (with its proprioceptive stimulus) is condi-tioned to a tone. In Stage 2, both light and its response-produced stimulus are conditioned stimuli for flexion elicited by shock. In Stage 3, the proprio-ceptive stimulus (evoked when the tone elicits its previously conditioned response to light) now elicits the flexion response. (After Bitterman, Reed, and Kubala, 1953).

It is to be noted that this explanation of the sensory preconditioning phenomenon leads the S-R theorist into a position which is somewhat out of character, in that he has been forced to abandon the simple con-cepts of environmental stimuli and overt responses. He had found it neces-sary to posit the existence of covert, difficult-to-recognize, responses and to rely in his explanation upon the sensory consequences of these re-sponses. In this shifting of ground, the S-R theorist moves, in effect, a step closer to expectancy theory in that the specification of the response is now in terms of implicit behavior. On the other hand, the mediation hypothesis appears to be worth everything it costs the S-R position in terms of theoretical concessions, because it suggests an explanation for some of the previous negative results obtained in preconditioning studies and provides a rationale for experiments which should clarify the issue. If the first phase of such studies is, indeed, an ordinary classical conditioning procedure, the variables important for classical conditioning should be important for it. Of these variables, the two which appear to be most worthy of examination are the temporal spacing of the two stimuli (interstimulus interval) and the relative intensities of the two stimuli.

In several of the sensory preconditioning studies the stimuli in Stage I have been presented simultaneously; in others they have been separated by two seconds or more. Neither of these conditions is very favorable to the formation of a classical CR, and this may account for the failure of some of these experiments to obtain positive results. In much the same vein, the best arrangement for classical conditioning seems to be one in which the CS (S_1, in sensory preconditioning) is relatively weak by comparison to the UCS (S_2); this suggests that such an arrangement might produce stronger preconditioning than has usually been obtained. Evidence from investigations manipulating these variables would go far toward substantiating or refuting the mediation hypothesis. Unfortunately there are very few experiments which are directly relevant.

Silver and Meyer (1954) compared the effectiveness of simultaneous, forward ("CS" - "UCS" interval 1.5 seconds), and backward ("UCS" - "CS" interval 1.5 seconds) presentation of the stimuli in the preconditioning phase of a typical experiment, using light and buzzer as the two stimuli, and using rats as subjects. After 3000 presentations of the stimuli, they conditioned a running response to one stimulus until 7 con-

TABLE 14

SUMMARY OF CONDITIONS IN COPPOCK'S (1958) EXPERIMENT

(Tone-light conditions represented were reversed for half of the subjects)

Group	Preconditioning	Pre-extinction	Training	Test
Control (c)	Tone and light each presented alone	—	Light — shock	Tone
Preconditioning (PC)	Tone — light	—	Light — shock	Tone
Standard pre-extinction (SPE)	Tone — light	Tone only	Light — shock	Tone
Inverted pre-extinction (IPE)	Tone — light	Light — tone	Light — shock	Tone
Inverted preconditioning (IPC)	Light — tone	—	Light — shock	Tone

ditioned responses occurred in a series of 10 trials. Finally there was a test consisting of 100 *reinforced* trials with the other stimulus. In this test the forward conditioning group was superior to the simultaneous and backward conditioning groups, which were, themselves, indistinguishable. All of the preconditioning groups were superior, however, to three appropriate control groups. The main support for the mediation hypothesis is in the superiority of the preconditioning group originally trained with the stimuli presented in a forward order.

Certain of W. J. Coppock's (1958) results, in a study using human subjects and the GSR, may be interpreted in a similar way. Coppock ran 5 groups in the experiment outlined in Table 14. Note that, in addition to running the usual control and conditioning groups, he ran two pre-extinction groups for the purpose of extinguishing the associations established during preconditioning and an inverted preconditioning group for which the procedure corresponds to Silver and Meyer's backward conditioning one. The results of the Coppock experiment appear in Figure 8.4. The most straightforward statement of the outcome is that the three preconditioning groups were all superior to the control and inverted (backward) conditioning groups. By the usual statistical stand-

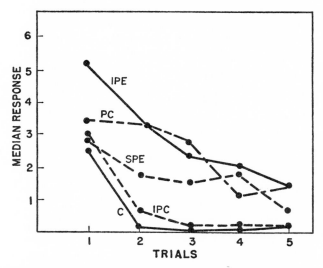

FIGURE 8.4. Results of W. J. Coppock's experiment on sensory preconditioning. The symbols are to be read: SPE = standard pre-extinction; IPE = inverted pre-extinction; C = control; PC = (standard) preconditioning; IPC = inverted preconditioning. Note that groups C and IPC are inferior to the other three groups. The inferiority of group IPC supports the hypothesis that for sensory preconditioning to occur, the order of stimuli during the preconditioning phase of the experiment must be in the forward-conditioning sequence. Graph from W. J. Coppock (1958).

ards there was no significant difference between the latter two groups individually or among the first three. In general these results, then, support the mediation hypothesis. They do, however, raise a problem as to why the pre-extinction procedure failed to accomplish its purpose.

Finally there is the parametric study of Hoffeld, Thompson, and Brogden (1958) which, although it was not conceived within the mediation hypothesis framework, is directly relevant. These investigators trained five experimental groups of cats in a preconditioning arrangement with tone and light as the first and second stimuli, separated by 0, 0.5, 1.2, 2.0, or 4.0 seconds for the different groups. There was also a control group which was placed in the apparatus for the same amount of time but received neither of the two stimuli. All of the cats were then trained to avoid a shock in a wheel-turning apparatus, with light as the CS, to a criterion of 90 per cent CR. Tests for sensory preconditioning followed, measured as number of responses to extinction. In these tests, the control group gave no CR's, but all of the experimental animals gave at least one. Median numbers of responses to extinction were: for the 0-, 0.5-, 1.2-, 2.0-, and 4.0-second groups, respectively, 2.5, 3.5, 3.0, 5.5, and 8.5 responses. This suggests that the function relating the amount of sensory preconditioning to the interstimulus interval is still increasing at 4.0 seconds, a curve which is very different from that obtained in studies of ordinary conditioning. This result calls into question the theory which demands that the optimal interval occur at about 0.5 second.

Other studies of the mediation hypothesis have attempted to manipulate the mediating process in some way. Seidel (1958) obtained sensory preconditioning in an experiment with rats and, by shifting drives, showed that the mediators are not responses specifically associated with hunger and thirst. Wickens and Briggs (1951) presented two stimuli, tone and light, in the preconditioning phase of their experiment and had their subjects respond with the word "now" under different conditions. For Group I, the stimuli were presented together and the subject responded to the combination. For Group II, the stimuli were presented separately and the subjects responded with the word "now" to both of them. For Groups III and IV the stimuli were also presented separately, but the subjects responded to only one of them, light or tone respectively. Following this, there were the typical conditioning (finger retraction to shock) and test periods. The results of the experiment in terms of the number of CR's in a 10-trial test session appear in Table 15. The differences between Groups I and II and the differences between Groups III and IV are insignificant. But there is a clear difference between these *pairs* of groups which can be summarized by saying that when a common mediating response was attached to the two stimuli transfer of a second response between them was facilitated.

TABLE 15

MEAN NUMBER OF RESPONSES ON TEST TRIALS WITH SHOCK OMITTED
(Wickens and Briggs, 1951)

Preconditioning Group	Mean
I "Now" to tone and light together	7.6
II "Now" to tone and light separately	7.1
III "Now" to light only	2.1
IV "Now" to tone only	0.2

Perceptual Learning

In discussing perceptual learning it will be well to keep two different meanings of the phase separate (Gibson and Gibson, 1955). On the one hand, perceptual learning may refer to the proposition that learning, or at least some learning, is a process closely related to perception and consists in a reorganization or integration of perceptual processes. S-S learning theory advocates such an interpretation. At other times, the expression *perceptual learning* refers to the fact that perception itself depends upon experience. It is this second sense of perceptual learning to which we turn briefly in this section.

There is evidence in considerable variety to indicate that a part of what we call perception is learned. It has been shown that: (1) practice or familiarity increases the speed with which materials can be recognized tachistoscopically, and this effect is upon speed of seeing and not upon the mere sensitization of a restricted range of motor responses (Neisser, 1954); (2) perceptions of the simplest properties of the visual world, both in animals and men, are acquired, and if experience with this environment is prevented, there may be a serious impairment of visual capacity (Senden, 1932; Riesen, 1947); (3) age improves size, shape, and brightness constancy (Brunswick, 1956); and (4) exposure to visual stimuli makes the organism more capable of dealing with these stimuli in a subsequent learning situation.

Some of the evidence in this last category comes from the field of verbal learning (Hovland and Kurtz, 1952) and is beyond the scope of this book; some of the rest is related to discrimination learning and will be treated later. The work of E. J. Gibson and her associates may be cited at this point to demonstrate the validity of the concept of perceptual learning. In the first of their studies, these investigators (E. J. Gibson and Walk, 1956) reared the rats in their experimental groups with distinctive stimuli, black circles and triangles, on the walls of their cages. Most of the other distinctive stimulation in a normal environment was excluded by surrounding the cages with blank white cardboard walls. The control group saw only the blank walls. At the age of about 90 days these two groups of rats were taught to discriminate the circles from the triangles in a typical discrimination procedure. In this procedure the animals were released from a starting box into a choice chamber which contained samples of the two stimuli, side by side, on the wall at the end opposite to that through which the animal entered. In order to prevent the subjects from learning a simple position preference, the stimuli were randomly shifted from side to side on various trials. The animal was rewarded with food if it nosed open a small door in the center of the correct stimulus, which was the triangle for some subjects and the circle for others. Learning curves for the experimental and control groups appear in Figure 8.5. Quite obviously previous exposure to the stimuli

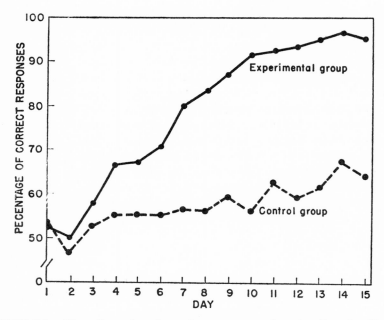

FIGURE 8.5. The effect of prolonged exposure to the stimuli to be discriminated upon the ease of the establishment of a discrimination (Gibson and Walk, 1956).

aided in the discrimination process. Subsequent research has confirmed this result and has, in addition, shown (1) that feeding in the presence of the forms is not responsible for the relative ease with which they are discriminated (Walk, E. J. Gibson, Pick, and Tighe, 1958) and (2) that the effect is probably limited to stimuli similar to those present in the cage (E. J. Gibson, Walk, Pick, and Tighe, 1958).[2]

From the S-R point of view the problem posed by these results is that

[2] See also Forgays and Forgays (1952); Forgus (1954, 1955a, 1955b); Meier and McGee (1959); Walk (1958); Walk, E. J. Gibson, and Tighe (1957).

it is difficult to see how overt, molar responses, even if they were conditioned to the stimuli, could be of much help in mastering the discrimination problem. Such responses transferred to the learning situation would be of no particular use, because the stimuli were shifted from side to side. Moreover, for half the animals, the circle was positive; and for the other half, the triangle was positive. Thus, to maintain the S-R position, it is necessary to say that some subtler form of behavior such as, perhaps, Wyckoff's (1952) observing responses were strengthened during the first part of the experiment; thus the experimental animals would be better prepared to "pay attention" to the relevant cues than the animals in the control group. Another S-R explanation might hold that perceptions have response properties and, like other responses, can be modified by learning.

Place Learning

In 1946 there appeared the first of a series of studies (Tolman, Ritchie, and D. Kalish, 1946a, 1946b, 1947a, 1947b; Ritchie, 1947)[3] which argued in favor of place learning, rather than response learning, as characteristic of the behavior of rats in a spatial maze. The second of these studies, for example, opposed the two kinds of learning in an attempt to provide a definitive comparison of their relative importance. The apparatus employed was the maze shown in Figure 8.6, which differed from most

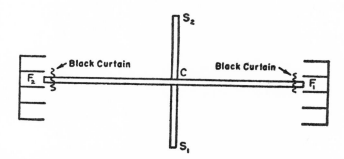

FIGURE 8.6.   Apparatus for the study of place and response learning. S_1 and S_2 are starting points. F_1 and F_2 are the locations of goal boxes containing food. In this experiment, rats began some trials at S_1 and others at S_2. Under conditions of place learning, food is always in the same place, say, F_1. In conditions of response learning, food is shifted from F_1 to F_2 in a way which requires the animal always to make the same response, say a right, turn in order to get food. (Tolman, Ritchie, and Kalish, 1946b).

[3] See also: Tolman and Gleitman (1949); Ritchie, Hay, and Hare (1951); Ritchie, Aeschliman, and Pierce (1950).

mazes in having two starting points, S_1 and S_2. In the experiment the rats sometimes began a trial at one starting point, sometimes at the other.

There were two groups of rats in the study. One group, a *response-learning group*, had to learn to make a right turn, no matter which was the starting point. If they began at S_1, they had to go to F_1 to be fed; if they began at S_2, they had to go to F_2. The other group was a *place-learning group*, which was always reinforced in the same place, say F_1, without respect to the starting point.

The latter, place-learning, group mastered the maze very much more rapidly than the response-learning group. Whereas the average rat in the response-learning group did not meet the criterion of 10 successive correct runs in 72 trials, the place-learning group met this criterion in only 2 trials. Obviously the place-learning conditions favored learning in a way the response-learning conditions did not. Again the simplest form of S-R theorizing fails to predict the outcome.

More sophisticated versions of S-R theorizing, however, suffer no embarrassment from the place-learning experiments. The problem, it should be clear, is with the term *place*. To use it, as Tolman and his collaborators clearly saw, is to identify a region of the environment in terms of specific stimuli. According to Tolman, Richie, and Kalish, one of the things a rat learns in a maze is "a disposition to orient towards the place where the food is located (under the window, to the left of the radiator, and so on)" (1946b, p. 221). And, in the demonstrations of the superiority of place learning over response learning, such distinctive stimuli (overhead lights, nearby wall, animal cages giving off distinctive odors) were always present in a way which made it possible to locate the food by reference to them (Ballachey and Buel, 1934b). Given this, it is but a short step to the interpretation of place learning as the result of generalized tendencies to approach certain stimuli and to avoid others. Such an explanation can be made quite detailed as Hull shows in his two discussions of behavior in open field situations (Hull, 1938, 1952). The general validity of such an account is attested to by the fact that, when there are no distinctive features in the environment, animals resort to response learning. The whole problem is highly reminiscent of the sensory control of the maze issue (Honzik, 1936) which led, after much research, to the discovery that rats are very efficient in making use of whatever sensory information is provided, and master a maze on this basis.

Learning without Responding

Another test of the S-S versus S-R positions theoretically might be provided by determining whether learning is possible without responding, as a result of mere perceptual (S-S) experience with the learning situation, or whether the response to be performed must, in some sense, occur.

Various attempts to eliminate the response from the learning situation have ranged all the way from giving rats a ride through a maze in a little cart (McNamara, Long, and Wike, 1956) to pharmacological and surgical immobilization of the response mechanism during sensory stimulation. Studies in this latter category have most often used the strategy of conducting "conditioning" trials when the subjects were immobilized by an administration of curare or a curare-like drug and then tested for the presence of a CR when the effects of the drug had worn off. The results of early studies of this sort[4] were sometimes positive and sometimes negative. It now seems that the negative results may have arisen from inadequacies in the training procedures, the drugs, or both. More recent investigations usually have been successful.

Using cats as subjects, Beck and Doty (1957) immobilized the flexion response to shock in various ways and paired a .2-second shock with a tone to determine whether conditioning would occur. For three cats immobilization was produced pharmacologically by injections of bulbocapnine; for three others the bulbocapnine injections were combined with crushing the motor nerves for the flexion response; and for two other cats, the immobilization was produced by bulbocapnine and midbrain lesions. Seven of these 8 animals showed substantial levels of conditioning when the effect of the drug had disappeared and the animals had recovered the use of the surgically immobilized limb. Light and Gantt (1936) and Kellogg, Scott, Davis, and Wolf (1940) had previously shown that conditioning can occur when the response is prevented by crushing the motor nerves.

In a related experiment, Black (1958) showed that extinction occurs if the CS is presented alone while the response is immobilized. Dogs were first trained to turn their head to one side, in response to a tone, to avoid shock. Following this training control subjects received 50 nonreinforced tone presentations in a normal, responsive state. Experimental subjects were injected with d-tubocurarine chloride, which produces a flaccid paralysis on the skeletal musculature, and given 50 extinction trials on which the response, of course, could not occur. The median number of trials necessary for extinction (counting the 50 under curare) was 91 for the experimental group; the control group animals did not, on the average, extinguish in 450 extinction trials. It should be noted that extinction is actually considerably faster under curare than in the normal mobile state. Such experiments bring the problem facing the S-R theorist into sharp focus. Obviously the conception of learning as involving an association between stimuli and responses, when the latter are conceived in terms of gross molar events is untenable.

[4] Girden (1940, 1942a, 1942b, 1942c), Girden and Culler (1937), Harlow (1940), Harlow and Settlage (1939), Harlow and Stagner (1933).

Latent Learning

The term *latent learning,* as it is used in experiments designed to test the relative merits of habit and expectancy interpretations of learning, refers to learning which occurs (*a*) without immediate consequences on performance and (b), according to the expectancy point of view, without reward. The argument is mainly about the second of these two propositions. The expectancy position is that learning can occur without reward, and that mere experience in a situation is sufficient. The translation of such learning into performance requires, in addition, the existence of an incentive. From such a point of view, the trouble with the typical learning situation is that these two processes are confounded in a way which makes it appear that the incentive is an essential condition of learning. The latent-learning experiment is a method for separating the two processes.

The reference experiment in the field of latent learning is that of Tolman and Honzik (1930) in which rats ran a maze for 10 days with (control group) or without (one experimental and one control group) reward. On the eleventh day reward was introduced for the experimental group previously run without reward. The results of this experiment appear in Figure 8.7, where it is quite obvious: (1) that the rewarded rats performed better than non-rewarded rats; (2) that, even without reward, there was some improvement; and (3) that the introduction of reward on the eleventh day of the experiment led to an immediate decrease in number of errors in the group treated in this way. This last observation is the most direct kind of evidence for the existence of latent learning. It was as if the rats in this group knew considerably more about the maze than their previous behavior had indicated, and all that was required to make them show it was an adequate reason (incentive). The crux of such an interpretation is in the assumption that reinforcement is a performance variable rather than one controlling learning.

Naturally the S-R reinforcement theorists did not take this apparent refutation of their main theoretical assumption lying down. They had a number of questions to ask; the two most important were the following:

1. Is the phenomenon of latent learning dependable? That is, can the effect be obtained routinely? Experiments began to be reported which showed that it did not always appear (for example, Reynolds, 1945c). Such demonstrations, however, are in the minority. MacCorquodale and Meehl (1954) reviewed 48 relevant studies and assigned 30 of them to the positive category. It seems, as Hilgard (1956) concludes, that the reality of the phenomenon can no longer be denied. Table 16 summarizes the studies yielding positive and negative results in terms of the classification developed below.

2. Has reward actually been eliminated from the situation? This ques-

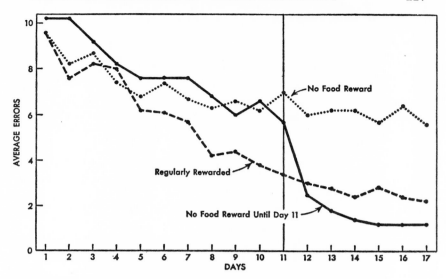

FIGURE 8.7. One of the classical demonstrations of latent learning. For description of experiment, see text. Data from Tolman and Honzik (1930).

tion may be asked from a number of different angles. For one thing, the initial improvement in performance in the Tolman and Honzik experiment can be made a source of embarrassment to expectancy theory. If the sudden drop after trial 11 is to be attributed to reward, is it completely logical to fail to interpret the previous, more gradual improvement in the same way? With this as an entering wedge, it is possible to suggest a number of sources of reward which might reinforce behavior on the first 10 trials. These include: secondary reinforcement through being handled by the experimenter or returned to the home cage, reinforcement provided by escape from confining culs-de-sac during the early trials, and reinforcement stemming from the satisfaction of curiosity or activity drives. Such possibilities led to a multiplication of the number of experimental designs employed in the study of latent learning. Mac-Corquodale and Meehl (1954) added one type of experiment to the list proposed by Thistlethwaite (1951a) and identified five varieties:

a. *Trials without reward followed by the introduction of a reward appropriate to the animal's motives.* This is the design employed in the Tolman and Honzik experiment taken as a reference. Similarly Karn and Porter (1946) ran rats to a food reward in a complex maze. For a control group with no previous experience in the maze, the number of trials required to learn it was 10.25. For an experimental group which had been given five unrewarded trials, the number was only 3.83.

b. *Free exploration followed by the introduction of reward.* Lashley as

TABLE 16

SUMMARY OF REPRESENTATIVE LATENT LEARNING EXPERIMENTS
CLASSIFIED IN TERMS OF TYPE OF EXPERIMENT AND OUTCOME

Type of Experiment	Outcome Positive	Negative
1 Trials without reward followed by introduction of reward.	Blodgett (1929), Elliott (1929), Herb (1940), Muenzinger, and Conrad (1953), Simmons (1924), Tolman and Honzik (1930), Wallace, Blackwell, and Jenkins (1941), Williams (1929), Meehl and MacCorquodale (1953)	Meehl and MacCorquodale (1951), Reynolds (1945c)
2 Free exploration followed by introduction of reward.	Buxton (1940), Daub (1933), Haney (1931), Karn and Porter (1946), Lashley (1918	
3 Trials satiated, goal objects present. Tests under relevant drive.	Kendler and Levine (1953), MacCorquodale and Meehl (1951, Meehl and MacCorquodale (1938), Seward, Levy, and Handlon (1950), Spence, Bergmann, and Lippitt (1950), Spence and Lippitt (1940), Szymanski (1918), Thistlethwaite (1951b)	Kendler (1947a), Maltzman (1950)
4 Trials under irrelevant drive followed by shift to relevant drive.	Bendig (1952), Christie (1952), Diesenroth and Spence (1941), Strange (1950), Thistlethwaite (1952b), Walker (1951), Walker, Knotter, and De-Valois (1950), Johnson (1952)	Christie (1951), Feher (1951), Gleitman (1950), Grice (1948a), Kendler (1947b), Kendler and Kanner (1950), Littman (1950), Shaw and Waters (1950), Spence and Lippitt (1946), Walker (1948)
5 Exploration followed by reinforcement in a distinctive goal box.	Gilchrist (1952), Iwahara and Marx (1950), Seward (1949), Strain (1953), Tolman and Gleitman (1949b)	Denny and Davis (1951), Levy (1952), Minturn (1954), Seward, Datel, and Levy (1952)

early as 1918 had reported an experiment of this sort. Later Haney (1931) repeated the experiment using a complex 14-unit maze and long periods of free exploration, and allowing his animals to live in the maze for four 18-hour periods. A control group received similar handling and exploratory experience, but in a simple rectangular maze. When both groups were tested in the maze in which the experimental group had lived, this group made fewer errors than the control group.

c. Trials while satiated, with goal objects present, followed by tests under the relevant drive. Thistlethwaite (1951b) ran rats, satiated for food and water, in a Y-maze which contained a dish of wet mash in one arm. Interspersed with these satiated trials, there were test trials in which the rats were 22-hours hungry and there was no food in the maze. On these test days there was a stronger tendency to take the food side than on the satiation days, indicating that under satiation the animals had learned the location of food.

d. Trials under a strong irrelevant drive followed by a shift to the relevant drive. Bendig (1952) ran 46 rats (Experiments II and III), satiated for food, in a two-choice water maze. Escape from water provided the reward in this portion of the study. In a series of free- and forced-choice trials, the runs (really swims) terminated sometimes at a landing platform covered with food which they never ate, sometimes at an empty landing platform. Then the rats received one additional trial under 23 hours of food deprivation. Thirty-five of the 46 animals swam directly to the platform which had contained food.

e. Exploration followed by reinforcement in a distinctive goal box. Seward (1949) allowed 32 rats, five or six at a time, to explore a T-maze for 30 minutes a day over a period of three days. On the fourth day he fed the animals in a distinctive goal box which had always been at the end of one arm of the T. Then he tested the rats in an ordinary trial in which they began the run at the starting point in the maze and chose the path to one goal box or the other. Of the 32 rats in the experiment, 28 went directly to the box where they had just been fed.

One of the few studies of latent learning involving negative reinforcement also belongs in this category. Strain (1953) first allowed rats to explore a runway divided by opaque swinging doors into six perceptually distinct compartments. Following six days of this without reinforcement, he shocked the rats in a duplicate of the end compartment. Then he reintroduced the rats to the apparatus. Four different groups entered the runway at the four middle compartments, as they had in the period of free exploration. The question was: When the animals left the compartment into which they were introduced on this test, would they now tend to leave in the direction leading away from the compartment in which they had just been shocked? Of the 80 rats in the experiment, 53 did exactly that. Moreover, the animals introduced into the compartment adjacent to the shock compartment showed this tendency to a greater degree than any of the others. Well-executed controls showed that the latent learning evidenced in this study must have depended upon memory for the sequence of compartments rather than upon extra-maze cues.

Variables Controlling Latent Learning. The foregoing experiments have all been ones with positive outcomes, stressing the point that latent learning occurs in enough different experimental settings to force the law-of-effect theorist to take the phenomenon seriously. To stop at this point, however, would be to overstate the case and to omit the facts: (1) that the latent-learning effect is frequently weak and transistory; and (2) that, in many experiments, it failed to appear at all. These considerations raise an obvious question: What are the conditions which favor the occurrence of latent learning? There has, as yet, been no definitive answer to this question. But there have been numerous suggestions as to important variables, most of which have been summarized by Thistlethwaite (1951). Some of the most important general classes of such variables are the following:

1. *The maze pattern.* Some of the most impressive of the demonstrations of latent learning have been in complex mazes. These include many of the studies in the first and second designs outlined in the previous section. The significance of this fact is that it is difficult to construct a complex maze without making the majority of true-path sections goal pointing. Thus, for latent learning to occur, it would be necessary only for the animal to learn the general location of food on its first reinforced run, in terms of some extra-maze cue. In attempting to go directly to that place a decrease in the number of errors would be inevitable. This might be called a place-learning explanation. One of the points to recommend this interpretation is that it accounts for the fact that, so far as latent learning is concerned, complex mazes appear to be easier to master than simple ones. Another line of evidence in support of such an explanation comes from the results of Type 5 experiments in which rats are first allowed to explore a maze and then fed in a distinctive goal box located somewhere other than at its previous and subsequent position in the maze (Leeper, 1935; Seward, 1949). This procedure (which might be thought of as misinforming the rats as to the location of food) leads to a failure of latent learning to appear. There are, however, data obtained in complex mazes which the place-learning interpretation will not explain. Blodgett (1929) ran one group of rats *backward* through a maze in the exploratory period. Then he reversed the direction for the rewarded runs. These animals failed to show latent learning in spite of the fact that all but one of the true path segments was goal pointing. Obviously, where latent learning does occur, experience with respect to intramaze cues must play some part. Goal-box stimuli may be particularly important in this regard. As evidence for this point, Seward (1949) showed that rats trained without reward in a maze with two identical goal boxes and then fed in one of them also failed to show latent learning.

2. *Motivation.* The motivational level of the subject during the training period in latent-learning studies is probably crucial in determining whether or not the phenomenon occurs. The effect, however, is not a simple one and no doubt varies from one form of the latent-learning experiment to another and from one motive to another. Tolman's (1948) position leads to the expectation that high motivation would interfere with latent learning, especially in Type 4 experiments, where the subject

is highly motivated for one goal object but, to show latent learning, would have to discover the location of a reward appropriate to another drive. The reason for this is that strong motivation, according to Tolman, narrows the rat's cognitive map and prevents his paying attention to objects other than those particularly relevant to his needs.

By and large the evidence is in support of this interpretation. For one thing, studies of latent learning of the Type 4 variety have been predominantly negative, whereas Type 3 studies (which are the same as Type 4 except that drive is low during the initial training) have been predominantly positive. More to the point is the study of Johnson (1952) who studied the role of drive in an experiment where groups of rats deprived of water for 0, 6, 12, or 22 hours ran a T-maze; there was no water but food was present in one arm. After seven days of training under these conditions, the rats were made hungry. On the initial hunger trial, the percentages of rats running to the food side were 93, 79, 50, and 57 for the four groups arranged from lowest to highest drive during training. Thus, training under low drive seems to be the most effective condition for the establishment of latent learning. Related, but less direct evidence to the same point comes from experiments which show that incidental learning, of which latent learning is a variety, is better under low drive than under high drive (Bruner, Matter, and Papanek, 1955).

A somewhat neglected aspect of the role of motivation in latent learning concerns the consequences of changing drives as must be done in a Type 3 or Type 4 study. Such changes have a variety of influences which may tend to assist or interfere with the appearance of latent learning. Some may even lead to the spurious appearance of what seems to be latent learning but is not learning at all. In this last category there is the phenomenon demonstrated by Kendler and his associates: that animals trained (in an ordinary learning experiment, not latent learning) under hunger with food reward tend, upon switching the drive to thirst, to avoid the previously reinforced side of a T-maze (Kendler, Levine, Altchek, and Peters, 1952), as if the "thought" of dry food were unpleasant to a thirsty rat. Thus, any procedure which involves a drive shift from hunger to thirst in a two-choice situation of the sort ordinarily used in Type 4 studies of latent learning would result in the animals' abandoning the side previously reinforced with food. The switch would occur for reasons which in no way demand that the animal know that water is on the previously non-reinforced side. This may account for the fact that latent learning occurs better when the original training is under food deprivation than under water deprivation (Vineberg, 1953).

The effects of altering motives might also influence latent-learning experiments in another way. Ordinarily in the life history of the laboratory rat, hunger and thirst occur together and are satisfied at about the same time. This probably accounts in part for the fact (Leeper, 1935; Hull,

1933) that rats sometimes have very great difficulty in discriminating their drive states. If this difficulty carried over to the Type 4 latent-learning experiment, the animal might not recognize the change from hunger to thirst or vice versa as a change at all, and for this reason, might continue to respond with the originally reinforced response. Operating on this assumption, Christie (1951) gave animals training in discriminating drives and then carried out a Type 4 latent-learning experiment to determine whether animals with such experience might not show more latent learning than rats without such a history. They did not, and Christie was led temporarily to reject the hypothesis that drive discrimination is an important factor in the latent-learning experiment.

3. *Previous experience.* A more general conception suggested by Christie's experiment is that the history of the organism may determine whether or not it is capable of displaying latent learning. Christie's earlier negative result, then, might only indicate that a history of deprivation is probably not the critical thing. Other possibilities are that the most effective kind of prior experience is that which creates a generalized exploratory drive, leads the animal to notice objects in the environment, diminishes the amount of fear aroused in a novel situation, or provides an irrelevant incentive with unusually powerful secondary reinforcement value. There is presently no very good reason to choose one of these interpretations over any other, but there are experiments which show, beyond much doubt, that previous experience does influence the outcome of latent-learning experiments. Christie (1952) repeated his earlier experiment adding some additional groups which had had exploratory experience in a non-maze situation prior to the latent-learning experiment. He found that the exploratory training contributed more impressively to the animal's ability to display latent learning than the history of deprivation did, although in this experiment the drive-discrimination procedure led to latent learning, too. Christie's results also suggest that exploration under satiation is, if anything, superior to exploration under high drive. A later experiment (Vineberg, 1953), however, throws doubt on this interpretation. In Vineberg's experiment animals given an opportunity to explore while they were highly motivated turned out to be better latent learners than those who explored while satiated.

Present Status of the Problem. The phenomenon of latent learning was originally conceived as an attempt to demonstrate learning without reward and, therefore, as a challenge to the validity of the law of effect. Reinforcement theorists accepted this interpretation of the phenomenon, and the battle was joined. Since then there have been scores of published articles on latent learning, reporting an even greater number of experiments conducted by some of psychology's finest craftsmen in the art of experimental design. In spite of the effort and resourcefulness devoted to the problem, however, one is forced to conclude that experiments on latent learning have contributed little or nothing *directly* to the issue they were designed to settle. It may be instructive to outline some of the reasons for this.

The basic reason, no doubt, is that the situations and behaviors involved in latent-learning studies are so complex that it is never possible to state with complete certainty that a given experiment has accomplished its primary objective, that of temporarily eliminating reinforcement for one group of subjects in the experiment. To get subjects to perform in the complete absence of drive is difficult, if not impossible. Thus, to say that a rat ran the maze is to say that it was at least minimally motivated. This raises the possibilities of the existence of uncontrolled rewards for such drives as activity (Kagan and Berkun, 1954; Desiderato, 1956), curiosity (Butler, 1953), exploratory (Montgomery, 1954), and restriction avoidance (MacCorquodale and Meehl, 1951). Then, without considering irrelevant drives, there are the possibilities (1) that there is incomplete satiation in Type 3 and Type 4 studies and (2) that reinforcement is provided by the sight of an incentive even though the subject is satiated (Wike and Casey, 1954; Hull, 1952, p. 148ff.). Thus it is impossible to rule out the possibility that reward was present in some form in any experiment on latent learning.

On the other hand, a mere demonstration of the existence of some sort of reward does not provide a complete explanation for the results of latent-learning experiments. What is still required is some way to translate this learning into performance. In this regard the problem of the S-R theorist becomes the same as that of the expectancy theorist. Hull's (1952) handling of the results of the Type 3 (training satiated, tests under relevant drive) form of the latent-learning experiment is typical of a number of such explanations. He begins with the assumption that the sight of food or water is mildly reinforcing even to a fully satiated organism, and that this comes about through the evocation of an $r_G \longrightarrow s_G$ mechanism. Moreover, he assumes that the $r_G \longrightarrow s_G$ mechanism evoked by the sight of food ($r_f \longrightarrow s_f$) is different from that elicited by water ($r_w \longrightarrow s_w$). To illustrate the application of these ideas consider the situation as it exists in the presence of the cues (S_c) at the choice point in a T-maze, where a left turn (R_L) leads to food and a right turn (R_R) leads to water. It is critical to this argument that the choice-point cues elicit, in addition to the final overt response, other responses of looking back and forth, which serve the function of providing discrete proprioceptive stimulation. They are, in Hull's earlier terminology, *pure stimulus acts,* or, in the terms of Muenzinger (1956), *vicarious trial and error* (VTE). Symbolizing the looking-to-the-right and looking-to-the-left responses as r_R and r_L we may begin the construction of a diagrammatic explanation of latent learning:

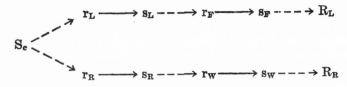

In brief this diagram says that the implicit behaviors elicited by S_c have distinctly different proprioceptive consequences (s_R and s_L) which, because they previously have been followed by food and water, now are capable of eliciting the appropriate fractional goal responses (r_F and r_W). This is possible in the absence of, and in anticipation of, the molar responses R_L and R_R, because the molecular, implicit, internal, nature of r_F and r_W permits them to occur covertly. Given this assumption, it is now possible to assume the important link in the conditioning process for the explanation of latent learning: that is $s_F - - \longrightarrow R_L$ and $s_W - - \longrightarrow R_R$.

If, now, the animal is made thirsty, the situation changes in the following way: The thirst drive and its associated drive stimuli S_T, in the past, have been conditioned to r_W, so that now:

$$S_T - - \longrightarrow r_W \longrightarrow s_W - - \longrightarrow R_R,$$

and the animal goes to water in the T-maze.

There are certain points about this explanation which need to be made: (1) It is limited to the Type 3 version of the latent-learning experiment. Other, probably different, explanations are required for other types. (2) Obviously it is a complicated explanation even in the oversimplified form just presented. This, however, is how it is with psychology. It seems quite clear that if behavior were to be explained simply, the simple explanations would have been discovered long ago. (3) The mechanism, $r_L \longrightarrow s_L - - \longrightarrow r_F \longrightarrow s_F$, is about as expectative as the expectancy concept itself. As we have seen several times before, in the face of contradictory data, the S-R theorist has frequently been forced to develop explanations which attempt to bring the cognitive phenomena within an S-R framework. Such developments have, today, nearly destroyed the sharp differences which once existed among the classical theories of reinforcement. There are, in fact, very few proponents remaining of the positions of the 1930's and probably none who believe that the issues will be settled by a single perfectly conceived experiment. The theories simply are not that exactly formulated. In the face of this impossibility, interest in the field of learning seems to have shifted toward a much more factually oriented set of problems. We turn to these in the next chapter.

SUMMARY

In the 1930's research in the psychology of learning was dominated by three major systematic points of view: (1) Contiguity theory which held that the conditions necessary for learning were simply the occurrence of a response in the presence of a stimulus. Later on that stimulus, theoretically, would evoke the response. No additional principle of reinforcement was hypothesized. (2) Effect theory which maintained that learning requires (a) stimulus-response contiguity and (b) reward in the form of satisfaction or drive reduction. (3) Expectancy theory according to which learning consists in the acquisition of knowledge and involves intersensory (S-S) associations, rather than the S-R connections hypothesized by the other two major positions. Expectancy theory was also typically a non-reward position.

The issues which divide these major theories are essentially two: (1) Is reward (effect) necessary for learning, or is mere contiguity (whether S-S or S-R) enough? (2) What is learned—stimulus-response connections, or knowledge in the form of S-S associations? These two questions, together with the alternative answers to each, gives rise to four possible general theories of learning: (1) S-R contiguity theory, (2) S-R effect theory, (3) S-S contiguity theory, and (4) S-S effect theory. No one has ever proposed the last of these for more than certain limited forms of learning. As this last statement implies, several theorists have maintained one position for some kinds of learning and another position for others. These multi-process theories will be described in the next chapter.

Experiments designed to settle the issues implicit in these various systematic positions have most often consisted of attempts on the part of the S-S theorists and non-reinforcement theorists to discredit the S-R effect position. More specifically, these efforts have involved experiments of six different kinds: (1) attempts to condition subjects without reinforcement, (2) sensory preconditioning, (3) perceptual learning, (4) place learning, (5) non-response conditioning, and (6) latent learning. Work on each may be summarized as follows:

1. *Conditioning without Reinforcement.* There have been a few attempts to produce conditioning without the use of a typical reinforcer at any point in the conditioning procedure, but they have been unsuccessful. In cases where conditioning has occurred, it has always been possible to demonstrate the presence of some reinforcer which the procedure has failed to eliminate. The reason there have been so few experiments of this sort is that it is very difficult to maintain behavior without the use of reinforcement.

2. *Sensory Preconditioning.* The sensory preconditioning experiment requires three phases which involve (a) the pairing of two neutral stimuli, (b) the conditioning of some response to one of these stimuli, and

(*c*) a test with the other of the two neutral stimuli. A successful demonstration of sensory preconditioning consists in showing that the response conditioned to one stimulus automatically transfers to the other, as if during the first phase of the experiment an equivalence had been formed between these two stimuli. It is to be noted especially that, if such an association has been formed, (*a*) it seems to be of a stimulus-stimulus variety, and (*b*) the presence of a reinforcer, in the sense the effect theorists use the term, is difficult to demonstrate.

There is no doubt that sensory preconditioning occurs, although, with adequate controls for cross-modal stimulus generalization and familiarity with the two stimuli, the magnitude of the phenomenon may be small. Attempts to explain sensory preconditioning by S-R effect theorists have concentrated more on the S-R aspect of the problem than they have on the difficulties it raises for the law of effect. These explanations have adopted a mediational approach and have taken the position that the original phase of the experiment is actually a true conditioning procedure in which undetected cue-producing responses ($r_G \longrightarrow s_G$) elicited by one stimulus are conditioned to the other. During the second phase of the experiment, the conditioned reaction is connected to the response-produced cues mentioned above. Then in the test, the first stimulus evokes the response which produces these cues. They, in turn, call out the CR. Although cumbersome and a departure from the traditional S-R position, this hypothesis has value. It suggests certain experiments, some of which have been done. They tend in a modest way to support the mediation hypothesis.

3. *Perceptual Learning.* If an organism is exposed to a given set of stimuli for an extended period of time, it becomes more capable of discriminating among these stimuli than animals without such a history. This fact is impossible to explain in terms of simple S-R terms. There is also evidence that reward probably has nothing to do with the development of this capacity.

4. *Place Learning.* There is much evidence that rats in a maze learn the general location of food whether or not they also acquire a set of specific motor reactions with which they traverse the maze. The analysis of such place learning leads to many of the same questions as were asked by the early investigators of animal behavior who were concerned with the sensory control of the maze. It seems that the cues to which the rat in this situation responds are partly intra-maze and partly extra-maze stimuli. Place learning may be nothing more than a generalized tendency to approach certain extra-maze cues.

5. *Learning without Overt Response.* There seems to be little reason to doubt that animals can form associations without making overt responses. The most impressive demonstrations of this fact come from experiments in which associations are established in curarized animals.

Advances in psychopharmacology and experimental instrumentation now make it possible to immobilize an animal's skeletal musculature completely, without interfering with the sensory mechanisms. Under these conditions associations between neutral stimuli and shock are readily established; and later on, in a normal state, the animal makes appropriate avoidant responses. The threat to any theory which demands the occurrence of a response in the sense of overt, skeletal motion is obvious.

6. *Latent Learning.* The term *latent learning* refers to the fact that, under certain circumstances, animals apparently can acquire habits which are not immediately translated into performance, either because of the absence of reward or because the animal is not motivated for a reward which is present. Investigators have performed experiments of five different kinds in the study of latent learning. In brief summary, these are:

   a. Trials without reward, followed by trials with reward present.

   b. Free exploration of a maze without reward, followed by trials with reward present.

   c. Trials with rewards present and the animal satiated, followed by trials under the appropriate drive state.

   d. Trials under one drive (such as thirst) with appropriate reward (water) under conditions where an unwanted reward (e.g. food) is present at one place in a maze. Tests are performed later when the animal motivated by the drive which was originally satiated (e.g. hunger).

   e. Exploration, followed by reward in a distinctive goal box, and then a series of trials in the maze.

All of these procedures except for method (*d*) have provided substantial evidence for latent learning. Attempting to explain this effect, S-R effect theorists again have turned to versions of the $r_G \longrightarrow s_G$ mechanism. The explanations thus generated seem successful for certain forms of the latent-learning experiment.

The effect of the argument and debate which has been carried on in connection with these problems seems to have been about as follows: In its preoccupation with the disproof of the S-R theory, S-S theory has actually contributed to the development of the position it set out to destroy. In the face of criticism from the cognitive theorists, the S-R theorists were forced to develop new concepts, new ways of looking at old problems, and new experimental approaches. With such theoretical and experimental advances, the general appearance of learning theory has now changed in two important ways: (1) multiprocess views are held much more commonly than they formerly were, and (2) interest has now shifted to a set of problems of much more limited scope. The problem of the nature of reinforcement is still central to these newer interests, but probably no one any longer expects to discover a single simple reinforcement mechanism. We turn next to the newer conceptions of reinforcement.

·9·

Mechanisms of Reward

WHEN IT IS EXAMINED more closely than we have hitherto paused to do, the reinforcement occasion seems to consist of three distinguishable aspects involving (1) the presentation of a *stimulus* to which the organism (2) *responds* in a way which typically contributes to (3) *tension reduction* of some sort. Such an analysis naturally raises a question: Is one of these the critical event in the reinforcement process? This question has been asked at least implicitly in the formulation of the newer conceptions of the nature of reinforcement which now have replaced the classical views discussed in the last chapter.

CONTEMPORARY VIEWS OF REINFORCEMENT

Modern conceptions of the nature of reinforcement differ from the earlier ones in being less general and in being oriented more concretely toward the specific factual questions suggested by the analysis of reinforcement outlined above: Is the basic nature of reinforcement to be found in its stimulus aspect, in consummatory behavior, in tension reduction, or in some combination of these components? In keeping with this more empirical approach to the problem, there is less tendency than in the past for the experiments conceived in one tradition to clash head-on with those derived from another. Possibly because the "crucial experiments" of the thirties actually settled no issues, more recent work on the nature of reinforcement has usually tended to remain modestly content with furthering the objectives of a single position, without attempting at the same time to destroy every rival hypothesis. The sections which follow sketch the main theoretical ideas guiding current research on the nature of reinforcement as organized in terms of the component aspects suggested above.

Tension Reduction

The concepts of tension reduction and reinforcement have always been so closely related that the two are often regarded as roughly synonymous.

And, for many psychologists, a "reinforcement theorist" is simply an individual who accepts some version of the tension-reduction interpretation of reinforcement; a "non-reinforcement theorist" is someone who does not. It may be well to comment on this matter before proceeding further.

As we have seen, reinforcement is basically an empirical term which covers the fact that there are conditions (reinforcers) which, when used appropriately, promote learning. The set of conditions which function in this way, however, is a very heterogeneous one. Reinforcing events are as different as providing food, administering a shock, and letting the organism explore a novel environment. In the face of such heterogeneity, the psychologist has naturally been led to look for properties which the various reinforcers may possess in common. To this end, different theorists have proposed that reinforcement is basically either a matter of stimulus change, the elicitation of a response, or tension reduction. It should be noted, however, that reinforcement remains an empirical fact; these latter proposals are merely attempts to reduce all of the different kinds of reinforcement to some single mechanism. In this sense, the tension-reduction hypothesis is, logically, the same sort of proposal as the other two and is no more "reinforcement theory" than they are.

Of the various tension-reduction views, those of Hull and his followers have been the most influential. In this tradition there have been three somewhat different formulations which have identified reinforcement with *need reduction, drive reduction,* and *drive-stimulus reduction.*

Need-reduction theory was a natural consequence of Hull's initial commitment to a Darwinian interpretation of behavior in that it emphasized the importance of reinforcement to the survival of the individual and the species. This theory was that reinforcement consisted in the reduction of *needs,* needs being defined as departures from optimal conditions for biological survival either in the direction of lacks, produced by deprivations, or excesses resulting from over-intense or over-prolonged stimulation. Such a conception seems to work very well in the case of reinforcement provided by escape from intense painful stimulation. But for other reinforcers basic problems arise. As an example, in the case of food reinforcement, given what is known about the delay-of-reinforcement function, the reduction of the need for food (in the ultimate biochemical sense) occurs so long after eating that it seems unlikely that this could be the essential mechanism of reinforcement. Similarly, it is improbable that secondary reinforcement, provided by a stimulus previously associated with food, produces need reduction at all. In fact, it is known that a secondary reinforcer has no effect upon food intake (p. 169). For these and other reasons, Hull (1943) abandoned the need-reduction theory (retaining the word need as a general term for "motivation") and adopted a *drive*-reduction theory, in which *drive* was conceived abstractly as an intervening variable whose value depends upon specific drive conditions, C_D, many of which correspond closely to need-establishing operations. In Hull's own writings the distinction between drive and need was never developed with complete sharpness; there was a tendency to use the terms *drive reduction, drive-stimulus reduction,* and *need reduction* more or less interchangeably.

N. E. Miller and his students, on the other hand, have emphasized the distinction between need and drive because both Miller's theory and certain of his experimental interests have brought the importance of the distinction into sharp focus. For Miller, *needs* are conceived, as they were by Hull, in terms of environmental lacks or excesses which, if uncorrected, lead the organism or the species to perish. Thus, an organism can be said to need water in the same sense as an automobile can be said to need water. If the lack continues, normal functioning collapses. *Drives,* on the other hand, are conceptualized mechanistically, rather than abstractly as Hull did, in stimulus terms: "A drive is a strong stimulus which impels action. Any stimulus can become a drive if it is made strong enough . . . The faint murmur of distant music has but little primary drive function; the infernal blare of the neighbor's radio has considerably more." (Miller and Dollard, 1941). Reinforcement in this theory is conceived as drive-stimulus reduction. Although this position does not deny the existence of need states or their biological importance, it lays little stress on needs in the definition of reinforcement.

Consummatory Behavior

There are, as we shall see in more detail later, many situations where learning occurs in the apparent absence of anything resembling tension reduction. These demonstrations raise questions which the tension-reduction theorists have been able to answer in some cases, but not in others. An example of an experiment which creates problems for tension-reduction theory is one on sexual behavior in the rat performed by Sheffield, Wulff, and Backer (1951). These investigators ran three groups of sexually inexperienced male rats down a 32-inch runway to sexual lures. On the basis of preliminary observation of sexual performance, the subjects had been divided into two main groups of copulators and noncopulators. In the experiment, the copulators were divided into matched groups and run either to a female in heat (experimental group) or to a male (control group). The noncopulators were divided into similarly matched groups and treated in the same way. In this study advantage was taken of the copulatory pattern of the rat which consists in a series of intromissions and withdrawals, terminating finally in ejaculation. Sheffield, Wulff, and Backer allowed the rat two intromissions or, if it did not attempt to copulate, two minutes in the goal box with the companion. Since ejaculation did not occur, these investigators argued that their procedure could have led only to an increase in tension and that the running response was followed by the opposite of drive reduction. The results of the experiment appear in Figure 9.1; data for the two groups of noncopulators are com-

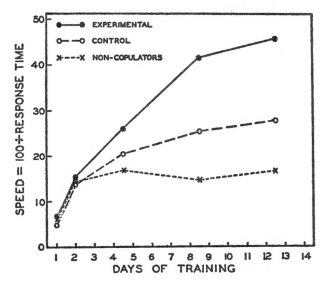

FIGURE 9.1. Performance of male rats run to sexual lures. Animals in the experimental group were run to females in heat. They were allowed to mount and penetrate the female, but not to ejaculate. Animals in the control group were run to a male companion. Subgroups of the noncopulators were run in each of the previous conditions; but since there was no difference in their performance under these conditions, the data were combined (Sheffield, Wulff, and Backer, 1951).

bined because their behavior was the same whether the lure was a male or a female in heat. Obviously, copulatory activity short of ejaculation is reinforcing. Since the rats were sexually naïve, there is no likelihood that secondary reinforcement is involved. One possible interpretation of these results is on the assumption that sexual consummatory *activity* is reinforcing.

Reinforcing Stimuli

A somewhat different interpretation of the same results is in terms of the *stimulation* attendant upon copulation, rather than in terms of the activity *per se*. This is an application of the stimulus view of reinforcement which assumes that certain forms of stimulation are innately rewarding. In addition to sexual stimulation, certain tastes, odors, tactual

stimuli, sights, and sounds seem, on common-sense grounds, to be reinforcing. There is also some suggestive experimental evidence (Ribble,
1944) that human infants respond pleasurably to such stimulation, and
Harlow (1958) presents data which seem to show that tactual stimulation
may provide the primary basis upon which the infant monkey develops
an affection for its mother.

Experimentally the distinction between the reinforcing-stimulus position and the one stressing consummatory responses is not easy to make,
because most of the stimuli which have been used as reinforcers elicit behavior. Whether it is their function as stimuli or the behaviors they evoke
which leads to their value as reinforcers is a question which requires for
its answer more evidence than is now available.

NEED REDUCTION AND THE PHYSIOLOGICAL
LOCUS OF REINFORCEMENT

Research on mechanisms of reinforcement most often has taken the
drive- or need-reduction theory as a point of reference and treated the
outcome of experimental studies as confirmations or disproofs of this position. One particularly important aspect of this line of investigation involves the search for the physiological bases of reinforcement. In such
studies experimenters have posed questions of two different general kinds
and have conducted different sorts of experiments in an effort to obtain an
answer to each. The questions are these: (1) Are there physiological effects without known drive- or need-reducing value which are capable of
reinforcing behavior? If there are, such evidence calls drive- and need-
reduction theory into question. (2) Is drive or need reduction, without
sensory stimulation or consummatory activity, capable of producing
learning? If it is, this means that drive or need reduction is at least sufficient for learning to occur. The experiments prompted by these questions have obtained affirmative answers to both, sometimes with respect
to the same reinforcer, such as food. Although such evidence necessarily
complicates the picture of the nature of reinforcement, it also leads to a
measure of clarification.

Mouth and Stomach Factors in Appetitional Reinforcement

Sometime around 1890, Pavlov performed an experiment which now
seems important in two ways: (1) it antedated the work on salivary conditioning and probably suggested it, and (2) it anticipated the outcome
of much subsequent work on the nature of reinforcement. By means of
an operation requiring considerable surgical skill, Pavlov was able to
segregate approximately one-tenth of a dog's stomach without disturbing
its nerve or blood supply, as shown in Figure 9.2. In this fashion he cre-

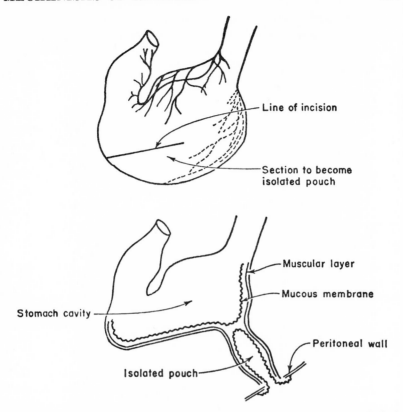

FIGURE 9.2. The Pavlov pouch. The two figures show the stomach before and after the construction of the pouch. A section of gastric mucosa was surgically isolated from the rest of the stomach, leaving its nerve and blood supply intact. This segregated portion of the stomach could be studied during digestion, but in the absence of food. (Adapted from Brazier, 1959a.)

ated a small artificial stomach whose activity, observed through a fistula, was uncomplicated by the presence of food, which never reached this part of the stomach. The activity of this artificial stomach, however, paralleled that of the main stomach, which food could reach. In some animals there also was an esophageal fistula preventing food eaten by the dog from reaching the stomach. In others, there was a fistula into the main part of the stomach so that food could be placed there directly. When a dog eats normally, chewing and swallowing its food, the effect on the stomach is to initiate the secretion of gastric juice, a process which follows a time course such as appears in the left-hand panel of Figure 9.3. Introducing food directly into the stomach produced the same effect, but in reduced magnitude (second panel of Figure 9.3). Sham feeding, in which food eaten by the dog does not reach the stomach, has a similar effect (third

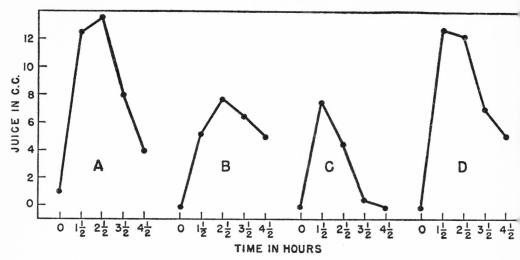

FIGURE 9.3. Gastric secretion in the stomach. Panel A depicts the pattern of secretion under normal conditions. Panel B is a plot of data obtained after introduction of food directly into the stomach. Panel C is for data obtained following sham feeding. Panel D is the sum of the functions presented in Panels B and C. The similarity of the pattern of secretion in Panels A and D suggests that the total effect results from the addition of two more elementary ones involving events in the stomach and in the mouth. Data from Pavlov (1910).

panel), again in a lessened degree, with some indication that the peak of the function is reached earlier. The fourth panel in Figure 9.3 shows the result of adding the two separate effects together. It is quite apparent that this essentially reproduces the total effect of normal feeding upon gastric secretion.

The results of this study suggest that the effect of food upon the digestive processes of the dog consists of two subprocesses, one of which involves taste and swallowing, the other acting more directly upon the stomach. Subsequent experimentation, more directly related to learning, has confirmed this general conclusion. Some 60 years later it was demonstrated with a single dog with an esophageal fistula that (1) under conditions of sham feeding the eating response extinguishes, suggesting that the effect of the mouth factors may depend upon learning, (2) that the dog could discriminate between real feeding (accomplished by connecting the cut ends of the esophagus with a plastic tube) and sham feeding, (3) that the dog preferred sham feeding to no feeding in a choice situation, and similarly (4) that it preferred esophageal feeding to no feeding (Hull, Livingston, Rouse, and Barker, 1951).

N. E. Miller and his associates have also done a number of experiments, which make a set of related points, using rats as subjects. In the first of these, Kohn (1951) began by training rats to press a panel in a Skinner-type apparatus for a liquid food on a three-minute fixed-interval schedule. Then he operated upon the rats and placed a permanent tube into their stomachs so that it was possible to insert liquids there directly. Regular oral ingestion was also possible. Finally, at different times, he tested the rats in the panel-pushing situation under three different conditions designed to alter the animals' drive state in different ways. One of these tests was performed following the oral ingestion of 14 cc. of milk (mouth milk). In a second condition, 14 cc. of milk was placed directly into the stomach via the tube, (stomach milk). This and the mouth-milk condition should have reduced drive to approximately the same degree, although in the stomach-milk condition the normal ingestion process was bypassed. The third condition, instituted as a partial control for the effect of stomach distension, involved the placing of 14 cc. of saline solution directly into the stomach (stomach saline). These treatments occurred just prior to a retest to determine their effect upon panel-pressing rate. In responses per minute the performances of the rats following these three treatments were: after mouth milk, 5.64; after stomach milk, 7.34; after stomach saline, 13.03. The only reasonable interpretation of these results is that the bar-pressing rates reflect the drive states of the animals. Specifically it seems that food introduced directly into the stomach decreased drive to some extent, and that drinking the milk decreased it slightly more. One aspect of these results is of particular interest and importance. The effects just described were obtained within 20 minutes of the administration of food. This is too soon for any important nutritive effect to have occurred. This points to the necessity for a sharp distinction between drive and need. Apparently in this study, and in other similar ones (Berkun, M. L. Kessen, and Miller, 1952; Miller, Sampliner, and Woodrow, 1957), drive reduction occurred in the absence of need reduction.

Although results of the sort obtained by Kohn seem to indicate that nutrients delivered directly to the stomach can reduce drive, they do not show that such drive reduction can function as a reinforcer for learning. Evidence favoring such a conclusion is, however, available. Miller and M. L. Kessen (1952) trained rats in a T-maze with three different kinds of reinforcement: (1) injection of 14 cc. of milk for a correct response and 14 cc. of saline for an incorrect one; (2) mouth reinforcement by 14 cc. of milk for a correct response and 14 cc. of saline for an incorrect one; (3) mouth milk and saline again but after a delay, 7 minutes and 35 seconds, which was the amount of time required for the injection of substances directly into the stomach. All of the rats learned. The group reinforced by mouth immediately was best; but the other two groups learned. The results of the experiment appear in Figures 9.4 and 9.5 for number of correct responses and speed of running, respectively.

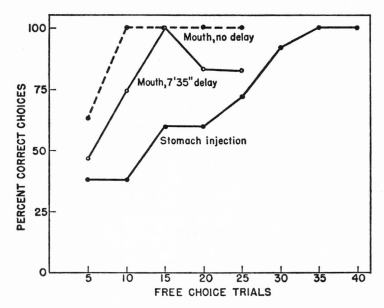

FIGURE 9.4.   Percentage of correct choices to the side reinforced with milk
on free-choice trials (N. E. Miller and M. L. Kessen, 1952).

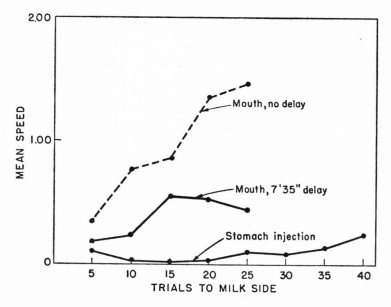

FIGURE 9.5.   Speed of running to the compartment in which milk was given
(Miller and Kessen, 1952).

The reason for presenting both of the measures obtained by Miller and Kessen is to call attention to an important difference. Although the rats reinforced by stomach injection attained 100 per cent correct responses, their speed of running hardly improved at all. A possible interpretation suggested by this discrepant effect upon number of correct choices and running speed is that the influence of the injection may be much more upon the habit mechanism than upon incentive. This speculation follows from the fact that speed measures depend much more upon motivational (incentive) factors than percentage of correct responses do. It is as if the animals ''knew'' where reinforcement occurred, but were not very ''eager'' for it.

Blood Sugar Level and Reinforcement

It is well known that starvation leads to a lowering of the level of sugar in the blood. Although this is not the complete physiological basis of hunger, it apparently is an important part of it and raises an interesting question about food reinforcement: What would happen if blood sugar level were to rise immediately after the performance of some particular response by a hungry animal? Would such ''reinforcement'' lead to a strengthening of the response in question? If it did, the suggestion would be that need reduction is a sufficient, if not necessarily an essential, condition of reinforcement. Several experiments of this sort have been reported. H. W. Coppock and Chambers (1954) showed that injection of a 10 per cent glucose solution into the tail vein was capable of reinforcing a head-turning response in rats. Chambers (1956a) attempted a similar experiment with dogs, but was unsuccessful, probably because the apparatus he used was poorly suited to this particular species. In the same study he was successful in reinforcing a response in rabbits with intravenous glucose injections. The apparatus was a cylindrical enclosure with a number of plates on the floor which, when pressed, closed electrical connections which recorded the response and, in some cases, administered reinforcement. After a preliminary determination of preference for the different floor plates, the rabbits were divided into two matched groups. For one group (glucose group) intravenous glucose was injected for a response to the least preferred plate, intravenous xylose (a nonnutritive monosaccharide) was injected for a response to the preferred plate, and a saline solution was injected for a response to any of the other five plates. For the other group (xylose group) xylose was paired with the nonpreferred plate and saline was paired with the other six. Different groups were tested under 0, 3, 4, and 6 days of starvation.

The results of the experiment appear in one form in Table 17, which shows the proportion of time spent on the rewarded (previously nonpreferred) plate by each group, together with the difference between the

TABLE 17

PROPORTION OF TIME SPENT BY GLUCOSE-REINFORCED AND XYLOSE-REINFORCED RATS ON THE REINFORCED PLATE

(From Chambers, 1956a)

Days of Starvation	Mean for Glucose Group	Mean for Xylose Group	Difference
0	32.00	22.23	9.77
3	52.75	26.55	26.20
4	64.27	31.95	32.32
6	56.08	35.78	20.30

two groups on this measure at each hunger level. Statistically speaking, this difference was significant for the deprived groups, but not for the satiated group. This shows that intravenous glucose is capable of reinforcing a response under conditions of hunger, where the reinforcement is appropriate to the drive state, but not otherwise.

At face value, the results of this experiment seem to provide strong support for the need- or drive-reduction view of reinforcement in that learning has been produced without consummatory behavior and without direct taste stimulation. As Chambers points out, however, the taste mechanism cannot be ruled out completely, because the injection of certain substances, including some which are chemically related to those used in this experiment, produces a sensation of taste within a few seconds. Conceivably this could have happened, and the animal could have experienced a sweet taste which might be either primarily or secondarily reinforcing. Moreover, even if this possibility were ruled out, there remains a question as to the exact physiological mechanism brought into operation by the injection of glucose into the blood stream. One possibility is that a temperature increase follows glucose injection and that this is at the basis of the reinforcing effect. In support of this hypothesis, Chambers reports that, in a follow-up study (Chambers, 1956b), glucose injection did lead to a slight, but reliable, temperature rise in certain parts of the body. (See also Chambers and Fuller, 1958.)

STIMULUS INTERPRETATIONS OF REINFORCEMENT

Various lines of evidence, including some of the materials just covered, make the conception of reinforcement as, at least in part, a stimulus function hard to resist.[1] Among the considerations leading to this conclusion

[1] The most complete theory relating behavior to stimulational factors is that of Young (1952). Young's theory, however, covers so much that it would be misleading to present it here as a theory merely of reinforcement. The interested reader should consult Young (1959) which presents a recent statement of his position and lists several relevant references.

are the following: (1) As has been shown, taste stimulation, and perhaps proprioceptive-feedback from chewing and swallowing, seem to contribute to the reinforcing value of food. (2) Reinforcers seem to display some typically stimulus attributes including absolute and difference thresholds (B. A. Campbell, 1955, 1956, 1957, 1958; B. A. Campbell and Kraeling, 1953; Guttman, 1954). (3) Secondary reinforcement is always a matter of stimulus presentation. (4) Studies presently to be described have provided evidence for a reinforcing effect of stimuli when other influences (such as drive reduction) seem to have been ruled out. The most important lines of experimentation in this last category are those concerned with the reinforcing effects of (a) taste stimulation, (b) exploration, and (c) electrical stimulation of the brain.

Taste Stimuli as Reinforcers

Up to a point, rats prefer a mild salt solution to plain tap water and show a peak preference in the neighborhood of the concentration of

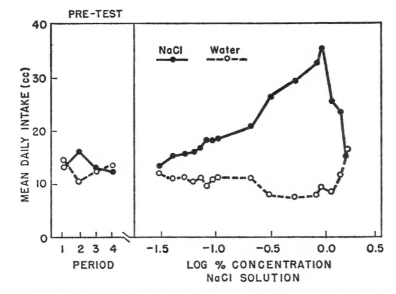

FIGURE 9.6. Graph showing the preference of the white rat for salt solutions of various strengths. The pre-test period provided a measure of the amount of plain water consumed from each of two bottles (Bare, 1949).

physiological saline, .9 per cent, as is illustrated in the intake functions in Figure 9.6. These facts have been demonstrated many times (Bare, 1949; Richter, 1939). From the point of view of reinforcement theory, the two most important considerations brought to light by research in this general area are the following: (1) Preference for mild salt solutions appears in animals whose diets contain enough sodium chloride for nutritional purposes and, thus, are in no state of need. (2) Salt deficiency, when it occurs, as with adrenalectomy, increases salt intake and may lower the preference threshold for salt solutions over plain water. This latter fact points to the importance of nutritional variables in the control of the rat's salt intake and is in line with a drive-reduction view.[2] For our present purposes, the former result is of greater interest, for it seems to mean that rats like the taste of weak salt solutions, and raises the question whether taste preferences alone might not provide an adequate basis for reinforcement. The most extensive line of evidence available for consideration in attempting to answer this question involves the results of experiments in which saccharine, a nonnutritive sweet substance, has been employed as a reinforcer. Sheffield and his associates have performed a number of such studies. In one (Sheffield and Roby, 1950), it was shown that rats preferred a .13 per cent saccharine solution to tap water and that such a solution, used as a reward in a T-maze, led to a performance which was nearly as efficient as that obtained with food reward, whether measured in terms of number of correct responses or in terms of error-reduction with practice. A later study (Sheffield, Roby, and Campbell, 1954) showed that the same saccharine solution was a more effective reinforcer in a runway situation than a nutritive, but less sweet, dextrose solution.

On the face of it, such results seem to prove that a sweet taste, by itself, is an adequate reinforcer. There have, however, been those who have refused to accept this obvious interpretation without an argument. Miller (1951), for example, ventures the guess that saccharine may be slightly drive- (not need-) reducing. He presents evidence to support this opinion in the form of the observation that rats eat less after the ingestion of saccharine than would be expected under the level of drive employed, as if the saccharine had reduced the animals' drive. M. P. Smith mentions an informal observation that mice were more likely to survive insulin shock if they were fed saccharine immediately after the insulin injection than if they were not (M. P. Smith and Capretta, 1956, p. 556n.). This fact points to a possible connection between saccharine and sugar metabolism. If, as this scanty evidence implies, saccharine does have some indirect influence on metabolism or on hunger, there remains

---

[2] In a more typical learning situation, evidence for such an interpretation is to be found in a study by Thomson and Porter (1953). These investigators tested sodium-deficient rats, which had been deprived of the sense of taste surgically, for the ability to learn the location of a salt solution in a T-maze. They found some evidence for such learning, indicated that reduction of the sodium need may function as an adequate reinforcer.

at least the possibility that the reinforcing effect of saccharine is traceable to a drive-reduction process.

Experiments investigating the effect of hunger upon responses reinforced with saccharine and other sweet-tasting substances are relevant at this point; because, if saccharine does have some indirect metabolic effect, it is at least possible that the reinforcing power of the substance would change with the level of this drive. Sheffield and Roby (1950) and M. Smith and M. Duffy (1957a) both have found that hungry rats in a free-drinking situation consume more saccharine water than satiated rats. There is, however, no good evidence that this effect carries over into more typical learning situations. Using sucrose, which also apparently secures its reinforcing value mainly because of its sweet taste (Young and Shuford, 1954, 1955), M. Smith and Kinney (1956) obtained no difference in bar-pressing rates for hungry and satiated rats reinforced with sugar water. This is to be contrasted with the very great effect that the sweetness of the solution has on bar-pressing rate (Guttman, 1953). Thus, there is reason to believe that it actually is the taste of sugar which provides it with its reinforcing power.

Even accepting this conclusion, however, a different interpretation of the results of experiments in this area is possible, in terms of secondary reinforcement. It could be argued that certain tastes, such as sweet tastes, are reinforcing because, in the past, they have been associated with eating and have acquired reinforcing power this way (Bare, 1949). Against such an interpretation there stands, first of all, the fact that Sheffield and Roby observed no diminution of the reinforcing power of saccharine, although they used the same rats in an extensive series of experiments and for a long period of time in their study. If the reinforcing power of saccharine were entirely a matter of secondary reinforcement, there should have been some evidence of extinction. On the other hand, M. P. Smith and Capretta (1956) have reasoned that the Sheffield and Roby experiment did not meet the conditions which would be necessary to extinguish the secondary reinforcing power of saccharine because of the possibility that the sweet taste of saccharine and digestive processes occurred together during some of the experimental tests. More specifically, if the animals were allowed to drink saccharine while the previously ingested food remained in the stomach, this would provide the opportunity for the taste of saccharine to be associated with drive reduction. Smith and Capretta proposed that saccharine would lose its secondary reinforcement value only when such an association with drive reduction or need reduction had been completely eliminated. Pursuing this hypothesis, they performed an experiment with six groups of rats which received 4, 8, or 15 one-hour exposures to saccharine after 2 or 21 hours of food deprivation. Following such training there was a test using a T-maze to determine the reinforcing power of saccharine in a learning situation. Two major results came out of this experiment. The first was that the animals deprived of food for two hours seemed to develop a stronger preference for saccharine than the hungrier animals which had been starved for 21 hours. Figure 9.7 shows this result in the form of curves depicting the decreasing amount of time required to consume 8 ml. of the solution. The second result was that, in the T-maze tests, in which all subjects had been with-

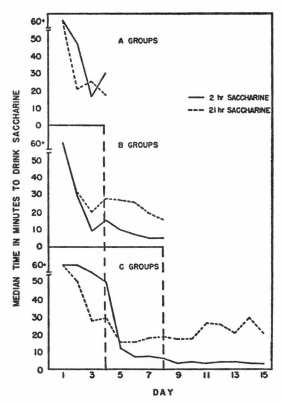

FIGURE 9.7. Median times required to drink 8 cc. of saccharine solution. For the 2-hour and 21-hour groups previous experience with saccharine had been under 2 or 21 hours of food deprivation. For the A, B, and C groups, respectively, this experience extended over 4, 8 or 15 days. Data from Smith and Capretta (1956).

out food for 10 hours, the animals whose previous experience with saccharine had been under 2 hours of food deprivation learned better than the other group. This phenomenon is shown in Table 18 which presents the number of errors made by each of the 6 groups in the T-maze test. Both of these results indicate that saccharine was a more powerful reinforcer for the animals whose original experience with saccharine had been under low drive. Moreover, Table 18 clearly indicates that increasing amounts of experience with saccharine produced opposite trends in the

TABLE 18

Mean Errors in T-Maze for Each Saccharine Group
(From M. P. Smith and Copretta, 1956)

Days of Experience with Saccharine	Hours of Deprivation	
	2	21
4	13.75	13.88
8	12.12	14.00
15	10.25	16.12

two sets of deprivation groups: an increase in the reinforcing power of saccharine (fewer errors) for the 2-hour group, a decreasing effectiveness for the 21-hour group. This last fact suggests that the taste of saccharine loses some of its power (extinguishes) when it is presented when the animal is hungry and not rewarded. If so, this means that at least a part of the reinforcing power of saccharine is learned. On the other hand, 15 hours of extinction was incapable of completely destroying the reward value of saccharine. Perhaps more experience would have had such an effect, as the trend displayed by the errors for the three 21-hour groups suggests. It is equally conceivable, however, that the taste of saccharine is primarily reinforcing and that the secondary reinforcement component is very small.

Reinforcement by Exploration

The thesis that reinforcement occurs only as a result of drive reduction has also been called into question by the outcomes of experiments which show that animals will learn for a reward which is apparently nothing more than the privilege of exploring a complex environment. For example, Montgomery (1954) ran rats in a Y-maze in which one arm of the Y terminated in a typical goal box and the other led to a Dashiell-type maze which the rat could explore. After 24 trials with the Dashiell maze on one side, the conditions were reversed and the Dashiell maze was placed on the other side. The animals learned to go to the side containing the Dashiell maze and reversed their preference with a change in conditions. In a later study Montgomery and Segall (1955) showed that rats could learn a black-white discrimination for a similar reinforcement, and A. K. Meyers and N. E. Miller have shown that rats will learn to press a bar in order to explore a compartment to which the bar-pressing response gains an entry. The threat to drive-reduction theory implicit in such findings is obvious. It looks very much as if a response is acquired with the arousal of an exploratory motive rather than with its reduction (Montgomery, 1954).[3]

Even more impressive results have been obtained in studies with monkeys. In one experiment, Butler (1953) tested monkeys in an enclosed box located in a large room in which there usually were people engaged in one sort of activity or another. The box contained two windows with a provision for putting a blue card in one window and a yellow card in the other and for changing the positions of the two cards from side to side. Pushing on one of the windows opened it, allowing the subjects to look out and observe the happenings in the room. All of the animals learned to open the door with the card which signified that it could be opened and kept at the task with great persistence. An average of 40 per cent of an animal's time may be spent in visual exploration of a situation if the choice is left up to the subject (Butler and Alexander, 1955). In later studies Butler showed that different incentives have different values. The sight of another monkey is possibly the most effective visual incentive; but the opportunity to watch an electric train, to observe a tray of food, or just to observe an empty box leads to learning (Butler, 1954). Moreover, the mere sound of a train running and the noises made by the other monkeys in the colony are also adequate reinforcers (Butler, 1957a). About the only kind of stimulation which a monkey will not learn to produce is a fear-eliciting one such as a large dog (Butler, 1958a, 1958b). It is of some interest that the effectiveness of visual reinforcers increases with up to 6 or 8 hours deprivation from the opportunity to engage in visual exploration (Butler, 1957b). In this regard, the exploratory motive resembles the homeostatic drives.

Another set of studies initiated by that of Kish (1955) has demonstrated the reinforcing power of mild visual stimulation. Kish tested mice in a modified Skinner box in which touching a metal bar turned on a dim light in the otherwise dark environment for one group of subjects, but did not do so for another. The effect of this procedure was to produce an increase in the rate of the response for the group with the light reinforcement. When the response no longer turned on the light, a gradual extinction process ensued. Essentially the same results were obtained later by a number of other investigators (Marx, Henderson, and C. L. Roberts,

---

[3] The inveterate curiosity of the white rat is well known to comparative psychologists, and even better known to the animal caretaker and trainer. One of the best of many stories about the affectionately remembered Fred Brown, for many years animal caretaker at Brown University, is the following: One of the graduate students appeared one day with a group of rats in a large iron pail which was being used for a carrying cage. The rats were milling about the bottom of the pail in an agitated way which made the student think they had ''whirling disease'' and would have to be destroyed. But Fred took one look and said, ''Naw, them rats ain't got the whirling disease. Them rats just want to see out.'' And, sure enough, cutting windows in the sides of the pail cured them. For other experiments on the exploratory drive of the rat, see Montgomery (1951, 1952, 1953;, 1953b, 1953c).

1955; Hurwitz, 1956; Kling, Horowitz, and Delhagen, 1956; C. L. Roberts, Marx, and Collier, 1958).

The study of C. L. Roberts, Marx, and Collier was concerned both with the cessation of light, which has long been known to function as a rein-forcer (See the studies by Keller, 1941 and Hefferline, 1950), and with light onset. Moreover, this investigation examined the conditions related to such reinforcement and to its mode of expression in much more detail than any experiment so far reported. The variables manipulated were (1) the level of illumination under which the rats lived, light or complete darkness (except for brief period once a day during feeding), (2) the condition of illumination associated with feeding, light or darkness, and (3) the light change (onset or cessation) used for reinforcement. Rates of responding to produce light onset or cessation were measured in a Skinner box in a period of nine 30-minute sessions, with the results shown in Figure 9.8. Obviously the onset of the light was a more effective rein-

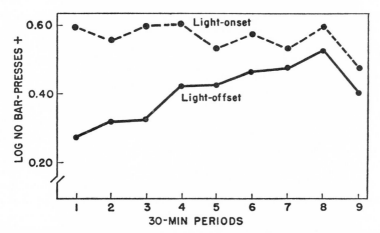

FIGURE 9.8. Light onset and cessation as reinforcers for bar-pressing (Roberts, Marx, and Collier, 1958).

forcer initially, but with practice, light offset became about equally as effective. An examination of the performances of the various subgroups showed that the condition associated with feeding had no effect upon rate of responding. There was, however, an interaction between the condition in which the rats had lived and the effectiveness of light onset or cessation as reinforcement. Rats reared in darkness performed better when a bar press led to darkness, and rats reared in the light performed better when a bar press turned the light on.

In addition to providing a large-scale demonstration of the effectiveness of light as a reinforcer, this study is important in two main ways: (1) It rules out the most obvious interpretation in terms of secondary reinforcement by showing that the reinforcing value of light exists over and above any influence producible by associating light with food and eating. (2) At the same time, it indicates that secondary reinforcement may play a subordinate role in that there is an interaction between maintenance illumination and the effect of the specific reinforcer.

Reinforcement by Brain Stimulation

By far the most spectacular evidence in favor of a stimulational theory of reinforcement is to be found in the discovery of numerous areas in the lower brain where weak electrical stimulation is capable of reinforcing behavior. Since the work of Olds and Milner (1954) [4] the phenomenon has been a matter of very great interest to psychologists. In their demonstration of this effect, Olds and Milner used as subjects rats that had

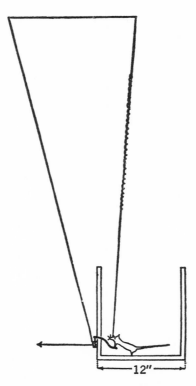

FIGURE 9.9. Schematic diagram to represent brain-stimulation apparatus (Olds, 1956).

[4] Also see Olds (1956a, 1956b, 1956c, 1956d, 1956e), Olds, Killam, and Bach-y-Rita (1956), Olds and Olds (1958).

electrodes chronically implanted in the limbic system which includes the septal area, the amygdala, the hippocampus, the cingulate cortex, the hypothalamus, and the anterior nucleus of the thalamus. A few days after the electrode was implanted the rat was tested in a Skinner box (see Figure 9.9) where a bar depression produced a brain shock. The startling fact was that many rats pressed the bar at very rapid rates to obtain this stimulation and showed little signs of satiation, ceasing to press the bar only after becoming physically exhausted (Olds, 1958b). Figure 9.10 shows a record which covers a period of several days. It is of particular interest to note the suddenness with which bar-pressing starts and stops depending upon whether or not it produces brain stimulation.

A phenomenon as spectacular as this raises a number of questions: (1) Since not all areas in the brain have this effect, what are the neuroanatomical locations of the areas which do? (2) Is it not possible that this method will provide a better brain-mapping method than any now available? (3) How does the reinforcing effect come about? Is it through the activation of sensory (pleasure) mechanisms or in some other way? (4) How general in terms of species and apparatus is this effect? (5) What are the parameters of the brain shock controlling its effectiveness? (6) What conventional psychological processes are involved? The first two of these questions are of more interest to the neuroanatomist and neurophysiologist than to the psychologist. We will, therefore, concentrate our attention upon the others.

Following the original demonstration performed on hooded rats, many studies with similar results have appeared using white rats, cats, and monkeys, indicating that the effect is obtainable in a wide range of species. Studies with apparatuses other than the Skinner box have also been successful. Rats have mastered runways and mazes for brain stimulation; cats have been trained to perform in shuttleboxes; and monkeys have been shown to prefer the side of the table on which such stimulation occurred. There seems to be little doubt that brain stimulation is an effective reinforcer in many different situations.

Stimulation of the lower brain structures, however, is not always positively reinforcing. In the earliest investigations it was found that some rats failed to learn to obtain brain stimulation or even to pay any apparent attention to it, suggesting that, for them, the stimulus was neutral or at least not reinforcing. Others pressed the bar once or twice and then ceased completely, indicating that the brain shock may have been painful. This latter observation means that, under some circumstances, brain stimulation may be a negative reinforcer. There have been several direct experimental demonstrations of this fact. Delgado, Roberts, and Miller (1954) first trained cats to rotate a wheel in response to a buzzer to avoid a strong shock to the feet. Then they paired the same buzzer with brain

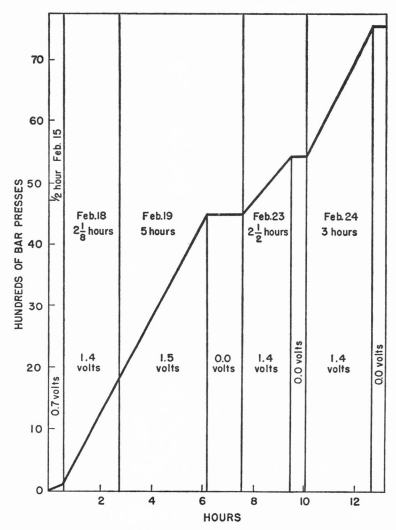

FIGURE 9.10. Smoothed cumulative response curve for a single rat working for brain stimulation. Note (a) that the rat continues to respond at a high rate over a period of several days. But also note (b) that turning off the shock produces an almost immediate cessation of responding (Olds and Milner, 1954).

shock delivered to the tectal area, lateral nuclear mass of the thalamus, or hippocampus, and showed that the cat rotated the wheel to avoid such stimulation. Delgado, Rosvold, and Looney (1956), using monkeys, first conditioned a fear response to a high tone by pairing it with painful shock to the feet. In a series of testing trials brain stimulation was sometimes substituted for the tone, with the result that the stimulation of certain areas led to an avoidance response indistinguishable from that elicited by the original CS. The areas reported as eliciting fear when stimulated were: ''medial nucleus of the amygdala and adjacent tissue in the rhinal fissure, trigeminal nerve at the Gasserian ganglion, rostral part of the pons, medial part of the mesencephalon in the vicinity of the central gray, nucleus ventralis posteromedialis, external part of the nucleus ventralis posterolateralis of the thalamus, and external medullary lamina of the pallidum.'' (Delgado, Rosvold, and Looney, 1956, p. 379). In another demonstration that brain stimulation may serve as a basis for avoidance learning (Cohen, G. W. Brown, and M. L. Brown, 1957), cats learned to run to avoid brain stimulation delivered to the anterior hypothalamus or to the median forebrain bundle when the onset of such stimulation was signalled by a tone. Thus we see that brain stimulation may be used either as a positive reinforcer or as a negative one which apparently elicits pain or fear. The question which naturally arises concerns the conditions under which brain stimulation is a fear elicitor and under which it is a positive reinforcer. It seems likely that one important factor would be the exact placement of the electrode. There is as yet, however, no definite mapping of the areas which are positively and negatively reinforcing.

Two characteristics of the shock, itself, are known to be important parameters in determining the effect of brain stimulation. They are shock intensity and duration.[5] In his early work, Olds (1955) reported that rats seemed to be positively reinforced by all intensities of brain stimulation, up to and including intensities which produced convulsions. More recent evidence suggests that high intensities of stimulation are, at least, less effective than lower intensities; and there is some evidence that still higher levels may become aversive. Reynolds (1958) studied the rate of bar pressing for brain shocks of .5-second duration and varying intensities delivered to the hypothalamus. A sample set of results, shown in Figure 9.11, indicate that increasing voltage is increasingly reinforcing up to a point and that, beyond this point, the stimulus is less so. For different rats the most effective voltage was from 1.9 to 3.8 volts. At higher shock intensities behavior appeared which might be interpreted as a response to pain; it included withdrawal from the bar and (sometimes successful) attempts to escape from the apparatus. The bearing of this upon the function of brain stimulation is that the experiments obtaining avoidance learning with brain stimulation have usually employed fairly high levels of shock. Cohen, Brown, and Brown, for example, set their shock at a level capable of eliciting certain emotion-like reactions from the cat including hissing, spitting, pilo-erection (hair standing on end), pupillary dilation, and aimless jumping. The intensities were 1.2 ma. and

---

[5] Reinforcement schedules also influence the rate of responding for brain stimulation (Sidman, Brady, Boren, Conrad, and Schulman 1955).

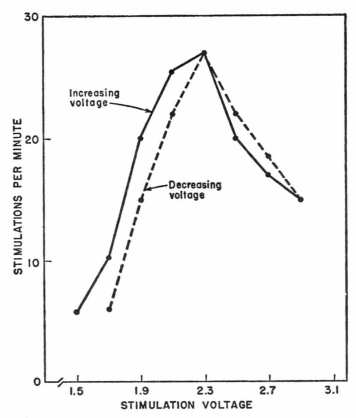

FIGURE 9.11. Rate of responding of a single rat reinforced with brain stimulations of different intensities. Data for the solid curve were obtained in a
series of tests which began with a low voltage. Data for the dashed curve
were obtained in a series of tests beginning with a high voltage. Other rats
showed similar patterns of behavior, although the details and specifically the
optimal voltage varied. (R. W. Reynolds, 1958).

3.5 v., which was high enough to be aversive for many rats in the study
by Reynolds.

Roberts (1958a) reports that the behavioral symptoms employed by
Cohen, Brown, and Brown (hissing, pilo-erection, and so on) are equally
diagnostic of two different brain stimulation effects which he refers to,
respectively, as "flight" and "alarm" reactions. The former of these
reactions was elicited by stimulation of a restricted area in the posterior
hypothalamus, the latter by stimulation in a heterogeneous collection of
areas in the midbrain and diencephalon. Animals which showed either of
these reactions learned to go from one side of a two-compartment shuttle

box to turn off (escape) the brain shock; but only the group which showed the alarm reaction learned to avoid the brain shock by responding anticipatorily. To Roberts this suggested that the brain stimulus may have had a dual effect. He reasoned that, for the animals showing the "flight" reaction, the shock was probably positively reinforcing at its onset but, when continued, it gradually became painful. If this analysis is correct it means that the animal was first reinforced by shock onset for doing nothing. Then after the shock had been on for long enough to become painful, the animal was reinforced for an escape response. To test this hypothesis, Roberts (1958b) performed an experiment in which he demonstrated (1) that cats would press a bar to receive a brief stimulation in the posterior hypothalamus, (2) that they learned an escape response to the same stimulus, but (3) that they did not learn an avoidance reaction which would have prevented the brain shock. The last two of these results are the same as those obtained in Roberts' first study. The first shows the hypothesized positively reinforcing effect of brief stimuli.

In stimulus terms, Roberts' hypothesis is that, in the area which his studies have concentrated upon, brief brain shocks are positively reinforcing and prolonged ones punishing. Bower and N. E. Miller (1958) made a direct test of this hypothesis. They showed that rats receiving stimulation in certain portions of the medial forebrain bundle learned to escape from brain shock but not to avoid it. These were referred to as reward-aversion animals. Rats with electrodes in other areas, by contrast, could learn to avoid brain stimulation as well as to escape from it. These results, thus, replicate those of Roberts. To test the hypothesis that stimulus duration is the important factor, the rats were allowed to press a bar in a Skinner box, receiving shock as long as the bar remained depressed. The mean duration of the reward-aversion animals' bar presses ranged from 0.15 to 0.80 seconds. For animals showing only a reward effect (electrodes placed differently), the mean duration was 0.33 to 5.19 seconds. There are, of course, animals with electrodes in other locations where the effect is entirely aversive; for these, durations could not be obtained.[5]

Psychological Significance of Brain-Stimulation Studies. The kind of interpretation which has most often been made of the brain-stimulation studies is that they have provided information about the neuroanatomical locus of reinforcement. It may be argued, however, that this is essentially an item of neurological information, and a somewhat limited one at that. For psychology it is important to ask how the effects produced by brain stimulation are related to familiar psychological processes.

Possibly the most interesting question of this sort is the following: What is the animal's experience like when it receives a brain shock. Given the location of positively effective electrodes, possibilities which suggest

[5] For related studies see Lilly (1957, 1958).

themselves are that brain stimulation might produce pleasant olfactory sensations, feelings of satisfaction like those which follow eating or drinking, or perhaps, sexy feelings either of arousal or satisfaction. But, phrased in this way, such speculations obviously violate the most basic rules of scientific methodology. They represent an operationally impossible invasion of the white rats "private experience" and are inaccessible to experimental test.

These methodologically unsatisfactory questions about the psychological processes related to brain stimulation do, however, lead to testable hypotheses if they are translated into more nearly behavioral terms. One might ask, for instance, whether the effectiveness of brain stimulation varies with the level of hunger, thirst, or sexual motivation of the animal. If it does, this fact would lend credence to the idea that brain stimulation is somehow related to these motives. Brady, Boren, Conrad, and Sidman (1957) have studied the effect of food and water deprivation upon rate of responding for brain stimulation, and Olds (1958a) has obtained evidence on the effect of hunger and sexual motivation. In this latter study sixteen male rats were first trained to press the bar in a Skinner apparatus for brain shock, hungry on some days and satiated for food on others. Then they were castrated to produce a low androgen (sex hormone) level and tested for rate of bar pressing under this condition which was assumed to produce a low level of sex drive. Finally, sexual motivation was restored by injections of testosterone propionate, and bar pressing for brain stimulation tested again. Depending upon the location of the electrode, increasing intensity of hunger or of the sex drive either elevated the rate of bar pressing, or depressed it. Moreover, there was a negative relationship between the androgen and hunger effects. The brain locations which, when stimulated, led to the greatest increases in response level under hunger suffered a relative decrease with a high androgen level, *and vice versa*.

At a general level, these last results show that brain stimulation is probably somehow related to commonly recognized motives, a fact which indirectly supports the hypothesis that research on the effects of brain stimulation has at least approached the discovery of the basic neurological mechanism of reinforcement. It seems to have been accepted as such by many psychologists (Zeigler, 1957). For this reason it may be well, as a final point, to sound a note of caution: In spite of the very great imporance of the facts of brain stimulation, there are certain difficulties in the way of accepting without further ado the proposition that the reinforcement process involves electrical stimulation of the brain areas, and nothing else. Some of the objections to such a conclusion will simply be listed without pursuing them further: (1) At bottom, nerve conduction, which must be involved in ordinary reinforcement, is not an electrical, but a chemical process (Eccles, 1953). (2) The fact that electrical stimulation of the limbic system produces a reinforcing effect does not prove that this is the normal function of this area, although it does, of course, suggest it. (3) The ability of certain areas either to reward or punish suggests that something more basic than mere neuroanatomical considerations is involved. (4) Similarly, the fact that brain stimulation sometimes has other side effects (Olds, 1955), such as making the animal vicious and hard to handle, remains to be explained and scarcely seems to be a part of the usual picture of reinforcement. (5) Brain stimulation which is capable of producing vigorous bar pressing is sometimes incapable of reinforcing maze running, although a food reinforcement of the same dimensions would surely do so (Olds, 1956d). (6) Extinction is much more rapid when brain shock is turned off than when the delivery of food is discontinued in the usual bar-pressing situation (Olds and Milner, 1954). Obviously the brain stimulation method is not yet in a position to make old-fashioned studies of reinforcement either unimportant or unnecessary.

RESPONSE INTERPRETATIONS OF REINFORCEMENT

Certain of the studies described in the previous section as favoring a stimulational account of reinforcement might be interpreted almost as easily in response terms; some of them were originally presented by their authors as evidence for such a theory. The possibility of such alternative interpretations exists because reinforcement always involves both stimulus and response elements. The animal reinforced with saccharine tastes it, as a stimulus theory would emphasize, but it also approaches, drinks, and swallows it. In the light-reinforcement studies, the organism receives the light stimulation and, in addition, looks at it or pays attention to it. It is conceivable that these response processes are the essential conditions of reinforcement. Response theories of reinforcement have taken two general forms which we may call *consummatory response* interpretations and *prepotent response* interpretations. The first is the commoner of the two positions. It holds that *motivated* behavior is reinforcing. For this reason, the evidence for it is often of the sort which can be explained rather easily in terms of drive reduction. The prepotent response interpretation, on the other hand, maintains that *any* dominant response is capable of strengthening a preceding weaker response.

Among the sources of support for a consummatory response theory is an incidental finding of one of the studies designed to show that saccharine is a reinforcer (Sheffield, Roby, and Campbell, 1954); namely, that the strength of the instrumental response and the vigor of the consummatory drinking response are strongly correlated. Figure 9.12 presents this relationship in the form of a scatter plot. Such evidence led

these investigators to adopt consummatory response theory of reinforcement and to attempt to demonstrate the reinforcing power of other
activities, such as copulation without ejaculation (Sheffield, Wulff, and
Backer, 1951). Kagan and Berkun (1954) found that rats learned to

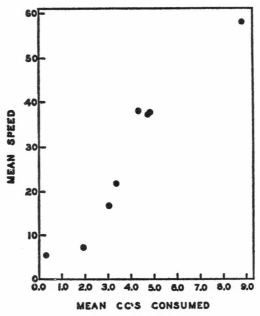

FIGURE 9.12. Correlation diagram to illustrate the relationship between
   consummatory behavior and response strength in a situation where the animal
   is performing for reinforcement in the form of a saccharine solution (Sheffield, Roby, and Campbell, 1954).

press a bar for the opportunity of running in a running wheel. And, in
an experiment suggested by the Sheffield, Wulff, and Backer study, Kagan
(1955) showed that rats can learn a T-maze for sexual reinforcement
which consisted only of the opportunity to mount and thrust at a receptive female whose vagina had been sewed shut.

   Harlow and his colleagues have reported several studies which demonstrate the existence of a manipulative drive of great strength in monkeys.
For example, Harlow, Harlow, and Myer (1950) and Harlow (1950b)
have shown that monkeys will master mechanical puzzles for the sheer
sake of doing them. A food reward made contingent upon the successful
solution of the puzzle actually interfered with performance. Closely
massed trials administered over a 10-hour period were found to produce
a performance decrement which suggests that the manipulation drive is
satiable. In still another demonstration of the strength of the manipula-

tion drive, Harlow and McClearn (1954) showed that monkeys learned to discriminate between different colors on the basis of this motive alone. The monkey was presented with a board containing 5 pairs of screw eyes of different colors. Those of one color were removable; those of the other color were not. The monkey learned which were removable, and practice led to a significant increase in the number of screw eyes removed.

The most recent statement of the more general, *prepotent response,* theory is that of Premack (1959) who holds that the essential condition of reinforcement is a rate differential between two responses in a situation where emitting the stronger is made contingent upon the prior occurrence of the weaker. For many reinforcement situations, the response with the higher rate is a consummatory response. In these situations the predictions of Premack's position and that of the conventional consummatory response position would be the same. The former theory, however, suggests an interesting experiment which might not occur to the proponents of the consummatory response theory: If it were possible to find a nonconsummatory act with a higher rate than a consummatory one, it should be possible to strengthen consummatory behavior by making it instrumental to the occurrence of the nonconsummatory act. One item of evidence which Premack cites is an experiment of this sort in which children increased their rate of eating candy when the operation of a pinball machine (a response whose rate was initially higher) was made contingent upon eating.

Of all the interpretations of reinforcement, the response theories have gained the fewest adherents, possibly because it is very difficult to state this position in a way which distinguishes clearly between it and either the stimulational or drive-reduction position. In the saccharine studies is it the consummatory act or the sweet taste that is reinforcing? In the experiments involving manipulative behavior does the reinforcement come from performing the responses required, or from kinesthetic and visual feedback from these responses? In the studies of exploratory behavior, is it running the maze or what the animal sees as it runs which functions as a reinforcer (Montgomery, 1953)? Or, on the other hand, if a monkey learns to open a door to see out of its cage, does this not indicate that the organism has a drive toward exploratory experience and that the reduction of this drive is reinforcing? If the children in Premack's experiment learned to eat in order to operate the pinball machine, does this not mean that the children *wanted* to operate the machine and that the eating response was reinforced by the satisfaction of this want? These translations of the evidence most often offered in support of response theories of reinforcement into stimulational and drive-reduction terms are listed merely to show that the definitional problems facing the response position are acute. No strengthening thereby of the latter two positions is implied.

TWO-PROCESS THEORIES OF REINFORCEMENT

If there is one most important conclusion to be drawn from the mass of evidence on the mechanisms of reward, it would seem to be that no single theory, as currently formulated, can cover all of the data. The experiments described in the previous sections succeeded in demonstrating the partial validity of several hypotheses, without seriously invalidating others. The inference to which this situation almost inevitably leads is that reinforcement must be much more complicated than the simple formulations of the single-process theories imply. Such a conclusion naturally leads to the idea that the nature of reinforcement may differ from one kind of learning situation to another. Theories which take this general point of view are called multiprocess theories.

Of the multiprocess theories, the most popular is a two-process theory which maintains that a tension-reduction explanation applies to instrumental learning and that a contiguity principle, like that described in the last chapter, applies to classical conditioning. The origin of this two-process position is in certain difficulties which arise when the learning theorist, especially the drive-reduction theorist, attempts to explain learning based on noxious stimulation.[6] The first discussion of the problems of negative reinforcers in a line which links directly to present-day accounts of escape and avoidance learning was by Hull (1929).[7] In this early paper, Hull outlined a very simple version of the theory which has since dominated learning-theoretical discussions of avoidance behavior. He also called attention to some of the problems which such behavior poses for the learning theorist. Arguing from a generally functionalist position, Hull emphasized the survival value of defense reactions and called attention to the necessity for the occurrence of these responses in anticipation of the noxious stimulus to be avoided. Then he proceeded to point out the dilemmas which seem to grow out of this fact. Specifically, a defense reaction to be maximally useful should be inextinguishable; but if it is, this seems to disprove the generality of the principle of experimental extinction and to leave the organism vulnerable to the acquisition of defensive reactions to all sorts of stimuli which accidentally happen to have

[6] Although two-process theory of the sort to be discussed here developed in connection with avoidance learning and, so far, has been applied almost exclusively within this context, evidence is beginning to accumulate that it may be fruitfully extended to situations involving positive reward. The theory which several investigators seem to be converging upon parallels that for avoidance learning: A classically conditioned component stemming from an association between neutral stimuli and reward provides a motivational element (incentive), which motivates performance and also provides reward (Powell and Perkins, 1957; Seward, 1951, 1952; Spence, 1956; Collier and Siskel, 1959). Mowrer (1960) recently has presented such a theory, worked out in some detail.

[7] For somewhat different interpretations of the role of negative reinforcement see Dinsmoor (1954, 1955), and Sidman (1953a, 1953b, 1954a, 1954b, 1955a, 1955b).

occurred in conjunction with painful stimuli. On the other hand, if fear responses *are* extinguishable, the organism's behavior with respect to painful stimuli should consist in a series of cycles in which the defense reaction undergoes gradual extinction until it is weakened to the point where it fails to prevent the noxious stimulus. This reminder would reinstate the defense reaction and initiate a new extinction phase in the history of the response. According to Hull: "From a biological point of view, the picture emerging from the above theoretical considerations is decidedly not an attractive one" (Hull, 1929, p. 510). Hull then proceeds to suggest that this unattractive picture may be the true one for avoidance reactions based upon weak noxious stimuli, but that, with stronger stimuli, experimental extinction may be held "progressively in abeyance as the gravity of the injury increases" (Hull, 1929, p. 510-511). A quarter of a century later Solomon and Wynne (1954) presented the most detailed and sophisticated theory of avoidance learning so far developed, incorporating precisely these same propositions.

The Two-Process Explanation of Avoidance Learning

In 1929 Hull had not yet developed his drive-reduction theory of learning, so the special difficulty created by avoidant behavior for such a view was not a matter of concern. Briefly, the problem is this: The drive-reduction theory assumes that the motive or drive operating in avoidance learning derives from the noxious unconditioned stimulus employed, and that reinforcement occurs when the unconditioned stimulus terminates. Since a successful avoidance response prevents the occurrence of the unconditioned stimulus, it eliminates not only the drive in the situation, but also the basis for reinforcement. This makes it difficult for the drive reductionist to explain how avoidance behavior could be learned in the first place or, once learned, how it could be maintained.

Two-process learning theory espoused by Mowrer (Mowrer, 1947, 1950) and Solomon and his associates (Solomon and Wynne, 1954) is devised to handle this problem in S-R terms. This theory proposes that a motive of fear is acquired on the basis of the pairing of neutral and noxious stimuli early in training, *drive reduction playing no part in the process,* and that presenting the previously neutral (now feared) stimulus is motivating. Acts leading to the removal of the feared stimulus are strengthened by a *drive-reduction mechanism of reinforcement.* As this brief statement shows, the two processes are (1) contiguity-learning (classical conditioning) which leads to the establishment of fear and (2) law-of-effect-learning (instrumental conditioning) through which instrumental responses leading to escape from the feared stimulus are reinforced. The nature of this theory may be illustrated concretely by reference to a study by May (1948) which was carried out in a series of stages corresponding to the subprocesses assumed to take place in avoidance learning. In this experiment, rats were first trained to escape from shock by crossing a barrier in a shuttle box. After they had learned this, the rats were confined in a limited area of the shuttle box and given a series of unavoidable shocks which were paired with a buzzer, after the manner of classical conditioning. Finally, with the escape response again possible, the buzzer was sounded to determine whether, in the absence of shock, the rats would cross the hurdle in response to it. In two slightly different replications of this experiment, approximately 80 per cent of the animals responded to the buzzer by crossing the barrier. Fewer than 10 per cent of control animals which had received buzzer only, shock only, or unpaired buzzer and shock in the second phase of the experiment responded in this way. Obviously the pairing of buzzer and shock was crucial in producing escape behavior on the test trials.

The two-process interpretation of the learning which occurred in this experiment may now be presented with the aid of a series of diagrams:

1. *Training to Escape Shock*

$$\text{S (shock)} \longrightarrow r_x \longrightarrow s_x \text{ (fear)} \dashrightarrow R \text{ (escape)}$$

The intention of this diagram is to show two things: (*a*) that shock, functioning as a CS and as an elicitor of escape behavior, soon becomes capable of calling out the escape response, indicated by the upper arrow, through instrumental conditioning, and (*b*) that shock also produces internal fear reactions, r_x, with consequent stimuli, s_x. These internal stimuli are assumed to be drive stimuli. And it is escape from them, rather than escape from shock *per se* which constitutes the reinforcement for this learning. In addition to functioning as a drive stimulus, s_x also becomes a CS for the escape response.

2. *Fear Conditioning*: *Buzzer Paired with Shock*

$$\text{Shock} \longrightarrow r_x \longrightarrow s_x \text{ (no escape response possible)}$$
$$\text{Buzzer} \nearrow$$

This is a straightforward case of classical conditioning. Two-process theory assumes that contiguity of the buzzer and r_x is all that is required for such conditioning to occur.

3. *Test Trials*: *Buzzer but no Shock*

$$\text{Buzzer} \dashrightarrow r_x \longrightarrow s_x \dashrightarrow R \text{ (escape)}$$

As a result of two previous conditioning processes (*a*) the internal mechanism, $r_x \longrightarrow s_x$ is capable of eliciting the escape reaction, and (*b*) the buzzer is capable of eliciting $r_x \longrightarrow s_x$. Thus the animal performs the escape reaction in response to the buzzer. There are two points of importance to be made in this connection: (*a*) Since s_x is capable of evoking the escape reaction, it provides a potential explanation for the occurrence of avoidant behavior in anticipation of a noxious stimulus. (b) Since s_x is assumed to have drive properties, there is also a device for the reinforcement of avoidant behavior through the elimination of s_x.

In ordinary avoidance-conditioning studies it is assumed that the three phases outlined above all occur together. On early trials, the warning signal and the stimulus to be avoided occur one after the other and continue to do so until the avoidance response appears. During this stage the animal is learning to escape from the noxious stimulus (stage 1 above) and also acquiring a fear of the signal (stage 2 above). When the avoidance response finally appears, it is elicited by response-produced stimuli and reinforced by escape from the CS (Miller, 1948). This corresponds to stage 3 in May's experiment described above.

The Nature of the Fear Response

The most important questions raised by the two-process theory of avoidance conditioning concern the details of the fear-conditioning process. One of the specific problems involves the nature of the classically conditioned fear reaction. Mowrer (1947) inclines toward the belief that the fear responses are exclusively autonomic. R. L. Solomon and Wynne (1954) believe that the response is more complicated, consisting of reactions of the autonomic nervous system which result in visceral responses of high magnitude, skeletal motor discharge, neuroendocrine responses, and activity of the higher central nervous system. This view is based in large part upon the results of an experiment (Wynne and R. L. Solomon, 1955) on avoidance learning in sympathectomized dogs. These animals, whose autonomic processes were effectively blocked, learned to avoid shock, although with greater difficulty than normal dogs. Moreover, dogs deprived of autonomic activity after avoidance conditioning were, if anything, more resistant to extinction than normal dogs. These facts appear to require an extension of Mowrer's interpretation to include these other processes, perhaps in the direction of nonmuscular neural responses. The most recent statements of the major learning theorists (Koch, 1959) seems to indicate that many of them currently favor this conception.

Reinforcement for the Acquisition of Fear

As regards the acquisition of fear itself, two-process theory makes two assumptions: (1) that fear is established by a process of conditioning and (2) that this conditioning is specifically a matter of contiguity learning. Of these the first is less a matter of dispute than the second. Two-process learning theory could, as in Hull's 1929 treatment, proceed without accepting either the effect or the contiguity theory for the development of fear. Such a theory would simply propose that fear is established according to the laws of classical conditioning, whatever they may be, and then concentrate on the role of fear in the establishment of avoidant behavior, confining its interest in fear conditioning to the variables which control the strength of fear. There is a considerable amount of research which conforms to this strategy. It has been shown (1) that the strength of the fear reaction increases with the number of pairings of neutral and noxious stimuli and decreases when the neutral stimulus is presented alone (Kalish, 1954), (2) that fear generalizes in much the same way as other CR's (for example, May, 1948), (3) that it shows spontaneous recovery following extinction (Brown and Jacobs, 1949), (4) that its intensity increases with the intensity of the UCS (Gwinn, 1951), and (5) that the function relating strength of fear to the time separating neutral and noxious stimuli probably resembles that for other classically conditioned responses.

Studies of this last sort require special comment. Investigations of the interstimulus-interval function (pp. 155 to 161) involving unavoidable painful UCS's and the classical conditioning paradigm have yielded optimal temporal intervals in the neighborhood of half a second. There have also been numerous other investigations in which the interval between signal and an *avoidable* shock has been manipulated. These studies (Warner, 1932; Kamin, 1954, 1956; Kish, 1955; F. R. Brush, E. S. Brush, and R. L. Solomon, 1955; Church, F. R. Brush, and R. L. Solomon, 1956) have, without exception, shown a tendency for the shortest interval employed to produce the best conditioning. Because of the interest in avoidant behavior, however, the intervals employed have usually been considerably longer than the optimal interval in classical conditioning, thereby providing time for the avoidant response to occur. Kish's (1955) study is an exception. In a study of the wheel-turning response in rats, he paired a light with a (theoretically) avoidable shock at intervals of 0.25, 1.0, and 5.0 seconds. The first two of these conditions were ones in which the rats were shocked on almost every trial because the latencies of typical avoidant responses in this situation are 1.5 to 2.0 seconds. Thus, for these two groups, the pairing of light and shock onset was essentially the same as in classical conditioning. The chief difference was that the animals' response terminated the shock. Figure 9.13 presents resistance to extinction plotted as a function of the interstimulus interval. The 0.25-second interval produced the highest level of conditioning. It thus seems possible that the interstimulus interval has much the same effect in the development of fear in the avoidance-learning situation as it does in other cases of classical conditioning.

The hypothesis that avoidant learning involves a classically conditioned motive of fear raises another problem of even more basic interest: How is the fear response itself reinforced? Common sense suggests that classical

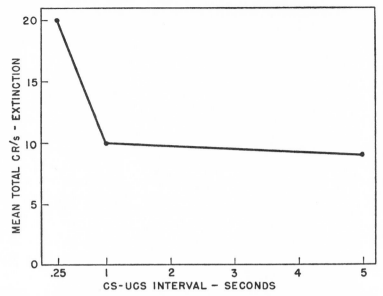

FIGURE 9.13.   Interstimulus-interval function obtained in avoidance training
(Kish, 1955).

conditioning employing a noxious unconditioned stimulus produces an
anticipation of the painful stimulus which occurs whenever the CS is
presented. Pushed a little further this position says that what is anticipated is the pain, and in more technical terms, that it is UCS-onset which
constitutes the essential condition of reinforcement. This is also the position of the two-process theory under discussion. Drive-reduction theorists
propose a different explanation, which is that the critical component of
reinforcement occurs with the going off of the noxious stimulus (Kendler
and Underwood, 1948). Thus, the difference between the two-process and
drive-reduction positions quickly reduces to the question whether the onset or cessation of the UCS is the reinforcer in conditioning of this type.
Translations of this question into experimental operations have taken
three different forms,[8] in which the magnitude, duration, and rate of
cessation of the UCS have been manipulated.

The first kind of experiment in its simplest form does not provide a

[8] For a time, it looked as if data on the conditioned heart rate response were going
to provide good support for the drive-reduction position. Many investigators have
found that, although heart rate is conditionable, the form of the response is sometimes
an acceleration, sometimes a deceleration (Notterman, Schoenfeld, and Bersh, 1952a,
1952b; Notterman, 1953; Bersh, Schoenfeld, and Notterman, 1953). Preliminary evidence (Zeaman and Wegner, 1954) seemed to indicate that whether the CR was an
acceleration or deceleration depended upon the response pattern at the moment of
shock termination. But subsequent evidence (Zeaman and Wegner, 1957) failed to
confirm the preliminary result.

crucial test of the two explanations, because positive results can be handled quite easily from either point of view, and because negative results would create problems for either of them. This point will be easy to make with the aid of an experimental example. Spence (1953), in a factorially designed experiment, first conditioned the eyelid reflexes of human subjects, using strong and weak airpuffs as the unconditioned stimuli for two different groups. On the second day of the experiment the UCS intensity remained the same for half of the subjects in each group, but for the other half, it was switched to the other intensity. The four groups thus created produced the numbers of CR's shown in Table 19

TABLE 19

MEAN NUMBER OF CR's IN FIRST 20 TRIALS ON DAY 2
(From Spence, 1953)

Day 1 UCS	Day 2 UCS weak	strong	Means reflecting learning differences
weak	5.65	8.80	7.23
strong	7.45	13.00	10.23
Means reflecting performance differences (drive)	6.55	10.90	

on the first 20 trials of the second day. Our particular interest is in the row means. As the results of factorially designed experiments are usually interpreted (p. 118), the difference between these values shows that the subjects in the strong UCS group had *learned* more on the first day of training than the subjects in the weak UCS group and that the effect was still present on day 2. The means of the columns, on the other hand, cannot reflect the level of learning because, averaged across day-1 conditions, the histories of these two groups are identical. Differences between the means of the columns, thus, must be attributed to *performance* factors (UCS intensities) operating on day 2, when these measures were obtained. In general, then, it is possible to interpret these results as evidence for an effect of UCS intensity upon learning *and* performance. The contention of the drive-reductionist would be that the stronger UCS leads to better learning because of the greater reinforcing value associated with the cessation of this stimulus.

As Spence points out, however, other interpretations are possible. Specifically, it might be argued that the stronger airpuff on day 1 elicited a reflex of greater vigor and that better learning occurred for this reason. Or, it might be proposed that the stronger UCS on day 1 created a stronger fear drive to be conditioned to the CS, and that this acquired fear was responsible for the superior performance of these subjects on day 2. Neither of these accounts, it will be noted, says anything about drive reduction or reward.

In an effort to develop a purer test of the effect of UCS intensity upon learning, Spence and his students subsequently turned to a different experimental design. In these studies (Ross and Hunter, 1959; Spence, Haggard, and Ross, 1958a, 1958b) groups were conditioned with unconditioned stimuli of different intensities. In order to equate drive strength, the subjects conditioned with the weaker UCS received interspersed trials with the strong UCS, and those conditioned with the stronger UCS received interspersed trials with the weak UCS. On these trials there was no CS. The results of one of these studies appear in Figure 9.14. The superiority of the group conditioned with the strong UCS is taken as evidence that the intensity of the unconditioned stimulus has an effect upon learning and not just performance. It should be noted, however, that even if these experiments demonstrate an effect of UCS intensity upon learning, they do not prove that drive reduction, produced by the

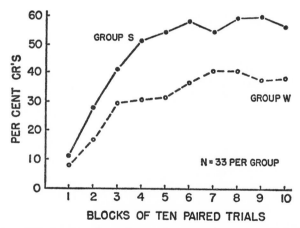

FIGURE 9.14. Percentage of conditioned responses obtained with strong (S) and weak (W) unconditioned stimuli when interpolated trials with the alternative UCS are used to equate experience with the different intensities (Ross and Hunter, 1959).

cessation of the UCS, is responsible for this effect. In fact, other tests of the drive-reduction hypothesis carried out in the context of classical defense conditioning cast serious doubt upon such an interpretation.

Since drive-reduction theory equates the cessation of a noxious stimulus with reinforcement, this theory predicts poor conditioning with a UCS of long duration because in this case reinforcement is delayed. Experiments manipulating duration of the UCS, however, have shown that the magnitude of that variable is of little or no importance in the case of the conditioned GSR (Bitterman, Reed, and Krauskopf, 1952), an acquired fear response in rats (Mowrer and L. N. Solomon, 1954), cardiac conditioning (Wegner and Zeaman, 1958), and the conditioned eyelid reflex (Runquist and Spence, 1959). Beyond this, drive-reduction theory maintains that the noxious stimulus must undergo an abrupt diminution for an acquired drive to be learned. More specifically, the rate at which a noxious stimulus goes off should affect the strength of fear. To test this proposition, Mowrer and L. N. Solomon (1954) paired the same CS, a 3-second blinking light, with shock under the four arrangements shown in Figure 9.15 for different groups of rats. After this training the effect

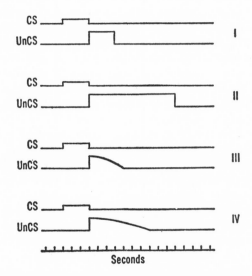

FIGURE 9.15. Various arrangements of CS and UCS (UnCS) employed in study designed to determine the effect of UCS duration and rate of cessation upon conditioned fear. (Mowrer and L. N. Solomon, 1954).

of the blinking light upon a previously established bar-pressing response was determined. To make this test, it was arranged that a bar-press, instead of delivering food as it had before, now turned on the danger signal. This change in the situation led to a very marked diminution of the rate of bar-pressing, presumably because of the arousal of fear. There was, however, no difference among the various groups, indicating that neither UCS duration nor rate of offset during conditioning had had any important effect upon the magnitude of the fear response. This indicates that the important factor controlling the strength of fear is UCS onset, a conclusion in favor of the contiguity assumption made for classical conditioning by the two-process theorist.

The Reinforcement of Avoidance Responses

In the most general sense, it seems that avoidant reactions are reinforced by the cessation of, or escape from, the once-neutral stimulus now associated with pain. One of the most impressive lines of evidence for this conclusion is that postponing the cessation of the feared CS beyond the moment of occurrence of the avoidant response (delay of reinforcement) retards the acquisition of conditioned avoidance reactions (Mowrer and Lamoreaux, 1942, 1946). It is also known that there is a delay-of-reinforcement gradient which resembles that obtained for positive reinforcers (Church and R. L. Solomon, 1956; Kamin, 1957a, 1957b; Wickens and Platte, 1954). Looking beyond this most general interpretation, however, we are immediately confronted with problems, all of which, in one way or another, involve the difficulty of extinguishing avoidant behavior (R. L. Solomon, Kamin, and Wynne, 1953). In the experiments performed by Solomon and his associates, the subjects have usually been dogs trained to avoid shock in a two-compartment apparatus. The conditioned stimulus, signalling the onset of a very strong (traumatic) shock, was a change in illumination and the lowering of a door, which made it possible for the dog to jump a shoulder-high hurdle and get into the other compartment to avoid the shock or escape from it in the early stages of learning. The interval between the signal and shock onset was 10 seconds.

Figure 9.16 shows the results obtained from what Solomon and Wynne (1953) describe as a fairly typical subject. Note the following facts about this dog's performance: (1) After seven trials with latencies longer than 10 seconds the dog avoids the shock on trial 8 and never experiences it again. (2) In spite of the fact that there is no shock, the dog improves its performance throughout the fifty-two remaining trials, rapidly at first and then more slowly. There is no evidence of extinction here, or of backsliding to receive the occasional reminder that the situation is dangerous. In fact, after 10 successive avoidances in this experiment, Solomon and Wynne discontinued the shock altogether. This procedure brought certain other important facts to light. (3) The occasional long-latency responses which occurred without shock never resulted in extinction, but if anything, strengthened the animal's behavior on the immediately following trials as if such procrastination enhanced the subject's fear of the situation. This observation should be coupled with another common one in avoidance training, (4) that indices of fear other than the avoidance response itself show a brief period of increase during the first three or four trials which is followed by marked decrease later in learning. Solomon and Wynne describe this fact for several fear indicators in their experiment. It has also been noted in the case of other responses in other species (Kessen, 1953; Mowrer and Lamoreaux, 1951). Adding a fifth fact (5) that the hurdle-jumping responses in Solomon's and Wynne's study per-

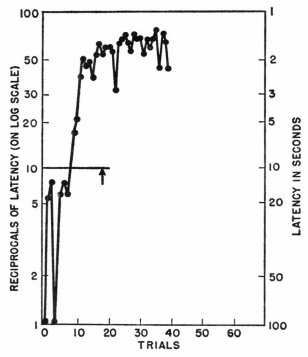

FIGURE 9.16.   Performance of a single, typical dog in avoidance conditioning
with traumatic shock as the UCS. The horizontal line is drawn at the level of
the CS-UCS interval. Thus responses below this line were escape trials; responses above it were avoidance trials. Shock was turned off permanently at
point indicated by arrow (Solomon and Wynne, 1953).

sisted without apparent diminution for hundreds of trials completes the
picture of the problem confronting the theorist interested in explaining
avoidance learning. How is the enormous persistence of such behavior to
be accounted for?

One fact of particular importance about the data presented in Figure
9.16 is that they seem to disprove one common explanation for the great
resistance of avoidant behavior to extinction. This explanation appeals to
the typical effect of partial reinforcement, during acquisition, upon later
performance in extinction. Conditioned avoidance is so resistant to extinction, according to this account, because it was established by a variable ratio schedule, brought about by the occasional lapses and consequent punishments which occur during conditioning. In this subject,
however, every trial was reinforced until the first avoidance occurred;
from then on, there were no reinforced trials at all. Whatever validity
the partial reinforcement interpretation has in explaining the results of

other studies, it is not applicable here. Such facts as this led Solomon and Wynne to propose an elaborated version of the two-factor theory to explain traumatic avoidance conditioning. The main elements in their position are those developed by Mowrer: the classical conditioning of fear by stimulus-response contiguity, and the subsequent establishment of instrumental avoidant behavior on the basis of drive (fear) reduction. Beyond this, however, they suggest two additional principles, the principle of anxiety conservation and the principle of partial irreversibility, which are descriptive hypotheses drawn from their conditioning data.

The typical asymptotic latency of the hurdle-jumping response, and also of the wheel-turning response in rats, is about 1.5 seconds. This latency is less than that of almost all visceral responses and certainly less than the time between the presentation of a feared stimulus and the reception of a feedback from such responses. This means that the avoidance reaction takes place too soon for some of the most important elements of the fear response to occur. And, if the response terminates the fear stimulus, these components of the response will never occur in the presence of the stimulus. It will, therefore, be difficult to extinguish the fear response. Because of its protracted latency, anxiety is in this way saved from extinction or, as Solomon and Wynne say, conserved.

On the other hand, occasional long-latency avoidance responses do occur with two effects. The first is that such a response allows the fear reaction to occur in greater intensity than on short-latency trials. This increase in motivation accounts for the fact that such responses, even if not punished, often lead to a faster reaction on the next trial. On the other hand, with such responses, there is also an opportunity for the extinction of the fear response to occur, and it is impossible to avoid the prediction that this will indirectly weaken avoidance behavior and ultimately result in its disappearance. To handle this problem, Solomon and Wynne offer their second principle, that of partial irreversibility. This principle, patterned after G. W. Allport's (1937) concept of functional autonomy, maintains that fear reactions are incapable of complete extinction and once learned are capable of motivating behavior forever. Some avoidance reactions, however, extinguish rather easily. Only those developed on the basis of traumatic unconditioned stimuli seem completely resistant to extinction. For this reason, Solomon and Wynne suggest, as Hull had earlier, that the intensity of the UCS is the important determiner of this irreversibility.

SUMMARY

Contemporary views on the nature of reinforcement tend to be of more limited scope than the general theories reviewed in the last chapter. The most important of these newer positions identify reinforcement with the reduction of tension, the evocation of a response, or the presentation of a stimulus.

Tension-Reduction Theory

There have been three important versions of the tension-reduction position. (1) The earliest of these was the theory of need reduction which held that reinforcement always entailed the satisfaction of a basic biological need. This theory had to be abandoned because of numerous exceptions to the general principle it proposed. The phenomenon of secondary reinforcement, as well as the facts that the onset of a light and the taste of saccharine are reinforcing are difficult to incorporate in such a theory. (2) The drive-reduction theory treats motives abstractly and relates them to appropriate antecendent conditions. Although many of the drive-establishing operations employed in the definition of drives are the same as those which produce states of biological need, the distinction between drive and need is possible in drive-reduction theory. (3) Finally there is drive-stimulus-reduction theory. In this view drives are regarded as intense stimuli and the reduction of this stimulation is considered to be reinforcing.

Alternatives to Tension Reduction

Tension-reduction theory has so dominated thinking about the nature of reinforcement that it is widely accepted as THE reinforcement theory, and alternative positions are incorrectly regarded as non-reinforcement theories. These alternative views of the nature of reinforcement are: (1) a response theory which holds that certain forms of behavior, most of them consummatory behavior, are reinforcing and (2) a stimulational theory which maintains that reinforcement reduces to a matter of stimulation. These positions have not been developed to the same extent as tension-reduction theory, being most applicable to certain experimental situations.

Physiological Studies of Need Reduction

Experiments designed to obtain data relevant to the role of need reduction have asked two questions which are essentially opposite: (1) Is drive or need reduction a sufficient condition for the production of learning? (2) Is it possible to obtain learning with reinforcers which reduce no drives or needs?

Experiments prompted by the first question have shown that food introduced directly into the stomach and glucose (which raises blood sugar) injected into the blood stream are adequate reinforcers. These results support a need-reduction interpretation of reinforcement. On the other hand experiments prompted by the second question have shown that saccharine, exploration, and electrical stimulation of the brain can also function as reinforcers. In none of these cases is there the reduction of any obvious drive or need. Such data, therefore, favor an interpretation in terms of stimulational effects.

Brain Stimulation and the Stimulus Theory

Of the results just mentioned the one of particular interest is that a mild electrical shock applied to certain areas of the brain (limbic system) through chronically implanted electrodes is capable of reinforcing many kinds of learning. This raises questions of interest to the neuroanatomist and neurophysiologist as well as to the psychologist. Experiments have shown that the effect of stimulating different areas of the brain varies and that, with some electrode placements, brain shock is a negative reinforcer. Whether a brain shock is a positive or a negative reinforcer also depends to a degree upon the intensity and duration of the electrical stimulus and upon the drive state of the animal. This last result provides the very strong suggestion that brain stimulation is related to the process of reinforcement as it normally occurs in conventional experiments on learning. At the same time, it must be recognized that the details of this relationship are not well worked out. Much additional research needs to be done on the operation of the usual reinforcers, as well as upon brain stimulation.

Response Theories of Reinforcement

Theories which treat reinforcement in terms of responses have never been very popular, possibly because of methodological difficulties which stand in the way of clearly separating them from stimulational theory and, in some cases, from drive reduction. There is, however, evidence which leads in the direction of such a theory. It has been shown that there is a very high correlation between the vigor of consummatory behavior and the vigor of the instrumental response in certain learning situations. There is also evidence that activity and manipulation will serve to reinforce learned acts.

Two-Process Theories

Avoidance learning creates problems for any theory of reinforcement. Since a successful avoidant response prevents the occurrence of the reinforcer, it is difficult to understand how such behavior could be maintained. Yet it is known that such responses can be highly resistant to extinction. Several writers have developed two-process theories to explain the characteristics of avoidant behavior. These theories assume that, early in the course of avoidance learning, a process of classical conditioning occurs in which a fear response, initially elicited by the noxious UCS, becomes conditioned to the CS. This acquisition of fear is assumed to take place without drive- or need-reduction. Once acquired, the conditioned fear is thought of as a drive, capable of motivating behavior. Escape from the fear-evoking CS is reinforcing through the mechanism of drive reduction.

This theory, though attractive, raises certain questions:

1. Is fear conditioning, as hypothesized, a case of learning by contiguity alone? Studies in which the duration and rate of cessation of the UCS have been manipulated in classical conditioning offer an affirmative answer. Since a UCS of long duration theoretically delays drive reduction and gradual cessation of the UCS means that drive reduction occurs gradually, learning, according to drive-reduction theory, should occur slowly under these conditions. It has been found, however, that neither of these variables has any effect. The most obvious predictions from drive-reduction theory, thus, turn out to be in error. Studies of the intensity of the UCS have demonstrated quite convincingly that this variable influences learning. But they have contributed little or nothing to the question whether classical conditioning is a process of contiguity learning.

2. Why is avoidant behavior so persistent? Since the avoidant response prevents the occurrence of the UCS, it might be expected that extinction would set in as soon as the response became at all consistent. In many experiments this does not happen. In order to explain the great resistance of avoidance behavior to experimental extinction, two additional principles have been proposed: (*a*) the principle of anxiety conservation, which is that fear is so resistant to extinction because the avoidant response occurs before fear can be aroused, thus protecting the fear from extinction; and (*b*) the principle of partial irreversibility, which is that fear is inextinguishable if it is based upon a very intense and traumatically painful stimulus.

·10·

The Nature of Extinction

IF THE CS is repeatedly presented unaccompanied by the usual reinforcer, the conditioned response undergoes a progressive decrement called extinction, and finally fails to occur. This reduction in the strength of the CR is not a spontaneous decay. Conditioned responses show only a very limited tendency to diminish with the passage of time. Studies of the retention of CR's have usually shown some decrease in strength with disuse, but a much more impressive retention. The numerous demonstrations of the great resistance to CR's to forgetting include reports of the retention of conditioned motor responses by sheep for two years (Liddell, W. T. James, and O. D. Anderson, 1934); conditioned eyelid reactions in dogs for 16 months (D. G. Marquis and Hilgard, 1936); conditioned eyelid reactions in man for 20 weeks (Hilgard and A. A. Campbell, 1936) and for 19 months (Hilgard and Humphreys, 1938b); conditioned flexion reflexes in the dog for 30 months (Wendt, 1937); conditioned salivation in man for 16 weeks (Razran, 1939a); various responses in dogs for 6 months (Kellogg and Wolf, 1939); and a pecking response in pigeons for four years (Skinner, 1950). From such evidence it is apparent that the elimination of a conditioned response in a brief extinction session must depend upon an active process or, perhaps, several of them.

The determination of the basic mechanisms which underly extinction is difficult because of the great complexity of the phenomenon. We have previously seen that resistance to extinction is a measure of learning, a fact which means that, to understand extinction, it will be necessary first of all to know how the conditions of training affect habits. To mention facts which appear to be of greatest significance for extinction, the omission of reinforcement always has at least some of the following consequences: (1) inhibition or adaptation of the response mechanism, (2) the instigation of interfering responses, (3) generalization decrement, resulting from changes in the stimulus situation, (4) decreases in the level of motivation, which is most obvious when extinction involves the omission of a negative reinforcer, and (5) frustration, which is most obvious when extinction involves the omission of a positive reinforcer. Various writers have stressed different aspects of extinction, each tending to favor one or two of the processes just listed. The result has been the development of a series of hypotheses to account for extinction. The most important of these hypotheses are described in the following sections.

INHIBITION THEORY

The central concepts in early theories of extinction were those of inhibition and interference, both of which were drawn from physiological work on simple reflexes (Sherrington, 1906) and from Pavlov's studies of conditioning. In these original contexts both concepts were employed. When they were taken over by psychologists, however, there was a strong tendency for one concept or the other to be emphasized. In this way two alternative theories of extinction gradually developed. One adopted the principle of inhibition and attempted to explain all extinction phenomena in terms of it. The other attempted to do the same thing using only the principle of interference (Guthrie, 1935; Wendt, 1936).

The most nearly contemporary version of classical inhibition theory is to be found in *a part* of Hull's (1943) explanation of extinction. In this theory, Hull assumed that every response of the organism, whether reinforced or not, left in the organism an increment of *reactive inhibition* (I_R), the magnitude of which was an increasing function of the rate of response elicitation and the effortfulness of the response. It was assumed to decay with rest. Hull further assumed that reactive inhibition is a primary negative drive resembling fatigue which leads to a cessation of the response which produces it. Formally, reactive inhibition was a performance variable in Hull's theory, subtracting from the combined effect of learning and motivation $(_sE_R)$ and, as a result, lowering response strength.

Before considering this theory as an explanation of extinction, certain more general observations need to be made about the concept of inhibition: (1) Since reactive inhibition theoretically develops with responding even when the response is reinforced, the effects of this variable will be discernible in a variety of performance situations. More or less successful applications of the I_R concept have been made to alternation behavior (Siegel, 1950; Zeaman and House, 1951), distribution of practice effects (p. 126) and inhibition of reinforcement (p. 127), as well as to extinction. (2) The conception of reactive inhibition as a drive leading to the cessation of a response contains in it the seeds of a very limited interfering-response theory which will be considered later.

The Effect of Distribution of Extinction Trials

The basic assumption of inhibition theory is that inhibition reduces the level of performance. Thus any conditions which increase the amount of inhibition should have a detrimental effect upon response strength. The two most important of such conditions are the distribution of extinction trials and the effortfulness of the response. As regards the first of these variables, the specific prediction to which inhibition theory leads is that extinction will occur more rapidly with massed than with distributed trials. The results of several of the most straight-forward tests of this prediction are summarized in Table 20. By "straight-forward" we mean that interest in these studies has centered exclusively, or nearly so, on the effect of the distribution of trials, while other factors, such as generalization decrement, have been left out of consideration. As Table

TABLE 20

RESULTS OF STUDIES OF EFFECT OF INTERTRIAL
INTERVAL ON THE RATE OF EXTINCTION

Investigator	Response and Subject	Conditions of Distribution	Results
Pavlov (1927, p. 53)	Salivation; dog	2, 4, 8, 16 min.	No effect on number of non-reinforced trials
Hilgard and Marquis (1935)	Eyelid CR, dog	60 trials per day versus 10 trials every other day	Faster extinction with massed trials
Porter (1938c)	Running 20-foot alley, rat	A few seconds, 5 minutes, 10 minutes	No effect
Porter (1939)	Eyelid CR, human subjects	10, 20, 40, 80, 180 seconds	No effect
Gagné (1941b) (Exp. 1 only. Exp. II complicated by different amounts of reinforcement)	Running 3-foot elevated maze, rat	.5, 1, 2, 3, 5, 10 minutes, in acquisition and extinction	Interpretation complicated by differences due to acquisition distribution and inhibition of reinforcement. Probably no effect.
Rohrer (1947)	Bar-pressing, rat	10, 90 seconds	In general, faster extinction with massed practice. Suggests increased effect with stronger responses.
Rohrer (1949)	Bar-pressing, rat	10, 90 seconds	Faster and more permanent extinction with massed trials.
Edmonson and Amsel (1954)	Running 6-foot alley to escape shock, rat	1, 5, or 15 trials a day	5- and 15-trial groups showed extinction tendency. Little difference between these 2 groups. One-trial group showed little extinction.

20 shows, the most common result has been for massed practice to speed up extinction. There have, however, been enough experiments in which this effect failed to occur to suggest that manipulating the distribution

variable must also produce changes in processes other than inhibition. The most likely additional process has to do with a relationship between the distribution of practice and the nature of the stimulus situation, a topic to be taken up later.

The Phenomenon of Spontaneous Recovery

Somewhat more substantial support for an inhibitory concept comes from studies of spontaneous recovery, although again the details of the evidence soon demonstrate that extinction must involve additional factors. It will be recalled that the phenomenon of spontaneous recovery is that, following extinction, rest produces an automatic increase in response strength. The most obvious explanation for this increase is that some temporary inhibitory state, produced by non-reinforcement, decays during the rest interval. There are, however, many difficulties in the way of explaining everything that is known about spontaneous recovery in terms of an inhibitory process. Some of the problems are these: (1) Spontaneous recovery seldom brings response strength back to the level it had attained prior to conditioning. Pavlov stated that, left to themselves, extinguished reflexes sooner or later returned to their full strength, and he presents evidence to support his claim (Pavlov, 1927, p. 58-59); but this finding seems to be the exception. More often spontaneous recovery restores something like 50 per cent of the response strength lost in extinction. From the inhibitory point of view this creates a difficulty, because no permanent negative process has been assumed. (2) The assumption that spontaneous recovery is the result of the dissipation of inhibition leads to the general prediction that procedures which increase inhibition will also increase the amount of spontaneous recovery. The massing of extinction trials is one condition which might bring this about. In a study concerned with several aspects of acquisition and extinction, D. J. Lewis (1956) extinguished the response of running a straight alley to food with 15 seconds or two minutes between extinction trials. He found no reliable evidence that spontaneous recovery was increased by massed extinction trials. (3) Repeated presentations of the CS, after the CR has completely disappeared, continue to reduce the amount of spontaneous recovery (Pavlov, 1927). This extinction "below zero" is hard to explain in terms of a response-produced inhibition. (4) There are some puzzling unexplained differences among curves of spontaneous recovery which seem difficult to attribute to the effects of a single process. Sometimes the upper limit of the function is reached within a few minutes after extinction (Pavlov, 1927, p. 58; Graham and Gagné, 1940); but in other experiments, it has sometimes been necessary to wait for an hour or several hours for the same degree of spontaneous recovery to occur (Ellson, 1938; D. J. Lewis, 1956). It seems improbable that the extended spontaneous-recovery functions result from the same process as those of shorter duration.[1]

Extinction and the Effortfulness of the Response

From the assumption that the amount of reactive inhibition varies with the effort required to perform a response, it follows that increased effort-fulness will result in quicker extinction of the response in question. Although Maatsch, Adelman, and Denny (1954) obtained negative re-sults, experiments testing this prediction have, more often than not, con-firmed the prediction (Mowrer and Jones, 1943; Solomon, 1948; Apple-zweig, 1951; Stanley and Aamodt, 1954; Capehart, Viney, and Hulicka, 1958). The experiment of Capehart, Viney, and Hulicka illustrates the typical procedure employed in such investigations. Rats were trained to press a bar in a Skinner box to obtain food. In order to balance out experience with the various degrees of effortfulness later to be compared, all animals received 30 trials with bar-weightings of 5, 40, or 70 gm. during the initial training. Then they were divided into three groups and extinguished under conditions where it took different amounts of pressure (5, 40, or 70 gm.) to press the bar. The results of this study appear in Figure 10.1. Quite clearly, increasing effort leads to increas-ingly rapid extinction.

Although the evidence seems clear on the point that effort does influ-ence extinction, the form of the function, and the importance of this variable, are still in doubt. This is because the problems of manipulating effort, but no other variable, in studies of extinction are greater than might have been anticipated. In the majority of investigations, which have used a Skinner apparatus and produced different degrees of effort by differential bar-weightings, two procedural difficulties arise: (1) In order to train the animal to press a heavy bar it is usually necessary to begin by teaching it to press a lighter bar first. Such training may, in effect, give the animals extinguished on the light bar more training than those extinguished on a heavier one. (2) The problem of partial responses is sometimes critical. Such responses, which consist of bar depressions of insufficient magnitude to operate the food release mechanism, occur more frequently with a heavy bar than with a light one. During training, the occurrence of these responses introduces uncontrolled schedule effects; and during extinction, one must decide whether to count them. If they are counted, the difference between groups extinguished with responses requiring different amounts of effort necessarily decreases (Applezweig, 1951; Stanley and Aamodt, 1954). Other ways of manipulating effort produce other difficulties. Solomon (1948), for example, increased and

[1] For further studies and discussion of spontaneous recovery see Estes (1942), Liberman, (1944, 1948), Murphy, Miller, and Finnochio (1956), Miller and Miles (1936), Miller and Stevenson (1936), Razran (1939b), and Youtz (1938a).

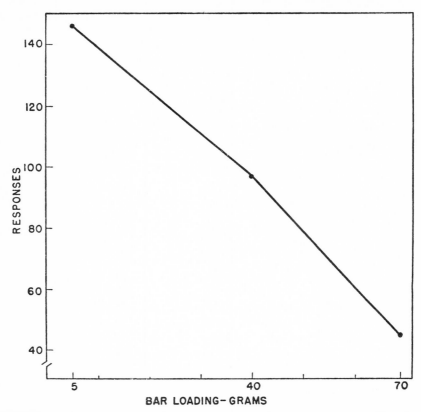

FIGURE 10.1. The effect of effort upon resistance to extinction (Capehart, Viney, and Hulicka, 1958).

decreased effort by varying the distance rats had to jump in a jumping stand. In this procedure increasing the length of the jump may very well increase the animals' fear.

The Problem of Partial and Varied Reinforcement

The most critical problem facing any theory of extinction is to explain the effect of partial reinforcement. And, for inhibition theory, the difficulties are particularly great. Although Skinner had previously described the effects of partial reinforcement upon extinction, the significance of this demonstration seems to have been recognized only after Humphreys' work. In 1939, Humphreys reported that a random alternation of reinforced and non-reinforced trials in eyelid conditioning led to a slight lowering of the rate of acquisition, by comparison with a continuous reinforcement schedule, and to a very much greater resistance to extinction.[2] To explain this finding Humphrey's offered an interpretation in terms of expectancy (Humphreys, 1939a, 1939b).

The impressive thing about the ''Humphreys' effect'' or ''Humphreys' paradox'' to investigators in the early forties was that it seemed to threaten two widely accepted principles, the law of effect and the inhibitory explanation of extinction. With respect to the first of these, the point was that an expected correlation between numbers of reinforcements and response strength (measured in resistance to extinction) failed to materialize. With respect to the second, the problem was to explain the fact that nearly identical levels of learning required for their extinction vastly different numbers of responses and, therefore, different amounts of inhibition.

Studies of what has come to be called *varied reinforcement* (McClelland and McGowan, 1953) are related to studies of partial reinforcement in that they are concerned with learning under circumstances where the conditions of reward change from trial to trial. But instead of omitting reward on certain trials, the procedure in these studies is to change other aspects of reinforcement according to some schedule. The possibilities are quite numerous, including the place where reinforcement is administered from trial to trial, the delay of reinforcement, the quantity or quality of reinforcement, the drive state of the animal, and the specific response leading to reward. Ordinary continuous and partial reinforcement conditions are sometimes included as control conditions. Mackintosh (1955) ran 12 different groups of subjects, varying three different sources of irregularity systematically among them. The sources of irregularity were: (1) Percentage of reinforcement, 80 or 100 per cent. (2) Number of response alternatives, 1, 2, or 3. The response possibilities were pulling a chain, pressing a horizontal bar, and pressing a vertical bar. For the different groups the correct response was always the same (chain pull), one of two responses (chain pull or horizontal bar-press), or one of three responses. (3) Number of reinforcers employed (one or two). Under one schedule the reinforcement was always food; on another it was food on some trials and water on others. The subjects were always both hungry and thirsty. The apparatus was that shown in Figure 10.2. The problem for the animal was to operate the correct mechanism, which opened a door allowing access to the reinforcement. The various reinforcement conditions combined in all possible ways yield a dimension of irregularity of reinforcement extending from 100 per cent reinforcement —one response—one reinforcement, to 80 per cent reinforcement—three response alternatives varied from trial to trial—two rewards varied from trial to trial. In general, number of trials to a strict extinction criterion

[2] For a variety of demonstrations of this point see Jenkins and Rigby, 1950; Jenkins, McFann, and Clayton (1950), Wike (1953), Notterman, Schoenfeld, and Bersh (1952), and Freides (1957).

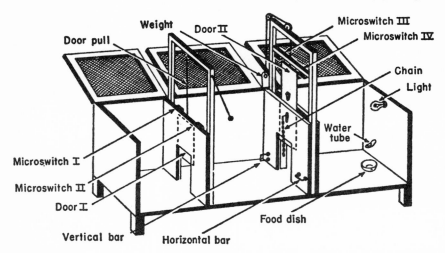

FIGURE 10.2. Apparatus employed in a study of the effects of irregular reinforcement upon extinction. See text for a description of the apparatus (Mac-
Kintosh, 1955).

increased with increases in irregularity, from about 45 trials, for the
most regular condition, to something like 200 for the most irregular.
Analysis of the contribution of the various sources of irregularity showed
that the type of reinforcer did not contribute to the increased resistance
to extinction. Schedule of reinforcement and number of response possibilities produced the entire effect. The fact that varying appropriate
reinforcers does not increase resistance to extinction has subsequently
been confirmed (Kendler, Pliskoff, D'Amato, and Katz, 1957).

Another experiment in this same tradition extends the range of conditions shown to affect extinction. In this study McNamara and Wike
(1958) first trained 5 different groups of rats to run a straight alley.
One, a control group, was trained under standard conditions, involving
little or no variation in the experimental situation or in the conditions
of reward from trial to trial. For other groups, variations in training
conditions were produced (1) by making a series of environmental
changes such as altering the level of illumination, changing the goal
box, and so on, (2) by varying the immediacy of reward, 0 seconds on
some trials and 20 seconds on others, (3) by combining the two previous
procedures, and (4) by manipulating delay of reinforcement, percentage
of reinforcement, drive state and reward, and environmental condition
simultaneously. This last procedure was an attempt to maximize irregularity. After 36 trials under these conditions, the animals were extinguished. Extinction curves for the 5 groups are presented in terms of
running time in Figure 10.3. Obviously, increasing the irregularity of
the training conditions increases resistance to extinction.

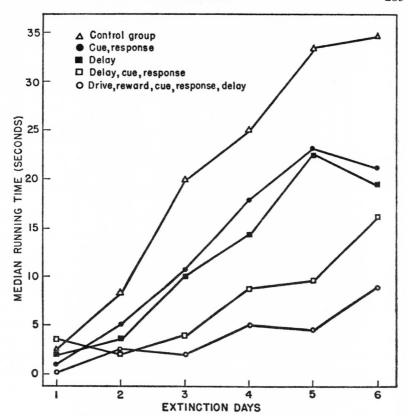

FIGURE 10.3. Median running time in seconds for groups trained under a variety of conditions of reinforcement. In the control group there was minimal variation in the conditions from trial to trial. The sources of variation from trial to trial are given in the legend. Cue and response variation was accomplished by inserting hurdles in the runway, changing illumination, and shifting goal boxes. Variations in delay of reinforcement were produced by administering reward immediately on some trials and after a delay of 20 seconds on others. To manipulate drive, animals were hungry on some days, thirsty on others, and both hungry and thirsty on still others. Reward was dry food pellets on hunger days, water on thirst days, and wet mash on hunger-thirst days. Note that, in general, the greater the number of sources of variation, the greater the resistance to extinction. After McNamara and Wike (1958).

Other investigators have studied the effect of varied reinforcement in a more analytic way, by manipulating the regularity of some single aspect of reinforcement (magnitude, delay, pattern). Crum, Brown, and Bitterman (1951) have reported the results of two experiments which show that varied temporal intervals of two sorts produce increased resistance to extinction. In the first of their experiments fear was condi-

tioned to a 6-second buzzer under three different conditions. In one
(control) condition, a 2-second shock came on at the cessation of the
buzzer. In a second (partial reinforcement) condition, the shock was
omitted on 50 per cent of the trials. In the last condition, shock occurred
on every trial but was delayed 30 seconds following the cessation of the
buzzer on half of the trials. Following this conditioning, all of the subjects learned to escape a shock by running from one section of a two-
compartment box to another. Finally the shock was omitted and the
buzzer reintroduced. On these trials the buzzer was at first capable of
eliciting the escape reaction. This tendency disappeared (extinguished)
in 12 trials for the control group, 95 for the partial reinforcement group
and 107 for the varied delay group. The implication is that varying the
interstimulus interval from trial to trial has at least as strong an effect
as a partial reinforcement condition.

In their second experiment, Crum, Brown, and Bitterman used food
reinforcement and a straight runway, a procedure which has been
employed in much later work. One of two groups received immediate
reinforcement on each trial; the other received immediate reinforcement
on half of the trials and reinforcement after a 30-second delay on the
other. The first of these groups required 13 trials to extinguish; the
second required 31, again showing that varied reinforcement produces
greater resistance to extinction than regular continuous reinforcement.
Scott and Wike (1956) repeated the Crum, Brown, and Bitterman
experiment and obtained the same results. Peterson (1956) and Logan,
Beier, and Kincaid (1956) have also found that extinction of a runway
response is retarded when training is under a variable delay schedule.
The latter investigators found such an effect only when training consisted of a random alternation of 0- and 30-second delays. Similar alternation of 0- and 9-second delays had no such effect.

Logan, Beier, and Kincaid also compared resistance to extinction
following varied and constant magnitudes of reinforcement. Specifically
they ran three groups of rats in a straight alley to (1) 9 pellets of food
on every trial, (2) 9 pellets on some trials and none on others (partial
reinforcement), or (3) 9 pellets on some trials and one on others (varied
reinforcement). In extinction the performances of the varied and partial groups were indistinguishable, and both were superior to that of
the group which had previously been reinforced on every trial.

In studies of varied reinforcement where appropriate comparisons can
be made, level of responding during training is usually similar under
the different reinforcement conditions. Thus these investigations raise
the same question as the partial reinforcement studies: Since response
strengths are similar at the end of training, how can inhibition theory
explain the fact that they are so different in resistance to extinction?

The Response-Unit Hypothesis

In the face of the facts of partial and varied reinforcement, most
theorists would probably agree that inhibition theory must be supple-
mented by other principles if the details of extinction are to be accounted
for adequately. There is, however, one interpretation which offers some
slight possibility of dealing at least with the partial reinforcement data
in terms of inhibition. This is the response-unit hypothesis. Mowrer and
Jones (1945) performed an experiment in which rats first received 80
continuous reinforcements for bar-pressing. Following this, one group
remained on the continuous schedule; three other groups were switched
to fixed-ratio schedules in which they had to press the bar 2, 3, or 4 times
to receive the reinforcement; and a final group was switched to a variable-
ratio schedule in which reinforcement occurred, on the average, after
2.5 responses. All groups received 140 reinforcements on the new schedule. Then they were extinguished, with the results shown in Figure 10.4.

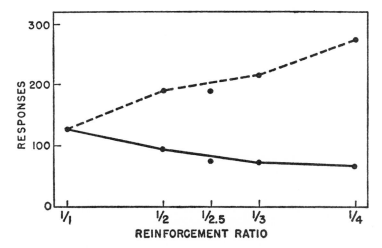

FIGURE 10.4.   Resistance to extinction as a function of ratio of reinforced to
non-reinforced responses. In the upper curve, responses are plotted directly.
Lower (response unit) curve was obtained by multiplying the values in the
upper curve by the reinforcement ratio. Points not included in the curve
itself are for the randomly reinforced group. See text. Mowrer and Jones
(1945).

As the upper curve in Figure 10.4 shows, the usual effect of partial reinforcement occurred. With increasing ratios, the number of responses
emitted in three days of extinction increased. Mowrer and Jones, however, argued that this trend appeared only because each bar depression

was counted as a response. If the concept of response were redefined so that a response becomes a behavioral sequence leading to reinforcement, it would be necessary to multiply the number of extinction bar depressions by the reinforcement ratio (1/1, 1/2, 1/2.5, and so on) in order to obtain the true number of responses. The effect of counting responses in this way is shown in the lower line of Figure 10.4. It will be noted that the trend in the results is now the opposite of that obtained by counting each bar depression as a response. Moreover, the downward slope of this function fits the necessary prediction from inhibition theory, that more effortful responses (consisting of more bar depressions) should extinguish more rapidly than less effortful responses. Thus, in this case, the response-unit hypothesis salvages the inhibition theory. It seems unlikely, however, that this explanation will always work, for two reasons: (1) The response-unit hypothesis does not seem to apply very well to trial-by-trial procedures, particularly if the trials are widely spaced. It is difficult to imagine the sense in which two successive responses separated by 24 hours, as occur in some experiments on partial reinforcement, constitute a unit. (2) Certain facts about extinction argue against it. For example, Capaldi (1958) gave rats 10 trials a day in an apparatus which consisted in an elevated runway terminating in a jump stand. To obtain food the subject had to run down the alley and jump across a gap. Capaldi ran, among others, two groups of rats which received reinforcement or alternate trials. One group received 70 trials; the other, 140. In terms of response-units, as defined by Mowrer and Jones, the first of these groups received 35 trials and the second, 70. This should produce greater response strength and greater resistance to extinction in the second group. The opposite, however, turned out to be the case. The animals with the smaller amount of training required about 67 trials to reach an extinction criterion; the group with more training required only 36. Capaldi interpreted this result in terms of the discrimination hypothesis, to be discussed later. The group with more training, he argued, found it easier to perceive the difference between training and extinction because of their more frequent exposure to the alternating reinforcement procedure. This is a sort of stimulus-unit hypothesis.

Evaluation of Inhibition Explanation of Extinction

Put as briefly as possible, the experiments reviewed so far show that inhibition of the sort postulated by the early proponents of inhibition, and by Hull, probably contributes to extinction, but cannot serve as a complete explanation. Evidence supporting inhibition theory includes the phenomenon of spontaneous recovery, the generally more rapid extinction under massed than distributed extinction trials, and the fact that the speed of extinction varies with the effortfulness of the response.

On the negative side, against the view that inhibition provides a complete explanation for extinction, are the rather numerous instances where the distribution of extinction trials fails to have the predicted effect, the fact that spontaneous recovery is seldom able to restore an extinguished response completely, the phenomenon of extinction below zero, and the impossibility of handling the influence of partial and varied reinforcement upon extinction, except in a limited number of cases.

The negative evidence just cited indicates the necessity for supplementing inhibition theory with other principles in order to explain a greater number of the facts of extinction. One source of such additional principles obviously is the rest of the theory which attempts to explain extinction in terms of inhibition. Hull's theory, which is the clearest case in point, contains numerous possibilities of this sort. According to this theory the extinction procedure might lead to a decrease in response strength through a reduction of incentive motivation or secondary reinforcement, through the reduction of habit strength with changes in the amount and delay of reinforcement (Dufort and Kimble, 1956), or through generalization decrement resulting from stimulus changes correlated with the shift from conditioning to extinction. Of these various possibilities the last has been the only one to have received much serious consideration. We shall turn to it next.

GENERALIZATION DECREMENT

All extinction procedures involve changes in the experimental situation in that the proprioceptive consequence of reinforcement, and eventually responding, are eliminated. If the conditioned response is at all under the control of these stimuli, it should lose strength as a result of such changes, and extinction should be hastened to a degree which depends upon the magnitude of these differences in stimulation between conditioning and extinction. The generalization-decrement hypothesis stresses this interpretation.

As was true of the concept of inhibition, generalization decrement has applications beyond the field of extinction. The general principle that changes in the learning situation result in response decrements has been verified in a variety of ways. One obvious example is in the phenomenon of external inhibition. It has also been shown that the drinking behavior of rats diminishes progressively as more and more of the customary environmental cues to drinking are eliminated (Fink and Patton, 1953). And the warm-up phenomenon characteristic of the performance of motor skills (Ammons, 1947) and rote learning (Thune, 1950) seems to be a matter of overcoming a decrement produced by the loss, with rest, of response-produced cues which control the learned response in some measure.

Generalization Decrement and the Distribution of Practice

This last example has important implications for extinction, especially when related to the concept of inhibition. Inhibition, as it is usually conceived, is a response process. Hull's term *reactive inhibition* suggests an effector-localized mechanism, as does his treatment of I_R as something analogous to fatigue. If this interpretation is accepted, it is important to recognize that responses, at least skeletal ones, almost always have stimulus consequences in the form of kinesthetic feedback (Solomon, 1948), and that these stimuli may play a very important part in the control of behavior.

The generalization-decrement hypothesis, together with the concept of response-produced stimuli, suggests a more detailed analysis of the effect upon extinction of the distribution of extinction trials. This analysis applies most directly to experiments which alter the conditions of distribution at the beginning of the extinction series. Responding, under a given distributional condition, would be expected to maintain kinesthetic feedback at some particular level. Changing the degree of distribution for extinction, or for further practice, would lead to a change in the level of response-produced stimulation and, therefore, to a loss of response strength through generalization decrement.

Experimental evidence in general support of such a theory comes

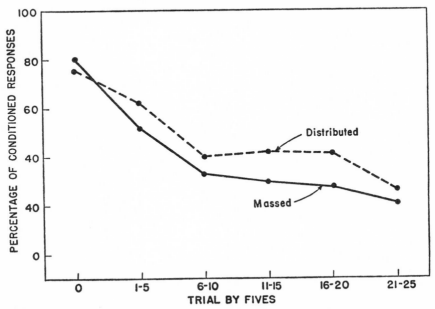

FIGURE 10.5. Extinction curves for the conditioned eyelid reflex obtained under massed and distributed practice (Reynolds, 1945b).

from several quarters. In one of the earliest demonstrations (Reynolds, 1945b), the eyelid reflexes of groups of human subjects were conditioned with an intertrial interval of either 15 or 90 seconds. Then, for extinction, these main groups were subdivided, half continuing under the original interval, half shifting to the other. An overall comparison of the groups being extinguished under massed and distributed practice appears in Figure 10.5, which shows that there is a slight tendency for the group being extinguished under massed practice to show a more rapid reduction in response strength than the group extinguished with distributed trials. Figure 10.6 presents a more detailed analysis of the same data with the performances of different acquisition groups being considered separately. In this figure, the performances of the groups conditioned with distributed practice show a wide divergence, with the distributed-extinction group displaying very much greater resistance to extinction than the massed group. For the group conditioned by massed trials the difference is smaller and, it should be noted, in the opposite direction.

The meaning of these data apparently is as follows. For subjects originally conditioned with distributed-acquisition trials, the switch to

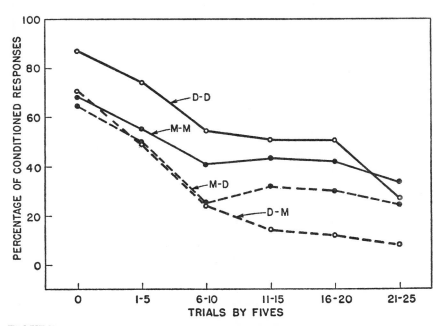

FIGURE 10.6. Extinction curves from Reynolds' experiment (Figure 10.5) plotted separately for groups conditioned by massed and distributed practice. The first letter in the label on each curve indicates condition of spacing of trials during acquisition (D=distributed; M=massed). The second letter indicates condition during extinction (Reynolds, 1945b).

massed practice during extinction produces (1) an increased accumulation of inhibition by comparison with the distributed-extinction group, and (2) a loss of response strength through generalization decrement. For the subjects conditioned and extinguished with massed trials, inhibition similarly accumulates at a rapid rate during extinction. But the massed-extinction procedure maintains the conditions of distribution which existed in training. Under these circumstances response strength does not suffer from generalization decrement. The importance of this second factor is indicated by the fact that extinction with distributed practice occurs slightly more rapidly than with massed practice following training under conditions of massing.

Various other investigators have made a similar interpretation of the role of the spacing of extinction trials and have presented evidence similar to that obtained by Reynolds. Teichner (1952) performed two experiments which, considered together, provided the data presented in Figure 10.7. In this study, the bar-pressing responses of rats were first condi-

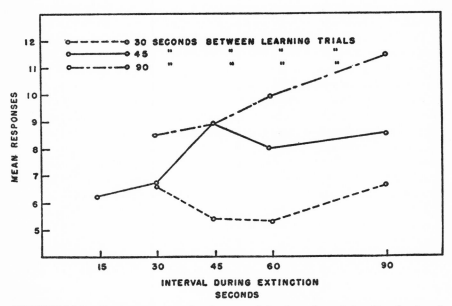

FIGURE 10.7. Resistance to extinction as a joint function of the distributional conditions during acquisition and extinction. Note the tendency for resistance to extinction to be greater when the acquisition and extinction occur with the same separation of trials (Teichner, 1952).

tioned at intertrial intervals of 30, 45, or 90 seconds. Then they were extinguished at intervals of 15 (first experiment only), 30, 45, 60, or 90 seconds. As Figure 10.7 shows, one effect of the distribution of extinction trials was to produce greater resistance to extinction with increasing time between trials. This finding illustrates the importance of inhibition in the sense in which we used the term in the previous section. Over and above this effect, however, there is an increase in resistance to extinction which occurs when extinction takes place at the same intertrial interval as had existed in training. This effect is quite clear in the curves for the groups conditioned at the 30- and 45-second intervals. Results similarly pointing to the significance of a generalization decrement factor have been obtained by V. F. Sheffield (1950) and Stanley (1952) for the straight-alley and T-maze situations, respectively. D. J. Lewis (1956) obtained negative results in a study which was well controlled and completely analyzed statistically. The reasons for such discrepancies are not clear.

Spontaneous Regression

With the conception of kinesthetic feedback as an entering explanatory wedge, many otherwise puzzling facts about conditioning and extinction become clear. If one considers the stimuli involved in the control of the CR, it becomes apparent that, in addition to the CS and the cues produced by the act of responding, two other classes of stimulation are important: (1) the stimulus aftereffects of the UCS and (2) the heterogeneous array of stimuli attendant upon being introduced to the experimental situation and remaining in it. If it is accepted that these stimuli in some measure control the occurrence of the CR, any interference with the pattern of these cues will lead to a loss of response strength, by the same generalization-decrement principle as was employed in the analysis of the effects of changing distributions of practice. Such a loss could occur without the appearance of a CR, as a sort of "automatic deconditioning" (Razran, 1956) or "spontaneous regression" (Estes, 1955).

Among the incidental facts which seem explainable in terms of an interference with the cues developed in the course of conditioning are the following: (1) When animals are tested for the retention of CR's, there is usually some loss, in spite of the remarkable stability of conditioning. This loss may represent the extent to which the response is controlled by the cues in question. (2) The beneficial effect of providing the rat with a taste of food prior to a maze run may result from the fact that this procedure restores an element of the stimulus situation ordinarily lost with the interruption of practice. (3) Kurke (1956) found that the resistance of a bar-pressing response to extinction was remarkably similar when measured in terms of the average number of experimental sessions required to meet a five-minute criterion, although the number of responses required ranged from less than 40 to more than 150 under various conditions. This suggests that a certain amount of the control of conditioned behavior resides in the stimuli associated with entering the experimental situation, and that this control extinguishes in a fairly regular manner as a function of the number of extinction sessions.

The portion of these stimuli contributed by the mere fact of being in the experimental situation presumably would disappear as soon as the organism leaves the situation; and the traces of them would be lost soon thereafter. Stimulus consequences of the UCS, particularly of a noxious one, conceivably might last longer, but they, too, might be expected to disappear within a matter of an hour or two at most. These considerations suggest that there should be a brief function relating a loss in response strength to the time the organism has been away from the experimental situation, and that, after some relatively short period, the function should be asymptotic. Moyer (1958) reports a set of results which support this expectation in a limited way. He conditioned rats in an avoidance situation and then extinguished them after a wait of 1 hour, 2 days, 4 days, 8 days, 16 days, or 32 days. The numbers of trials to extinction for these six groups, respectively, were: 15.1, 4.5, 7.9, 5.4, 7.8, and 4.2. The pattern of these points is what would be expected. Unfortunately, the differences among them turned out not to be significant when tested by the methods of analysis of variance. The trend, however, is reassuring, and a study with more subjects might well produce the expected result in a more dependable way, especially if time intervals shorter than one hour were sampled.

Indirect evidence on the dissipation of response-produced stimulation has come from an experiment by Rothkopf (1955) in which he first trained rats to run an elevated runway for food on a one-trial-a-day schedule and, later on, shifted to two trials a day. The reasoning behind this method was that, with trials occurring at the rate of one a day, traces of the previous response or reinforcement would not be a part of the cue pattern controlling the running response. Introducing a second trial soon after the first in the later portion of the experiment would lead to relatively poorer performance on this second trial because the stimuli produced by the responses on the first trial, if still present, would function as external inhibitors and disrupt the conditioned running response.

One difficulty in this argument clearly is that the introduction of the second response in the second part of the experiment will have two effects: (1) It will provide the desired measure of the stimulus consequences of the response on the first trial; but, at the same time, (2) the second response will be weakened by response-produced inhibition generated on the first trial. Since these influences operate in the same direction, Rothkopf took measures designed to separate them. The experiment proceeded as follows: training, with trials at the rate of 1 trial a day, continued for 10 days. Then, from the eleventh day on, the animals received two trials a day with the trials separated by different amounts of time, 5, 15, 30, or 120 seconds. Some of the animals continued to receive two trials a day at the same spacing for the rest of the experiment. Others were shifted from one interval to another and, in the course of the study, had blocks of trials at each of the intervals mentioned above.

The results of the experiment appear in two learning curves based on response latency on the first and second trials separately. Figure 10.8 shows a set of such functions for the groups receiving all of their second trials at the same interval following the first. The points of importance in this graph are the following: (1) As predicted, the second-trial latencies were increased, in a way which depended upon the intertrial interval. This is most clearly apparent on the first test. (2) With practice the disruptive effect disappeared. By the end of the experiment, the animals were responding as if the cues produced by the response on the first trial had become a part of the stimulus situation controlling the response on the second trial. (3) The fact that the 5-second group continues to be inferior suggests that, in this group, an additional effect, response-produced inhibition, continued to depress performance. Figure 10.9 presents results for the groups whose second trials were at several different intervals during the experiment. Again it is obvious that practice at a given spacing of trials reduced the disruptive effect. Successive shifts in the interval, it will be noted, produced less and less disruption. This seems to indicate that learning to respond at one interval (and with one set of response-produced stimuli) generalized to others.

The Generalization-Decrement Hypothesis and Partial Reinforcement

The generalization-decrement hypothesis asumes that the heightened resistance to extinction following partial reinforcement occurs because such training increases the similarity in the stimulus situation between the learning and extinction, with the result that there is less generalization decrement when extinction begins. Specifically, the effects of non-reinforcement persist for partially reinforced subjects, in the form of a stimulus trace, and become a part of the stimulus situation on subsequent trials. For continuously reinforced subjects, by contrast, the stimulus traces controlling behavior on each trial after the first always include the traces of the reinforcement. Thus, in extinction, when all trials are non-reinforced, there is less change in the stimulus situation if training has been with intermittent reinforcement than if it has been with continuous reinforcement. The result should be a greater resistance to extinc-

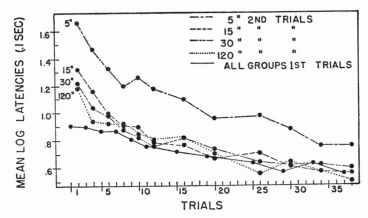

FIGURE 10.8. Learning curves showing the effect of introducing a second trial at varying times after the first. For explanation, see text (Rothkopf, 1955).

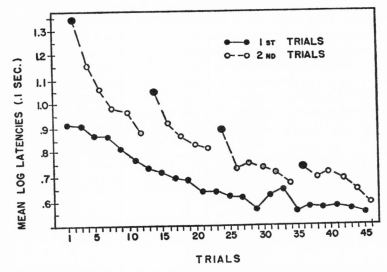

FIGURE 10.9. Learning curves showing decreased response strength with introduction of a second trial when rats are accustomed to running one trial a day. Note that the effect disappears with increased amounts of training. For a more detailed explanation, see text (Rothkopf, 1955).

tion under the former conditions. This theory was devised by Hull but was not published until the appearance in 1949 of V. F. Sheffield's doctoral dissertation.

To test the generalization-decrement explanation, one additional assumption becomes important: that the stimulus traces of reinforcement and non-reinforcement dissipate in time. This assumption means that, with highly distributed training trials, the superiority of partial reinforcement should disappear. In an experiment specifically designed to test this hypothesis, Sheffield ran rats down a straight alley to food; some were reinforced on every trial, others were reinforced randomly on half the trials. Each of these major groups was subdivided; half received trials at the rate of one every 15 seconds (massed group), the other half received trials at the rate of one every 15 minutes (spaced group). In extinction, the previously partially reinforced group showed superior resistance to extinction only when training had been massed. There was no difference between the two spaced-training groups. Similar data in support of the generalization-decrement hypothesis have been obtained by Rubin (1953) who showed that distributing training trials by 40 minutes and also eliminating the complicating effects of secondary reinforcement led to greater resistance to extinction following continuous reinforcement.

Weinstock (1954) and Wilson, Weiss, and Amsel (1955), on the other hand, have obtained evidence against the generalization-decrement hypothesis. The latter investigators attempted to repeat the Sheffield experiment with different drive-reward conditions. They found that partial reinforcement during training always led to greater resistance to extinction, whatever the intertrial interval. Weinstock ran hooded rats to food in an L-shaped maze under several percentages of reinforcement (30, 50, 80, and 100 per cent) and at the rate of one trial a day, which would surely be enough to allow for the complete dissipation of the stimulus traces of the previous trial. Yet in extinction the perform-

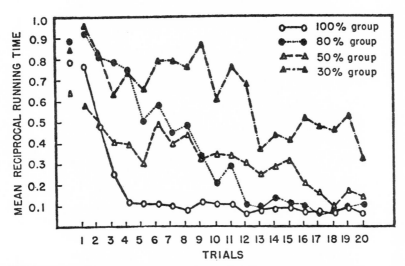

FIGURE 10.10. Extinction curves obtained following training at one trial a day under several percentages of reinforced trials (Weinstock, 1954).

ance of the subjects, expressed in terms of speed of running, was as shown in Figure 10.10. Clearly there were differences in resistance to extinction under conditions where the generalization-decrement theory says that there should be none. To account for this, Weinstock proposed a variety of interference theory which will be discussed in connection with other explanations of the same sort.

INTERFERENCE THEORY

The interference theory assumes that extinction occurs when the CS comes to elicit a response other than the conditioned response. In its original form, the interference theory came from the same sources as inhibition theory, from reflex physiology, particularly the studies of the reduction of one reflex by the elicitation of another, and from Pavlovian conditioning, in which an interference concept appeared in the form of external inhibition. In this connection, Pavlov had pointed out that the presentation of an additional stimulus often led to a response decrement, that the most effective external inhibitors were strong and unusual stimuli which evoked marked investigatory reflexes, and that repeated presentation of the extra stimulus led to a progressive loss of the inhibitory effect. All of these observations suggest a decremental mechanism in which the CR is weakened by a competing response (Guthrie, 1935; Wendt, 1936).

Other evidence favoring such a view is to be found in a small amount of available information regarding the fate, during conditioning and extinction, of the unconditioned response to the conditioned stimulus. Many conditioned stimuli evoke a natural reflex at the outset of conditioning. This response will decrease and disappear as learning proceeds if it is antagonistic to the newly developing conditioned response. If no antagonism exists between the two responses there will be no interference effect. Examples of both results were found in some experiments on conditioned eyelid responses of dogs (Hilgard and D. G. Marquis, 1935). Before training, the CS (a light) evoked a short latency (90 msec.) lid *opening* of very small magnitude and a longer latency (200 msec.) partial lid *closure*. During the acquisition of the conditioned blink, reinforced by an air-puff, there was no significant decrement in the original opening response, which did not interfere because of its short latency. The partial closure response, however, occurred at about the same latency as the conditioned response and, during conditioning, was gradually reduced in frequency, to return during extinction (Figure 10.11).

A similar illustration of interference was given by Pavlov (1932b) in his description of the formation of a conditioned salivary response to the ringing of a bell. The conditioned stimulus originally evoked typical listening movements; the dog turned its head and pricked up its ears.

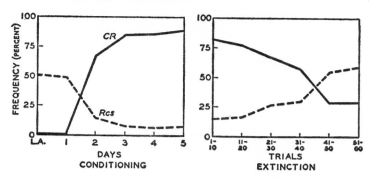

FIGURE 10.11. Antagonistic relation of conditioned response and original bilateral partial lid closure in dogs during conditioning and extinction. The bilateral closure (R_{cs}), present before conditioning, gave way during conditioning to a unilateral closure (CR) of similar latency. The decrease in the bilateral response during conditioning, and increase during extinction, reflect an interference between the two responses (Hilgard and D. G. Marquis, 1935).

The listening movements gradually disappeared as the dog came to respond to the bell by licking its chops and turning toward the food pan. A more dramatic instance of the same phenomenon was afforded by an experiment, also with dogs, in which an electric shock was employed as a signal for the presentation of food (Erofeeva, 1916). The struggling and yelping elicited by the shock were not compatible with the conditioned responses which were acquired on the basis of food reinforcement, and the original responses gradually diminished until after many training sessions almost no trace of them remained.

In other cases the interfering response may be one established in some earlier learning experience which reappears during extinction. Hull (1934b) has described an instance of this sort. Rats were first trained to run down a 20-foot straight alley to receive food. When the alley was lengthened to 40 feet, they showed a tendency to halt at the 20-foot point, but with continued training this tendency disappeared and the animals ran steadily down the entire path. During extinction of the later habit by omission of food reinforcement at the end of the alley, the tendency to halt at the 20-foot point again reappeared. A study by Kellogg and E. L. Walker (1938a) provides still another example. Dogs were trained to lift the right leg to a conditioned stimulus (buzzer) by shocking the right foot. Then the electrodes for shocking were transferred to the left foot, and the conditioning of the left leg response to the same buzzer stimulus was undertaken. The initial effect of the new situation was to intensify the conditioned response of the right leg. In the particular apparatus used the dog was able to lift both legs together by supporting its weight on a wooden stock enclosing its neck, and this double response was common, persisting for as many as 100 trials. Eventually the right leg response disappeared and the dog responded only with the left foot.

Early Arguments against the Interference Theory

The foregoing evidence appears to make a fairly strong case for the interference interpretation and raises a question as to why such a theory was not more generally accepted than it was. There seemed to be several reasons for this: (1) It was not always clear where the competing response came from. Although it could sometimes be identified as an unconditioned response to the CS or the product of learning, explaining why it came to be made in extinction posed a problem. It was necessary to supply some other mechanism to weaken the conditioned response to the point where the interfering response could appear. (2) Once the response did appear its strengthening was a problem for reinforcement theory, since extinction was specifically a non-reinforcement situation. For this reason, pure interference theories were generally held by non-reinforcement theorists. (3) There were certain factual difficulties involving (a) the phenomenon of spontaneous recovery, (b) the effects of distribution of practice, and (c) the influence of drugs.

Spontaneous recovery, according to the interference theory, could occur only to the extent that the competing response is weakened during the interval by forgetting. Experimental data, however, indicate that spontaneous recovery is much more rapid, being measured ordinarily in terms of minutes or hours, whereas forgetting is measured in terms of days or months and in many cases is not appreciable over even longer periods. If extinction occurs through interference by a learned response, the spontaneous recovery would be expected to be just as slow as the forgetting of this newly acquired antagonistic response.

The other lines of evidence against interference theory were derived from the fact that such theorizing held that conditioning and extinction were basically one process, namely, conditioning. As such, it was argued, conditioning and extinction should respond in the same way to experimental variables, such as the distribution of practice; but they do not. Massing of trials results in more rapid extinction, but conditioning is retarded by the same process. Similar evidence for the functional dissimilarity of extinction and conditioning came from the differential effects of certain drugs. Sodium bromide and other drugs of a depressant character retard the rate of conditioning, but accelerate the rate of extinction. Excitants such as caffeine and benzedrine have been found to increase the strength of conditioned responses, but to decrease the rate of extinction.

The conclusion to which this analysis led was that, although interference was possibly a factor in extinction, it was not a complete explanation

(Hilgard and Marquis, 1940). The situation remains much the same to-day. Two major lines of development have occurred since 1940 which make the interference conception potentially more generally acceptable. These are (1) a clearer insight into several possible origins of interfering responses, and (2) the discovery of a variety of sources of reinforcement which might strengthen the interfering response. The initial development of a *type* of theory which deals with these issues was Hull's theory of conditioned inhibition.

Hull's Theory of Conditioned Inhibition

It will be recalled that, among the properties assigned by Hull to his concept of reactive inhibition, were the following three: (1) It was a negative drive which (2) led to the cessation of the response which produced it and (3), after evocation, diminished with inactivity. These three assumptions, together with Hull's commitment to a drive-reduction theory of reinforcement, logically demanded the development of a second inhibitory concept, which he called *conditioned inhibition*, $_sI_R$. The necessity for such a concept comes about as follows: Since I_R is a drive, the reduction of I_R is a reinforcement and, as such, is capable of strengthening any response which precedes it closely in time. In the original development of the I_R concept, a particular response, the cessation of activity, was assumed to occupy such a position. Such reasoning provided the mechanism for the conditioning of a resting response to the stimuli in the learning situation, a resting response evoked by I_R and reinforced by I_R-reduction. Hull referred to this process as the conditioning of I_R to the stimuli in the learning situation, hence the name *conditioned inhibition* and the symbol $_sI_R$.

Formally, Hull proposed a two-factor theory of extinction, in which I_R added to $_sI_R$ to produce total inhibition, $\bar{I}_R$. This, in turn, was hypothesized to subtract from $_sE_R$ and to reduce response strength. Thus, extinction was conceived as occurring because of the development of I_R, a response-localized temporary inhibitory state, and $_sI_R$, a habit, which would be permanent unless specifically subjected to extinction.

The advantages of the $_sI_R$ concept to Hull's theory were very great: (1) It made it possible to explain permanent extinction, which the temporary inhibitory process could not. (2) It made it understandable that spontaneous recovery was seldom complete, in terms of the fact that $_sI_R$ does not dissipate. (3) It provided for the generalization of extinction to similar stimuli, which the effector process, I_R, could not. (4) It made it possible to explain the phenomena of external inhibition and disinhibition by means of a single hypothesis. External inhibition theoretically occurred because the introduction of the novel stimulus during conditioning changed the situation and reduced the strength of the CR through generalization decrement. Disinhibition was explained in the same way. In this case, the new stimulus presented during extinction was assumed to lead, through generalization decrement again, to a reduction in the magnitude of $_sI_R$. This afforded the CR being subjected to extinction the opportunity to reappear. Adding the explanatory power of the $_sI_R$ concept to that of I_R obviously covers many of the most important facts of experimental extinction.

Evaluation of Hull's Theory

In spite of these strengths, Hull's theory has been subjected to very harsh criticism. It is demonstrably weak on methodological grounds (Koch, 1954) and is also inadequate in the face of certain extinction phenomena (Gleitman, Nachmias, and Neisser, 1954). These latter difficulties include the following: (1) It is hard to see how this theory can explain the extinction of relatively effortless responses, such as the GSR, which presumably would develop little if any inhibition. (2) It is equally difficult to understand the complete resistance to extinction of. certain very effortful responses, such as jumping a hurdle to escape shock. (3) Extinction at the rate of one trial a day is probably incapable of treatment in this theory. (4) The facts of latent extinction (see below) and other cases of extinction without responding (for example, under curare) are particularly embarrassing. (5) During extinction, the subject is very often not merely withholding the conditioned response, but is actively doing something else. Monkeys trained to open a door on signal to obtain food show, during extinction, an increase of other activities such as vocalization, biting and pulling the door, and racing about the cage (Wendt, 1936). (6) The facts of extinction following reinforcement schedules are hard to bring in line with this theory.

These and other difficulties lead to the recognition that Hull's inhibition theory, even with the useful addition of the concept of conditioned inhibition, is not an adequate explanation for many of the facts of extinction. On the other hand, the *kind of reasoning* employed by Hull in the development of the concept, $_sI_R$, may represent the form which a more complete extinction theory might take.

Sources of Motivation and Reward in Extinction

In developing the concept of conditioned inhibition, Hull addressed himself to the two most difficult problems facing an interference theory of extinction, the origin of the interfering response and the mechanism by which such a response could be strengthened. The answers to which Hull came, that the response was to a drive state generated in extinction and that reinforcement depends upon the reduction of this drive, provide instructive leads, in spite of the fact that the particular drive and reinforcement mechanism Hull proposed do not seem generally applicable. The suggestion is that it may be fruitful to look for other possible motives and rewards for interfering behavior in the extinction situation. Within this general orientation some of the possibilities which suggest themselves are the following: (1) Responses produced by frustration, reinforced by the escape from frustration; (2) the I_R, I_R-reduction hypothesis proposed by Hull; (3) investigatory behavior, stimulated by novel stimuli; (4) interfering responses resulting from persisting stimuli such as those arising from an irritating injury, distension of the bladder, and sexual excitement (Pavlov, 1927, p. 47), and (5) in fear-conditioning experiments, responses based on fear, reinforced by fear reduction. We shall deal with this possibility first.

The Extinction of Avoidance Behavior

As we have seen, avoidant behavior is often highly resistant to extinction. Yet there are individual exceptions to this, and with an embarrassing frequency, such behavior is found to extinguish after just one or two extinction trials. Occasionally extinction even occurs without any non-reinforced trials at all (Moyer, 1958). This fact, in and of itself, raises the crucial question: Avoidance behavior is generally considered to be motivated by an acquired drive of fear. Does this no-trial "extinction" mean that the fear has somehow disappeared with the end of training? It seems unlikely that this is the case, because animals which "extinguish" precipitously in this way may just previously have been thoroughly conditioned, suggesting the existence of a high level of fear.

The alternative to the unlikely explanation in terms of the spontaneous reduction of fear is that the fear is still there, but that the organism has learned some other response to reduce it. In other words, extinction occurs because the organism has acquired interfering responses. The results obtained by Page (1955) may be cited in support of such an interpretation. In an earlier study, Page and Hall (1953) had trained rats to go from one side of an apparatus to the other to avoid shock and, following training to a criterion, extinguished the rats in two different ways. One (control) group received ordinary extinction trials beginning immediately after conditioning. For the other (experimental) group the first 5 trials were blocked. These animals were put in the starting box on each trial and restrained there for 15 seconds. Following these 5 trials, the experimental animals were extinguished in the same way as the control group. The number of trials required to produce extinction was 38 for the control group and 13 for the experimental group. Quite clearly the restraining procedure had produced some measure of extinction. The question is whether this extinction consisted in the reduction of fear, or whether it involved learning a new interfering response. Page's later (1955) experiment shows that at least part of what is involved is the second of these processes. This study was a repetition of the earlier one in its first stage, and the results were the same. The numbers of trials to extinction for the control and experimental groups were 30 and 8, respectively. In a second stage of the experiment, the rats of both groups were trained to run from the previous goal compartment to the starting box to obtain food, the reasoning being that performance under these circumstances would reflect residual fear still conditioned to the starting box stimuli. If the animals were still afraid of the starting box, they would hesitate before going there to get food. An adequate test of this idea required the use of a second control group which had not previously been shocked in the experimental situation. Results of the experiment suggested that, so far as *fear* was concerned, the blocking procedure had, if anything, increased it. Average latencies (geometric means) for the first 5 training trials estimated from a graph published by Hall were approximately 25, 60, and 110 seconds for the control, normal extinction, and blocked groups respectively. This increase in fear with blocking seems to agree with the report of Solomon and Wynne (1954) that animals showing a long latency (which would be like restraining them) are apt to respond very rapidly on the next several trials, as if their fear had increased.

The important fact for our present discussion is the evidence in this study that fear had not extinguished under the experimental condition, although the avoidant response had. This means that the fear, which originally motivated avoidant behavior, was at least available to instigate other habits, and that fear reduction might conceivably have reinforced them. In short, the possibility exists that, following avoidance conditioning, interfering responses may be reinforced in exactly the same way as the response subjected to extinction originally was.

At least two objections may be raised to this explanation: (1) It is entirely *ad hoc*. Yet it probably makes sense to anyone who has run rats in an avoidance-training experiment. It is fairly common, in extinction, to observe an animal, apparently paralyzed with fear, frozen in a position which makes the avoidant response impossible. And if the animal is still in the same position at the start of the next trial, it will probably not respond. It is as if the animal had been reinforced for immobility by avoiding the shock. Animals responding this way in extinction tend to extinguish precipitously and sometimes after a very few trials. (2) There is no precise explanation of the source of the interfering responses. In this connection it is probably important to recognize that the typical avoidance-training situation is poorly suited to the discovery of the origin of such responses. Denny, Koons, and Mason (1959), however, have obtained data which suggest that, sometimes, these interfering responses may occur as a result of stimulus generalization. These investigators trained rats to jump out of a box to avoid shock. The escape area, for different groups, was either a box like the starting box where shock was administered or an open area which was perceptually much different from the starting box. Extinction was found to be faster when the start and escape areas were similar. It, thus, may be that "safe" responses occurring in the similar escape box generalized to the starting situation and interfered with the avoidance response.

There is also one more general point which needs to be made. The usefulness of this specific explanation is probably limited to the extinction of responses based on negative reinforcers. On common sense grounds it seems unlikely that interfering responses in a situation employing a food reward can ever be reinforced in extinction in the same way as the correct response was during training. This suggests that, if the interference hypothesis outlined above is to have general applicability, it will be necessary to discover, in the extinction procedure, still other sources of motivation and reward.

The Frustration Hypothesis

At the present time frustration produced by the omission of reward seems to provide the most promising lead as to the source of interfering responses in the extinction of positively reinforced habits. The frustration hypothesis differs from the explanation in terms of anxiety described in the previous section in that the motivating and rewarding processes are peculiar to extinction; they are not carried over as a residual from training. In the application of the frustration hypothesis to extinction, the assumption has been that frustration provides the motivation for interfering responses, and that these responses are strengthened by escape from frustration. The assumption that extinction sometimes creates a motivational state of frustration has led to predictions of three general kinds: (1) Since it is assumed to be a motive, frustration should be capable of energizing behavior; that is, performance following frustration should be more vigorous than would have occurred without it. (2) Most if not all motives have associated drive stimuli. Frustrating an animal, therefore, might be expected to produce cues which could be made the condition for some learned act. (3) Since frustration, introspectively, is aversive, analogues to escape and avoidance should be demonstrable.

Possibly the first clear demonstration of the energizing function of frustration on learned behavior was that of Amsel and Roussel (1952). These investigators employed a type of apparatus which might be called a two-stage straight runway. The first stage led to the first goal box; the second stage led to the second goal box. Hungry rats first ran from the starting box to the first goal box, in which they were rewarded with food (or not rewarded when the object was to frustrate them). Then they ran the second stage of the maze to a second goal box where they were always rewarded. The standard procedure consisted of first running a long series of trials with reward available in both goal boxes, and then switching to a situation in which reward was omitted in the first goal box on half the trials (that is, to partial reinforcement). The assumption that non-reward is frustrating leads to the prediction of faster running in the second stage of the maze following non-reinforced trials. The results of the experiment which appear in Figure 10.12 supported this expectation. Alternative

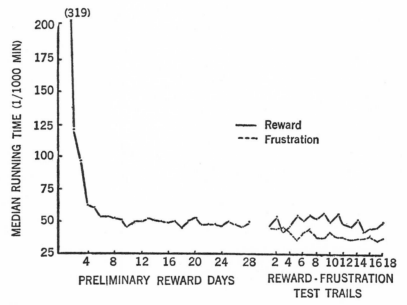

FIGURE 10.12.   Graph showing the effect of frustration upon the running time
of rats (Amsel and Roussel, 1952).

explanations which might be developed, capitalizing upon a lowering of motivation produced by the consumption of the food pellet in the first goal box (Seward, Pereboom, Butler, and Jones, 1957), seem to have been ruled out by later experiments (Wagner, 1959).

The second implication of the assumption of a frustration drive, that frustration will have associated drive stimuli which can serve as cues for learning, has also been investigated. Amsel and J. Ward (1954) performed a series of experiments in which the procedure initially was like that just described. In a final phase of the experiment, however, they removed the second stage of the double runway and replaced it with a T-maze. In this phase of the experiment, the animal first ran from the starting box of the maze to the first goal box where it found food or no food, depending upon the trial. Then it was allowed access to the T-maze. Following reinforcement a left turn led to food; but following non-reinforcement (frustration) a right turn led to food. The animals learned this discrimination in five somewhat different experiments. Whether such data provide evidence favoring the hypothesis that frustration stimuli can control behavior remains a question. Tyler, Marx, and Collier (1959) have argued that the stimulation supplied by the presence or absence of food at the end of the first maze segment, and by the proprioceptive consequences of eating, could easily guide the animals' subsequent right or left turn, and that no added frustration concept is necessary. To test this hypothesis these investigators performed an experiment patterned after that of Amsel and Ward. Among the groups of subjects in the experiment were one which found no food on the "frustration" trials and another which found inaccessible food on the same trials. Tyler, Marx, and Collier proposed that this latter group, if anything, should have been more frustrated than the no-food group, that the frustration stimuli should have been more intense, and that the learning of this group should have been superior to that of the no-food group. As it turned out, however, the no-food group was superior. This led to the conclusion that the discrimination between available and unavailable food was more difficult than that between food and no food, and that performance suffered under the more difficult discrimination. Such an explanation does not invoke the concept of frustration stimuli at all.

Frustration in Extinction

Returning to the question of whether frustration contributes to resistance to extinction, the experiment of Adelman and Maatsch (1956) provides a demonstration that it does. In this study, the response investigated was that of jumping out of a box 10 inches high for rewards of three different kinds, satisfaction of curiosity, food, and release from frustration. For the food-reinforced group the procedure was as follows: After 37 habituation trials without food and without an opportunity to escape from the box, these animals received 30 trials in which jumping out of the box, and up onto a ledge, was reinforced with food. The animals in the group rewarded with the satisfaction of curiosity were treated in the same way, except that there was no food; that is, there were 37 habituation trials and 30 trials in which the rats jumped out of the box. These latter trials, however, were unreinforced except by escape from the box and the possible satisfaction of exploratory and curiosity drives. The frustrated subjects were treated somewhat differently. Instead of 37 habituation trials they received 37 trials in a runway which terminated in the jump box. On these trials they were reinforced with food, in order to provide a basis for frustration later on in the experiment. They were not allowed to jump out of the box. In the later phase, the frustration animals, as usual, ran the straight alley into the box; but in this case they found no food there. They were confined for 5 minutes and then allowed to escape from this theoretically frustrating situation by jumping out of the box.

There were vast differences in the effectiveness of the three reinforcers used in this experiment. One reflection of this is in terms of average latencies during acquisition. For the curiosity-rewarded, food-rewarded, and frustration groups they were, respectively, 168, 20, and 5 seconds. There were even greater differences in extinction behavior. The curiosity-rewarded animals were, in effect, "extinguished" at the end of the acquisition phase of the experiment; the food-reinforced animals required about 60 non-reinforced trials to reach a criterion of extinction. The animals rewarded by escape from frustration, however, showed no signs of extinction in 100 trials. This attests to what appears to be the tremendous strength of escape from frustration as a reinforcement, a point to which we shall return later.

One matter upon which Adelman and Maatsch did not comment was the runway behavior of their animals. Since frustration is aversive, it might be supposed that there would be some tendency to avoid the frustrating situation. W. B. Holder, Marx, E. E. Holder, and Collier (1957) report such an effect. These investigators used a maze situation not unlike that employed by Amsel and Roussel (described above) and a procedure similar to Amsel and Roussel's frustration procedure. They ran three different groups of rats down a 90-inch runway to food, delaying the different groups for different amounts of time halfway down the runway. One group was delayed for 1 second (essentially no delay); two other groups were delayed for 15 and 45 seconds. The effect of the delay was to retard both starting time and running time in the maze section before the delay, as if the delay were an anticipated noxious aversive stimulus. In the second maze segment, the effect was the opposite; both starting time and running time were faster. The second result was similar to that of Amsel and Roussel, with the difference that, in this study, the amount of frustration apparently increased with practice. This last result suggests that either the frustration drive or the responses elicited by it can be conditioned to stimuli in the learning situation.

Some of the most impressive evidence that the frustration produces very persistent learning comes from the work of Maier on "abnoral fixations" in rats. In these studies the procedure is to confront the rat in the Lashley jumping stand (Figure 10.13) with an insoluble problem. Two stimuli (for example, a white circle on a black background and a black circle on a white background) are placed randomly right and left in the apparatus, and responses to each are randomly reinforced half the time.

Under these circumstances, any course of action adopted by the rat leads to reinforcement on half the trials. On the other half of the trials, the animal jumps against a locked door and falls into a net. Maier regards this situation as highly frustrating. Some evidence that he is right appears in the fact that the animals soon develop a marked tendency not to jump at all. When this happens, they are forced to jump by electric shock applied to the feet or by an air jet applied to the base of the tail. These

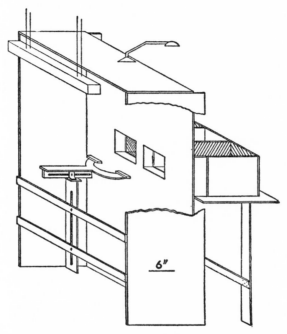

FIGURE 10.13. A modification of the Lashley Jumping Stand used to investigate discrimination learning. A rat must jump from one of the starting platforms at the end of the Y to stimuli placed in the opening of the goal box (Ehrenfreund, 1949).

unpleasant stimuli probably make the situation even more frustrating. In any event, the rats studied by Maier and his colleagues do develop very strong and persistent adjustments to the situation. Most often these are right or left position habits; but sometimes they are other modes of adjustment such as brightness preferences or tendencies to alternate. What has been termed the "compulsive nature" of these habits attests to their strength.

After an abnormal fixation has been established, attempts to break it, by making the problem soluble and consistently reinforcing jumps to one card, fail with about 75 per cent of the animals. They continue to jump right or left unless special "therapeutic" techniques are introduced (Maier and Ellen, 1952; Maier and Klee, 1945). This is in spite of the fact that other evidence may indicate that the animals actually have solved the discrimination problem. This persistence of the maladaptive behavior in spite of the fact that the animal apparently "knows" the solution to the problem is why the fixated behavior is called "compulsive." Feldman (1953), for example, compared the latencies of fixated jumps to the positive and negative cards and found the latencies very much longer to the negative cards after a certain amount of training (Figure 10.14). It has also been found that the animals can respond correctly once the problem is made soluble if the situation is changed so that a response to the correct stimulus does not differ too much from the compulsive, fixated response (Ellen, 1956).

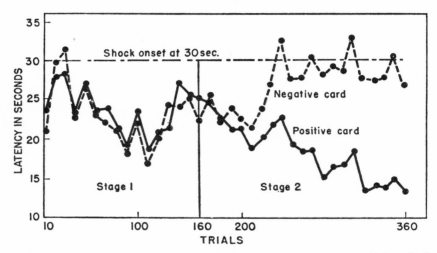

FIGURE 10.14. Evidence for the compulsive nature of fixations. Although the rat jumps in a rigidly stereotyped ("compulsive") way, it is obviously discriminating correctly between positive and negative stimuli as is evidenced by the latencies of response to these two stimuli. Stage 1 was the frustration stage of the experiment designed to produce fixated behavior. In Stage 2, the problem was solvable, but all subjects which solved it were discarded. The data, thus, are for animals behaving in a compulsive way. Subjects not responding in 30 seconds were shocked with an electric "wand" to make them jump (Feldman, 1953).

Maier regards abnormal fixations as a natural (that is, unlearned) consequence of frustration. It seems possible, however, that the great resistance to change of the fixated response comes about because Maier's experimental situations are arranged so that three separate factors are all made to operate in favor of resistance to extinction: (1) Original learning involves partial reinforcement (Wilcoxon, 1952); (2) a noxious, anxiety-evoking stimulus is one of the sources of motivation, an arrangement which often leads to very persistent behavior; and (3) frustration from non-reinforcement and frustration reduction, the factor which Maier stresses, may contribute to the persistence of the response. It seems quite possible that a series of jumps (say) to one side of the apparatus, occurring at first more or less by accident, is powerfully reinforced by these three sets of factors. After that, intermittent reinforcement of the same powerful sort would continue to support the fixated response. This argument, if correct, reduces the abnormal fixations to the expression of perfectly normal processes. There is, however, no suggestion in this that the behavior of Maier's rats is not analogous to human compulsive behavior. It is entirely possible that it is, because human compulsions, too, are no doubt established by normal learning principles.

The Frustration Hypothesis and the Effect of Partial Reinforcement

The explanation of the partial-reinforcement effect in terms of frustration relies upon the fact previously demonstrated, that frustration is capable of strengthening the response which follows non-reinforcement. Since partial reinforcement introduces frustration on non-reinforced trials, this should strengthen behavior during training; and, if the frustration drive is conditionable, as there is reason to believe it is, this conditioned frustration would carry over into extinction and increase the persistence of behavior there. The first part of this interpretation raises a problem: the usual outcome of partial-reinforcement studies is that behavior during training is slightly *weakened*, whereas frustration theory seems to require a strengthening of the response as a result of heightened drive. How is the low performance level during training to be accounted for? Two lines of reasoning, one hypothetical, the other factual, may be offered by the frustration theorist in response to this question: (1) Increased drive theoretically would increase the strength of the organism's responses indiscriminately. If one effect of partial reinforcement is to evoke competing responses, these would be strengthened and the response being measured thereby weakened. (2) In some cases the predicted strengthening effect has occurred. Goodrich (1959) and Weinstock (1958) have both obtained superior performance with partial reinforcement. Weinstock ran 6 groups of approximately 40 rats each for a total of 108 training and 60 extinction trials in a runway at the rate of one trial a day. For different groups, acquisition was under six different schedules of reinforcement. The results of this investigation, thus, provide some of our most substantial data on the effects of partial reinforcement in the runway situation. In terms of numbers of non-reinforced trials in blocks of 12 trials, the schedules of partial reinforcement were 0 (continuous reinforcement), 2, 4, 6, 8, and 10. The response measure employed was speed of leaving the starting box. Briefly the results were these: (1) Early in learning, performance was superior for the groups receiving relatively consistent reinforcement. This result conforms to that obtained in the great majority of other experiments, which have typically used relatively brief periods of training. (2) Later in training, however, the groups receiving infrequent reinforcement performed best. (3) Extinction behavior conformed to the usual pattern. Groups with low proportions of reinforced trials during training continued, throughout extinction, to run faster than groups with high frequencies of reinforcement during training.

The essentials of the explanation of these results, proposed both by Goodrich and by Weinstock, are as follows: The effect of frustration is to increase motivation. Early in training, before the running response is firmly established, the effect of this motivational increase is mainly to strengthen irrelevant and interfering responses produced by frustration. This accounts for the lowered performance under intermittent schedules early in training. With increased practice, however, the interfering responses tend to disappear because they are never reinforced, and the animal's behavior is limited fairly strictly to the running response which is the one most consistently reinforced. When this happens, the motivation produced by frustration has only the correct response to act on, with the result that partial reinforcement now improves performance. In extinction, animals previously trained with continuous reinforcement are frustrated for the first time, producing interfering responses long since abandoned by partially reinforced subjects. As a result, the running response of the former group extinguishes quickly.

The acceptance of such an explanation entails two difficulties. One is a general methodological problem encountered by any version of an interference theory. The interfering responses proposed in an explanation of this sort are in the nature of intervening variables, seldom being observed directly or manipulated experimentally. The study of Adelman and Maatsch (1955), however, suggests that this difficulty is not insurmountable. These investigators ran 30 rats in a straight alley to a food reward and then extinguished them by three different procedures. One subgroup of 10 rats received a normal extinction series in which they were simply confined in the goal box for 20 seconds following the response. A second group was allowed to jump out of the goal box, theoretically escaping from a frustrating situation. The animals in the third group were allowed to escape from the goal box by running back into the alley through the door to the goal box which had been left open. This group was called a "recoil" group. Results of the experiment in terms of running time appear in Figure 10.15. The response elicited in the goal box obviously makes a great deal of difference in determining resistance to extinction. In the recoil group the response following non-reinforcement is directly incompatible with running, and extinction proceeds very rapidly. For the jump group, making a compatible response, extinction is very greatly retarded. The normal group, whose responses were uncontrolled, fell in between.

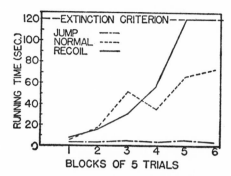

FIGURE 10.15.   Behavior in extinction as determined by the response which occurred to the empty goal box (Adelman and Maatsch, 1955).

These results lend support to an interference interpretation of extinction, but they also raise the other question: How are responses (even incompatible responses) elicited in a goal box able to interfere with the learned response, which is measured elsewhere in the learning situation? Obviously some mechanism must be supplied to make the interferences occur at points in learning when they actually interfere. It is to be noted that this problem is exactly the same as the one previously encountered in connection with incentive motivation. Adelman and Maatsch report, in the case of their jump group, that they sometimes saw jump responses occurring in the starting box. This is some evidence that responses to non-reinforcement do generalize to other portions of the maze. It is of some interest that this took place in spite of the fact that the goal box and starting box were quite different, suggesting that general situational cues, or perhaps internal cues, provided the basis for generalization.

EXPECTANCY THEORY

Tolman's original statement of the expectancy hypothesis was that conditioning consisted of the establishment of an expectancy that the UCS will follow the CS, and that for extinction to occur, all that was necessary was to prove to the animal that this correlation no longer existed. As with other aspects of expectancy theory, the development of this counter-expectancy was assumed to be a perceptual matter and not to require the performance of an overt response. From this general orientation, two hypotheses have emerged which have guided much of the research conceived in the expectancy framework: (1) the discrimination hypothesis, and (2) the prediction that a latent-extinction effect comparable to latent learning is possible.

The Discrimination Hypothesis

In the same paper in which they offered the response-unit hypothesis to account for the effects of partial reinforcement upon extinction, Mowrer and Jones (1945) also outlined what has come to be known as the discrimination hypothesis. According to this hypothesis, extinction is retarded by any acquisition procedure which makes it difficult for the subject to distinguish between training and extinction. The conditions of training which have since come to be regarded as making such discriminations easy are (1) continuous reinforcement, (2) regular patterns of reinforcement in the partial-reinforcement situation, and (3) alterations in the stimulus conditions at the beginning of extinction.

1. *The Discrimination Hypothesis and Partial Reinforcement.* One of the original arguments in favor of the expectancy theory was based on the effect of partial reinforcement. In terms of the discrimination hypothesis, this argument is that extinction following partial reinforcement is slow because the expectancy developed during learning includes the subexpectancy that reinforcement will not occur on every trial. For this reason the beginning of extinction, after which reinforcement never occurs, is more difficult to perceive than when extinction occurs after consistent reinforcement. Although this reasoning leads to predictions which fit the facts, it provided no critical support for expectancy theory because other theories were also able to explain the effects of partial reinforcement with the aid of the concepts of secondary reinforcement and generalization decrement. Probably for this reason, the expectancy theorist was led to look elsewhere for evidence in support of his position.

2. *The Effect of Patterned Reinforcement.* Within a partial-reinforcement schedule, reinforcements may be administered either irregularly or regularly, according to some pattern, such as on every second, third, or fourth trial. In general, extinction following irregular reinforcement is much slower than following regular reinforcement. Longnecker, Krauskopf, and Bitterman (1952) conditioned the galvanic skin responses of two groups of human subjects, using two different partial-reinforcement schedules. One schedule omitted shock on half of the trials in an irregular order; the other schedule consisted of a regular alternation of reinforced and non-reinforced trials. Following 22 trials administered according to these schedules there were 30 extinction trials. Three important results came from this study: (*a*) During training, the performance of the ran-

dom group was somewhat superior to that of the alternation group, although this effect was less than has been obtained in other studies. (*b*) During training, the magnitude of the conditioned GSR alternated appropriately in the case of the regular alternation group, being large on shock trials and small on non-shock trials. No such effect appeared in the random group. (*c*) During extinction, performance was much superior in the group conditioned on the random schedule. Tyler, Wortz, and Bitterman (1953) and Capaldi (1958) have obtained essentially the same results in experiments where rats were required to run down a straight runway and then jump to a goal box.

The conditioned eyelid response also displays greater resistance to extinction following an irregular schedule of reinforced trials than following a regular schedule, at least when the measure of performance is the percentage of conditioned responses (Kimble, Mann, and Dufort, 1955). With measures based upon magnitude of the response the extinction curves have been found to differ in form following irregular and regular (single alternation and double alternation) reinforcement, making resistance to extinction difficult to compare (Grant, Riopelle, and Hake, 1950). In the eyelid conditioning experiment, there has been no tendency for the conditioned response to follow the pattern of reinforced and non-reinforced trials in spite of the fact the subjects typically are able to describe the sequence. The reason for this may be that the short intervals usually employed in eyelid conditioning studies effectively preclude the occurrence of mediating responses necessary for such matching of response to reinforcement condition.

3. *Changes in the Learning Situation.* A final line of evidence favoring the discrimination hypothesis comes from experiments directed against the explanation of the effect of partial reinforcement in terms of secondary reinforcement (Bitterman, Fedderson, and Tyler, 1953; Elam, Tyler, and Bitterman, 1954). In the first of these experiments rats were trained, on a combination elevated runway and single window jump stand, to run to the end of the end of the runway and jump to food. They were reinforced on 50 per cent of the trials and not on the others on an irregular pattern. During the acquisition phase of the experiment, there were two main groups. One, a discrimination group, received reinforcements and non-reinforcements, respectively, in goal boxes of different colors (black or white). The other main group, a nondiscrimination group, entered the same goal box on both reinforced and non-reinforced trials. In extinction each of the main groups was divided into two subgroups. One of these, a secondary-reinforcement subgroup, was extinguished using the goal box previously associated with reinforcement. The other group, a non-secondary-reinforcement subgroup, was extinguished with the previously negative goal box in the case of the discrimination group, and with a new goal box, opposite in color to that used in training, in the

case of the nondiscrimination group. The results obtained from the four groups thus produced appear in Table 21. Considering first the results

TABLE 21

GEOMETRIC MEAN OF TIME PER TRIAL (SECONDS) IN
15-DAY EXTINCTION PERIOD
(Bitterman, Fedderson, and Tyler, 1953)

| | | Extinction Condition | |
		Secondary Reinforcement	Non-secondary Reinforcement
Training	Discrimination	38	30
Condition	Nondiscrimination	27	40

for the nondiscrimination groups, it is clear that the usual effect of secondary reinforcement appeared. The rats run to the previously reinforced goal box ran faster. In the case of the discrimination groups, however, the results were the opposite. Resistance to extinction was reduced by using the previously reinforced goal box.

The discrimination theory handles these results, without reference to the concept of secondary reinforcement, as follows: For the nondiscrimination groups, the introduction of the new goal box changes the situation markedly, leading to easy discrimination of the difference between training and extinction. For the discrimination groups, entering the previously reinforced goal box, where there is now no food, is a much more "impressive" thing to the rat than entering the always negative goal box where there never was any food. This again makes it easy for the rat to recognize that some important change in procedures has occurred.

Latent Extinction

Latent extinction (sometimes called indirect extinction, goal extinction, or non-response extinction) refers to a reduction in response strength, achieved without the occurrence of the response itself, by exposing the animal to the goal situation in the absence of reinforcement. It is the parallel, in extinction, of latent learning discussed in Chapter 8. Latent extinction seems unexplainable in terms of inhibition theory but offers no difficulty to expectancy theory. Experimental demonstrations of latent extinction typically begin by teaching the animal some response such as running a straight maze (Seward and Levy, 1949), pressing the bar in the Skinner box (Coate, 1956), making the correct choice in a brightness discrimination situation (Deese, 1951), or running a maze (W. L. Brown and Halas, 1957a, 1957b, 1957c; Moltz, 1955). After such training, animals in an experimental group are placed directly into the empty goal box a number of times. Those in a control group are placed elsewhere, without reward, or merely handled. The demonstration of latent extinction consists in the fact that the subjects in the experimental group reach a criterion of extinction more rapidly than animals without the latent-extinction experience. Moltz' experiment is typical. Sixty rats received 40 trials in a T-maze and then were extinguished in one of three ways. One (control) group was subjected to ordinary extinction. The other two groups received four one-minute latent-extinction trials in the goal box. For one of these groups the food cup, a powerful secondary reinforcer, was present during latent extinction. For the other latent-extinction group, it was not. In subsequent tests these groups displayed quite different resistance to extinction. The numbers of correct responses required to meet a criterion of extinction were 4.7 for the control group, 5.4 for the group given latent extinction without the food cup, and 2.2 for the group given latent extinction with the food cup. The only significant differences were between the group subjected to latent extinction with the food cup present and the other two groups.

The results of this experiment are important in the following ways: (1) They provide a typical illustration of latent extinction. (2) They suggest that one of the important variables determining whether or not latent extinction occurs is the discriminability of the positive and negative goal boxes. The evidence for this is in the fact that the performances of the control group and the no-food-cup group were not different. Presumably this is because the positive goal box without the food cup is indistinguishable from the negative goal box which never contained one. Studies which failed to obtain latent extinction (Bugelski, Coyer, and Rogers, 1952; Scharlock, 1954) have employed situations where this discrimination was difficult to make. Denny and Ratner (1959) found that the elimination of distinctive environmental cues destroyed the phenomenon of latent extinction. (3) They indicate the possibility of explaining latent extinction in terms of the loss, through extinction, of the value of goal-box stimuli as secondary reinforcers.

The results of an experiment by Moltz and Maddi (1956) seem to attest to the essential validity of such an interpretation. These investigators gave 60 rats training in a straight alley runway with a food reward. In this part of the experiment the animals received 7 reinforced and 3 non-reinforced trials per day. The goal boxes on the two kinds of trials were distinctly different. The purpose of this training was to provide the goal-box stimuli with strong secondary reinforcing power. In the second part of the experiment, half of the animals received four latent-extinction trials in the previously positive goal box. Different subgroups received these trials under 0, 22, or 44 hours of food deprivation. The other half of the animals were divided into subgroups and subjected to the same deprivation conditions, but they were given no latent-extinction training. Finally all animals received 15 trials in a T-maze with the positive and negative goal boxes placed on the two ends. The results obtained in this portion of the experiment appear in Table 22. It will be noted that the control groups

TABLE 22

MEAN NUMBERS OF RESPONSES TO PREVIOUSLY POSITIVE GOAL BOX
FOR EACH GROUP

(after Moltz and Maddi, 1956)

Deprivation During Experimental Treatment	Experimental Groups (Latent Extinction)	Control Groups (No Latent Extinction)
0 hours	9.30	9.30
22 hours	7.10	9.90
44 hours	6.30	9.80

all showed evidence that the positive goal box was secondarily reinforcing. The latent-extinction procedure, however, had destroyed the secondary reinforcing value of the goal box, except for the satiated group.

Studies of latent extinction in the Skinner situation have also consisted of direct attempts to extinguish the secondary reinforcing value of the stimuli associated with the delivery of primary reinforcement. Ratner (1956)[3] trained rats to press a bar to obtain water which was delivered with the characteristic click of the magazine. Following this training, different groups of animals received three different treatments. One experimental group (click group) was subjected to a latent-extinction procedure in which the empty magazine was operated repeatedly to extinguish responses to the click. The bar was absent from the box during this procedure. A second group (no-click group) was placed in the Skinner box for the same amount of time as the click group, with the bar removed. In this group, however, the magazine did not operate, and the animals' approach responses were extinguished in the absence of the click. A third (control) group was merely handled during the time the two experimental procedures were carried out. On the following day all animals

TABLE 23

MEAN NUMBER OF BAR PRESSES AND DIPPER APPROACHES
FOR EACH GROUP DURING EXTINCTION

Group	Bar Presses	Dipper Approaches
Control	87.7	99.2
Click	65.2	65.8
No-click	72.3	60.5

[3] See Coate (1956) and Rozeboom (1959) for similar studies with similar results.

were extinguished. Each bar depression produced the click during this phase of the experiment, and it was possible to obtain separate records of bar presses and dipper approaches. The results of the experiment appear in Table 23. Quite clearly the two experimental groups produced fewer responses of both kinds than the control group. There is, however, no good evidence for a difference between the two experimental groups themselves. This indicates that the important process in latent extinction, at least in this situation, is the elimination of the approach response to food.

CONCLUDING OBSERVATIONS

The chief impression left by a survey of the literature on extinction is one of enormous complexity. A part of the explanation for this seems to be a great lack of parametric data in the field. With certain notable exceptions, the investigations cited have intended to support or refute some particular theoretical point; relatively few of them have been designed to determine the effect upon extinction of some variable throughout a substantial portion of its manipulable range.

Another reason for the impression of complexity is that the variables controlling extinction seem to interact in ways which limit the generality of statements about extinction. This occurs to a greater extent than in the control of learning. In certain cases these interactions create a situation in which the manipulation of a single variable has one effect under one set of conditions and the opposite effect under another. A few examples of this have been cited earlier in the chapter: (1) Massed trials may increase or decrease resistance to extinction, depending upon considerations relating to generalization decrement. (2) Resistance to extinction is usually greater following partial reinforcement; but it may be less if secondary reinforcement and generalization decrement are adequately controlled, or (3) if the partial-reinforcement schedule involved a regular succession of reinforced and non-reinforced trials. (4) Extinction, with secondary reinforcers present, is usually retarded, but it may be hastened if conditions are arranged to make the presence of the secondary reinforcer during extinction increase the ease of making a discrimination between training and extinction. Some additional interactive complexities have been demonstrated in an experiment by Hulse (1958) who studied the effects upon runway performance of a number of variables among which were quantity and certainty of reinforcement. In extinction he found that the effect of the partial-reinforcement schedule depended upon the amount of reinforcement. Resistance to extinction following partial reinforcement was much greater if the amount of reinforcement was large than if it was small. Similarly, large amounts of reinforcement increased resistance to extinction following partial reinforcement, but *decreased* it following continuous reinforcement.

A second impressive suggestion in the literature on extinction is that extinction is not a unique phenomenon. Instead it is simply the result of the operation of factors which may have exactly the same influence during reinforced practice. Inhibition, frustration, alterations in the stimulus situation, interfering responses, and changes in secondary reinforcement are all conditions which, in this chapter or elsewhere, have been treated as operating during learning as well as in extinction. This is not to say that the principles of learning as they are now understood are capable of handling the facts of extinction. But it seems a mistake to ignore variables known to be important in learning, when it is perfectly obvious that extinction involves the manipulation of a number of them.

Adopting this line of reasoning inevitably means that it is no longer possible to hold a simple one-factor theory of extinction. In general, investigators in the field seem to have accepted this conclusion. With a few exceptions, there are no longer any proponents of the classical inhibition, expectancy, or interference theories of extinction. This has come about in two ways. As in the field of learning, there have been theoretical concessions on both sides with the result that the lines separating rival theories have become blurred. For example, S-R theory has assimilated latent extinction with relative ease, reducing it to the extinction of secondary reinforcement and sometimes specifically evoking the $r_G \longrightarrow s_G$ mechanism as a part of the explanation. Beyond this, theorists of all schools have tended to increase the number of principles used to explain extinction. Individuals sympathetic to a Hullian position have incorporated the concepts of frustration and generalization decrement into their theories; and at least some expectancy theorists have admitted the possible usefulness of the concept of reactive inhibition (Robinson and Capaldi, 1958).

SUMMARY

The term *extinction* refers to the gradual weakening and eventual disappearance of the CR which occurs if the CS is repeatedly presented without reinforcement. Since conditioned responses show little or no tendency to be forgotten with the mere passage of time, it is evident that extinction must be the result of some active process associated with nonreinforcement. The nature of this process is a matter upon which there are many very different opinions. Hypotheses which have been advanced to explain extinction have employed concepts as varied as those of inhibition, response competition, discrimination, frustration, and generalization decrement. The first two of these are older views of extinction. The others have appeared as it has become increasingly clear that the classical theories are inadequate.

Inhibition Theory

The inhibition hypothesis maintains that every response elicited during extinction adds to the strength of an inhibitory tendency which opposes that response. Furthermore it is assumed that inhibition increases with the number of responses and the effortfulness of the response, and that it dissipates or decays with rest. Experimental predictions to which this theory leads are the following: (1) Extinction will occur more rapidly with massed than with distributed extinction trials. (2) The rate at which extinction progresses will vary directly with the effortfulness of the response. (3) Spontaneous recovery will occur as inhibition dissipates with rest. Experimental evidence supports these predictions in a general way, but it also shows that some of the details of the evidence are not as inhibition theory requires: (1) Sometimes widely spaced extinction trials produce faster extinction than massed extinction trials. (2) Spontaneous recovery seldom restores response strength to the level it had attained prior to extinction. (3) Resistance to extinction is greater following partial reinforcement than following continuous reinforcement. These facts are sufficient to show that the explanation of extinction will require assumptions in addition to those made by inhibition theory.

Generalization Decrement

The first additional assumption adopted by the inhibition theorists was that of generalization decrement. If it is recognized that the conditioned response is, to some degree, controlled by stimuli provided by the mere fact of being in the experimental situation and by traces of the rewards and the responses which occurred on previous trials, it becomes clear that changing any of these stimuli would lead to a loss of response strength. For example, altering the time between trials in extinction should lead to relatively more rapid extinction than would be obtained had the conditions of distribution used in training been maintained. Experiments performed to test this prediction have supported it. Other evidence from investigations carried out in connection with partial reinforcement and spontaneous regression indicate that the concept of generalization decrement is of considerable value in the understanding of extinction. As was true of inhibition theory, however, it does not provide a complete explanation of extinction.

Interference Theory

The idea which is basic to the interference theory of extinction is that of response competition. Extinction occurs, according to this theory, when a new and incompatible response is conditioned to the CS. Although evidence for such an interpretation has existed for a long time, the difficulties with interference theory have always been very great. Some of these difficulties are the following: (1) The origin of the interfering response requires explanation. (2) Even if the source of the interfering response were known, it would still be difficult to account for the strengthening of this response during nonreinforced extinction trials. (3) The effects of the distribution of practice, and the phenomenon of spontaneous recovery, are difficult to explain by the interference hypothesis. Facts like these led Hull to develop a two-factor explanation of extinction which combined inhibition theory with a very limited form of interference theory.

According to Hull's theory unreinforced practice results in the development of reactive inhibition which is a negative drive capable of instigating the response of resting. Resting, however, leads to the dissipation of reactive inhibition. The reduction of inhibition is reinforcing (drive reducing) with the result that a conditioned resting response is acquired during extinction. This conditioned resting response (conditioned inhibition) interferes with the CR and produces a permanent extinction.

The Frustration Hypothesis

Although Hull's two-factor theory contains many defects, the strategy which Hull adopted in the development of that theory seems very promising. In more general terms the idea is that it may be fruitful to look for other motives and sources of reward in the extinction situation which may instigate and reinforce interfering responses. In the case of avoidance learning, the acquired fear established during learning may function in this way. In situations where extinction occurs because of the omission of a positive reinforcer, the frustration hypothesis is applicable.

The basic assumption in the frustration hypothesis is that the omission of a positive reinforcer is frustrating. Frustration is conceived as a drive which (a) energizes behavior and (b) produces interfering responses which might interfere with the conditioned response. Experiments on frustration have provided evidence that frustration is a drive and that the responses produced by this drive determine the resistance of a response to extinction. Among the accomplishments of a frustration theory, which takes account of specific responses, is an explanation of the great resistance to extinction of habits established under conditions of partial reinforcement.

Expectancy Theory

The expectancy theorist's explanation of extinction resembles interference theory in that it involves new learning. In expectancy theory, however, the assumption is that extinction occurs when the organism develops an expectancy that reinforcement will no longer follow the CS or the occurrence of the instrumental response. As with the expectancy theorist's treatment of learning in general, perceptual variables occupy a position of central importance in this theory. This emphasis has led to the specific hypothesis, the discrimination hypothesis, to explain the major phenomena of extinction. The essential point in this hypothesis is that conditions which make it difficult for the organism to recognize that training has ended and extinction begun will lead to great resistance to extinction. Among the conditions leading in this direction are partial reinforcement and irregularly patterned reinforcement. Changes in the physical situation with the beginning of extinction should hasten extinction. This idea is obviously the same as part of what is stressed in the generalization-decrement hypothesis.

Just as expectancy theory leads to the prediction of latent learning, it also predicts an analogous phenomenon of latent extinction. Experiments on latent extinction have often been conducted using mazes. After animals have mastered the maze, they are extinguished with one of two procedures. Animals in a control group are extinguished in the normal way. Those in an experimental group receive a series of trials in the empty goal box before receiving regular extinction trials. The majority of these studies have shown that the animals in the experimental group extinguish more rapidly than those in the control group. The expectancy theorist attributes this result to negative expectancies developed through the experience with the empty goal box. S-R theorists have explained the fact of latent extinction in terms of the extinction of secondary reinforcement.

·11·

Generalization

WHEN AN ORGANISM has been conditioned to respond to a particular stimulus it can be shown that other similar stimuli will also elicit the response, even though these other stimuli have not been used in training. This ability of different stimuli to evoke a conditioned response is known as *stimulus generalization*. There is also a comparable phenomenon on the response side which is called *response generalization*. A stimulus which has come, through training, to elicit a particular response may, under some circumstances, elicit a related response without special training. It is evident that generalization is important in the adaptive economy of the organism because environmental situations never recur in nature without at least some changes. If situations had to be repeated in absolutely identical form in order for previous experience to be effective, learned adjustments would be of little service.

The basic facts of stimulus and response generalization are not limited to conditioned reactions, but are true of unconditioned reflexes and of complex voluntary behavior. Every response is elicitable, not just by one stimulus, but by a class of similar stimuli. Correspondingly, every stimulus elicits, not just one response, but one of a class of responses. In the case of unlearned reflexes, the degree of generalization is determined by the inherited structural organization of the nervous system. With learned responses, however, the degree of generalization can be modified by experience. The study of the generalization of conditioned responses provides the opportunity of determining the fundamental principles of such modification in simple, experimentally controlled situations.

DEMONSTRATIONS OF STIMULUS GENERALIZATION

A brief summary of some of the studies demonstrating stimulus generalization appears in Table 24. These experiments are ones which were designed merely to show the existence of the phenomenon. Investigations involving other parameters or attempts to establish some particular view of the nature of generalization have, for the most part, been omitted. Even these limited materials, however, suggest certain important points

TABLE 24

STUDIES DEMONSTRATING GENERALIZATION

Experimenter	Subjects, Response, Method	Stimuli	Results
Anrep (1923)	Dogs, classically conditioned salivation.	Tactile stimuli in different locations on dog's body.	Demonstrated generalization. Amount of salivation decreased with distance of test stimulus from CS.
Noble (1950)	Human, GSR, classical conditioning.	Nonsense syllables, *volvap* (CS), *nostaw* (generalization stimulus) spoken silently by the subject.	Demonstrated generalization to subvocal stimulus.
Hovland (1937a)	Human, GSR, classical conditioning.	Pitch. 4 tones separated by 25 j.n.d.'s and equated for loudness.	Demonstrated generalization for conditioning and extinction. Decelerated decreasing function.
Littman (1949)	Human, GSR, classical conditioning.	Same as Hovland, above.	Demonstrated generalization. Function flatter than Hovland's.
Philip (1947)	Human, judgment of "color-mass".	11 cards with different proportions of green and blue dots.	Demonstrated generalization.
Grandine and Harlow (1948)	Monkeys, Wisconsin General test apparatus (see p. 386).	Height and brightness; 5 values of each. Training stimulus paired with all for test. 4 steps of increasing difference from training point.	Demonstrated generalization; function not different from a straight line; trend (not significant) for steeper generalization following non-reinforcement.
Brown (1942)	Rats, non-reinforced running response to food. Measured in terms of latency and strength of pull.	Brightness. Three lights. 0.02, 5, and 5,000 foot candles. Extremes used as training stimuli for different groups.	Generalization demonstrated. Steeper gradient for higher intensity. Gradient steepened during extinction.
Schlosberg and Solomon (1943) (Experiment I only)	Rats. Latency of choice response following discrimination training on black-white discrimination, white positive.	Brightness. 5 pairs of stimuli, of which previously negative was always one: white-black; light gray-black; midgray-black; dark gray-black.	Mean log latency a linear increasing function of brightness.

TABLE 24—*Continued*

Experimenter	Subjects, Response, Method	Stimuli	Results
Miller and Dollard (1941)	Imitative response in rats and children.	Leader's "color" changed white to black rat; white to Negro leader.	Demonstrated generalization.
Watson and Rayner (1920)	Child. Fear response conditioned to rat.	Other furry objects, Santa Claus mask, fur coat, cotton.	Demonstrated generalization.
Brown, Bilodeau, and Baron (1951); Brown, Clarke, and Stein (1958)	Voluntary key pressing response in human subjects.	Lights arranged on a spatial dimension.	Demonstrated generalization.
Bass (1958)	Verbal "betting" responses of human subjects.	Silhouettes of different shades of gray.	Demonstrated generalization.
Grant and Schiller (1953)	Human, GSR, classical.	Height (area) of rectangles. 3 points above and 3 below CS.	Demonstrated generalization. Function convex upward for lower stimuli. For higher shows an inversion. Suggestion of stimulus intensity dynamism effect.
Bass and Hull (1934)	Human, GSR, classical.	Place on body, shoulder, back thigh, ankle. Extreme spots CS. Tested at other points.	Demonstrated generalization and generalization of extinction.
Hovland (1937b)	Human, GSR, classical.	Loudness. 4 tones separated by 50 j.n.d.'s.	Demonstrated generalization. Loudness gradient flatter than pitch gradient.
Guttman and Kalish (1956)	Instrumental pecking response in pigeons. Measure: rate of response.	Hues. 11 wave lengths varying over a range of 70 mu on either side of CS wavelength. 4 different CS's.	Demonstrated generalization. Function essentially linear to operant level. Demonstration of generalization in individual subjects.
Grice and Saltz (1950)	Extinction of door pushing response in rats.	Areas of circles. Training at 20- and 79- square-centimeter circles. Tests at 20-, 32-, 50-, 63-, (one group only) and 79- square-centimeter circles.	Generalization gradients different for tests to larger and smaller circles.

and raise issues to which we will return later. (1) Generalization has been demonstrated in many species and in a variety of conditioning situations, both classical and instrumental. No striking differences in generalization appear to characterize habits established in these two ways. (2) In many of these demonstrations, *generalization gradients* have appeared, with response strength decreasing in a regular fashion with increasing differences between test and training stimuli. (3) Generalization gradients have been demonstrated for individual subjects (Guttman and Kalish, 1956), establishing the reality of the phenomenon as a process characteristic of individual organisms. At one time there was good reason to question this point (Razran, 1949). (4) The form which generalization gradients most often have taken has been of the concave upward variety. Gradients of other forms, however, have been obtained. Such variables as the schedule of reinforcement during training, number of previous generalization tests, the dimension involved, and individual differences have all been shown to influence the shape of the gradient. Consequently statements of the exact form of some hypothetical universal gradient are unwarranted or, at best, premature. (5) The generalization of extinction has also been demonstrated. This fact has made it possible to construct a theory of discrimination learning which has been very influential. This is the theory developed by Spence, in which the concepts of the generalization of excitation and inhibition are basic. We will describe this theory in the next chapter.

Methods of Investigation

Hovland's (1937a) study of the generalization of the conditioned galvanic skin response along a pitch dimension provides a reference experiment. In this investigation, four tones were selected by psychophysical methods as separated in pitch by 25 just noticeable differences (j.n.d.'s). The frequencies chosen were 153, 468, 1000, and 1967 cycles. The tones, after being equated for loudness, represented a scale of approximately equal units on a dimension of pitch similarity, as judged by the verbal reports of subjects. One group of subjects was conditioned to the lowest tone and then tested, in extinction, on the others to determine the magnitude of the generalized responses. A second group was conditioned to the highest tone and, afterwards, tested on the three lower tones. Permutational orders of presentation made possible the pooling of the results obtained from all subjects into a single curve representing the generalization of tones separated in pitch by 25, 50, and 75 j.n.d.'s. The curve, reproduced in Figure 11.1, shows that the degree of generalization decreases progressively with greater differences in pitch, producing, when plotted, a concave gradient.

This study illustrates the characteristic features of experiments on

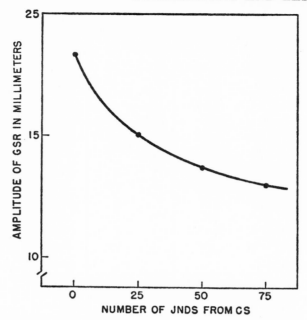

FIGURE 11.1. Stimulus generalization gradient for the galvanic skin response
conditioned to a tone of 1000 cycles per second (Hovland, 1937a).

stimulus generalization. The typical investigation begins by conditioning
subjects to a CS of some particular value. To test for generalization, other
stimuli are then presented, usually in extinction. Unless separate subgroups are extinguished at each stimulus value to be tested, difficulties
arise at this point. Since the tests are carried out in extinction, and since
the effects of extinction generalize, the measure obtained at a given stimulus point will be reduced by the effects of extinction trials carried out
with the other stimuli. This is the reason for the permutational orders of
stimuli during the test. They are employed in the hope that such effects
will be balanced out and that the gradient obtained will provide a faith-
ful representation of the underlying function.

Other possible procedures for conducting generalization tests might
involve the use of reinforced or non-reinforced trials, with the test stimuli
interspersed among the training trials with the CS. These methods introduce somewhat different difficulties. If reinforced test trials were used,
the subjects would soon learn that they were reinforced and come to
respond to the test stimuli in the same way as to the CS. If non-reinforced
test trials were used the subjects would begin to discriminate the reinforced trials from the generalization tests, and this would complicate the
measures. In addition the use of non-reinforced trials imposes a partial-
reinforcement schedule upon the training situation, and partial reinforce-

ment is known to alter the form of the generalization gradient (see below).

The Generalization of Extinction

Many of the classical studies of generalization (Bass and Hull, 1934; Hovland, 1937a, 1937b) included tests for the generalization of extinction. In the experiment described above, Hovland investigated the generalization of extinction in a separate group of subjects. CR's were first established in equal strength to the four frequencies. Extinction was then carried out for half of the subjects by presenting the highest tone without reinforcement. For the other half of the subjects, extinction was carried out with the lowest tone. The generalization of extinction was determined by the amount of reduction of response to the other frequencies. The curve of generalization of extinction was found to be similar to that for the generalization of conditioning, as is shown in Figure 11.2.

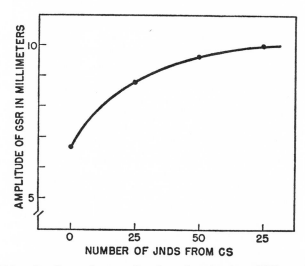

FIGURE 11.2. Gradient of generalization of extinction. GSR was conditioned to all tones and then extinguished to an extreme tone. Finally tests were conducted with all tones (Hovland, 1937a).

More recently Kling (1952) has investigated the generalization of extinction in an instrumental situation in the following way: Groups of rats were trained to respond to either of two stimuli to obtain food. The stimuli were circles of metal of different sizes. For one major group one stimulus had an area of 79 square centimeters and the other stimulus was 20, 32, 50, or 79 square centimeters in area. For the other major group one stimulus had an area of 20 square centimeters and the other had an area of 20, 32, 50, or 79 square centimeters. It is important to remember that the animals were reinforced for responding to both stimuli. In all, then, there were eight groups, trained to respond to the following pairs of stimuli: 79-20, 79-32, 79-50, 79-79, 20-20, 20-32, 20-50, 20-79. Following such training, the response to the 79-square-centimeter circle was extinguished for the subjects in one of the major groups. The response to the 20-square-centimeter circle was extinguished in the other. Then the animals were tested on the other member of the original pair. Note that the more similar the two original stimuli, the more generalization of extinction should interfere with responding in this test. The results of the experiment, presented in Figure 11.3, fully confirm this expectation. The

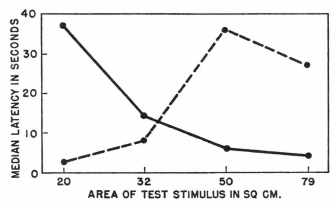

FIGURE 11.3. The generalization of extinction of an instrumental response in rats (Kling, 1952).

response measure plotted there is median latency on the test trial. The decreasing function is for subjects in the four groups which shared the small stimulus. The increasing function is for those which had had the large stimulus as one of the pair. Generalization of extinction is clearly in evidence under both sets of conditions. A question of great theoretical importance concerns the similarities and differences between the forms of the generalization gradients of learning and extinction. The early classical conditioning studies (Bass and Hull, 1934; Hovland, 1937a) suggested that the two gradients may be quite similar in terms of shape and breadth. Kling's results, when compared with those of Grice and Saltz (see below) using the same apparatus, lead to the same impression.

VARIABLES CONTROLLING THE AMOUNT OF STIMULUS GENERALIZATION

With the validity of the phenomenon of stimulus generalization established, we may turn to the question of the variables which control the degree of generalization. Since these variables are almost always ones which are introduced during training, they characteristically affect the strength of response during acquisition as well as the range, slope, or shape of the generalization gradient.

Generalization and the Number of Reinforcements

With continuing reinforcement, the range of stimulus generalization shows an initial increase. Beyond this point, it has sometimes been found to show a further increase (Margolius, 1955) and sometimes to show a decrease (Beritov, 1924, p. 123; Hovland, 1937d). On the basis of a summary of 67 Pavlovian experiments, Razran (1949) suggests that the initial increase may be followed by a decrease and then a second increase. The magnitudes of response strength providing the basis for this conclusion are small, however, and the reality of the details of this postulated function is, by no means, certain.

Most of the results of studies of the acquisition function for generalized response strength are complicated by the fact that they are presented in terms of *relative generalization* as opposed to *absolute generalization*. The distinction between these two terms is as follows: Absolute generalization is response strength expressed directly in terms of the measure employed in the experiment. Relative generalization is generalized response strength expressed as a percentage of response strength to the CS. The relationship between these measures can be made more concrete by reference to the results of Hovland's (1937d) experiment on the conditioned GSR. The results of that experiment, presented in these two different ways, appear in Figures 11.4 and 11.5. Figure 11.4 is a representation of absolute generalization. It depicts the changes in the amplitudes of reinforced and generalized responses as a function of practice. The upper curve shows the (ungeneralized) amplitude of response to the CS, and the lower curve depicts the changes in magnitude of the generalized responses to test stimuli. This way of presenting the data suggests that generalized response strength increases up to about 16 trials and then levels off. Figure 11.5 presents the same data in terms of relative generalization. The values in the lower function of Figure 11.4 have been expressed as a percentage of those in the upper curve. This derived function in Figure 11.5 behaves differently, showing an increase up to a point, and then a decrease. Functions of this form, when they have been reported, have always been for relative generalization, never for absolute generalization.

Presenting these two measures together as they appear in Figures 11.4 and 11.5 sheds some useful light on the nature of the function relating relative generalization to the number of reinforcements. Since the measure is derived from two others (the strength of the response to the CS, and the strength of the response to some other stimulus used to elicit a gener-

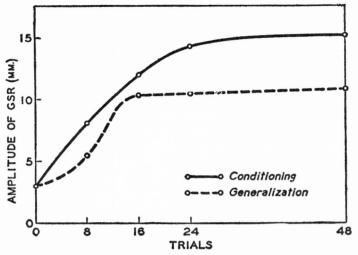

FIGURE 11.4. Strength of generalized responses during the course of acquisition. The solid line represents the amplitude of the galvanic skin response to the conditioned stimulus at successive stages of conditioning. The broken line represents the amplitude of the same response to the generalized stimulus. (From Hovland, 1937d.) •

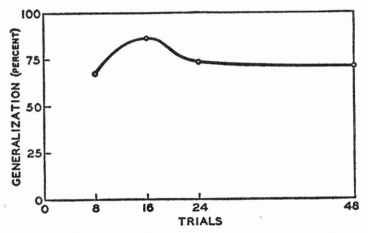

FIGURE 11.5. Relative generalization as a function of number of acquisition trials. The data of Figure 11.4 have been replotted to show the percentage of generalization at successive stages of conditioning. Each point on the curve represents the ratio of the strength of generalized responses to the strength of conditioned responses. (Hovland, 1937d).

alized response) the function in question will depend upon the shapes of these two more basic functions. Moreover, since the learning curves are, themselves, likely to be quite different, it seems most improbable that different learning situations and different response measures will produce identical relative-generalization functions. In fact, in the absence of measures relating various response indices to the underlying learning mechanism, questions about the "true" nature of the relative-generalization function are unanswerable. Thus differences among these functions should occasion no quarrels among the individuals who obtain them.

Hull (1952, p. 70) has proposed that changes in the form of the generalization gradient with practice depend upon the extent to which the response is conditioned to incidental stimuli in the learning situation. Such stimuli (apparatus noises, movements of the experimenter, sounds of the heating or cooling equipment in the room, distinctive odors, and so on) are often present at the time of reinforcement and should acquire a certain degree of potential for eliciting the conditioned response early in learning. Later on, these stimuli would be expected to lose their power to evoke the CR, through extinction, since they are apt to be present between, as well as during, trials. Thus, early in learning, a generalization test should yield an increasing response strength as these nongeneralized incidental stimuli undergo conditioning. With further practice there should be a relative weakening of the generalized response as a result of the extinction of the same conditioned response. It will be noted that this pattern of acquisition and subsequent extinction is exactly what appears in Figure 11.5. Presumably under other conditions where the incidental stimuli play either a more or a less important role the course of the function depicted in Figure 11.5 would change.

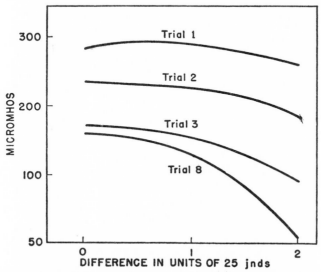

FIGURE 11.6. Smoothed generalization gradients at various stages in extinction. (Wickens, Schroder, and Snide, 1954).

Changes in Generalization with Extinction

Another way of changing response strength is through extinction. Thus alterations of the generalization gradient with non-reinforcement also have a bearing upon the relationship between the strength of conditioning and the process of generalization. Studies of this problem have, with exceptions to be considered in the next section, found that the generalization function steepens during extinction (Hovland, 1937d; Brown, 1942). In an experiment directly concerned with this problem, Wickens, Schroder, and Snide (1954) conditioned the GSR of human subjects and tested for generalization along a pitch dimension during extinction, using three of the tones previously scaled by Hovland. The experimental procedure consisted of 16 training trials followed by 8 extinction trials. Separate groups of subjects were extinguished at the CS and at two test points. Figure 11.6 presents the generalization gradients obtained on trials 1, 2, 3, and 8. It shows that, as extinction proceeds, the generalization gradient sharpens. The forms of the gradients are, however, convex upward, rather than concave as they were in Hovland's experiment (See Figure 11.1).

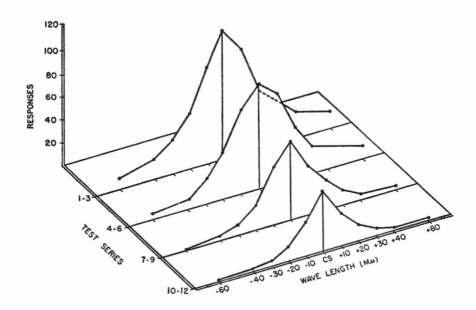

FIGURE 11.7. Changes in the form of the generalization gradient in the course of extinction for the key-pecking response in pigeons (Guttman and Kalish, 1956).

Guttman and Kalish (1956) trained pigeons to peck at a light of a certain hue, using a variable-interval reinforcement schedule to build up great response strength. Following this training, the birds were tested with the previously reinforced color and a range of others. The generalization gradients produced by the pigeons in successive fourths of the extinction test appear in Figure 11.7. It will be noted that, in this case, the range of generalization does not decrease with extinction, but seems instead to remain about the same. As a result the gradient itself becomes flatter. The reason for this difference between the results obtained by Guttman and Kalish and those obtained by others might be due to any of a number of conditions. Perhaps the most likely is the variable-interval schedule of reinforcement employed in training.

Individual Differences

In the study just described, Guttman and Kalish also compared the generalization gradients for pigeons showing a high response rate with those for birds showing an intermediate or low response rate. These gradients appear in Figure 11.8. At least in this situation, lowered overall rate does not markedly decrease the range of generalization. Guttman and Kalish stress the fact that the effect of response strength upon gener-

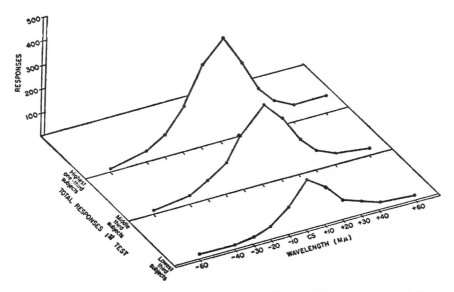

FIGURE 11.8. Generalization gradients for subjects differing in overall level of response strength (Guttman and Kalish, 1956).

alization seems to be much the same whether the variations are obtained by an extinction procedure or by selecting subjects with different rates of responding.

Partial Reinforcement

It has been known for some time that the gradient of generalization following intermittent reinforcement is flatter than that following continuous reinforcement (Humphreys, 1939c). There is also reason to believe that the schedule of reinforcement must be taken into account in considering the changes in the form of the generalization gradient which occur during extinction. In the main, the experiments reviewed so far seem to indicate that the range of generalization decreases as response strength weakens during extinction. The one study which fails to support this conclusion is that of Guttman and Kalish, who investigated generalization in extinction following training under a variable-interval reinforcement schedule. It thus becomes a distinct possibility that the changes in the generalization gradient observed in extinction vary with the schedule of reinforcement employed during acquisition. Wickens, Schroder, and Snide (1954) obtained evidence supporting this interpretation in the experiment described earlier. In one part of this study, they introduced a number of non-reinforced trials with a click during the conditioning of the GSR to tone. In extinction following this procedure, there was no tendency for the gradient to become steeper as response strength became weaker. This result, it will be noted, is different from that obtained following continuous reinforcement, but resembles the finding reported by Guttman and Kalish.

Generalization and Motivation

The results of experiments on the effect of motivation upon generalization have been consistent, showing that increased drive broadens the generalization gradient, both in the classical and instrumental conditioning situations. In one study (Bersh, Notterman, and Schoenfeld, 1956) a cardiac depression was classically conditioned in human subjects by pairing a shock of either 20 or 28 volts with a tone of 1920 cycles per second. Following conditioning, the tests for generalization were carried out at 1920, 1020, 480, or 180 cycles per second. The results for the groups conditioned with high and low shock appear in Figure 11.9. Clearly the generalization gradient is broader following conditioning with the stronger shock.

A similar effect has been obtained in experiments employing instrumental procedures and using lower animals for subjects. Jenkins, Pascal,

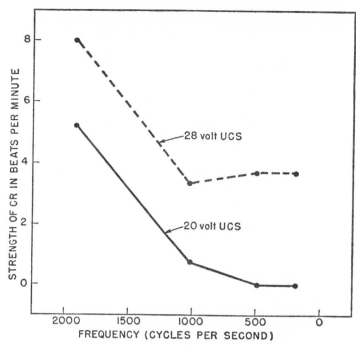

FIGURE 11.9. Generalization gradients for the conditioned heart response in man following training with relatively weak (20 volts) and relatively strong (28 volts) UCS (Bersh, Notterman, and Schoenfeld, 1956).

and R. W. Walker (1958), for example, trained pigeons to peck at an illuminated circle 1.4 centimeters in diameter and tested them later, with this stimulus and six other larger and smaller circles which differed from the training stimulus in steps of 0.4 centimeters. During training and the subsequent test, some of the subjects were maintained at 70 per cent of their normal weight and others were maintained at 90 per cent. In order to eliminate overall differences in level of responding resulting from the differences in the deprivation condition, a relative generalization measure was used. The number of responses to each stimulus (including the CS) during the test period was expressed as a percentage of the number of responses to the CS during a previous training period of equal length. The results appear in Figure 11.10. Again the effect of increasing motivation is to increase response strength to the test stimuli. Similarly, Rosenbaum (1953), using human subjects, found that threat of a strong shock led to greater generalization of a voluntary response than threat of a weak shock; he also found (Rosenbaum, 1956) that highly anxious subjects, for whom the threat of shock might be very highly motivating, showed broader generalization gradients than less anxious subjects.

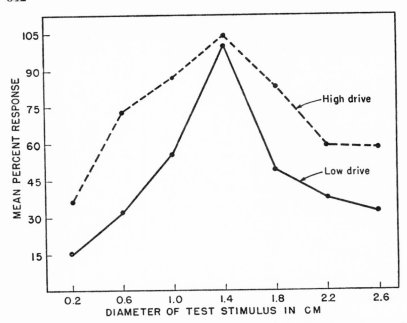

FIGURE 11.10.   Effect of level of hunger upon generalization of the key-pecking response in pigeons (W. O. Jenkins, G. R. Pascal, and R. W. Walker, 1958).

Stimulus Intensity

Since increased stimulus intensity increases the vigor of at least some conditioned responses, the factor of stimulus intensity enters to complicate the generalization function for such responses. Intensities lower than the CS will lead to lessened response strength because of generalization decrement and the directly weakening effect of the lower intensity. With higher intensities, these two factors act against each other. Increasingly higher intensities will tend to strengthen responses through a dynamogenic effect, which Hull (1949) calls stimulus intensity dynamism, at the same time that generalization decrement tends to weaken the response.

The form of the generalization function produced by variations in intensity will depend upon the relative contributions of these two processes. At the very least, it is to be predicted that the generalization gradient for stimuli more intense than the CS will be flatter than the one obtained with weaker stimuli. In classical conditioning, the bulk of the evidence suggests that the intensity function is more important than the generalization function, with the result that increasing intensities beyond the CS produces increases in response strength with no sign of diminution. Razran (1949) summarizes the results of 54 Pavlovian studies which manipulated stimulus intensity. A composite generalization gradient derived from these data appears in Figure 11.11. Hovland (1937b) obtained essentially similar results in his study of intensity

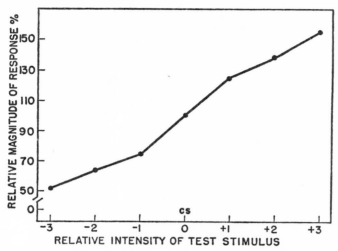

FIGURE 11.11. "Generalization" of salivary response to stimuli of intensities higher and lower than the CS. Data are weighted averages reported by Razran (1949) in his summary of Russian literature on generalization.

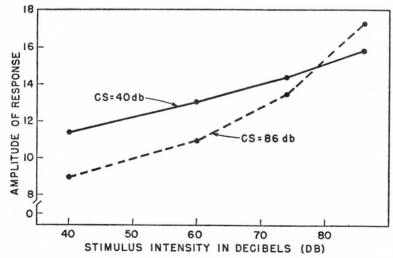

FIGURE 11.12. Strength of conditioned GSR as a function of the intensity of the eliciting auditory stimulus. Although the experiment was an investigation of stimulus generalization employing different intensities of tone as the generalization stimuli, it is clear that the main effect is directly attributable to intensity (Hovland, 1937b).

generalization. Two groups, each of 16 subjects, were conditioned to tones of 86 and 40 decibels, respectively, and then tested to this and to tones of 40, 60, 74, and 86 decibels. Figure 11. 12 presents the results in terms of amplitude of the GSR. Again tests with stimuli more intense than the CS reflect only an increase in response strength. See also Hovland and Riesen (1940).

Studies using motor responses and instrumental conditioning procedures have usually obtained somewhat different results: generalization decrement occurs to stimuli above and below the CS, but the amount of such decrement is typically greater when generalization tests are carried out with stimuli weaker than the CS than when they involve stronger stimuli (W. C. Miller and Greene, 1954). Grice and Saltz (1950) trained rats to open a small door located in the center of a white circle to obtain food. For different major groups the circles were 20 or 79 square centimeters in area. After training, subgroups of animals were tested in extinction to determine the form of the generalization functions for larger and smaller areas. The results of the study appear in Figure 11.13,

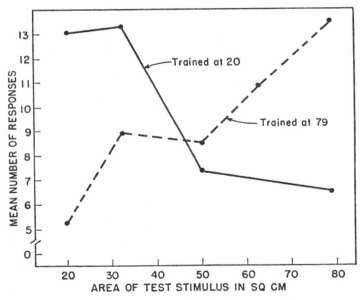

FIGURE 11.13.   Generalization of an instrumental response in rats along a size dimension (Grice and Saltz, 1950).

in the form of generalization gradients. Note particularly the slight increase in performance of the group trained on the 20 square-centimeter stimulus when the extinction stimulus is 32 square centimeters. This may have resulted from the fact that the larger stimulus reflects more light and is more intense; or it may simply mean that area functions as does an intensity dimension.

The Effect of Changing more than One Aspect of the Stimulus

The stimuli employed in conditioning experiments are always complex in that they at least exist on more than one dimension, and they may involve more than one sensory modality. Tests for generalization, however, usually consist of altering only one carefully controlled aspect of the stimulus. Obviously it would be possible to change more than one aspect of the stimulus in order to compare the effect of such a manipulation with that produced by changing just one. Experiments of this sort unfortunately are rare. Fink and Patton (1953) controlled certain characteristics of the stimulus situation (visual, auditory, and tactile) in which rats were allowed to drink, until the animals were accustomed to this procedure. Then these investigators altered one or more of the elements of the situation under their control. They found that any change led to a decrement in drinking, but that changing two or three of the stimuli produced a progressively larger decrement. White (1958) taught children to pull a handle to get marbles, using a card of a certain hue and saturation as a discriminative stimulus. Then, for different groups of subjects, he changed the color of the stimulus card, its saturation, or both in a series of unreinforced test trials. Changing both dimensions produced a greater decrement than changing just one. Butter (1959) trained pigeons to peck at a key which carried a vertical strip of a certain color. In extinction tests, the color was changed, the line was tilted, or both of these alterations were introduced. Changes in two dimensions were found to produce greater decrements than changes in just one. The most accurate quantitative expression for response strength (expressed as response probability) remaining with changes in two dimensions simultaneously turned out to be the product of response probabilities obtained when the two changes were made independently.

The Effect of Discrimination Training on Generalization

The conception that discrimination will alter the form of the generaliation gradient comes from a variety of sources. Hull (1953) predicts a steepening of the gradient in the region between the reinforced and non-reinforced stimuli and a decrease in the total amount of generalized response strength. The reason for this is that extinctive inhibition, conditioned to the non-reinforced stimulus, would generalize, reducing net response strength for a considerable range along the stimulus dimension.

This argument and the experimental evidence are developed more fully in the next chapter. (See pp. 364 to 369 and especially Figure 12.1.)

Lashley and Wade (1946, p. 74) have taken an even stronger position declaring that "the 'dimensions' of a stimulus series do not exist for

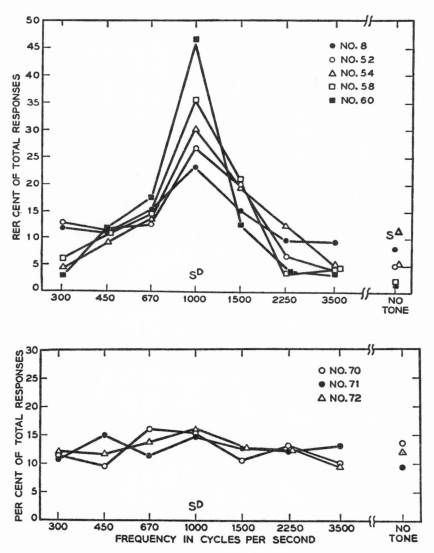

FIGURE 11.14. Generalization gradients for individual pigeons under two conditions. In the condition represented by the lower graph the training tone (S^D) was continuously present. In the condition represented in the upper graph the tone was present only part of the time, and reinforcement occurred only in the presence of the tone (H. M. Jenkins and Harrison, 1958).

the organism until established by differential training." Although the bulk of the evidence (Grandine and Harlow, 1948; Grice, 1948) appears to be against this view, Jenkins and Harrison (1958) have obtained supporting data. These investigators trained pigeons to peck at a key in the presence of a 1000 cycles per second tone under two conditions. In non-differential training the tone was continuously present and the subjects were reinforced on a variable-interval schedule. In differential training, the tone was present some of the time and absent some of the time, reinforcement occurring only in the presence of the tone. The generalization gradients following these two training procedures appear in Figure 11.14. Quite clearly, experience with the differential procedure led to the appearance of a gradient which non-differential training did not. Jenkins and Harrison suggest that other experiments, which appear to have produced gradients on the basis of training with nondifferential procedures, may have capitalized on the fact that the positive stimulus was typically a visual one isolated in space, so that the comparison of the stimulus with its background was always possible. It is to be noted that the changes in the generalization gradient during extinction can also be made to fit such an interpretation, since the subject is exposed to a new point on the stimulus dimension for the first time with the beginning of the extinction series.

The Extinction of Generalized Responses

Some interest centers in the ease with which generalized responses can be extinguished, for this bears upon the rapidity with which a discrimination can be established. Hovland (1937c) has reported data on this problem. After 16 presentations of a vibrator followed by a shock, when the generalization should be at its maximum, the conditioned galvanic skin response was tested both by the stimulus used in training and by one differing in intensity. Half of the subjects were trained with each stimulus, to control the effect of the difference in strength of stimuli. The conditioned responses to the reinforced stimulus were found to extinguish more slowly than the generalized conditioned responses to the other stimulus. After four extinction trials, the response to the original CS remained at 89 per cent of its original magnitude, while the generalized response had fallen to 60 per cent of its original magnitude. The more rapid extinction of the generalized response was followed by greater spontaneous recovery, so that, 24 hours after extinction, the difference between generalized and conditioned responses was no longer statistically significant.

This last result is probably related to the fact that generalized responses apparently increase in strength with time, a phenomenon which Bindra and Cameron (1953) describe as an *incubation effect* and Perkins and Weyant (1958) call the *reminiscence* of generalized responses. These latter investigators trained four groups of rats to run down an elevated runway to obtain food. Half of the rats were later tested in the same runway and half on a new runway which differed in color. Moreover, each of these groups was subdivided, half being tested immediately, half tested after a week's delay. The results of the experiment in terms of speed of running appear in Figure 11.15, which shows that the delay

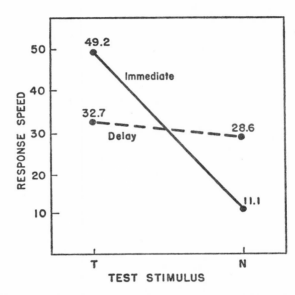

FIGURE 11.15.   The effect of an interval between training and test upon the slope of the generalization gradient. Animals were trained to traverse a runway of a particular color to obtain food. Following this training either by 60 seconds or one week the animals were tested either in the training alley (T) or a novel alley (N) differing in color. The delay of one week leads to a weaker response in the tests with the training stimulus, but a stronger response in tests with the novel stimulus (Perkins and Weyant, 1958).

produced a loss in response strength when the test was in the training runway. When it was in the new runway, however, there was an increase in strength.

The Summation of Generalized Responses

One of the important theoretical points associated with the concept of generalization is that it solves what Hull (1943) called the *stimulus-learning* and *stimulus-evocation paradoxes*. These closely related problems both stem from the fact that stimulus situations in learning are probably never repeated in exactly identical form from trial to trial. There are always differences, produced by equipment variation or changes in the subject's posture or attention. This fact poses two basic problems for any strict formulation of stimulus-response theory: (1) If more than one stimulus-response sequence is needed for learning to occur, how is it possible for learning to take place, since the stimuli differ from trial to trial? This is the stimulus-learning paradox. (2) Assuming that this problem is solved, for example, by the postulation of one-trial learning, how could this learning ever be made manifest, again because the stimulus situation would never reappear exactly? This is the stimulus-evocation paradox.

To handle these two problems, Hull assumed that habit strengths, including generalized habit strengths, summated. A graphical representation of this hypothesis appears in Figure 11.16. Experimental tests of

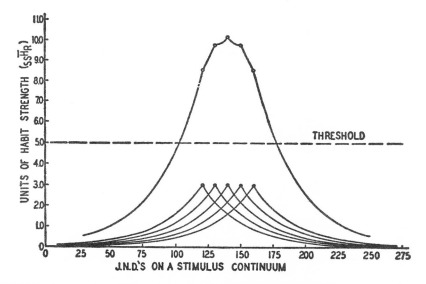

FIGURE 11.16. Graphic representation of Hull's hypothesis of the summation of generalized habit strength (Hull, 1943). The idea is that, although single reinforcements produce habit strengths of subliminal value, which are too weak to mediate a response, the summation of these response strengths leads to the development of supra threshold habit strength.

Hull's summation hypothesis have been only partially confirmatory. Bilodeau, Brown, and Meryman (1956) obtained a small amount of summation in an experiment involving the generalization of a voluntary response along a size dimension. Generalization gradients following such conditioning were elevated in the region between the two stimuli, but not elsewhere. Kalish and Guttman (1957) obtained similar results with pigeons trained to peck at lights of two different colors (Figure 11.17). It seems clear that the amount of summation is considerably less than Figure 11.16 suggests.

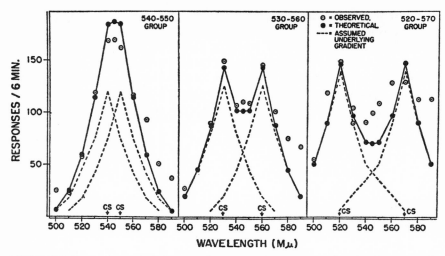

FIGURE 11.17. Empirical data on the summation of generalized habit strength. Pigeons were trained to peck at the two CS's indicated in each graph. Then they were tested on a wide range of hues. Assumed gradients centered about the training stimuli are indicated by the dashed lines. Derived theoretical functions are indicated by the solid circles connected by continuous lines. Actual empirical points are depicted by open circles with black points in their centers (Kalish and Guttman, 1957).

THE PROBLEMS OF STIMULUS EQUIVALENCE AND SIMILARITY

One way of interpreting the results of stimulus-generalization experiments is in terms of the hypothesis that the degree of generalization between two stimuli is a measure of the extent to which they are perceived as similar. This is an attractive conception because of the implied possibility of building, at this point, a connecting bridge between the fields of learning and perception. Such an idea seems, directly or indirectly, to have been at the base of a certain amount of research on generalization. For example, we perceive pitches separated by an octave as similar and might expect responses conditioned to a certain tone to generalize quite strongly to tones bearing an octave relationship to the tone employed in training. The evidence supports this expectation. Humphreys (1939c) established a conditioned galvanic skin response to a tone of 1967 cycles and tested the magnitude of the generalized response to other tones. The response to a tone of 984 cycles, which is an octave below the reinforced tone, was reliably greater than that to a tone of 1,000 cycles, which is more similar to the reinforced tone in terms of physical frequency. Similarly, Blackwell, and Schlosberg (1943) trained rats to respond to a 10,000-cycle tone by crossing an uncharged grid to obtain food. Responses to other tones (8, 7, 5, and 3 kilocycles) were punished and partially extinguished by means of a mild shock administered through the grid and omitting food reinforcement. During this period, the 5,000-cycle tone, an octave below the reinforced tone, elicited responses more regularly than any tone except the reinforced one. Percentage of responses are plotted in Figure 11.18. The hump in the

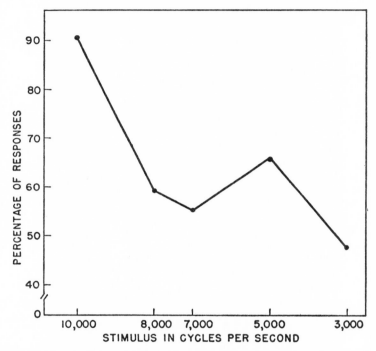

FIGURE 11.18.   A demonstration of octave generalization in the rat. See text for a description of the experiment and an interpretation of this figure (Blackwell and Schlosberg, 1943).

curve at 5,000 cycles is the evidence for octave generalization. The important point is that the phenomenon of octave generalization supports the hypothesis that generalization and the perception of similarity are parallel processes.

Classical psychophysical studies of perception tend to center their interest, not in the perception of similarity, but in the perception of differences. With this minor difference, the procedures in certain psychophysical experiments have a pronounced similarity to those in generalization. Stimuli differing by certain amounts are presented to subjects to determine whether they are responded to as the same or as different. The basic product yielded by such investigations is a *difference threshold,*

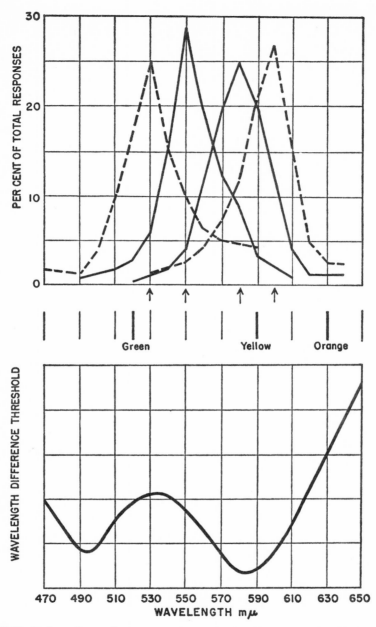

FIGURE 11.19. Generalization gradients with varying wavelengths in the pigeon (upper curves) compared with a function showing the sensitivity of the pigeon to differences in wavelength. The birds were trained to the points indicated by the arrows and tested to the others. In the curve of spectral sensitivity, low values mean high sensitivity (Guttman and Kalish, 1956).

representing, in physical terms, the smallest difference which can be perceived with reliability.

The theory that generalization reflects the extent to which stimuli are perceived as similar leads to the prediction that generalization gradients will be related to the size of the difference threshold: Where the difference threshold is large, the gradient should be relatively flat. Where the difference threshold is small, the gradient should be steeper. Guttman and Kalish (1956) (in the study previously described) tested this prediction for generalization along a hue dimension in pigeons, training the animals to peck at lights of certain colors and testing them in extinction at other colors. Figure 11.19 presented the results of their experiment, together with a graph relating the difference threshold to wave length. Careful examination of Figure 11.19 will show that there is very little correspondence between the two functions.

This fact means either that the theory connecting generalization and perceived similarity is wrong, or that the pigeons' difference thresholds are actually much smaller than the bottom half of Figure 11.18 suggests. There is some reason to believe that the second alternative is the correct one. Kalish (1958) performed a second study, with human subjects, and obtained a remarkably good correspondence between discriminability and generalization. The conclusion suggested by the Kalish experiment is that, at least in certain cases, the generalization function is the result of a failure to discriminate. Several other investigators (Lashley and Wade, 1946; Schlosberg and Solomon, 1943; Philip, 1947) have also proposed such a theory to account for stimulus generalization. Others have developed theories which merely suggest that discriminability is a factor in stimulus generalization. These theories (Hull, 1943; Shepard, 1957, 1958) of which Hull's is the best known, propose that generalized response strength is some nonlinear (for example, exponential) function of stimulus differences expressed in units of discriminability (j.n.d.'s). The use of discrimination units suggests that the perception of similarity is involved in discrimination. The use of a nonlinear function indicates that additional processes are involved.

As a way of approaching the obvious next question, concerning the nature of these additional processes, it may be well to consider first some of the experiments in which generalization has occurred in spite of the fact that confusion of stimuli seems, on common sense grounds, to have been extremely improbable. Some of these demonstrations involve the classical studies of generalization. Hovland (1937b) obtained almost complete generalization with test tones 150 j.n.d.'s away from the training tone in loudness. In the Bass and Hull (1934) experiment responses conditioned to stimulation of the shoulder generalized to stimuli applied to the calf. Brown, Bilodeau, and Baron (1951) observed generalization of a voluntary response trained to one light to other lights several inches away. In none of these cases does it seem very likely that the subjects were ever confused as to the identity of the stimuli.

Certain other demonstrations are even harder to force into a failure-of-discrimination schema. Lundholm (1928, 1932) showed that it was possible to use hallucinated stimuli in hypnosis as a basis for conditioning. Responses produced in the presence of hallucinated lights were given as CR's to genuine lights. In quite a different way, Razran (1949) presents data which contribute to this point. Describing Russian studies of *cross-modal generalization,* he reports that a response conditioned to (say) a light transfers, with a strength of about 40 per cent on the average, to auditory or tactile stimuli. Again, the proposition that the subjects confused the stimuli is hard to accept.

Semantic Generalization

Another set of materials which argue strongly against a failure-of-discrimination explanation is to be found in studies of *semantic generalization* in which the meaning of a stimulus has been shown to provide the basis for generalization (Osgood, 1953, pp. 701-705). For example, a response conditioned to a blue light generalizes to the word BLUE. In other studies of semantic generalization both CS and test stimuli have been words. Diven (1936) performed an experiment, which, though weak on methodological grounds, suggested that a GSR conditioned to the word BARN generalized to other rural words. This result has since been verified by J. D. Lacey and his associates. In these latter experiments (Lacey and Smith, 1954; Lacey, Smith, and Green, 1955), subjects were required to free associate for 15 seconds to each word of a list containing, among others, the words COW and PAPER. For two different groups, a strong electric shock followed one or the other of these words. The critical words appeared six times in the list, providing six conditioning trials. The list also contained eight other words with rural connotations (PLOW, CORN, TRACTOR, and so on). The response measure was an autonomic lability score (Lacey, 1956) based upon heart rate. It was shown that conditioning occurred to the CS and, as Diven had found, that there was generalization to other rural words, mediated presumably by some process which equated the rural words for meaning.

Since language habits are involved in semantic generalization, it is to be expected that the process will be enormously complicated. The evidence fully confirms this expectation. Semantic generalization has been demonstrated in experiments employing a wide range of semantic relationships, including the species-genus relationship (Goodwin, Long, and Welch, 1945), and synonyms, antonyms, and homophones (Razran, 1939c). Moreover, there is some evidence that generalization is most readily mediated by different relationships at different ages. Reiss (1946), using a conditioned GSR procedure and words (for example, RIGHT) as the CS, found that for 7- to 9-year-olds generalization was greatest to homophones (WRITE); for 10- to 12-year-olds generalization was best to antonyms (WRONG); and for 14- to 20-year-olds it was best to synonyms (CORRECT).

The Mediation Hypothesis

The foregoing materials indicate that, although some generalization apparently occurs as the result of a failure to discriminate, there are many cases in which other explanations must be invoked. One of the most fruitful hypotheses available to account for such generalization is through an application of Guthrie's (1935) conception, which Osgood (1953) refers to as a mediation hypothesis. Specifically Guthrie's idea is that all conditioning, and therefore all generalization, is mediated by responses of looking at, listening for, or paying attention to stimuli. Diagrammatically:

$$S \longrightarrow r \longrightarrow s \longrightarrow R.$$

S, the training stimulus, produces a characteristic observing response (r) with proprioceptive consequences (s). In this interpretation, s plays the crucial role in the elicitation of behavior (R). It, rather than S, is the true conditioned stimulus. Stimuli (S') which differ from S may elicit different responses (r') with different proprioceptive consequences (s'). The extent to which s and s' differ will theoretically depend upon the difference between S and S'. If one assumes that response strength diminishes directly with the difference between s and s', this provides an explanation of the generalization gradient. In Guthrie's view all generalization is *mediated*, in the sense that S only initiates a sequence of events which includes the true stimulus to which responses are conditioned.

Others, notably Dollard and Miller (1950) and Goss (1955), have extended such a view to situations in which the physical similarity among stimuli is slight. Suppose that two different stimuli (S_A and S_B) evoke the same initial response. It might then be that these two stimuli, however different, would be responded to in the same way, or that behavior learned to one would transfer (generalize) to the other. Again, diagrammatically:

$$\text{If}: S_A \longrightarrow r_1 \longrightarrow s_1 \longrightarrow R_A$$

$$\text{And}: S_B \longrightarrow r_1 \longrightarrow s_1$$

$$\text{It follows that}: S_B \longrightarrow r_1 \longrightarrow s_1 \longrightarrow R_A$$

It will be noted that this is exactly the paradigm employed previously (p. 217) in connection with sensory preconditioning. It should also be noted that, if the initial responses to S_A and S_B are different (however similar S_A and S_B may be physically) the final response to the two stimuli should be different. Thus, in addition to a mechanism for describing the mediated equivalence of cues, there is a similar one which will deal with mediated distinctiveness. We will develop this latter mechanism further in the next chapter.

The most direct implication of the mediation hypothesis is that the amount of generalization between two stimuli will increase if the subject makes the same initial response to them. Grice and Davis (1958) put this implication to a test, using a conditioned eyeblink procedure. They used, as conditioned stimuli, three tones which differed widely in pitch. Only one, the middle tone, was positive and always reinforced. The subjects in this experiment also made a manual response to each of the CS's, consisting of pushing or pulling a lever. For one of the non-reinforced stimuli the lever response was the same as to the reinforced CS; for the other negative stimulus it was different. The subjects made significantly more generalized CR's to the non-reinforced stimulus involving the same motor response as the CS than they did to the stimulus requiring a different reaction.

A somewhat different demonstration of the role of mediating reactions in learned stimulus equivalence is provided by an experiment on indirect conditioning. Following a procedure employed earlier by Shipley (1933, 1935), Lumsdaine (1939) established conditioned eyeblinks in human subjects by pairing a light (CS) with a blow of a mechanical striker (UCS) on the cheek near the eye. Later a finger withdrawal was conditioned by combining the striker (now a CS) with shock to the finger. After this course of training it was found that the light evoked finger reactions in a large proportion of the subjects, although it had never been followed by shock. A diagrammatic analysis of a mediational explanation of this result appears in Figure 11.20. In this explanation, it is assumed that the proprioceptive consequences (s) of the eyeblink are common to the finger withdrawal and eyelid conditioning situation, thus providing mediating stimuli. It can be seriously doubted, however, that all learned stimulus equivalence is mediated by proprioceptive stimuli arising from intermediate reactions. In Lumsdaine's experiment (as in a related study by J. Miller and Cole, 1936), the finger response did not always wait for the eyelid response but in a few instances coincided with it or preceded it. This suggests the possibility that the eyelid response may not be an essential step in the sequence, but merely an overt indicator of a central "set" which is common to both the light and the striker stimuli. Grice and Davis (1958) in the experiment mentioned previously also obtained some evidence that the set to respond was enough to mediate generalization. The tendency in this direction was not, however, statistically dependable, and the result is only suggestive.

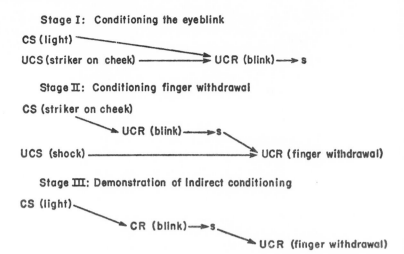

Stage I: Conditioning the eyeblink

CS (light)

UCS (striker on cheek) ⟶ UCR (blink) ⟶ s

Stage II: Conditioning finger withdrawal

CS (striker on cheek)

UCR (blink) ⟶ s

UCS (shock) ⟶ UCR (finger withdrawal)

Stage III: Demonstration of Indirect conditioning

CS (light)

CR (blink) ⟶ s

UCR (finger withdrawal)

FIGURE 11.20. The mediational explanation of Lumsdaine's (1939) results. The light, without previous pairing with shock or finger withdrawal, comes to evoke this response because of proprioceptive stimulation produced by the eyeblink which had been conditioned to the light.

Other scattered evidence on the importance of mediating responses comes from studies of long trace conditioning. It has already been pointed out that these responses probably involve mediating activity (p. 200). It is of particular interest that they seem to generalize very widely. According to Pavlov (1927, p. 113) they exhibit "a permanent and universal generalization of the analyzers." And according to Evans (1925) the longer the latency of a CR, the greater its tendency to generalize. Assuming that long-latency responses involve mediation, this again provides evidence for the importance of such processes in generalization.

If one accepts this interpretation of stimulus generalization, as mediated, certain questions naturally arise as to the nature of the organism's mediating responses and the way in which such responses participate in the generalization process. Such considerations seem to lie at the base of Lashley and Wade's (1946) proposal that the dimensions of stimuli do not exist for the organism until it has had a chance to make comparisons among sample stimuli differing on the dimension. Razran (1949), going a step further, takes the position that, even with experience, dimensions never emerge. Instead the organism forms crude categories on some similarity-dissimilarity scale, with the result that generalization gradients, for individual subjects, are usually uneven and stepwise. Data presented by Razran in support of this argument show that many of the gradients in the early studies were, indeed, smooth only because the results of several individuals were averaged. Mednick (1960) suggests that the organism may sometimes form ordinal scales as a result of experience with a stimulus series, and that generalization may be a function of the number of units on such a scale separating the training and test stimuli. Such a theory leads to the prediction that the amount of response strength generalized to the same stimulus will vary with the number of units between the stimulus and the CS. Both Mednick and W. O. Evans (1959) have shown that the strength of a generalized voluntary response to a stimulus a given distance away from the training stimulus depends upon the number of test stimuli intervening.

RESPONSE GENERALIZATION

The principle of stimulus generalization, stated somewhat abstractly, is that an organism which has learned to respond in a certain way to stimulus S, has thereby learned also to respond in a similar way to a different stimulus S'. The counterpart of the response side is as follows: if an organism has learned to react with response R to a stimulus S, it has also learned thereby to react with a response R', which is unlike R, but in some respects equivalent to it. Wickens (1943, 1948) has described two experiments on response generalization involving conditioned finger withdrawal. In these studies an extensor response was first conditioned by pairing a tone with a mild shock to the finger. During this original conditioning the subject sat at the apparatus with the palm down, the middle finger resting on the shock-administering electrode. After conditioning, the subject turned his hand over so that the palm was now up. Under these circumstances most of the subjects responded to the CS with a flexor response, demonstrating response generalization. In addition, one of these experiments (Wickens, 1948) successfully demonstrated stimulus generalization of the generalized response. That is, the flexor response transferred in reduced strength to tones other than the specific one used as a CS. Other studies of response generalization have been conducted by Antonitis (1951), Arnold (1945), and by Williams (1941).

SUMMARY

An organism which has learned to respond to a given stimulus will tend to respond in the same way to stimuli which resemble the training stimulus. This phenomenon is called stimulus generalization. Often the amount of stimulus generalization decreases with increasing differences between the CS and the test stimulus. When response strength is plotted as a function of this difference, the result is a decreasing gradient, the form of which is frequently concave upward.

Variables Controlling the Amount of Stimulus Generalization

At the most general level, there is good evidence that the breadth of the generalization gradient increases with increases in the strength of the conditioned response. The evidence for this conclusion is to be found in the facts that: (1) increasing numbers of reinforcements broaden the generalization gradient (although a subsequent narrowing may occur), (2) the generalization gradient steepens with extinction, unless training was under conditions of intermittent reinforcement, (3) increased motivation increases the range of the generalization gradient, and (4) the generalization gradient is flatter following intermittent reinforcement than following continuous reinforcement.

It has also been shown that the form of the generalization gradient can be influenced by the intensity of the test stimuli. If a response is conditioned to a particular stimulus and then tested with stimuli which are both weaker and stronger than the training stimulus, the amount of generalization will be greater for the stronger stimuli than it will be for the weaker. In experiments on the generalization of classically conditioned responses, this stimulus-intensity effect may be so powerful as to obscure the generalization gradient.

Finally, the extent of generalization depends upon the conditions of training. If a response is established with the procedures of discrimination learning, the generalization gradient is steeper than it is following training in which no discrimination is required.

Methodological Issues

Since stimulus generalization occurs on a dimension of stimulus similarity, a question arises as to the relationship between generalization and the dimensions obtained in the classical studies of psychophysics. There is reason to believe that a part of what is reflected in the generalization gradient is the extent to which the organism distinguishes among stimuli. Some investigations have yielded generalization gradients which were essentially linear when plotted on a dimension of discriminability. Moreover, the phenomenon of octave generalization suggests that a stimulus which is perceived as similar to the CS tends to evoke a relatively strong generalized response in spite of great physical dissimilarity. On the basis of such evidence, most theories of generalization include some reference to the discriminability of stimuli.

On the other hand, it is quite clear that it is necessary to give consideration to processes other than discriminability in any complete account of stimulus generalization. This is evident from the fact that many demonstrations of generalization are to be found in studies where the stimuli were so different that there is almost no probability that they could have been confused. Included in this category are cross-modal and semantic generalization, in which the CS and test stimuli do not exist on the same physical dimension.

Semantic generalization is generalization which occurs on the basis of the meaning of stimuli. A subject conditioned to respond to the word BARN for example, may show a tendency to make the same response to other words with rural connotation, for example, TRACTOR. But the response does not occur to nonrural words such as PAPER. In generalization of this sort the suggestion is that the response requires some intervening activity on the part of the subject. On this basis such generalization may be referred to as mediated.

It seems quite likely that *all* generalization is mediated in some degree and that an important, if difficult, consideration involves the extent to which mediation enters in different instances of generalization. The transfer of the conditioned GSR from a tone of one pitch to a tone of another probably requires only the minimal degree of mediating behavior involved in perceiving the tones. Semantic generalization, at the other extreme, would depend upon a process of mediation in a very important way. Finding means of controlling and specifying the amount of mediating activity in studies of stimulus generalization is an important unsolved problem.

Response Generalization

Response generalization refers to the fact that, when a certain response is conditioned to a particular stimulus, related responses are also automatically conditioned to the same stimulus. The process is the counterpart on the response side of stimulus generalization. Experimental studies of response generalization have been of very different sorts and, so far, have not gone far beyond a demonstration of the points that (*a*) the phenomenon of response generalization is real, (*b*) there seems to be a gradient of response generalization resembling that which occurs in the case of stimulus generalization, and (*c*) it is entirely possible for stimulus and response generalization to occur at the same time.

·12·

Discrimination

ALTHOUGH THE TENDENCY for a response to generalize has adaptive value in many situations, there are some circumstances which present an obvious necessity for inhibiting this tendency. One does not with impunity respond to all men in uniform, all aces in a card deck, or all mushroom-shaped fungi in the same way. As this implies, there must be an influence which restricts the range of generalization and restrains the organism from making the same response to all physically similar stimuli. This influence is called *discrimination*.

All learning seems to involve discrimination at least to some degree. A response acquired in one situation does not generalize universally. A response conditioned to a tone, for example, usually does not appear to lights or even to all tones. Sometimes it may not occur if just the location of the original tone is changed (Girden, 1938). In cases where cross-modal generalization does occur the amount of it is typically small. The 40 per cent value mentioned in the previous chapter is probably somewhat large. Beyond this, most learning experiments require a primitive sort of discrimination between the situation when the signal to respond is present and the same situation when the signal is absent. The importance of this fact has been stressed by Mowrer and Lamoreaux (1951) and by C. C. Perkins (1953).

Training of the sort just described does not result in very fine discrimination. To produce a more precise discrimination among stimuli it is necessary to employ some special procedure which makes reinforcement contingent upon a response to one of two or more stimuli. When such procedures are introduced, the differentiating power of mammalian organisms can be demonstrated to be remarkably great, extending to a wide range of stimuli. With proper training, discriminations between drive levels, amounts of work (Thompson, 1944), delays of reinforcement (Logan, 1952), as well as among the obvious exteroceptive stimuli, have been established.

EXPERIMENTAL METHODS

The general method required to produce a discrimination involves the extinction of generalized responses by non-reinforcement, while the strength of the response to some particular stimulus is maintained by reinforcement. Two more specific procedures may be identified. These have been called the methods of *successive* and *simultaneous* presentation of stimuli by certain investigators (W. S. Hunter, 1914).

The Method of Successive Presentation of Stimuli (Contrasts)

In Pavlov's method of contrasts, now more often called the method of successive presentation of stimuli, only one of two stimuli to be discriminated is presented on each trial. Reinforcement follows one stimulus and not the other, with the result that the subject comes to respond to one of the two stimuli and to inhibit the response to the other. As originally conceived, the method was applied within the framework of the classical conditioning procedure and used to establish discriminations between different stimuli in the same modality, such as two tones of different pitches. It is also the technique basic to the establishment of conditioned inhibition in which a CS is reinforced if presented alone but not if presented with another (conditioned inhibitor). Similarly, the demonstration of *patterning* involves the method of successive presentation. In this procedure there are two stimuli. Presented together, they are reinforced, but either of them presented alone is not (Hull, 1940, 1945a).

Experiments on discrimination of the instrumental conditioning variety, using the method of successive presentation, have been carried out by Elder (1934, 1935), Wendt (1934), Verplank (1942), and by Antoinetti (1950). Elder taught chimpanzees to react to a telegraph key following a ready signal, provided a tone was present. The animals learned to refrain from response after the ready signal when the tone was absent. In Wendt's study, monkeys learned to open a drawer which contained food following the positive auditory stimulus. The drawer was locked following the negative (that is, absent) stimulus, and the animal learned to withhold reaction. Antoinetti's experiment, in which rats were used as subjects, was similar in conception. First the animals learned to open a door containing a black card to get out of a starting box and obtain food. Following this initial training, discrimination learning began. The black card continued to be followed by reinforcement, but on randomly alternated trials a white card was substituted and this card was not reinforced. As a result of this training a discrimination gradually developed. The rats responded very quickly to the black door, but they responded slowly or refused to leave the starting box on trials with the white door. Verplank's procedure was similar to Antoinetti's, except that the apparatus was the Graham-Gagné runway and reinforced and non-reinforced trials were alternated according to the regular schedule.

Skinnerian methods of discrimination training are also modified versions of the method of successive presentation of stimuli. Responses in the presence of a positive discriminative stimulus (S^D) are reinforced; and responses in the presence of a negative discriminative stimulus (S^Δ), which is usually the absence of S^D, are not reinforced. With training, high rates of responding are established to S^D and very low ones to S^Δ (M. H. Smith and Hoy, 1954).

The Method of Simultaneous Presentation of Stimuli (Choice Reaction)

In instrumental learning situations, the development of discriminations is more commonly studied in experiments where the positive and negative stimuli are present simultaneously. The simplest of these is the *position discrimination* required in simple T- or Y-mazes in which the animal is reinforced for going to one side or the other. In somewhat more complicated experiments using other stimuli, the apparatus is very often an adaptation of the T- or Y-maze; but the positive stimulus, which may be a card of a certain color or pattern, a light, a floor of distinctive texture, or an alley of a certain width, is shifted randomly from side to side on different trials. If the subject responds to this stimulus, it is rewarded. If it does not respond correctly there is no reward and punishment may be administered. Using adaptations of this basic plan, many different kinds of apparatus and reactions have been used in studies of discrimination learning. Subjects have been trained to pull a string on the left or right, which will bring food if correct (Kluver, 1933), to open one of two possible boxes to secure food (Spence, 1934), to jump through an opening (Lashley, 1930b), to push open a door (Munn, 1931), and so forth.

There are two important differences between the successive and simultaneous procedures for studying discrimination learning. (1) Since the two stimuli are presented simultaneously in the latter procedure, the relational characteristics of the stimuli may be easier for the subject to notice than when the stimuli are present separately. (2) In simultaneous discrimination the choice is usually between two reactions (for example, turning right or left) rather than between reaction and restraint. Each of the reactions, thus, may have a double determination, being an approach to one of the stimuli and at the same time a reaction away from the other (Nissen, 1951). The first of these differences has been most stressed in theoretical discussions of discrimination learning. Theorists who hold that discrimination involves a response to a relationship have argued that the method of simultaneous presentation should lead to quicker learning than the method of successive presentation. Empirical studies on this point will be reviewed in a later section.

DISCRIMINATION AS COMBINED CONDITIONING AND EXTINCTION

Looked at in operational terms, one fact about discrimination learning is inescapable: The procedure is a combination of two simpler procedures. Trials with the positive, or reinforced, stimulus (S+) are conditioning trials; trials with the negative, or non-reinforced, stimulus (S—) are extinction trials. Given this fact it is not surprising that several theorists have proposed explanations of discrimination learning which involve the concepts of conditioning and extinction. Among such conditioning-extinction theories, the most important are those of Spence (1936, 1937a, 1937b) and Hull (1939b, 1943, 1950, 1952). Conditioning-extinction theory, as originally developed by Spence and Hull, entails the following assumptions: (1) that every reinforcement leads to an increment in the (excitatory) tendency to repeat the reinforced response, (2) that every non-reinforcement leads to an increment in the (inhibitory) tendency not to respond, (3) that both of these tendencies generalize to other stimuli, (4) that the magnitude of the inhibitory tendency is less than that of the excitatory tendency (otherwise learning could not occur in any partial-reinforcement situation, S+ and S— being the same stimulus, where reinforced and non-reinforced trials occur in a ratio of 1:1 or less), (5) that the excitatory and inhibitory tendencies interact algebraically; and (6) that discriminatory reactions are based on the resolution of the competing tendencies in favor of the reaction to the stimulus which has the stronger tendency conditioned (or generalized) to it. In experiments involving the method of successive presentation of stimuli, a discrimination is said to have been established when the subject characteristically responds to S+, but does not respond to S—. The theoretical account explains such discriminations by the assumption that the processes of reinforcement and extinction have provided S+ and S— with habit loadings which, respectively, are predominantly positive and negative. In experiments involving the simultaneous presentation of stimuli or choice reactions, the response theoretically occurs to the stimulus with the stronger excitatory strength conditioned to it.

In order to make predictions about the outcome of specific experiments, it is necessary to add a seventh assumption to the list above: (7) that the stimuli manipulated by the experimenter are in fairly direct control of the subject's behavior. In situations where mediating stimulus-producing reactions are important, it would be necessary to know more than we usually do about the functioning of such stimuli to explain the results of a discrimination experiment. As we shall see, studies which maximize the role of such responses cannot always be explained by conditioning-extinction theory without modification.

Figure 12.1 provides us with a concrete representation of Hull's

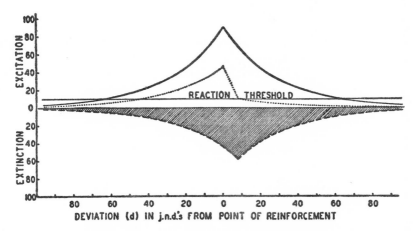

FIGURE 12.1. Hull's theory of discrimination learning. The upper curve is a hypothetical generalization gradient established by conditioning a response to the stimulus corresponding to point zero on the baseline. The lower, shaded, gradient represents the generalization of extinction carried out with a non-reinforced stimulus 8 j.n.d.'s away from the positive stimulus on the baseline. The smaller, asymmetrical function represents the difference between the two other functions (Hull, 1943).

(1943) version of the conditioning extinction position, in the form of three generalization gradients. The upper curve is the excitation function generated by reinforcing a stimulus (S+) at the point marked zero on the baseline. The lower, shaded, curve is the inhibitory function developed as a result of non-reinforcement of a stimulus (S—) 8 j.n.d.'s away from S+ on some stimulus dimension. The intermediate dotted curve is the residual obtained by subtracting the points of the inhibitory function from those on the excitatory one. This has been called a *post-discrimination gradient* (Hull, 1952) and represents the form which a generalization gradient obtained after discrimination training theoretically should take (Passey and Herman, 1955).

Formulated in this way, conditioning-extinction theory leads to a variety of predictions, some of which have been tested in a differential eyelid conditioning experiment by Gynther (1957). In this study the positive and negative stimuli were small lights about two inches apart directly ahead of the subject. The right-hand light was followed by an air puff; the left-hand light was not. The first prediction from Hull's theory which Gynther set out to test involved the level of conditioning attainable in discrimination learning. Reference to the dotted line in Figure 12.1 will show that the generalization of inhibition from the negative stimulus to the positive one theoretically should reduce the level of performance to the positive stimulus. To test this deduction Gynther ran two groups of subjects. One was conditioned in the ordinary way, receiving 50 presentations of only one stimulus which was always followed by the air puff. The other group received the same number of reinforced trials with the same stimulus, but there was an equal number of non-reinforced trials with the negative stimulus. The results for these two groups appear in Figure 12.2. The upper curve is for the regularly

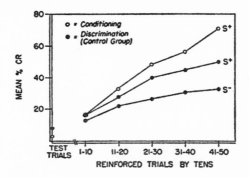

FIGURE 12.2. A comparison of performance in eyelid conditioning under conditions of discrimination and straight conditioning (Gynther, 1957).

conditioned group. The lower two curves show the responses to the positive and negative stimuli obtained from the discrimination group. In correspondence with the theory, the discrimination group gave fewer conditioned responses to S+ than the conditioning group. Passey's (1957) data also support this deduction for the running response of rats.

It will also be observed in Figure 12.2 that there was a substantial level of responding to S—. This result has typically occurred in studies of differential eyelid conditioning and theoretically can happen under circumstances where (1) the excitatory process conditioned to S+ is greater than the inhibitory process conditioned to S—, and (2) the positive and negative stimuli are close together on the stimulus dimension. The first of these conditions is assumed by the theory. The second is a matter of experimental manipulation. Other evidence in Gynther's study suggests that S+ and S— are, as these results indicate, close together on the generalization gradient.

The discrimination group in this portion of Gynther's experiment served as a control group against which the effects of a number of other

procedures could be compared. One of these involved the ratio of reinforced to non-reinforced trials. To understand the result of this manipulation, suppose that the gradients of excitation and inhibition in Figure
12.1 are those which exist after 50 reinforced and 50 non-reinforced trials,
as in the case of Gynther's discrimination control group. Administering
50 reinforced trials with S+ and only 17 with S— (a ratio of 3:1) would
leave the gradient of excitation unchanged, but the inhibitory gradient
would be weakened considerably. The effect of this weakening of the
inhibitory gradient should be two-fold: (1) There should be a higher
level of response to S+ because of the smaller amount of inhibition
generalizing to S+. (2) At the same time, there should also be a higher
level of response to S—, because the excitation which generalizes to S—
will suffer less from inhibition. The results of the comparison implied in
these predictions appear in Figure 12.3. It will be observed that the

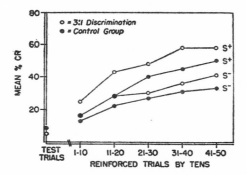

FIGURE 12.3. Performance in differential eyelid conditioning under conditions where the reinforced stimulus and unreinforced stimulus are presented
in a ratio of 3:1 or 1:1 (control group). The data are from Gynther (1957).

predictions were confirmed. Moreover, it appears that the increased
response strength to S+ and S— in the 3:1 group was about the same
to each of these two stimuli. The degree of discrimination (responses to
S— subtracted from responses to S+) did not differ for the two groups.
G. N. Cantor and Spiker (1954) obtained essentially the same result in
an experiment where preschool children learned to discriminate between
toy cars of different colors, receiving reinforced and non-reinforced trials
in the ratio of 2:2 or 2:1.[1]

To introduce a third prediction suppose that a subject has been conditioned to respond to S+ before discrimination training begins. In terms

[1] Two other investigations of this problem (Birch, 1955; Fitzwater, 1952) used the
procedure of keeping total number of trials constant and varying the number of reinforced and non-reinforced trials within this total. This procedure makes the results
hard to interpret in terms of Figure 12.1, because, theoretically, both the excitatory
and inhibitory gradients are manipulated in ways which cannot be assessed.

of Figure 12.1, this is to say that the gradient of excitation is established
without setting up the inhibitory one. With the beginning of discrimination training, inhibition develops and generalizes to S+. The result should
be a decrement in response strength to S+. To test this prediction
Gynther gave another group of subjects 20 conditioning trials before
initiating discrimination training. At the end of the preliminary conditioning trials, the subjects were giving approximately 60 per cent CR's.
During the first 10 conditioning trials the level of response to S+
dropped to less than 50 per cent. Similar results, usually of lesser magnitude have been reported by Antoinetti (cf. Hull, 1952, p. 62), Spence
and Beecroft (1954), and Hilgard, Campbell, and Sears (1938).

One of the most obvious predictions from Hull's theory is that psycho-
physically dissimilar stimuli will be more easily discriminated than similar stimuli. (In Figure 12.1, this would be represented by separating the
two gradients on the stimulus dimension). To test this prediction,
Gynther increased the difference between stimulus lights S+ and S— by
covering the latter with a red filter which changed its color and reduced
its intensity. Figure 12.4 shows the result of this procedure. Note that

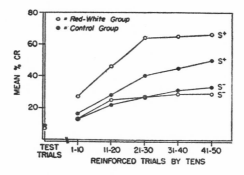

FIGURE 12.4. Performance in differential eyelid conditioning with two different degrees of similarity of positive and negative stimuli (Gynther, 1957).

the difference in response level to S+ and S— increases, and that the
absolute level of responding to S+ also increases. Both of these findings
are consistent with the theory.

At the other extreme as regards degree of similarity is the partial-
reinforcement situation in which S+ and S— are identical. In terms of
Figure 12.1, this would involve drawing the shaded inhibitory gradient
as a shortened mirror image of the excitatory gradient, with the peaks
of the two functions opposite each other on the baseline. Subtracting
values on the inhibitory gradient from those on the excitatory gradient
in this case would produce a residual gradient with a smaller maximum
than could be produced by any other combination of positive and nega-

tive gradients. In behavioral terms, response strength should be lower under a partial-reinforcement schedule than under any other. A group run under these conditions confirmed this prediction. In their last 10 of 100 trials, the percentage of CR's was 39 per cent. The same values for the discrimination group (responses to S+) and the conditioning group were 50 per cent and 66 per cent, respectively. Obviously, and in line with the theory, response strength to S+ is reduced in proportion to the similarity of S+ and S—. This same prediction has been tested by Raben (1949) in an experiment which employed rats as subjects and the Graham-Gagné runway as the apparatus. As in Gynther's study there was clear evidence that the ease of discrimination varied directly with the difference between the stimuli.

Criticisms and Alternative Formulations of Conditioning-Extinction Theory

In spite of its obvious utility in suggesting experiments and in predicting the outcomes of certain of them, conditioning-extinction theory has been subjected to considerable criticism. In some cases this has led to a reinterpretation of the basic processes supposed to lie behind discrimination. In other cases, experiments suggested by the criticisms have led to a strengthening of the underlying assumptions. In still others, new and useful ways of looking at discrimination learning have emerged as an indirect result of the criticism. Let us look at some of these criticisms and problems and then observe the effect that they have had upon the theory.

1. *The Lashley-Wade Criticism.* As a part of their attack on "neo-Pavlovian" psychology, particularly as it uses the concept of generalization, Lashley and Wade (1946) criticized the conditioning-extinction explanation of discrimination learning very severely both on theoretical and empirical grounds. As a crucial test of this theory, they proposed the following experiment: Two groups of rats were to be trained in a discrimination situation. One group was to be rewarded for responding to a 5-cm. circle as opposed to a black card. The other was to be rewarded for responding to an 8-cm. circle as opposed to the same black card. Then the two groups were to be trained to discriminate between the two circles with the 8-cm. circle being positive. Conditioning-extinction theory would predict that the animals previously trained to the 8-cm. circle would transfer this learning to the new discrimination situation and learn it more quickly than the group trained previously on the 5-cm. circle. Experiments reported by Lashley and Wade, however, produced the opposite outcome. That is, learning was more rapid by the group previously trained on the 5-cm. circle. Although it is by no means clear that any other theory would predict the results which were obtained,

such data do pose obvious difficulties for the theories of Hull and Spence.

Attempting to answer the criticisms implicit in the Lashley-Wade studies, Grice (1948c, 1951) performed two experiments which followed the Lashley-Wade plan; but he also made certain changes designed to eliminate complicating aspects of the original procedure. The most important complications were the following: (*a*) Lashley and Wade had used punishment for incorrect responses. On trials when an error occurred the rat jumped against a locked door and fell into a net. Thus, if the animals originally trained with the 5-cm. circle had transferred a tendency to respond to it to the second discrimination situation, they would have been punished oftener than the 8-cm. animals early in this second phase of training. Such punishment might, then, have led to their abandoning the response to the 5-cm. circle very quickly. (*b*) Lashley and Wade had used the so-called correction method (Hull and Spence, 1938) in which a trial is counted only after the animal makes a correct response, no matter how many errors occur in such a trial. Grice used a non-correction method and allowed only one correct or incorrect response per trial. Under these conditions Grice obtained the results appearing in Figure 12.5, which are clearly in line with the results of conditioning-extinction theory in that response strength acquired in one situation was shown to transfer to another, benefiting the development of a discrimination.

In his second experiment, Grice (1951) provided the same sort of evidence for the transfer of extinction. Two groups of rats were trained to respond to a black square rather than to an 8- or 5-cm. circle, respec-

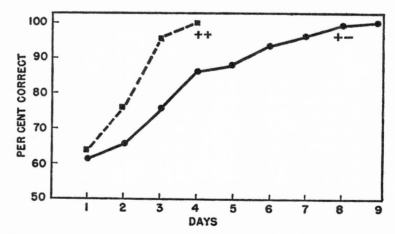

FIGURE 12.5.   The formation of a discrimination following reinforced training with a single stimulus. In one case (Group + +) the positive stimulus was the same as the previously reinforced stimulus. In the other case (Group + —) the previously reinforced stimulus is now the negative stimulus (Grice, 1948c).

tively. Then both groups were trained to discriminate the two circles with the 5-cm. circle positive and 8-cm. circle negative. The group originally trained with the 8-cm. circle negative made only 3.7 errors in learning the new discrimination, whereas those trained with the 5-cm. circle made 11.7 errors. These results, again, conform to the predictions from conditioning-extinction theory.

For reasons which may be attributable merely to slight procedural variations or to differences in strain of rats, learning in Grice's second experiment was much more rapid (3.7 and 11.7 errors for the two groups) than it was for the first experiment (12.9 and 27.0 errors). The difference seems worth mentioning, however, because it is in line with F. K. Graham's earlier (1943) discovery that what is transferred in the transfer of a discrimination is chiefly a tendency not to respond, in conditioning-extinction terms, the extinctive or inhibitory tendency.

2. *The Problem of Motivation.* One of the most obvious predictions from the original Spence-Hull version of conditioning-extinction theory is that increasing motivation will facilitate the development of a discrimination. In Hull's (1943, 1952) terms this is expressed abstractly by saying that drives (D) and the difference between net habit strengths (H) to S+ and S— interact multiplicatively. That is:

$$R_{s+} - R_{s-} = f(D) \times f(H_{s+} - H_{s-})$$

Clearly, increasing drive should increase the preference for R_{s+} whenever $H_{s+} > H_{s-}$. Experimental evidence on this point is inconsistent. Some investigators (Buchwald and Yamaguchi, 1955; Tolman and Gleitman, 1949; Powlowski, 1953; Dinsmoor, 1952; Eisman, 1956; Eisman, Asimow, and Maltzman, 1956) have obtained evidence that increased drive improves discrimination. Others have obtained either no effect (Teel, 1952; Teel and Webb, 1951; Miles, 1959; Meyer, 1951) or an indication that, under certain conditions, increased drive may actually interfere (Bruner, Matter, and Papanek, 1955; Yerkes and Dodson, 1908). Results of the latter two kinds pose an obvious problem for conditioning-extinction theory.

This difficulty could be removed if there were a reasonable basis for making the assumption that the experiments in which drive failed to benefit discrimination were ones in which H_{s+} and H_{s-} were equal. Under these conditions, drive should theoretically have no beneficial effect upon discrimination. A revision of conditioning-extinction theory outlined by Spence (1958) makes such an assumption tenable for certain forms of learning. Whereas Spence's earlier writings had at least implied that the law of effect applies to all learning, he was led, in 1956, to alter this position and to propose a variety of two-process theory. This was apparently due, in part, to the difficulties encountered by uniprocess reinforcement theory in dealing with the effects of motivation on discrimination. In Spence's revised theory, classical conditioning is assumed to obey the law of effect, and instrumental learning is thought of as involving only a contiguity principle. It will be noted that this theory is exactly the opposite of the more conventional two-process position.

The implications of the revised theory for the outcomes of experiments investigating the effect of drive on discrimination differ somewhat depending upon whether the discrimination is established by classical or instrumental conditioning procedures. In classical differential conditioning, habit strength accrues to S+ only on reinforced trials, and S— receives no habit strength except through generalization. Thus there is always a difference in the strength of H_{S+} and H_{S-}. In theory, drive multiplies this difference, and the straightforward prediction is that increased motivation will improve discrimination. In their total effect, classical differential conditioning experiments support this prediction (Runquist, Spence, and Stubbs, 1958; Spence and Beecroft, 1954; Spence and Farber, 1953, 1954), although there are exceptions (Hilgard, Jones, and Kaplan, 1951) and the differences in individual experiments have usually not been statistically significant. This latter fact may be the result of a phenomenon considered in the last chapter, where we saw that increasing motivation increases the breadth of the generalization gradient. This effect would reduce somewhat the difference to be multiplied by drive, thereby working against the prediction.

For instrumental conditioning experiments, the situation is different because the law of effect, according to Spence's new theory, does not operate. In such an experiment, the habit strength associated with the positive and negative stimuli will be equal if these stimuli have been responded to (rewarded or not) an equal number of times in the discrimination experiment, and drive changes should have no effect upon discriminative performance. Experiments in which drive has had no effect upon discrimination appear to have approximated this condition. Such reasoning has led Spence and his associates (Ramond, 1954; Spence, Goodrich, and Ross, 1959) to perform a series of experiments in which an attempt was made to manipulate the relative strengths of H_{S+} and H_{S-} simultaneously with the manipulation of drive, and to observe the effect of such procedures upon performance. In the latter of these studies, for example, rats learned a black-white discrimination under 3 or 40 hours of food deprivation. In one subcondition free- and forced-choice trials were arranged so that the numbers of responses to the positive and negative stimuli were equal. In a second subcondition there were twice as many responses to the positive stimulus as to the negative. Speed of responding increased with drive under both subconditions; but discrimination improved only when the arrangement of trials favored the development of relatively stronger habit strength to S+. Thus, at the cost of a major theoretical concession, conditioning-extinction theory can be made to explain the results of at least some experiments which manipulated motivation.

3. *Discrimination Learning with Two Reinforced Stimuli.* Studies bearing on this revised, non-reinforcement, theory of discrimination are also to be found in investigations where the two stimuli are both associated with reward, but where a less effective reward is used for the "incorrect" stimulus. Logan (1952) trained rats in a position discrimination with short and long delays of reinforcement following the two responses. In this study, the animals learned to press either of two bars, one on the right of the apparatus and one on the left, to obtain food. One response, however, was reinforced after 1 second; the other was reinforced after 5 seconds. Responses to the two bars were carefully equated through the use of a series of free and forced trials. Under these conditions, the rats responded faster to the bar with the short delay and, on free-choice trials, selected it in preference to the bar with the long delay. Reversal of the delay conditions led to an appropriate reversal of both of these tendencies. The speed results appear in Figure 12.6. In experiments of this sort,

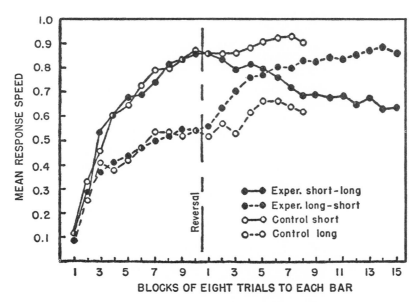

FIGURE 12.6. Discrimination and reversal of a discrimination in a situation where responses to both stimuli were reinforced. Animals were run in an apparatus where touching a bar produced food; but the time between pressing the bar and the delivery of food differed, being one second for one bar and five seconds for the other. The graph above shows speed of responding to the short- and long-delay bars for two groups of subjects. For one group the delay conditions were reversed after 80 trials. For the other there was no reversal (Logan, 1952).

Spence's revised theory would require that the habit strength associated with the two responses be equal because of the equivalent numbers of trials with each response. If this interpretation is correct, the differential performance must have resulted from an incentive mechanism (p. 170) derived from a classical conditioning of responses during the delay to stimuli associated with the right and left sides of the apparatus. This suggests the intriguing possibility that, with trials equated, in instrumental conditioning discriminations may be established through the classical conditioning mechanism involved in the development of incentive motivation or secondary reinforcement. The implications of this idea are largely unexplored.

4. *The Learning-Performance Distinction in Discrimination Learning.* As a part of the revision of his general theory of learning, Spence has also (1956, 1958) brought an important aspect of the learning-performance distinction to bear on behavior in selective learning. Specifically, he argues that the curves shown in Figure 12.1 (and comparable ones which might be constructed to represent the new contiguity interpretation) are reflections of the underlying learning process. There is good reason to believe that behavior in the selective learning situation will not mirror these functions in anything like a one-to-one fashion. Employing a modification of Hull's assumption of an oscillatory process, Spence sometimes uses a transformation which makes the probability of choosing S+ in selective learning a normal integral (z-score) function of the difference in response strengths conditioned to S+ and S—. At the same time, however, he (Spence, 1958) claims that this procedure probably provides but a poor first approximation to an adequate statement of the transformation involved.

RELATIONAL THEORY

Particularly in the case where the stimuli to be discriminated are presented simultaneously and in situations involving choice reactions, an alternative explanation of discrimination seems possible. This is relational theory, which is closely related to the cognitive view of learning in general. It holds that the development of a discrimination depends upon a comparison of the stimuli to be discriminated, and that the response of the organism is to the relationship between them. The most important empirical predictions to which this theory leads are that (*a*) simultaneous presentation of stimuli, which favors the act of comparing stimuli, will lead to the more rapid development of a discrimination than the successive presentation of stimuli; and (*b*) since the discrimination is a response to a relationship transposition, or transfer, the response will occur to pairs of stimuli not involved in the original discrimination but standing in the same relationship to each other. In addition, relational theorists often hold (*c*) that the development of discrimination involves, on the part of the organism, the adoption of a series of hypotheses which are successively discarded until the correct one is hit upon. This non-continuity position, however, is not limited to discrimination learning. It is a theory about the nature of learning in general and, as such, has been discussed earlier (p. 136).

Simultaneous and Successive Discrimination Learning

The proposition that discrimination learning involves an act of comparison suggests that such learning should proceed most rapidly under conditions which maximize the opportunity for such comparing behavior to occur. A direct test of this idea seems to be provided by the relative speeds of mastering simultaneous and successive discriminations. In simultaneous discrimination, positive and negative stimuli are presented together, ordinarily in some sort of random spatial arrangement from trial to trial. The learner's task is to choose between the two stimuli, both of which are present for inspection and comparison. In successive discrimination, however, only one stimulus (or a pair of identical ones) is present. The stimuli differ from trial to trial, and the organism must make one response in the presence of one stimulus (or pair of stimuli) and the other response in the presence of the other.[2] In this procedure it is obviously not possible for the organism to make a direct comparison of stimuli. Relational theory holds that a comparison actually does occur, between the stimulus now present and a memory trace of the alternative stimulus, and that such comparison is harder to make than one with both stimuli physically present. This, more exactly, is the reason that relational theory predicts relatively greater difficulty with successive discriminations. Absolute stimulus theory predicts no difference.

Experimental comparisons of the two forms of discrimination learning have produced all possible results. In some experiments (Spence, 1952; North and Jeeves, 1956) simultaneous discriminations have, as predicted by relational theory, been easier than successive discriminations. In others there has been no difference (Grice, 1949). In still others the successive discrimination has been found to be easier (Bitterman and Wodinsky, 1953; Weise and Bitterman, 1951; Teas and Bitterman, 1952). The implications of these various outcomes for discrimination learning theory seem to be as follows: (1) Both of the initial theoretical alternatives, relational theory and absolute stimulus theory, lead to erroneous predictions, indicating that both must be modified in order to explain the results of these studies. (2) Since opposite outcomes have been obtained, it would seem that the relative effectiveness of the two procedures must depend

---

[2] This procedure differs from the method described earlier in that it is possible to make a correct response and obtain reward on each trial.

upon the operation of other variables. Of such variables, one of the most important appears to be the similarity of the stimuli to be discriminated. In easy discriminations, there is little or no difference between the two procedures, but in difficult discriminations the simultaneous method is superior (Loess and Duncan, 1952; McCaslin, 1954). (3) In certain experiments deriving from the simultaneous-successive discrimination issue, another problem has been raised. This problem involves the nature of the stimuli controlling responses in the discrimination situation.

This last problem is basic and has plagued students of discrimination learning for a long time. All theories in this area begin with the implicit assumption that the organism perceives the stimuli presented. If it does not, no theorist would expect the discrimination to be learned. This simple statement, however, obscures certain differences of emphasis which separate absolute stimulus theory and relational theory. Absolute stimulus theory holds that it is sufficient if the stimulus energy reaches appropriate receptors. Relational theory, on the other hand, assumes that the animal must, in addition, "pay attention" to the stimuli in question, a conception which modern physiological research makes less mysterious than it once was (Lindsley, 1957).

In experimental terms, the absolute stimulus theory seems to say that all stimuli impinging upon the receptors of the organism should control the response in some measure. Some relational theorists have extended this conception, perhaps unfairly, and have attempted to put the absolute stimulus theorists in the position of saying that small incidental differences between two stimuli will be discriminated, even if reinforcement is in no way contingent upon a response to one of these stimuli as opposed to the other. To illustrate: Teas and Bitterman (1952, Experiment II) trained two groups of rats in the following way: Original training for both groups consisted of two successive discriminations in a Lashley jumping apparatus, as outlined in Table 25. In this phase of the experiment, two similar cards marked with vertical stripes were present on certain trials. The two cards differed in that the stripes on one (always on the

TABLE 25

EXPERIMENTAL PROCEDURE
(From Teas and Bitterman, 1952)

Problem	Stimuli in Left/Right Order	Rewarded Response Group I	Group II
I	a. thin/thick	left	left
	b. light/dark	right	right
II	a. thin/thick	left*	right
	b. light/dark	right*	left
	c. thick/thin	left	right*
	d. dark/light	right	left*

left) were thin, and the stripes on the other (always on the right) were thick. On trials with these two cards a correct response was a jump to the left. On other trials, the stimuli were two plain gray cards which differed in brightness and the correct response was a jump to the right. One way of describing this problem is to say that the animals were rewarded for jumping to the thin lines and to the dark gray.

Following training of this sort the groups were subdivided and given training with the same stimuli; but, on half of the trials, each card was switched to the side it had not previously occupied. The various possible arrangements of the cards yield the four conditions indicated in Table 25 as problems IIa, IIb, and so on. For this problem, the conditions of reinforcement were reversed for Groups I and II. Group I was required to jump to the left on trials with the striped cards and to the right on trials with the gray cards. The other group was required to jump to the right on trials with the striped cards and to the left on trials with the gray cards. In this part of the experiment the problem was exactly the same as it previously had been on half the trials, while on the other half the lateral arrangement of the stimuli was reversed. Now, if the specific previously positive stimuli (thin lines and dark gray) were in complete control of the rats' jumping response, this would suggest that the two groups would show a substantial, but equal, decrement on Problem II.

Another way of looking at the experiment, however, leads to quite a different prediction. It might be argued that, in the original training, the rat merely learns to respond left on trials with the striped cards and right on trials with the gray cards, and that no discrimination between thick and thin stripes or between the two shades of gray need have occurred at all. On such an assumption, it will be observed that Problem II continues this arrangement for Group I and reverses it for Group II. Thus the shift to Problem II should produce little or no decrement for Group I, but a marked one for Group II.

The results of the experiment appear in Figure 12.7. There was, it will be noted, a small and relatively temporary disruption of the behavior of the animals in Group I with the beginning of Problem II. This means that the exact stimulus conditions employed in Problem I had exercised some control over the rats' behavior, and that changing these conditions produced an interference through the mechanism of generalization decrement. Studies by Bitterman, Calvin, and Elam (1953) and Grice (1952) have independently suggested this conclusion. The effect on Group II, however, was much more marked, producing an immediate and persistent reduction in the number of correct responses. This seems to indicate that the chief thing the rats had learned in the first phase of the experiment was to jump one way in the presence of the striped stimuli and the other in the presence of the gray stimuli, and that the reversal of reinforced responses had produced a substantial decrement through habit interference.

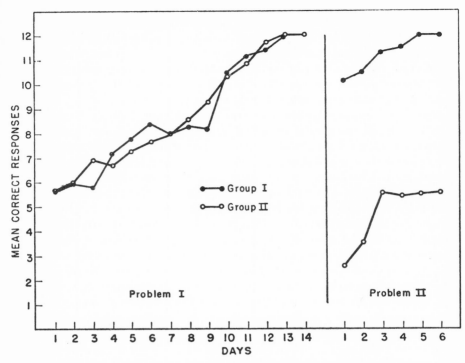

FIGURE 12.7.   Results of experiment by Teas and Bitterman (1952). See text
for explanation.

The importance of the Teas and Bitterman study is in the stress it
places on the perceptual control of discrimination learning. Clearly, to
predict the results of the study, it would have been necessary to know that
the animal was responding to the general configuration (stripes or grays)
and not to the differences between the two similar stimuli. In the Teas and
Bitterman experiment, common sense predicts that the discrimination
would be of this primitive configurational sort, and that the discrimination would be easy on this basis. In other experiments, however, it is
harder to arrive at such an anthropomorphic understanding of the discrimination situation or to predict which discrimination will be easier
(Wodinsky and Bitterman, 1952; Bitterman, Tyler, and Elam, 1955;
Saldanha and Bitterman, 1951; Turbeville, Calvin, and Bitterman, 1952).

Transposition

If an animal is trained to discriminate between two stimuli, such as two
shades of gray, by reinforcing a response to (say) the lighter, it is a
typical finding that this discrimination will transfer to other pairs of

stimuli and that the animal will continue to select the lighter. Moreover, this effect occurs even if the originally positive stimulus is paired with a still lighter one. That is, instead of choosing the originally reinforced stimulus, the animal now selects the new stimulus which bears the same relationship to the originally positive stimulus as the originally positive stimulus did to the negative stimulus. This transfer of discrimination to new pairs of stimuli is called *transposition*.

The first experimental work on transposition was done by Kinnaman (1902) who demonstrated transposition in monkeys. Since then there have been scores of studies of transposition, which have shown that the phenomenon is real and that it occurs on a wide range of stimulus dimensions and in a variety of species. In the course of these studies, one other fact of importance has come to light. As the test stimuli are made more and more different from the training stimuli, there is a gradual weakening of the transposition effect. This phenomenon has been crucial in the development of a nonrelational explanation of transposition, an explanation based upon the generalization of excitation and extinction.

Building on this relationship between the degree of transposition and the difference between training and test stimuli, Spence (1936, 1937b) developed the theory suggested in Figure 12.8. This representation depicts theoretical generalization gradients for excitation and inhibition along a size dimension. It is similar in conception to that presented in Figure 12.1 although the form of the generalization gradients is different. It should, perhaps, be emphasized that certain of Spence's deductions are independent of the exact form of the generalization gradients. Spence, himself, has since suggested other shapes (Spence, 1942a). It also seems very probable that different species, different stimulus dimensions, different discrimination measures, and, perhaps, different individual organisms will require different generalization functions.

The numbers on the baseline of Figure 12.8 have purely hypothetical meaning, although in Spence's example, they were assumed to represent areas of visual stimuli. As is indicated in the caption to Figure 12.8 the gradients of excitation and inhibition are established by training with stimulus 256 as S+ and stimulus 160 as S—. Suppose now that a test for transposition is made with the pair of stimuli 256 and 409. From the diagram it is evident that the strength of the tendency to react to 409 (6.5) is greater than the tendency to react to 256 (4.8). Therefore, the organism will choose 409 in spite of the fact that 256 was the positive stimulus during training. For this pair of stimuli, transposition should occur. This is predicted, however, without any assumption that the organism perceives the relationship ''relatively larger.'' Suppose, now, that the pair of stimuli 655 and 1049 are presented. The response strengths to these stimuli are 6.7 for 655 and 2.5 for 1049. In this case, the reaction

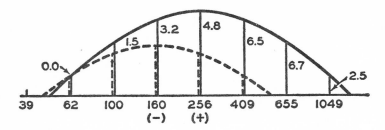

FIGURE 12.8. Spence's theoretical treatment of discrimination. Areas of the visual stimuli used in the experiment are represented along the baseline. During the training, response to 256 is rewarded, response to 160 extinguished. As a result of reinforcing 256 the generalization represented by the solid lines results. That is, tendencies to react positively are generalized to the neighboring stimuli in proportion to the heights of the solid lines above each stimulus size. The non-reinforcement of 160 leads to a generalization of inhibition represented by the broken lines, extending also to stimuli on either side of 160. The resulting reaction tendencies, obtained by subtracting the negative from the positive, are indicated by the figures above each stimulus size. (Spence, 1937b). The use of the diagram to explain the results of transposition experiments is described in the text.

should be to the smaller of the two stimuli. That is, the opposite of transposition should occur.

The crucial test of Spence's theory, as opposed to relational theory, obviously lies in the results of experiments designed to examine the details of transposition behavior as a function of the difference between training and test stimuli. Early demonstrations of the fact that transposition fails to occur under certain conditions are to be found in the studies of Gulliksen (1932), Kluver (1933), and Spence (1937a). This supplies indirect support for Spence's theory. More recently several studies have demonstrated that the tendency for an animal to respond relationally in a transposition test decreases with the difference between test and training stimuli and may show the predicted reversal (T. S. Kendler, 1950; Ehrenfreund, 1952). The strongest support for Spence's theory comes from the experiment by Ehrenfreund. In this investigation, two groups of rats were trained in a T-maze to respond to the lighter (Experiment I) or darker (Experiment II) of two stimuli. For one group the positive stimulus was the darker of two bright stimuli. For the other the positive stimulus was the lighter of two dark intensities. After initial training, transposition tests were made with individual groups of animals. For those trained with the bright stimuli, the tests were with darker pairs; for those trained with dark stimuli, the tests were with brighter pairs. The results of the experiment appear in Figure 12.9 in terms of the percentage of relational responses in the transposition tests. It is quite clear

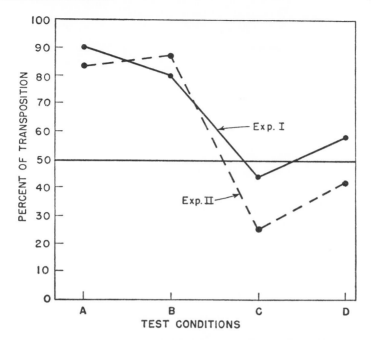

FIGURE 12.9. Amount of transposition as a function of the difference between training and test stimuli. The test conditions, A, B, C, and D represent a series of approximately equal steps away from the training stimuli (Ehrenfreund, 1952).

that the results are in excellent agreement with predictions derivable from Spence's theory: (1) There is a general tendency for the amount of transposition to decrease with increases in the difference between training and test stimuli. (2) There is also a point at which the opposite of transposition occurs in that the curves fall below the 50 per cent point. This reversal was significant in the case of Experiment II, but not in the case of Experiment I.

Results much less favorable to Spence's theory have come from an experiment by Lawrence and DeRivera (1954). These investigators used the Lashley jumping stand (Figure 10.13, p. 313) and a novel procedure to test for transposition. The stimuli were cards made up of two shades of gray, selected from a series of seven grays ranging from number 1 (white) to number 7 (black). The bottom half of the training stimulus was always a mid-gray, number 4. The top half was lighter on half of the trials and darker on the other half. The method was a variation of the successive-presentation procedure. When the top half of the card was lighter, a correct response was a jump to the right; when the top half was darker, the correct response was a jump to the left. Training consisted of practice to a criterion on six different stimuli. Represented as a fraction with the numbers of the upper and lower grays on the stimulus cards as numerator and denominator, respectively, the stimuli were: 1/4, 2/4, 3/4, 5/4, 6/4, and 7/4. To the first three of these, a right jump was correct; to the second three, a left jump was correct.

Tests for transposition were carried out over a long series of trials with 24 new cards which had a different shade of gray on the bottom. To illustrate, one test stimulus, 3/1, was a card with a relatively light gray on the top half and white on the bottom half. Relational theory and absolute stimulus theory make different predictions regarding the response to this stimulus. Since both of the grays had previously been associated with a right jump, a theory of the type proposed by Spence would predict a right jump. Relational theory, on the other hand, predicts a left jump, since the upper part of the stimulus was darker than the lower and preserves the relationship previously requiring a left jump. On 12 pairs of stimuli in which the two thoeries make opposed predictions, 65 per cent were in favor of relational theory; and this figure may be too low because the failures of the relational hypothesis occurred most conspicuously in cases where the upper and lower stimuli were fairly similar (for example, 6/7).

The two experiments described above present results which may be summarized as follows: Ehrenfreund's data are generally favorable to an absolute stimulus theory, supporting it in rather considerable detail. Lawrence and DeRivera, on the other hand, obtain results which support the relational interpretation, though with occasional failures for the predictions from this theory to hold. One possibility is that some combination of the two theories will ultimately have to be developed (Stevenson and Bitterman, 1955).

Another way of handling transposition in somewhat different terms has been suggested by a number of writers who propose to do so by means of a redefinition of the stimulus concept. If a stimulus is anything which can serve as a cue to which a response can be conditioned (Miller, 1959), it is an open question as to whether relationships can function in this way. If it turns out that they can, however, then the phenomenon of transposition would be nothing more than a special case of stimulus generalization in which the stimulus dimension is one of similarity of relationships. In more mechanistic terms, this idea could be reduced to a matter of mediated generalization. Suppose that an organism learns to respond to the relationship, S_1/S_2, in which S_1 and S_2 are either different stimuli presented to an animal simultaneously, or are two different parts of a single stimulus when the correct response depends upon the relationship between these parts. If it is assumed that the act of comparing these two stimuli, r_o, provides proprioceptive stimuli which function as discriminative stimuli, the following S-R analysis applies:

$$S_1/S_2 \longrightarrow r_o \longrightarrow {}^sS_1/S_2 \longrightarrow R$$

This merely assumes that the response (R) is mediated by an internal stimulus (${}^sS_1/S_2$) which is somehow peculiar to the relationship involved. Obviously, to say that the organism "recognizes" or "perceives" the relationship is little different from making this assumption. Now, if the organism is confronted with a new pair of stimuli (S_3 and S_4) bearing the same relationship to each other as S_1 did to S_2, it could be argued that the following holds:

$$S_3/S_4 \longrightarrow r_p \longrightarrow {}^sS_3/S_4$$

If ${}^sS_3/S_4$ is on some continuum with ${}^sS_1/S_2$ but differs in absolute value, there should be generalization of the response (R) to the new relationship, and the degree of transposition should depend upon the similarity of training and test stimuli. There should, however, be no reversal of the transposition function with increasing differences between training and test pairs, as Spence's theory requires.

If the mediating response is one of observing or comparing, it might be, as suggested in connection with the simultaneous-successive discrimination discussed earlier, that the former of these procedures would lead to better transposition than the latter. There is some evidence that this is the case. Baker and Lawrence (1951) trained rats to discriminate between circles of two different sizes and then tested for transposition. They found that animals trained by the simultaneous method showed reliable evidence of transposition; those trained by the successive method did not. A possibility since suggested by Wertheimer (1959) is that the traces of relationships (s_1/s_2) are better retained than the traces of single stimuli, making transposition more likely following training on a simultaneous discrimination simply because the animal is more likely to remember the relevant cue.

In much human behavior, implicit verbal labeling is a possible cue-producing response of the sort just described. On this basis it might be expected that responses to relationships would exhibit transposition to the extent that such responses occur. Kuenne (1946) and Alberts and Ehrenfreund (1951) have both reported studies which support this expectation. Kuenne ran four groups of children in a discrimination study, using positive and negative stimuli which differed in size. Then she tested for transposition with stimuli similar to the training stimuli ("near test") and very different ("far test"). The children in the four groups had mental ages of 3, 4, 5, and 6 years. Their transposition scores were all very similar on the near test of transposition; but, as a function of mental age, they gave 50, 60, 80, and 100 per cent relational responses on the far test. Moreover, children who verbalized the relationship showed 100 per cent transposition, whereas those who did not behaved in nearly a chance manner.[3]

Acquired Distinctiveness of Cues

The general point made in the foregoing discussion is that responses which occur to the stimuli in discrimination learning may provide cues which are capable of equating pairs of stimuli in terms of relationships. These responses, it may be said, mediate the relational response. With the concepts of mediational responses and response-produced stimulation developed, a number of questions arise as to the conditions which govern the functioning of this process. One possibility, considered by Lawrence (1949, 1950) is very similar to the Lashley-Wade proposal described earlier (p. 347). Lawrence hypothesized that experience with particular stimuli made the response-produced cues initiated by them more discriminable, so that discriminations involving these stimuli would be facilitated. To test this prediction, Lawrence (1949) trained rats on a simultaneous discrimination problem and then transferred them to a successive one. Although there was a total of 18 different combinations of conditions in the experiment, the principal findings can be made clear if we describe the procedure as if there were only three. In the simultaneous discrimination, these three different groups learned, respectively, to differentiate black versus white alleys, rough versus smooth floors, or wide versus narrow alleys in a special choice apparatus. Adopting the standard procedure in such experiments, the positive cue was switched randomly from one side of the apparatus to the other. Because of this, no specific, overt, right- or left-going response could be learned in the stage of the experiment. The later, successive, discrimination was carried out in a T-maze. The relevant cue was brightness (black vs. white). Both arms of the T were black on some trials and white on others, and the animals were required to respond by going to one side when the arms were white and to the other when the arms were black. During this test rough and smooth floors were present randomly from trial to trial and uncorrelated with reward. For the three original groups, for which the relevant cue had been brightness, alley width, and smoothness of floors, this procedure should have quite different effects: (1) For the group trained with the black-white discrimination in the simultaneous procedure, the relevant cue continues to be relevant, and it should be easy for this group to learn the discrimination. (2) For the group originally trained to make the rough-smooth discrimination, the texture cue is still present, but irrelevant. It should be more difficult for this group to learn the new discrimination. (3) The group originally trained with wide and narrow alleys should perform at a level between the other two. No positive or negative effect should transfer from the earlier experience, since the cues involved in the simultaneous situation are both new. The results of the experiment showed the predicted beneficial effect of the original training on the black-white discrimination, but failed to show the negative transfer expected in the case of the rough-smooth group.

On the basis of this and subsequent evidence Lawrence proposed a two-process theory of discrimination learning, part of which is suggested by the schema in Figure 12.10. End-organ stimulation, according to this

FIGURE 12.10

view, initiates a mediating process which modifies the pattern of internal stimuli received by the organism. It is assumed that this modification occurs gradually with learning, making the internal pattern of stimuli more discriminable after such experience. This acquired distinctiveness is thus available to aid later learning, even if no instrumental response is available to transfer to the new situation.

THE FORMATION OF LEARNING SETS

In many areas of learning, practice on a series of learning tasks leads to an improvement of the organism's ability to deal with learning situations involved. This is a general statement which apparently applies at all levels of task complexity. Repeated conditioning and extinction increase the rapidity with which these processes occur (Bullock and Smith, 1953). The number of trials required to learn a list of nonsense syllables decreases by about 50 per cent with practice on a series of a dozen lists (Meyer and Miles, 1953). And there is a remarkable improvement in the ability of organisms of several species to master discrimination problems with practice at making such discriminations. Harlow (1949, 1959) refers to such improvements as the formation of *learning sets* and explains learning sets in terms of *error factor theory,* which will be treated later.

The classic study of learning sets (Harlow, 1949) was one in which monkeys learned a series of over 300 discriminations in the Wisconsin General Test Apparatus (WGTA, Figure 12.11), each presented for 6 trials. The changes in performance within these 6 trials for various blocks of discriminations are shown in Figure 12.12. What is striking is the great improvement in performance over the series of problems. On the final block the typical performance is chance (50 per cent on the first trial and nearly perfect from then on. Occasional errors do occur, for reasons to be discussed later. But these are relatively infrequent and appear only once in about 20 trials, as is indicated by the leveling of the function for problems 201-312 at about 95 per cent.

For the discrimination-learning situation, the development of learning sets is a case in which insightful behavior occurs as the end result of a great deal of experience with the sort of problem eventually handled insightfully. This may be true of insightful behavior in general. Harlow (1959) citing a variety of evidence (Birch, 1945; Schiller, 1952) comes to the conclusion that, at the present time, there is no good evidence for the existence of unlearned insightful behavior.

Learning sets of this sort described by Harlow have been demonstrated in several primate genera (Miles and Meyer, 1956; Miles, 1957; Riopelle, 1958), in rats (Koronakos and Arnold, 1957), in cats (Warren and Baron, 1956), and in both normal and mentally defective children (Kaufman

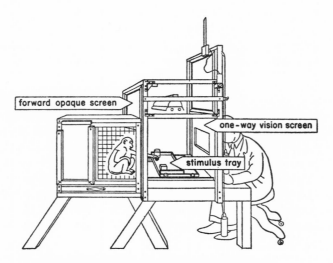

WISCONSIN GENERAL TEST APPARATUS

Showing: Stimulus tray
One-way vision screen in lowered position
Forward opaque screen in raised position

FIGURE 12.11. The Wisconsin General test apparatus (Harlow, 1949).

DISCRIMINATION LEARNING CURVES

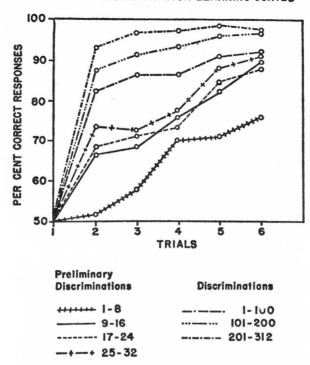

Preliminary Discriminations	Discriminations
┼┼┼┼┼ 1-8	—·——· 1-luO
——— 9-16	···——··· 101-200
-------- 17-24	—·—·—·— 201-312
—┼—┼ 25-32	

FIGURE 12.12. Performance on Trials 1-6 in a series of discriminations. The improvement with practice depicts the development of a learning set (Harlow, 1949).

and Peterson, 1958).[4] In general, the speed with which learning sets develop, and perhaps the level to which they can develop, depend upon the phylogenetic level of the learner. Figure 12.13 presents data for the Rhesus monkey, squirrel monkey, and marmoset which support this conclusion. The results obtained by Kaufman and Peterson indicate that the formation of learning sets is more rapid in either normal or mentally defective (IQ 50-75) children than it is in any of these species. K. S. Hayes, R. Thompson, and C. Hayes (1953) obtained data to suggest that learning sets in chimpanzees may develop at about the same rate as the

[4] The literature on learning sets is quite large. The reader interested in a more extensive coverage of these materials would do well to begin with Harlow's (1959) paper. Some related papers, selected to cover a range of tasks, procedures and species are: Barnett and Cantor (1957), Cotterman, Meyer, and Wickens (1956), Darby and Riopelle (1955), Gatling (1951, 1952) and Hayes, Thompson, and Hayes (1953a, 1953b). Although they are not commonly treated in this connection, it seems possible that the studies demonstrating a transfer of a discrimination along some physical dimension will provide leads to additional factors contributing to the formation of learning sets (Baker and Osgood, 1954; Lawrence, 1952).

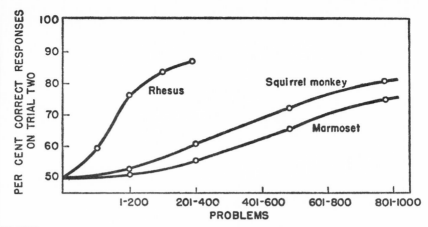

FIGURE 12.13.   Curves showing the formation of learning sets in the Rhesus
monkey, squirrel monkey, and marmoset (Miles, 1957).

mentally retarded children in Kaufman and Peterson's study, and somewhat less rapidly than in normal children.

A special form of learning set occurs in discrimination-reversal experiments. In these studies the positive stimulus in one series of trials becomes the negative stimulus in a subsequent series, and the previously
negative stimulus becomes positive. Most of these studies have been done
using rats as subjects, and either black-white or spatial discriminations.
With a few exceptions (for example, Fritz, 1930) these studies have
shown progressive improvement in the speed with which the discrimination can be reversed (Krechevsky, 1932c; North, 1950a, 1950b). At least
two have shown the rat to be capable of learning a one-trial discrimination reversal in the relatively simple spatial discrimination situation
(Buytendijk, 1930; Dufort, Guttman, and Kimble, 1954). And one study
has shown that the process is remarkably similar in low-grade mental
defectives (House and Zeaman, 1959). See Figure 12.14.

Both the ordinary learning set and the reversal set just described are
a form of learning, that is, learning to learn. Although research has not
gone far in this direction, it is clear that learning to learn displays some
of the characteristics of other learning. In a sense, the process can be
brought under stimulus control. Riopelle and Copelan (1954) trained 5
Rhesus monkeys to perform discrimination reversals without making a
wrong response, by changing the color of the tray in the WGTA on which
the positive and negative stimuli were placed. There is also some evidence
that learning sets may generalize. It has been shown, for example, that
improvement in discrimination ability established with flat stimulus
objects transfers with little loss to objects much different in height
(Harlow and Warren, 1952).

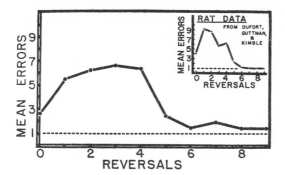

FIGURE 12.14. Performance in a discrimination-reversal experiment compared for feebleminded human subjects and rats. In both experiments subjects first learned to respond to one position (for example, right) as correct. Then the problem was reversed, and the alternative position (left) became correct. When this was mastered the original response was again correct, and so on. Larger curve is for mental retardates. (House and Zeaman, 1959).

Error Factor Theory and the Uniprocess Learning Concept

To account for the learning-set phenomenon, Harlow has developed a theoretical treatment which he believes applies to all learning but is most appealing in the context of discrimination learning (Harlow, 1950, 1959). This theory is, first of all, a uniprocess theory; but it differs from other single-factor theories, such as those of Hull and Guthrie, in that the one mechanism is not, strictly speaking, learning at all. It is, rather, extinction or the suppression of incorrect responses. According to Harlow's view, the learner comes to the learning situation with the correct habit already available, but also with a number of other competing tendencies which obscure the correct response. The mastery of the discrimination by the organism consists in the elimination of these interfering tendencies. In his original analysis of discrimination learning, Harlow (1950) identified five of these interfering tendencies or *error factors,* four of which seemed most important to the understanding of the development of learning sets.

1. *Stimulus Perseveration.* Stimulus-perseveration errors presumably reflect preferences which the organism has for the incorrect stimulus. These tendencies may generalize from previous learning (Jarvik, 1953) or, like the preference for darkness commonly observed in rats, they may be innate. If they exist at all, they appear as a tendency for the animal to choose the negative stimulus on the first trial and to continue choosing it on subsequent trials. This source of errors is most important early in a series of discriminations. With increasing numbers of discriminations, the size of the effect diminishes as does the number of trials on which it can be detected (Harlow, 1959, p. 514; Riopelle, 1953).

2. *Differential Cue.* In 1936, Spence pointed out a second potential source of errors in many discrimination experiments. In a black-white discrimination, with black positive, the first reinforced response is not only to black, but also to (say) the left. Thus, there is an inherent ambiguity concerning the reinforcement contingency, and it is necessary for the response strength conditioned to the spatial cue to extinguish before a perfect brightness discrimination can occur. Operationally, this factor leads to a greater number of errors on trials in which the spatial position of the positive stimulus is changed than on trials where it is the same as on the previous correct trial. The influence of the differential-cue factor has been demonstrated in several studies and has also been shown to be a highly persistent source of errors (Braun, Patton, and Barnes, 1952).

3. *Response Shift.* It is a common observation in learning experiments of most sorts that absolutely perfect performance is difficult to obtain. The subject may go for a long series of trials without error and then, for no apparent reason, make a mistake. Harlow attributes this response-shift tendency to exploratory drive and reports that it seems incapable of complete suppression, at least in studies with the WGTA and food-incentives (Harlow, 1959, p. 517).

4. *Position Preferences.* In discrimination experiments, responses may perseverate in a way that parallels stimulus perseveration described earlier. The source of such perseveration is often in "handedness," which applies to lower animals as well as to man. In experiments where the positive and negative stimuli are shifted from side to side, such preferences will lead to errors. The evidence is that position preferences are relatively unimportant as sources of errors in primate discrimination learning. They may determine the animal's choice on the first trial in a new discrimination, but they are rapidly and easily suppressed (Riopelle, 1953). In rats, on the other hand, such tendencies are sometimes very powerful. It is often reported, in descriptions of discrimination experiments, that position habits are so strong in certain subjects that the intended discrimination is never learned.

The application of error factor theory to the development of learning sets involves the assumption that error tendencies can be suppressed fairly permanently, and that such suppression transfers at least to all new discriminations in the same general apparatus. If this is the case, the development of a learning set consists simply in the gradual elimination of error factors so that they do not have to be suppressed with each new discrimination. This explanation also appears to handle a certain puzzling fact about discrimination reversal. It has been shown (Reid, 1953) that overtraining on a black-white discrimination actually facilitates the learning of the reversed white-black discrimination. In error-factor terms this means that the suppression of error tendencies may go on after a discrimination is learned. Since the elimination of such tendencies is as appropriate to the reversed discrimination as to the original one, it should assist the discrimination reversal. Put in these terms, it becomes apparent that error factor theory is really very similar to Krechevsky's theory of hypotheses. The idea which is basic in both formulations is that the responses of the organism are determined at first by tendencies which are irrelevant to the solution of the problem. Obviously a perseverative tendency to respond by going to the left is operationally equal to a left-going hypothesis. Similarly, Harlow and Krechevsky both assume a sort of conceptual independence of error tendencies and the correct response, so that the elimination of one of these tendencies (hypotheses) is useful whatever the correct solution to the discrimination problem. The only important difference between the two positions seems to lie in the point that, according to Krechevsky, the animal does acquire a kind of knowledge in the situation, whereas Harlow does not regard the organism as learning anything, the entire "learning" process being attributed to extinction. Given Krechevsky's adherence to the noncontinuity view of learning, it might be said that he has a one-trial learning theory and that Harlow has a no-trial learning theory.

SUMMARY

Although all learning involves a minor element of discrimination, special procedures are required to establish a fine differentiation between stimuli. In general it is necessary to maintain the strength of a response to one stimulus by reinforcement and, at the same time, to extinguish by non-reinforcement responses generalized to an alternative stimulus. Two somewhat different techniques for accomplishing this objective are to be found in the methods of successive and simultaneous presentation of stimuli.

The method of successive presentation of stimuli is Pavlov's method of contrasts and is especially well suited to the study of discrimination in the classical conditioning situation. The reinforced (positive) and non-reinforced (negative) stimuli are presented on randomly alternated trials, but never together. Under this procedure the animal gradually comes to respond on trials with the positive stimulus and not to respond on trials with the negative stimulus.

In the method of simultaneous presentation of stimuli, the reinforced and non-reinforced cues are presented at the same time, and the situation is arranged so that the animal may respond to one of them, by approaching it or manipulating it. If the subject responds to the stimulus arbitrarily designated as correct (positive), it is rewarded. The most important difference between this method of establishing a discrimination and the method of successive presentation of stimuli is that the simultaneous method affords a greater opportunity for the comparison of the positive and negative stimuli. This is a point to which we shall return.

Conditioning-Extinction Theory

Looked at operationally, discrimination learning procedures are a combination of two simpler procedures, those of conditioning and extinction. This fact has led several investigators to propose theories of discrimination learning in which the processes of conditioning and extinction provide the central concepts. These conditioning-extinction theories also take account of the fact that the relationship between positive and negative stimuli necessitates a consideration of the process of stimulus generalization.

Among the predictions to which conditioning-extinction theory leads are the following: (1) In discrimination learning, the level of responding to the reinforced stimulus should be less than would be obtained by the same number of reinforcements in an ordinary conditioning situation where no inhibition, generated by trials with the negative stimulus, would develop. (2) There will be a substantial level of responding to the non-reinforced stimulus whenever this stimulus is enough like the positive stimulus to receive, through stimulus generalization, response strength conditioned to the positive stimulus. (3) Increasing the ratio of reinforced to non-reinforced trials, with the appropriate stimuli, should increase response level to both stimuli; but there should be no improvement in the differentiation of the stimuli. (4) If an organism has acquired a response to a particular stimulus, the effect of beginning discrimination training should be to lower response strength to the positive stimulus. (5) The ease of developing a discrimination should vary directly with the psychophysical difference between the stimuli to be discriminated. Studies which vary widely in procedure have provided data in affirmation of all these deductions.

Relational Theory

In spite of the obvious power of the conditioning-extinction theory of discrimination learning, it has not gone uncriticized. As an alternative, many writers have favored a relational theory of discrimination. The central conception in relational theory is that the learning of a discrimination involves an active act of comparison, either between stimuli which are physically present, or between one stimulus which is present and the memory trace of another. One of the most direct deductions from such a theory appears to be that it would be easier to establish discriminations by the method of simultaneous presentation of stimuli than by the method of successive presentation. Studies of the sort implied have sometimes yielded the predicted results, but with an embarrassing frequency the two methods have either produced no difference, or the successive method has actually been superior. There seems to be no simple or single explanation for this variety of outcomes.

A second deduction from the relational theory of discrimination is that the transposition of a discrimination should be possible. Transposition is a variety of transfer of training in which a discrimination formed between stimuli bearing a certain, objectively specifiable, relationship to each other will transfer appropriately to stimuli other than those involved in original training. To illustrate, an animal which has been trained to choose the larger of two particular circles will, if it exhibits the phenomenon of transposition, also choose the larger of two different circles Transposition has been demonstrated in many experimental situations It has been shown that an animal will actually reject a formerly positive stimulus in favor of a new one which bears the same relationship to this formerly positive stimulus as it did to the original negative stimulus. There is also evidence that the magnitude of the difference between the training pair of stimuli and test stimuli is important in determining whether transposition will occur. This last fact has provided the basis for the development of an S-R theory of transposition. This theory explains transposition in terms of interacting gradients of generalized excitation and inhibition. Experimental evidence specifically relevant to the question "Which of these theories is correct?" is mixed. In order to obtain an adequate explanation of transposition, it will ultimately be necessary to develop a different theory, perhaps one which begins with some assumption capable of making a relationship a cue. Another set of extremely important considerations stems from the fact that the initial discriminability of stimuli is partly determined by previous experience with these stimuli.

Learning Sets

A final set of factors which increase the difficulties involved in understanding discrimination learning derives from the fact that the ability to deal with discrimination problems improves with practice. Animals develop learning sets. In order to account for the formation of learning sets, Harlow has proposed a theory of discrimination learning in general, in which the correct response is assumed to be present at the beginning of training in a particular discrimination situation, but suppressed by error tendencies. The appearance of the correct response is accounted for in terms of the extinction of these erroneous responses. Among the important error tendencies to be considered are preferences for particular stimuli or responses, tendencies to alternate, and confusion stemming from the fact that, in most discrimination-learning experiments, the aspect of the correct response which determines its correctness is ambiguous. The development of learning sets theoretically depends upon the extinction of these error tendencies and the transfer of this extinction to new discriminations.

·13·

Motivation and Learning

THE TOPIC OF MOTIVATION is an increasingly important field of investigation in its own right and has been the subject of several book-length expositions (for example, Young, 1936; Bindra, 1959). Discussions of motivation differ widely in their overall treatment of the subject, and also in the relationship which motivation is assumed to have to learning. Because of this diversity, it may be well to begin what we have to say with a brief statement of the general position to be adopted.

METHODOLOGICAL STATUS OF THE CONCEPT OF MOTIVE

It is important to recognize at the outset that motivation is a *concept* (Koch, 1941a, 1941b), a concept suggested by certain characteristics of behavior which are a matter both of everyday observation and of experimental manipulation in the laboratory. The two features of behavior which seem to demand the development of some such concept as that of motivation are (1) certain variations in the behavior of the same individual from time to time, and (2) certain extreme individual differences in response to the same situation, including differences in the apparent speed of learning. If, for example, we observe that a 10-year-old youngster loiters and dallies along his way to school and, a few hours later, rushes pell mell on his way to the playground, we are apt to infer that his *motives* differ on the two occasions. Or if we watch two small children in the presence of a large dog and see that one of them runs in apparent terror to its mother, while the other shows strong interest or at least no alarm, it again seems reasonable to think in terms of different motives and to say that the first child was afraid of the dog.

In order to make either of these inferences with certainty, it is essential, first, to be able to exclude an alternative explanation in terms of capacity, skill, or learning. In the first example, it is necessary to be certain that the boy has not learned to run faster in the interval separating the two observations; in the second example, we must be willing to assume that the two children do not differ in their innate responsiveness to dogs. This requirement implies a distinction between motivation on the one hand, and the capacities of the organism on the other. In theories such as Hull's, where this distinction is sharply made, the assumption is that motives are relatively temporary conditions of the organism which serve to energize relatively permanent habits or capacities.

Drive and Drive Stimulus

The motivation of behavior comes about through the existence of conditions (drive-establishing operations) which release energy originating in the organism's metabolic processes. This energy, in and of itself, is directionless and may serve any of a variety of motivational objectives. As Hebb puts it, ". . . drive is an energizer, but not a guide; an engine, but not a steering gear." (Hebb, 1955, p. 249). Against this view of motivation as directionless there stands a considerable body of evidence that motivated behavior is directed. The hungry rat, given all three opportunities, eats rather than drinks or copulates, suggesting that motives somehow provide for the direction of activity. The mechanism commonly accepted as subserving this function of guiding motivated behavior is that of drive stimulation (S_D). There is good reason to believe that most drives have associated drive stimuli. Some of the evidence will be presented later in this chapter. For the present, there are several methodological observations which need to be made.

The basic question to be answered is whether drive and drive stimuli are two separate processes or two reflections of a single one. Our view is that they are two processes and that it is important to keep them separate. It has sometimes been urged that only one process is involved, and that the concept of drive stimulus is superfluous. Because the conditions for producing drive stimuli are the same as those for creating a drive, the argument is that this fact makes drive and drive stimulus operationally indistinguishable. This point does not seem well taken because, (a) even admitting the identity of establishing operations, it is entirely possible for drive and drive stimulus to differ with respect to other characteristics. Presumably, drive stimuli would share the properties of other stimuli and would function in such a way as to make the discrimination among drives and drive-stimulus generalization possible. Drive, considered solely as an energizer would not serve such functions. (b) There is also the strong likelihood that the functions which relate drive and drive stimuli to these identical determining conditions will be different. In the case of hunger, for example, there is evidence that stomach contractions, which represent the source of drive stimulation (Cannon, 1934), reach their maximal strengths within a few hours, although the energizing effect of drive continues to increase for considerably longer. (c) Furthermore, if one of these two concepts is superfluous, it is at least as likely to be drive, itself, as it is to be drive stimulus. Estes (1958) makes a good case for this point. (*d*) Finally it is important to point out that recognizing the existence of drive stimuli does not require the postulation of a steering or guiding function of drive per se. The two processes, as Hebb cogently argues, may profitably be considered separately, with the drive or motive concept being reserved for the energizing function.

Drive as an Intervening Variable

As we mentioned earlier, drive is a concept, or an intervening variable. It is an unobservable construct employed as a logical link between manipulated antecedent drive-establishing operations and the effect of these operations upon behavior. In this respect the concept, drive, is like that of learning. We assume that it is produced by certain environmental circumstances and reflected in certain effects upon behavior. Figure 13.1 is a diagrammatic representation of this general point. It depicts the logical status of drive as seen by different theorists, and it also shows how they think of the concept of drive stimulus as fitting into this scheme.

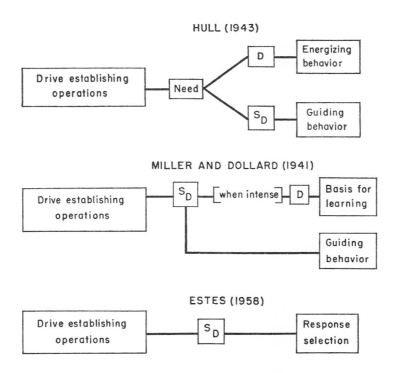

FIGURE 13.1. Status of drive (D) and drive stimulation (S$_D$) as intervening variables in several theoretical systems.

As Figure 13.1 shows, drive and drive stimulation are intervening variables in all of these conceptions. There is, however, little agreement as to
the "true nature" of drive, and even less on the nature of the relationship
between drive and drive stimuli. Hull's conception was that drive-establishing operations are such as to create a state of need in the organism,
and that drive and drive stimulation both derive from it (Hull, 1943,
p. 72). Miller and Dollard propose a stimulus theory of drive according
to which motives result from high intensities of drive stimulation. Estes
goes a step farther and develops a theory in which the only considerations
are the stimuli produced by drive-establishing operations and the responses conditioned to them. In this theory no special concept of drive is
necessary.

S-R and R-R Concepts of Motive

In various places, Spence (for example, 1944, 1948) has distinguished
between two forms of psychological law which he refers to as S-R and
R-R laws. S-R laws have terms on the independent-variable side, which
refer to manipulations of the environment (loosely, "stimuli"). The R-R
laws, in contrast, are formulated between independently observable aspects of a single organism's behavior. Corresponding to the difference
between S-R and R-R laws, it is possible to distinguish two general classes
of operations for introducing concepts into the language of psychology.
On the one hand, there are concepts which are defined in terms of antecedent conditions, in Spence's treatment, "stimuli." On the other hand,
there are other concepts which are defined in terms of the organism's
behavior or of its physiological state. The essential difference seems to be
that the R-type concepts require a reference to characteristics of the organism. The S-type concepts do not.

It often happens that definitions of both types are available for terms
bearing the same construct name. This is true of the concept, "motive."
There are times, particularly in the case of complex human motives, when
it is important to remember the operational dictum that different operations define different concepts, and that the equivalence of differently
defined concepts requires demonstration. Whether anxiety produced by
a traumatic experience (an example of an S-defined concept) is the same
as anxiety reflected in a clinical interview (an example of an R-defined
concept) is a question of fact, which the terminological identity of the
concepts does nothing to resolve. Table 26 is an attempt to clarify the
nature of the concept of motive still further, by including additional
details and by dealing with a selection of specific motives. The S-R and
R-R types of concept are treated separately, and an attempt has been
made to illustrate the main independent variables involved in the definition of each. An effort has also been made to categorize the important

manifestations of motives on the response side. The general categories which seem to be important in this last connection have been indicated in detail only for hunger. It seems likely, however, that the same categories apply to other forms of motivated behavior.

TABLE 26

SUMMARY OF SOME DIFFERENT CONCEPTIONS OF MOTIVATION

Independent Variable (S)	*A. S-R Conceptions* *Intervening Variable* *(Motive Defined)*	*Dependent Variable (R)*
1. Time (for example, food deprivation)	Hunger	Consummatory Response (eating) Instrumental Response (Performance in maze situation) Substitute Response (Thinking about food)
2. Stimulus intensity (for example, shock)	Pain Avoidance	Escape
3. History of organism (for example, avoidance conditioning)	Anxiety	Avoidant Behavior
Independent Variable (R₁)	*B. R-R Conceptions* *Intervening Variable* *Motive Defined*	*Dependent Variable (R₂)*
1. Response strength (for example, eating)	Hunger	Maze performance.
2. Score on test (for example, anxiety scale)	Anxiety	Performance on learning task.
3. Physiological condition (for example, androgen level)	Sexuality	Performance for a sexual lure.

The most important points suggested by Table 26 are the following: (1) Whether a particular item of observation appears as an independent or dependent variable in the diagram depends upon the use to which it is put. Consummatory behavior may function in either way, as the two examples employing the motive, hunger, show. (2) It seems quite likely, in the case of the S-type specification, that all three of the major classes of independent variables are involved in determining the strengths of these motives. The evidence on this point is clearest for the appetitive drives. The strength of a hunger-motivated response depends upon deprivation, the desirability of the particular food, and the organism's previous experience with it (Ghent, 1951, 1957). Similarly the strength of sexual behavior depends upon deprivation, upon the attractiveness of the sexual lure, and upon sexual experience. (3) The categorization of motivational expressions into consummatory, instrumental, and substitute modes is offered only very tentatively, but there is evidence from a wide range of motives that something like such a classification may be useful. The consummatory and instrumental categories probably require no further comment, but the generality of substitute or indirect expressions of motives may not be so obvious. At the human level, the fact that unsatisfied drives are expressed in substitute, indirect, and imagined ways is well established. According to the ethologists, such substitute behavior also occurs in lower animals. For example, a wild bird raised in captivity may display a complicated pattern of behavior appropriate for catching insects, even in its cage where there are no insects (Lorenz, 1952). Similarly, male rats have been observed to make sexual advances toward other males, or even toward inanimate objects when no female is available.

The Importance of the Response Measure

The existence of this variety of motivational expressions of course raises the question whether all of them reflect motive strength in the same way. The evidence points very clearly to the conclusion that they do not. Although most measures of the strength of hunger increase with deprivation, many show a decrease with long periods of deprivation (Skinner, 1938, p. 396), and some show little change or even a decrease from the beginning (Campbell and Sheffield, 1953; Strong, 1957). Analysis of the factors which produce these differences indicates that the main effect of hunger upon the responses of the rat is to increase the amount of locomotor activity displayed. Smaller responses, such as grooming and biting at the cage, are much less affected. Thus, indices which reflect the level of gross actions of the whole body tend to increase with deprivation; those reflecting fine, nonlocomotor, responses do not (Strong, 1957).

Even among measures which increase with deprivation, there are differences in their sensitivity and in their ability to reflect differences at all levels of drive. Common sense would probably say that consummatory behavior would be the most accurate indicator and that other responses would reflect drive level less faithfully. In this case, common sense turns out to be misleading, as has been shown very effectively in a series of studies by N. E. Miller and his associates (N. E. Miller, Bailey, and Stevenson, 1950; N. E. Miller, 1955, 1956, 1957). The first of these experiments was an investigation of the behavior of rats made hyperphagic by a brain lesion. It had previously been discovered (Hetherington and Ranson, 1942) that animals with lesions in the region of the ventromedial nuclei of the hypothalamus overeat enormously. The evidence leads one to conclude that the hypothalamic lesions must have had a pronounced effect upon the hunger of these animals, and that their motivation would be higher than that of normal subjects. To test this hypothesis, Miller, Bailey, and Stevenson compared operated animals with normal controls on a number of tasks and found exactly the opposite to be true. On any task which required the animal to overcome an obstacle to get food, the hypothalamic subjects were much inferior to normals. The tests included rate of bar pressing, the force with which the animals would pull toward food in a straight alley, the amount they would eat when they had to lift a heavily weighted lid of a food receptacle to obtain food, and the amount of quinine (which made the food bitter) in their food which they would tolerate.

The fact that all of these measures revealed decreased drive in the hyperphagic animals, whereas food intake had suggested increased drive, seems to mean that food intake depends upon different factors from those controlling performance on the other measures. The results of other studies support this interpretation. Up to about 24 hours of deprivation, various measures of the hunger drive agree quite well (Horenstein, 1951). Beyond this point, marked discrepancies occur. The bar-pressing and quinine measures previously mentioned continue to increase for as much as 4 days. Food intake, on the other hand, seldom increases beyond 24 hours and may even show a decrease, which is often taken as showing a weakening (inanition) component resulting from starvation.

A set of results obtained on rats (Miller, 1956), illustrating the changes in various measures with deprivation, appears in Figure 13.2. One of the measures included in this presentation is an index of the activity of the stomach. To obtain this measure an inflated balloon on the end of a plastic

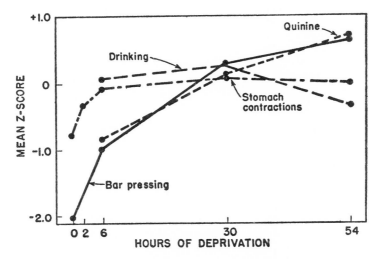

FIGURE 13.2. Graph showing changes in several measures of hunger as a function of number of hours of food deprivation (N. E. Miller, 1956).

fistula was permanently implanted in the stomach. This made it possible to obtain a graphic record of stomach movement. It is of particular interest that this measure shows no increase beyond the first 6 hours of deprivation, a fact which fits in with a proposal of Eisman's to be considered later.

Similar evidence, showing that consummatory behavior is not always a good indicator of motive strength, has come from studies employing the thirst drive. Water deprivation ordinarily leads to increased water consumption (Stellar and Hill, 1952), and, within limits, to an increase in the speed of learning. As with hunger, there is a rough relationship between the strength of the consummatory response and other motivational indices. When thirst is produced in another way, however, the relationship disappears. Subcutaneous injections of hypertonic salt solutions have been found to increase drinking in much the same way as deprivation does (Heyer, 1951a). But, under these circumstances, learning for a water reward is very poor (Heyer, 1951b; O'Kelly and Heyer, 1948, 1951). This suggests, for another drive, that the relationship between deprivation and the consummatory response may turn out to be quite different from that relating other indicators of drive to the same variable.

FUNCTIONS RELATING DRIVE TO DETERMINING CONDITIONS

Much of the research carried out in the field of motivation is directed at determining the nature of the relationships which exist between response strength and the level of drive. The accomplishment of this objective is complicated in a number of ways. As we have just seen, changes in one response measure will probably never exactly parallel those in another. Even within a given class of measures, the functions are complex and the number of variables involved is large. For these reasons our discussion of this problem will be confined to a consideration of the hunger drive, where the evidence is most substantial.

One representative study of the relationship between drive level and deprivation is that carried out by Yamaguchi (1951). This investigator trained 219 rats to press the bar in the Skinner box to obtain food. Then he extinguished different groups of them under 3, 12, 24, 48, or 72 hours of deprivation. Median numbers of responses to extinction, for these groups were, respectively, 12.0, 14.0, 22.0, 28.5, and 28.0. The pattern formed by these values is one most easily represented as an S-shaped, increasing function. It is of interest that a substantial response level was obtained at the shortest deprivation level employed. This last result was also obtained by Perin (1942) in an earlier study of motivation and extinction. In *Principles of Behavior,* Hull (1943) made a considerable point of this fact and, extrapolating the function to zero, concluded that, under conditions of satiation, something like 25 per cent of maximal response strength remained. Later studies (Koch and Daniel, 1945; Saltzmann and Koch, 1948) have shown this conclusion to be in error. With less than two or three hours of deprivation the empirical function shifts sharply downward, and response strength at very low levels of motivation is considerably weaker than Hull's extrapolation had led him to suppose it would be.

In a study which sampled a number of deprivation points and also investigated the effects of prefeeding upon performance, Kimble (1951) trained rats to push open a small swinging door to obtain food and used the speed of this response as a measure of the effect of drive on performance. Tests were carried out under a variety of motivational conditions, some of them produced by allowing the rats to eat a portion of their daily meal just before the panel-pushing test. In other cases the tests were administered after some amount of food deprivation up to 24 hours, which was the training deprivation. The results of the experiment appear in Figure 13.3 in terms of response speed. Clearly, prefeeding progres-

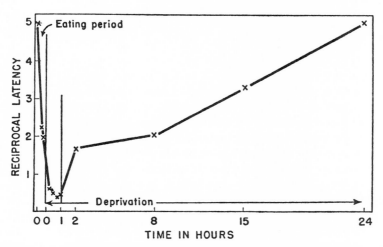

FIGURE 13.3.   Changes with response strength as a function of the ingestion of food (left-hand portion of the graph) and food deprivation (Kimble, 1951).

sively slows up the speed of responding, and deprivation leads to faster reactions. The reason for the various discontinuities which appear in Figure 13.3 are not clear. It may be that the initial horizontal, or perhaps slightly downward, trend lasts as long as food remains in the stomach and distends it. The time values are about right. The sudden spurt at 2-3 hours may be a residual reflection of the fact that rats allowed *ad libitum* access to food put themselves on a roughly rhythmical, 2-4 hour, feeding schedule. This schedule may, in turn, result from the fact that stomach contractions and hunger pangs become intense at about this interval.

Considerations of this sort led Eisman (1956) to propose a theory in which the hunger drive is hypothesized to depend upon two parameters, one controlled by the maintenance schedule of the animal, the other by deprivation in the usual sense. The second factor is regarded specifically as depending upon hunger contractions and reaching an asymptote early in the deprivation period. Eisman's guess was that the upper limit occurred in 4 hours or so. Miller's evidence (Figure 13.2) indicates that the limit of this function may occur slightly later. In a general way, the predictions to which Eisman's theory leads is that increasing the deprivation period within some fixed interval will increase motivation and, therefore, response strength. This results from the influence of the first hunger parameter. With values of this parameter constant, there should be no effect of deprivation beyond approximately the first four hours (Eisman, Asimow, and Maltzman, 1956).

To investigate the validity of this explanation, Eisman (1956) ran 5 groups of rats in a black-white discrimination problem. Three of the groups were starved for 47 out of every 48 hours and run 4, 22, or 45 hours after feeding. The prediction was that these three groups would perform equally well, since the first parameter was the same for all groups and the value of the second was, in every case, asymptotic. One of the other two groups was starved 24 hours out of every 48 and run 22 hours after feeding. The last group was starved 5 hours out of every 48 and run 4 hours after feeding. These last groups were, thus, run under conditions when the second parameter was asymptotic, but the first would have a decreased value. These animals should perform less well than any of the animals on the 47-hour maintenance schedule. There was no difference in performance among the animals in the first three groups. The animals starved 24 hours out of 48 were somewhat inferior, and the animals starved only 5 hours out of 48 were poorest of all.

These results support Eisman's theory for the particular learning situation he employed and show the importance of the feeding schedule in determining level of drive. They do not, however, agree at all with the results obtained by other investigators, some of whom have obtained differences in drive level where Eisman's hypothesis would indicate that there should be none. Yamaguchi, in the study described above, employed such conditions. Specifically, all of his animals were starved for 72 hours out of 120 and were tested at the appropriate time within this interval. Since this procedure equated the subjects on the first parameter there should have been no differences among groups tested at deprivation intervals greater than four hours. There were such differences, however, a fact which seems to refute Eisman's theory about the second drive parameter. The importance of the first (maintenance schedule), however, remains and deserves more study than it has received.

The Role of Competing Responses

The most likely explanation of the differences between Eisman's results and those of others is in the response measure employed. We have had a number of occasions to call attention to the fact that motivational variables seem to have more influence on speed than on measures of accuracy in learning. This, in turn, may come about as a result of the fact that the measures which vary most with drive are particularly susceptible to disruption by the effects of competing responses. The suggestion is that at least a part of the increase in speed of responding, and in measures which involve speed, is to be attributed to the fact that less time is spent in extraneous activity. Cotton (1953) studied the runway behavior of rats under different conditions of hunger. After 44 initial training trials, the same animals were observed under 0, 6, 16, or 22 hours of food deprivation and run under each drive condition until they made at least 49 responses without competing responses. A competing response was defined as any response which interfered with progress toward the goal. Stopping to wash, sniffing at the side of the alley, and other exploratory activity are typical examples. The procedure made it possible to obtain functions of hunger from the trials on which competing responses did and did not occur. The running time measures obtained under these two conditions are presented in Figure 13.4. These results are instructive in a number of ways. (1) It is obvious, in the first place, that the animals running under low drive indulge in much more extraneous behavior than animals running under high drive. (2) The fact that the two curves nearly come together at the highest drive level means that competing responses have been almost completely eliminated at this drive level. (3) Although the drive function is considerably reduced in magnitude when competing responses are eliminated, the slight slope appearing in the lower function of Figure 13.4 is significant. (4) Together these facts mean that increasing drive has two effects upon the running behavior of the rat in the straight maze. The first of these is a strengthening of the running response. The second is the elimination of competing responses. Recent research suggests that the first of these effects is more important than Cotton's results indicate. R. A. King (1959) performed an experiment which replicated the Cotton study in most respects, except that he used independent groups of rats at each drive level. King's results are shown in Figure 13.5. Again the elimination of competing responses decreases the slope of the drive function, but in this case much less than in Cotton's study. In King's experiment, in fact, the main

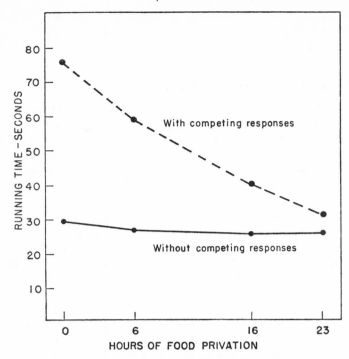

FIGURE 13.4. Response strength as a function of number of hours of food deprivation measured on trials with (upper curve) and without (lower curve) competing responses (Cotton, 1953).

influence of drive increase appears to be upon the running response itself.

The recognition of the fact that drive level may control the qualitative characteristics of behavior has a number of important consequences, one of which is that it introduces a completely new dimension into the analysis of the effect of drive upon behavior. This dimension, in the absence of a commonly accepted name, is one which we may call *response compatibility,* by which we mean the degree to which the responses occurring under a given level of drive are consistent with those required by the learning or performance situation. To illustrate the importance of this variable, we borrow an example from the Gestalt psychologists, the *umweg* or *detour* problem.

Consider the situation represented in Figure 13.6 in which an animal, in the classical experiments a chicken, is placed before a fence on the other side of which there is a dish of grain. In order to get to the grain it is necessary to turn directly away from it and take the detour around the enclosure. The chicken, being of somewhat limited intellectual capacities, finds this solution difficult. Instead of trying to find ways around

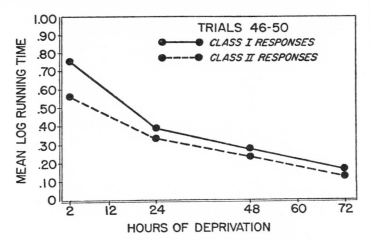

FIGURE 13.5. Response strength as a function of food deprivation measured with competing responses included (Class I responses) and excluded (Class II responses). Adapted from R. A. King (1959).

the barrier, it tends to keep on making futile efforts to get through the fence and directly to the goal. Learning occurs, but only slowly.

Now consider the effect of increasing hunger upon the chicken's behavior. As in the case of Cotton's rats, the chicken tends to restrict its actions more and more to those which seem to lead directly to food. But, where this effect improves performance in the straight runway, it does exactly the opposite in the detour situation. Increasing motivation interferes with performance because the behavior associated with increased motivation is incompatible with that required by the problem.

The concept of response compatibility has an obvious implication for the function relating drive to performance, namely, that there is no

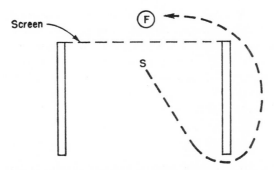

FIGURE 13.6. The *umweg* (detour) problem. The organism at point S must take the path indicated by the dashed line to food which is visible through the screen.

single function which can be expected to apply to learning situations in general. The performance curve may be constantly increasing, constantly decreasing, or curvilinear, depending upon relationships of the sort considered above. At the same time, it is important to recognize that, behind this statement, there lies the assumption that the function of drive on behavior is *basically* an increasing one. The responses given increased energy may, however, be either appropriate or inappropriate as far as the demands of a particular situation are concerned. It is this latter characteristic which makes possible what superficially appears to be a multiplicity of functions.

In a more formal way the sense of this interpretation may be expressed in terms of Hull's (1943) theory. Hull proposed that drive (D) multiplies with (energizes) habit strength (H) to produce excitatory potential (E), and that response strength (R) depends upon the value of E. In summary:

$$R = f(E) = f(D) \times f(H).$$

This statement, however, applies only to single-response situations. Where more than one response is possible, an equation of the same sort is necessary for each. That is:

$$R_1 = f(E_1) = f(D) \times f(H_1), \text{ and}$$
$$R_2 = f(E_2) = f(D) \times f(H_2).$$

When more than one response is possible, the one which will probably occur in the choice situation depends upon which E is stronger, and since D multiplies both habits, this will depend upon which habit is stronger. For the same reason the difference between E_1 and E_2 depends upon the difference between H_1 and H_2. Specifically:

$$E_1 - E_2 = f(D) \times f(H_1 - H_2).$$

With this last equation formulated it is possible to make two important points: (1) The difference between E_1 and E_2 will increase with D, thus increasing the probability of occurrence of the response depending upon the stronger habit. (2) Whether this is beneficial or hindering so far as learning is concerned depends upon whether the stronger response is correct or incorrect. Such theorizing is important in much of the current work on human motivation, some of which will be discussed in the next chapter.

Behavior in the Absence of the Acquisition Drive

There is evidence from a considerable variety of experiments that a habit acquired under a certain drive will sometimes appear when that drive is satiated (Teel and Webb, 1951). Naturally this raises the question of the conditions responsible for this phenomenon. Webb (1952) has surveyed the literature in this field and has suggested a three-fold classification of the explanations for responses which occur in the absence of the acquisition motive. Certain of these explanations are merely *nominal* and only provide another name for the phenomenon. Woodworth's (1918) proposal that well-learned habits become ends in themselves and G. W. Allport's (1937) concept of functional autonomy are examples. A second set of explanations are referred to as *acquired-tendency* theories. In these explanations it is assumed either that training serves to condition the original drive state to stimuli in the learning situation, so that a motive is actually present when the training drive is satiated, or that drive is not necessary for the elicitation of a response once it is learned. Finally there is *irrelevant-drive* theory which assumes that drives other than those under which a given habit was acquired are capable of giving it energy.

Theorists as diverse in their views as Freud and Hull have held the irrelevant-drive position. Freud, in particular, made much of the point that libidinal energy was capable of expression in substitute form and could be made to serve nonsexual purposes. Hull postulated that all drives, relevant (D) and irrelevant ($\dot{D}$), added to produce a generalized drive state ($\bar{D}$). The further assumption that reaction potential ($_sE_R$) was a multiplicative function of habit strength ($_sH_R$) and generalized drive ($\bar{D}$) leads to the prediction that irrelevant drives can energize behavior.

Experimental evidence on this particular point is mixed. Both positive and negative results have been reported. On the positive side, Spence and his associates have had considerable success in demonstrating that manifest anxiety, measured by a paper and pencil test, functions as an irrelevant motive in learning situations ranging from eyelid conditioning (Taylor, 1951) to verbal learning (Montague, 1953) and stylus maze learning (Farber and Spence, 1953). Amsel (1950) found that rats performed a running habit motivated by fear better when they were hungry than when they were satiated. On the negative side, Franks (1957) failed to find an increase in the rate of eyelid conditioning when drive was increased by deprivation from food, drink, and tobacco. And it has been found that injections of cocaine produce no increase in the resistance to extinction of a bar-pressing response over and above that which can be attributed to heightened general activity (Miles, 1958).

A series of studies begun by Webb (1949) seemed at first to show that responses acquired under food motivation could be energized by thirst. Webb trained hungry rats to push open a small swinging door to get food and then tested them in extinction trials under different degrees of water deprivation. He found that increasing thirst led to increasing resistance to extinction, a finding later confirmed by Brandauer (1953). These studies, however, have been severely criticized on the ground that thirsty rats do not eat as much as nonthirsty ones (Verplanck and Hayes, 1953) and therefore must have been somewhat hungry in the extinction tests in the Webb and Brandauer investigations. To test this possibility Grice and J. D. Davis (1957) repeated the Webb experiment using four different groups of rats. All of the animals learned the panel-pushing response hungry, but they were extinguished under four different conditions. During extinction one group was hungry; one was satiated for food and water; one was thirsty but allowed free access to food; and one was deprived of water with food available until just before the extinction test and then it was allowed to drink. The important group is this last one. If thirst inhibits eating and allows the animal to get hungry, the opportunity to drink just before extinction might be expected to eliminate the inhibition, causing the rat to respond in terms of its hunger. This is what seems to have happened in this experiment. Table 27 presents median numbers of responses to extinction, speeds of

TABLE 27

RESULTS DURING EXTINCTION TESTS
(From Grice and Davis, 1957)

Group	Median Number of Responses	Median Speed	Median Responses Per Minute
Hungry	26.5	246	4.68
Satiated	13.5	105	1.29
Thirsty	13.0	71	1.18
Thirsty-drink	22.0	218	3.62

the first 10 responses, and overall response rates. In each case it is quite clear that the last (thirsty-drink) group responded much more vigorously than the thirsty group. Thus for this particular situation, the indication is that the irrelevant thirst drive does not actually energize the response learned on the basis of hunger. Instead the suggestion is that thirst, in the earlier studies, had merely prevented satiation of hunger, which was responsible for the apparent effect of the irrelevant motive.

Although the Grice and Davis demonstration casts considerable doubt upon the validity of the particular idea that thirst is capable of energizing habits originally learned under a hunger drive, it should not be concluded that this negates the entire concept of irrelevant drive. The positive evidence cited earlier still stands. Obviously much remains to be learned about the conditions under which such motives may energize behavior or fail to do so.

THE EFFECT OF DRIVE ON LEARNING

A problem of great theoretical interest concerns the relationship between motivation and learning. The basic question is the following: Is drive one of the variables determining the strength of habit, or is it exclusively a performance variable? The experimental procedure for determining the answer to this question is essentially the two-phase method previously discussed in connection with conditioned stimulus intensity (p. 119). Different groups of subjects are trained initially under two or more different levels of motivation. Then, at some point, each of these groups is subdivided. Some of the subjects continue under the original drive condition; others switch to the alternative drive levels. For the simplest situation, where only two drive levels are involved, this procedure generates the 2x2 factorial design represented in Table 28,

TABLE 28

EXPERIMENTAL DESIGN FOR SEPARATING EFFECTS OF DRIVE ON
PERFORMANCE FROM EFFECTS OF DRIVE ON LEARNING

		Later Test Drive			
		High	Low		
Initial Training Drive	High	Measures obtained in test condition	Measures obtained in test condition	M_{High}	Means reflecting habit differences
	Low	Measures obtained in test condition	Measures obtained in test condition	M_{Low}	
		M_{High}	M_{Low}		
		Means reflecting performance differences			

in which the rows represent the conditions of original training and the columns represent conditions after drive levels have been switched for some of the subjects. As with the CS-intensity example, differences in the column means represent performance differences, and differences in the row means reflect learning differences; that is, differences due to the original training drives are now reflected with drives equated.

There are six points which should be emphasized with respect to this diagram: (1) It is to be noted that the measures in the table are those obtained in the second phase of the experiment. (2) This second phase has taken a number of different forms in different studies. The test has sometimes been in extinction, sometimes in recall, and sometimes in a series of further reinforced trials. (3) The measures of behavior employed have included resistance to extinction, running time and its various derivatives, and errors in a maze. (4) Interest in these experiments has centered about the question of the differences in the row means, which reflect learning differences. The fact that the column (performance) means differ in almost all experiments of this sort merely reflects the point, on which there is no disagreement, that motives influence behavior. (5) Not all of the experiments attempting to answer this question have employed a complete factorial design. Particularly in the earlier studies, the procedure sometimes was to train subjects under a variety of drive levels and then to test with drive equated for all groups. This creates problems because shifting from a high drive to an intermediate one may not be the same as shifting from a low drive to an intermediate one. (6) Especially in these latter experiments there sometimes seems to be a residual effect of the earlier drive level which enters and complicates the interpretation of the results in the second phase of the experiment (Deese and Carpenter, 1951).

The theoretical framework for experiments on the effects of drive on learning has, in recent times, most often been provided by Hull's (1943) theory developed in *Principles of Behavior*. In that book, Hull formalized the distinction between learning and performance, and he introduced constructs corresponding to each. The learning construct, habit ($_sH_R$), was hypothesized to be a function of such variables as the number of reinforced trials, the amount of reinforcement, delay of reinforcement, and stimulus-response asynchronism. Drive was not included. It entered as a multiplier of habits in the determination of the strength of the performance variable, excitatory potential ($_sE_R$). Thus, Hull made drive a performance variable and proposed that it had no effect upon learning.

Experiments which may be regarded as tests of this theory have produced results both for and against Hull's hypothesis. That is, some have obtained no performance differences attributable to drive at the time of learning. This is the result predicted by Hull. Others have obtained such differences. Those in the latter category have usually found that higher drive at the time of original learning leads to better learning; but a few have found learning to be most efficient at some intermediate or lower level of motivation (Finan, 1940; Reynolds, 1949).

A tabular summary of some of the results obtained in experiments on the question under discussion appears in Table 29. Careful inspection of this table will show that the number of experiments which have obtained positive results is just about equal to the number obtaining negative results. Moreover, there seems to be no breakdown by procedure, type of drive, or response measure which provides a certain indication of the factors responsible for the discrepant results. The only discernible tendency is for experiments involving complex mazes to show an effect of drive on learning oftener than other procedures. All except one of these studies (Hillman, Hunter, and Kimble, 1954) have obtained such results.

At the most general level it would seem that the condition determining whether drive apparently influences learning in a given experiment is not among those reflected in the table. What this variable is (if, indeed, there is only one) remains a matter of speculation. The most likely possibility is that certain detailed features of the behavior occurring in original training may be involved. Campbell and Kraeling were the first to call attention to this possibility.

As is shown in Table 29, Campbell and Kraeling obtained evidence for an effect of training drive upon learning. In their discussion of this fact, these investigators mentioned that it was their impression that the rats learning under low drive behaved differently from those behaving under high drive. Specifically, the subjects under high drive appeared to have acquired a marked readiness to leave the starting box, which the low-drive group had not. In behavioral terms the high-drive animals tended to maintain an orientation toward the door leading from the starting chamber and to leave the box as soon as it was opened. The low-drive animals, by contrast, developed no such tendency. If this interpretation is correct, two points follow: The first is that drive will show an effect upon learning whenever the training situation evokes different behavior under different drive levels. On mainly common sense grounds, complex situations might be expected to maximize such effects. In the complex maze, for example, exploratory tendencies might dominate the behavior of low-drive subjects, with the result that such subjects would learn somewhat different habits from high-drive subjects who explored less. In this connection, it has already been noted that the use of complex mazes, more often than any other procedure, tends to yield results indicating an effect of drive on learning. Moreover, the one experiment producing the opposite result (Hillman, Hunter, and Kimble, 1954) differed from the others in one very important respect: the rats used as subjects were blind. This might very well eliminate exploratory tendencies if, as seems to be the case, such tendencies depend upon visual stimulation. In support of this interpretation, Hillman, Hunter, and Kimble report that there were no differences in error scores during phase 1 of the experiment, suggesting that the animals' behavior was similar in both drive groups.

The same line of reasoning also leads to the conclusion that the effect of drive on learning, when such an effect occurs, would not always have to be uniformly increasing. If some intermediate drive level elicited behavior better adapted to the requirements of the situation, then the most efficient learning would occur under these conditions. This sort of argument, already developed in connection with the energizing effect of motives on behavior, will not be amplified upon further, except to point out that, in a highly speculative and *ad hoc* way, the results obtained by Finan and by Reynolds can be made to fit such a scheme.

The second major point suggested by the emphasis upon drive-produced

TABLE 29

SUMMARY OF EXPERIMENTS USING RATS AS SUBJECTS ON LEARNING AS A FUNCTION OF DRIVE

Experimenter	Procedure	Motive Studied	Response Measures	Effect of Drive on Learning
Barry, 1958	straight runway	hunger, 2½ vs. 26½ hrs.	running speed	has an effect
J. L. Brown (1956)	Skinner box with secondary reinforcement	hunger, 8 hrs. vs. 12 hrs. deprivation 2 gm. vs. 18 gm. prefeeding	no. bar presses	no effect
B. A. Campbell and Kraeling, 1954	straight runway	hunger, 12 vs. 60 hrs.	running speed, resistance to extinction	has an effect on speed; none on resistance to extinction
Eisman, Asimow, and Maltzman, 1956	black-white discrimination	hunger, 4, 72, 46 hrs.	errors; trials and reinforcements to criterion; resistance to extinction	no effect on any measure
Deese and Carpenter, 1951	straight runway	hunger, 1 vs. 23 hrs., (approx.)	latency	results equivocal
Finan, 1940	Skinner box	hunger, 1, 12, 24 or 48 hrs.	resistance to extinction	12 hrs. of deprivation superior to 1, 24 or 48 hrs.
Hillman, Hunter, and Kimble, 1953	complex maze	thirst, 2 or 22 hrs.	errors running time	no effect on any measure
Kendler, 1945b	Skinner box, T-maze	irrelevant thirst drive	resistance to extinction, errors	no effect

414

TABLE 29—Continued

Experimenter	Procedure	Motive Studied	Response Measures	Effect of Drive on Learning
Lewis and Cotton, 1957	straight runway	hunger, 1, 6, or 22 hrs.	running time in extinction, responses to extinction	higher acquisition drives strengthened both measures
King, 1959	straight runway	hunger, 12 and 60 hrs.	running speed	no effect
MacDuff, 1946	6-unit and 16-unit T-maze	hunger, 12, 24, and 48 hrs.	retention over two and six weeks, for two mazes	higher drive led to better retention
Heyer, 1951b	5-choice T-maze	thirst produced by NaCl injection; thirst produced by deprivation	relearning errors, trials to criterion	thirst produced by deprivation has an effect; thirst by injection has none
O'Kelley and Heyer, 1951	5-choice T-maze	thirst produced by NaCl injection and deprivation	relearning errors, trials to criterion	has an effect
O'Kelley and Heyer, 1948	straight runway	thirst, 12 and 36 hrs.	running time	36 hrs. superior to 12 hrs.
Strassburger, 1950	Skinner box	hunger in deprivation range from 0.5 to 47 hrs.	resistance to extinction	no effect
Teel, 1952	single-unit T-maze	1, 7, 15, 22 hrs. of hunger	resistance to extinction	no effect
Reynolds, 1949	panel pushing	hunger controlled by prefeeding	resistance to extinction	low-drive superior to high drive

415

behavior is more basic. Insofar as Hull's theory is concerned, the implication is that the theory has not been refuted. Such a refutation would come from an experiment in which (1) drive at the time of learning were shown to have an effect later, with drives equated, and (2) the responses elicited during original training were shown to be exactly the same for the two groups. Thus far, no experiment meeting the second of these requirements has been reported. The one attempt at such an experiment failed because the first condition was not met. In this experiment (R. A. King, 1959), animals were trained in a straight runway, at first under 12 and 60 hours of food deprivation; then, in extinction, drives were reversed for half the animals. It will be noted that this is exactly the set of conditions used by Campbell and Kraeling in their experiment which obtained an effect of drive on learning. To evaluate the importance of competing responses in such experiments, King used two different response measures. One measure was running time in the usual sense; the other was running time with the time spent performing competing responses subtracted out. The expectation was that the first measure would yield results which seemed to show an effect of drive on learning, and that the second measure would not, thus assigning the influence of drive to the mechanism of competing responses. The results, however, failed to show an effect of drive on learning in either measure. It thus appears that an important experiment remains to be done.

DRIVE STIMULI AND LEARNING

The concept of drive stimulus was introduced in a preliminary, methodological, way earlier in this chapter. The main concern of this section will be with experimental studies of its role in the learning process. In general, such investigations have been planned on the assumption that drive stimuli will influence behavior in the same way as other stimuli do, and that such processes as discrimination and generalization apply to drive stimuli (Webb, 1955).

Discrimination Among Drive Stimuli

The classical experiment demonstrating the discriminability of drive stimuli was done by Hull (1933). He ran rats in a simple maze, hungry on some days and thirsty on others. On the hunger days one turn in the maze was rewarded with food; on the thirst days the opposite turn was rewarded with water. Over a series of 1,200 trials, the animals showed some learning, although most of them continued to make errors even after this amount of training. A part of the reason the task proved to be so difficult was that Hull had used a maze in which the thirst and water runs terminated in the same final common path and in the same

goal box. Leeper (1935) showed that the problem could be made somewhat easier by using separate goal boxes and very much easier by other
procedural alterations favoring the discriminability of the two reinforcement locations. From the nature of his results, Leeper argued that what
was important in such learning was the development of cognitions concerning the location of reward. Seeman and H. Williams (1952), on the
other hand, have proposed that the Hullian concepts of secondary reinforcement and r_G can handle Leeper's results. They performed an experiment comparing the speed of learning to respond in terms of drive state
when the final path in the maze and the goal box were the same for the
two drives and when they were different. To produce this difference Seeman and Williams used a maze in which the final common path was
always in the same physical location. For a control group of rats, it was
also perceptually the same whether the drive was hunger or thirst. For an
experimental group, however, this path and the goal box were black on
hunger days and white on thirst days. The experimental subjects learned
much better than the control subjects, supporting the argument for
secondary reinforcement.

Still other conditions related to the speed of learning a discrimination
between drive stimuli have been described by Bolles and Petrinovich
(1954). These investigators called attention to the following differences
between the procedures used to study discrimination between drives and
procedures employed in the investigation of discriminations between external environmental cues: (1) In the ordinary discrimination-learning
procedure, the stimuli to be discriminated are presented rather suddenly,
for example, at the choice point in a maze. In drive discrimination, the
intensity of the stimuli increases gradually, and these stimuli are present
outside the choice situation. (2) In the ordinary discrimination situation,
the discriminanda are absent when the animal is taken from the apparatus. In drive discrimination studies, they are still present. (3) In ordinary discrimination learning, the stimuli are usually physically separate.
In drive discrimination studies hunger and thirst have probably always
been present at the same time. Bolles and Petrinovich performed an experiment in which animals learned to go one way in a modified T-maze when
hungry and the other way when thirsty. In order to reduce the differences
described above to a practicable minimum, they employed the following
special procedures: (a) The animal's home cage was the choice point of
the maze, so that the drives to be discriminated developed in the choice
situation. (b) The animals were run one trial a day and were allowed 30
minutes or more in the correct goal box with food or water so that the
drive stimuli would have been eliminated when the subject was removed
from the goal box at the end of the trial. (c) A special deprivation
schedule described by Verplanck and Hayes (1953) was used to separate
hunger and thirst as sharply as possible. Under these conditions the

subjects required an average of only 4.5 trials to reach a criterion of 9 correct responses in 10 trials.

There have been very few experiments in which animals were required to learn to discriminate between the stimuli provided by drives other than hunger and thirst. In one example of such a study, however, Amsel and McDonnell (1951) were moderately successful in training rats to go one way in a T-maze to escape shock and the opposite way to escape the stimuli associated with shock. This suggests that the motives of escape from pain and fear can be distinguished in somewhat the same way as hunger and thirst.

With the discriminability of the stimuli provided by different drives demonstrated, the next question to arise is whether different intensities of the same drive are also discriminable. There is evidence (Bloomberg and Webb, 1949; Jenkins and Hanratty, 1949) to indicate that they are. Jenkins and Hanratty, for example, ran rats in a single-unit T-maze alternately under 11.5 and 47.5 hours of deprivation, with a right turn correct under one drive level and a left turn correct under the other. The animals learned this discrimination in a matter of 100 trials or so. At the end of the experiment the subjects were tested under 4 and 72 hours of deprivation, with the result that they responded under the lower drive as they had at 11.5 hours of deprivation and under the higher drive as they had at 47.5 hours of deprivation. In a somewhat novel way, this shows the generalization of a habit along a dimension of drive stimulus intensity.

The fact that rats could learn to discriminate these particular drive intensities has a bearing on a related problem. Heron (1949) obtained, as had Hull and Leeper, a discrimination between hunger and thirst. A series of control tests, however, suggested that the subjects in this experiment had not discriminated the distinctive drive stimuli, but may have responded to relative fullness of the stomach which could have differed under the two drive conditions. The Jenkins and Hanratty demonstration casts doubt upon this as a general interpretation, because, under both of their conditions, the stomach would have been completely empty. See also Bailey and Porter, 1955.

The Selective and Nonselective Theories of Drive Stimulation

In interpreting the results of his early study, Hull had proposed that learning to discriminate among drive stimuli is possible on the basis of stimulus patterning. That is, the animal learns to go right to food and left to water by responding one way to the pattern of choice-point cues plus hunger stimuli and the other way to the pattern of choice-point cues plus thirst stimuli.

Some years later, Kendler (1946) set out to test the validity of Hull's theory by the following experiment. Rats, simultaneously hungry and thirsty were run in a T-maze with essentially forced trials which led them sometimes in one direction to water and an equal number of times in the other direction to food. Specifically, there were four trials a day. The first and third trials were free; but on the second and fourth trials, the animal was forced to go in a direction opposite to that on the preceding trial. In this manner, experience with each maze path and each reward was equalized. Following this training there was a series of four tests. On some days the animal was only hungry; on other days it was only thirsty. The point in question was whether the animal would now behave appropriately, going to water on thirst days and to food on hunger days.

Hull's theory, strictly applied, predicts that no such learning could occur because the hunger and thirst stimuli had been simultaneously present and should have been conditioned to the right and left responses in approximately equal degrees. When only one drive state was present there would be no stronger tendency to go in one direction than in the other. The behavior of the rats gave no support for such a hypothesis. On thirst days they ran correctly to water on 98 per cent of their trials; on hunger days they ran to food on 73 per cent of the trials. In order to explain this result, Kendler proposed what he called a selective principle of association of drive stimuli which stated that "only those drive stimuli which are themselves reduced become connected to the rewarded response." (Kendler, 1946, p. 220). This is to be contrasted with Hull's nonselective principle according to which all stimuli become connected to the rewarded response.

Although some experiments have produced results modestly supporting the selective association principle (Kendler, 1949; Kendler and Law, 1950), the most convincing studies have obtained negative results. With an occasional exception (Woodbury and Wilder, 1954; Porter and N. E. Miller, 1957) these studies have adopted a strategy which differs somewhat from that of Kendler's original experiment. Where Kendler, following the lead of Hull and Leeper, had tested the effectiveness of the stimuli provided by relevant drives, more recent investigations have made the critical cues the stimuli provided by irrelevant drives. In all of these investigations animals have learned different responses in the presence of hunger and thirst stimuli, but the responses led to the satisfaction of another motive through anxiety reduction (Amsel, 1949) or light avoidance (Winnick, 1950; Levine, 1953; Bailey, 1955).

Bailey used five groups of 10 rats each in an escape-training procedure in which pushing one of two panels would turn off a noxious light. The correct panel differed from day to day in a manner which depended upon the particular group. For three groups, variations in drive provided the cue stimuli; for the two other groups, presence or absence of a tone served the same purpose. Specifically, the five conditions required the subjects to discriminate between (a) hunger and thirst, (b) hunger and satiation, (c) thirst and satiation, (d) presence or absence of a tone sounded after the animals were placed in the apparatus (short-sound group), and (e) presence or absence of a tone which, when used, was continuously present over a long period of time (long-sound group). All the animals except those in the long-sound group learned to respond correctly. This demonstrated that drive stimuli can serve as cues although they are not reduced by the rewarded response, thus providing strong evidence against the selective association principle. Moreover, the drive stimuli were about as effective as cues as the short tone. Bailey attributed the fact that long tone provided so poor a cue to the operation of a principle suggested by Hull, that unchanging (static) stimuli are less effective cues than changing (dynamic) ones (Hull, 1943, p. 207). Since hunger and thirst stimuli show periodic fluctuations in intensity, they would be more dynamic than the tone which was continuously present at a constant level.

Generalization on a Dimension of Drive Stimulation

Another direct implication of the drive-stimulus concept is that alterations in drive will lead to a relative loss of response strength because changing drive changes a part of the stimulus complex to which the response had been conditioned. Data which support this prediction have come from a variety of sources. Heathers and Arakelian (1941) found that a bar-pressing response extinguished more rapidly if two extinction sessions involved the same degree of hunger than if the two sessions involved different drive levels. Barry (1958) found that changing drives led to less rapid running early in extinction, although, later in extinction, the effect of changing drives was the opposite. Elliott (1929), in a famous study, showed that changing drives midway in the course of maze learning produced a temporary disruption of behavior. In this experiment a control group of 32 thirsty rats learned a maze for water. An experimental group began with the thirst-water condition but on the tenth of 20 trials were shifted to a hunger-food regime. The effect of this manipulation is shown in Figure 13.7 for error scores. There was a similar but relatively smaller effect on running time. Although the concept of drive stimulus is not directly involved, it is worth mentioning that alterations in level of motivation produced in other ways sometimes have a similar disruptive effect. Changing incentives in the middle of learning a maze, for example, produces even a greater disturbance in performance than changing drives (Elliott, 1928).

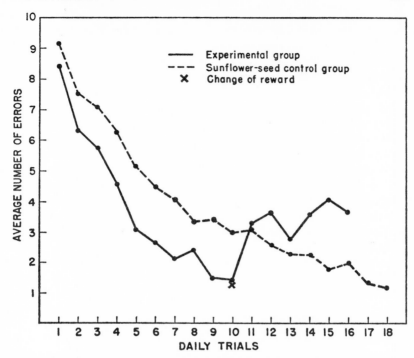

FIGURE 13.7. Learning curves showing effect of a changed reward upon the performance of rats in a maze. The control group was rewarded with sunflower seed from the beginning. The experimental group received a wet mash as reward for the first nine days and sunflower seeds after that. Note that this change disrupted the rats' behavior and produced a response level which was much inferior to that of the control group. (Elliott, 1928).

Since, theoretically, the mechanism by which alterations in drive disrupt learning is that of stimulus generalization, it should be possible to demonstrate a generalization gradient along a dimension of drive stimulus intensity. A response conditioned at one drive level and tested at several others should show a diminution in strength, and the amount of this diminution should increase with the difference between training and test drives. Although the prediction is a straightforward one, testing it proves quite difficult. The most important consequence of changing drive (which is essential in the performance of the necessary experiment) is to increase or decrease the vigor of response. Raising drive level increases response strength, and lowering it decreases response strength. Moreover, these effects ordinarily are of greater magnitude than any that can be produced merely by changing drive stimulation. Taking this fact into account, however, it is possible to make a general prediction about the form of the generalization gradient along a drive-stimulus dimension.

To illustrate, consider the case of a rat conditioned to press a bar to obtain food at an intermediate drive level, say 24 hours of deprivation, and tested at the training drive and several others, for example, 3, 12, 48, and 72 hours of deprivation. Tests at 3 and 12 hours, which are below the level of deprivation during training, may be expected to lead to lowered response strength for two reasons: (*a*) drive is lower, and the response will be weakened for this reason; (*b*) the drive stimuli are different, and response strength should be reduced as a result of generalization decrement. Tests at 48 and 72 hours, which are above the level of deprivation during training, pit these two effects against each other. The increased deprivation should raise response strength; the altered stimulus situation should lower it. These considerations lead to the prediction that the generalization gradient obtained when drive is lowered will be steeper than that obtained when drive is increased (Meehl and MacCorquodale, 1948).

The only extensive evidence on this point is from an experiment by Yamaguchi (1952) in which rats were trained to press the bar in a Skinner box at one drive level and tested at the same drive level and certain others. Table 30 presents a set of results in terms of reaction

TABLE 30

MEDIAN LATENCIES OF BAR-PRESS RESPONSE DURING TESTING
(Numbers in bold type are for conditions in which test
and training conditions were the same. Yamaguchi, 1952)

Hours of Hunger During Testing	*Hours of Hunger During Training*			
	3	24	48	72
3	**.97**	1.05	1.19	1.65
24	.93	**.85**	.90	.96
48	.88	.89	**.87**	.95
72	.97	.83	.89	**.85**

latency. The generalization gradients for each training drive level are represented by the numbers in the columns. Close inspection of these data will show that the expected relationships occur. For the subjects trained at 3 hours of deprivation, the main effect of changing drive is to improve performance. It is only with the very largest change in drive (72-hour condition) that the effect of generalization decrement is sufficient to overcome the opposite effect of raising drive level. For the other conditions it is to be noted that, with a single exception, the most rapid reaction occurs at the drive level used in training. And, as expected, the decrease in response strength (increase in latency) is much greater with lowered drive than with increased drive.

The Intensity of Drive Stimulation and the Range of Behavior

There is, as we have seen, considerable evidence that one of the effects of increasing drive is to eliminate competing responses. It becomes important at this point to ask why this should be. Classical S-R and cognitive theory suggest two rather different-sounding answers. S-R theorists have held that any response in the process of being learned competes with alternative responses, and that increases in drive increase the differences among the strengths of the various response tendencies. Thus, when the response being measured is dominant, increasing drive will eliminate competing responses because the correct response is strengthened relative to them. In most instrumental conditioning situations (for example, Skinner box and runway) the apparatus is arranged so as to make the measured response dominant either from the beginning or very early in learning. Thus, it follows that increased drive will increase the strength of the dominant response and eliminate its competitors.

The cognitive theorist, on the other hand, reasons as follows. Increases in drive strength make the motivational situation so important that it dominates the organism's behavior, and the animal responds to its drive state (S_D) to the exclusion of everything else. Tolman (1948) has put this argument most clearly. He referred to heightened drive as a narrower of cognitive maps, meaning by this that intense motivation tends to limit the animal's perceptions and to restrict them to stimuli directly involved in the satisfaction of the drive in question. Other events in the environment, having no significance, are not noticed.

Bruner, Matter, and Papanek (1955) performed an experiment which was designed as a direct test of Tolman's theory. The procedure involved three stages. In the first stage, rats learned a black-white discrimination in a linear maze with four choice points. In this stage of the experiment, the position of the black and white stimuli were randomly varied from choice point to choice point. Stage two was a continuation of the black-white discrimination problem, but in this series of trials, the positive (for example, black) stimulus was alternately on the right and left at successive choice points for the experimental groups. For a series of control groups the positive cue continued to be randomly right or left. In the third and final phase of the experiment all subjects were required to learn the single-alternation pattern introduced incidentally for the experimental group in phase two of the experiment. Gray doors were substituted for the black and white ones, and the only available cue marking the correct choice was position.

Throughout the experiment, some of the animals had been kept 12-hours hungry; others had been 36-hours hungry. The general prediction made from Tolman's theory was that the 12-hour animals would learn the single alternation faster than the 36-hour animals in stage three of the experiment, for the following reason : During the second phase of the experiment, being less dominated by their drive state, the 12-hour animals would have tended to perceive the single-alternation sequence of correct choices and would be able to transfer this information to the later test phase of the experiment. The results supported this prediction, although the differences were not large. It seems possible that the 12-hour deprivation condition may have made the subjects too hungry for the effect to appear in maximal proportions. A group of subjects only about 2-hours hungry would have provided a clearer differentiation of the high and low drive levels.

LEARNED MODIFICATIONS OF MOTIVES

Up to this point our discussion has been focussed on learning, and motivation has been viewed as a contributor to it. It must be recognized, however, that the reverse perspective is possible. Motives, themselves, depend upon learning; and, especially in recent years, there has been an increasing interest in the topic of acquired drive or secondary motivation.

Instinct and Secondary Motivation

Watson's (1925) behaviorism, as is well-known, represented a break from previous tradition, in its adoption of an extreme environmentalism. Man, in the eyes of the environmentalist, is born with a limited number of unconditioned reflexes which, by conditioning and chaining, eventually produce the elaborate set of skills which are typical of the adult. The behaviorist's view of motivation was also very similar to this. Besides his innate reflexes, the infant possesses, Watson thought, a few unconditioned emotional reactions to certain specific stimuli, and the richness of adult emotional experience develops, by conditioning, out of these primitive raw materials. As a sort of case demonstration, Watson and Rayner (1920) did the experiment which is now a classic. A rat (CS) was shown to a child, Albert, simultaneously with a loud and unpleasant sound (UCS) produced by striking a steel bar behind the child's head. The sound caused the child to cry (UCR). After a few repetitions, the child cried at the sight of the rat (CR) and this fear generalized to other furry objects, such as a fur neckpiece or a Santa Claus mask. Attempts to repeat the Watson and Rayner study (English, 1929; Bregman, 1934) were not always successful; and Valentine (1930) made the cogent point that Watson's case was probably overstated. Specifically, Valentine presented evidence to suggest that fears might be much more easily conditioned to furry objects, such as a caterpillar or a rat, than to others, such as a pair of opera glasses. But, in spite of the limitations suggested by these later studies, the effect of the Watson and Rayner study upon the immediately subsequent history of psychology was very great. It demonstrated a general methodology which has been used in many more recent fear conditioning studies. It also suggested that what have been called instinctive reactions may be responses conditioned to previously neutral stimuli. With time this last point has undergone a subtle transformation, with the result that one seldom hears of the conditionability of instinctive reactions. Instead, the point has become that the responses once thought to be instinctive are actually learned.

Whatever the merits of this way of phrasing it, the reformulation precludes the asking of an interesting question: are instinctive reactions, strictly conceived, conditionable? Recent years have seen the reacceptance of the instinct concept by psychologists, mainly as a result of the work of a group of zoologists of whom the best known are Lorenz (1952) and Tinbergen (1951). These two men in particular have advocated theories which have certain parallels to psychological theory. They have also made behavioral studies which have important psychological implications.

The instinct concept is central in these theories. Instinctive behavior is defined as an unlearned, relatively stereotyped act or series of acts (of which the most elementary seem almost exactly the same as unconditioned responses) which is tied to some specific environmental stimulus (paralleling the psychological concept of UCS). The energy (psychologically, drive) for instinctive behavior is thought of as existing in the nervous system as *action specific energy*. Instinctive behavior is elicited by a highly specific stimulus, or *releaser*, which initiates the action of a neurological *innate releasing mechanism*. Except in the presence of a releaser, the action specific energy is held in check or blocked, so that the instinctive act ordinarily occurs only to the biologically appropriate stimulus. Occasionally it does break through this inhibiting barrier and appears in response to the wrong stimulus, in which case the response is referred to as *displacement activity*, or to no apparent stimulus at all, in which case it is referred to as *vacuum activity*. As the parenthetical expressions in the description above indicate, instinct theory contains an obvious parallel to the concepts of drive, unconditioned stimulus, and unconditioned response. In some of the literature the distinction between instrumental and consummatory behavior made previously in this chapter also appears (Thorpe, 1954).

Although the emphasis in the recent instinct literature is upon unlearned acts, the importance of learning is not only admitted, but is of prime importance in connection with at least two concepts, *instinct-training interlocking* and *imprinting*. The former of these refers to the fact that sequences of instinctive acts (for example, the complicated series of responses involved in the flight of birds) are apparently bound together by the effects of stimuli which have acquired significance as a result of learning. The latter concept, imprinting, refers to the emotional attachments which the infants of many species seem to invest in the first large, moving object they see.

Although the description of such learning is seldom put in conditioning terms, it seems possible that the conditioning of released responses can occur. Lorenz (1952) describes what is probably a case in point in the behavior of the jackdaw. This bird instinctively attacks any animal, including man, carrying a dark limp object of appropriate size, such as a wounded jackdaw or a pair of dark swimming trunks. Lorenz himself was attacked on several occasions when carrying a pair of black swimming trunks and reports that, afterward, the jackdaws would attack him, *even without the trunks.* This seems to be a clear case of conditioning. If it turns out to be fairly dependable, it will be possible to bring the phenomenon under a degree of laboratory control which has so far not been typical of studies in this area.

The phenomenon of imprinting is an exception to this last statement. Several investigators have done laboratory work on imprinting. Jaynes (1956, 1957), for example, has performed a series of studies showing that baby chicks can readily be imprinted by making the first large moving object they see a colored cube or cylinder. After such experience, the chicks follow the object and remain near it much as they would if it were their mother. Moreover, Jaynes has also shown that such phenomena as acquisition and generalization apply to imprinted behavior, suggesting that there is a close relationship between it and other learning. There remains the question whether what is learned is a motive. The answer will come in the form of experiments to determine whether the conventional criteria of motivation apply. Some observations of Hess (1958) suggest that they will: ducklings will overcome obstacles in order to get to a decoy on which they have been imprinted.

Fear as an Acquirable Drive

It has been necessary at previous points in this book to explain the mechanism by which a number of different theorists believe that fear develops (pp. 267-277). Briefly, this theory is that stimuli associated with painful events come, by a process of classical conditioning, to evoke fear. The status of fear as a motive is then inferred from the fact that it has the same properties as other motives, those of providing the basis for learning and of influencing the vigor of behavior.

Effects in this latter category are of two opposite sorts. Sometimes the presentation of a feared stimulus augments a response; sometimes it interferes. Brown, Kalish, and Farber (1951), using the apparatus shown in Figure 13.8, demonstrated the facilitating effect of fear in the follow-

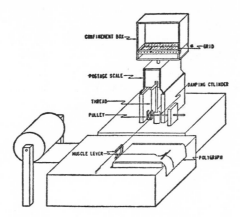

FIGURE 13.8. Stabilimeter for measuring startle response. Activity in the confinement box is registered in graphic form on the polygraph (Brown, Kalish, and Farber, 1951).

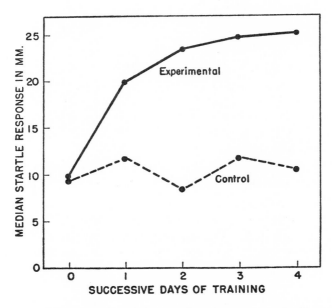

FIGURE 13.9. Augmentation of the startle response to a loud sound by the addition of a conditioned fear stimulus. The increasing trend in the magnitude of the startle response for the experimental group shows the acquisition of fear as a result of continued pairing of the CS with shock (Brown, Kalish, and Farber, 1951).

ing way. An experimental group of rats received four days of training with 10 trials each day. Seven of these trials consisted of the pairing of a CS (light and buzzer) with shock at a 3-second interval. On the other three trials the shock was omitted and the sound of a pop-gun substituted for it. Ordinarily the sound of the pop-gun produced a startle response. Presenting the fear stimulus prior to the startle stimulus increased the magnitude of the startle. This effect increased during the experiment as is shown in Figure 13.9. A control group which received the same number of CS presentations and the same number of shock trials showed no systematic trend in the magnitude of the startle response. Following the series of days represented in Figure 13.9 there were three extinction days in which the CS and the sound of the pop-gun were presented together but the rats were never shocked again. Results obtained in this part of the study exhibited an extinction trend within days and a spontaneous recovery between days, showing that these processes, as well as acquisition, apply to the conditioned fear drive.

A series of studies beginning with one by Estes and Skinner (1941) has shown that a fear-eliciting stimulus sometimes has quite a different effect upon behavior, that of producing an interruption of ongoing activity. H. F. Hunt, Brady, and their associates have reported a number of demonstrations of this fact in a series of studies more centrally concerned with the effect of electroconvulsive shock upon fear than with the properties of fear itself. The procedure involved in a typical study is as follows: Rats are first trained in a Skinner box to press a bar for water on a variable-interval schedule. When this response has been thoroughly established, the fear conditioning begins. This conditioning process consists of the presentation of a 16-per-second click for a period of three minutes, followed by a brief, but fairly strong, shock as the clicking sound terminates. Initially the clicker has no effect upon the animal's behavior, but, with a few presentations, it acquires the ability to inhibit bar pressing completely. During the three-minute CS presentation, the animal typically crouches in the apparatus and often defecates or urinates.[1]

[1] The rather extensive literature concerned with the effect of electroconvulsive shocks (ECS) upon conditioned emotional responses (CER) is beyond the scope of this book. It has been shown that ECS reduces CER (Brady and Hunt, 1951) and that this effect is of long duration (Brady, 1951, 1952). Although CER may show some recovery following ECS (Hunt, Jernberg, and Brady, 1952), this can be prevented by additional ECS treatments (Brady, Stebbins, and Hunt, 1953). There is good reason to believe that the convulsion produced in ECS is critical in the alleviation of CER in that other convulsion-producing procedures can reduce CER. These include audio-genic seizures (Brady, Stebbins, and Galambos, 1953) and CS_2 convulsions (Hunt, Jernberg, and Otis, 1953). Moreover, anesthesics which prevent the convulsions reduce the value of ECS for the alleviation of CER (Hunt, Jernberg, and Lawlor, 1953). For further discussion of these general areas see, in addition to the references above, Brady, Hunt, and Geller (1954), Brady and Hunt (1955), Hunt and Brady (1955), Geller, Sidman, and Brady (1955), Thompson and Dean (1955).

The fact that conditioned fears have different, and opposite, effects upon behavior poses no particular problem of interpretation. We have seen in connection with motives in general that their effects cannot be predicted without taking into account the responses elicited by the drive-establishing operation and the relationship of these responses to the responses they influence. The same sort of reasoning applies here. A series of experiments by Amsel and his associates may be cited to make this point. These studies involve the effect of fear upon the consummatory response of drinking. In the first investigation in this series (Amsel and Maltzman, 1950) rats were first trained to drink for 10 minutes each day in individual drinking cages. After the animals' intake had stabilized, they were given an electric shock just before the drinking test *in a situation which was different from that in which they were tested.* In the subsequent test there was an increase in the amount the animals drank. Amsel and Maltzman reasoned that the shock had increased the animals' fear and that this fear had served to energize the dominant response in the situation, namely, drinking. In this interpretation the fact that the shock occurred outside the drinking situation is of first importance. Later studies demonstrated that giving the shock in the drinking cages, or in compartments like the drinking cages, interfered with consummatory behavior (Amsel, 1950b) and that the degree of interference depended upon the degree of similarity between the drinking situation and the shock situation (Amsel and Cole, 1953). Together these results suggest that the shock leads to the conditioning of responses incompatible with drinking to the cues in the shock situation. If the shock and drinking situations are similar, these responses generalize to the latter and interfere with consummatory behavior. If they are quite different, all that generalizes is a heightened degree of emotionality which increases intake.[2]

The ability of a conditioned fear to motivate new learning may be illustrated by the study of J. S. Brown and Jacobs (1949). These investigators (experiment II) used two groups of 8 rats each and subjected the experimental group to a fear-conditioned procedure which consisted of the pairing of a CS (tone and light) with shock for 22 trials. The CS lasted for a total of 9 seconds on each trial, and the shock was presented during the last 6 seconds of this period. This training took place in one side of a two-compartment box, access to the other side having been prevented by a door. To test for the drive value of the CS, this door was raised and the subjects received 40 trials in which they could escape from the tone and light by jumping a little hurdle into the other side of the box. Results of the experiment appear in Figure 13.10 for the experimental group and for a control group, which had received no fear condi-

[2] Related studies are those of Lichtenstein (1950a, 1950b), Siegel and Brantley (1951), and Siegel and Siegel (1949).

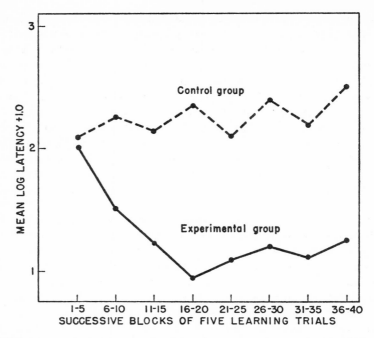

FIGURE 13.10. **Learning motivated by the presentation of a feared stimulus and reinforced by the cessation of the same stimulus (Brown and Jacobs, 1949).**

tioning. It is evident that the experimental animals learned and the controls did not.

Other Acquired Drives

Although the majority of the work on acquired drives has involved fear, there has been some investigation of other similarly developed motives. The motives with which such further investigation have dealt have comprised three clusters: (1) incentive motivation, (2) the "externalized" hunger drive, and (3) what Tolman called social techniques. We have considered the first of these previously (p. 170) and, so, will discuss only the second two here.

1. *The "Externalization" of the Hunger Drive.* Beginning with the theoretical article of E. E. Anderson (1941a) there has been a continuing interest in whether the hunger drive can be conditioned to environmental cues or, as Anderson put it "externalized."[3] There seems little reason to doubt that the performance of animals in a particular situation is different if that situation has been associated with hunger than if it has

[3] E. E. Anderson (1941a, 1941b, 1941c, 1941d).

not. To illustrate, Calvin, Bicknell, and Sperling (1953) showed that rats which had been placed in a striped box when they were hungry, over a period of 24 days, subsequently ate slightly more there than a group which had had the same experience when they were not hungry. Such evidence, however, only serves to raise the important question: Precisely what effect does the association between environmental cues and hunger have upon the organism? The answer to this question is not known. It is clear that, if conditioning is involved, it is not, strictly speaking, *drive* that is conditioned, inasmuch as only responses are conditionable. Denny and Behan (1956) have considered the possibility that demonstrations of conditioned hunger drive often reduce to instances of conditioned approach behavior. In other cases, learning may not be involved at all. Myers and Miller (1954) have called attention to the fact that learning thought to be motivated by an acquired hunger drive is sometimes motivated by an exploratory tendency. And Hall (1956) has shown that the animal's normal increase in activity in the presence of distinctive environmental stimulation is enhanced by food deprivation. Thus, for a final time, a basic question about the functioning of motives comes down to a question of the responses produced by the drive-establishing operations.

2. *Social Techniques.* The studies of the acquisition of motives reviewed in the previous sections were all ones in which a drive was established by a routine which followed a classical conditioning paradigm. That is, in each, the attempt was to provide a neutral stimulus with the properties of a drive by pairing it with an existing motive. It may be, of course, that the association developed was between the previously neutral stimuli and the *responses* produced by the drive state; but this does not alter the nature of the process involved.

There exists a parallel literature on acquired motivation in which the underlying mechanism is more like instrumental learning. Tolman (1942, 1943) has given us an account which is fairly representative. Figure 13.11 summarizes his view. The essential idea in this theory is that, in infancy, the individual has only a set of biological drives. Inevitably these drives are subjected to frustration and new techniques are developed to satisfy them. Whatever techniques lead to relief from frustration are learned, and by principles which are more typical of Hull's theory than of Tolman's, they become characteristic of the individual's repertory of responses to the world. As the drive-conversion diagram also suggests, these first primitive adjustments achieved by the individual are not adequate to deal with all situations. They, too, are frustrated with the result that new learning occurs and the individual's reactions to the world are modified further.

It should be noted that, so far, nothing has been said about motives. Yet a glance at Figure 13.11 will reveal that several of the social techniques are ones which we often describe in motivational terms. Aggres-

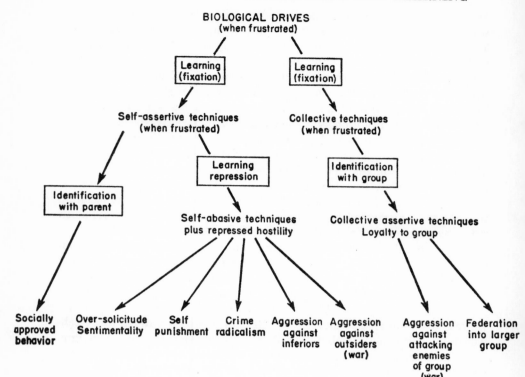

FIGURE 13.11. Tolman's drive-conversion diagram. The idea is that the social techniques develop as a result of the frustration, first, of the biological drives and, later, from the frustration of first-order techniques. The specific social techniques listed are merely illustrative. The variety of mechanisms acquirable in this way is theoretically very large. (After Tolman, 1942).

sion, hostility, social approval, loyalty, identification, and self-punishment are all terms which probably occur more often in the psychological literature in the context of motive than in the context of habit. The problem which this point creates introduces a somewhat different conception of the relationship between habits and drives. There is little doubt that social techniques develop according to a scheme like that described by Tolman. Miller and Dollard (1941) have produced an imitative tendency in rats, and Winterbottom (1958) has related the achievement motive in children to circumstances which appear to fit the requirements of such a theory. At a factual level, this seems to provide good evidence for a developmental process of the general sort described by Tolman. Two further questions remain: (1) are the results of these processes motives? and (2) if they are motives, how do they acquire this status?

So far, neither of these questions has received an answer which satisfies very many people. An answer to the first question will require a set of experiments devised so as to determine whether the social techniques possess the properties of other motives. It will be necessary to find means of increasing and decreasing the strengths of these motives to determine whether their effects upon behavior are appropriate. Is it possible, for example, to show that the strength of aggression increases when an aggressive individual is deprived of the opportunity to satisfy his motive in the same way as hunger increases with food deprivation? Conversely, can aggression be satiated in the same way as hunger? Scanty evidence indicates that the answer to these questions may be affirmative. Feshbach (1955) aroused the hostility of college students and found that an opportunity to express this aggression in a projective test reduced this motive, after the manner of consummatory responses in general. Similarly, Gewirtz and his associates have shown that deprivation and satiation of the need for social companionship have appropriate influences on the behavior of children learning for reward in the form of expressions of approval (Gewirtz and Baer, 1958a, 1958b; Gewirtz, Baer, and Roth, 1958). Confirmation of such results will do much to establish the motivational status of the social needs.

The answer to the second question is even more difficult. One form of answer was suggested by Woodworth (1918) in his proposal that habits can become drives. Essentially the same answer is to be found in Allport's (1937) conception of functional autonomy, according to which habits become ends in themselves, that is, drives. We have already seen, however, that such answers are, at best, descriptive and leave the main problem still unsolved.

SUMMARY

Variations in the intensity of activity in a single individual from time to time, as well as from individual to individual, suggest the desirability of developing a concept to deal with the energy characteristics of behavior. Motivation is such a concept.

The General Properties of Motives

In addition to its capacity to provide behavior with energy, it has sometimes been proposed that motivation also guides or directs behavior. There is no doubt that motivated behavior is directed, and there is general agreement that the mechanism through which this guidance is accomplished is that of drive stimulation. There is less agreement, however, on the relationship between drive and drive stimulation. Some writers have maintained that one or the other of these two conceptions is dispensable. We have taken the position that both of them are of value, but

that it is important to distinguish between the guidance and the ener-
getics of behavior. The term *motive* should, we think, be reserved for the
latter function.

Functions Relating Motives to Behavior

Since motivation is conceptualized in terms of energy, it is natural to
expect that increasing the strength of a motive will always produce an
increase in the vigor of behavior. In the majority of cases, the effect of
increased motivation is probably in the expected direction; but there are
enough exceptions to raise questions. In numerous instances, increased
motivation has been found to produce first an increase and then a decrease in response strength. In a few others the effect has been entirely
interfering.

Careful examination of these functions leads to two important points:
(1) Basically, the effect of increased drive probably is to increase the
vigor of behavior. The responses so energized, however, may not be
those under observation in a particular experiment. In that event, the
effect of increased drive will vary depending upon the compatibility between the energized response and the response being measured. (2) Even
where the effect is to produce a uniform increase in the magnitude of
several measures of the strength of a particular drive, the functions may
be quite different for the different measures.

The Effect of Drive on Learning

One of the most important theoretical questions in the field of learning
is whether the level of learning (as distinguished from performance)
varies with the level of motivation at the time of learning. Superficially
considered, experiments designed to answer this question appear to have
yielded positive and negative answers with about equal freqency. Further
examination of the evidence, however, suggests another interpretation.
It may be that experiments which have seemed to demonstrate that drive
does affect learning are actually irrelevant, because somewhat different
responses were learned under the different training drives. Thus the
hypothesis that motivation has no effect upon learning is yet to be dis-
proved.

Drive Stimuli and Learning

Although we have thought it wise to maintain a sharp conceptual
separation of drive and drive stimulus, this should not be allowed to
obscure the fact that drive stimulation plays an important role in learning. It has been demonstrated, for example, that different drives can

provide distinctive stimuli to which the organism can learn to respond, and that such learning can occur quite quickly under optimal conditions. There is reason to believe that these drive stimuli provide satisfactory cues for the guidance of behavior which is unrelated to the drive with which they are associated. Moreover, it has been shown that drive stimuli provide a dimension along which stimulus generalization occurs.

Acquired Drives

At least from the time of Watson, the idea that drive and emotions are largely acquired has been very popular in American psychology. Today it seems probable that there has been a serious tendency to overestimate the importance of learning in relation to motives. But this is not to say that motives are never acquired or uninfluenced by learning, because they obviously are. In the study of acquired motivation, it is possible to identify four somewhat separate lines of approach to the problem:

1. *The Modification of Instinct.* There is no doubt that the biological drives such as hunger, thirst, and sex depend upon experience, at least for their mode of expression. There is also a very small amount of informal evidence that instinctive reactions are conditionable.

2. *Incentive Motivation.* In previous chapters (p. 170) the point has been made that rewards produce motivational effects. Operating in this way rewards are called incentives. The mechanism underlying the development of incentive motivation seems to be a matter of conditioning goal responses to previously neutral aspects of the learning situation.

3. *Fear as an Acquirable Drive.* By far the largest amount of experimental work has been done on conditioned fears, which are capable of motivating behavior. Beginning with the classical study of Watson and Rayner, there have been numerous investigations to show (*a*) that conditioned fears display the various characteristics of other classically conditioned responses, (*b*) that fear will serve as a motive for learning, and (*c*) that fear-reduction is a reinforcer. There is some evidence that the arousal of positive motives in a particular situation also influences behavior in that same situation on later occasions. There is still a question, however, as to whether this effect is properly considered motivational.

4. *Social Techniques.* Finally, it is quite obvious that such tendencies in human behavior as those toward imitation, aggression, achievement, and loyalty are learned. And, in common speech, they are often spoken of as motives. Whether they qualify psychologically as motives remains a question. They should, we think, be regarded as motives if they show the same properties as other motives; for example, if they increase in strength with deprivation and are satiated with consummatory behavior. There is fragmentary evidence that they do display these characteristics.

·14·

Applications to Personality

ALTHOUGH THE laws of conditioning are important in their own right, as statements of the nature of learning in specially devised experimental situations, most psychologists probably feel that these laws would be much more important if it could be demonstrated that they also apply to complex behavior nearer to everyday human activity. Accordingly, there have been numerous attempts to apply the principles of simple learning to such behavior. The most recent efforts in this direction have extended the principles of conditioning and simple learning to rote memorization (Hull, Hovland, Ross, Hall, Perkins, and Fitch, 1940), the acquisition of motor skill (Ammons, 1947; Kimble, 1949), social behavior (Miller and Dollard, 1941), and personality and psychotherapy (Dollard and Miller, 1950; Shoben, 1949). Attempts such as these raise basic questions about the relationship between conditioning and other forms of behavior. On the one hand, some writers have argued that all behavior must be an expression of a single set of laws which apply at all levels of complexity, from the conditioned response in lower animals to the most elaborate mental functioning of man. To others it has seemed that new principles will be required to deal with complex behavior and that no combination of the principles of conditioning could ever serve to explain the complete range of human activity. At the present time it would be a mistake to accept either of these positions. It may, some day, be known whether the laws of conditioning do or do not explain (say) psychopathological behavior. But that day is still far in the future. For the time being all that is possible is to attempt the explanation of complex phenomena in simpler terms. It is to be expected that the resulting explanations will be incomplete and imperfect. Complex behavior, if it is explainable at all in these terms, certainly involves the simultaneous operation of many principles of conditioning. Unfortunately these principles are not exactly known, and we know even less about the way in which they combine and function together. These facts, together with the consideration that knowledge in the field of personality is also in a very primitive stage of development, mean that there will be many points at which learning theory can offer only the grossest of speculations in dealing with problems of personality. And there will be other cases in which conditioning principles suggest ideas which do not appear in personality theory. Such disagreements and lacunae define problems for future research in both areas.

GENERAL NATURE OF THE LEARNING THEORY APPROACH

One of the salient features of the learning theorists' approach to the topic of personality has been a tendency to try to co-ordinate psychiatric (most often psychoanalytic) concepts to the familiar concepts in the field of learning. Thus personality has been defined in terms of habit (Guthrie, 1938) and such processes as generalization, discrimination, reinforcement, extinction, and partial reinforcement have been advanced in an effort to explain the adjustment mechanisms familiar to the psychiatrist by means of concepts familiar to the learning theorist. Experimental analogues of psychoanalytic phenomena have been demonstrated, often in studies with lower animals. These studies have included efforts to produce concrete instances of the processes regarded as important for therapy.

The Influence of Psychoanalysis

At first blush the fact that the learning theorists have drawn quite heavily from Freudian theory seems strange, because of what appear to be vast differences in approach to psychological problems. Although attempts have been made to represent Freud as an experimentalist, they have not been convincing; Freud's great contribution is his penetrating insights into the dynamics of human behavior. The learning theorists, on the other hand, have always remained close to the laboratory and have insisted on more objective evidence than Freud usually had for his interpretations.

A closer look at Freud's psychology, however, reveals a number of strong similarities which the learning theorist finds appealing. The most general of these is the commonly shared assumption that behavior is determined in part by the events in an organism's past. Even more importantly, the *concepts* of both systems are historical in nature. Although other systematists, notably Lewin (1935) and his followers (for example, J. F. Brown, 1936), admit that behavior is, as a matter of fact, historically determined, such theorists have developed ahistorical theories and deny the usefulness of attempting to understand contemporary behavior in terms of past causes. Thus, the learning theorist has been drawn to psychoanalytic thinking by a basic commitment implicit in the nature of his subject matter.

Beyond this large and pervasive parallel between Freudian psychology and learning, a parallel involving matters of general strategy, there are numerous other more limited similarities which give this theory appeal for the learning theorist:

1. Freud's approach to motivation is a kind of variation on the concept of *homeostasis* which has been implicit in the thinking of many learning theorists. In the field of physiology, homeostasis refers to the regulative tendencies of the body by which certain constancies are maintained. The mechanisms for the control of body temperature, salt content of the body fluids, and water balance in the cells are typical examples. When this concept is applied to motivation, drives become tendencies to correct imbalances produced by lacks or excesses in the organism's environment. Freud's treatment of motives took this form and the adjustive behavior of the organism was regarded as conservative in this homeostatic sense.

2. As a similarity closely related to the point above, Freud's concept of the *pleasure principle* obviously paraphrases the law-of-effect. The energies of the *id*, in Freud's theory, are conceived as throwing the individual into a state of painful tension. Adjustive behavior is such as to relieve this tension. In Freudian theory both normal and abnormal behavior serve the same end, tension reduction. This is obviously very similar to the principle advocated by Hull in his drive-reduction theory of reinforcement. In what appears to be a contrast to Hull, Freud held that the ideal state of the organism is not the complete absence of tension, but rather one of tension at a mild and optimal level.

3. Certain aspects of Freud's description of the developing personality seem easily translatable into the concepts of classical and instrumental conditioning. The psychological development of the individual involves two mechanisms, which Freud called primary and secondary processes. Briefly the essentials of these processes are as follows:

a. Primary process. The infant's first reactions to the world are governed by the *pleasure principle* and are motivated by selfish needs for immediate bodily satisfaction. When satisfaction occurs, the objects which produce it become associated with tension reduction. As a result, the infant, when frustrated, is able to call up an image of the conditions (food, fondling, rocking, dryness) which will relieve its tension. Up to this point, the concept of primary process seems to be little more than classical conditioning described in terms somewhat similar to those employed by theorists who accept the idea of perceptual learning. Along the same lines, Freud held that, because of its immaturity, the infant is unable to distinguish between object and image, with the result that the mere thought of satisfaction is somewhat tension-reducing. This extension of the concept seems to be almost exactly the same thing as was involved in the extension of classical conditioning principles to cover the phenomenon of secondary reinforcement (p. 170).

b. *Secondary process.* The primary process provides a poor basis for adjustment to the environment. The demand for immediate satisfaction and the inability to distinguish wish from object are clearly maladaptive in many situations. With his increasing intellectual powers and better control over the environment, the infant develops in directions which tend to correct this state of affairs. This development is the secondary process, as a result of which the infant comes to distinguish between self and environment, learns techniques for obtaining desired goals, and is able to forego immediate pleasure. He reacts more and more in terms of the *reality principle* rather than the pleasure principle. The secondary process is quite plainly analogous to instrumental learning. Indeed the picture of instrumental behavior sketched by the psychoanalysts is not much different from that of the S-R reinforcement theorists. Through the primary process the organism is capable of knowing what will satisfy its needs. The secondary process provides the means through which satisfaction becomes a reality (Hall, 1954, p. 29).

4. Elements of the personality dynamics proposed by Freud bear a resemblance to the conflict analysis developed by N. E. Miller. In psychoanalytic terms, there is continual friction between the demands of the id, which are primitive, asocial, biological motives, and the superego which contains the mores and taboos of one's society. This is essentially an internalized approach-avoidance conflict in which an individual's tendencies toward sex and aggression clash with tendencies to feel guilty about exactly these impulses.

5. Anxiety is important in Freud's thinking (Freud, 1926) in many of the ways in which learning theory tends to use the concept. Anxiety provides a motivational basis for adjustment since it is experienced as unpleasant. And relief from anxiety is regarded as an important goal. Moreover, anxiety was thought of as providing the cues (drive stimuli) which evoke the various mechanisms of adjustment.

6. Certain of the basic phenomena of learning are represented, at least approximately, in psychoanalytic thought. Generalization, for example, is clearly a part of what is referred to in *predicate thinking,* a process involved in symbol development. A knife becomes a symbol for the male organ because both are long and pointed. Habit appears in the Freudian conception of *repetition compulsion.* The individual's behavior tends to be consistent, and his various adjustments to the world tend to take similar forms from one occasion to another, even though the details may change: "An adult may change his job or his wife or his hobbies quite frequently, but the new job or wife or hobby bears a close resemblance to the old one" (Hall, 1954, p. 117). Acquired drives are represented

much as Tolman (1943) does as *instinct derivatives* or new *object cathexes*. The id cannot always achieve its aims directly and must make compromises, which take the form of displacements or sublimations of the primitive urge. Attempts to satisfy sexual tensions by physical activity or verbal expressions of aggression are examples. Because such indirect expressions do partially relieve tension they become a part of the individual's characteristic adjustment and constitute the basis for the development of very persistent motive states.

It thus becomes clear that Freudian psychology contains much that is directly translatable into the concepts of learning. Partly for this reason the learning theorist interested in personality has tended to develop theories and experimental ideas closely in touch with psychoanalytic thought. There are however certain historical and methodological points which need to be made: (1) The interpretation of psychoanalysis in terms of the psychology of learning has not occurred as a grand hypothetico-deductive tour de force. What has so far been accomplished has been done in a piecemeal and fragmentary way, with much looking to the writings of Freud after the experimentally verified facts are in. The process is still going on. (2) Both psychoanalysts and psychologists recognize that learning theory has managed to deal only with the most superficial aspects of personality as interpreted from the analytic point of view (Kris, 1951). This is largely because the psychology of learning, at the present time, has much difficulty in dealing with symbolically mediated behavior, although progress in this direction has been made (Dollard and Miller, 1950).

EXPERIMENTAL NEUROSIS

Still another parallel between the learning theorist's approach and that of Freud has been a greater interest in neurotic than in psychotic forms of maladjustment. One of the earliest laboratory attacks on problems of personality consisted in the study of *experimental neuroses,* a term which has often been criticized but continues to be used (Liddell, 1956). This field of application for conditioning procedures and theories began with some experimental observations by Shenger-Krestovnikova in Pavlov's laboratory in 1914 (Pavlov, 1927, p. 291ff.). A dog was trained to salivate when a luminous circle was projected on a screen. After the conditioned response was well established, a discrimination was obtained between the circle and an ellipse with a ratio between the semi-axes of 2 :1. The discrimination was acquired comparatively quickly. The shape of the ellipse was then changed by stages, until it was almost that of a circle. During these manipulations the discrimination training continued : the circle was followed by reinforcement, but the ellipse was not. Finally an ellipse with a ratio of the semi-axes of 9 :8 was reached. At this point discrimination not only did not improve, but throughout three weeks of training it became worse.

At the same time the whole behavior of the animal underwent a marked change. The hitherto quiet dog began to squeal in its stand, kept wriggling about, tore off with its teeth the apparatus for mechanical stimulation of the skin, and bit through the tubes leading from the animal's room to the observer's, all behavior which had never occurred before. On being taken into the experimental room the dog now barked violently, which was also contrary to its earlier tranquility. In short, it presented symptoms of a condition which, in a human being, we would call neurosis. Among the additional symptoms reported by later investigators have been (1) signs of anxiety such as whining and trembling, (2) a breakdown of the precision of the CR, with the latency of the response becoming extremely variable, (3) refusal of the dog to eat in the experimental apparatus or room, (Dworkin, 1939), and (4) signs of strong "inhibition" such as yawning drowsiness and sleep (Muncie and Gantt, 1938). There are three circumstances under which the neuroses are said to arise: the application of a strong conditioned stimulus after the animal has become accustomed to a weak one (overstrained excitatory processes); protracted inhibition, as in excessive delays (overstrained inhibitory processes); and clash of excitation and inhibition, as in an overly difficult discrimination.

Experimental Neuroses in the Sheep

Liddell and his co-workers at Cornell have studied conditioned responses in sheep for many years and have observed experimental neuroses since 1926. Generally speaking, there is good agreement between their observations and those of Pavlov. Experimental neuroses have been produced in a number of ways which include: (1) requiring a difficult discrimination (Pavlov's clash of excitation and inhibition), (2) employing a long series of extinction trials or too long a delay between CS and UCS (Pavlov's overstrained inhibitory process), and (3) carrying out a long series of alternating reinforced and non-reinforced trials at a regular seven-minute intertrial interval. Among the symptoms of neurotic behavior are the following: (1) hyperirritability, (2) resistance to entering the laboratory, (3) motor abnormalities including persistent tic-like movements and tremors, (4) changes in social behavior, including refusals to join the flock and symptoms of "suspicion" and "aggressiveness," (5) loss of ability to withhold responses to negative conditioned stimuli, (6) loss of the ability to delay responses to positive stimuli, (7) autonomic symptoms including abnormalties of respiration, eliminative function, and heart action, and (8) abnormal effects of drugs (Liddell, 1938; Anderson and Parmenter, 1941). One of the striking facts reported by the group at Cornell is that experimental neuroses are very persistent, lasting for 13 years or more (Liddell, 1956). On the other hand, Liddell (1956) also reports that experimental neurosis in the sheep is frequently so incapacitating that the experimental animals die early. In particular, they become easy prey for marauding dogs.

Experimental Neurosis in the Rat

Successful development of experimental neurosis in the rat has been reported by Cook (1939). From among a group of six rats, three developed disorders of behavior in a situation described as follows:

The rats were strapped to a stand so that the only sizeable limb movement possible was a flexion of the right foreleg. Under certain conditions such a flexion was rewarded with a food pellet; under other conditions it was punished with an electric shock. Observations indicated that the animals experienced two principal stresses: the first, when they were required to delay the food-bringing flexion until they received a bright-light stimulus; the second, when they were required to make a very difficult discrimination between a bright-light stimulus which permitted a food-bringing flexion and a dim-light stimulus which prohibited such a flexion on pain of shock. Because, under such conditions, the organism was receiving simultaneously stimuli to the excitation and inhibition of the same response, the stresses experienced have been characterized as comprising a "clash" between the neural activity of initiating a response and the neural activity of inhibiting the same response. (Cook, 1939, pp. 307-308)

Cook points out that restraint of activity is an essential feature of the experimental situation leading to abnormal behavior. In three other conflict problems, which permitted more freedom in bodily activity, no disturbance was produced.

Experimental Neurosis in the Cat

Studies of experimental neurosis in cats have been reported by Masserman and his associates (for example, Masserman, 1943). In these experiments cats were trained to operate a switch to produce a signal that food was available and then to get food delivered into a receptacle by an automatic delivery mechanism. Then, at the moment of feeding, an unpleasant airblast was directed across the animal's face or a shock was delivered to the feet. The conflict thus produced led to a variety of behavioral changes including (1) restlessness and agitation, or, sometimes, passivity, (2) fear responses to the feeding signals such as trembling, rapid and irregular pulse and respiration, crouching, hiding, and attempting to escape from the apparatus, (3) refusal to eat, (4) "compulsively" stereotyped behavior, and (5) "regressive" behavior such as preening, "immature" aggression, or kittenish playfulness.

Evaluation of Research on Experimental Neurosis

A question which occasionally arises in connection with the experiments just described is whether they have produced a real neurosis. Without further specification of the meaning of the term *neurosis* this question has no answer. If the implication in such questions is that there exists some disease entity, neurosis, which, like poliomyelitis, people get and lower animals can also get, the answer must be a rejection of this idea. On the other hand, the behavior which we call neurotic has certain characteristics which seem to be represented in the studies of experimental neurosis: (1) Neurotic behavior is the product of stress and conflict. It will be observed that in most of the demonstrations cited above a conflict is plainly evident between reinforced and non-reinforced, or punished, action tendencies. (2) Neurotic behavior is characterized by anxiety. This implies punishment of some sort; and, again, it will be noted that a noxious stimulus has usually figured in the studies of experimental neurosis. (3) Neurotic behavior occurs, in part, because of conflict which is inescapable. In the animal experiments, physical restraint has always been a part of the procedure, and one of the typical results has been a resistance of the subjects against entering the situation where conflict occurs. (4) Neurotic behavior is marked by a set of symptoms that are frequently very unusual by social standards and always only partially a solution to the conflict. Analogous behavior has often been observed in the studies of experimental neurosis. On all of these counts, the term *experimental neurosis* seems justified and not unduly anthropomorphic. But, in one respect, the studies of experimental neurosis do deserve sharp criticism: the procedures employed have typically been haphazard, the number of subjects run under strictly comparable conditions small, and the behavioral measures at best unquantified and often grossly subjective. In addition to this, the phenomenon itself is exceedingly complex. The characteristics of neurotic behavior just listed suggest some more particular lines of investigation with relevance to personaliity. These involve the topics of anxiety, conflict, and symptom formation. A short section will be devoted to each.

ANXIETY

In applications of learning theory to problems of personality the concept of anxiety occupies a central position. The general point of view parallels that of psychoanalysis in assuming that anxiety plays a double role, being on the one hand a drive, and on the other, a source of reinforcement through its reduction. Studies cited earlier show that this is a reasonable assumption. Anxiety is capable of producing restless activity, and elements of such activity leading to anxiety reduction are learned.

Types of Anxiety

Drawing his ideas from laboratory experimentation almost exclusively, the learning theorist attributes anxiety to a conditioning process in which neutral stimuli have come to stand for punishment, pain, and fear. The nature of the evidence for this conception leads to a limited view of anxiety for two reasons.

1. The noxious unconditioned stimuli in most experiments have produced physical pain, which means that it is dangerous to generalize to fears based upon other noxious stimuli. It seems clear, however, that many other forms of stimulation are innately fear producing. Some of the stimuli which have been shown to be unconditioned fear stimuli are: (*a*) in birds of certain species, the shadow of a hawk (Tinbergen, 1951); (*b*) in monkeys, the decapitated head of another monkey (Hebb, 1946) and even certain toys (Harlow, 1958); (*c*) in cats, air blasts in the face (Masserman, 1943); (*d*) in the human infant, sudden loud noises and loss of support (Watson, 1925); and (*e*) in rats, being placed in a large open field. These stimuli are, of course, in addition to painful stimuli, which appear to be negative stimuli for all species. Hebb (1946) classifies innate fears into three categories: (*a*) fears due to conflict which include fears induced by pain, sudden loud noises, dead or mutilated bodies, and strange persons or animals, (*b*) fears due to sensory deficit, which include fears based on loss of support, darkness, and solitude, and (*c*) fear produced by physiological disturbances. Examples of the latter are provided by the psychotic fears frequently associated with pellagra. It may be that endocrine disturbances also sensitize fearful reactions which individuals without the disturbance do not display. Beyond this, it is quite clear that certain acquired fears also can serve as the motivational basis for much adjustive behavior. Phobias and fear of loss of love are two examples.

2. Conceptions of anxiety based exclusively upon laboratory research tend to overemphasize the importance of the fear of objective situations. The psychoanalytic literature contains evidence that anxiety occurs in many different forms. Freud distinguished three varieties of anxiety, *objective, neurotic,* and *moral.* Objective anxiety is anxiety about events in the real world and includes anxieties about physical harm and economic privation. The cues provided by these forms of anxiety ordinarily lead the individual to take measures to avoid the threatening danger. He looks for a hiding place, a job, or a means of defense, depending upon the nature of the threat. Neurotic anxiety (which is not the exclusive property of neurotic people) is an anxiety prompted by desires of the id; it is a fear of expressing antisocial, sexual, aggressive urges in the form of some impulsive act. Its symptoms, according to Freudian psychology, are found in free-floating anxiety, phobias, and panic. Moral anxiety, experienced as guilt, shame, or a pang of conscience, comes from the superego.

In the past certain sorts of behavior were punished by the parents. Instigation to similar behavior now calls up the anxiety thus established. This is moral anxiety.

In terms of practical adjustment, it is clear that moral and neurotic anxiety will be harder to deal with than objective anxiety. It is usually possible to escape from objective anxiety by running away, but in the case of the other two it is not. In any environment, performing the guilty act, almost performing the guilty act, or even thinking about it, are able to elicit unpleasant anxiety. There is a tendency among the psychoanalysts to distinguish more sharply between objective anxiety and the other two than between moral and neurotic anxiety. In psychoanalytic thinking, these latter two are intrapsychic. In the concepts of the learning theorist, they are conditioned to aspects of the individual's behavior, whereas objective anxiety is occasioned by stimuli in the external world. In this case the concepts of the learning theorist may provide the means of making a distinction where Freudian psychology finds it difficult. From the descriptions of moral and neurotic anxiety, it sounds very much as if the difference is in terms of the stimuli to which the anxiety is conditioned. If neurotic anxiety is a fear of expressing antisocial *urges,* the suggestion is that, in this case, the anxiety-evoking stimuli are drive stimuli. A fear of performing certain *acts,* as is said to be the case in moral anxiety, on the other hand, may be elicited by response-produced stimuli.

The Origin of Anxiety

Anxiety is an inevitable by-product of socialization. In infancy the child has no way of knowing what behavior society rewards and punishes; it responds in terms of its selfish needs. Some of these are socially taboo and are punished by the parents. Quite obviously, from the point of view of the child, the adjustive thing to do is to inhibit the unacceptable behavior and, thereby, avoid punishment. Inevitably this is the child's solution to the problem. The solution, however, is, at best, imperfect for several reasons: (1) It leaves the original drive unsatisfied. It must be put aside or even forgotten. This is a point which the psychoanalysts stress, in their view that acute anxiety is always symptomatic of repression. (2) The reinforced and punished acts to be discriminated create real problems. The child must distinguish between rewarded forthrightness and punished aggression, between proper respect and sissified timidity, between craven cowardice and graceful concession, between brotherly affection and incestuous lust, between the joys of male companionship and homosexuality, between standing up for one's rights and selfish hostility. Probably no one learns to recognize all the necessary nuances in his own behavior, or to achieve a satisfactory correlation of the ones he does discriminate to the requirements of the environment. (3) The origin of much anxiety is to be found in incidents which occurred before the child had learned to talk. Punishment for soiling during toilet training, for infantile sexuality, for lapses of table manners, and for early aggression all instill anxiety for behavior which bears no verbal label. In later life such verbal labels are of great assistance in developing discriminations between tabooed and nontabooed acts. The labels are usually easier to discriminate than the stimuli arising from the acts themselves. In early childhood, however, anxiety may be conditioned to vague, poorly differentiated aspects of behavior. (4) In a sense it is impossible for the child to make completely accurate discriminations and to develop responses perfectly calculated to avoid all punishment. Too much depends upon the inconsistent moods and insensitive perceptions of parents and others in control of the child's life. Sometimes certain acts (for example, boisterous play) are encouraged; sometimes they are punished. Beyond this, there is no guarantee that such consistency as parents show will be matched by a similar predictability in the behavior of nurses, babysitters, grandparents, or teachers.

Avoidable vs. Unavoidable Punishment and the Strength of Anxiety

It is a common-sense opinion that unavoidable punishments, where the individual has no control over the situation, lead to greater fear than avoidable punishment. There is also experimental evidence to support this idea. In avoidance conditioning experiments, the subjects frequently show decreased general anxiety as they learn the response which avoids punishment. Particularly in experiments using the wheel-turning apparatus, there tends to be a great deal of instrumental activity between trials. The animal "rehearses" the avoidant response of wheel turning with great persistence, although the danger signal is absent. With practice, however, this behavior disappears almost completely. It is as if the original high level of between-trial activity arose from a "feeling of helplessness" and that learning the avoidant response created a "sense of mastery" with a resulting diminution of fear of the general situation (Coppock and Mowrer, 1947; Mowrer and Lamoreaux, 1951).

In a different approach to the relationship between fear and the avoidability of punishment, Mowrer and Viek (1948) employed, as a measure, inhibition of eating. Their procedure consisted of offering the rat food on the end of a stick and, 10 seconds later, whether the rat ate or not, turning on a shock. The animals in one group had control over the duration of the shock because it was terminated as soon as the rat jumped off the electrified grid. Another group received exactly the same treatment, except that the animals in this group had no control over the shock. Each subject in this latter group was paired with one in the former and on each trial, given the same amount of shock received by its partner. The difference in behavior in the two groups of animals was very striking. The 10 subjects in the first group with control over shock duration failed to eat on an average of only 1.6 of 14 trials on which meaningful comparisons can be made. The animals in the group with no control over shock duration failed to eat on 8.5 trials. It thus appears that the unavoidable shock increased the strength of fear. In other studies the same effect may occur because of a difficulty in recognizing the significant environmental cues. This would also make punishment unavoidable.

Effects of Anxiety on Behavior

Anxiety is commonly recognized as an unpleasant experience and as a disrupter of behavior. The learning theorist takes it as his task to explain these familiar influences within his own conceptual framework. The following two ideas have dominated research in this area: (1) Anxiety is conceived as a drive, with anxiety reduction playing the role of reinforcer; and (2) as with other drives, anxiety has distinctive stimuli associated with it. These stimuli serve as cues to which responses can be conditioned, with the result that the individual whose anxiety is aroused may be expected to show a characteristic set of responses. Although individuals who favor one or the other of these views sometimes have argued as to which is correct, it should be recognized that, as with other drives, anxiety almost certainly functions both as a motive and as a producer of stimulation.

Most of the research on anxiety carried out by psychologists interested in learning has been done to test the implications of the first of these propositions, the idea that anxiety is a drive. The line of reasoning behind such studies was developed in some detail in the previous chapter (p. 408). In very brief review, the assumption of a multiplicative relationship between drive and habit strength leads to the following predictions: (1) In simple, uncomplicated learning situations, such as classical conditioning, where only one response is elicited, anxiety should facilitate performance. This is because anxiety, as an irrelevant drive, contributes to the total motivational level of the subject and increases the quantity obtained when habit strength and drive are multiplied. (2) In complex, even two-choice situations, the effect of increased drive depends upon two further considerations: (a) the nature of the dominant habit evoked in the learning situation, and (b) whether the response which corresponds to this habit is right or wrong. If it is right, increased motivation (high anxiety) should facilitate performance, just as in the case of noncompetitional learning. If it is wrong, the situation becomes more complicated. Initially anxiety should interfere with performance, since it energizes incorrect responses. As the correct responses are mastered, however, there should be a point at which these latter responses become dominant; and from then on, anxiety again may be expected to facilitate. In complex learning situations, thus, the effects of anxiety upon behavior may be facilitating, interfering, or first interfering and then facilitating, depending upon the correctness of the original response tendencies of the subject and the manner in which these tendencies change with practice.

Tests of these deductions about the effect of anxiety on learning have most often made use of Taylor's (1953) Manifest Anxiety Scale (MAS). The MAS consists of a selection of items from an objective test, the Minnesota Multiphasic Personality Inventory, judged by clinicians to be diagnostic of anxiety. In the main, the items are one-sentence descriptions of anxiety symptoms, and the subject is asked to indicate whether each is characteristic of him. The measure of anxiety is the number of such symptoms to which the individual admits. In typical experiments, subjects with scores indicating very low and very high anxiety are compared in their performances on some learning task.

The original studies of the effect of anxiety upon learning (Spence and Taylor, 1951; Taylor, 1951) employed eyelid conditioning as the learning procedure. The results of one of these appears in Figure 14.1. The predicted difference in favor of high-anxiety subjects occurs and its magnitude increases with practice. This result has been obtained in a number of studies (Spence, Farber, and E. Taylor, 1954; Spence and Ross, 1957). Studies involving tasks which are more complex than eyelid conditioning have employed, to mention a variety, verbal maze learning (Taylor and Spence, 1952), stylus maze learning (Farber and Spence, 1953), serial rote learning (Montague, 1953), paired-associates learning (Ramond, 1953), discriminative eyelid conditioning (Hilgard, L. V. Jones, and Kaplan, 1951; Spence and Beecroft, 1954; Spence and Farber, 1954), problem solving (Maltzman, Fox, and Morrissett, 1953), and concept formation (Wesley, 1953). The support for a drive theory of anxiety from these studies, although generally positive, has been less impressive than that obtained in the studies of eyelid conditioning. In certain notable cases (for example, Montague, 1953; Taylor and Chapman, 1955) high-anxiety subjects have performed better on noncompetitional tasks and poorer on competitional ones, as it was predicted they would. But a more typical finding is simply that high-anxiety subjects are inferior on complex tasks, whatever the strengths of correct and incorrect tendencies. This suggests that complex learning situations evoke interfering responses in highly anxious subjects, and this tends to override whatever beneficial effects anxiety may have upon learning in situations of this sort.

Much of the discussion in the literature on anxiety has stressed the fact that the influence of anxiety on behavior is exceedingly complex,

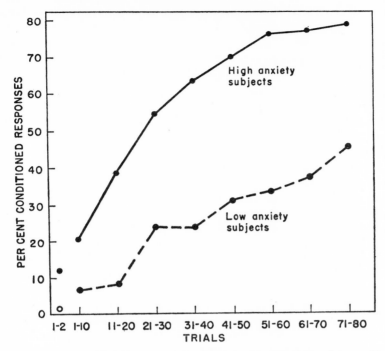

FIGURE 14.1.   Conditioning curves for high- and low-anxiety subjects (Taylor, 1951).

an emphasis which seems wholly justified on the basis of research. It has been found that the effect of anxiety depends upon individual difference variables such as sex (L'Abate, 1956) and the intelligence of the subjects (Spielberger and Katzenmeyer, 1959). It has also been suggested that subjects with different scores on the MAS probably differ in other ways, too, and that these differences complicate the interpretation of results. The importance of this fact depends upon whether the main interest is in the role of drive (anxiety) in learning, as it has been in the most important research carried out with the MAS, or whether the main interest is in the intrinsic nature of anxiety. In the latter case the need for a purer measure is obviously imperative.

What the Anxiety Scales Measure

Studies of the relationship between MAS scores and clinicians' judgments of anxiety have yielded correlation coefficients ranging from .16 to .68 (Taylor, 1956) with a median in the neighborhood of .40. This suggests that what the MAS measures may be only partly anxiety. Other possibilities which have been suggested are general neuroticism (Franks,

1956), introversion (Eysenck, 1955), psychasthenia and absence of hysteria (Eriksen, 1954; Eysenck, 1955), and emotional responsivity (Spence, 1958). The one study which is most directly pertinent to the view of anxiety as an emotional response is that of Runquist and Ross (1959). These investigators obtained a low, but significant, correlation of .22 between physiological measures of emotionality, heart rate and GSR changes, and MAS scores. They also compared eyelid conditioning performances of two extreme groups selected in terms of the physiological indicators. Their results indicated that subjects who were highly responsive in physiological terms showed superior conditioning.

One of the questions sometimes raised about anxiety, however measured, concerns its relationship to environmental stimulation. The early studies, emphasizing the concept of anxiety as a drive, conveyed the impression (intended or otherwise) that anxiety, like hunger, was something which the organism carried around with him to energize any and all habits. This might be called a "chronic" interpretation of anxiety. An alternative view, which held that anxiety occurred only in response to threatening situations, might be called an "acute" interpretation. With Spence's recent interpretation of anxiety as an emotional response (Spence, 1956, 1958), the "acute" view seems to have become the accepted one. Since it is a response, it presumably occurs as a reaction to stimulation, and the conventional laws of the evocation of responses should apply. Among these would be the proposition that anxiety, since it was acquired through punishment, would appear most markedly in situations which symbolize or portend punishment. Experimental support for such an interpretation comes from the facts that: (1) Eyelid conditioning, where the MAS has had its most conspicuous successes in predicting the outcome of experiments, involves a noxious stimulus. (2) High- and low-anxiety subjects apparently perform equally well in classical conditioning studies where there is no threat (Bindra, Paterson, and Strzelecki, 1955). (3) In several studies, stress and failure have been found to disrupt the performance of high-anxiety subjects (Gordon and Berlyne, 1954; Lucas, 1952).

Evaluation of the Anxiety as Drive Conception

The amount of research which has been instigated by the anxiety-as-drive conception is enormous. Since the original studies in 1951, the number of articles containing the word *anxiety* in their titles has increased steadily. Despite the fact that the outcomes of these experiments have not always supported the original theory, they have led to constructive reformulations involving the conception of anxiety as an emotional response conditioned to previously neutral stimuli.

Perhaps the main shortcoming of research on anxiety is that too little attention has been devoted to the stimuli which normally control anxiety. In the most important cases, these stimuli are internal and response-produced. The problems implicit in this fact are almost completely untouched by experimentation, although they are in principle solvable. Animals are able to discriminate internal drive states including fear and anxiety (Amsel and McDonnell, 1951). They also show some capacity to discriminate between self-produced and other anxiety signals. Masserman (1943, p. 84) reports that some of the cats in his studies of experimental neurosis displayed the neurotic behavior only if they themselves pressed the key which administered the feeding-airblast signal. If these signals were turned on by the experimenter, little or no neurotic behavior appeared. An even more fascinating fact is that deliberate training made it possible to reverse this relationship. One cat was made neurotic ("bodily manifestations of anxiety, self-starvation, exaggerated startle reaction . . .") by a procedure in which the experimenter delivered the signals. When the cat was trained to administer the signals itself, no signs of disturbance appeared, although it continued to cower at all signals given by the experimenter. Further research along these lines could contribute much to our understanding of response-produced anxiety.

CONFLICT

Conflict occurs when two or more incompatible reaction tendencies are instigated[1] simultaneously. This means that conflict is characteristic of all choice situations, and that it can be understood in terms of the principles which apply to any case where competing habits are aroused. Two such cases involving the conflict between short and long paths to a goal (p. 142) and between alternative reinforced responses in a discrimination situation (p. 373) have been discussed previously.

Types of Conflict

The classical literature recognizes four types of conflict: approach-approach, avoidance-avoidance, approach-avoidance, and multiple approach-avoidance. It is obvious at once that these categories derive from the two basic action tendencies discussed earlier in connection with instrumental learning and reinforcement: approach tendencies based on positive reinforcement, and avoidance tendencies based on negative reinforcement. Thus, *approach-approach* conflict occurs when two approach tendencies occur at the same time. Sometimes these two tendencies in-

---

[1] The term *instigation,* in its various forms, is a very useful one in that it provides a means of referring to the combined effect of drive and stimulation by a single word. An act is instigated if the stimuli and motivation for it are simultaneously present.

volve different goals, and selecting one means giving up the other. This is *divergent* approach-approach conflict. In other situations the two lines of action are directed at the same goal, as in the case where the rat chooses between long and short paths to food. This is a version of *convergent* approach-approach conflict.

Avoidance-avoidance conflict occurs in situations where one of two undesirable lines of action is required. It may be necessary, for example, to do one of two undesirable tasks but not both.

Approach-avoidance conflict occurs when the same object or situation is both attractive and repelling. A child wants to pet a strange dog but he has been warned not to. The pigeons in the park seem attracted by peanuts held out to them, but unable to take them from the hand because of what appears to be fear. It is characteristic of these conflicts that they involve fear or anxiety as one of the response tendencies.

Multiple approach-avoidance conflict occurs in situations where important choices must be made; for example, between careers, job offers, roommates, colleges, new homes, or scientific theories. In these cases, neither alternative is wholly attractive or unattractive; each has its desirable and undesirable features.

Experimental Analysis of Conflict

Although there has been some experimental work on approach-approach and avoidance-avoidance conflicts (Hovland and Sears, 1938) greatest interest has been in the approach-avoidance variety. N. E. Miller and his colleagues have provided a series of theoretical and experimental studies of approach-avoidance conflict in which basic learning concepts are made to play a crucial explanatory role. The experimental studies with the laboratory rat have involved conflict produced by giving it food and electric shocks in the same goal box. Specifically, hungry rats are first trained to run down an alley to obtain food and are then given shocks in the same place. By the principles of classical conditioning, this means that the goal becomes simultaneously a positive and negative secondary reinforcer, involving conflict. The advantages of this procedure are that (1) the separate components of the conflict (hunger-food and shock-escape) are relatively easy to control, (2) the behavior of the rat in conflict is easily described in physical terms, and (3) this experimental situation seems to contain many of the features of psychologically important conflicts. In particular, human conflict is often of the approach-avoidance variety and the resulting behavior is frequently describable in terms of nearness to the ambivalent situation or goal.

In his most recent description of his work on conflict, Miller (1959, pp. 204-234) has approached his materials formally, presenting a series of postulates and deductions. With minor changes, the postulates are reproduced as follows:

A. *The tendency to approach a goal is stronger the nearer the subject is to it.*
This is an application of the goal-gradient principle described earlier
(pp. 140). In the description of conflict behavior, it is called an *approach
gradient.*

B. *The tendency to avoid a feared object is stronger the nearer the individual
is to it.* This is an extension of the gradient-of-reinforcement idea to avoidance learning. In this context, the function is called the *avoidance gradient.*

C. *The strength of avoidance increases more rapidly with nearness to the goal
than does the strength of approach.* In other words, the avoidance gradient
is steeper than the approach gradient.

D. *The strength of the tendency to approach or avoid varies directly with the
strength of the drive upon which it is based.* In other words, an increase in
drive raises the gradient throughout its length.

E. *Below the asymptote of learning, increasing the number of reinforced trials
will increase the strength of the response tendency that is reinforced.* To this
it should be added that any of the variables known to influence the strength
of a learned response should contribute to the strength of the approach or
avoidance tendency. Such factors as the amount, delay, and scheduling of
reinforcement have not been thoroughly investigated. What evidence there
is supports the expectation that these variables will have the same effect in
the conflict situation as they do in simple learning (Berkun, 1957).

F. *When two incompatible responses are in conflict, the response corresponding
to the stronger tendency will occur.* This is an application of the assumption
discussed earlier (pp. 142) in dealing with the results of experiments involving choices to two paths to a goal. (By permission from *Psychology:
A study of a science,* by S. Koch (Editor). Copyright 1959. McGraw-Hill
Book Company, Inc.)

Figure 14.2 presents the first three of these postulates in graphic form.
The baseline in this representation is distance from the ambivalent goal
situation. The vertical axis is strength of the tendency to approach or
avoid. The functions themselves are the approach and avoidance gradients with the avoidance gradient represented as steeper, as the postulates
require. The linear form of the functions is purely for the sake of simplicity of representation. Goal-gradient data suggest that the functions are
actually curvilinear; but the deductions will be qualitatively the same
from any two gradients which are monotonically decreasing (Miller,
1959, p. 206).

It will be noted, in Figure 14.2, that the approach and avoidance
gradients cross. Most of Miller's deductions involve this set of conditions.
There are, of course, situations in which the two tendencies are both
present; but one is stronger than the other at all distances from the goal.
In the classical Columbia-obstruction-box studies, for example, rats ran

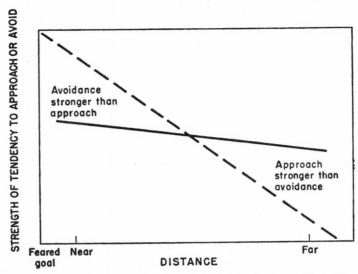

FIGURE 14.2. Graphical analysis of approach-avoidance conflict. Where the approach gradient is stronger, the organism advances toward the goal; where the avoidance gradient is stronger it retreats. (This and Figures 14.3 and 14.4 adapted from Neal E. Miller, "Experimental studies of conflict" in *Personality and behavior disorders*, edited by J. McV. Hunt. Copyright 1944, The Ronald Press Company.)

across an electrified grid to get to food or some other goal object (Warden, 1931). This situation contains all the elements of that involved in Figure 14.2 except the crossing of gradients. Whether it is to be called conflict or something else is entirely a matter of preference.

Figures 14.3 and 14.4 show the effects which the level of drive and the number of reinforcements are assumed to have upon the gradients. Figure 14.3 shows the hypothesized effect of two levels of hunger with the strength of the avoidance tendency held constant. Figure 14.4 shows the effect of varying the strength of the avoidance tendency, with the strength of the approach tendency kept constant. These two figures, together with Figure 14.2, lead to the following five deductions. As with the postulates these are taken from Miller (1959, p. 207-208) with only minor changes:

1. *The subject should approach part way to the goal and then stop.* Stopping should occur at the point where the gradients cross. Nearer the goal, the avoidance tendency is stronger and avoidance should occur. Further away, the approach tendency is stronger and approach should occur.

2. *Increasing the strength of hunger should cause the subjects to approach nearer to the goal.* (Figure 14.3)

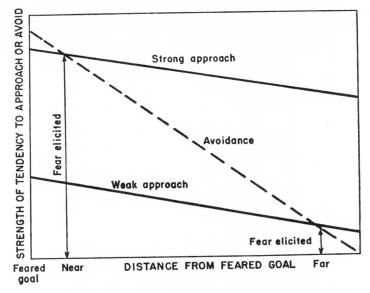

FIGURE 14.3. Graphical analysis of approach-avoidance conflict: the effect of raising the approach gradient. When the approach tendency increases, the point of intersection moves closer to the goal and the animal will approach nearer to the ambivalent object. (Adapted from N. E. Miller, 1944).

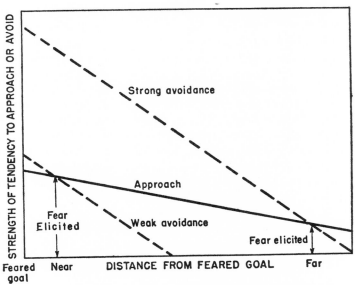

FIGURE 14.4. Graphical analysis of approach-avoidance conflict: the effect of lowering the avoidance gradient. (Adapted from N. E. Miller, 1944).

3. *Increasing the number of training trials reinforced with food (below the asymptote) should cause the subject to approach nearer to the goal.* This is because increasing numbers of training trials increase the height of the approach gradient, with essentially the same effect as increasing hunger.

4. *Increasing the strength of fear by using a more intense shock should cause the subjects to remain farther away from the goal.* This is because the more intense shock increases the avoidance gradient. See Figure 14.4.

5. *Increasing the strength of fear by increasing the number of reinforced avoidance trials (below the asymptote) should cause the subjects to remain further from the goal.* The reasoning is the same as in connection with the third deduction.

Tests of this theory of conflict have been of two general sorts: (1) Those concerned with the validity of the postulates. These have dealt with the approach and avoidance gradients separately. (2) Those designed as tests of the deductions. These have investigated the influence of the two gradients working in combination. The major study in the first category is that of J. S. Brown (1948). He trained some rats to approach a goal box to get food and trained others to leave it to escape from shock. Then, to demonstrate the approach and avoidance tendencies, he measured the strength with which the animals would pull against a harness either in the direction of the goal or away from it, depending upon whether they had been trained to approach or to avoid. The results of this study demonstrated the following points: (1) Approach and avoidance gradients exist as shown by the fact that strength of pull varied appropriately with training condition and distance from the goal. (2) The avoidance gradient is steeper than the approach gradient. (3) The height of the gradient varies with drive, whether hunger or shock-avoidance. This study verifies postulates A through D above. Evidence supporting the others has come from studies involving actual conflicts, rather than just one or the other of the two separate tendencies.

In an early study of this second sort, Miller, Brown, and Lewis (cited in Miller, 1959, p. 212), studied the effects of degree of hunger and shock intensity, using nearness of approach to the goal as a measure. They found that (1) the animals would go part of the way to the goal and stop, and (2) the animals would approach nearer if they were run either with strong hunger or weak shock. Subsequently Kaufman and Miller (1949) showed that there is a positive relationship between number of positively reinforced training trials and the number of animals which ran all the way to the goal. Conflict was established by giving 1, 3, 9, 27, or 81 runway trials reinforced with food and then 3 shock trials with a stronger shock on each succeeding trial. Figure 14.5 presents a graph showing the number of animals in each group reaching the goal

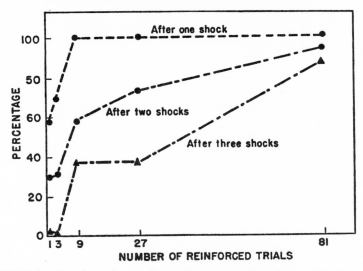

FIGURE 14.5. Number of animals reaching a feared goal as a joint function of the number of positively reinforced trials and the number of shock trials (Kaufman and N. E. Miller, 1949).

after 1, 2, and 3 shocks. With increasing numbers of reinforcements it is clear that more animals reached the goal following any number of shocks. The apparent relationship between number of shocks and number of animals reaching the goal depends upon number of shocks and shock level jointly, since the intensity of the shock was increased systematically on' successive trials.

Displacement and Substitute Behavior

One of Freud's great insights into human behavior was his recognition that much of it is of a substitutive nature. Since society so often prohibits direct expression of the urges of the id, these impulses seek indirect outlets which range from such simple expressions as day-dreams and slips of the tongue to the most highly constructive and artistic creations. The energies of the id are said to be displaced onto these activities. In terms of learning theory, displacement can be understood as another consequence of approach-avoidance conflict. The chief new idea required by such an interpretation is that the gradients in question are formed on a dimension of stimulus similarity rather than spatial distance. This conception makes the approach and avoidance gradients special cases of the generalization gradient. Both Spence (1947) and Miller (1959) have made a case for this interpretation even for spatial gradients.

To illustrate the application of conflict theory to displacement phe-

nomena, consider the consequences of punishment as it is involved in
child-rearing practices. A child, let us say, is punished physically for
some misdeed. Since punishment serves to frustrate some line of motivated activity there follows a strong, probably learned, tendency to
aggression directed at the parent who does the punishing (Dollard, Doob,
Miller, Mowrer, and Sears, 1939). The aggression, however, does not
materialize, because the punishment has also led to the conditioning of
a fear of the parent. But it may appear, seemingly with little or no
provocation, in some other situation typically against a sibling to whom
the aggression generalizes. The concept of generalization is basic to the
S-R interpretation of displacement.

Miller and Kraeling (1952) have performed an experiment designed
to test this interpretation of displacement, using the straight-alley conflict situation previously described. In this experiment, rats were first
trained to approach and obtain food in an alley of a distinctive color
and width. After this habit had been thoroughly learned, the animals
received increasingly strong shocks at the moment of touching the food
until they refused to take it. At this point it was assumed that a conflict
had been established. In order to study the phenomenon of displacement,
different groups of rats were tested either in the original alley or in one
of two others which were increasingly different from the original alley.
In this test only 23 per cent of the animals tested in the original alley
went all the way to the goal box. Instead they showed the typical behavior
of the rat in conflict in this situation. They went only part of the way to
the goal and stopped. Thirty-seven per cent of the animals tested in the
alley of intermediate similarity to the training alley reached the goal,
whereas 70 per cent of those tested in a very different alley responded
in this way. In short, as the test situation became more and more different a greater and greater proportion of the subjects performed the punished response.

Evaluation of S-R Conflict Theory

From the foregoing discussion, it is clear that the main postulates in
the stimulus-response theory of conflict have been verified, as have some
of the more straightforward deductions. The theory has also been extended with some success to situations more nearly resembling real life
(Miller, 1948b; Murray, 1954; Murray and Berkun, 1955; Whiting and
Child, 1953). On the other hand, S-R conflict theory as presented so far
has certain shortcomings which presumably will have to be remedied
before a completely adequate translation can be made. As is true of
other extensions of S-R theory, concepts designed to handle symbolic
behavior have been introduced relatively recently. Whether these attempts will be successful remains to be seen. Such developments seem

particularly important in connection with the topic of human conflict because the competing response tendencies are usually internalized (intrapsychic) and involve a large element of symbolic representation. Presumably because of the central importance of this problem it has been one of the first to which proponents of this kind of conflict theory have addressed themselves (Dollard and Miller, 1950).

Other problems involve the details of the theory. The following set of examples provides a sample: (1) One of the basic assumptions in conflict theory is that the avoidance gradient is steeper than the approach gradient. Why should this be? One possibility (Brown, 1948; Miller and Murray, 1952) is that the internal stimuli arising from hunger make the stimulus situation more nearly the same at various distances from the goal than it is in the case of fear. Although this argument seems to have some merit for the hunger-fear conflict used in experimental studies with lower animals, it seems less plausible when extended to human behavior. (2) Conflict seems to have a particularly disruptive effect upon behavior. Why is this? Specifically it has been demonstrated (Masserman, 1943) that a fear-conditioning situation alone produces avoidance, but does not produce the symptoms of experimental neurosis. Apparently the conflict between fear and hunger is critical. It may be that the effect of conflict comes about through the addition of drives, but this seems unlikely. It is more probable that conflict itself is a negative drive and that learning to avoid conflict occurs. Little, if any, research has been done on this problem. Guthrie's (1938) interpretation suggests that conflict may have its effect by keeping the individual in a constant state of heightened tension resulting in physical exhaustion. (3) Conflict, so far, has been described grossly in terms of competing reaction tendencies, a description which eventually will have to be refined (Haner and P. A. Brown, 1955). The concept, reaction tendency, is a performance concept; and we have seen that performance is jointly determined by habit and (mainly) motivational mechanisms. From this, it follows that conflicts between equally strong reaction tendencies may come about in a variety of ways. They may represent conflicts of motives, as the introductory text books usually imply; they may derive from strong competing habits; or they may occur in situations where one tendency involves a weak habit operating under intense drive, and the other involves a strong habit and weak drive. No doubt the influences of these different forms of conflict upon behavior will differ. The implications for eliminating the conflict differ even more, since the procedures required for reducing motives and extinguishing habits are essentially opposites of each other. For a hunger-motivated response, one feeds the animal to reduce the drive and fails to feed it to destroy the habit (Kimble, 1956). It seems very likely that the concept of conflict might profit from being thought of in quantitative terms. Employing Miller's graphical analysis of conflict, it is possible to construct a great variety of approach and avoidant gradients, all of which lead to the prediction that the rat will stop (say) halfway to the goal. This can be accomplished by raising and lowering the heights of the avoidance gradients together, so that the point of intersection does not change. It seems quite likely that the conflict produced by two strong tendencies might have very different behavioral consequences from one produced by two weak ones.

THE ORIGIN OF MALADJUSTMENT

At one level or another, all theorists regard behavior as adjustive in the sense of satisfying needs and resolving conflicts. Most human behavior is quite well suited to the attainment of these objectives. But there are some people whose behavior is much less than adequate. There are also cases in which the behavior of the well-adjusted person is maladaptive. This section deals with the attempts which have been made to understand such behavior in terms of learning theory.

Symbols, Language, and Cue-Producing Responses

The main problem which the learning theorist faces in attempting to understand complex human behavior is that such activity is mediated. That is, between the occurrence of a stimulus and the response to it, there intervenes a series of internal events which are subtle and difficult to investigate. The individual "plans his line of action," "thinks about what to say next," "decides whether or not to respond," "wonders whether he is on the right track," "feels guilty about wanting to do the wrong thing"—all covertly, with little or no visible sign that all of this is going on within him. Much, but not all, of this intervening behavior is verbal.

Because of the intimate connection between verbal behavior and adjustment, it will be necessary, before proceeding further, to present a brief outline of a psychology of language which employs the concepts of conditioning. It seems useful to begin by noting that the distinction between classical and instrumental conditioning applies to verbal behavior. Language, on the one hand, is a complex set of responses used by the individual to provide cues (communicate) to others. On the other hand, it is also a set of stimuli to which one has learned to respond. With respect to the former (response) function, language seems to develop in the same way as other instrumental acts (Skinner, 1957). Certain combinations of words and intonations of voice are strengthened through reward and are gradually made to occur in appropriate situations by the processes of discrimination learning.

In the other (stimulus) function of language, the principles of classical and instrumental conditioning both seem to apply. Words supply cues to action and, in this case, serve as discriminative stimuli in a practical application of the procedures of *instrumental learning*. When we are told to "hurry up," we probably do so because in the past we have been rewarded for such behavior and punished for failing to obey. But words also have signal and symbol values which seem to result from their having occupied the position of conditioned stimuli in practical analogues to a *classical conditioning* experiment of the higher order sort. As a result, words acquire the same cue and secondary reinforcing functions as the stimuli in any classical conditioning study. Pavlov (1927) reported that one of his dogs, conditioned to salivate to a light, licked the light as if it were food. Zener (1937), in contrast, pointed out that such behavior is not at all common and that more often animals respond to the CS with a response in preparation for the occurrence of the UCS. Today it seems quite likely that Pavlov's observation and Zener's were both correct. The behavior described by Pavlov appears to be an unusually direct reflection of the incentive value of a CS. The more typical behavior described by Zener reflects the cue function of a CS. Words, because of a history of association with significant events, acquire the properties of incentives and secondary reinforcers, typified by the terms, "good," "bad", and their synonyms. They also acquire signal properties. When the dentist says, "This is going to hurt a little," we respond by habitual actions in preparation for pain.

Thinking Repression and the Unconscious

Just as language can supply cues to guide the behavior of other people, it is also a means by which one can direct his own responses, for example, when one verbalizes the steps in a problem. Similar behavior occurs in lower animals, overtly, in the form of vicarious trial and error. In human behavior it, more often, occurs covertly as what we call thought. The responses involved in thinking may be of any sort, but they are predominantly verbal. Among the important functions of thought is that of supplying cues to subsequent behavior.

In childhood, thinking often occurs aloud and the relationship between it and language is quite clear. Confronted with a problem, the three-year-old may verbalize his solution ("Maybe I could stand on a chair to get it."). Age and practice, however, lead to two significant changes: (1) The overt verbalization disappears, although the responses may continue to occur subvocally. This is probably partly because the child learns that certain plans, such as competitive ones, and certain feelings, such as those of guilt or smugness, are better left unsaid (Guthrie, 1938). (2) As with other sequences of behavior, the verbal chain tends to be shortened and compressed. Thought is as rapid as it sometimes is because of this feature. The complex sequence of verbal items is replaced by some fragment. The advantages of this lie in a saving of time and energy.

The fact that thoughts are capable of providing cues means that, theoretically, they can provide the same conditions for the control of behavior as environmental events do. At a street intersection the thought, "I must either go straight ahead or turn left," has exactly the same effect as does a sign which reads "no right turn." From the same general fact it follows that thoughts can be punishing or rewarding if they have been associated with rewards or punishments in the past. The most important application of this idea is to the Freudian concept of *repression*, which refers to the inability to remember some traumatic event.

Personality maladjustment always contains an element of conflict which is unverbalizable or unconscious. In part, this is because the conflicts often have occurred before the age of talking, making clear representation in thought impossible (see below). But it is also partly a matter of repression. A person in a highly dangerous or guilt-provoking situation responds to it in many ways, with the skeletal musculature, autonomically, and verbally. These responses produce stimuli which then may become conditioned to the anxiety evoked in the situation. On later occasions talking about the frightening experience, or even thinking about it, leads to the reproduction of these stimuli and therefore to anxiety. The only response which prevents the uncomfortable arousal of anxiety is to cease thinking about the unpleasant occasion. If one does discontinue such thoughts, reinforcement in the form of anxiety reduction follows and strengthens the tendency not to think of the topic. With time, the tendency to repression spreads until all of the stimuli which might serve as a reminder only evoke avoidance of the unpleasant thought. No question, hint, or suggestion will stimulate recall. What is lost in repression is the ability to produce any of the responses which provide the stimuli conditioned to intense anxiety.

The Development of Neurosis

The materials presented up to this point contain the main principles necessary to describe neurotic maladjustment in terms of learning theory. Such disorders have their origin in conflict which remains unresolved, producing great anxiety. Since the elements of the conflict are repressed and unconscious, the neurotic person cannot form a reasonable plan of action to cope with his discomfort. Conflicts of this sort occur, of course, in normally adjusted individuals, too. The difference between normal and neurotic conflict appears to be partly the result of the stimuli in control of action. In neurotic conflict, these stimuli seem to be produced by aspects of the person's own behavior. To illustrate the importance of this point, consider sexual tendencies, which are so often involved in neurotic behavior. The monograph of Ford and Beach (1952) suggests that, in normal male sexual behavior, the most important factor is the availability of an attractive female. That is, the strength of instigation to sexual behavior depends upon the presence of a sexual goal object. In neurotic behavior, however, there is often a preoccupation with sex which indicates a control of sexual tendencies by other factors, probably internal and response-produced. This means that the neurotic person can carry his conflict around with him in a way which the normal individual does not. It is possible to conceive of two individuals with equally strong urges in the direction of socially prohibited sexuality and with equally strong guilt reactions providing restraint. For one of these individuals, the urge arises only with opportunity because it is controlled by external stimuli; for the other, however, it is constantly present because it is called forth by proprioceptive stimulation. For the first of these individuals, anxiety arises only in a few situations; for the other, it is a continual problem.

If almost any person is put into a highly conflictful situation and forced to remain there, the equivalent of neurotic maladjustment may occur under conditions where the conflicting action tendencies are under external stimulus control. War neuroses develop under circumstances where there is intense conflict between fear and the demands of battle (Grinker and Spiegel, 1945). Normally a person avoids such situations and leaves them if he can. The inescapability of the battle situation is one of the conditions leading to neurosis. The conflicts of other neuroses are also inescapable, but for a different reason, because the elements of conflict are in the individual's behavior.

Another important difference between neurotic and other conflict is that the former is usually unconscious, at least in part. This comes about for three reasons: (1) Anxiety reactions are acquired by a process of classical, rather than instrumental, conditioning. This means that the response is elicited rather than emitted and, being out of voluntary control, less likely to contain an element of verbalization in the first place. (2) Anxiety-producing responses, including memories and thoughts, tend to be repressed for the reasons developed earlier. (3) The traumatic situations responsible for neurotic conflict are often unverbalizable, repressed events in the distant past. Among the earliest adaptations required of the child are those connected with feeding himself, keeping clean, and avoiding expressions of aggression and sexuality. It is necessary to eat at certain times, in certain places, and in certain ways called "manners." One must learn to bring the sphincters controlling elimination under voluntary control, a rather considerable physical accomplishment. Aggression must be inhibited or modulated. And sexual impulses must be curbed. These are hard lessons for the child, learned under punishment or threat of punishment and resulting in a great deal of anxiety. Since this training begins early in life, before the child can talk, the punishment is for unlabeled acts and is probably very confusing. The connection between this point and the unconscious element of conflict is that unverbalized situations are very difficult to remember. Punishment has occurred in the presence of vague urges which are only felt and are not identified as ''sexuality,'' ''aggression,'' or ''anal-erotic tendencies.'' Later on these same feelings may evoke anxiety on bases that cannot be recalled because they were never put into words. The punishment situation itself has long since faded from consciousness. This unlabeled, unconscious, feature of conflict renders it inaccessible to reason. Since thinking is mainly a matter of manipulating verbal symbols, the neurotic cannot cope with his conflict on an intellectual level. There are no symbols to manipulate and, in areas which touch upon his conflict, he shows what Dollard and Miller (1950) have called ''neurotic stupidity.''

Symptom Formation

To summarize the preceding materials as briefly as possible, the origin of neurosis is in conflict between powerful primitive drives and equally powerful restraints or inhibitions, either or both of which may be partly unconscious. The result is misery which cannot be lessened by reasoned courses of action. Symptoms develop as unreasonable solutions to this problem, solutions which yield at least a partial reduction of conflict and escape from anxiety. Such learning differs from that behind normal modes of adjustment in that the deviant forms of behavior (symptoms) produce less tension reduction and frequently create problems nearly as difficult as those they solve. A closer analysis of neurotic anxiety suggests a reason for this.

Reflection tells us that anxiety functions in two somewhat different ways: (1) On the one hand, anxiety sometimes is a currently present motivating state which instigates action designed to alleviate it. (2) On the other hand, anxiety is also a negative incentive and something, therefore, to be avoided. This is the fear of fear discussed earlier, and it is the process which seems particularly important in neurotic maladjustment, especially in symptom formation. The outstanding characteristic of neurotic symptoms is that they prevent anxiety arousal. Phobias, for example, prevent the phobic individual from ever getting into situations where his unreasonable fear will be aroused. A person with a phobia for high places keeps away from such places. Similarly, obsessions and compulsions keep guilt-producing thoughts from consciousness. A compulsive need to count one's heart beats effectively keeps one's mind away from sexy thoughts (Dollard and Miller, 1950), and an obsessive concern to avoid anything related to the number 13 serves the same function (T. A. Ross, 1937). Hysterical symptoms typically prevent the individual from getting into situations where he may fail or have a painful conflict aroused. A pianist whose hand is paralyzed cannot play (and perhaps be criticized). A man who is blind cannot see his new (and unwanted) baby. A woman with intense abdominal pains cannot very well be expected to submit to her husband's sexual advances. Fugue (amnesia) allows the neurotic to shed all of the anxieties and conflicts associated with his identity. A man with no name cannot carry on the wartime responsibilities which properly belong to some other individual.

Thus the partially adjustive value of neurotic symptomatology is quite apparent. There are, however, equally obvious disadvantages. Having no name or home address creates numerous problems. Hysterical symptoms are as "real" as if they had a physiological basis. Obsessions and compulsions so occupy the individual's mind as to make him useless for any worthy enterprise.. And phobias leave the patient in a state of constant apprehension. The symptoms produce some degree of relief from tension, but they are far from wholly successful. Since the symptoms are considerably less than completely successful, the motivation for their continuation persists. In this way, a vicious circle is established in which the neurotic symptoms develop great strength although, in the long run, they produce nothing but continued conflict and misery.

Symptom Selection

Masserman (1943, pp. 67-71) reports that the cats in his studies of experimental neurosis developed a variety of symptoms. Some responded with intense phobic reactions consisting of crouching, hiding, attempting to escape from the apparatus, trembling, and exhibiting very rapid, irregular pulse and respirations. Others developed sterotyped behavior suggestive of compulsions. Still others responded with kittenish, playful, or withdrawing behavior resembling human regressive reactions. An important question, of course, is, why did these animals react in such widely different ways?

It seems certain that a part of the answer resides in innate individual differences. Pavlov believed that it was possible to distinguish among various "types" of dogs in terms of the ease with which they formed conditioned reactions, and that neurotic behavior differed with different types of animal. At one extreme, there is the excitable dog which, according to Pavlov, develops positive CR's with ease and inhibitory CR's with difficulty or not at all. Under stress, dogs of this type develop behavior likened by Pavlov to the symptoms of neurasthenia. At the other extreme, there are dogs of the inhibitable type which form conditioned responses with great difficulty; but their inhibitory responses, once formed, are very stable. Under strain these animals, according to Pavlov, respond with an experimental neurosis resembling hysteria.

Although the importance of presumably innate tempermental factors should not be underemphasized, it seems quite likely that situational conditions and the history of the individual are more important in determining the form that symptoms take. Conflict, it will be recalled, is a condition in which goal-directed activity is frustrated. When frustration occurs, the frustrated response must be abandoned and another substituted for it. Sometimes the new response will be an earlier response employed in the same or in a similar situation. For this reason responses to frustration, and therefore neurotic symptoms, are often regressive. The process of growing up, as we have seen, involves a series of conflicts between the urges of the child and the requirements of society. At each stage in development, more mature adjustment consists of replacing an older habit with a newer and better one. Acquiring the new habit, however, does not mean that the old one is completely obliterated. It still exists as an alternative to the new behavior and may appear in times of stress. In Freudian terms, the individual remains *fixated* at a certain level of development. In the terms of learning theory, the old habit remains as a part of the *habit-family hierarchy*. Numerous studies (Hamilton and Krechevsky, 1933; Sanders, 1937; Martin, 1940; Mowrer, 1940) have demonstrated regression to former habits in lower animals. Martin, for example, trained rats to make a choice in a T-maze and gave three different groups three different numbers of trials on this habit. Then he reversed the problem and required the rats to learn to take the opposite turn. In the course of learning this second habit, a shock was administered at the choice point. As a result, many of the animals showed a tendency to regress to the first habit. The proportion regressing varied directly with the amount of training on the first response. This is exactly as Freud had said: The stronger the fixation in the path of development, the more easily the function yields before external obstacles by regressing onto those fixations.

The behavior of the human organism under stress differs from this in being much more complex, because of the wide array of habits at his disposal. Early in the development of neurosis, there is often a profusion of symptoms which appear one after another, only to be abandoned. In time, the symptom picture becomes stable and most of the symptoms disappear permanently, leaving behind only a few. The reason for this apparently is that the symptoms remaining, however inadequate, are those which are most consistently reinforced. The reinforcement is always a matter of lowered anxiety, at least in part. But sometimes secondary gains are a contributing factor, as in the case of the neurotic veteran whose pension is dependent upon the continuance of his symptoms (Dollard and Miller, 1950, p. 196). Once the symptom has been established, it tends to spread by what appears to be a complex application of stimulus generalization. T. A. Ross (1937) describes a classic case in which a compulsive fear of the number 13 gradually spread to the thirteenth tread of a stair, the thirteenth day of the month, and salutations containing thirteen letters.

PSYCHOTHERAPY

Early applications of conditioning principles to psychiatric problems employed direct applications of conditioning technique to diagnosis and treatment. The detection of sensory function in cases of hysterical anesthesia by such methods has been carried out successfully for a long time. Bekhterev early reported his success with hysterical deafness (1912), and his procedure was confirmed later by Myasishchev (1929). R. R. Sears and Cohen (1933) studied a case of hysterical anesthesia, analgesia, and astereognosis by conditioning methods. They found that when conditioned responses were established to stimulation of supposedly anesthetic areas the anesthesia disappeared. Cohen, Hilgard, Wendt (1933) were able to demonstrate visual sensitivity in a patient with hysterical blindness, but the symptoms did not disappear as a result of conditioning.

In addition to being used in diagnosis, conditioning was occasionally used in therapy. The following case illustrates the kind of clinical application which is feasible. The patient, an unmarried school-teacher of 32, had been in a motor car accident six years before coming for treatment. During these six years her left arm had been entirely useless to her, being totally paralyzed and anesthetic. Neurological examination showed the anesthesia to be of the glove type, with a line of demarcation at the shoulder. The symptoms were thus shown to be functional. The arm and hand showed considerable atrophy from disuse. Attempts by a psychiatrist to give the patient insight into the functional nature of the abnormality met with great resistance, although the fact that the patient had returned to the hospital voluntarily in the hope of a cure was considered a hopeful sign. The psychiatrist arranged to have the patient treated by conditioning methods in the psychological laboratory which adjoined the psychiatric unit.

A finger-withdrawal experiment was arranged. Two electrodes were used, one for each hand. The first series of experiments consisted in presenting a shock to the anesthetic hand as the conditioned stimulus and a shock to the normal hand as the unconditioned stimulus. This was designed to give evidence of sensitivity in the anesthetic hand, since a shock to it served as the signal for withdrawal of the normal hand. Although little conditioning occurred, the desired effect was produced and sensitivity gradually returned in the insensitive hand and arm. Experiments were repeated daily, and the improvement was gradual. After recovery of sensitivity, the conditioning procedure was reversed for purposes of developing voluntary control. The normal hand was given a light shock which served as the conditioned stimulus. For the unconditioned stimulus, the paralyzed hand was given a more severe shock, to which it was now fully sensitive. Presently movement began to occur in the paralyzed hand at the signal given to the normal hand. This was the beginning of control, and voluntary movement was gradually restored. At this stage, the patient was given physiotherapy to strengthen the muscles which had been so long unused. The symptoms had not returned two years later, nor were any additional symptoms reported.

This case illustrates the feasibility of conditioning procedures in the treatment of psychoneurotic symptoms. The experimental situation was one that permitted the patient to eliminate her symptoms without loss of face. She believed the machine to be making the cure. Although the conditioning procedure was the effective means for bringing the symptoms to an end, other dynamic factors in the situation were probably of great importance. In most cases, it is necessary to treat basic mechanisms, as well as symptoms, in order to effect a permanent cure.

Obstacles to Psychotherapy

From the point of view of the learning theorist, maladjustment consists of a set of inadequate habits designed to reduce the anxiety associated with conflict. From the same point of view, therapy is a matter of finding other ways of reducing anxiety. As we shall see, there are several alternative possibilities. Before considering these, however, we may note that the translation into the concepts of learning contributes to an understanding of the great difficulties often associated with the achievement of a psychiatric cure.

We have previously seen that learned behavior does not spontaneously disappear with rest. Extinction occurs only when there is some active interference with behavior. In the case of the responses involved in personality disorder, the difficulty of extinction is increased by the fact that the behavior to be eliminated is based upon fear. In at least some quarters, there is a disposition to question whether fear can ever be eliminated, and it is certain that fear can be very resistant to extinction. This means (1) that therapeutic tactics must, in the main, be directed at the response rather than the motive behind it, (2) that the original motive responsible for maladjustment remains and often creates new symptoms as the original ones are destroyed, and (3) that society's main disciplinary agent, punishment, will probably be of little value in treating personality difficulties. Since they are based on fear in the first place, punishment, which also elicits fear, only provides the occasion for the punished response. The experimental evidence supports this line of reasoning. When punishment is accompanied by a clearcut alternative response leading to the original goal, it sometimes hastens the abandonment of the punished response (Whiting and Mowrer, 1943). In cases where no available response leads to the original goal (Estes, 1944) punishment apparently does not expedite extinction. And, avoidance responses based upon shock (Gwinn, 1955) become more persistent when animals are shocked for performing them. This suggests that the therapist must either (*a*) resort to other motive-reinforcement combinations, or (*b*) attempt to reduce anxiety, realizing that in some cases this may turn out to be impossible.

Another set of conditions standing in the way of successful psychotherapy involves the cues controlling maladaptive behavior. For one thing these cues are very pervasive. Through a process of stimulus generalization, one's behavior tends to extend itself to all areas of life. This is what makes the individual's responses predictable and dependable. When the aim is to alter behavior, however, this fact also makes it very difficult to eliminate the responses in question. As Guthrie (1935) has stressed, it is necessary to disconnect an act from all of the stimuli which control it before it can be regarded as completely extinguished. The therapist has one ally in the accomplishment of this formidable objective, namely, the generalization of extinction. Responses eliminated in one situation should show a diminished tendency to appear in others. It will be recalled, however, that the generalization of extinction can be counted on only for some weakening of the response, not for its complete obliteration. Moreover, if it is correct that the generalization gradient for extinction is narrower than that for excitation, this limits the usefulness of the mechanism.

Still considering stimulus variables related to the accomplishment of psychotherapy, it is important to recognize that these are internal, subtle, minimal cues which are difficult for the patient to recognize. Accordingly, one of the main goals of psychotherapy is to get the patient to recognize these cues. This requires that he be forced to recall all-but-forgotten past experiences and to label the dimly recognized impulses which supply the cues to the undesirable behavior. Psychotherapy must make these cues more distinct and conspicuous in order to facilitate the conditioning of new and better responses to them. The task of making these cues available to the patient is impeded by the process of repression. Recalling a traumatic experience or recognizing a tabooed impulse calls up cues associated with powerful anxiety reactions. Thus, as the therapist gets close to significant problem areas, anxiety often becomes acute and much evasive behavior ensues. The patient forgets appointments, decides that his case is hopeless, or finds that he has to visit a relative in a distant city. In each case the behavior is calculated to escape from the therapeutic situation where these anxiety-evoking stimuli are apt to appear.

Therapeutic Possibilities

Looked at as a problem in learning, psychotherapy becomes a matter of equipping the patient with responses to relieve the misery he experiences as a result of conflict and anxiety. Even considered abstractly, it is clear that the problem is one of enormous complexity. In such terms there are four possible courses of action to be considered. The possibilities emerge from the fact that neurotic conflict is of the approach-avoidance variety, and the approach and avoidance components each comprise a habit and a drive factor. Thus the four conceivable lines of therapeutic action are the following:

1. *Relieve the intensity of the drive toward the positive goal.* Masserman (1943) makes the point that the cats in his studies of experimental neurosis showed little or none of their neurotic behavior if they were satiated when placed in the apparatus. Speaking in terms of conflict this means that the approach gradient was lowered to the point where no conflict existed. To the extent that this is possible in cases of human conflict, it represents a constructive point of departure. Where conflict involves unrealistic aspirations, say, to enter a scientific or other exacting career, it may be sound therapeutic tactics to try to get the person to abandon his unrealistic goals. In cases of sexual conflict, on the other hand, it seems unlikely that reducing the level of sexual drive would be practical, because of the anxiety which would be associated with almost all available outlets.

2. *Alter the habits mediating attempts to attain the positive goal.* The behavior of the neurotic is ill-considered and impulsive. It often lacks the elements of hesitation and restraint which are characteristic of normal adjustive behavior (Guthrie, 1938). Or it sometimes is over-cautious. In either case, one aspect of therapy obviously must be to provide the patient with better means of dealing with his desires.

3. *Reduce the intensity of conflict by reducing anxiety.* Implicitly or explicitly, traditional psychotherapy seems to have concentrated on this possibility. The patient is urged to recall and relive traumatic experiences. In this way anxiety is elicited and subjected to extinction. As the therapist well knows, one implication of this procedure is that painful anxiety must occur during therapy if a cure is to occur. This fact is responsible for the main practical problems which arise in psychotherapy. As we have seen, the patient goes to great lengths to prevent having such anxiety aroused in him. The learning theorist might also raise a question about this procedure on other grounds. If it is correct that very traumatic anxiety is inextinguishable, it would be impossible to eliminate certain conflicts by reducing the avoidance gradient.

4. *Alter the habits mediated by anxiety.* One of the main points here is that the complete elimination of anxiety, even if it were possible, would

be undesirable. Anxiety provides the individual with a set of moderating influences which control normal behavior, and it would be a mistake to rob the patient of these controls. What he needs instead is some more constructive means of handling his anxiety. As with the habits mediated by the patient's positive motives, it is important to give him a method for dealing with his fears.

As a final point in connection with these brief comments on therapeutic possibilities, it should be mentioned that they are merely theoretical alternatives. Whether they are all equally useful, either in individual cases or as a general rule, is something which only more detailed analysis of the psychotherapeutic process can determine. It seems quite clear that the practicing therapist uses all of them, employing at every point the technique which his evaluation of the situation suggests.

Drive, Cue, Response, Reward

The most complete treatment of psychotherapy in learning terms is that of Dollard and Miller (1950) who deal with the problem along the same lines as they used in their analyses of social behavior (Miller and Dollard, 1941). The essentials of this analysis may be presented quickly: For learning to occur, a *response*, stemming from an important *drive*, must take place in the presence of a relevant stimulus or *cue; reward*, in the form of drive-stimulus reduction, must follow immediately. The paradigm is that of instrumental reward learning, and it is assumed that psychotherapy can be conceived in these terms.

1. *Drive.* The motives for therapy are the same as those which underly maladjustment, the powerful drives comprising the conflict and, in addition, an element of misery coming from the conflict itself. Since these motives are the same as those which originally produced the symptoms, a great deal depends upon how effective the symptoms have been. If they have proven quite successful, the patient's drive level may have been reduced to a point where there is little motivational basis for a cure.

2. *Reward.* Reinforcement for the new response also derives at least in part from the same mechanism as that which led to the development of the neurosis. For therapy to be successful it is necessary for the new responses to be more satisfying than the symptoms. Otherwise the laws of reinforcement indicate that the symptoms will persist. In this connection, considerations extraneous to maladjustment are often important. A person from the upper social and economic levels, one who is natively intelligent and is physically attractive, usually obtains greater benefit from improved psychological adjustment than one who does not possess these advantages. Conversely, patients who derive secondary gains (such as pensions) from their symptoms have less to gain from successful treat-

ment. For these reasons, psychotherapists use such criteria in deciding whether or not to accept a given patient.

3. *Response.* In the final analysis, the patient must find the new and more adjustive behavior within himself. Some forms of therapy, usually called non-directive (Rogers, 1942), stress this fact particularly. In other forms of therapy, the therapist takes a more direct hand in suggesting lines of action. He may encourage the patient to cast around for his own solution to problems; but, at the same time, he makes suggestions and calls attention to the examples of what others have done. He tries to get the patient to test his new and tentative adjustments, first in safe situations such as his office and then in nondangerous outside situations. After attempting to build confidence and to reinforce appropriate behavior in these' situations, the therapist relies on generalization to carry it to still wider application. The method is not unlike the method of successive approximations employed in the preliminary training in many animal experiments.

4. *Cue.* From the point of view of learning theory, the most difficult problems of psychotherapy involve the stimulus concept. This is because the cues in neurotic conflict are internal, response-produced, and hard to isolate. Such problems develop in a number of different ways. First, the problem of leading the patient to understand his conflict seems mainly a matter of getting him to recognize and to label certain urges and fears which hitherto have been unclearly perceived, if they have been perceived at all. The patient must bring to the present events which were poorly understood and unlabeled when they occurred. Naturally, this is hard to do. Once recalled, however, it is usually possible to label these memories in ways which make them less threatening. Next the patient, having recognized the problem, must be made to distinguish between word and deed, to see that having a certain thought is really quite a different thing from translating the content of that thought into action. Simple as this seems, it should be recognized that thoughts are fractions of acts, and this may make the discrimination difficult.

Finally, the whole success of therapy depends upon considerations involving the stimuli which control the patient's behavior. The basic question is this: How can solutions arrived at in mere consultation have any effect upon actions outside the therapeutic situation? Obviously there must be some way in which therapy provides the patient with a set of cues by means of which he transfers his new learning from the therapist's office to real life. What seems to happen is that the patient comes to respond to threatening situations with mediating responses (initially verbal labels) which produce the cues to adaptive behavior. Situations which once evoked anxiety and *its* stimulus consequences now produce labeling responses which set off more appropriate action. The result is sometimes a stage of too deliberate, unspontaneous, overly intellectualized adjustment in which the patient plans his actions with care, expresses alternatives, and verbalizes his emotions. With practice these mediational links tend to shorten and to disappear.

Evaluation of the Learning Theorist's Analysis of Therapy

It is important, finally, to make this point: Learning theory is not a theory of psychotherapy. It is a position which attempts to interpret simple learning. The analyses in this chapter have extended certain of the theory's experimentally derived concepts in what appear to be suggestive directions. Whether such extension is fruitful will depend upon two things: (1) Whether there is any sense in which this analysis produces a valid description of personality processes. This is a matter which experts in the fields of personality and psychopathology will be able to judge. And (2) whether the analysis leads to effective ways of dealing with personality problems in experimental and practical, psychotherapeutic terms. It is still too early to evaluate the interpretation in terms of learning theory from this point of view.

SUMMARY

One of the basic questions connected with the study of conditioning concerns the range of applicability of the principles discovered in these simple learning situations. In this chapter we have explored the possibility of applying these principles to materials in the field of personality.

Freud's Contribution

Somewhat surprisingly there are numerous parallels between the approach to the problem of personality taken by the learning theorist and that of the psychoanalyst. Among these parallels are the following: (1) Psychoanalytic theory, although not itself a theory of learning, is historical in orientation. Thus it shares with learning theory a common initial commitment. (2) Freudian theory contains, in the concepts of primary and secondary process, ideas which seem potentially translatable into the basic learning mechanisms of classical and instrumental conditioning. (3) Psychoanalysis also contains, in figuratively presented form, the essentials of such learning phenomena as acquisition, stimulus generalization, and acquired drive.

Experimental Neurosis

Another contribution to the learning theorist's interest in personality stems from the laboratory investigation of experimental neurosis. It was originally discovered in Pavlov's laboratory that certain dogs developed strange and seemingly maladaptive behavior if they were forced to make too fine a discrimination. Subsequently other procedures for establishing experimental neuroses were also discovered. In the terms of Pavlov's theory, any circumstance which evoked unusually strong excitatory or inhibitory responses, or led to a clash of excitation and inhibition, could produce an experimental neurosis. Later experimentation was successful in developing experimental neuroses in animals of other species. The disorders reported as being characteristic of experimental neurosis have included a variety of motor, autonomic, emotional, and social symptoms.

Studies of Anxiety

A condition basic to maladjustment, which was stressed by Freud and is also apparent in cases of experimental neurosis, is anxiety. For the learning theorist, anxiety is the conditioned form of reactions to painful stimuli. As a result of this view, investigations of anxiety in the laboratory have been largely limited to what Freud called objective anxiety, that is, anxiety about real, physical situations. The learning theorist recognizes, however, that anxiety may be conditioned to drive stimuli or to response-produced stimuli. Anxiety conditioned to such stimuli may correspond to the psychoanalytic processes of neurotic and moral anxiety.

One advantage of the view that anxiety is a conditioned pain reaction is that it leads to the search, in the life history of the individual, for traumatic occasions which may provide the origin of anxiety. This has led to the emphasis on certain events in childhood which are often responsible for the development of anxiety. These events include some of the same episodes stressed by the psychoanalysts in their theory of psychosexual development, such as toilet training and the inhibition of infantile sexuality and aggression. One of the important points about such fears is that they are acquired before the child can talk. This appears to contribute to the difficulties encountered later on in trying to remember traumatic events which led to the development of anxiety.

Experimental studies of the development of anxiety in lower animals were discussed in the last chapter. In this chapter we have concentrated on studies of the functioning of anxiety in human subjects. Much of this research has employed the strategy of selecting subjects with very different levels of manifest anxiety and studying the differences in learning displayed by such subjects in a variety of situations. The assumption behind many of these investigations is the familiar one that anxiety is a drive and should have the same effect upon behavior as is obtained by manipulating other drives. The results of relevant experiments support this assumption in a general way; but, as with other motives, it turns out that a very important consideration involves the responses elicited by anxiety.

Conflict

Conflict occurs when incompatible action tendencies are instigated simultaneously. Although many different varieties of conflict are described in the literature, the kind which is of greatest interest in a discussion of personality is approach-avoidance conflict, which is basic to much human maladjustment. An approach-avoidance conflict is one in which the same goal object elicits tendencies toward approach and avoidance at the same time. At the human level such conflicts often center about sex and aggression.

Stimulus-response psychology has made an effort to deal with approach-avoidance conflict in terms of a formal theory. In this theory both the approach and the avoidance tendencies are conceived as depending upon the conventional variables studied in experiments on learning. They are also considered to increase in strength with increasing proximity to the ambivalent goal object. These assumptions have been demonstrated to be capable of handling certain elementary forms of conflict, particularly in experiments with lower animals. Application at the level of human behavior has just begun.

The Importance of Language

One of the chief difficulties involved in any attempt to deal with human activity in terms of the concepts provided by simple conditioning experiments stems from the fact that so much human behavior involves language as a mediating link between stimulus and response. This is not to say that such an account is impossible. Applications of S-R theory to verbal behavior stress the fact that words are cue-producing responses. These responses acquired from childhood on are, at first, overt. With age, however, the responses become covert and occur as thoughts.

The fact that words (and, therefore, thoughts) are cue-producing responses makes it potentially possible to understand such difficult concepts as repression and the unconscious in terms of learning theory. Repression, for example, becomes a case of avoidance learning in which one acquires the habit of avoiding certain thoughts because the stimuli provided by these thoughts are the occasion for intense anxiety. The avoidance response of not thinking about the topic is reinforced by anxiety reduction.

Maladjustment and Psychotherapy

The materials presented so far contain the main principles necessary to describe maladaptive behavior in S-R terms. The important elements are conflict, anxiety, and the inability to deal with either of these by means of reason (repression). The result in some people is a break from conventional modes of adjustment and the development of neurotic symptomatology in their place. These symptoms are learned because they provide occasional and temporary relief from conflict and anxiety. They are maladaptive because, besides being unconventional, the relief they bring is neither consistent nor permanent.

The analysis of maladjustment in terms of conflict, anxiety, and repression points the direction in which therapy might proceed. Its method might be to bring traumatic events to consciousness so that the fear they evoke might extinguish. This would make it possible to develop better ways to deal with anxiety as well as with more positive urges.

A Final Word

It is important to stress the nature of our attempt to deal with personality and adjustment in terms of the concepts of conditioning. We do not feel that the psychology of learning, as it now exists, contains all, or even very many, of the answers to the questions which arise in the study of personality. In fact we cannot be sure that the psychology of learning can ever supply these answers. On the other hand, it is at least possible that such topics as repression, the unconscious, and psychotherapy will be understandable in terms of the processes of conditioning. Explorations of this possibility appear to be worth an occasional try.

GLOSSARY

PROMINENT in the glossary are terms specific to conditioning, including translations of Pavlov's terms, which are designated by his name. The index may serve in locating the usage of words and expressions not included in the glossary.

adaptation. The decrement in a response which is a consequence of its repeated elicitation. (Cf. internal inhibition; contrast with extrinsic inhibition, interference)

alpha conditioning (Hull). Augmentation by reinforcement of the original response to the conditioned stimulus. Not often observed. A more usual effect is adaptation of this response. (Cf. sensitization, pseudoconditioning)

alpha response. Original response to the conditioned stimulus. (Cf. alpha conditioning)

association. The establishment of functional relations between psychological activities and states in the course of individual experience. A broader term which includes conditioning. (Cf. conditioning)

associative shifting (Thorndike). Considered by Thorndike to be the more general case of which the conditioned response is a special case.

avoidance training. A training procedure in which the learned movement circumvents or prevents the appearance of a noxious stimulus.

backward conditioning. The experimental arrangement in which the conditioned stimulus is presented after the cessation of the unconditioned stimulus.

beta response (Grant). In eyelid conditioning, an unconditioned eyeblink to light sensitized by dark adaptation.

classical conditioning experiment. An experiment after the prototype of Pavlov, which consists in the repeated presentation of the conditioned and unconditioned stimuli in a controlled relationship so that there occur alterations in reaction tendencies with respect to the conditioned stimulus which would not arise except for its relationship to the unconditioned stimulus and response. Distinguished from instrumental conditioning.

concentration (Pavlov). I. The focussing of the hypothetical nervous processes of excitation and inhibition within restricted cortical areas. (Contrast with irradiation) 2. Behaviorally, restricted generalization. (Cf. generalization)

conditioned inhibition (Pavlov). A variety of internal inhibition defined by the experimental arrangements under which it is obtained. The negative, non-reinforced, combination to be differentiated from the positive conditioned stimulus consists of the positive stimulus plus an added stimulus known as the conditioned inhibitor.

conditioned response. A response which appears or is modified as a consequence of the occurrence of a conditioned stimulus in proximity to reinforcement. (Syn. conditioned reflex or conditional reflex—Pavlov; association reflex—Bekhterev; individual reflex—Beritov)

conditioned stimulus (Pavlov). The experimental stimulus to which a new or modified response becomes related through the process of conditioning. (Syn. conditional stimulus, inadequate stimulus, substitute stimulus)

conditioning. The process of training which results in the formation of conditioned responses. (Cf. association)

contiguity theory. The hypothesis that, for learning to occur, it is necessary only for two stimuli (CS and UCS) or a stimulus and a response to occur closely together in time. (Contrast with effect theory and expectancy theory)

continuity theory. Any theory of learning which incorporates the assumption that learning occurs gradually. (Contrast with non-continuity theory)

counter conditioning. Extinction under circumstances in which the response decrement is hastened by the reinforcement of a response which displaces the original conditioned response. (Distinguish from adaptation and inhibition; cf. interference)

delayed conditioning (Pavlov). The conditioned stimulus begins from 5 seconds to several minutes before the unconditioned, and continues until reinforcement occurs. (Distinguish from trace conditioning)

differential inhibition (Pavlov). A form of internal inhibition arising in respect to the negative stimulus when stimuli are discriminated by the method of contrasts. (Cf. discrimination)

discrimination. The inferred basis for differential responses to unlike stimuli. Discrimination is always measured by differential responses, but absence of a specified differential response is not necessarily an indication of lack of discriminatory capacity.

disinhibition (Pavlov). A temporary increase in the strength of an extinguished conditioned response as the result of an extraneous stimulus. While called by Pavlov an "inhibition of inhibition," the term may be used in a strictly behavioral sense.

dominance (Ukhtomsky). A physiological description of the interaction of certain reflexes, whereby following repeated stimulation, the dominant one is evoked by stimuli appropriate to other reflexes, while at the same time the normal responses to these stimuli are inhibited.

effect, empirical law of. A statement of the fact that certain events placed appropriately with respect to a response leads to the strengthening of that response. (Contrast with effect, theoretical law of)

effect, theoretical law of. The hypothesis that some satisfying or rewarding consequence is necessary for learning. (Contrast with effect, empirical law of; cf. effect theory)

effect theory. Any theory of learning which stresses the theoretical law of effect.

elicited behavior (Skinner). A response to a specifiable stimulus (Contrast with emitted behavior, operant; cf. involuntary behavior)

emitted behavior (Skinner). Spontaneous behavior in response to no specifiable stimulus. (Contrast with elicited behavior, respondent; cf. voluntary behavior)

error factor theory (Harlow). A theory designed to account for the phenomena of discrimination learning, particularly for learning sets (q.v.). The basic assumptions are (1) that the correct response is already in the response repertoire of the organism, but (2) that it fails to appear at once because of errors of certain specified kinds. Discrimination learning consists in the extinction of these tendencies. Learning sets develop because of the transfer of such extinction to similar problems.

escape training. An instrumental conditioning procedure in which the response terminates a noxious stimulus. (Contrast with avoidance training)

excitation (Pavlov). One of two hypothetical nervous processes in the cortex, interacting with inhibition, its opposite. (Cf. inhibition)

expectancy theory. The theory which interprets the animal's learned behavior as consonant with anticipated (expected) events or consequences. (Syn. sign learning—Tolman; distinguish from effect theory, contiguity theory)

experimental extinction. See extinction.

experimental neurosis (Pavlov). A disturbed state appearing in some animals as a result of conditioning procedures, such as too difficult discriminations or prolonged periods of delay. The animal is unsuitable for experimentation, but may or may not appear to be disturbed when outside the experimental situation.

external inhibition (Pavlov). A temporary reduction in the strength of a conditioned response as a result of the occurrence of an extraneous stimulus. (Contrast with disinhibition)

extinction (Pavlov). The specific procedure of presenting the conditioned stimulus unaccompanied by the usual reinforcement; also the decrement in a conditioned response which results from that procedure.

extinctive inhibition (Pavlov). The variety of internal inhibition which appears with non-reinforcement of a conditioned response. (Cf. extinction)

facilitation. A temporary nonlearned increase in strength of response as a result of the occurrence of a second stimulus or response. (Distinguish from reinforcement)

fixed-interval schedule. A schedule in which reinforcement occurs for the first response after a certain amount of time following the preceding reinforcement. (Contrast with variable-interval, variable-ratio, and fixed-ratio schedules)

fixed-ratio schedule. A schedule in which reinforcement occurs regularly on every n^{th} trial. (Contrast with fixed-interval, variable-interval, and variable-ratio schedules)

fractional anticipatory (or antedating) goal response. A component of the consummatory or goal response which can occur in the absence of the goal stimulus or reinforcer. Often used as a theoretical concept by S-R theorists to explain expectant behavior. Symbolized r_G.

goal gradient (Hull). (1) The delay-of-reinforcement gradient. (2) A performance gradient in which parts of a serial act are reinforced by a common goal situation, acts being more vigorous the nearer they lie to the reinforcing state of affairs. The goal gradient so defined is explained in part by the gradient of reinforcement, but is a gradient of strength of response rather than of strength of conditioning and is modified by factors other than proximity of individual responses to the reinforcement.

habit. A term used formally (Hull) or informally to refer to the result produced in the organism by training. Sometimes employed as a synonym for learning.

habit-family hierarchy (Hull). A number of habitual alternative behavior sequences having in common the initial stimulus situation and the final reinforcing state of affairs, the alternative sequences having a preferential order which produces the hierarchy.

higher-order conditioned response (Pavlov). A conditioned response based on reinforcement by another conditioned stimulus and response. A first-order response is reinforced by an unconditioned stimulus, a second-order response (or secondary response) by a first-order conditioned stimulus, and so on. (Cf. secondary reinforcement)

hypothetico-deductive method. Method of theory construction in which a known (for example, mathematical) system is co-ordinated to a less well-known empirical one, in the hope that deductions in the known system will yield testable theorems in the more poorly understood one. Hull's use of this method was not truly hypothetico-deductive, in that the formal process of co-ordination was not employed.

inhibition. 1. (Pavlov). One of the two hypothetical cortical processes, interacting with excitation, its opposite. 2. Behaviorally, any decrease in the strength of a response which is occasioned by positive stimulation, either of the response itself (as in extinction) or of some other response (as in external inhibition). (Cf. conditioned inhibition, external inhibition, extinctive inhibition, inhibition of delay, inhibition of reinforcement, internal inhibition)

inhibition of delay (Pavlov). That form of internal inhibition manifested during the latent period of a delayed or trace conditioned response. That the interval of delay is inhibitory is evidenced by (1) the ease with which disinhibition may be demonstrated, and (2) secondary inhibition of weak conditioned responses if the attempt is made to elicit them during the period of delay (Rodnick).

inhibition of inhibition. (Cf. disinhibition)

inhibition of reinforcement (Hovland). The diminution of a conditioned response which may occur within reinforcement trials if such trials are repeated at short intervals. The phenomenon is like adaptation in that it is temporary and may be recovered from by rest.

inhibition with reinforcement (Pavlov). (Cf. inhibition of reinforcement)

inhibition theory. A theory of extinction which relies heavily upon a concept of extinctive inhibition.

interference. The decrement in a response which is a consequence of the elicitation of another incompatible response.

interference theory. A theory of extinction which relies heavily upon the concept of interference.

intermittent reinforcement. A training procedure in which the reinforcement occurs on only a fraction of the trials. Under some circumstances random alternation of reinforcement and non-reinforcement leads to a normal acquisition rate and, at the same time, increases resistance to extinction. Special forms of intermittent reinforcement have different consequences. (Cf. fixed-ratio schedule, variable-ratio schedule, fixed-interval schedule, variable-interval schedule)

internal inhibition (Pavlov). That form of inhibition which depends upon stimulation by a conditioned stimulus. (Contrast with external inhibition)

interoceptive conditioning (Razran). Conditioning in which either stimuli or responses are internal.

investigatory reflex (Pavlov). (Cf. pure-stimulus act)

irradiation (Pavlov). 1. The wave-like spread of excitation and inhibition through the cortex, the inferred physiological basis of generalization. (Contrast with concentration). 2. Behaviorally, the phenomenon of stimulus generalization. Little used in this latter sense.

latent extinction. Extinction without responding which occurs as a result of non-reinforced experience with the goal box in a maze. Also called indirect extinction, goal extinction, and non-response extinction. (Cf. latent learning)

latent learning. 1. Learning not made manifest in performance. 2. Learning which is latent in sense 1 (above) but, in addition, has occurred without reinforcement, appearing only with the introduction of reward.

learning. A relatively permanent change in response potentiality which occurs as a result of reinforced practice.

learning set. The improved ability to master certain kinds of learning problems which occurs as a result of previous experience with problems of the same sort. Has been demonstrated most often in experiments on discrimination learning, but has also been demonstrated in other learning situations.

micromolar theory (Hull, Logan). Any theory of learning which makes the primary assumption that responses with different quantitative values must be treated as different responses.

method of simultaneous presentation of stimuli. A procedure for the study of discrimination learning. Positive and negative stimuli are presented together, and the organism must select one or the other. Sometimes called the method of choice reaction.

method of successive presentation of stimuli. A procedure for the study of discrimination learning. Positive and negative stimuli are presented one at a time. Responses to the positive stimulus are reinforced; responses to the negative stimulus are not reinforced. Pavlov called this the method of contrasts.

mosaic of functions (Pavlov). A conception of localization of functions in the cortex. For Pavlov, the mosaic is determined in part anatomically (the analyzers), in part functionally, as a result of the integration of conditioned excitation and inhibition.

negative conditioned stimulus. A conditioned stimulus which, through repeated presentation, either alone or in combination, without being followed by reinforcement, tends to be followed by reduced or inhibited conditioned responses.

negative induction (Pavlov). The intensification of inhibition under the influence of preceding excitation. (Contrast with positive induction)

non-continuity theory. Any theory of learning which assumes that learning occurs in a single exposure of the organism to the situation. (Contrast with continuity theory)

observing response. (Cf. pure-stimulus act)

omission training. A little used training procedure in which positive reinforcement occurs unless the organism makes a specified response.

operant (Skinner). An act which first appears as a random movement. The operant commonly becomes related to a discriminated stimulus, which then sets the occasion for the operant behavior, but, strictly speaking, does not elicit it. (Cf. emitted behavior; contrast with respondent, elicited behavior)

orienting reflex. (Cf. pure-stimulus act)

paradoxical phase (Pavlov). A state of the cortical processes lying between that of equalization and complete inhibition in which only weak conditioned stimuli lead to responses and strong stimuli either elicit no responses at all or have a barely noticeable effect. (Cf. phase of equalization; ultra-paradoxical phase)

partial reinforcement. See intermittent reinforcement.

phase of equalization (Pavlov). A state of the cortical processes lying between that of normal waking and sleeping in which all conditioned stimuli, independent of their intensities, are equally effective. (Cf. paradoxical phase; ultra-paradoxical phase)

positive induction (Pavlov). The intensification of excitation under the influence of preceding inhibition. (Contrast with negative induction)

preparatory response. A form of conditioned response within classical conditioning, often unlike the unconditioned response, which may be appropriately characterized as a response in readiness for the appearance of the unconditioned stimulus.

presolution period. In discrimination learning, the period during which the animal responds in a chance fashion. A question of great theoretical interest is whether learning of the correct habit occurs during this period. (See continuity and non-continuity theory)

primary reinforcement (reward). A stimulus with innate reinforcing value which does not depend upon the fact of prior association with other reinforcing stimuli. (Cf. secondary reinforcement)

pseudoconditioning (Grether). The strengthening of a response to a previously neutral stimulus through the repeated elicitation of the response by another stimulus without paired presentation of the two stimuli. (Cf. dominance; sensitization)

punishment training. An instrumental training procedure in which a specified response is followed by the presentation of a noxious stimulus.

pure-stimulus act (Hull). An act which serves no biological function other than to provide stimuli which aid in the integration of the organism's behavior.

recency principle (Guthrie). An explanatory principle of associative learning which states that an organism when next confronted with a stimulating situation closely resembling an earlier one tends to react as it last did in such a situation. To be distinguished from that form of the "law of recency" which states that associative strength is a function of the time elapsed since the association was established. Guthrie's principle is that of recency in order of occurrence, not of recency in time.

receptor-exposure act. (Cf. pure-stimulus act)

reconditioning. The re-establishment of a conditioned response by reinforcement after it has been diminished by extinction or forgetting.

redintegration. The arousal of a response by a fraction of the stimuli whose combination originally aroused it.

reinforcement (Pavlov). 1. The experimental arrangement of presenting the conditioned stimulus accompanied by the unconditioned stimulus, or, more generally, the arrangement of following the conditioned stimulus and response by reward or punishment, or some substitute for these. 2. The process which increases the strength of conditioning as a consequence of these arrangements. (Distinguish from facilitation; cf. primary reinforcement, secondary reinforcement, intermittent reinforcement)

respondent (Skinner). That form of response which is elicited by a stimulus, and hence to be distinguished from an operant. (Contrast with operant)

response. A stimulus-occasioned act. A general term for acts correlated with stimuli, whether the correlation is untrained or the result of training.

response differentiation. The modification of the quantitative characteristics of a response by reinforcing only limited forms of it.

response generalization. The behavioral fact that following the conditioning of one response, other responses may be elicited by the same conditioned stimulus although there has been no specific training to establish a relationship between this stimulus and these responses. (Cf. stimulus generalization)

response tendency. A tendency to respond which is inferred from other responses. The tendency may be expressed in units of behavior if it is inferred from measured behavior.

reward training. An instrumental conditioning procedure in which a specified response is followed by a positive reinforcer.

r_G. (Cf. fractional anticipatory goal response)

secondary extinction (Pavlov). The extinction of other conditioned responses which results when any one conditioned response undergoes extinction. (Syn. generalized extinction; cf. generalization)

secondary reinforcement (reward). A stimulus which derives its reinforcing value from prior conditioning in which it has been associated with a primary reward.

sensitization (Wendt). The increase in the strength of a reflex originally evoked by a conditioned stimulus through its conjunction with an unconditioned stimulus and response. Differs from conventional conditioning in that the response which is strengthened is appropriate to the conditioned stimulus, not to the unconditioned stimulus. (Syn. alpha conditioning—Hull; cf. pseudoconditioning—Grether)

sensory conditioning. (Cf. sensory preconditioning)

sensory preconditioning. Two stimuli, S_1 and S_2, are presented closely together in time for a number of trials. Then a response is conditioned to one of these two stimuli. Finally the other stimulus is presented to determine whether the CR transfers to it. Sensory preconditioning is used to refer (a) to the experimental procedure and (b) to the fact of transfer of the CR from one stimulus to the other. (Cf. latent learning)

sign learning (Tolman). The formation of an expectation that a first stimulus-object is going to be followed by a second stimulus-object, as testified by behavior preparatory to the second stimulus-object. (Syn. S-S learning, cognitive learning)

spontaneous recovery (Pavlov). The return in strength of a conditioned response, whether partial or complete, brought about by lapse of time following its diminution by extinction.

stimulus. An external or internal object or event which occasions an alteration in the behavior of the organism.

stimulus generalization (Pavlov). The behavioral fact that a conditioned response formed to one stimulus may also be elicited by other stimuli which have not been used in the course of conditioning. If one stimulus is like another except for a difference in a single dimension (for example, pitch or loudness of tones as determined by psychophysical experiments) the degree of generalization will vary inversely with the distance of the stimuli from each other along this dimension. The function expressing this relationship is called the generalization gradient. Its form varies with circumstances of experimentation. There is a corresponding gradient of generalization of extinction resulting when each of several similar stimuli evokes a conditioned response, and then the response to one of them is extinguished. Stimuli otherwise unlike may participate in generalization through the equivalence of the responses which they evoke. Such generalization is known as mediated generalization. (Cf. irradiation; response generalization)

strength of conditioning. The extent to which a conditioned stimulus tends to evoke a given conditioned response, as inferred from the strength of response to the conditioned stimulus. Strength of response is not, however, a direct measure of strength of conditioning, for in inferring strength of conditioning, due regard must be paid to prior and subsequent responses. Thus, of two responses equal in magnitude, one may represent an inhibited response, another may be facilitated, and strength of conditioning may differ accordingly. Similarly, responses unequal in magnitude may represent equal strengths of conditioning if the conditioned stimuli differ in intensity. (Syn. associative strength; distinguish from strength of response)

strength of response. Any descriptive characteristic of single responses (such as latency or amplitude) or of groups of responses (such as percentage frequency or rate) which may be expressed quantitatively and hence enter as data with respect to magnitude or vigor of response. Which measures of strength of response are most serviceable must be determined empirically. (Distinguish from strength of conditioning)

subgoal. A stimulus regularly reacted to in the series of events leading up to the goal, so that this stimulus derives reinforcing value from its association with the goal. It is, therefore, a secondary reinforcer (q.v.).

summation. The additive effect observed when stimuli which have been separately conditioned to the same response are presented together.

temporal conditioned response. When an unconditioned stimulus is presented at regular intervals, a conditioned response may appear at or near the usual time of appearance of the unconditioned stimulus, even if the unconditioned stimulus is omitted. Such response is known as a temporal conditioned response.

test trial. A trial with the usual reinforcer omitted introduced into a series of reinforced trials to determine whether a response occurs.

top capability of the cortical cells (Pavlov, Konorski). The theoretical upper limit of the excitatory response of the cortical elements.

trace conditioning (Pavlov). The conditioned stimulus is permitted to act and then is removed before the onset of the unconditioned stimulus. Trace conditioned responses are more difficult to establish than delayed conditioned responses. In short-trace conditioning the conditioned stimulus is terminated a few seconds before the unconditioned stimulus is presented; in long-trace conditioning the conditioned stimulus is terminated a minute or more before the unconditioned stimulus begins to act. (Distinguish from delayed conditioning)

token. A secondary reward characterized by the fact that it must be manipulated in a prescribed manner in order to produce the primary reward. (Cf. secondary reinforcement)

trial-and-error learning (Thorndike). The mode of learning in which the learner tries various movements in its repertory, apparently in a somewhat random manner and without explicit recognition of the connection between the movement and the resolution of the problem situation. Tentative movements which succeed are more frequently repeated in subsequent trials, and those which fail gradually disappear. (Syn. selecting and connecting—Thorndike; contrast with associative shifting—Thorndike)

types of nervous system (Pavlov). A classification of individual differences in conditioning on the basis of the relative susceptibility to excitation and inhibition. The final types, with their correspondence to the ancient Greek classifications of temperaments, are as follows: (1) excitable type (choleric), (2) central type, with two subtypes, lively type (sanguine), and stolid type (phlegmatic), (3) inhibitable type (melancholic).

ultra-paradoxical phase (Pavlov). A transitory state of the cortical processes sometimes occurring before complete inhibition, in which only inhibitory agents have a positive effect. (Cf. phase of equalization; paradoxical phase)

unconditioned stimulus (Pavlov). That experimental stimulus in a classical conditioning experiment which evokes the unconditioned response and hence serves as the reinforcing agent. (Syn. unconditional stimulus; conditioning stimulus—Razran; original stimulus—Guthrie)

variable-ratio schedule. A schedule in which reinforcement occurs irregularly, but on the average, after n responses. (Contrast with variable interval, fixed-interval, and fixed-ratio schedules)

variable-interval schedule. An irregular schedule in which reinforcement, occurs on the average after a certain amount of time. (Contrast with fixed-interval, fixed-ratio, and variable-ratio schedules)

vicarious trial and error. The tentative behavior of looking back and forth often observed in the behavior of rats at the choice points of mazes.

Vincent curve. A technique for constructing learning curves in which performance measures for each subject are computed for constant fractions of the total number of trials required to reach a criterion of learning. This method permits the construction of average learning curves for groups of subjects which differ in number of trials to learn.

REFERENCES

AAMODT, MARJORIE S. *See* Stanley and Aamodt (1954).

ABE, M. *See* Iwama and Abe (1952) (1953).

ADAMS, D. K. (1929) Experimental studies of adaptive behavior in cats. *Comp. Psychol. Monogr., 6,* No. 27.

ADAMS, D. K. (1931) A restatement of the problem of learning. *Brit. J. Psychol., 22,* 150-178.

ADAMS, D. K. (1937) Note on method. *Psychol. Rev., 44,* 212-218.

ADAMS, J. K. *See* Grant and Adams (1944).

ADAMS, Pauline A. *See* Postman and Adams (1954) (1956a) (1956b), Postman, Adams, and Bohm (1956).

ADELMAN, H. M. *See* Denny and Adelman (1955), Maatsch, Adelman, and Denny (1954).

ADELMAN, H. M., and MAATSCH, J. L. (1955) Resistance to extinction as a function of the type of response elicited by frustration. *J. exp. Psychol., 50,* 61-65.

ADELMAN, H. M., and MAATSCH, J. L. (1956) Learning and extinction based upon frustration, food reward, and exploratory tendency. *J. exp. Psychol., 52,* 311-315.

AESCHLIMAN, B. *See* Ritchie, Aeschliman, and Pierce (1950).

AIKEN, E. G. *See* Mowrer and Aiken (1954).

ALBERTS, Elizabeth, and EHRENFREUND, D. (1951) Transposition in children as a function of age. *J. exp. Psychol., 41,* 30-38.

ALEXANDER, H. M. *See* Butler and Alexander (1955).

ALLEN, M. K. *See* Hilgard and Allen (1938).

ALLPORT, F. H. (1924) *Social psychology.* Boston: Houghton Mifflin.

ALLPORT, G. W. (1937) The functional autonomy of motives. *Amer. J. Psychol., 50,* 141-156.

ALTCHECK, E. *See* Kendler and others (1952).

AMMONS, R. B. (1947) Acquisition of motor skill: I. Quantitative Analysis and theoretical formulation. *Psychol. Rev., 54,* 263-281.

AMSEL, A. (1949) Selective association and the anticipatory goal response mechanism as explanatory concepts in learning theory. *J. exp. Psychol., 39,* 785-799.

AMSEL, A. (1950a) The combination of a primary appetitional need with primary and secondary emotionally derived needs. *J. exp. Psychol., 40,* 1-14.

AMSEL, A. (1950b) The effect upon level of consummatory response of the addition of anxiety to a motivational complex. *J. exp. Psychol., 40,* 709-715.

AMSEL, A. *See also* Edmonson and Amsel (1954), Vandermeer and Amsel (1952), Wilson, Weiss, and Amsel (1955).

AMSEL, A., and COLE, K. F. (1953) Generalization of fear-motivated interference with water intake. *J. exp. Psychol., 46,* 243-247.

AMSEL, A., and HANCOCK, W. (1957) Motivational properties of frustration: III. Relation of frustration effect to antedating goal factors. *J. exp. Psychol., 53,* 126-131.

AMSEL, A., and MALTZMAN, I. (1950) The effect upon generalized drive strength of emotionality as inferred from the level of consummatory response. *J. exp. Psychol., 40,* 563-569.

AMSEL, A., and MCDONNELL, R. (1951 Discrimination of pain from conditioned pain in the rat. *J. comp. physiol. Psychol., 44,* 457-461.

AMSEL, A., and ROUSSEL, Jacqueline. (1952) Motivational properties of frustration: I. Effect on a running response of the addition of frustration to the motivational complex. *J. exp. Psychol., 43,* 363-368.

AMSEL, A., and WARD, J. S. (1954) Motivational properties of frustration: II. Frustration drive stimulus and frustration reduction in selective learning. *J. exp. Psychol.,* 48, 37-47.

ANDERSON, A. C. (1933) Runway time and the goal gradient. *J. exp. Psychol., 16,* 423-428.

ANDERSON, E. E. (1941a) The externalization of drive. I. Theoretical considerations. *Psychol. Rev., 48,* 204-224.

ANDERSON, E. E. (1941b) The externalization of drive. II. The effect of satiation and removal of reward at different stages in the learning process of the rat. *J. genet. Psychol., 59,* 359-396.

ANDERSON, E. E. (1941c) The externalization of drive. III. Maze learning by non-rewarded and by satiated rats. *J. genet. Psychol., 59,* 397-426.

ANDERSON, E. E. (1941d) The externalization of drive. IV. The effect of prefeeding on the maze performance of hungry non-rewarded rats. *J. comp. Psychol., 31,* 349-353.

ANDERSON, O. D. *See* Liddell, James, and Anderson (1934).

ANDERSON, O. D., and PARMENTER, R. (1941) A long-term study of the experimental neurosis in the sheep and in the dog. *Psychosom. Med. Monogr., 2,* Nos. 3 and 4.

ANREP, G. V. (1920) Pitch discrimination in the dog. *J. Physiol., 53,* 367-385.

ANREP, G. V. (1923) The irradiation of conditioned reflexes. *Proc. roy. Soc., 94B,* 404-426.

ANTOINETTI, J. A. (1950) The effect of discrimination training upon generalization. Unpublished Ph.D. thesis. Yale University.

ANTONITIS, J. J. (1951) Response variability in the white rat during conditioning, extinction, and reconditioning. *J. exp. Psychol.*, *42*, 273-281.

ANTONITIS, J. J. *See also* Schoenfeld, Antonitis, and Bersh (1950).

APPLEZWEIG, M. H. (1951) Response potential as a function of effort. *J. comp. physiol. Psychol.*, *44*, 225-235.

ARAKELIAN, P. *See* Heathers and Arakelian (1942).

ARNOLD, W. J. (1945) An exploratory investigation of primary response generalization. *J. comp. Psychol.*, *38*, 87-102.

ARNOLD, W. J. (1947a) Simple reaction chains and their integration. I. Homogeneous chaining with terminal reinforcement. *J. comp. physiol. Psychol.*, *40*, 349-364.

ARNOLD, W. J. (1947b) Simple reaction chains and their integration. II. Heterogeneous chaining with terminal reinforcement. *J. comp. physiol. Psychol.*, *40*, 427-440.

ARNOLD, W. J. (1948) Simple reaction chains and their integration. III. Heterogeneous chaining with serial reinforcement. *J. comp. physiol. Psychol.*, *41*, 1-10.

ARNOLD, W. J. (1951) Simple reaction chains and their integration. IV. Homogeneous chaining with serial reinforcement. *J. comp. physiol. Psychol.*, *44*, 276-282.

ARNOLD, W. J. *See also* Herbert and Arnold (1947), Koronakis and Arnold (1957).

ASIMOW, Adele. *See* Eisman, Asimow, and Maltzman (1956).

BACH-Y-RITA, P. *See* Olds, Killam, and Bach-Y-Rita (1956).

BACKER, R. *See* Sheffield, Wulff, and Backer (1951).

BAER, D. M. *See* Gewirtz, Baer, and Roth (1958), Gewirtz and Baer (1958a) 1958b).

BAHRICK, H. P. (1952) Latent learning as a function of the strength of unrewarded need states. *J. comp. physiol. Psychol.*, *45*, 192-197.

BAILEY, C. J. (1955) The effectiveness of drives as cues. *J. comp. physiol. Psychol. 48*, 183-187.

BAILEY, C. J. *See also* Miller, Bailey, and Stevenson (1950).

BAILEY, C. J., and Porter, L. W. (1955) Relevant cues in drive discrimination in cats. *J. comp. physiol. Psychol.*, *48*, 180-182.

BAIR, J. H. (1901) Development of voluntary control. *Psychol. Rev.*, *8*, 474-510.

BAKAN, D. (1954) A generalization of Sidman's results on group and individual functions and a criterion. *Psychol. Bull.*, *51*, 63-64.

BAKER, L. E. (1938) The pupillary response conditioned to subliminal auditory stimuli. *Psychol. Monogr.*, *50*, No. 223, 32 pp.

BAKER, L. E. *See also* Metzner and Baker (1939).

BAKER, R. A., and LAWRENCE, D. H. (1951) The differential effects of simultaneous and successive stimuli presentation on transposition. *J. comp. physiol. Psychol., 44,* 378-382.

BAKER, R. A., and OSGOOD, S. W. (1954) Discrimination transfer along a pitch continuum. *J. exp. Psychol., 48,* 241-246.

BALLACHEY, E. L., and BUEL, J. (1934a) Centrifugal swing as a determinant of choice-point behavior in the maze running of the white rat. *J. comp. Psychol., 17,* 201-223.

BALLACHEY, E. L., and BUEL, J. (1934b) Food orientation as a factor determining the distribution of errors in the maze running of the rat. *J. genet. Psychol., 45,* 358-370.

BARE, J. K. (1949) The specific hunger for sodium chloride in normal and adrenalectomized white rats. *J. comp. physiol. Psychol., 42,* 242-253.

BARKER, A. N. *See* Hull and others (1951).

BARLOW, J. A. (1956) Secondary motivation through classical conditioning: A reconsideration of the nature of backward conditioning. *Psychol. Rev., 63,* 406-408.

BARNES, G. W. (1956) Conditioned stimulus intensity and temporal factors in spaced-trial classical conditioning. *J. exp. Psychol., 51,* 192-198.

BARNES, H. W. *See* Braun, Patton, and Barnes (1952).

BARNETT, C. I. , and Cantor, G. N. (1957) Discrimination set in defectives. *Amer. J. Ment. Defic., 62,* 334-337.

BARON, A. *See* Warren and Baron (1956).

BARON, M. R. *See* Brown, Bilodeau, and Baron (1951).

BARRY, H., III. (1958) Effects of strength of drive on learning and extinction. *J. exp. Psychol., 55,* 473-481.

BASS, Bettina (1958) Gradients in response percentages as indices of non-spatial generalization. *J. exp. Psychol., 56,* 278-281.

BASS, M. J., and HULL, C. L. (1934) The irradiation of a tactile conditioned reflex in man. *J. comp. Psychol., 17,* 47-65.

BAUER, F. J., and LAWRENCE, D. H. (1953) Influence of similarity of choice-point and goal cues on discrimination learning. *J. comp. physiol. Psychol., 46,* 241-252.

BEACH, F. A. *See* Ford and Beach (1952).

BECK, E. C., and DOTY, R. W. (1957) Conditioned flexion reflexes acquired during combined catalepsy and de-efferentiation. *J. comp. physiol. Psychol., 50,* 211-216,

BECK, L. H. (1939) Conditioning and the co-ordination of movements. *J. gen. Psychol., 20,* 375-397.

BEECROFT, R. S. *See* Spence and Beecroft (1954).

BEER, T., BETHE, A., and v. UEXKÜLL, J. (1899) Vorschlage zu einer objektivierenden Nomenklatur in der Physiologie des Norvensystems *Biol. Zbl., 19,* 517-521.

BEHAN, R. A. (1953) Expectancies and Hullian theory. *Psychol. Rev., 60,* 252-256.

BEHAN, R. A. *See also* Denny and Behan (1956).

BEIER, Eileen M. *See* Logan, Beier, and Ellies (1955), Logan, Beier, and Kincaid (1956).

BEKHTEREV, V. M. (1908) Die objective Untersuchung der neuropsychischen Tatigkeit. *Congr. int. Psychiat. Neurol., Amsterdam,* 20-27.

BEKHTEREV, V. M. (1909) Die objektive Untersuchung der neuropsychischen Sphare der Geisteskranken. *Z. Psychother, med. Psychol., 1,* 257-290.

BEKHTEREV, V. M. (1912) Die Anwendung der Methode der motorischen Assoziationsreflexe zur Aufdeckung der Simulation. *Z. ges. Neurol. Psychiat., 13,* 183-191.

BEKHTEREV, V. M. (1913a) *La psychologie objective.* Paris: Alcan.

BEKHTEREV, V. M. (1913b) *Objektive Psychologie oder Psychoreflexologie. Die Lehre von den Assoziationsreflexen.* Leipzig: Teubner.

BEKHTEREV, V. M. (1923a) Die Perversitaten und Inversitaten vom Standpunkt der Reflexologie. *Arch. Psychiat. Nervenkr., 68,* 100-213.

BEKHTEREV, V. M. (1923b) Studium der Funktionen der Praefrontal und anderer Gebitete der Hirnrinde vermittelst der assoziativmotorischen Reflexe. *Schweiz. Arch. Neurol. Psychiat., 13,* 61-76.

BEKHTEREV, V. M. (1923c) Die Krankheiten der Personlichkeit vom Standpunkt der Reflexologie. *Z. ges. Neurol. Psychiat., 80,* 265-309.

BEKHTEREV, V. M. (1928) *General principles of human reflexology.* Translated by E. and W. Murphy. New York: International.

BEKHTEREV, V. M. (1932) *General Principles of Human Reflexology.* New York: International.

BENDIG, A. W. (1952) Latent learning in a water maze. *J. exp. Psychol., 43,* 134-137.

BERGMANN, G. (1956) The contribution of John B. Watson. *Psychol. Rev., 63,* 265-276.

BERGMANN, G. *See also* Spence, Bergmann, and Lippitt (1950).

BERGMANN, G., and SPENCE, K. W. (1941) Operationism and theory in psychology. *Psychol. Rev., 48,* 1-14.

BERGMANN, G., and SPENCE, K. W. (1944) The logic of psychophysical measurement. *Psychol. Rev., 51,* 1-24.

BERITOV, I. S. (1924) On the fundamental nervous processes in the cortex of the cerebral hemispheres. *Brain, 47,* 109-148; 358-376.

BERKUN, M. M. (1957) Factors in the recovery from approach-avoidance conflict. *J. exp. Psychol., 54,* 65-73.

BERKUN, M. M. *See also* Kagan and Berkun (1954), Murray and Berkun (1955).

BERKUN, M. M., KESSEN, M. L., and MILLER, N. E. (1952) Hunger-reducing effects of food by stomach fistula versus food by mouth measured by a consummatory response. *J. comp. physiol. Psychol., 45,* 550-554.

BERLYNE, D. E. *See* Gordon and Berlyne (1954).

BERNSTEIN, A. L. (1934) Temporal factors in the formation of conditioned eyelid reactions in human subjects. *J. gen. Psychol., 10,* 173-197.

BERSH, P. J. (1951) The influence of two variables upon the establishment of a secondary reinforcer for operant responses. *J. exp. Psychol., 41,* 62-73.

BERSH, P. J. *See also* Notterman, Schoenfeld, and Bersh (1952), Schoenfeld, Antonitis, and Bersh (1950).

BERSH, P. J., NOTTERMAN, J. M., and SCHOENFELD, W. N. (1956) Generalization to varying tone frequencies as a function of intensity of unconditioned stimulus. Air Univ., School of Aviation Medicine, U.S.A.F., Randolph AFB, Texas, pp. 4.

BERSH, P. J., SCHOENFELD, W. N., and NOTTERMAN, J. M. (1953) The effect upon heart-rate conditioning of randomly varying the interval between conditioned and unconditioned stimuli. *Proc. Nat. Acad. Sci., 39,* 563-570.

BETHE, A. *See* Beer, Bethe, and v. Uexküll (1899).

BEVAN, W., and DUKES, W. F. (1955) Effectiveness of delayed punishment on learning performance when preceded by premonitory cues. *Psychol. Rep. 1,* 441-448.

BICKNELL, E. A. *See* Calvin, Bicknell, and Sperling (1953a) and (1953b).

BIEL, W. C. *See* Hilgard and Biel (1937).

BILODEAU, E. A. *See* Brown, Bilodeau, and Baron (1951).

BILODEAU, E. A. BROWN, J. S., and MERYMAN, J. J. (1956) The summation of generalized reactive tendencies. *J. exp. Psychol., 51,* 293-298.

BINDRA, D. (1959) *Motivation.* New York: Ronald.

BINDRA, D., and CAMERON, Lois (1953) Changes in experimentally produced anxiety with the passage of time: incubation effect. *J. exp. Psychol., 45,* 197-203.

BINDRA, D., PATERSON, A. L., and STRZELECKI, Joanna (1955) On the relation between anxiety and conditioning. *Canad. J. Psychol., 9,* 1-6.

BIRCH, D. (1955) Discrimination learning as a function of the ratio of nonreinforced to reinforced trials. *J. comp. physiol. Psychol., 48,* 371-374.

BIRCH, H. G. (1945) The relation of previous experience to insightful problem-solving. *J. comp. Psychol., 38,* 367-383.

BIRCH, H. G., and BITTERMAN, M. E. (1949) Reinforcement and learning: The process of sensory integration. *Psychol. Rev., 56,* 292-308.

BITTERMAN, M. E. *See* Birch and Bitterman (1949), Crum, Brown, and Bitterman (1951), Tyler, and Bitterman (1954), Longnecker, Krauskopf, and Bitterman (1952), Stevenson and Bitterman (1955), Saldanha and Bitterman (1951), Teas and Bitterman (1952), Tyler, Wortz, and Bitterman (1953),

Weise and Bitterman (1951), Elam, Turbeville, Calvin, and Bitterman (1952), Wodinsky and Bitterman (1952).

BITTERMAN, M. E., CALVIN, A. D., and ELAM, C. B. (1953) Perceptual differentiation in the course of nondifferential reinforcement. *J. comp. physiol. Psychol., 46,* 393-397.

BITTERMAN, M. E., FEDDERSON, W. E., and TYLER, D. W. (1953) Secondary reinforcement and the discrimination hypothesis. *Amer. J. Psychol., 66,* 456-464.

BITTERMAN, M. E., and HOLTZMAN, W. H. (1952) Conditioning and extinction of the galvanic skin response as a function of anxiety. *J. abnorm. soc. Psychol., 47,* 615-623.

BITTERMAN, M. E., REED, P., and KRAUSKOPF, J. (1952) The effect of the duration of the unconditioned stimulus upon conditioning and extinction. *Amer. J. Psychol., 65,* 256-262.

BITTERMAN, M. E., REED, P. C., and KUBALA, A. L. (1953) The strength of sensory preconditioning. *J. exp. Psychol., 46,* 178-182.

BITTERMAN, M. E., TYLER, D. W., and ELAM, C. B. (1955) Simultaneous and successive discrimination under identical stimulating conditions. *Amer. J. Psychol., 68,* 237-248.

BITTERMAN, M. E., and WODINSKY, J. (1953) Simultaneous and successive discrimination. *Psychol. Rev., 60,* 371-376.

BLACK, A. H. (1958) The extinction of avoidance responses under curare-like drugs. *J. comp. physiol. Psychol., 51,* 519-

BLACKWELL, H. R., and SCHLOSBERG, H. (1943) Octave generalization, pitch discrimination, and loudness thresholds in the white rat. *J. exp. Psychold., 33,* 407-419.

BLACKWELL, M. G. *See* Wallace, Blackwell, and Jenkins (1941).

BLODGETT, H. C. (1929) The effect of the introduction of reward upon the maze performance of rats. *Univ. Calif. Publ. Psychol., 4,* 113-134.

BLOOMBERG, R., and WEBB, W. B. (1949) Various degrees within a single drive as cues for spatial response learning in the white rat. *J. exp. Psychol., 39,* 628-636.

BLUM, J. S. *See* Blum and Blum (1949).

BLUM, R. A., and BLUM, J. S. (1949) Factual issues in the "continuity controversy." *Psychol. Rev., 56,* 33-50.

BOGOSLOVSKI, A. I. (1937) An attempt at creating sensory conditioned reflexes in humans. *J. exp. Psychol., 21,* 403-422.

BOHM, A. M. *See* Postman, Adams, and Bohm (1956).

BOLLES, R., and PETRINOVICH, L. (1954) A technique for obtaining rapid drive discrimination in the rat. *J. comp. physiol. Psychol., 47,* 378-380.

BONEAU, C. A. (1958) The interstimulus interval and the latency of the conditioned eyelid response. *J. exp. Psychol., 56,* 464-472.

BOREN, J. J. *See* Brady, Boren, Conrad, and Sidman (1957), Sidman and others (1955).

BOREN, J. J., Sidman, M., and Herrnstein, R. J. (1959) Avoidance, escape, and extinction as a function of shock intensity. *J. comp. physiol. Psychol., 52,* 420-425.

BOSLOV, G. L. *See* Gerall, Sampson, and Boslov (1957).

BOSWORTH, L. L. *See* Brown, Gentry, and Bosworth (1949).

BOWER, G., and MILLER, N. E. (1958) Rewarding and punishing effects from stimulating the same place in the rat's brain. *J. comp. physiol. Psychol., 51,* 669-674.

BRADY, J. V. (1951) The effect of electro-convulsive shock on a conditioned emotional response: The permanence of the effect. *J. comp. physiol. Psychol., 44,* 507-511.

BRADY, J. V. (1952) The effect of electro-convulsive shock on a conditioned emotional response: The significance of the interval between the emotional conditioning and the electro-convulsive shock. *J. comp. physiol. Psychol., 45,* 9-13.

BRADY, J. V. (1955) Extinction of a conditioned "fear" response as a function of reinforcement schedules for competing behavior. *J. Psychol., 40,* 25-34.

BRADY, J. V. *See also* Geller, Sidman, and Brady (1955), Hunt and Brady (1955), Hunt, Jernberg, and Brady (1952), Sidman and others (1955).

BRADY, J. V., BOREN, J. J., CONRAD, D., and SIDMAN, M. (1957) The effect of food and water deprivation upon intracranial self-stimulation. *J. comp. physiol. Psychol., 50,* 134-137.

BRADY, J. V., and HUNT, H. F. (1951) A further demonstration of the effect of electro-convulsive shock on a conditional emotional response. *J. comp. physiol. Psychol., 44,* 204-209.

BRADY, J. V., and HUNT, H. F. (1955) An experimental approach to the analysis of emotional behavior. *J. Psychol., 40,* 313-324.

BRADY, J. V., HUNT, H. F., and GELLER, I. (1954) The effect of electro-convulsive shock on a conditioned emotional response as a function of the temporal distribution of the treatments. *J. comp. physiol. Psychol., 47,* 454-457.

BRADY, J. V., STEBBINS, W. C., and GALAMBOS, R. (1953) The effect of audiogenic convulsions on a conditioned emotional response. *J. comp. physiol. Psychol., 46,* 363-365.

BRADY, J. V., STEBBINS, W. C., and HUNT, H. F. (1953) The effect of electro-convulsive shock (ECS) on a conditioned emotional response: The effect of additional ECS convulsions. *J. comp. physiol. Psychol., 46,* 368-372.

BRAGIEL, R. M., and PERKINS, C. C., Jr. (1954) Conditioned stimulus intensity and response speed. *J. exp. Psychol., 47,* 437-441.

BRANDAUER, C. M. (1953) A confirmation of Webb's data concerning the action of irrelevant drives. *J. exp. Psychol., 45,* 150-152.

BRANTLEY, J. J. *See* Siegel and Brantley (1951).

BRAUN, H. W., and GEISELHART, R. (1959) Age differences in the acquisition and extinction of the conditioned eyelid response. *J. exp. Psychol., 57,* 386-388.

BRAUN, H. W., PATTON, R. A., and BARNES, H. W. (1952) Effects of electroshock convulsions upon the learning performance of monkeys: I. Object-quality discrimination learning. *J. comp. physiol. Psychol., 45,* 231-238.

BRAZIER, M. A. B. (Ed.) (1959a) *The Central Nervous System and Behavior; Transactions of the First Conference.* New York: Josiah Macy Jr. Foundation.

BRAZIER, M. A. B. (Ed.) (1959b) *The Central Nervous System and Behavior; Transactions of the Second Conference.* New York: Josiah Macy Jr. Foundation.

BREGMAN, E. O. (1934) An attempt to modify the emotional attitudes of infants by the conditioned response technique. *J. genet. Psychol., 45,* 169-198.

BRELAND, K., and BRELAND, M. (1951) A field of applied animal psychology. *Amer. Psychologist, 6,* 202-204

BRELAND, M. *See* Breland and Breland (1951).

BRIGGS, G. E. *See* Wickens and Briggs (1951).

BROGDEN, W. J. (1939a) The effect of frequency of reinforcement upon the level of conditioning. *J. exp. Psychol., 24,* 419-431.

BROGDEN, W. J. (1939b) Unconditioned stimulus-substitution in the conditioning process. *Amer. J. Psychol., 52,* 46-55.

BROGDEN, W. J. (1939c) Sensory preconditioning. *J. exp. Psychol., 25,* 323-332.

BROGDEN, W. J. (1939d) Higher order conditioning. *Amer. J. Psychol., 52,* 579-591.

BROGDEN, W. J. (1947) Sensory preconditioning of human subjects. *J. exp. Psychol., 37,* 527-539.

BROGDEN, W. J. (1949) Acquisition and extinction of a conditioned avoidance response in dogs. *J. comp. physiol. Psychol., 42,* 296-302.

BROGDEN, W. J. (1950) Sensory conditioning measured by the facilitation of auditory acuity. *J. exp. Psychol., 40,* 512-519.

BROGDEN, W. J., and GANTT, W. H. (1937) Cerebellar conditioned reflexes. *Amer. J. Psysiol., 119,* 277-278.

BROGDEN, W. J. *See also* Chernikoff and Brogden (1949), Culler, Finch, Girden, and Brogden (1935), Roessler and Brogden (1943), Hoffeld, Thompson, and Brogden (1958).

BROGDEN, W. J., and GREGG, L. W. (1951) Studies of sensory conditioning measured by the facilitation of auditory acuity. *J. exp. Psychol., 42,* 384-389.

BROGDEN, W. J., LIPMAN, E. A., and CULLER, E. (1938) The role of incentive in conditioning and extinction. *Amer. J. Psychol., 51,* 109-117.

BROMILEY, R. B. (1948) Conditioned responses in a dog after removal of neocortex. *J. comp. physiol. Psychol., 41,* 102-110.

BROMILEY, R. B. *See also* Pinto and Bromiley (1950).

BROWN, G. W. *See* Cohen, Brown, and Brown (1957).

BROWN, H. C. (1916) Language and the associative reflex. *J. Phil. Psychol. sci. Meth., 13,* 645-649.

BROWN, J. F. (1936) *Psychology and the social order.* New York: McGraw-Hill.

BROWN, Janet L. (1956) The effect of drive on learning with secondary reinforcement. *J. comp. physiol. Psychol., 49,* 254-260.

BROWN, J. S. (1942) The generalization of approach responses as a function of stimulus intensity and strength of motivation. *J. comp. Psychol., 33,* 209-226.

BROWN, J. S. (1948) Gradients of approach and avoidance responses and their relation to level of motivation. *J. comp. physiol. Psychol., 41,* 450-465.

BROWN, J. S. *See also* Bilodeau, Brown, and Meryman (1956).

BROWN, J. S., BILODEAU, E. A., and BARON, M. R. (1951) Bidirectional gradients in the strength of a generalized voluntary response to stimuli on a visual-spatial dimension. *J. exp. Psychol., 41,* 52-61.

BROWN, J. S., CLARKE, F. R., and STEIN, L. (1958) A new technique for studying spatial generalization with voluntary responses. *J. exp. Psychol., 55,* 359-362.

BROWN, J. S., and JACOBS, A. (1949) The role of fear in the motivation and acquisition of responses. *J. exp. Psychol., 39,* 747-759.

BROWN, J. S., KALISH, H. I., and FARBER, I. E. (1951) Conditioned fear as revealed by magnitude of startle response to an auditory stimulus. *J. exp. Psychol., 41,* 317-328.

BROWN, M. L. *See* Cohen, Brown, and Brown (1957).

BROWN, Patricia A. *See* Haner and Brown (1955).

BROWN, W. L. *See* Crum, Brown, and Bitterman (1951), Gentry, Brown, and Kaplan (1949).

BROWN, W. L., and DALRYMPLE, H. B. (1951) The effects of intra-maze delay. 6. Different extra-maze cues between anterior and posterior sections. *J. comp. physiol. Psychol., 44,* 604-607.

BROWN, W. L., and GENTRY, G. (1948) The effects of intra-maze delay. *J. comp. physiol. Psychol., 41,* 403-407.

BROWN, W. L., GENTRY, G., and BOSWORTH, L. L. (1949) The effects of intra-maze delay: 4. A gap in the maze. *J. comp. physiol. Psychol., 42,* 182-191.

BROWN, W. L., GENTRY, G., and KAPLAN, S. J. (1948) The effects of intra-maze delay. 1. Delay enforced by a revolving wheel. *J. comp. physiol. Psychol., 41,* 258-268.

BROWN, W. L., and HALAS, E. S. (1957a) Terminal extinction in a multiple-T maze within a heterogeneous environment. *J. genet. Psychol., 90,* 89-95.

BROWN, W. L., and HALAS, E. S. (1957b) Terminal extinction in a multiple-T maze within a homogeneous environment. *J. genet. Psychol., 90,* 97-101.

BROWN, W. L., and HALAS, E. S. (1957c) Latent extinction in a multiple-T maze with heterogeneous and homogeneous environments. *J. genet. Psychol., 90,* 259-266.

BROWN, W. L., and SJOBERG, W. E., Jr. (1950) The effects of intra-maze delay. V. Tetanizing shock during various intervals of delay. *J. comp. physiol. Psychol., 43,* 272-280.

BROWNSTEIN, A. *See* Goodson and Brownstein (1955).

BRUNER, J. S., MATTER, Jean, and PAPANEK, Miriam L. (1955) Breadth of learning as a function of drive level and mechanization. *Psychol. Rev., 62,* 1-10.

BRUNSWIK, E. (1959) Probability as a determiner of rat behavior. *J. exp. Psychol., 25,* 175-197.

BRUNSWIK, E. (1956) *Perception and the representative design of psychological experiments.* Berkeley: University of California Press.

BRUSH, Elinor S. *See* Brush, Brush, and Solomon (1955), Solomon and Brush 1956).

BRUSH, F. R. *See* Church, Brush, and Solomon (1956).

BRUSH, F. R., BRUSH, Elinor S., and SOLOMON, R. L. (1955) Traumatic avoidance learning: the effects of CS-UCS interval with a delayed-conditioning procedure. *J. comp. physiol. Psychol., 48,* 285-293.

BRYAN, W. L., and HARTER, N. (1897) Studies in the physiology and psychology of the telegraphic language. *Psychol. Rev., 4,* 27-53.

BUCHANAN, G. *See* Smith and Buchanan (1954).

BUCHWALD, A. M., and YAMAGUCHI, H. G. (1955) The effect of change in drive level on habit reversal. *J. exp. Psychol., 50,* 265-268.

BUEL, J. *See* Ballachey and Buell (1934a) and (1934b).

BUGELSKI, R. (1938) Extinction with and without sub-goal reinforcement. *J. comp. Psychol., 26,* 121-134.

BUGELSKI, B. R. (1956) *The psychology of learning.* New York: Henry Holt.

BUGELSKI, B. R., COYER, R. A. and ROGERS, W. A. (1952) A criticism of preacquisition and pre-extinction of expectancies. *J. exp. Psychol., 44,* 27-30.

BULLOCK, D. H., and SMITH, W. C. (1953) An effect of repeated conditioning-extinction upon operant strength. *J. exp. Psychol., 46,* 349-352.

BURNHAM, W. H. (1917) Mental hygiene and the conditioned reflex. *J. genet Psychol., 24,* 449-488.

BURNHAM, W. H. (1924) *The normal mind.* New York: Appleton-Century Croft.

BUTLER, B. *See* Seward and others (1957).

BUTLER, R. A. (1953) Discrimination by Rhesus monkeys to visual-exploration motivation. *J. comp. physiol. Psychol., 46,* 95-98.

BUTLER, R. A. (1954) Incentive conditions which influence visual exploration *J. exp. Psychol., 48,* 19-23.

BUTLER, R. A. (1957a) The effect of deprivation of visual incentives on visua exploration motivation in monkeys. *J. comp. physiol. Psychol., 50,* 177-179.

BUTLER, R. A. (1957b) Discrimination learning by Rhesus monkeys to auditor incentives. *J. comp. physiol. Psychol., 50,* 239-241.

BUTLER, R. A. (1958a) Exploratory and related behavior: A new trend in animal research. *J. Indiv. Psychol., 14,* 111-120.

BUTLER, R. A. (1958b) The differential effect of visual and auditory incentives on the performance of monkeys. *Amer. J. Psychol., 71,* 591-593.

BUTLER, R. A., and ALEXANDER, H. M. (1955) Daily patterns of visual exploratory behavior in the monkey. *J. comp. physiol. Psychol., 48,* 247-249.

BUTLER, R. A., and HARLOW, H. F. (1954) Persistence of visual exploration in monkeys, *J. comp. physiol. Psychol., 47,* 257-263.

BUTTER, C. M. (1959) Stimulus generalization along the dimensions of wavelength and angular orientation. Unpublished Ph.D. dissertation. Duke University.

BUTTER, C. M. and THOMAS, D. R. (1958) Secondary reinforcement as a function of the amount of primary reinforcement. *J. comp. physiol. Psychol., 51,* 346-348.

BUXTON, C. E. (1940) Latent learning and the goal-gradient hypothesis. *Contr. psychol. Theor., 2,* No. 2.

BUYTENDIJK, F. J. J. (1930) Uber das Umlernen. *Arch. neerl. Physiol., 15,* 283-310.

BYKOV, K. M. (1957) *The cerebral cortex and the internal organs.* Translated and edited by W. H. Gantt. New York: Chemical Publishing Co.

CALVIN, A. D. *See* Bitterman, Calvin, and Elam (1953), Turbeville, Calvin, and Bitterman (1952).

CALVIN, J. S. (1939) Decremental factors in conditioned response learning. Ph.D. dissertation, Yale University.

CALVIN, J. S., BICKNELL, E. A., and SPERLING, D. S. (1953a) Establishment of a conditioned drive based on the hunger drive. *J. comp. physiol. Psychol., 46,* 173-175.

CALVIN, J. S., BICKNELL, E. A., and SPERLING, D. S. (1953b) Effect of a secondary reinforcer on consummatory behavior. *J. comp. physiol. Psychol., 46,* 176-179.

CAMERON, Lois. *See* Bindra and Cameron (1953).

CAMPBELL, A. A. (1938) The interrelations of two measures of conditioning in man. *J. exp. Psychol., 22,* 225-243.

CAMPBELL, A. A. (1939) A reply to Dr. Razran. *J. exp. Psychol., 24,* 227-233.

CAMPBELL, A. A. *See also* Hilgard and Campbell (1936), Hilgard, Campbell, and Sears (1938).

CAMPBELL, A. A., and HILGARD, E. R. (1936) Individual differences in ease of conditioning. *J. exp. Psychol., 19,* 561-571.

CAMPBELL, B. A. (1955) The fractional reduction in noxious stimulation required to produce "just noticeable" learning. *J. comp. physiol. Psychol., 48,* 141-148.

CAMPBELL, B. A. (1956) The reinforcement difference limen (RDL) function for shock reduction. *J. exp. Psychol., 52,* 258-262.

CAMPBELL, B. A. (1957) Auditory and aversive thresholds of rats for bands of noise. *Science, 125,* 596-597.

CAMPBELL, B. A. (1958) Absolute and relative sucrose preference thresholds for hungry and satiated rats. *J. comp. physiol. Psychol., 51,* 795-800.

CAMPBELL, B. A. *See also* Sheffield and Campbell (1954), Sheffield, Roby, and Campbell (1954).

CAMPBELL, B. A., and KRAELING, Doris (1953) Response strength as a function of drive level and amount of drive reduction. *J. exp. Psychol.*, *45*, 97-101.

CAMPBELL, B. A., and KRAELING, Doris (1954) Response strength as a function of drive level during training. *J. comp. physiol. Psychol.*, *47*, 101-103.

CAMPBELL, B. A., and SHEFFIELD, F. D. (1953) Relation of random activity to food deprivation. *J. comp. physiol. Psychol.*, *46*, 320-322.

CAMPBELL, B. J. *See* Long, Hammack, and Campbell (1959).

CANNON, W. B. (1932) *The wisdom of the body.* New York: Norton.

CANNON, W. B. (1934) Hunger and thirst. In C. Murchison (ed.) *Handbook of general experimental psychology.* Worcester: Clark University Press.

CANNON, W. B. (1939) *The wisdom of the body.* (Rev. Ed.) New York: Norton.

CANTOR, G. N., and SPIKER, C. C. (1954) Effects of non-reinforced trials on discrimination learning in preschool children. *J. exp. Psychol.*, *47*, 257-258.

CANTOR, G. N. *See also* Barnett and Cantor (1957).

CAPALDI, E. J. (1958) The effect of different amounts of training on the resistance to extinction of different patterns of partially reinforced responses. *J. comp. physiol. Psychol.*, *51*, 367-371.

CAPALDI, E. J. *See* Robinson and Capaldi (1958).

CAPEHART, J., Viney, W., and Hulicka, I. M. (1958) The effect of effort upon extinction. *J. comp. physiol. Psychol.*, *51*, 505-507.

CAPRETTA, P. J. *See* Smith and Capretta (1956).

CARLTON, P. L. (1955) Response strength as a function of delay of reward and physical confinement. *Proc. Iowa Acad. Sci.*, *62*, 438-444.

CARPENTER, J. A. (1952) Anticipatory behavior in the rat following frontal lesions. *J. comp. physiol. Psychol.*, *45*, 413-418.

CARPENTER, J. A. *See also* Deese and Carpenter (1951).

CARTER, L. F. (1941) Intensity of conditioned stimulus and rate of conditioning. *J. exp. Psychol.*, *28*, 481-490.

CASEY, A. *See* Wike and Casey (1954a) (1954b).

CASON, H. (1922a) The conditioned pupillary reaction. *J. exp. Psychol.*, *5*, 108-146.

CASON, H. (1922b) The conditioned eyelid reaction. *J. exp. Psychol.*, *5*, 153-196.

CASON, H. (1925b) The physical basis of the conditioned response. *Amer J. Psychol.*, *36*, 371-393.

CASON, H. (1932) The pleasure-pain theory of learning. *Psychol. Rev.*, *39*, 440-466.

CASON, H. (1935) Backward conditioned eyelid reactions. *J. exp. Psychol.*, *18*, 599-611.

CASON, H. (1936) Sensory conditioning. *J. exp. Psychol.*, *19*, 572-591.

CHAMBERS, R. M. (1956a) Effects of intravenous glucose injections on learning, general activity, and hunger drive. *J. comp. physiol. Psychol.*, *49*, 558-564.

CHAMBERS, R. M. (1956b) Some physiological bases for reinforcing properties of reward injections. *J. comp. physiol. Psychol.*, *49*, 565-568.

CHAMBERS, R. M. *See also* Coppock and Chambers (1954).

CHAMBERS, R. M., and FULLER, J. L. (1958) Conditioning of skin temperature changes in dogs. *J. comp. physiol. Psychol.*, *51*, 223-226.

CHAPMAN, J. P. *See* Taylor and Chapman (1955).

CHERNIKOFF, R., and BROGDEN, W. J. (1949) The effect of instructions upon sensory preconditioning of human subjects. *J. exp. Psychol.*, *39*, 200-207.

CHILD, I. L. *See* Whiting and Child (1953).

CHRISTIE, R. (1951) The role of drive discrimination in learning under irrelevant motivation. *J. exp. Psychol.*, *42*, 13-19.

CHRISTIE, R. (1952) The effect of some early experiences in the latent learning of adult rats. *J. exp. Psychol.*, *43*, 281-288.

CHURCH, R. M., BRUSH, F. R., and SOLOMON, R. L. (1956) Traumatic avoidance learning: The effects of CS-US interval with a delayed conditioning procedure in a free-responding situation. *J. comp. physiol. Psychol.*, *49*, 301-308.

CHURCH, R. M., and SOLOMON, R. L. (1956) Traumatic avoidance learning: the effects of delay of shock termination. *Psychol. Rep. 2*, 357-368.

CLARKE, F. R. *See* Brown, Clarke, and Stein (1958).

CLAYTON, Frances L. (1956) Secondary reinforcement as a function of reinforcement scheduling. *Psychol. Rep. 2*, 377-380.

CLAYTON, Frances L. *See also* Jenkins and Clayton (1949), Jenkins, McFann, and Clayton (1950).

COATE, W. B. (1956) Weakening of conditioned bar-pressing by prior extinction of its subsequent discriminated operant. *J. comp. physiol. Psychol.*, *49*, 135-138.

COHEN, B. D., BROWN, G. W., and BROWN, M. L. (1957) Avoidance learning motivated by hypothalamic stimulation. *J. exp. Psychol.*, *53*, 228-233.

COHEN, B. D., KALISH, H. I., THURSTON, J. R., and COHEN, E. (1954) Experimental manipulation of verbal behavior. *J. exp. Psychol.*, *47*, 106-110.

COHEN, E. *See* Cohen, Kalish, Thurston, and Cohen (1954).

COHEN, J. (1950) Observations on strictly simultaneous conditioned reflexes. *J. comp. physiol. Psychol.*, *43*, 211-216.

COHEN, L. H. *See* Sears and Cohen (1933).

COHEN, L. H., HILGARD, E. R., and WENDT, G. R. (1933) Sensitivity to light in a case of hysterical blindness studied by reinforcement-inhibition and conditioning methods. *Yale J. Biol. Med.*, *6*, 61-67.

COLE, K. F. *See* Amsel and Cole (1953).

COLE, L. E. *See* Miller and Cole (1936).

COLLIER, G. *See* Holder and others (1957), Roberts, Marx, and Collier (1958), Tyler, Marx, and Collier (1959).

COLLIER, G., and MARX, M. H. (1959) Changes in performance as a function of shifts in the magnitude of reinforcement. *J. exp. Psychol., 57*, 305-309.

COLLIER, G., and SISKEL, M., Jr. (1959) Performance as a joint function of amount of reinforcement and inter-reinforcement interval. *J. exp. Psychol., 57*, 115-120.

CONRAD, D. *See* Brady, Boren, Conrad, and Sidman (1957).

CONRAD, D. G. *See* Meunzinger and Conrad (1953), Sidman and others (1955).

COOK, S. W. (1939b) The production of "experimental neurosis" in the white rat. *Psychosom. Med., I*, 293-308.

COPELAN, E. L. *See* Riopelle and Copelan (1954).

COPPOCK, H. W., and CHAMBERS, R. M. (1954) Reinforcement of position preference by automatic intravenous injections of glucose. *J. comp. physiol. Psychol., 47*, 355-357.

COPPOCK, H., and MOWRER, O. H. (1947) Inter-trial responses as 'rehearsal': A study of 'overt thinking' in animals. *Am. J. Psychol., 60*, 608-616.

COPPOCK, W. J. (1958) Pre-extinction in sensory preconditioning. *J. exp. Psychol., 55*, 213-219.

COTTERMAN, T. E., MEYER, D. R., and WICKENS, D. D. (1956) Discrimination-reversal learning in marmosets. *J. comp. physiol. Psychol., 49*, 539-541.

COTTON, J. W. (1953) Running time as a function of amount of food deprivation. *J. exp. Psychol., 46*, 188-198.

COTTON, J. W. *See also* Lewis and Cotton (1957).

COWLES, J. T. (1937) Food-tokens as incentives for learning by chimpanzees. *Comp. Psychol. Monogr., 14*, No. 71.

COYER, R. A. *See* Bugelski, Coyer, and Rogers (1952).

CRASILNECK, H. B., and McCRANIE, E. J. (1956) On the conditioning of the pupillary reflex. *J. Psychol., 42*, 23-27.

CRAWFORD, M. P., FULTON, J. F., JACOBSEN, C. F., and WOLFE, J. B. (1948) Frontal lobe ablations in chimpanzees: a resume of "Becky" and "Lucy." *Res. Publ. Ass. nerv. ment. Dis., 27*, 1-58.

CRESPI, L. P. (1942) Quantitative variation of incentive and performance in the white rat. *Amer. J. Psychol., 55*, 467-517.

CRESPI, L. P. (1944) Amount of reinforcement and level of performance. *Psychol. Rev., 51*, 341-357.

CRISLER, G. (1930) Salivation is unnecessary for the establishment of the salivary conditioned reflex induced by morphine. *Amer J. Physiol., 94*, 553-556.

CRISLER, G. *See also* Kleitman and Crisler (1927).

CRUM, Janet, BROWN, W. L., and BITTERMAN, M. E. (1951) The effect of partial and delayed reinforcement on resistance to extinction. *Amer. J. Psychol., 64*, 228-237.

CRUTCHFIELD, R. S. *See* Krech and Crutchfield (1948).

CULLER, E. (1937) Observations on the spinal dog. *Psychol. Bull. 34*, 742-743.

CULLER, E. *See* also Brogden, Lipman, and Culler (1938), Finch and Culler (1935), Girden and Culler (1937), Girden and others (1936), Shurrager and Culler (1938) (1940) (1941).

CULLER, E., FINCH, G., GIRDEN, E., and BROGDEN, W. J. (1935) Measurements of acuity by the conditioned-response technique. *J. gen. Psychol., 12*, 223-227.

CULLER, E., and METTLER, F. A. (1934) Conditioned behavior in a decorticate dog. *J. comp. Psychol., 18*, 291-303.

DALRYMPLE, H. B. *See* Brown and Dalrymple (1951).

D'AMATO, M. R. (1955a) Secondary reinforcement and magnitude of primary reinforcement. *J. comp. physiol. Psychol., 48*, 378-380.

D'AMATO, M. R. (1955b) Transfer of secondary reinforcement across the hunger and thirst drives. *J. exp. Psychol., 49*, 352-356.

D'AMATO, M. R. *See also* Kendler and others (1957).

DANIEL, W. J. *See* Koch and Daniel (1945).

DARBY, C. L., and RIOPELLE, A. J. (1955) Differential problem sequences and the formation of learning sets. *J. Psychol., 39*, 105-108.

DATEL, W. E. *See* Seward, Datel, and Levy (1952).

DAUB, C. T. (1933) The effect of doors on latent learning. *J. comp. Psychol., 15*, 49-58.

DAVIS, J. D. *See* Grice and Davis (1957) (1958).

DAVIS, R. C. *See* Kellogg and others (1940).

DAVIS, R. H. *See* Denny and Davis (1951).

DAVIS, R. T. *See* Harlow and others (1952).

DEAN, W. *See* Thompson and Dean (1955).

DEESE, J. (1951) The extinction of a discrimination without performance of the choice response. *J. comp. physiol. Psychol., 44*, 362-366.

DEESE, J. *See* also Kellogg and others (1947), Kellogg, Pronko, and Deese (1946).

DEESE, J., and CARPENTER J. A. (1951) Drive level and reinforcement. *J. exp. Psychol., 42*, 236-238.

DEESE, J., and KELLOGG, W. N. (1949) Some new data on the nature of 'spinal conditioning.' *J. comp. physiol. Psychol., 42*, 157-160.

DELGADO, J. M. R., ROBERTS, W. W., and MILLER, N. E. (1954) Learning motivated by electrical stimulation of the brain. *Amer. J. Physiol., 179*, 587-593.

DELGADO, J. M. R., ROSVOLD, H. E., and LOONEY, E. (1956) Evoking conditioned fear by electrical stimulation of subcortical structures in the monkey brain. *J. comp. physiol. Psychol., 49*, 373-380.

DELHAGEN, J. E. *See* Kling, Horowitz, and Delhagen (1956).

DENNY, M. R. (1946) The role of secondary reinforcement in a partial reinforcement learning situation. *J. exp. Psychol., 36*, 373-389.

DENNY, M. R. (1948) The effect of using differential end boxes in a simple T-maze learning situation. *J. exp. Psychol., 38,* 245-249.

DENNY, M. R. *See also* Maatsch, Adelman, and Denny (1954).

DENNY, M. R., and ADELMAN, H. M. (1955) Elicitation theory: I. An analysis of two typical learning situations. *Psychol. Rev., 62,* 290-296.

DENNY, M. R., and BEHAN, R. A. (1956) Conditioned hunger drive or conditioned approach? *Psychol. Rep. 2,* 192-193.

DENNY, M. R., and DAVIS, R. H. (1951) A test of latent learning for a non-goal significate. *J. comp. physiol. Psychol., 44,* 590-595.

DENNY, M. R. and DUNHAM, M. D. (1951) The effect of differential non-reinforcement of the incorrect response on the learning of the correct response in the simple T-maze. *J. exp. Psychol., 41,* 382-389.

DENNY, M. R., and KING, G. F. (1955) Differential response learning on the basis of differential size of reward. *J. genet. Psychol., 87,* 317-320.

DENNY, M. R., KOONS, P. B., and MASON, J. E. (1959) Extinction of avoidance as a function of the escape situation. *J. comp. physiol. Psychol., 52,* 212-214.

DENNY, M. R., and RATNER, S. C. (1959) Distal cues and latent extinction. *Psychol. Rec., 9,* 33-35.

DERIVERA, J. *See* Lawrence and DeRivera (1954).

DESIDERATO, O. (1956) The interaction of several variables in latent learning. *J. exp. Psychol., 52,* 244-250.

DETERLINE, W. A. *See* Katz and Deterline (1958).

DEVALOIS, R. L. *See* Walker, Knotter, and DeValois (1950).

DIESENROTH, C. F., and SPENCE, K. W. (1941) An investigation of latent learning in the white rat. *Psychol. Bull., 38,* 706 (abstract).

DINSMOOR, J. A. (1950) A quantitative comparison of the discriminative and reinforcing functions of a stimulus. *J. exp. Psychol., 40,* 458-472.

DINSMOOR, J. A. (1952a) The effect of hunger on discriminated responding. *J. abnorm. soc. Psychol., 47,* 67-72.

DINSMOOR, J. A. (1952) Resistance to extinction following periodic reinforcement in the presence of a discriminative stimulus. *J. comp. physiol. Psychol., 45,* 31-35.

DINSMOOR, J. A. (1954) Punishment: I. The avoidance hypothesis. *Psychol. Rev., 61,* 34-46.

DINSMOOR, J. A. (1955) Punishment: II. An interpretation of empirical findings. *Psychol. Rev., 62,* 96-105.

DINSMOOR, J. A., KISH, G. B., and KELLER, F. S. (1953) A comparison of the effectiveness of regular and periodic secondary reinforcement. *J. gen. Psychol., 48,* 57-66.

DITTMER, D. G. *See* Grant and Dittmer (1940a) (1946).

DIVEN, K. (1936) Certain determinants in the conditioning of anxiety reactions. *J. Psychol., 3,* 291-308.

DODGE, R. (1926) a pendulum-photochronograph. *J. exp. Psychol.*, *9*, 155-161.

DODSON, J. D. *See* Yerkes and Dodson (1908).

DOLLARD, J. C. *See* Miller and Dollard (1941).

DOLLARD, J. C., DOOB, L. W., MILLER, N. E., MOWRER, O. H., SEARS, R. R., FORD, C. S., HOVLAND, C. I., and SOLLENBERGER, R. T. (1939) *Frustration and aggression.* New Haven: Yale University Press.

DOLLARD, J., and MILLER, N. E. (1950) *Personality and psychotherapy.* New York: McGraw-Hill.

DOOB, L. W. *See* Dollard, Doob, Miller, Mowrer, Sears, Ford, Hovland, and Sollenberger (1939).

DOTY, R. W. *See* Beck and Doty (1957).

DOTY, R. W., RUTLEDGE, L. T., Jr., and LARSEN, R. M. (1956) Conditioned reflexes established to electrical stimulation of cat cerebral cortex. *J. Neurophysiol.*, *19*, 401-415.

DREW, G. C. (1939) The speed of locomotion gradient and its relation to the goal gradient. *J. comp. Psychol.*, *27*, 333-372.

DUFFY, M. *See* Smith and Duffy (1957).

DUFORT, R. H. *See* Kimble and Dufort (1956), Kimble, Mann., and Dufort (1955).

DUFORT, R. H., GUTTMAN, N., and KIMBLE, G. A. (1954) One-trial discrimination reversal in the white rat. *J. comp. physiol. Psychol.*, *47*, 248-249.

DUFORT, R. H., and KIMBLE, G. A. (1956) Changes in response strength with changes in amount of reinforcement. *J. exp. Psychol.*, *51*, 185-191.

DUFORT, R. H., and KIMBLE, G. A. (1958) Ready signals and the effect of UCS presentations in eyelid conditioning. *J. exp. Psychol.*, *56*, 1-7.

DUKES, W. F. *See* Bevan and Dukes (1955).

DUNCAN, C. P. (1945) The effect of electroshock convulsions on the maze habit in the white rat. *J. exp. Psychol.*, *35*, 267-278.

DUNCAN, C. P. (1949) The retroactive effect of electroshock on learning. *J. comp. physiol. Psychol.*, *42*, 32-44.

DUNCAN, C. P. *See also* Loess and Duncan (1952).

DUNHAM, B. (1957) The formalization of scientific languages. Part 1. The work of Woodger and Hull. *IBM J. Res. and Develpm. 1*, 341-348.

DUNHAM, M. D. *See* Denny and Dunham (1951).

DURYEA, R. A. (1955) Stimulus response asynchronism and delay of reinforcement in selective learning. *Amer. J. Psychol.*, *68*, 343-357.

DUSSER, DE BARENNE, J. G., and McCULLOCH, W. S. (1938) Functional organization in the sensory cortex of the monkey (Macaca mulatta). *J. Neurophysiol.*, *I*, 69-85.

DUTTON, C. E. *See* Hilgard, Dutton, and Helmick (1949).

DWORKIN, L. (1939) Conditioning neuroses in dog and cat. *Psychosom. Med.*, *1*, 388-390.

DYKMAN, R. A. *See also* Shurrager and Dykman (1951).

DYKMAN, R. A., and Shurrager, P. S. (1956) Successive and maintained conditioning in spinal carnivores. *J. comp. physiol. Psychol., 49,* 27-35.

DYMOND, S. *See* Warden and Dymond (1931).

EBELING, E. *See* Ritchie, Ebeling, and Roth (1950).

ECCLES, J. C. (1953) *The neurophysiological basis of mind.* Oxford: Clarendon Press.

EDMONSON, Barbara W., and AMSEL, A. (1954) The effects of massing and distribution of extinction trials on the persistence of a fear-motivated instrumental response. *J. comp. physiol. Psychol., 47,* 117-123.

EHRENFREUND, D. (1948) An experimental test of the continuity theory of discrimination learning with pattern vision. *J. comp. physiol. Psychol., 41,* 408-422.

EHRENFREUND, D. (1949) Effect of a secondary reinforcing agent in black-white discrimination. *J. comp. physiol. Psychol., 42,* 1-5.

EHRENFREUND, D. (1952) A study of the transposition gradient. *J. exp. Psychol., 43,* 81-87.

EHRENFREUND, D. (1954) Generalization of secondary reinforcement in discrimination learning. *J. comp. physiol. Psychol., 47,* 311-314.

EHRENFREUND, D. *See also* Alberts and Ehrenfreund (1951).

EISMAN, E. (1956) An investigation of the parameters defining drive (D). *J. exp. Psychol., 52,* 85-89.

EISMAN, E., ASIMOW, Adele, and MALTZMAN, I. (1956) Habit strength as a function of drive in a brightness discrimination problem. *J. exp. Psychol.. 51,* 58-64.

ELAM, C. B. *See* Bitterman, Calvin, and Elam (1953), Bitterman, Tyler, and Elam (1955).

ELAM, C. B., TYLER, D. W., and BITTERMAN, M. E. (1954) A further study of secondary reinforcement and the discrimination hypothesis. *J. comp. physiol. Psychol., 47,* 381-384.

ELDER, J. H. (1934) Auditory acuity of the chimpanzee. *J. comp. Psychol., 17,* 157-183.

ELDER, J. H. (1935) The upper limit of hearing in chimpanzee. *Amer J. Physiol., 112,* 109-115.

ELDER, J. H. *See* also Nissen and Elder (1935).

ELLEN, P. (1956) The compulsive nature of abnormal fixations. *J. comp. physiol. Psychol., 49,* 309-317.

ELLEN, P. *See also* Maier and Ellen (1952).

ELLINGSON, R. J. (1956) Brain waves and problems of psychology. *Psychol. Bull., 53,* 1-34.

ELLIOTT, M. H. (1928) The effect of change of reward on the maze performance of rats. *Univ. Calif. Publ. Psychol., 4,* 19-30.

ELLIOTT, M. H. (1929a) The effect of appropriateness of reward and of complex incentives on maze performance. *Univ. Calif. Publ. Psychol., 4,* 91-98.

ELLIOTT, M. H. (1929b) The effect of change in drive on maze performance. *Univ. Calif. Publ. Psychol., 4,* 185-188.

ELLIS, R. A. *See* Logan, Beier, and Ellis (1955).

ELLSON, D. G. (1938) Quantitative studies of the interaction of simple habits. I. Recovery from specific and generalized effects of extinction. *J. exp. Psychol., 23,* 339-358.

ELLSON, D. G. *See also* Humphreys, Miller, and Ellson (1940).

ENGLISH, H. B. (1929) Three cases of the "conditioned fear response." *J. abnorm. soc. Psychol., 24,* 221-225.

ENINGER, M. U. (1952) Habit summation in a selective learning problem. *J. comp. physiol. Psychol., 45,* 604-608.

ERIKSEN, C. W. (1954) Some personality correlates of stimulus generalization under stress. *J. abnorm. soc. Psychol., 49,* 561-565.

EROFEEVA, M. (1916) Contributions a l'etude des reflexes conditionnels destructifs. *C. R. Soc. Biol. Paris, 79.,* 239-240.

ESTES, W. K. (1942) Spontaneous recovery from extinction in maze-bright and maze-dull rats. *J. comp. Psychol., 34.,* 349-351.

ESTES, W. K. (1943) Discriminative conditioning. I. A discriminative property of conditioned anticipation. *J. exp. Psychol., 32.,* 150-155.

ESTES, W. K. (1944) An experimental study of punishment. *Psychol. Monogr., 47,* whole No. 263, pp. 40.

ESTES, W. K. (1948) Discriminative conditioning. II. Effects of a Pavlovian conditioned stimulus upon a subsequently established operant response. *J. exp. Psychol., 38.,* 173-177.

ESTES, W. K. (1949a) A study of the motivating conditions necessary for secondary reinforcement. *J. exp. Psychol., 39.,* 306-310.

ESTES, W. K. (1949b) Generalization of secondary reinforcement from the primary drive. *J. comp. physiol. Psychol., 42,* 286-295.

ESTES, W. K. (1950a) Toward a statistical theory of learning. *Psychol. Rev., 57,* 94-107.

ESTES, W. K. (1950b) Effects of competing reactions on the conditioning curve for bar pressing. *J. exp. Psychol., 40,* 200-205.

ESTES, W. K. (1954) Individual behavior in uncertain situations: an interpretation in terms of statistical association theory. Ch. IX in *Decision Processes,* 127-137.

ESTES, W. K. (1955a) Theory of elementary predictive behavior: an exercise in the behavioral interpretation of a mathematical model. *Mathematical models of human behavior—proceedings of a symposium,* 63-67.

ESTES, W. K. (1955b) Statistical theory of spontaneous recovery and regression. *Psychol. Rev., 62,* 145-154.

ESTES, W. K. (1956a) Learning. *Annu. Rev. Psychol., 7,* 1-38.

ESTES, W. K. (1956b) The problem of inference from curves based on group data. *Psychol. Bull., 53,* 134-140.

ESTES, W. K. (1958) Stimulus-response theory of drive. In Jones, M. R. *Nebraska Symposium on motivation.* Lincoln: University of Nebraska Press.

ESTES, W. K., KOCH, S., MacCORQUODALE, K., MEEHL, P., MUELLER, C. G., Jr., SCHOENFELD, W. N., and VERPLANCK, W. S. (1954) *Modern Learning Theory.* New York: Appleton-Century-Crofts.

ESTES, W. K., and SKINNER, B. F. (1941) Some quantitative properties of anxiety. *J. exp. Psychol., 29,* 390-400.

ESTES, W. K., and STRAUGHAN, J. H. (1954) Analysis of a verbal conditioning situation in terms of statistical learning theory. *J. exp. Psychol., 47,* 225-234.

EVANS, C. A. L. (1925) *Recent advances in physiology.* London: Churchill.

EVANS, W. O. (1959) The dimensional bases of stimulus generalization. Unpublished Ph.D. thesis. Duke University.

EYSENCK, H. J. (1955) A dynamic theory of anxiety and hysteria. *J. Ment. Science, 101,* 28-51.

FARBER, I. E. *See* Brown, Kalish, and Farber (1951), Spence and Farber (1953) (1954), Spence, Farber, and Taylor (1954).

FARBER, I. E., and SPENCE, K. W. (1953) Complex learning and conditioning as a function of anxiety. *J. exp. Psychol., 45,* 120-125.

FEDDERSON, W. E. *See* Bitterman, Fedderson, and Tyler (1953).

FEHER, E. (1951) Latent learning in the sophisticated rat. *J. exp. Psychol., 42,* 409-416.

FEINBERG, M. *See* Kellogg and others (1947).

FELDMAN, R. S. (1953) The specificity of the fixated response in the rat. *J. comp. physiol. Psychol., 46,* 487-492.

FELSINGER, J. M. *See* Gladstone and others (1947), Hull and others (1947).

FELSINGER, J. M., GLADSTONE, A. I., YAMAGUCHI, H. G., and HULL, C. L. (1947) Reaction latency ($_s t_r$) as a function of the number of reinforcements (N). *J. exp. Psychol., 37,* 214-228.

FERSTER, C B. (1951) The effect on extinction responding of stimuli continuously present during conditioning. *J. exp. Psychol., 42,* 443-449.

FERSTER, C. B. (1953) Sustained behavior under delayed reinforcement. *J. exp. Psychol., 45,* 218-224.

FERSTER, C. B., and SKINNER, B. F. (1957) *Schedules of reinforcement.* New York: Appleton-Century-Crofts.

FESHBACH, S. (1955) The drive-reducing function of fantasy behavior. *J. abnorm. soc. Psychol., 50,* 3-11.

FINAN, J. L. (1940) Quantitative studies in motivation. I. Strength of conditioning in rats under varying degrees of hunger. *J. comp. Psychol., 29,* 119-134.

FINCH, G. (1938a) Pilocarpine conditioning. *Amer. J. Psychol., 124,* 679-682.

FINCH, G. (1938b) Salivary conditioning in atropinized dogs. *Amer. J. Physiol., 124,* 136-141.

FINCH, G. *See also* Culler, Finch, Girden, and Brogden (1935), Girden and others (1936).

FINCH, G., and CULLER, E. (1935) Relation of forgetting to experimental extinction. *Amer. J. Psychol., 47,* 656-662.

FINGER, F. W. *See* Mote and Finger (1952).

FINK, J. B., and PATTON, R. M. (1953) Decrement of a learned drinking response accompanying changes in several stimulus characteristics. *J. comp. physiol. Psychol., 46,* 23-27.

FINOCCHIO, D. V. *See* Murphy, Miller, and Finocchio (1956).

FITCH, F. B. *See* Hull and others (1940).

FITTS, P. M. (1940) Preservation of non-rewarded behavior in relation to food-deprivation and work-requirement. *J. genet. Psychol., 57,* 165-191.

FITZWATER, M. E. (1952) The relative effect of reinforcement and non-reinforcement in establishing a form discrimination. *J. comp. physiol. Psychol., 45,* 476-481.

FITZWATER, M. E., and REISMAN, M. N. (1952) Comparison of forward, simultaneous, backward, and pseudo-conditioning. *J. exp. Psychol., 44,* 211-214.

FITZWATER, M. E., and THRUSH, R. S. (1956) Acquisition of a conditioned response as a function of forward temporal contiguity. *J. exp. Psychol., 51,* 59-61.

FLEURE, H. J., and WALTON, C. (1907) Notes on the habits of some sea anemones. *Zool. Anz., 31,* 212-220.

FORD, C. S. *See* Dollard and others (1939).

FORD, C. S., and BEACH, F. A. (1952) *Patterns of sexual behavior.* New York: Harper and Brothers.

FORGAYS, D. G., and FORGAYS, J. W. (1952) The nature of the effect of free environmental experience in the rat. *J. comp. physiol. Psychol., 45,* 322-328.

FORGAYS, J. W. *See* Forgays and Forgays (1952).

FORGUS, R. H. (1954) The effect of early perceptual learning on the behavioral organization of adult rats. *J. comp. physiol. Psychol., 47,* 331-336.

FORGUS, R. H. (1955a) Influence of early experience on maze-learning with and without visual cues. *Canad. J. Psychol., 9,* 207-214.

FORGUS, R. H. (1955b) Early visual and motor experience as determiners of complex maze-learning ability under rich and reduced stimulation. *J. comp. physiol. Psychol., 48,* 215-220.

Fox, J. *See* Maltzman, Fox, and Morrisett (1953).

FRANKS, C. M. (1956) Conditioning and personality: A study of normal and neurotic subjects. *J. abnorm. soc. Psychol., 52,* 143-150.

FRANKS, C. M. (1957) Effect of food, drink, and tobacco deprivation on the conditioning of the eyeblink response. *J. exp. Psychol., 53,* 117-120.

FRANZ, S. I. (1939) The neurology of learning. In Moss, F. A. (Ed.) *Comparative psychology*. New York: Prentice-Hall.

FREIDES, D. (1957) Goal-box cues and pattern of reinforcement. *J. exp. Psychol., 53,* 361-372

FRENCH, J. W. (1940) Trial-and-error learning in the paramecium. *J. exp. Psychol., 26,* 609-617.

FREUD, S. (1926) *The problem of anxiety*. Translation, 1936. New York: Norton.

FRITZ, M. F. (1930) Long time training of white rats on antagonistic visual habits. *J. comp. Psychol., 11,* 171-184.

FULLER, J. L. *See* Chambers and Fuller (1958).

FULTON, J. F. *See* Crawford, Fulton, Jacobsen, and Wolfe (1948).

GAGNÉ, R. M. (1941) The effect of spacing trials on the acquisition and extinction of a conditioned operant response. *J. exp. Psychol., 29,* 201-216.

GAGNÉ, R. M. *See also* Graham and Gagné (1940).

GAKKEL, L. B., and ZININA, N. V. (1953) Changes of higher nerve function in people over 60 years of age. *Fiziolog. Zhurnal. 39,* 533-539.

GALAMBOS, R. *See* Brady, Stebbins, and Galambos (1953).

GALAMBOS, R., SHEATZ, G., and VERNIER, V. G. (1956) Electrophysiological correlates of a conditioned response in cats. *Science, 123,* 376-377.

GANTT, W. H. *See* Brogden and Gantt (1937), Kupalov and Gantt (1927), Light and Gantt (1936), Loucks and Gantt (1938), Muncie and Gantt (1938).

GATLING, F. P. (1951) A study of the continuity of the learning process as measured by habit reversal in the rat. *J. comp. physiol. Psychol., 44,* 78-83.

GATLING, F. (1952) The effect of repeated stimulus reversals on learning in the rat. *J. comp. physiol. Psychol., 45,* 347-351.

GEISELHART, R. *See* Braun and Geiselhart (1959).

GELBER, Beatrice (1952) Investigations of the behavior of paramecium aurelia: I. Modification of behavior after training with reinforcement. *J. comp. physiol. Psychol., 45,* 58-65.

GELBER, Beatrice (1954) Investigations of the behavior of paramecium aurelia: IV. The effect of different training schedules on both young and aging cultures. *Amer. Psychologist, 9.* 374 (abstract).

GELBER, Beatrice (1956a) Investigations of the behavior of paramecium aurelia: II. Modification of a response in successive generations of both mating types. *J. comp. physiol. Psychol., 49,* 590-593.

GELBER, Beatrice (1956b) Investigation of the behavior of paramecium aurelia: III. The effect of the presence and absence of light on the occurrence of a response. *J. genet. Psychol., 68,* 31-36.

GELBER, Beatrice, and RASCH, Ellen (1956c) Investigations of the behavior of paramecium aurelia: V. The effects of autogamy (nuclear reorganization). *J. comp. physiol. Psychol., 49,* 594-599.

GELLER, I. *See* Brady, Hunt, and Geller (1954).

GELLER, I., SIDMAN, M., and BRADY, J. V. (1955) The effect of electro-convulsive shock on a conditioned emotional response: A control for acquisition recency. *J. comp. pysiol. Psychol., 48*, 130-131.

GENTRY, G. *See* Brown and Gentry (1948), Brown, Gentry, and Bosworth (1949), Brown, Gentry, and Kaplan (1948).

GENTRY, G., BROWN, W. L., and KAPLAN, S. J. (1949) The effects of intra-maze delay: 3. A delay box. *J. comp. physiol. Psychol., 42*, 81-86.

GERALL, A. A., SAMPSON, P. B., and BOSLOV, G. L. (1957) Classical conditioning of human pupillary dilation. *J. exp. Psychol., 54*, 467-474.

GEWIRTZ, J. L., BAER, D. M., and ROTH, C. H. (1958) A note on the similar effects of low social availability of an adult and brief social deprivation on young children's behavior. *Child Develpm., 29*, 150-152.

GEWIRTZ, J. L., and BAER, D. M. (1958a) The effect of brief social deprivation on behaviors for a social reinforcer. *J. abnorm. soc. Psychol., 56*, 49-56.

GEWIRTZ, J. L., and BAER, D. M. (1958b) Deprivation and satiation of social reinforcers as drive conditions. *J. abnorm. soc. Psychol., 57*, 165-172.

GHENT, Lila (1951) The relation of experience to the development of hunger. *Canad. J. Psychol., 5*, 77-81.

GHENT, Lila (1957) Some effects of deprivation on eating and drinking behavior. *J. comp. physiol. Psychol., 50*, 172-176.

GIBSON, E. J. *See* Walk and others (1958), Walk, Gibson, and Tighe (1957).

GIBSON, E. J., and WALK, R. D. (1956) The effect of prolonged exposure to visually presented patterns on learning to discriminate them. *J. comp. physiol. Psychol., 49*, 239-242.

GIBSON, E. J., WALK, R. D., PICK, H. L., Jr., and TIGHE, T. J. (1958) The effect of prolonged exposure to visual patterns on learning to discriminate similar and different patterns. *J. comp. physiol. Psychol., 51*, 584-587.

GIBSON, Eleanor. *See* Gibson and Gibson (1955).

GIBSON, J. J., and GIBSON, Eleanor J. (1955) Perceptual learning: Differentiation or enrichment? *Psychol. Rev., 62*, 32-41.

GILCHRIST, J. C. (1952) Characteristics of latent and reinforcement learning as a function of time. *J. comp. physiol. Psychol., 45*, 198-203.

GIRDEN, E. (1938) Conditioning and problem-solving behavior. *Amer. J. Psychol., 51*, 677-686.

GIRDEN, E. (1940) Cerebral mechanisms in conditioning under curare. *Amer. J. Psychol., 53*, 397-406.

GIRDEN, E. (1942a) Generalized conditioned responses under curare and erythroidine. *J. exp. Psychol., 31*, 105-119.

GIRDEN, E. (1942b) The dissociation of blood pressure conditioned responses under erythroidine. *J. exp. Psychol., 31*, 219-231.

GIRDEN, E. (1942c) The dissociation of pupillary conditioned reflexes under erythroidine and curare. *J. exp. Psychol., 31*, 322-332.

GIRDEN, E. *See also* Culler, Finch, Girden, and Brogden (1935).

GIRDEN, E., and CULLER, E. (1937) Conditioned responses in curarized striate muscle in dogs. *J. comp. Psychol., 23,* 261-274.

GIRDEN, E., METTLER, F. A., FINCH, G., and CULLER, E. (1936) Conditioned responses in a decorticate dog to acoustic, thermal, and tactile stimulation. *J. comp. Psychol., 21,* 367-385.

GLADSTONE, A. I. (1948) Reactively homogeneous compound trial-and-error learning with distributed trials and serial reinforcement. *J. exp. Psychol., 38,* 289-297.

GLADSTONE, A. I. *See* also Felsinger and others (1947), Hull and others (1947).

GLADSTONE, A. I., YAMAGUCHI, H. G., HULL, C. L., and FELSINGER, J. M. (1947) Some functional relationships of reaction potential ($_sE_R$) and related phenomena. *J. exp. Psychol., 37,* 510-526.

GLEITMAN, H. (1950) Studies in motivation and learning: II. Thirsty rats trained in a maze with food but no water, then run hungry. *J. exp. Psychol., 40,* 169-174.

GLEITMAN, H. *See also* Tolman and Gleitman (1949a) (1949b).

GLEITMAN, H., NACHMIAS, J., and NEISSER, U. (1954) The S-R reinforcement theory of extinction. *Psychol. Rev., 61,* 23-33

GOLDMAN, H. M. *See* Grice and Goldman (1955).

GOODRICH, K. P. (1959) Performance in different segments of an instrumental response chain as a function of reinforcement schedule. *J. exp. Psychol., 57,* 57-63.

GOODRICH, K. P. *See also* Goodrich, Ross, and Wagner (1957), Spence, Goodrich, and Ross (1959).

GOODRICH, K. P., ROSS, L. E., and WAGNER, A. R. (1957) Performance in eyelid conditioning following interpolated presentations of the UCS. *J. exp. Psychol., 53,* 214-217.

GOODSON, F. E., and BROWNSTEIN, A. (1955) Secondary reinforcing and motivating properties of stimuli contiguous with shock onset and termination. *J. comp. physiol. Psychol., 48,* 381-386.

GOODWIN, J., LONG, L., and WELCH, L. (1945) Generalization in memory. *J. exp. Psychol., 35,* 71-75

GORDON, W. M., and BERLYNE, D. E. (1954) Drive-level and flexibility in paired-associate nonsense-syllable learning. *Quart. J. exp. Psychol., 6,* 181-185.

GOSS, A. E. (1955) A stimulus-response analysis of the interaction of cue-producing and instrumental responses. *Psychol. Rev., 62,* 20-31.

GRAHAM, C. H., and GAGNÉ, R. M. (1940) The acquisition, extinction, and spontaneous recovery of a conditioned operant response. *J. exp. Psychol., 26,* 251-280.

GRAHAM, Frances K. (1943) Conditioned inhibition and conditioned excitation in transfer of discrimination. *J. exp. Psychol., 33,* 351-368.

GRANDINE, Lois, and HARLOW, H. F. (1948) Generalization of the characteristics of a single learned stimulus by monkeys. *J. comp. physiol. Psychol., 41,* 327-338.

GRANT, D. A. (1943a) The pseudo-conditioned eyelid response. *J. exp. Psychol., 32,* 139-149.

GRANT, D. A. (1943b) Sensitization and association in eyelid conditioning. *J. exp. Psychol., 32,* 201-212.

GRANT, D. A. A sensitized eyelid reaction related to the conditioned eyelid response. *J. exp. Psychol., 35,* 393-402.

GRANT, D. A. *See also* Norris and Grant (1948), Prokasy, Grant, and Meyers (1958).

GRANT, D. A., and ADAMS, J. K. (1944) 'Alpha' conditioning in the eyelid. *J. exp. Psychol., 34,* 136-142.

GRANT, D. A., and DITTMER, D. G. (1940a) An experimental investigation of Pavlov's cortical irradiation hypothesis. *J. exp. Psychol., 26,* 299-310.

GRANT, D. A., and DITTMER, D. G. (1940b) A tactile generalization gradient for a pseudo-conditioned response. *J. exp. Psychol., 26,* 404-412.

GRANT, D. A., HAKE, H. W., and HORNSETH, J. P. (1951) Acquisition and extinction of a verbal conditioned response with differing percentages of reinforcement. *J. exp. Psychol., 42,* 1-5.

GRANT, D. A., HORNSETH, J. P., and HAKE, H. W. (1950) The influence of the inter-trial interval of the Humphreys' 'random reinforcement' effect during the extinction of a verbal response. *J. exp. Psychol., 40,* 609-612.

GRANT, D. A., and NORRIS, Eugenia B. (1947) Eyelid conditioning as influenced by the presence of sensitized Beta-responses. *J. exp. Psychol., 37,* 423-433.

GRANT, D. A., RIOPELLE, A. J., and HAKE, H. W. (1950) Resistance to extinction and the pattern of reinforcement. I. Alternation of reinforcement and the conditioned eyelid response. *J. exp. Psychol., 40,* 53-60.

GRANT, D. A., and SCHILLER, J. J. (1953) Generalization of the conditioned galvanic skin response to visual stimuli. *J. exp. Psychol., 46,* 309-313.

GRANT, D. A., and SCHIPPER, L. M. (1952) The acquisition and extinction of conditioned eyelid responses as a function of the percentage of fixed-ratio random reinforcement. *J. exp. Psychol., 43,* 313-320.

GRANT, D. A., SCHIPPER, L. M., and ROSS, B. M. (1952) Effect of inter-trial interval during acquisition on extinction of the conditioned eyelid response following partial reinforcement. *J. exp. Psychol., 44,* 203-210.

GRANT, D. A., and SCHNEIDER, D. E. (1948) Intensity of the conditioned stimulus and strength of conditioning. I. The conditioned eyelid response to light.

GRANT, D. A., and SCHNEIDER, D. E. (1949) Intensity of the conditioned stimulus and strength of conditioning. II. The conditioned galvanic skin response to an auditory stimulus. *J. exp. Psychol., 39,* 35-40.

GREEN, A. *See* Lacey, Smith, and Green (1955).

GREENE, J. E. (1953) Magnitude of reward and acquisition of a black-white discrimination habit. *J. exp. Psychol., 46,* 113-119.

GREENE, J. E. *See also* Miller and Greene (1954).

GREENSPOON, J. (1955) The reinforcing effect of two spoken sounds on the frequency of two responses. *Amer. J. Psychol., 68,* 409-416.

GREGG, L. W. *See* Brogden and Gregg (1951).

GRETHER, W. F. (1938) Pseudo-conditioning without paired stimulation encountered in attempted backward conditioning. *J. comp. Psychol., 25,* 91-96.

GRICE, G. R. (1942) An experimental study of the gradient of reinforcement in maze learning. *J. exp. Psychol., 30,* 475-489.

GRICE, G. R. (1948a) An experimental test of the expectation theory of learning. *J. comp. physiol. Psychol., 41,* 137-143.

GRICE, G. R. (1948b) The relation of secondary reinforcement to delayed reward in visual discrimination learning. *J. exp. Psychol., 38,* 1-16.

GRICE, G. R. (1948c) The acquisition of a visual discrimination habit following response to a single stimulus. *J. exp. Psychol., 38,* 633-642.

GRICE, G. R. (1949) Visual discrimination learning with simultaneous and successive presentation of stimuli. *J. comp. physiol. Psychol., 42,* 365-373.

GRICE, G. R. (1951) The acquisition of a visual discrimination habit following extinction of response to one stimulus. *J. comp. physiol. Psychol., 44,* 149-153.

GRICE, G. R. (1952) Simultaneous acquisition of differential response strength to two stimulus dimensions. *J. gen. Psychol., 47,* 65-70.

GRICE, G. R., and DAVIS, J. D. (1957) Effect of irrelevant thirst motivation on a response learned with food reward. *J. exp. Psychol., 53,* 347-352.

GRICE, G. R., and DAVIS, J. D. (1958) Mediated stimulus equivalence and distinctiveness in human conditioning. *J. exp. Psychol., 55,* 565-571.

GRICE, G. R., and GOLDMAN, H. M. (1955) Generalized extinction and secondary reinforcement in visual discrimination learning with delayed reward. *J. exp. Psychol., 50,* 197-200.

GRICE, G. R., and SALTZ, E. (1950) The generalization of an instrumental response to stimuli varying in the size dimension. *J. exp. Psychol., 40,* 702-708.

GRINDLEY, G. C. (1929) Experiments on the influence of the amount of reward on learning in young chickens. *Brit. J. Psychol., 20,* 173-180.

GRINKER, R. R., and SPIEGEL, J. P. (1945) *War neuroses.* New York: Blakiston.

GULLIKSEN, H. (1932) Studies of transfer of response I. Relative versus absolute factors in the discrimination of size by the white rat. *J. genet. Psychol., 40,* 37-51

GULLIKSEN, H., and WOLFLE, D. L. (1938a) A theory of learning and transfer: I. *Psychometrika, 3,* 127-149.

GULLIKSEN, H., and WOLFLE, D. L. (1938b) A theory of learning and transfer. II. *Psychometrika, 3,* 225-251.

GUTHRIE, E. R. (1935) *The psychology of learning.* New York: Harper.

GUTHRIE, E. R. (1938) *The psychology of human conflict.* New York: Harper.

GUTHRIE, E. R. (1952) *The psychology of learning.* Revised. New York: Harper.

GUTHRIE, E. R. *See* Smith and Guthrie (1921), Yacorzynski and Guthrie (1937).

GUTHRIE, E. R., and HORTON, G. P. (1946) *Cats in a puzzle box.* New York: Rinehart.

GUTTMAN, N. (1953) Operant conditioning, extinction, and periodic reinforcement in relation to concentration of sucrose used as reinforcing agent. *J. exp. Psychol., 46,* 213-224.

GUTTMAN, N. (1954) Equal-reinforcement values for sucrose and glucose solutions compared with equal-sweetness values. *J. comp. physiol. Psychol., 47,* 358-361.

GUTTMAN, N. *See also* Dufort, Guttman, and Kimble (1954), Kalish and Guttman (1957).

GUTTMAN, N. and KALISH, H. I. (1956) Discriminability and stimulus generalization. *J. exp. Psychol., 51,* 79-88.

GUTTMAN, N., and KALISH, H. I. (1958) Experiments in discrimination. *Sci. Amer., 198,* 77-82.

GWINN, G. T. (1949) The effects of punishment on acts motivated by fear. *J. exp. Psychol., 39,* 260-269.

GWINN, G. T. (1951) Resistance to extinction of learned fear-drives. *J. exp. Psychol., 42,* 6-12

GYNTHER, M. D. (1957) Differential eyelid conditioning as a function of stimulus similarity and strength of response to the CS. *J. exp. Psychol., 53,* 408-416.

HADLEY, H. D., Jr. *See* Knott, Platt, and Hadley (1944).

HAGGARD, D. F. *See* Spence, Haggard, and Ross (1958a) (1958b).

HAKE, H. W. *See* Grant, Hake, and Hornseth (1951), Grant, Hornseth, and Hake (1950), Grant, Riopelle, and Hake (1950).

HALAS, E. S. *See* Brown and Halas (1957a, 1957b, 1957c).

HALL, C. S. (1951) The genetics of behavior. In S. S. Stevens (Ed.) *Handbook of experimental psychology.* New York: Wiley.

HALL, C. S. (1954) *A primer of Freudian psychology.* Cleveland: World Publishing Co.

HALL, J. F. (1951a) Studies in secondary reinforcement: I. Secondary reinforcement as a function of the frequency of primary reinforcement. *J. comp. physiol. Psychol., 44,* 246-251.

HALL, J. F. (1951b) Studies in secondary reinforcement: II. Secondary reinforcement as a function of the strength of drive during primary reinforcement. *J. comp. physiol. Psychol., 44,* 462-466.

HALL, J. F. (1956) The relationship between external stimulation, food deprivation, and activity. *J. comp. physiol. Psychol., 49,* 339-341.

HALL, J. F. *See also* Page and Hall (1953).

HALL, J. F., and KOBRICK, J. L. (1952) The relationships between three measures of response strength. *J. comp. physiol. Psychol., 45,* 280-282.

REFERENCES 515

HALL, M. *See* Hull and others (1940).

HAMEL, I. A. (1919) A study and analysis of the conditioned reflex. *Psychol. Monogr., 27,* No. 118.

HAMILTON, J. A., and KRECHEVSKY, I. (1933) Studies in the effect of shock upon behavior plasticity in the rat. *J. comp. Psychol., 16,* 237-253.

HAMMACK, J. T. *See* Long, Hammack, and Campbell (1959).

HANCOCK, W. *See* Amsel and Hancock (1957).

HANDLON, J. H. *See* Seward and Handlon (1952), Seward, Levy, and Handlon (1950) (1953).

HANER, C. F., and BROWN, Patricia A. (1955) Clarification of the instigation to action concept in the frustration-aggression hypothesis. *J. abnorm. soc. Psychol., 51,* 204-206.

HANEY, G. W. (1931) The effect of familiarity on maze performance of albino rats. *Univ. Calif. Publ. Psychol., 4,* 319-333.

HANRATTY, Jacqueline A. *See* Jenkins and Hanratty (1949).

HANSON, H. M. (1957) Discrimination training effect on stimulus generalization gradient for spectrum stimuli. *Science, 125,* 888-889.

HANSON, H. M. (1959) Effects of discrimination training on stimulus generalization. *J. exp. Psychol., 58,* 321-334.

HARE, Rachel. *See* Ritchie, Hay, and Hare (1951).

HARKER, George S. (1956) Delay of reward and performance of an instrumental response. *J. exp. Psychol., 51,* 303-310.

HARLOW, H. F. (1939) Forward conditioning, backward conditioning and pseudoconditioning in the goldfish. *J. genet. Psychol., 55,* 49-58.

HARLOW, H. F. (1940) The effects of incomplete curare paralysis upon formation and elicitation of conditioned responses in cats. *J. genet. Psychol., 56,* 273-282.

HARLOW, H. F. (1949) The formation of learning sets. *Psychol. Rev., 56,* 51-65.

HARLOW, H. F. (1950a) Analysis of discrimination learning by monkeys. *J. exp. Psychol., 40,* 26-39.

HARLOW, H. F. (1950b) Learning and satiation of response in intrinsically motivated complex puzzle performance by monkeys. *J. comp. physiol. Psychol., 43,* 289-294.

HARLOW, H. F. (1952) Learning. *Ann. Rev. Psychol., 3,* 29-54.

HARLOW, H. F. (1958a) The evolution of learning. In A. Roe and G. G. Simpson (Ed.) *Behavior and evolution.* New Haven: Yale University Press.

HARLOW, H. F. (1958b) The nature of love. *Amer. Psychologist. 13,* 673-685.

HARLOW, H. F. (1959) Learning set and error factory theory. In Koch, S. (Ed.) *Psychology: A study of a science.* Vol. II. New York: McGraw-Hill.

HARLOW, H. F. *See also* Butler and Harlow (1954), Grandine and Harlow (1948), Settlage and Harlow (1936).

HARLOW, H. F., DAVIS, R. T., SETTLAGE, P. H., and MEYER, D. R. (1952) Analysis of frontal and posterior association syndromes in brain-damaged monkeys. *J. comp. physiol. Psychol., 45,* 419-429.

HARLOW, H. F., HARLOW, M. K., and MEYER, D. K. (1950) Learning motivated by a manipulation drive. *J. exp. Psychol., 40,* 228-234.

HARLOW, H. F., and McCLEARN, G. E. (1954) Object discriminations learned by monkeys on the basis of manipulation motives. *J. comp. physiol. Psychol., 47,* 73-76.

HARLOW, H. F., and SETTLAGE, P. H. (1939) The effect of curarization of the fore part of the body upon the retention of conditioned responses in cats. *J. comp. Psychol., 27,* 45-48.

HARLOW, H. F., and STAGNER, R. (1933) Effect of complete striate muscle paralysis upon the learning process. *J. exp. Psychol., 16,* 283-294.

HARLOW, H. F., and TOLTZIEN, F. (1940) Formation of pseudo-conditioned responses in the cat. *J. gen. Psychol., 23,* 367-375.

HARLOW, H. F., and WARREN, J. M. (1952) Formation and transfer of discrimination learning sets. *J. comp. physiol. Psychol., 45,* 482-489.

HARLOW, M. K. *See* Harlow, Harlow, and Myer (1950).

HARRIS, J. D. (1941) Forward conditioning, backward conditioning, and pseudo-conditioning, and adaptation to the conditioned stimulus. *J. exp. Psychol., 28,* 491-502.

HARRISON, R. H. *See* Jenkins and Harrison (1958).

HARTER, N. *See* Bryan and Harter (1897).

HAY, Alice. *See* Ritchie, Hay, and Hare (1951).

HAYES, C. *See* Hayes, Thompson, and Hayes (1953a) (1953b).

HAYES, J. R. *See* Verplanck and Hayes (1953).

HAYES, K. J. (1953) The backward curve: A method for the study of learning. *Psychol. Rev., 60,* 269-275.

HAYES, K. J., THOMPSON, R., and HAYES, C. (1953a) Discrimination learning set in chimpanzees. *J. comp. physiol. Psychol., 46,* 99-104.

HAYES, K. J., THOMPSON, R., and HAYES, C. (1953b) Concurrent discrimination learning in chimpanzees. *J. comp. physiol. Psychol., 46,* 105-107.

HEATHERS, G. L., and ARAKELIAN, P. (1942) The relationship between strength of drive and rate of extinction of a bar-pressing reaction in the rat. *J. gen. Psychol., 24,* 243-248.

HEBB, D. O. (1946) On the nature of fear. *Psychol. Rev., 53,* 259-276.

HEBB, D. O. (1955) Drives and the C.N.S. (Conceptual Nervous System). *Psychol. Rev., 62,* 243-254.

HEFFERLINE, R. F. (1950) An experimental study of avoidance. *Genet. Psychol. Monogr., 42,* 231-234.

HEILBRONNER, K. (1912) Uber Gewohnung auf normalem und pathologischem Gebiete. *Grenzfr. Nerv.-u. Seelenleb., 13,* No. 87.

HELMICK, J. S. *See* Hilgard, Dutton, and Helmick (1949).

HENDERSON, R. L. *See* Marx, Henderson, and Roberts (1955).

HENRY, C. E. *See* Knott and Henry (1941).

HERB, Frances H. (1940) Latent Learning—non-reward followed by food in blinds. *J. comp. Psychol., 29*, 247-255.

HERBERT, M. J., and ARNOLD, W. J. (1947) A reaction-chaining apparatus. *J. comp. physiol. Psychol., 40*, 227-230.

HERMAN, P. N. *See* Passey and Herman (1955).

HERON, W. T. (1949) Internal stimuli and learning. *J. comp. physiol. Psychol., 42*, 486-492.

HERRNSTEIN, R. J. *See* Boren, Sidman, and Herrnstein (1959).

HESS, E. H. (1958) "Imprinting" in animals. *Sci. Amer., 198*, 81-90.

HETHERINGTON, A. W., and RANSON, S. W. (1942) The relation of various hypothalamic lesions to adiposity in the rat. *J. comp. Neurol., 76*, 475-499.

HEYER, A. W., Jr. (1951a) Studies in motivation and retention. III. A methodological approach to the independent manipulation of tissue dehydration and duration of water deprivation. *Comp. Psychol. Monogr. 20*, 251-272.

HEYER, A. W., Jr. (1951b) Studies in motivation and retention. IV. The influence of dehydration on acquisition and retention of the maze habit. *Comp. Psychol. Monogr., 20*, 273-286.

HEYER, A. W., Jr. *See also* O'Kelly and Heyer (1948) (1951).

HILDEN, A. H. (1937) An action-current study of the conditioned hand withdrawal. *Psychol. Monogr., 49*, No. 217, 173-204.

HILGARD, E. R. (1931) Conditioned eyelid reactions to a light stimulus based on the reflex wink to sound. *Psychol. Monogr., 41*, No. 184, 50 pp.

HILGARD, E. R. (1933a) Modification of reflexes and conditioned reactions. *J. gen. Psychol., 9*, 210-215.

HILGARD, E. R. (1933) Reinforcement and inhibition of eyelid reflexes. *J. gen. Psychol., 8*, 85-113.

HILGARD, E. R. (1938a) A summary and evaluation of alternative procedures for the construction of Vincent curves. *Psychol. Bull., 35*, 282-297.

HILGARD, E. R. (1938b) An algebraic analysis of conditioned discrimination in man. *Psychol. Rev., 45*, 472-496.

HILGARD, E. R. (1956) *Theories of Learning*, (second edition). New York: Appleton-Century-Crofts.

HILGARD, E. R. *See also* Campbell and Hilgard (1936), Cohen, Hilgard, and Wendt (1933), Marquis and Hilgard (1936).

HILGARD, E. R., and ALLEN, M. K. (1938) An attempt to condition finger reactions based on motor point stimulation. *J. gen. Psychol., 18*, 203-207.

HILGARD, E. R., and BIEL, W. C. (1937) Reflex sensitization and conditioning of eyelid responses at intervals near simultaneity. *J. gen. Psychol., 16*, 223-234.

HILGARD, E. R., and CAMPBELL, A. A. (1936) The course of acquisition and retention of conditioned eyelid responses in man. *J. exp. Psychol., 19*, 227-247.

HILGARD, E. R., CAMPBELL, R. K., and SEARS, W. N. (1938) Conditioned discrimination: the effect of knowledge of stimulus-relationships. *Amer. J. Psychol., 51*, 498-506.

HILGARD, E. R., DUTTON, C. E., and HELMICK, J. S. (1949) Attempted pupillary conditioning at four stimulus intervals. *J. exp. Psychol., 39*, 683-689.

HILGARD, E. R., and HUMPHREYS, L. G. (1938a) The effect of supporting and antagonistic voluntary instructions on conditioned discrimination. *J. exp. Psychol., 22*, 291-304.

HILGARD, E. R., and HUMPHREYS, L. G. (1938b) The retention of conditioned discrimination in man. *J. gen. Psychol., 19*, 111-125.

HILGARD, E. R., JONES, L. V., and KAPLAN, S. J. (1951) Conditioned discrimination as related to anxiety. *J. exp. Psychol., 42*, 94-99.

HILGARD, E. R., and MARQUIS, D. G. (1935) Acquisition, extinction, and retention of conditioned lid responses to light in dogs. *J. comp. Psychol., 19*, 29-58.

HILGARD, E. R., and MARQUIS, D. G., (1936) Conditioned eyelid responses in monkeys, with a comparison of dog, monkey, and man. *Psychol. Monogr., 47*, No. 212, 186-198.

HILGARD, E. R., and MARQUIS, D. G. (1940) *Conditioning and learning*, New York: Appleton-Century-Crofts.

HILGARD, E. R., MILLER, J., and OHLSON, J. A. (1933) Three attempts to secure pupillary conditioning to auditory stimuli near the absolute threshold. *J. exp. Psychol., 16*, 283-294.

HILL, C. J. (1939 Goal gradient, anticipation, and perseveration in compound trial-and-error learning. *J. exp. Psychol., 25*, 566-585.

HILL, J. H. *See* Stellar and Hill (1952).

HILLMAN, Beverly, HUNTER, W. S., and KIMBLE, G. A. (1953) The effect of drive level on the maze performance of the white rat. *J. comp. physiol. Psychol., 46*, 87-89.

HOFFELD, D. R., THOMPSON, R. F., and BROGDEN, W. J. (1958) Effect of stimuli time relations during preconditioning training upon the magnitude of sensory preconditioning. *J. exp. Psychol., 56*, 437-442.

HOLDER, E. E. *See* Holder and others (1957).

HOLDER, W. B., MARX, M. H., HOLDER, E. E., and COLLIER, G. (1957) Response strength as a function of delay of reward in a runway. *J. exp. Psychol., 53*, 316-323.

HOLLINGWORTH, H. L. (1928) *Psychology, its facts and principles*. New York: Appleton-Century.

HOLT, E. B., (1914) *The concept of consciousness*. New York: Macmillan.

HOLT, E. B. (1931) *Animal drive and the learning process*. New York: Holt.

HOLTZMAN, W. H. *See* Bitterman and Holtzman (1952).

HONZIK, C. H. *See* Tolman and Honzik (1930).

HOPKINS, C. O. (1955) Effectiveness of secondary reinforcing stimuli as a function of the quantity of quality of food reinforcement. *J. exp. Psychol., 50*, 339-342.

HORENSTEIN, Betty R. (1951) Performance of conditioned responses as a function of strength of hunger drive. *J. comp. physiol. Psychol.*, *44*, 210-224.

HORNSETH, J. P. *See* Grant, Hake, and Hornseth (1951), Grant Hornseth, and Hake (1950).

HOROWITZ, L. *See* Kling, Horowitz, and Delhagen (1956).

HORTON, G. P. *See* Guthrie and Horton (1946).

HOUSE, Betty J. *See* Zeaman and House (1951).

HOUSE, Betty J., and ZEAMAN, D. (1958) Reward and nonreward in the discrimination learning of imbeciles. *J. comp. physiol. Psychol.*, *51*, 615-618.

HOUSE, Betty J., and ZEAMAN, D. (1959) Position discrimination and reversals in low-grade retardates. *J. comp. physiol. Psychol.*, *52*, 564-565.

HOVLAND, C. I. (1936) "Inhibition of reinforcement" and phenomena of experimental extinction. *Proc. nat. Acad. Sci.*, *22*, 430-433.

HOVLAND, C. I. (1937a) The generalization of conditioned responses. I. The sensory generalization of conditioned responses with varying frequencies of tone. *J. gen. Psychol.*, *17*, 125-148.

HOVLAND, C. I. (1937b) The generalization of conditioned responses. II. The sensory generalization of conditioned responses with varying intensities of tone. *J. genet. Psychol.*, *51*, 279-291.

HOVLAND, C. I. (1937c) The generalization of conditioned responses. III. Extinction, spontaneous recovery, and disinhibition of conditioned and of generalized responses. *J. exp. Psychol.*, *21*, 47-62.

HOVLAND, C. I. (1937d) The generalization of conditioned responses. IV. The effects of varying amounts of reinforcement upon the degree of generalization of conditioned responses. *J. exp. Psychol.*, *21*, 261-276.

HOVLAND, C. I. *See also* Dollard and others (1939), Hull and others (1940).

HOVLAND, C. I., and KURTZ, K. H. (1952) Experimental studies in rote learning theory: X. Pre-learning syllable familiarization and the length-difficulty relationship. *J. exp. Psychol.*, *44*, 31-39.

HOVLAND, C. I., and RIESEN, A. H. (1940) Magnitude of galvanic and vasomotor response as a function of stimulus intensity. *J. gen. Psychol.*, *23*, 103-13.

HOVLAND, C. I., and SEARS, R. R. (1938) Experiments on motor conflict. I. Types of conflict and their modes of resolution. *J. exp. Psychol.*, *23*, 477-492.

HOY, W. J. *See* Smith and Hoy (1954).

HUDGINS, C. V. (1933) Conditioning and the voluntary control of the pupillary light reflex. *J. gen. Psychol.*, *8*, 3-51.

HUDGINS, C. V. (1935) Steckle and Renshaw on the conditioned iridic reflex: a discussion. *J. gen. Psychol.*, *12*, 208-214.

HUGHES, B., and SCHLOSBERG, H. (1939) Conditioning in the white rat. IV. The conditioned lid reflex. *J. exp. Psychol.*, *23*, 641-650.

HULICKA, I. M. *See* Capehart, Viney, and Hulicka (1958).

HULL, C. L. (1929) A functional interpretation of the conditioned reflex. *Psychol. Rev.*, *36*, 498-511.

HULL, C. L. (1930a) Knowledge and purpose as habit mechanisms. *Psychol. Rev., 37,* 511-525.

HULL, C. L. (1930b) Simple trial-and-error learning: a study in psychological theory. *Psychol. Rev., 37,* 241-256.

HULL, C. L. (1932) The goal-gradient hypothesis and maze learning. *Psychol. Rev., 39,* 25-43.

HULL, C. L. (1933) Differential habituation to internal stimuli in the albino rat. *J. comp. Psychol., 16,* 255-273.

HULL, C. L. (1934a) The concept of the habit-family hierarchy and maze learning. *Psychol. Rev., 41,* 33-54, 134-152.

HULL, C. L. (1934b) The rat's speed-of-locomotion gradient in the approach to food. *J. comp. Psychol., 17,* 393-422.

HULL, C. L. (1934c) Learning: II. The factor of the conditioned reflex. In C. Murchison, (Ed.)., *A handbook of general experimental psychology.* Worcester, Mass.: Clark University Press.

HULL, C. L. (1935a) The conflicting psychologies of learning—A way out. *Psychol. Rev., 42,* 491-516.

HULL, C. L. (1935b) The influence of caffeine and other factors on certain phenomena of rote learning. *J. gen. Psychol., 13,* 249-274.

HULL, C. L. (1935c) The mechanism of the assembly of behavior segments in novel combinations suitable for problem solution. *Psychol. Rev., 42,* 219-245.

HULL, C. L. (1937) Mind, mechanism, and adaptive behavior. *Psychol. Rev., 44,* 1-32.

HULL, C. L. (1938) The goal-gradient hypothesis applied to some "field-force" problems in the behavior of young children. *Psychol. Rev., 45,* 271-299.

HULL, C. L. (1939b) The problem of stimulus equivalence in behavior theory. *Psychol. Rev., 46,* 9-30.

HULL, C. L. (1940) Explorations in the patterning of stimuli conditioned to the G.S.R. *J. exp. Psychol., 27,* 95-110.

HULL, C. L. (1943) *Principles of behavior.* New York: Appleton-Century-Crofts.

HULL, C. L. (1945) The discrimination of stimulus configurations and the hypothesis of afferent neural interaction. *Psychol. Rev., 52,* 133-142.

HULL, C. L. (1947a) Reactively heterogeneous compound trial-and-error learning with distributed trials and terminal reinforcement. *J. exp. Psychol., 37,* 118-135.

HULL, C. L. (1947b) The problem of primary stimulus generalization. *Psychol. Rev., 54,* 120-134.

HULL, C. L. (1949) Stimulus intensity dynamism (V) and stimulus generalization. *Psychol. Rev., 56,* 67-76.

HULL, C. L. (1950a) Behavior postulates and corollaries—1949. *Psychol. Rev., 57,* 173-180.

HULL, C. L. (1950b) Simple qualitative discrimination learning. *Psychol. Rev.*, *57*, 303-313.

HULL, C. L. (1951) *Essentials of behavior.* New Haven: Yale University Press.

HULL, C. L. (1952) *A behavior system.* New Haven: Yale University Press.

HULL, C. L. *See also* Bass and Hull (1934), Felsinger and others (1947), Gladstone and others (1947).

HULL, C. L., FELSINGER, J. M., GLADSTONE, A. I., and YAMAGUCHI, H. G. (1947) A proposed quantification of habit strength. *Psychol. Rev.*, *54*, 237-254.

HULL, C. L., HOVLAND, C. I., ROSS, R. T., HALL, M., PERKINS, D. T., and FITCH, F. B. (1940) *Mathematico-deductive theory of rote learning.* New Haven: Yale University Press.

HULL, C. L., LIVINGSTON, J. R., ROUSE, R. O., and BARKER, A. N. (1951) True, sham, and esophageal feeding as reinforcements. *J. comp. physiol. Psychol.*, *44*, 236-245.

HULL, C. L., and SPENCE, K. W. (1938) "Correction" vs. "non-correction" method of trial-and-error learning in rats. *J. comp. Psychol.*, *25*, 127-145.

HULSE, S. H., Jr. (1958) Amount and percentage of reinforcement and duration of goal confinement in conditioning and extinction. *J. exp. Psychol.*, *56*, 48-57.

HUMPHREYS, L. G. (1939a) The effect of random alternation of reinforcement on the acquisition and extinction of conditioned eyelid reactions. *J. exp. Psychol.*, *25*, 141-158.

HUMPHREYS, L. G. (1939b) Acquisition and extinction of verbal expectations in a situation analogous to conditioning. *J. exp. Psychol.*, *25*, 294-301.

HUMPHREYS, L. G. (1939c) Generalization as a function of method of reinforcement. *J. exp., Psychol.*, *25*, 361-372.

HUMPHREYS, L. G. *See* also Hilgard and Humphreys (1938a) (1938b).

HUMPHREYS, L. G., MILLER, J., and ELLSON, D. G. (1940) The effect of intertrial interval on the acquisition, extinction, and recovery of verbal expectation. *J. exp. Psychol.*, *27*, 195-202.

HUNT, E. L. (1949) Establishment of conditioned responses in chick embryos. *J. comp. physiol. Psychol.*, *42*, 107-117.

HUNT, H. F. *See* Brady and Hunt (1951) and (1955), Brady, Hunt, and Geller (1954), Brady, Stebbins, and Hunt (1953).

HUNT, H. F., and BRADY, J. V. (1955) Some effects of punishment and intercurrent "anxiety" on a simple operant. *J. comp. physiol. Psychol.*, *48*, 305-310.

HUNT, H. F., JERNBERG, P., and BRADY, J. V. (1952) The effect of electroconvulsive shock ECS on a conditioned emotional response: The effect of post-ECS extinction on the reappearance of the response. *J. comp. physiol. Psychol.*, *45*, 589-599.

HUNT, H. F., JERNBERG, P., and LAWLOR, W. G. (1953) The effect of electroconvulsive shock on a conditioned emotional response: The effect of electroconvulsive shock under ether anesthesia. *J. comp. physiol. Psychol.*, *46*, 64-68.

HUNT, H. F., JERNBERG, P., and OTIS, L. S. (1953) The effect of carbon disulphide convulsions on a conditioned emotional response. *J. comp. physiol. Psychol., 46,* 465-469.

HUNT, J. McV. *See* Winnick and Hunt (1951).

HUNTER, I. M. L. (1952) Discrimination learning and transposition behavior of rats in a water-tank apparatus. *Quart. J. Psychol., IV,* 91-100.

HUNTER, I. M. L. (1953) The absolute and relative theories of transposition behavior in rats. *J. comp. physiol. Psychol., 46,* 493-497.

HUNTER, I. M. L. (1954) Children's reactions to bivariant stimuli. *Brit. J. Psychol., 45,* 288-293.

HUNTER, J. J. *See* Ross and Hunter (1959).

HUNTER, W. S. (1914) The auditory sensitivity of the white rat. *J. Anim. Behav., 4,* 215-222.

HUNTER, W. S. (1928) *Human behavior.* Chicago: University of Chicago.

HUNTER, W. S. (1930) A further consideration of the sensory control of the maze habit in the white rat. *J. genet. Psychol., 38,* 3-19.

HUNTER, W. S. (1934) Learning: IV. Experimental studies of learning. In Murchison, C., *A handbook of general experimental psychology.* Worcester: Clark University Press.

HUNTER, W. S. (1935) Conditioning and extinction in the rat. *Brit. J. Psychol., 26,* 135-148.

HUNTER, W. S. (1937) Muscle potentials and conditioning in the rat. *J. exp. Psychol., 21,* 611-624.

HUNTER, W. S. *See also* Hillman, Hunter, and Kimble (1953), Prosser and Hunter (1936).

HURWITZ, H. M. B. (1956) Conditioned responses in rats reinforced by light. *Brit. J. Anim. Behav., 4,* 31-33.

HUTT, P. J. (1954) Rate of bar pressing as a function of quality and quantity of food reward. *J. comp. physiol. Psychol., 47,* 235-239.

HUZIMORI, B. *See* Motokawa and Huzimori (1949).

IRION, A. L. *See* McGeoch and Irion (1952).

IRWIN, O. C. (1939) Toward a theory of conditioning. *Psychol. Rev., 46,* 425-444.

ISCOE, I. *See* Stevenson and Iscoe (1954) (1955), Stevenson, Iscoe, and McConnel (1955).

IWAHARA, S., and MARX, M. (1950) Cognitive transfer in discrimination learning. *Amer. Psycologist, 5,* 479.

IWAMA, K. (1950) Delayed conditioned reflex in man and brain waves. *Tohoku J. Exp. Med., 52,* 53-62.

IWAMA, K., and ABE, M. (1952) Electroencephalographic study of conditioned salivary reflexes in human subjects. *Tohoku J. Exp. Med., 56,* 345-355.

IWAMA, K., and ABE, M. (1953) Conditioned galvanic skin reflex and electroencephalogram. *Tohoku J. Exp. Med., 57,* 327-335.

JACKSON, T. A. *See* Jacobsen, Wolfe, and Jackson (1935).

JACOBS, A. *See* Brown and Jacobs (1949).

JACOBSEN, C. F. *See* Crawford, Fulton, Jacobsen, and Wolfe (1948).

JACOBSEN, C. F., WOLFE, J. B., and JACKSON, T. A. (1935) An experimental analysis of the functions of the frontal association areas in primates. *J. nerv. ment. Dis., 82,* 1-14.

JAMES, W. (1890) *Principles of psychology.* New York: Holt.

JAMES, W. T. *See* Liddell, James, and Anderson (1934).

JARVIK, M. E. (1953) Discrimination of colored food and food signs by primates. *J. comp. physiol. Psychol., 46,* 390-392.

JASPER, H., and SHAGASS, C. (1941a) Conditioning the occipital alpha rhythm in man. *J. exp. Psychol., 28,* 373-388.

JASPER, H. and SHAGASS, G. (1941b) Conscious time judgments related to conditioned time intervals and voluntary control of the alpha rhythm. *J. exp. Psychol., 28,* 503-508.

JASPER, H. H. *See* Morrell and Jasper (1956), Morrel, Roberts, and Jasper (1956).

JAYNES, J. (1956) Imprinting: The interaction of learned and innate behavior: I. development and generalization. *J. comp. physiol. Psychol., 49,* 201-206.

JAYNES, J. (1957) Imprinting: The interaction of learned and innate behavior: II. the critical period. *J. comp. physiol. Psychol., 50,* 6-10.

JEEVES, M. *See* North and Jeeves (1956).

JENKINS, G. *See* Wallace, Blackwell, and Jenkins (1941).

JENKINS, H. M., and HARRISON, R. H. (1958) Auditory generalization in the pigeons. Washington: Air Research and Development command. TN No. 58-443; Astia Document No. 158248.

JENKINS, J. J. and HANRATTY, Jacqueline A. (1949) Drive intensity discrimination in the albino rat. *J. comp. physiol. Psychol., 42,* 228-232.

JENKINS, T. N. *See* Warden, Jenkins, and Warner (1940).

JENKINS, W. O. (1950) A temporal gradient of derived reinforcement. *Amer. J. Psychol., 63,* 237-243.

JENKINS, W. O., and CLAYTON, Frances L. (1949) Rate of responding and amount of reinforcement. *J. comp. physiol. Psychol., 42,* 174-181.

JENKINS, W. O., McFANN, H., and CLAYTON, Frances L. (1950) A methodological study of extinction following aperiodic and continuous reinforcement. *J. comp. physiol. Psychol., 43,* 155-167.

JENKINS, W. O., PASCAL, G. R., and WALKER, R. W., Jr. (1958) Deprivation and generalization. *J. exp. Psychol., 56,* 274-277.

JENKINS, W. O., and RIGBY, Marilyn K. (1950) Partial (periodic) versus continuous reinforcement in resistance to extinction. *J. comp. physiol. Psychol., 43,* 30-40.

JENKINS, W. O., and STANLEY, J. C., Jr. (1950) Partial reinforcement: A review and critique. *Psychol. Bull.*, 47, 193-234.

JENSEN, D. D. (1957) Experiments on "learning" in Paramecium. *Science, 125,* 191-192.

JERNBERG, P. *See* Hunt, Jernberg, and Brady (1952), Hunt, Jernberg, and Lawlor (1953), Hunt, Jernberg, and Otis (1953).

JOHNSGARD, K. W. (1957) The role of contrast in stimulus intensity dynamism (V). *J. exp. Psychol.*, 53, 173-179.

JOHNSON, E. E. (1952) The role of motivational strength in latent learning. *J. comp. physiol. Psychol.*, 45, 526-530.

JOHNSON, E. P. *See* Shagass and Johnson (1943).

JONES, F. N. *See* Wenger, Jones, and Jones (1956).

JONES, H. J. *See* Wenger, Jones, and Jones (1956).

JONES, Helen M. *See* Mowrer and Jones (1943) (1945).

JONES, L. V. *See* Hilgard, Jones, and Kaplan (1951).

JONES, M. R. (Ed.) (1954, 1955, 1956, 1957, 1958, 1959) *Nebraska Symposium on Motivation.* Lincoln: University of Nebraska Press.

JONES, R. B. *See* Seward and others (1957).

KADYKOV, B. I. *See* Zeliony and Kadykov (1938).

KAGAN, J. (1955) Differential reward value of incomplete and complete sexual behavior. *J. comp. physiol. Psychol.*, 48, 59-65.

KAGAN, J., and BERKUN, M. M. (1954) The reward value of running activity. *J. comp. physiol. Psychol.*, 47, 108.

KALISH, D. *See* Tolman, Ritchie, and Kalish (1946a, 1946b, 1947a, 1947b).

KALISH, H. I. (1954) Strength of fear as a function of the number of acquisition and extinction trials. *J. exp. Psychol.*, 47, 1-9.

KALISH, H. I. (1958) The relationship between discriminability and generalization: a re-evaluation. *J. exp. Psychol.*, 55, 637-644.

KALISH, H. I. *See also* Brown, Kalish, and Farber (1951), Cohen and others (1954), Guttman and Kalish (1956) (1958), Tolman, Ritchie, and Kalish (1946a) (1946b) (1947a) (1947b).

KALISH, H. I., and GUTTMAN, N. (1957) Stimulus generalization after equal training on two stimuli. *J. exp. Psychol.*, 53, 139-144.

KAMIN, L. J. (1954) Traumatic avoidance learning: The effects of CS-US interval with a trace conditioning procedure. *J. comp. physiol. Psychol.*, 47, 65-72.

KAMIN, L. J. (1956) The effects of termination of the CS and avoidance of the US on avoidance learning. *J. comp. physiol. Psychol.*, 49, 420-424.

KAMIN, L. J. (1957a) The gradient delay of secondary reward in avoidance learning. *J. comp. physiol. Psychol.*, 50, 445-449.

KAMIN, L. J. (1957b) The delay of secondary reward gradient in avoidance learning tested on avoidance trials only. *J. comp. physiol. Psychol., 50,* 450-456.

KAMIN, L. J. (1959) The delay of punishment gradient. *J. comp. physiol. Psychol., 52,* 434-437.

KAMIN, L. J. *See also* Solomon, Kamin, and Wynne (1953).

KANNER, J. H. (1954) A test of whether the "nonrewarded" animals learned as much as the "rewarded" animals in the California latent learning study. *J. exp. Psychol., 48,* 175-183.

KANNER, J. H. *See* Kendler and Kanner (1950).

KANTROW, R. W. (1937) An investigation of conditioned feeding responses and concomitant adaptive behavior in young infants. *Univ. Ia. Stud. Child Welf., 13,* No. 337, 64 pp.

KAPLAN, S. J. *See* Brown, Gentry, and Kaplan (1948), Gentry, Brown, and Kaplan (1949).

KAPPAUF, W. E., and SCHLOSBERG, H. (1937) Conditioned responses in the white rat. III. Conditioning as a function of the length of the period of delay. *J. genet. Psychol., 50,* 27-45.

KARN, H. W. (1947) Sensory preconditioning and incidental learning in human subjects. *J. exp. Psychol., 37,* 540-544.

KARN, H. W., and PORTER, J. M., Jr. (1946) The effect of certain pretraining procedures upon maze performance and their significance for the concept of latent learning. *J. exp. Psychol., 36,* 461-469.

KATTSOFF, L. O. (1939) Philosophy, psychology, and postulational technique. *Psychol. Rev., 46,* 62-74.

KATZ, M. S., and DETERLINE, W. A. (1958) Apparent learning in the Paramecium. *J. comp. physiol. Psychol., 51,* 243-247.

KATZ, S. *See* Kendler and others (1957).

KATZENMEYER, W. G. *See* Spielberger and Katzenmeyer (1959).

KAUFMAN, Edna L., and MILLER, N. E. (1949) Effect of number of reinforcements on strength of approach in an approach-avoidance conflict. *J. comp. physiol. Psychol., 42,* 65-74.

KAUFMAN, M. E., and PETERSON, W. M. (1958) Acquisition of a learning set by normal and mentally retarded children. *J. comp. physiol. Psychol., 51,* 619-621.

KELLER, F. S. (1941) Light-aversion in the white rat. *Psychol. Rec., 4,* 235-250.

KELLER, F. S. *See also* Dinsmoor, Kish, and Keller (1953), Wilson and Keller (1953).

KELLER, F. S., and SCHOENFELD, W. N. (1950) *Principles of psychology.* New York: Appleton-Century-Crofts.

KELLOGG, W. N. (1938) Evidence for both stimulus-substitution and original anticipatory responses in the conditioning of dogs. *J. exp. Psychol., 22,* 186-192.

KELLOGG, W. N. (1939) "Positive" and "negative" conditioning, without contraction of the essential muscles during the period of training. *Psychol. Bull.*, *36*, 575.

KELLOGG, W. N. (1947) Is 'spinal conditioning' conditioning? Reply to 'a comment.' *J. exp. Psychol.*, *37*, 263-265.

KELLOGG, W. N. (1949) 'Superstitious' behavior in animals. *Psychol. Rev.*, *56*, 172-175.

KELLOGG, W. N. *See also* Deese and Kellogg (1949), Pronko and Kellogg (1942), Spooner and Kellogg (1947).

KELLOGG, W. N., DEESE, J., PRONKO, N. H., and FEINBERG, M. (1947) An attempt to condition the *chronic* spinal dog. *J. exp. Psychol.*, *37*, 99-117.

KELLOGG, W. N., PRONKO, N. H., and DEESE, J. (1946) Spinal conditioning in dogs. *Science*, *103*, 49-50.

KELLOGG, W. N., SCOTT, V. B., DAVIS, R. C., and WOLF, I. S. (1940) Is movement necessary for learning. *J. comp. Psychol.*, *29*, 43-74.

KELLOGG, W. N., and WALKER, E. L. (1938a) "Ambiguous conditioning," a phenomenon of bilateral transfer. *J. comp. Psychol.*, *26*, 63-77.

KELLOGG, W. N., and WALKER, E. L. (1938b) An analysis of the bilateral transfer of conditioning in dogs, in terms of the frequency, amplitude, and latency of the responses. *J. gen. Psychol.*, *18*, 253-265.

KELLOGG, W. N., and WOLF, I. S. (1939) The nature of the response retained after several varieties of conditioning in the same subjects. *J. exp. Psychol.*, *24*, 366-383.

KELLY, E. L. (1934) An experimental attempt to produce artificial chromaesthesia by the technique of the conditioned response. *J. exp. Psychol.*, *17*, 315-341.

KENDLER, H. H. (1945a) Drive interaction: I. Learning as a function of the simultaneous presence of the hunger and thirst drives. *J. exp. Psychol.*, *35*, 96-109.

KENDLER, H. H. (1945b) Drive interaction: II. Experimental analysis of role of drive in learning theory. *J. exp. Psychol.*, *35*, 188-198.

KENDLER, H. H. (1946) The influence of simultaneous hunger and thirst drives upon the learning of two opposed spatial responses of the white rat. *J. exp. Psychol.*, *36*, 212-220.

KENDLER, H. H. (1947a) An investigation of latent learning in a T-maze. *J. comp. physiol. Psychol.*, *40*, 265-270.

KENDLER, H. H. (1947b) A comparison of learning under motivated and satiated conditions in the white rat. *J. exp. Psychol.*, *37*, 545-549.

KENDLER, H. H. (1949) An experimental examination of the nonselective principle of association of drive stimuli. *Amer. J. Psychol.*, *62*, 382-391.

KENDLER, H. H. (1950) "What is learned?"—A theoretical blind alley. *Trans. N. Y. Acad. Sci.*, *13*, 73-77.

KENDLER, H. H. (1952) "What is learned?"—A theoretical blind alley. *Psychol. Rev.*, *59*, 269-277.

KENDLER, H. H., and KANNER, J. H. (1950) A further test of the ability of rats to learn the location of food when motivated by thirst. *J. exp. Psychol., 40,* 762-765.

KENDLER, H. H., and LAW, Florence E. (1950) An experimental test of the selective principle of association of drive stimuli. *J. exp. Psychol., 40,* 299-304.

KENDLER, H. H., and LEVINE, S. (1953) A more sensitive test of irrelevant-incentive learning under conditions of satiation. *J. comp. physiol. Psychol., 46,* 271-273.

KENDLER, H. H., LEVINE, S., ALTCHEK, E., and PETERS, H. (1952) Studies of the effect of change of drive: II. From hunger to different intensities of a thirst drive in a T-maze. *J. exp. Psychol., 44,* 1-3.

KENDLER, H. H., and MENCHER, Helen C. (1948) The ability of rats to learn the location of food when motivated by thirst—an experimental reply to Leeper. *J. exp. Psychol., 38,* 82-88.

KENDLER, H. H., PLISKOFF, S. S., D'AMATO, M. R., and KATZ, S. (1957) Non-reinforcements versus reinforcements as variables in the partial-reinforcement effect. *J. exp. Psychol., 53,* 269-276.

KENDLER, H. H., and UNDERWOOD, B. J. (1948) The role of reward in conditioning theory. *Psychol. Bull. 55,* 209-215.

KENDLER, Tracy S. (1950) An experimental investigation of transposition as a function of the difference between training and test stimuli. *J. exp. Psychol., 40,* 552-562.

KESSEN, M. L. *See* Berkun, Kessen, and Miller (1952), Miller and Kessen (1952).

KESSEN, W. (1953) Response strength and conditioned stimulus intensity. *J. exp. Psychol., 45,* 82-86.

KILLAM, K. F. *See* Olds, Killam, and Bach-Y-Rita (1956).

KIMBLE, G. A. (1947) Conditioning as a function of the time between conditioned and unconditioned stimuli. *J. exp. Psychol., 37,* 1-15.

KIMBLE, G. A. (1949) An experimental test of a two-factor theory of inhibition. *J. exp. Psychol., 39,* 15-23.

KIMBLE, G. A. (1951) Behavior strength as a function of the intensity of the hunger drive. *J. exp. Psychol., 41,* 341-348.

KIMBLE, G. A. (1955) Shock intensity and avoidance learning. *J. comp. physiol. Psychol., 48,* 281-284.

KIMBLE, G. A. (1956) Behavior theories and a counseling case: A symposium. Reinforcement theory. *J. counsel. Psychol., 3,* 112-115.

KIMBLE, G. A. *See also* Dufort, Guttman, and Kimble (1954); Dufort and Kimble (1956) and (1958), Hillman, Hunter, and Kimble (1953).

KIMBLE, G. A., and DUFORT, R. H. (1956) The associative factor in eyelid conditioning. *J. exp. Psychol., 52,* 386-391.

KIMBLE, G. A., MANN, Lucie I., and DUFORT, R. H. (1955) Classical and instrumental eyelid conditioning. *J. exp. Psychol., 49,* 407-417.

KIMBLE, G. A., and OST, J. W. P. (1961) A conditioned inhibitory process in eyelid conditioning. *J. exp. Psychol.*, (in press).

KINCAID, W. D. *See* Logan, Beier, and Kincaid (1956).

KING, G. F. *See* Denny and King (1955).

KING, H. E., and LANDIS, C. (1943) A comparison of eyelid responses conditioned with reflex and voluntary reinforcement in normal individuals and psychiatric patients. *J. exp. Psychol.*, *33*, 210-220.

KING, R. A. (1959) The effects of training and motivation on the components of a learned instrumental response. Unpublished Ph.D. dissertation. Duke University.

KINNAMON, A. J. (1902) Mental life of two macacus rhesus monkeys in captivity. *Amer J. Psychol.*, *13*, 98-148.

KINNEY, G. C. *See* Smith and Kinney (1956).

KISH, G. B. (1955b) Avoidance learning to the onset and cessation of conditioned stimulus energy. *J. exp. Psychol.*, *50*, 31-38.

KISH, G. B. (1955a) Learning when the onset of illumination is used as reinforcing stimulus. *J. comp. physiol. Psychol.*, *48*, 261-264.

KISH, G. B. *See also* Dinsmoor, Kish, and Keller (1953).

KJERSTAD, C. L. (1919) The form of the learning curves for memory. *Psychol. Monogr.*, *26*, No. 116, pp. 89.

KLEE, J. B. *See also* Maier and Klee (1945).

KLEITMAN, N. (1927) The influence of starvation on the rate of secretion of saliva elicited by pilocarpine, and its bearing on conditioned salivation. *Amer. J. Physiol.*, *82*, 686-692.

KLEITMAN, N. *See also* Whatmore and Kleitman (1946), Whatmore, Morgan, and Kleitman (1946).

KLEITMAN, N., and CRISLER, G. (1927) A quantitative study of a salivary conditioned reflex. *Amer. J. Physiol.*, *79*, 571-614.

KLING, J. W. (1952) Generalization of extinction of an instrumental response to stimuli varying in the size dimension. *J. exp. Psychol.*, *44*, 339-346.

KLING, J. W., HOROWITZ, L., and DELEHAGEN, J. E. (1956) Light as a positive reinforcer for rat responding. *Psychol. Rep. 2*, 337-340.

KLUVER, H. (1933) *Behavior mechanisms in monkeys.* Chicago: Univ. of Chicago Press.

KNOTT, J. R., and HENRY, C. E. (1941) The conditioning of the blocking of the alpha rhythm of the human electroencephalogram. *J. exp. Psychol.*, *28*, 134-144.

KNOTT, J. R., PLATT, E. B., and HADLEY, H. D., Jr. (1944) A preliminary neurophysiological investigation of the behavioral concept of stimulus trace. *J. exp. Psychol.*, *34*, 104-112.

KNOTTER, Margaret C. *See* Walker, Knotter, and DeValois (1950).

KOBRICK, J. L. *See also* Hall and Kobrick (1952).

KOCH, S. (1941a) The logical character of the motivation concept. I. *Psychol. Rev., 48,* 15-38.

KOCH, S. (1941b) The logical character of the motivation concept. II. *Psycho. Rev., 48,* 127-154.

KOCH, S. (1944) Hull's Principles of Behavior. A special review. *Psychol. Bull., 41,* 269-286.

KOCH, S. (1954) Clark L. Hull. In Estes, et al. *Modern learning theory.* New York: Appleton-Century-Crofts.

KOCH, S. (1959) *Psychology, a study of a science.* Vol. 2. New York: McGraw Hill.

KOCH, S. *See also* Estes and others (1954), Saltzman and Koch (1948).

KOCH, S., and DANIEL, W. J. (1945) The effect of satiation on the behavior mediated by a habit of maximum strength. *J. exp. Psychol., 35,* 167-187.

KOFFKA, K. (1924) *The growth of the mind.* New York: Harcourt Brace.

KOFFKA, K. (1929) *The growth of the mind* (second edition). New York: Harcourt Brace.

KÖHLER, W. (1925) *The mentality of apes.* New York: Harcourt Brace.

KÖHLER, W. (1929) *Gestalt psychology.* New York: Liveright.

KOHN, M. (1951) Satiation of hunger from food injected directly into the stomach versus food ingested by mouth. *J. comp. physiol. Psychol., 44,* 412-422.

KONORSKI, J. (1948) *Conditioned reflexes and neuron organization.* New York: Cambridge University Press.

KONORSKI, J. (1950) *Mechanisms of learning.* Vol. 4, *Soc. Exp. Biol. Symposium on physiological mechanisms in animal behavior.* New York: Academic Press.

KONORSKI, J. *See also* Miller, and Konorski (1928).

KONORSKI, J., and MILLER, S. (1937a) On two types of conditioned reflex. *J. gen. Psychol., 16,* 264-272.

KONORSKI, J., and MILLER, S. (1937b) Further remarks on two types of conditioned reflex. *J. gen. Psychol., 17,* 405-407.

KOONS, P. B. *See* Denny, Koons, and Mason (1959).

KORONAKIS, C., and ARNOLD, W. J. (1957) The formation of learning sets in rats. *J. comp. physiol. Psychol., 50,* 11-14.

KOTLIAREVSKY, L. I. (1935) The formation of pupillary conditioned reflexes and of a differentiation in response to both direct and verbal stimuli. *Arkh. Biol. Nauk, 39,* 477-489. (*Biol. Abstr.,* 1937, 11, No. 13724).

KRAELING, Doris. *See* Campbell and Kraeling (1953) (1954), Miller and Kraeling (1952).

KRASNOGORSKI, N. I. (1909) Uber die Bedingungsreflexe in Kindesalter. *Jb. Kinderheilk, 69,* 1-24.

KRASNOGORSKI, N. I. (1913) Uber die Grundmechanismen der Arbeit der Gross-hirnrinde bie Kindern. *Jb. Kinderheilk, 78,* 373-398.

KRAUSKOPF, J. *See* Bitterman, Reed, and Krauskopf (1952), Longnecker, Krauskopf and Bitterman (1952).

KRECH, D., and CRUTCHFIELD, R. S. (1948) *Theory and problems of social psychology.* New York: McGraw-Hill.

KRECHEVSKY, I. (1932a) "Hypotheses" in rats. *Psychol. Rev., 39,* 516-532.

KRECHEVSKY, I. (1932b) "Hypotheses" versus "chance" in the pre-solution period in sensory discrimination-learning. *Univ. Calif. Publ. Psychol., 6,* 27-44.

KRECHEVSKY, I. (1932c) Antagonistic visual discrimination habits in the white rat. *J. comp. Psychol., 14,* 263-277.

KRECHEVSKY, I. (1933a) Hereditary nature of "hypotheses." *J. comp. Psychol., 16,* 99-116.

KRECHEVSKY, I. (1933b) The docile nature of "hypotheses." *J. comp. Psychol., 15,* 429-443.

KRECHEVSKY, I. (1938) A study of the continuity of the problem-solving process. *Psychol. Rev., 45,* 107-133.

KRECHEVSKY, I. *See also* Hamilton and Krechevsky (1933).

KRIS, E. (1951) Psychoanalytic propositions. In M. H. Marx (Ed.) *Psychological theory.* New York: MacMillan.

KUBALA, A. L. *See* Bitterman, Reed, and Kubala (1953).

KUENNE, Margaret R. (1946) Experimental investigation of the relation of language to transposition behavior in young children. *J. exp. Psychol., 36,* 471-490.

KUPALOV, P. S., and GANTT, W. H. (1927) The relationship between the strength of the conditioned stimulus and the size of the resulting conditioned reflex. *Brain, 50,* 44-52.

KUPALOV, P. S., LYMAN, R. S., and LUKOV, B. N. (1931) The relationship between the intensity of tone-stimuli and the size of the resulting conditioned reflexes. *Brain, 54,* 85-98.

KURKE, M. I. (1956) Extinction rate as a function of distribution of practice and of practice sessions. *J. comp. physiol. Psychol., 49,* 158-160.

KURTZ, K. H. *See* Hovland and Kurtz (1952).

L'ABATE, L. (1956) Transfer and manifest anxiety in paired-associate learning. *Psychol. Rep., 2,* 119-126.

LACEY, J. I. (1956) The evaluation of autonomic responses: toward a general solution. *Ann. N. Y. Acad. Sci., 67,* 123-164.

LACEY, J. I., and SMITH, R. L. (1954) Conditioning and generalization of unconscious anxiety. *Science, 120,* 1045-1052.

LACEY, J. I., SMITH, R. L., and GREEN, A. (1955) Use of conditioned autonomic responds in the study of anxiety. *Psychosom. Med., XVII,* 208-217.

LACHMAN, S. J. (1956) Absolute and relational stimulus training in discrimination learning. *Psychol. Monogr.*, No. 5.

LAMBERT, W. W., and SOLOMON, R. L. (1952) "Extinction of a running response as a function of distance of a block point from the goal. *J. comp. physiol. Psychol.*, *45*, 269-279.

LAMOREAUX, R. R. *See* Mowrer and Lamoreaux (1942) (1946) (1951).

LANDIS, C. *See* King and Landis (1943).

LANG, J. M., and OLMSTED, J. M. D. (1923) Conditioned reflexes and pathways in the spinal cord. *Amer. J. Physiol.*, *65*, 603-611.

LARSEN, R. M. *See* Doty, Rutledge, and Larsen (1956).

LASHLEY, K. S. (1916a) The human salivary reflex and its use in psychology. *Psychol. Rev.*, *23*, 446-464.

LASHLEY, K. S. (1916b) Reflex secretion of the human parotid gland. *J. exp. Psychol.*, *1*, 461-493.

LASHLEY, K. S. (1918) A simple maze: with data on the relation of the distribution of practice to rate of learning. *Psychobiol.*, *1*, 353-367.

LASHLEY, K. S. (1924) Studies of cerebral function in learning. V. The retention of motor habits after destruction of the so-called motor area in primates. *Arch. Neurol. Psychiat., Chicago*, *12*, 249-276.

LASHLEY, K. S. (1929) *Brain mechanisms and intelligence.* Chicago: Univ. of Chicago Press.

LASHLEY, K. S. (1930a) Basic neural mechanisms in behavior. *Psychol. Rev.*, *37*, 1-24.

LASHLEY, K. S. (1930b) The mechanism of vision: I. A method for rapid analysis of pattern-vision in the rat. *J. genet. Psychol.*, *37*, 453-460.

LASHLEY, K. S. (1942) An examination of the "continuity theory" as applied to discriminative learning. *J. gen. Psychol.*, *26*, 241-265.

LASHLEY, K. S., and WADE, M. (1946) The Pavlovian theory of generalization. *Psychol. Rev.*, *53*, 72-87.

LAW, Florence E. *See* Kendler and Law (1950).

LAWLOR, W. G. *See* Hunt, Jernberg, and Lawlor (1953).

LAWRENCE, D. H. (1949) Acquired distinctiveness of cues: I. Transfer between discriminations on the basis of familiarity with the stimulus. *J. exp. Psychol.*, *39*, 770-784.

LAWRENCE, D. H. (1950) Acquired distinctiveness of cues: II. Selective association in a constant stimulus situation. *J. exp. Psychol.*, *40*, 175-188.

LAWRENCE, D. H. (1952) The transfer of a discrimination along a continuum. *J. comp. physiol. Psychol.*, *45*, 511-516.

LAWRENCE, D. H., and DeRIVERA, J. (1954) Evidence for relational transposition. *J. comp. physiol. Psychol.*, *47*, 475-471.

LAWRENCE, D. H. *See also* Baker and Lawrence (1951), Bauer and Lawrence (1953).

LAWSON, R. (1953) Amount of primary reward and strength of secondary reward. *J. exp. Psychol., 46,* 183-187.

LAWSON, R. (1957) Brightness discrimination performance and secondary reward strength as a function of primary reward amount. *J. comp. physiol. Psychol., 50,* 35-39.

LEBEDINSKAIA, S. I., and ROSENTHAL, J. S. (1935) Reactions of a dog after removal of the cerebral hemispheres. *Brain, 58,* 412-419.

LEEPER, R. (1935) The role of motivation in learning; a study of the phenomenon of differential motivational control of the utilization of habits. *J. genet. Psychol., 46,* 3-40.

LEEPER, R. (1944) Dr. Hull's Principles of Behavior, *J. genet. Psychol., 64,* 3-52.

LEVIN, S. (1959) The effects of awareness on verbal conditioning. Unpublished Ph.D. dissertation. Duke University.

LEVINE, S. (1953) The role of irrelevant drive stimuli in learning. *J. exp. Psychol., 45,* 410-416.

LEVINE, S. *See also* Kendler and Levine (1953), Kendler and others (1952).

LEVY, N. (1957) An experimental comparison of secondary inhibition and secondary reinforcement. *J. comp. physiol. Psychol., 50,* 29-34.

LEVY, N. *See also* Seward, Datel, and Levy (1952), Seward and Levy (1949) (1953), Seward, Levy, and Handlon (1950) (1953).

LEWIN, K. (1933) Environmental forces. In C. Murchison (Ed.), *A handbook of child psychology.* Worcester, Mass.: Clark University Press.

LEWIN, K. (1935) *A dynamic theory of personality.* Translated by D. K. Adams and K. E. Zener, New York: McGraw-Hill.

LEWIN, K. (1942) Field theory and learning. Chapter 4 in *The psychology of learning.* Nat'l. Soc. Stud. Educ., 41st Yearbook, Part II, 215-242.

LEWIS, D. J. (1956) Acquisition, extinction, and spontaneous recovery as a function of percentage of reinforcement and intertrial intervals. *J. exp. Psychol., 51,* 45-53.

LEWIS, D. J. (1960) Partial reinforcement: A selective review of the literature since 1950. *Psychol. Bull., 57,* 1-28.

LEWIS, D. J., and COTTON, J. W. (1957) Learning and performance as a function of drive strength during acquisition and extinction. *J. comp. physiol. Psychol., 50,* 189-194.

LIBERMAN, A. M. (1944) The effect of interpolated activity on spontaneous recovery from experimental extinction. *J. exp. Psychol., 34,* 282-301.

LIBERMAN, A. M. (1948) The effect of differential extinction on spontaneous recovery. *J. exp. Psychol., 38,* 722-733.

LICHTENSTEIN, P. E. (1950a) Studies of anxiety: I. The production of a feeding inhibition in dogs. *J. comp. physiol. Psychol., 43,* 16-29.

LICHTENSTEIN, P. E. (1950b) Studies of anxiety: II. The effects of lobotomy on a feeding inhibition in dogs. *J. comp. physiol. Psychol., 43,* 419-427.

LIDDELL, H. S. (1926a) A laboratory for the study of conditioned motor reflexes. *Amer. J. Psychol., 37,* 418-419.

LIDDELL, H. S. (1926b) The effect of thyroidectomy on some unconditioned responses of the sheep and goat. *Amer. J. Physiol., 75,* 579-590.

LIDDELL, H. S. (1934) The conditioned reflex. In F. A. Moss (Ed.), *Comparative psychology.* New York: Prentice-Hall.

LIDDELL, H. S. (1938) The experimental neurosis and the problem of mental disorder. *Amer. J. Psychiat., 94,* 1035-1043.

LIDDELL, H. S. (1956) *Emotional hazards in animals and man.* Springfield: Charles C. Thomas.

LIDDELL, H. S., JAMES, W. T., and ANDERSON, O. D. (1934) The comparative physiology of the conditioned motor reflex: based on experiments with the pig, dog, sheep, goat, and rabbit. *Comp. Psychol. Monogr., 11,* No. 51.

LIGHT, J. S., and GANTT, W. H. (1936) Essential part of reflex arc for establishment of conditioned reflex. Formation of conditioned reflex after exclusion of motor peripheral end. *J. comp. Psychol., 21,* 19-36.

LILLY, J. C. (1957) Learning elicited by electrical stimulation of subcortical regions in the unanesthetized monkey: The "start" and the "stop" patterns of behavior. *Science, 125* No. 3251:748.

LILLY, J. C. (1958) Learning motivated by subcortical stimulation: The 'start' and the 'stop' patterns of behavior. *International symposium on reticular formation of the brain.* Boston: Little, Brown.

LINDSLEY, D. B. (1957) Psychophysiology and motivation. In M. R. Jones (Ed.) *Nebraska symposium on motivation* (Vol. V). Lincoln, Neb.: Univ. Nebraska.

LIPMAN, E. A. *See* Brogden, Lipman, and Culler (1938).

LIPPITT, R. A. *See* Spence, Bergmann, and Lippitt (1950), Spence and Lippitt (1940) (1946).

LITTMAN, R. A. (1949) Conditioned generalization of the galvanic skin reaction to tones. *J. exp. Psychol., 39,* 868-882.

LITTMAN, R. A. (1950) Latent learning in a T-maze after two degrees of training. *J. comp. physiol. Psychol., 43,* 135-147.

LIVINGSTON, J. R. *See* Hull and others (1951).

LOESS, H. B., and DUNCAN, C. P. (1952) Human discrimination learning with simultaneous and successive presentation of stimuli. *J. exp. Psychol., 44,* 215-221.

LOGAN, F. A. (1951) A comparison of avoidance and non-avoidance eyelid conditioning. *J. exp. Psychol., 42,* 390-393.

LOGAN, F. A. (1952) The role of delay of reinforcement in determining reaction potential. *J. exp. Psychol., 43,* 393-399.

LOGAN, F. A. (1956) A micromolar approach to behavior theory. *Psychol. Rev., 63,* 73.

LOGAN, F. A., BEIER, Eileen M., and ELLIS, R. A. (1955) Effect of varied reinforcement on speed of locomotion. *J. exp. Psychol., 49,* 260-266.

LOGAN, F. A., BEIER, Eileen M., and KINCAID, W. D. (1956) Extinction following partial and varied reinforcement. *J. exp. Psychol., 52,* 65-70.

LONG, E. R., HAMMACK, J. T., and CAMPBELL, B. J. (1959) Intermittent reinforcement of operant behavior in children. *J. exp. anal. Beh., 1,* 315-339.

LONG, J. B. *See* McNamara, Long, and Wike (1956).

LONG, L. *See* Goodwin, Long, and Welch (1945).

LONGNECKER, E. G., KRAUSKOPF, J., and BITTERMAN, M. E. (1952) Extinction following alternating and random reinforcement. *Amer. J. Psychol., 65,* 580-587.

LOONEY, E. *See* Delgado, Rosvold, and Looney (1956).

LORENZ, K. Z. (1952) *King Solomon's Ring.* New York: Crowell.

LOUCKS, R. B. (1933) An appraisal of Pavlov's systematization of behavior from the experimental standpoint. *J. comp. Psychol., 15,* 1-47.

LOUCKS, R. B. (1934) A technique for faradic stimulation of tissues beneath the integument in the absence of conductors penetrating the skin. *J. comp. Psychol., 18,* 305-313.

LOUCKS, R. B. (1935) The experimental delimitation of neural structures essential for learning: the attempt to condition striped muscle responses with faradization of the sigmoid gyri. *J. Psychol., I,* 5-44.

LOUCKS, R. B. (1938) Studies of neural structures essential for learning II. The conditioning of salivary and striped muscle responses to faradization of cortical sensory elements, and the action of sleep upon such mechanisms. *J. comp. Psychol., 25,* 315-332.

LOUCKS, R. B., and GANTT, W. H. (1938) The conditioning of striped muscle responses based upon faradic stimulation of dorsal roots and dorsal columns of the spinal cord. *J. comp. Psychol., 25,* 415-426.

LUCAS, J. D. (1952) The interactive effects of anxiety, failure, and interserial duplication. *Amer. J. Psychol., 65,* 59-66.

LUKOV, B. N. *See* Kupalov, Lyman, and Lukov (1931).

LUMSDAINE, A. A. (1939) Conditioned eyelid responses as mediating generalized conditioned finger reactions. *Psychol. Bull., 36,* 650.

LUNDHOLM, H. (1928) An experimental study of functional anesthesias as induced by suggestion in hypnosis. *J. abnorm. soc. Psychol., 23,* 337-355.

LUNDHOLM, H. (1932) A hormic theory of hallucinations. *Brit. J. med. Psychol., 11,* 269-282.

LYMAN, R. S. *See* Kupalov, Lyman, and Lukov (1931).

McALLISTER, W. R. (1953a) Eyelid conditioning as a function of the CS-UCS interval. *J. exp. Psychol., 45,* 417-422.

McALLISTER, W. R. (1953b) The effect on eyelid conditioning of shifting the CS-US interval. *J. exp. Psychol., 45,* 423-428.

McAllister, W. R. (1953c) Adaptation of the original response to a conditioned stimulus. *Iowa Acad. Sci., 60,* 534-539.

McClearn, G. E. *See* Harlow and McClearn (1954).

McClelland, D. C., and McGown, D. R. (1953) The effect of variable food reinforcement on the strength of a secondary reward. *J. comp. physiol. Psychol., 46,* 80-86.

McConnell, Claudia. *See* Stevenson, Iscoe, and McConnell (1955).

McConnell, J. *See* Thompson and McConnell (1955).

McCranie, E. J. *See* Crasilneck and McCranie (1956).

McCulloch, T. L. (1934) Performance preferentials of the white rat in force-resisting and spatial dimensions. *J. comp. Psychol., 18,* 85-111.

McCulloch, T. L. (1939a) Comment on the formation of discrimination habits. *Psychol. Rev., 46,* 75-85.

McCulloch, T. L. (1939b) Reply to a note on discrimination habits. *Psychol. Rev., 46,* 304-307.

McCulloch, T. L. (1939c) The role of clasping activity in adaptive behavior of the infant chimpanzee: III. The mechanism of reinforcement. *J. Psychol., 7,* 305-316.

McCulloch, T. L., and Pratt, J. G. (1934) A study of the pre-solution period in weight discrimination by white rats. *J. comp. Psychol., 18,* 271-290.

McCulloch, W. S. *See* Dusser de Barenne and McCulloch (1938).

McDonnell, R. *See* Amsel and McDonnell (1951).

McFann, H. *See* Jenkins, McFann, and Clayton (1950).

McGee, R. K. *See* Meier and McGee (1959).

McGeoch, J. A., and Irion, A. L. (1952) *The psychology of human learning.* New York: Longmans Green.

McGown, D. R. *See* McClelland and McGown (1953).

McNamara, H. J., Long, J. B., and Wike, E. L. (1956) Learning without response under two conditions of external cues. *J. comp. physiol, Psychol., 49,* 477-480.

McNamara, H. J., and Wike, E. L. (1958) The effects of irregular learning conditions upon the rate and permanence of learning. *J. comp. physiol. Psychol., 51,* 363-366.

Maatsch, J. L. *See also* Adelman and Maatsch (1955) and (1956).

Maatsch, J. L., Adelman, H. M., and Denny, M. R. (1954) Effort and resistance to extinction of the bar-pressing response. *J. comp. physiol. Psychol., 47,* 47-50.

MacCaslin, E. F. (1954) Successive and simultaneous discrimination as a function of stimulus similarity. *Amer. J. Psychol., 67,* 308-314.

MacCorquodale, K. (1955) Learning. *Ann. Rev. Psychol., 6,* 29-62.

MacCorquodale, K., *See also* Estes and others (1954), Meehl and MacCorquodale (1948) (1951) (1953).

MacCorquodale, K., and Meehl, P. E. (1948) On a distinction between hypothetical constructs and intervening variables. *Psychol. Rev., 55,* 95-107.

MacCorquodale, K., and Meehl, P. (1949) "Cognitive" learning in the absence of competition of incentives. *J. comp. physiol. Psychol., 42,* 383-390.

MacCorquodale, K., and Meehl, P. E. (1951) On the elimination of cul entries without obvious reinforcement. *J. comp. physiol. Psychol., 44,* 367-371.

MacCorquodale, K., and Meehl, P. E. (1954) Edward C. Tolman. In Estes, et al. *Modern learning theory.* New York: Appleton-Century-Crofts.

MacDonald, Annette (1946) The effect of adaptation to the unconditioned stimulus upon the formation of conditioned avoidance responses. *J. exp. Psychol., 36,* 1-12.

MacDuff, M. M. (1946) The effect on retention of varying degrees of motivation during learning in rats. *J. comp. Psychol., 39,* 207-240.

Mackintosh, Irene (1955) The resistance to extinction of responses acquired under irregular conditions of learning. *J. comp. physiol. Psychol., 48,* 363-370.

Maddi, S. R. *See* Moltz and Maddi (1956).

Maher, Winifred B., and Wickens, D. D. (1954) Effect of differential quantity of reward on acquisition and performance of a maze habit. *J. comp. physiol. Psychol., 47,* 44-46.

Maier, N. R. F., and Ellen, P. (1952) Studies of abnormal behavior in the rat. XXIII. The prophylactic effects of guidance in reducing rigid behavior. *J. abnorm. soc. Psychol., 47,* 109-116.

Maier, N. R. F., and Klee, J. B. (1945) Studies of abnormal behavior in the rat. XVII. Guidance versus trial and error in the alteration of habits and fixations. *J. Psychol., 19,* 133-163.

Maier, N. R. F., and Schneirla, T. C. (1935) *Principles of animal psychology.* New York: McGraw Hill.

Maltzman, I. (1950) An experimental study of learning under an irrelevant need. *J. exp. Psychol., 40,* 788-793.

Maltzman, I., Fox, J., and Morrisett, L., Jr. (1953) Some effect of manifest anxiety on mental set. *J. exp. Psychol., 46,* 50-54.

Maltzman, I. *See also* Amsel and Maltzman (1950), Eisman, Asimow, and Maltzman (1956).

Mann, Lucie I. *See* Kimble, Mann, and Dufort (1955).

Margolius, G. (1955) Stimulus generalization of an instrument response as a function of the number of reinforced trials. *J. exp. Psychol., 49,* 105-111.

Marquis, D. G. *See* Hilgard and Marquis (1935) (1936) 1940).

Marquis, D. G., and Hilgard, E. R. (1936) Conditioned lid responses to light in dogs after removal of the visual cortex. *J. comp. Psychol., 22,* 157-178.

Marquis, D. G., and Porter, J. M., Jr. (1939) Differential characteristics of conditioned eyelid responses established by reflex and voluntary reinforcement. *J. exp. Psychol., 24,* 347-365.

MARQUIS, D. P. (1931) Can conditioned responses be established in the newborn infant? *J. genet. Psychol., 39,* 479-492.

MARTIN, R. F. (1940) "Native" traits and regression in rats. *J. comp. Psychol., 30,* 1-16

MARTINO, G. (1939) The conditioned reflex of blinking. *J. Neurophysiol., 2,* 173-177.

MARX, M. H. *See* Collier and Marx (1959), Holder and others (1957), Iwahara and Marx (1950), Roberts Marx, and Collier (1958), Tyler, Marx, and Collier (1959).

MARX, M. H., HENDERSON, R. L., and ROBERTS, C. L. (1955) Positive reinforcement of the bar-pressing response by a light stimulus following dark operant pre-tests with no aftereffect. *J. comp. physiol. Psychol., 48,* 73-76.

MASON, J. E. *See* Denny, Koons, and Mason (1959).

MASSERMAN, J. H. (1943) *Behavior and neurosis.* Chicago: University of Chicago Press.

MATEER, F. (1918) *Child behavior, a critical and experimental study of young children by the method of conditioned reflexes.* Boston: Badger.

MATTER, Jean. *See* Brunner, Matter, and Papanek (1955).

MAY, M. A. (1946) The psychology of learning from demonstration films. *J. educ. Psychol., 37,* 1-12.

MAY, M .A. (1948) Experimentally acquired drives. *J. exp. Psychol., 38,* 66-77.

MEDNICK, S. A. (1960) Stimulus generalization: A review of the literature. *Psychol. Bull.* (in press).

MEEHL, P. E. (1950) On the circularity of the law of effect. *Psychol. Bull., 47,* 52-75.

MEEHL, P. E. *See also* Estes and others (1954), MacCorquodale and Meehl (1948) (1949) (1951) (1954).

MEEHL, P. E., and MACCORQUODALE, K. (1948) A further study of latent learning in the T-maze. *J. comp. physiol. Psychol., 41,* 372-396.

MEEHL, P. E., and MACCORQUODALE, K. (1951) A failure to find the Blodgett effect and some secondary observations on drive conditioning. *J. comp. physiol. Psychol., 44,* 178-183.

MEEHL, P. E., and MACCORQUODALE, K. (1953) Drive conditioning as a factor in latent learning. *J. exp. Psychol., 45,* 20-24.

MEIER, G., and MCGEE, R. K. (1959) A re-evaluation of the effect of early perceptual experience on discrimination performance during adulthood. *J. comp. physiol. Psychol., 52,* 390-395.

MELCHING, W. H. (1954) The acquired reward value of an intermittently presented neutral stimulus. *J. comp. physiol. Psychol., 47,* 370-374.

MENCHER, Helen C. *See* Kendler and Mencher (1948).

MENZIES, R. (1937) Conditioned vasomotor responses in human subjects. *J. Psychol., 4,* 75-120.

MERRELL, Margaret (1931) The relationship of individual growth to average growth. *Human Biol., 3,* 37-70.

MERYMAN, J. J. *See* Bilodeau, Brown, and Meryman (1956).

METTLER, F. A. *See* Culler and Mettler (1934), Girden and others (1936).

METZNER, C. A., and BAKER, L. E. (1939) The pupillary response conditioned to subliminal auditory stimuli: a control experiment. *Psychol. Bull., 36,* 625.

MEYER, D. R. (1951) Food deprivation and discrimination reversal learning by monkeys. *J. exp. Psychol., 41,* 10-16.

MEYER, D. R. *See also* Cotterman, Meyer, and Wickens (1956), Harlow and others (1952), Harlow, Harlow, and Meyer (1950), Miles and Meyer (1956), Silver and Meyer (1954).

MEYER, D. R., and MILES, R. C. (1953) Intralist-interlist relations in verbal learning. *J. exp. Psychol., 45,* 109-115.

MEYERS, N. A. *See* Prokasy, Grant, and Meyers (1958).

MICHELS, K. M. (1955) The effects of fixed-ratio random reinforcement on response latency of monkeys. *J. comp. physiol. Psychol., 48,* 32-36.

MILES, R. C. (1956a) The relative effectiveness of secondary reinforcers throughout deprivation and habit-strength parameters. *J. comp. physiol. Psychol., 49,* 126-130.

MILES, R. C. (1956b) Secondary-reinforcement stimulation throughout a series of spontaneous recoveries. *J. comp. physiol. Psychol., 49,* 496-498.

MILES, R. C. (1957) Learning-set formation in the squirrel monkey. *J. comp. physiol. Psychol., 50,* 356-357.

MILES, R. C. (1958) The effect of an irrelevant motive on learning. *J. comp. physiol. Psychol., 51,* 258-261.

MILES, R. C. (1959) Discrimination in the squirrel monkey as a function of deprivation and problem difficulty. *J. exp. Psychol., 57,* 15-19.

MILES, R. C. *See also* Meyer and Miles (1953), Miller and Miles (1936).

MILES, R. C., and MEYER, D. R. (1956) Learning sets in marmosets. *J. comp. physiol. Psychol., 49,* 219-222.

MILES, R. C., and WICKENS, D. D. (1953) Effect of a secondary reinforcer on the primary hunger drive. *J. comp. physiol. Psychol., 46,* 77-79.

MILLER, J. (1939) The effect of facilitatory and inhibitory attitudes on eyelid conditioning. Ph.D. dissertation, Yale University. (Abstr. in *Psychol. Bull., 36,* 577-578.)

MILLER, J. *See also* Hilgard, Miller, and Ohlson (1933), Humphreys, Miller, and Ellson (1940).

MILLER, J., and COLE, L. E. (1936) The influence of a "voluntary" reception upon the development and the extinction of the conditioned eyelid reaction. *J. genet. Psychol., 48,* 405-440.

MILLER, J. G. (1939) Symbolic technique in psychological theory. *Psychol. Rev., 46,* 464-479.

REFERENCES 539

MILLER, N. E. (1944) Experimental studies of conflict. In Hunt, J. McV. *Personality and the behavior disorders.* New York: Ronald.

MILLER, N. E. (1948a) Studies of fear as an acquirable drive: I. Fear as motivation and fear reduction as reinforcement in the learning of new responses. *J. exp. Psychol., 38,* 89-101.

MILLER, N. E. (1948b) Theory and experiment relating psychoanalytic displacement to stimulus-response generalization. *J. abnorm. soc. Psychol., 43,* 155-178.

MILLER, N. E. (1951a) Comments on theoretical models. Illustrated by the development of a theory of conflict behavior. *J. Pers., 20,* 82-100.

MILLER, N. E. (1951b) Comments on multiple-process conceptions of learning. *Psychol. Rev., 58,* 375-381.

MILLER, N. E. (1951c) Learnable drives and rewards. In S. S. Stevens (Ed.) *Handbook of experimental psychology.* New York: Wiley.

MILLER, N. E. (1955) Shortcomings of food consumption as a measure of hunger; results from other behavioral techniques. *Ann. N. Y. Acad. Sci., 63,* 141-143.

MILLER, N. E. (1956) Effects of drugs on motivation: the value of using a variety of measures. *Ann. N. Y. Acad. Sci. 65,* 318-333.

MILLER, N. E. (1957) Experiments on motivation. *Science, 126,* 1271-1278.

MILLER, N. E. (1959) Liberalization of basic S-R concepts: Extensions to conflict behavior, motivation, and social learning. In S. Koch (Ed.), *Psychology, a study of a science.* Vol. 2. New York: McGraw-Hill.

MILLER, N. E. *See also* Berkun, Kessen, and Miller (1952), Delgado, Roberts, and Miller (1954). Bower and Miller (1958), Dollard and others (1939), Dollard and Miller (1950), Kaufman and Miller (1949), Murray and Miller (1952), Meyers and Miller (1954), Porter and Miller (1957).

MILLER, N. E., BAILEY, C. J., and STEVENSON, J. A. (1950) Decreased "hunger" but increased food intake resulting from hypothalamic lesions. *Science, 112,* 256-259.

MILLER, N. E., and DOLLARD, J. C. (1941) *Social learning and imitation.* New Haven: Yale University Press.

MILLER, N. E., and KESSEN, M. L. (1952) Reward effects of food via stomach fistula compared with those of food via mouth. *J. comp. physiol. Psychol., 45,* 555-564.

MILLER, N. E., and KRAELING, Doris (1952) Displacement: Greater generalization of approach than avoidance in generalized approach-avoidance conflict. *J. exp. Psychol., 43,* 217-221.

MILLER, N. E., and MILES, W. R. (1936) Alcohol and removal of reward. An analytical study of rodent maze behavior. *J. comp. Psychol., 21,* 179-204.

MILLER, N. E., and MURRAY, E. J. (1952) Displacement and conflict: Learnable drive as a basis for the steeper of avoidance than of approach. *J. exp. Psychol., 43,* 227-231.

MILLER, N. E., SAMPLINER, R. I., and WOODROW, P. (1957) Thirst-reducing effects of water by stomach fistula vs. water by mouth measured by both a consummatory and an instrumental response. *J. comp. physiol. Psychol., 50,* 1-5.

MILLER, N. E., and STEVENSON, S. S. (1936) Agitated behavior of rats during experimental extinction and a curve of spontaneous recovery. *J. comp. Psychol., 21,* 205-231.

MILLER, R. E. *See* Murphy, Miller, and Finocchio (1956), Murphy and Miller (1957).

MILLER, S. *See* Konorski and Miller (1937a) (1937b).

MILLER, S., and KONORSKI, J. (1928) Sur une forme particuliere des reflexes conditionnels. *C. R. Soc. Biol. Paris, 99,* 1155-1157.

MILLER, W. C., and GREENE, J. E. (1954) Generalization of an avoidance response to various intensities of tone. *J. comp. physiol. Psychol., 47,* 136-139.

MILNER, P. *See* Olds and Milner (1954).

MINTURN, L. (1954) A test for sign-gestalt expectancies under conditions of negative motivation. *J. exp. Psychol., 48,* 98-100.

MOELLER, G. (1954) The CS-UCS interval in GSR conditioning. *J. exp. Psychol., 48,* 162-166.

MOLTZ, H. (1955) Latent extinction and reduction of secondary reward value. *J. exp. Psychol., 49,* 395-400.

MOLTZ, H. (1957) Latent extinction and the fractional anticipatory response mechanism. *Psychol. Rev.,* 229-241.

MOLTZ, H., and MADDI, S. R. (1956) Reduction of secondary reward value as a function of drive strength during latent extinction. *J. exp. Psychol., 52,* 71-76.

MONTAGUE, E. K. (1953) The role of anxiety in serial rote learning. *J. exp. Psychol., 45,* 91-96.

MONTGOMERY, K. C. (1951) The relation between exploratory behavior and spontaneous alteration in the white rat. *J. comp. physiol. Psychol., 44,* 582-589.

MONTGOMERY, K. C. (1952) Exploratory behavior and its relation to spontaneous alternation in a series of maze exposures. *J. comp. physiol. Psychol., 45,* 50-57.

MONTGOMERY, K. C. (1953a) Exploratory behavior as a function of "similarity" of stimulus situations. *J. comp. physiol. Psychol., 46,* 129-133.

MONTGOMERY, K. C. (1953b) The effect of the hunger and thirst drives upon exploratory behavior. *J. comp. physiol. Psychol., 46,* 315-319.

MONTGOMERY, K. C. (1953c) The effect of activity deprivation upon exploratory behavior. *J. comp. physiol. Psychol., 46,* 438-441.

MONTGOMERY, K. C. (1954) The role of the exploratory drive in learning. *J. comp. physiol. Psychol., 47,* 60-64.

MONTGOMERY, K. C., and SEGALL, M. (1955) Discrimination learning based upon the exploratory drive. *J. comp. physiol. Psychol., 48,* 225-228.

MONTPELLIER, G. De (1933) An experiment on the order of elimination of blind alleys in maze learning. *J. genet. Psychol., 43,* 123-139.

MORGAN, C. L. (1894) *Introduction to comparative psychology.* London: Scott.

MORGAN, E. A. *See* Whatmore, Morgan, and Kleitman.

MORGAN, J. J. B. *See* Watson and Morgan (1917).

MORGAN, J. J. B., and MORGAN, Sarah S. (1944) Infant learning as a developmental index. *J. genet. Psychol., 65*, 281-289.

MORGAN, Sarah S. *See* Morgan and Morgan (1944).

MORGULIS, S. *See* Yerkes and Morgulis (1909).

MORRELL, F., and JASPER, H. H. (1956) Electrographic studies of the formation of temporary connections in the brain. *EEG Clin Neurophysiol., 8*, 201-215.

MORRELL, F., ROBERTS, L., and JASPER, H. H. (1956) Effect of focal epileptogenic lesions and their ablation upon conditioned electrical responses of the brain in the monkey. *EEG. Clin. Neurophysiol., 8*, 217-236.

MORRISETT, L. *See* Maltzman, Fox, and Morrisett (1953).

MOTE, F. A., and FINGER, F. W. (1942) Exploratory drive and secondary reinforcement in the acquisition and extinction of a simple running response. *J. exp. Psychol., 31*, 57-68.

MOTOKAWA, K. (1949) Electroencephalograms of man in the generalization of differentiation of conditioned reflexes. *Tohoku J. Exp. Med., 50*, 225-234.

MOTOKAWA, K., and HUZIMORI, B. (1949) Electroencephalograms and conditioned reflexes. *Tohoku J. exp. Med., 50*, 215-223.

MOWRER, O .H. (1938) Preparatory set (expectancy)—a determinant in motivation and learning. *Psychol. Rev. 45*, 62-91.

MOWRER, O. H. (1939) A stimulus-response analysis of anxiety and its role as a reinforcing agent. *Psychol. Rev., 46*, 553-565.

MOWRER, O. H. (1940) An experimental analogue of "regression" with incidental observations on "reaction-formation." *J. abnorm. soc. Psychol., 35*, 56-87.

MOWRER, O. H. (1947) On the dual nature of learning—A re-interpretation of "conditioning" and "problem-solving." *Harv. educ. Rev., 17*, 102-148.

MOWRER, O. H. (1950) Pain, punishment, guilt, and anxiety. *Anxiety*, Grune & Stratton, p. 27-40.

MOWRER, O. H. (1956) Two-factor learning theory reconsidered, with special reference to secondary reinforcement and the concept of habit. *Psychol. Rev., 63*, 114-128.

MOWRER, O. H. (1960) *Learning theory and behavior.* New York: Wiley.

MOWRER, O. H. *See also* Coppock and Mowrer (1947), Dollard and others (1939), Whiting and Mowrer (1943).

MOWRER, O. H., and AIKEN, E. G. (1954) Contiguity vs. drive-reduction in conditioned fear: temporal variations in conditioned and unconditioned stimulus. *Amer. J. Psychol., 67*, 26-38.

MOWRER, O. H., and JONES, Helen M. (1943) Extinction and behavior variability as functions of effortfulness of task. *J. exp. Psychol., 33*, 369-386.

MOWRER, O. H., and JONES, Helen M. (1945) Habit strength as a function of the pattern of reinforcement. *J. exp. Psychol., 35*, 293-311.

Mowrer, O. H., and Lamoreaux, R. R. (1942) Avoidance conditioning and signal duration—a study of secondary motivation and reward. *Psychol. Monogr., 54,* No. 247.

Mowrer, O. H., and Lamoreaux, R. R. (1946) Fear as an intervening variable in avoidance conditioning. *J. comp. Psychol., 39,* 29-50.

Mowrer, O. H., and Lamoreaux, R. R. (1951) Conditioning and conditionality (discrimination). *Psychol. Rev., 58,* 196-212.

Mowrer, O. H., and Solomon, L. N. (1954) Contiguity vs. drive-reduction in conditioned fear; the proximity and abruptness of drive-reduction. *Amer. J. Psychol., 67,* 15-25.

Mowrer, O. H., and Viek, P. (1948) An experimental analogue of fear from a sense of helplessness. *J. abnorm. soc. Psychol., 43,* 193-200.

Moyer, K. E. (1958) Effect of delay between training and extinction on the extinction of an avoidance response. *J. comp. physiol. Psychol., 51,* 116-118.

Mueller, C. G. (1950) Theoretical relationships among some measures of conditioning. *Proc. Nat. Acad. Sci., 36,* 123-130.

Mueller, C. G. *See also* Estes and others (1954).

Muenzinger, K. F. (1956) On the origin and early use of the term vicarious trial and error (VTE). *Psychol Bull., 53,* 493-494.

Muenzinger, K. F., and Conrad, D. G. (1953) Latent learning observed through negative transfer. *J. comp. physiol. Psychol., 46,* 1-8.

Muncie, W., and Gantt, W. H. (1938) Effect on behavior of inhibition of different forms of excitation. *Amer. J. Physiol., 123,* 152-158.

Munn, N. L. (1931) An apparatus for testing visual discrimination in animals. *J. genet. Psychol., 39,* 342-358.

Munn, N. L. (1939) The relative effectiveness of two conditioning procedures. *J. gen. Psychol., 21,* 119-136.

Munn, N. 'L. (1955) *The evolution and growth of human behavior.* Boston: Houghton-Mifflin.

Murphy, J. V., Miller, R. E., and Finocchio, D. V. (1956) Spontaneous recovery of an avoidance response over an extended time interval in the monkey. *J. genet. Psychol., 89,* 119-125.

Murphy, J. V., and, Miller, R. E. (1957) Higher-order conditioning in the monkey. *J. gen. Psychol., 56,* 67-72.

Murray, E. J. (1954) A case study in a behavioral analysis of psychotherapy. *J. abnorm. soc Psychol., 49,* 305-310.

Murray, E. J. *See also* Miller and Murray (1952).

Murray, E. J., and Berkun, M. M. (1955) Displacement as a function of conflict. *J. abnorm. soc. Psychol., 51,* 47-56.

Murray, E. J., and Miller, N. E. (1952) Displacement: Steeper gradient of generalization of approach than avoidance in generalized approach-avoidance conflict. *J. exp. Psychol., 43,* 222-226.

MYASISHCHEV, V. (1929) Experimental evidence on the problem of objective indices in sensory disorders. *Nov. Refl. Fiziol. Nerv. Sist.*, 3, 458, 480. (*Psychol. Abstr.*, 1930, 4, No. 4349.)

MYERS, A. K., and MILLER, N. E. (1954) Failure to find a learned drive based on hunger; evidence for learning motivated by "exploration." *J. comp. physiol. Psychol.*, 47, 428-436.

MYERS, J. L. (1958) Secondary reinforcement: A review of recent experimentation. *Psychol. Bull.*, 55, 284-301.

NACHMIAS, J. *See* Gleitman, Nachmias, and Neisser (1954).

NAGATY, M. O. (1951a) The effect of reinforcement on closely following S-R connections: I. The effect of a backward conditioning procedure on the extinction of conditioned avoidance. *J. exp. Psychol.*, 42, 239-246.

NAGATY, M. O. (1951b) The effect of reinforcement on closely following S-R connections: II. Effect of food reward immediately preceding performance of an instrumental conditioned response on extinction of that response. *J. exp. Psychol.*, 42, 333-340.

NEFZGER, M. D. (1957) The properties of stimuli associated with shock reduction. *J. exp. Psychol.*, 53, 184-188.

NEISSER, U. (1954) An experimental distinction between perceptual process and verbal response. *J. exp. Psychol.*, 47, 399-402.

NEISSER, U. *See also* Gleitman, Nachmias, and Neisser (1952).

NISSEN, H. W. (1951) Analysis of a complex conditional reaction in chimpanzee. *J. comp. physiol. Psychol.*, 44, 9-16.

NISSEN, H. W., and ELDER, J. H. (1935) The influence of amount of incentive on delayed response performances of chimpanzees. *J. genet. Psychol.*, 47, 49-72.

NOBLE, C. E. (1950) Conditioned generalization of the galvanic skin response to a subvocal stimulus. *J. exp. Psychol.*, 40, 15-25.

NOLAN, C. Y. *See* Webb and Nolan (1953).

NORRIS, Eugenia B. *See* Grant and Norris (1947), Spence and Norris (1950).

NORRIS, Eugenia B., and GRANT, D. A. (1948) Eyelid conditioning as affected by verbally induced inhibitory set and counter reinforcement. *Amer J. Psychol.*, 61, 37-49.

NORTH, A. J. (1950a) Improvement in successive discrimination reversals. *J. comp. physiol. Psychol.*, 43, 442-460.

NORTH, A. J. (1950b) Performance during an extended series of discrimination reversals. *J. comp. physiol. Psychol.*, 43, 461-470.

NORTH, A. J., and JEEVES, M. (1956) Interrelationships of successive and simultaneous discrimination. *J. exp. Psychol.*, 51, 54-58.

NOTTERMAN, J. M. (1951) A study of some relations among aperiodic reinforcement, discrimination training, and secondary reinforcement. *J. exp. Psychol.*, 41, 161-169.

NOTTERMAN, J. M. (1953) Experimental anxiety and a conditioned heart rate in human beings. *Trans. N. Y. Acad. Sci., 16,* 24-33.

NOTTERMAN, J. M. *See also* Bersh, Notterman, and Schoenfeld (1956), Bersh, Schoenfeld, and Notterman (1953).

NOTTERMAN, J. M., SCHOENFELD, W. N., and BERSH, P. J. (1952) Partial reinforcement and conditioned heart rate response in human subjects. *Science, 115,* 77-79.

O'KELLY, L. I., and HEYER, A. W., Jr. (1948) Studies in a motivation and retention. I. Retention of a simple habit. *J. comp. physiol. Psychol., 41,* 466-478.

O'KELLY, L. I., and HEYER, A. W., Jr. (1951) Studies in motivation and retention. V. The influence of need duration on retention of a maze habit. *Comp. Psychol., Monogr., 20,* 287-301.

OHLSON, J. A. *See* Hilgard, Miller, and Ohlson.

OLDS, J. (1955) Physiological mechanisms of reward. In M. R. Jones (Ed.) *Nebraska symposium on motivation.* Lincoln: University of Nebraska Press.

OLDS, J. (1956a) A preliminary mapping of electrical reinforcing effects in the rat brain. *J. comp. physiol. Psychol., 49,* 281-285.

OLDS, J. (1956b) Runway and maze behavior controlled by basomedial forebrain stimulation in the rat. *J. comp. physiol. Psychol., 49,* 507-512.

OLDS, J. (1956c) Pleasure centers in the brain. *Sci. Amer., 195,* 105-116.

OLDS, J. (1956d) Neurophysiology of drive. *Psychiatric Research Reports, 6,* 15-20.

OLDS, J. (1956e) *The growth and structure of motives: psychological studies in the theory of action.* Glencoe, Ill., The Free Press.

OLDS, J. (1958a) Effects of hunger and male sex hormone on self-stimulation of the brain. *J. comp. physiol. Psychol., 51,* 320-324.

OLDS, J. (1958b) Satiation effects in self-stimulation of the brain. *J. comp. physiol. Psychol., 51,* 675-678.

OLDS, J., KILLAM, K. F., and BACH-Y-RITA, P. (1956) Self-stimulation of the brain used as a screening method for tranquilizing drugs. *Science, 124,* 265-266.

OLDS, J., and MILNER, P. (1954) Positive reinforcement produced by electrical stimulation of septal area and other regions of rat brain. *J. comp. physiol. Psychol., 47,* 419-427.

OLDS, J., and OLDS, M. E. (1958) Positive reinforcement produced by stimulating hypothalamus with iproniazid and other compounds. *Science, 127,* 1175-1176.

OLDS, M. E. *See* Olds and Olds (1958).

OLMSTED, J. M. D. *See* Lang and Olmsted (1923).

OSGOOD, C. E. (1953) *Method and theory in experimental psychology.* New York: Oxford University Press.

OSGOOD, S. W. *See* Baker and Osgood (1954).

Ost, J. W. P. (1960) Interstimulus interval and proportion of non-reinforced trials in differential eyelid conditioning. Unpublished Ph.D. dissertation. Duke University.

Ost, J. W. P. *See also* Kimble and Ost (1961).

Otis, L. S. *See* Hunt, Jernberg, and Otis (1953).

Page, H. A. (1955) The facilitation of experimental extinction by response prevention as a function of the acquisition of a new response. *J. comp. physiol. Psychol.*, *48*, 14-16.

Page, H. A., and Hall, J. F. (1953) Experimental extinction as a function of the prevention of a response. *J. comp. physiol. Psychol.*, *46*, 33-34.

Papanek, Miriam L. *See* Bruner, Matter, and Papanek. (1955).

Parmenter, R. *See* Anderson and Parmenter (1941).

Pascal, G. R. *See* Jenkins, Pascal, and Walker (1958).

Passenti, R. G. *See* Passey and Possenti (1956).

Passey, G. E. (1948) The influence of intensity of unconditioned stimulus upon acquisition of a conditioned response. *J. exp. Psychol.*, *38*, 420-428.

Passey, G. E. (1957) Net discriminatory reaction potential as a function of stimulus separation along an intensive stimulus continuum. *J. gen. Psychol.*, *56*, 59-66.

Passey, G. E., and Herman, P. N. (1955) The shape of the discrimination gradient for two intracontinuum stimulus separations. *J. exp. Psychol.*, *49*, 273-277.

Passey, G. E., and Passenti, R. G. (1956) The effect of conditioned stimulus intensity upon a simple running response. *J. genet. Psychol.*, *89*, 27-33.

Paterson, A. L. *See* Bindra, Paterson, and Strzelecki (1955).

Patton, R. A. *See* Braun, Patton, and Barnes (1952).

Patton, R. M. *See* Fink and Patton (1953).

Pavlov, I. P. (1902) *The work of the digestive glands.* (Translated by W. H. Thompson) London: Charles Griffin.

Pavlov, I. P. (1906) The scientific investigation of the psychical faculties or processes in the higher animals. *Science, 24,* 613-619. Also in *Lancet, 2,* 911-915.

Pavlov, I. P. (1927) *Conditioned reflexes.* (Translated by G. V. Anrep) London: Oxford University Press.

Pavlov, I. P. (1928) *Lectures on conditioned reflexes.* (Translated by W. H. Gantt) New York: International.

Pavlov, I. P. (1930) A brief outline of the higher nervous activity. In C. Murchison (Ed.) *Psychologies of 1930.* Worcester, Mass.: Clark University Press.

Pavlov, I. P. (1934) An attempt at a physiological interpretation of obessional neurosis and paranoi. *J. ment. Sci.*, *80*, 187-197.

Pavlov, I. P. (1941) *Conditioned reflexes and psychiatry.* (Translated by W. H. Gantt) New York: International Publishers.

PAVLOV, I. P. (1955) *Selected Works* (Translated by S. Belsky; edited by J. Gibbons) Moscow: Foreign Languages Publishing House.

PEREBOOM, A. C. *See* Seward and others (1957).

PERIN, C. T. (1942) Behavior potentiality as a joint function of the amount of training and degree of hunger at the time of extinction. *J. exp. Psychol., 30,* 93-113.

PERIN, C. T. (1943a) A quantitative investigation of the delay-of-reinforcement gradient. *J. exp. Psychol., 32,* 37-51.

PERIN, C. T. (1943b) The effect of delayed reinforcement upon the differentiation of bar responses in white rats. *J. exp. Psychol., 32,* 95-109.

PERKINS, C. C. Jr. (1947) The relation of secondary reward to gradients of reinforcement. *J. exp. Psychol., 37,* 377-392.

PERKINS, C. C. Jr. (1953) The relation between conditioned stimulus intensity and response strength. *J. exp. Psychol., 46,* 225-231.

PERKINS, C. C. Jr. *See also* Bragiel and Perkins (1954), Powell and Perkins (1957).

PERKINS, C. C., Jr., and WEYANT, R. G. (1958) The interval between training and test trials as a determiner of the slope of generalization gradients. *J. comp. physiol. Psychol., 51,* 596-600.

PERKINS, D. T. *See* Hull and others (1940).

PETERS, H. *See* Kendler and others (1952).

PETERSON, L. R. (1956) Variable delayed reinforcement. *J. comp. physiol. Psychol., 49,* 232-234.

PETERSON, W. M. *See* Kaufman and Peterson (1958).

PETRINOVICH, L. *See* Bolles and Petrinovich (1954).

PICK, H. L. *See* Gibson and others (1958), Walk and others (1958).

PINTO, Teresa, and BROMILEY, R. B. (1950) A search for 'spinal conditioning' and evidence that it can become a reflex. *J. exp. Psychol., 40,* 121-130.

PFAFFMANN, C., and SCHLOSBERG, H. (1936) The conditioned knee jerk in psychotic and normal individuals. *J. Psychol., I,* 201-208.

PHILIP, B. R. (1947) Generalization and central tendency in the discrimination of a series of stimuli. *Canad. J. Psychol., 1,* 196-204.

PHILLIPS, Laura W. *See* Postman, Adams, and Phillips (1955), Postman and Phillips (1954).

PIERCE, P. *See* Ritchie, Aeschliman, and Pierce (1950).

PLATT, E. B. *See* Knott, Platt, and Hadley (1944).

PLATTE, C. E. *See* Wickens and Platte (1954).

PLISKOFF, S. S. *See* Kendler and others (1957).

POLTYREV, S. S. (1936) Die Rolle der Rinde und Subrindeknoten in der Bildung der bedingten Reflexe. *Z. Biol., 97,* 180-186.

POLTYREV, S. S., and ZELIONY, G. P. (1930) Grosshirnrinde und Assoziationsfunktion. *Z. Biol., 90,* 157-160.

PORTER, J. M., Jr. (1938a) Adaptation of the galvanic skin response. *J. exp. Psychol.*, *23*, 553-557.

PORTER, J. M., Jr. (1938b) Backward conditioning of the eyelid response. *J. exp. Psychol.*, *23*, 403-410.

PORTER, J. M., Jr. (1938c) Extinction of an acquired response as a function of the interval between successive non-rewarded trials. *J. comp. Psychol.*, *26*, 261-270.

PORTER, J. M., Jr. (1939) Experimental extinction as a function of the interval between successive non-reinforced elicitations. *J. gen. Psychol.*, *20*, 109-134.

PORTER, J. M., Jr. *See also* Karn and Porter (1946), Marquis and Porter (1939).

PORTER, L. W., and MILLER, N. E. (1957) Training under two drives, alternately present, vs. training under a single drive. *J. exp. Psychol.*, *54*, 1-7.

PORTER, P. B. *See* Thompson and Porter (1953).

POSTMAN, L. (1947) The history and present status of the law of effect. *Psychol. Bull.*, *44*, 489-563.

POSTMAN, L. *See also* Talman and Postman (1954).

POSTMAN, L., and ADAMS, Pauline A. (1954) Performance variables in the experimental analysis of the law of effect. *Amer. J. Psychol.*, *67*, 612-631.

POSTMAN, L., and ADAMS, Pauline A. (1956a) Studies in incidental learning: III. Interserial interference. *J. exp. Psychol.*, *51*, 323-328.

POSTMAN, L., and ADAMS, Pauline A. (1956b) Studies in incidental learning: IV. The interaction of orienting tasks and stimulus materials. *J. exp. Psychol.*, *51*, 329-333.

POSTMAN, L., ADAMS, Pauline A., and BOHM, A. M. (1956) Studies in incidental learning: V. Recall for order and associative clustering. *J. exp. Psychol.*, *51*, 334-342.

POSTMAN, L., ADAMS, Pauline A., and PHILLIPS, Laura W. (1955) Studies in incidental learning: II. The effects of association value and the method of testing. *J. exp. Psychol.*, *49*, 1-10.

POSTMAN, L., and PHILLIPS, Laura W. (1954) Studies in incidental learning: I. The effects of crowding and isolation. *J. exp. Psychol.*, *48*, 48-56.

POWELL, D. R., Jr., and PERKINS, C. C., Jr. (1957) Strength of secondary reinforcement as a determiner of the effects of duration of goal response on learning. *J. exp. Psychol.*, *53*, 106-112.

POWLOWSKI, R. F. (1953) The effects of combining hunger and thirst motives in a discrimination habit. *J. comp. physiol. Psychol.*, *46*, 434-441.

PRATT, C. C. (1948) *The logic of modern psychology.* New York: Macmillan.

PRATT, Cornelia H. *See* Schlosberg and Pratt (1956).

PRATT, J. G. *See* McCulloch and Pratt (1934).

PREMACK, D. (1959) Toward empirical behavior laws: I. Positive reinforcement. *Psychol. Rev.*, *66*, 219-233.

PROKASY, W. F. (1958) Extinction and spontaneous recovery of conditioned eyelid responses as a function of amount of acquisition and extinction training. *J. exp. Psychol., 56,* 319-323.

PROKASY, W. F., Jr., GRANT, D. A., and MEYERS, N. A. (1958) Eyelid conditioning as a function of unconditioned stimulus intensity and intertrial interval. *J. exp. Psychol., 55,* 242-246.

PROKOFIEV., G., and ZELIONY, G. P. (1926) Des modes d'associations cerebrales chez l'homme et chez les animaux. *J. de Psychol, 23,* 1020-1028.

PRONKO, N. H. *See* Kellogg, Pronko, and Deese (1946).

PRONKO, N. H., and KELLOGG, W. N. (1942) The phenomenon of the muscle twitch in flexion conditioning. *J. exp. Psychol., 31,* 232-238.

PROSSER, C. L., and HUNTER, W. S. (1936) The extinction of startle responses and spinal reflexes in the white rat. *Amer. J. Physiol., 117,* 609-618.

PUPKO, L. K. *See* Yuschenka, Rolle, and Pupko (1934).

RABEN, Margaret W. (1949) The white rat's discrimination of differences in intensity of illumination measured by a running response in the white rat. *J. comp. physiol. Psychol., 42,* 254-272.

RAEVA, N. V., and RAPPOPORT, E. J. (1934) The sensory pathways in motor activity. *Fiziol. Zh. S.S.S.R., 17,* 636-652. (*Psychol. Abstr.,* 1935, *9,* No. 1691).

RAMOND, C. K. (1953) Anxiety and tasks as determiners of verbal performance. *J. exp. Psychol., 46,* 120-124.

RAMOND, C. K. (1954) Performance in selective learning as a function of hunger. *J. exp. Psychol., 48,* 265-270.

RANSON, S. W. *See* Hetherington and Ranson (1942).

RAPPOPORT, E. J. *See* Raeva and Rappoport (1934).

RASCH, Ellen. *See* Gelber and Rasch (1956c).

RATNER, S. C. (1956) Effect of extinction of dipper approaching on subsequent extinction of bar pressing and dipper approaching. *J. comp. physiol. Psychol., 49,* 576-581.

RATNER, S. C. *See also* Denny and Ratner (1959).

RAUP, R. B. (1925) *Complacency, the foundation of human behavior.* New York: Macmillan.

RAYNER, R. *See* Watson and Rayner (1920).

RAZRAN, G. H. S. (1930) Theory of conditioning and related phenomena. *Psychol. Rev., 37,* 25-43.

RAZRAN, G. H. S. (1933) Conditioned responses in children. *Arch. Psychol., N. Y., 23,* No. 148.

RAZRAN, G. H. S. (1938) Transposition of relational responses and generalization of conditioned responses. *Psychol. Rev., 45,* 532-538.

RAZRAN, G. H. S. (1939a) Studies in configural conditioning. VI. Comparative extinction and forgetting of pattern and of single-stimulus conditioning. *J. exp. Psychol., 24,* 432-438.

RAZRAN, G. H. S. (1939b) Extinction, spontaneous recovery, and forgetting. *Amer. J. Psychol., 52,* 100-102.

RAZRAN, G. H. S. (1939c) A quantitative study of meaning by a conditioned salivary technique (semantic conditioning). *Science, 90,* 89-90.

RAZRAN, G. H. S. (1939d) The law of effect or the law of qualitative conditioning. *Psychol. Rev., 46,* 445-463.

RAZRAN, G. (1949) Stimulus generalization of conditioned responses. *Psychol. Bull., 46,* 337-365.

RAZRAN, G. (1955a) Operant vs. classical conditioning. *Amer. J. Psychol., 68,* 489-490.

RAZRAN, G. (1955b) A direct laboratory comparison of Pavlovian conditioning and traditional associative learning. *J. abnorm. soc. Psychol., 51,* 649-652.

RAZRAN, G. (1955c) Partial reinforcement of salivary CR's in adult human subjects: preliminary study. *Psychol. Rep., 1,* 409-416.

RAZRAN, G. (1955d) A note on second-order conditioning—and secondary reinforcement. *Psychol. Rev., 62,* 327-332.

RAZRAN, G. (1956a) Backward conditioning. *Psychol. bull., 53,* 55-69.

RAZRAN, G. (1956b) Avoidant vs. unavoidant conditioning and partial reinforcement in Russian laboratories. *Amer. J. Psychol., 69,* 127-129.

RAZRAN, G. (1956c) Extinction re-examined and re-analyzed: A new theory. *Psychol. Rev., 63,* 39-52.

RAZRAN, G. (1957) The dominance-contiguity theory of the acquisition of classical conditioning. *Psychol. Bull., 54,* 1-46.

REED, P. *See* Bitterman, Reed, and Krauskopf (1952), Bitterman, Reed, and Kubala (1953).

REESE, W. G. (1953) Certain aspects of conditioning in the human. *Ann. N. Y. Acad. Sci., 56,* 330-341.

REID, L. S. (1953) Development of non-continuity behavior through continuity learning. *J. exp. Psychol., 46,* 107-112.

REID, L. S., and SLIVINSKE, A. J. (1954) A test for generalized secondary reinforcement during extinction under a different drive. *J. comp. physiol. Psychol., 47,* 306-310.

REISMAN, M. N. *See* Fitzwater and Reisman (1952).

REISS, B. F. (1946) Genetic changes in semantic conditioning. *J. exp. Psychol., 36,* 143-152.

RENSHAW, S. *See* Steckle and Renshaw (1934).

RETHLINGSHAFER, Dorothy. (1941) The learning of a visual discrimination problem under varying motivating conditions. *J. comp. Psychol., 32,* 583-591.

REXROAD, C. N. (1932) Outline of the conditions under which learning occurs. *Psychol. Rev., 39,* 174-183.

REYNOLDS, B. (1945a) The acquisition of a trace conditioned response as a function of the magnitude of the stimulus trace. *J. exp. Psychol., 35,* 15-30.

REYNOLDS, B. (1945) Extinction of trace conditioned responses as a function of the spacing of trials during the acquisition and extinction series. *J. exp. Psychol.*, *35*, 81-95.

REYNOLDS, B. (1945c) A repetition of the Blodgett experiment on 'latent learning.' *J. exp. Psychol.*, *35*, 504-516.

REYNOLDS, B. (1949) The relationship between strength of a habit and the degree of drive present during acquisition. *J. exp. Psychol.*, *39*, 296-305.

REYNOLDS, R. W. (1958) The relationship between stimulation voltage and rate of hypothalamic self-stimulation in the rat. *J. comp. physiol. Psychol.*, *51*, 193-198.

REYNOLDS, W. F. (1958) Acquisition and extinction of the conditioned eyelid response following partial and continuous reinforcement. *J. exp. Psychol.*, *55*, 335-341.

RIBBLE, M. A. (1944) Infantile experience in relation to personality development. In J. McV. Hunt, *Personality and the behavior disorders.* New York: Ronald.

RICHTER, C. P. (1939) Salt-taste thresholds for normal and adrenalectomized rats. *Endocrinology*, *24*, 367-371.

RIESEN, A. H. (1947) The development of visual perception in man and chimpanzee. *Science*, *106*, 107-108.

RIESEN, A. H. *See also* Hovland and Riesen (1940).

RIGBY, Marilyn K. *See* Jenkins and Rigby (1950).

RIOPELLE, A. J. (1953) Transfer suppression and learning sets. *J. comp. physiol. Psychol.*, *46*, 108-114.

RIOPELLE, A. J. (1955) Rewards, preferences, and learning sets. *Psychol. Rep.*, *1*, 167-173.

RIOPELLE, A. J. *See also* Darby and Riopelle (1955), Grant, Riopelle, and Hake (1950).

RIOPELLE, A. J., and COPELAN, E. L. (1954) Discrimination reversal to a sign. *J. exp. Psychol.*, *48*, 143-145.

RITCHIE, B. F. (1947) Studies in spatial learning. III. Two paths to the same location and two paths to two different locations. *J. exp. Psychol.*, *37*, 25-38.

RITCHIE, B. F. *See also* Tolman and Ritchie (1943).

RITCHIE, B. F., AESCHLIMAN, B., and PIERCE, P. (1950) Studies in spatial learning: VIII. Place performance and the acquisition of place dispositions. *J. comp. physiol. Psychol.*, *43*, 73-85.

RITCHIE, B. F., EBELING, E., and ROTH, W. (1950) Evidence for continuity in the discrimination of vertical and horizontal patterns. *J. comp. physiol. Psychol.*, *43*, 168-180.

RITCHIE, B. F., HAY, Alice, and HARE, Rachel (1951) Studies in spatial learning: IX. A dispositional analysis of response performance. *J. comp. physiol. Psychol.*, *44*, 442-449.

ROBERTS, C. L. *See* Marx, Henderson, and Roberts (1955).

ROBERTS, C. L., MARX, M. H., and COLLIER, G. (1958) Light onset and light offset as reinforcers for the albino rat. *J. comp. physiol. Psychol., 51*, 575-579.

ROBERTS, L. *See* Morrell, Roberts, and Jasper (1956).

ROBERTS, W. W. (1958a) Rapid escape learning without avoidance learning motivated by hypothalamic stimulation in cats. *J. comp. physiol. Psychol., 51*, 391-399.

ROBERTS, W. W. (1958b) Both rewarding and punishing effects from stimulation of posterior hypothalamus of cat with same electrode at same intensity. *J. comp. physiol. Psychol., 51*, 400-407.

ROBERTS, W. W. *See also* Delgado, Roberts, and Miller (1954).

ROBINSON, D. E., and CAPALDI, E. J. (1958) Spontaneous recovery following nonresponse extinction. *J. comp. physiol. Psychol., 51*, 644-646.

ROBY, T. B. *See* Sheffield and Roby (1950), Sheffield, Roby, and Campbell (1954).

ROESSLER, R. L., and BROGDEN, W. J. (1943) Conditioned differentiation of vasoconstriction to subvocal stimuli. *Amer. J. Psychol., 56*, 78-86.

ROGERS, C. R. (1942) *Counseling and psychotherapy: newer concepts in practice.* Boston: Houghton-Mifflin.

ROGERS, W. A. *See* Bugelski, Coyer, and Rogers (1952).

ROHRER, J. H. (1947) Experimental extinction as a function of the distribution of extinction trials and response strength. *J. exp. Psychol., 37*, 473-493.

ROHRER, J. H. (1949) A motivational state resulting from non-reward. *J. comp. physiol. Psychol., 42*, 476-485.

ROLLE, S. D. *See* Yuschenka, Rolle, and Pupko (1934).

ROSENBAUM, G. (1953) Stimulus generalization as a function of level of experimentally induced anxiety. *J. exp. Psychol., 45*, 35-43.

ROSENBAUM, G. (1956) Stimulus generalization as a function of clinical anxiety.

ROSENTHAL J. S. *See* Lebedinskai and Rosenthal (1953).
J. abnorm. soc. Psychol., 53, 281-285.

ROSS, L. E. (1959) The decremental effects of partial reinforcement during acquisition of the conditioned eyelid response. *J. exp. Psychol., 57*, 74-82.

ROSS, L. E. *See also* Goodrich, Ross, and Wagner (1957), Runquist and Ross (1959), Spence, Goodrich, and Ross (1959), Spence, Hoggard, and Ross (1958a) (1958b), Spence and Ross (1957) (1959).

ROSS, L. E., and HUNTER, J. J. (1959) Habit strength parameters in eyelid conditioning as a function of UCS intensity. *Psychol. Rec., 9*, 103-107.

ROSS, R. T. *See* Hull and others (1940).

ROSS, T. A. (1937) *The common neuroses.* Baltimore: William Wood & Co.

ROSVOLD, H. E. *See* Delgado, Rosvold, and Looney (1956).

ROTH, C. H. *See* Gewirtz, Baer, and Roth (1958).

ROTH, W. *See* Ritchie, Ebeling, and Roth (1950).

ROTHKOPF, E. Z. (1955) Distribution of practice and the temporal decay of response-produced stimuli. *J. exp. Psychol., 49,* 33-38.

ROUSE, R. O. *See* Hull and others (1951).

ROUSSEL, Jacqueline. *See* Amsel and Roussel (1952).

ROZEBOOM, W. W. (1957) Secondary extinction of lever-pressing behavior in the albino rat. *J. exp. Psychol., 54,* 280-287.

ROZEBOOM, W. W. (1958) "What is learned?"—an empirical enigma. *Psychol. Rev., 65,* 22-23.

RUNQUIST, W. N., and ROSS, L. E. (1959) The relation between physiological measures of emotionality and performance in eyelid conditioning. *J. exp. Psychol., 57,* 329-332.

RUNQUIST, W. N., SPENCE, K. W., and STUBBS, D. W. (1958) Differential conditioning and intensity of the UCS. *J. Exp. Psychol., 55,* 51-55.

RUTLEDGE, L. T. *See* Doty, Rutledge, and Larsen (1956).

SALDANHA, E. L., and BITTERMAN, M. E. (1951) Relational learning in the rat. *Amer. J. Psychol., 64,* 37-53.

SALTZ, E. *See* Grice and Saltz (1950).

SALTZMAN, I. J. (1949) Maze learning in the absence of primary reinforcement: A study of secondary reinforcement. *J. comp. physiol. Psychol., 42,* 161-173.

SALTZMAN, I. J. (1950) Generalization of secondary reinforcement. *J. exp. Psychol., 40,* 189-193.

SALTZMAN, I., and KOCH, S. (1948) The effect of low intensities of hunger on the behavior mediated by a habit of maximum strength. *J. exp. Psychol., 38,* 347-370.

SAMPLINER, R. I. *See* Miller, Sampliner, and Woodrow (1957).

SAMPSON, P. B. *See* Gerall, Sampson, and Boslov (1957).

SANDERS, M. J. (1937) An experimental demonstration of regression in the rat. *J. exp. Psychol., 21,* 493-510.

SCHARLOCK, D. P. (1954) The effects of a pre-extinction procedure on the extinction of place and response performance in the T maze. *J. exp. Psychol., 48,* 31-36.

SCHILLER, J. J. *See* Grant and Schiller (1953).

SCHILLER, P. H. (1952) Innate constituents of complex responses in primates. *Psychol. Rev., 59,* 177-191.

SCHIPPER, L. M. *See* Grant, Schipper, and Ross (1952), Grant and Schipper (1952).

SCHLOSBERG, H. (1928) A study of the conditioned patellar reflex. *J. exp. Psychol., 11,* 468-494.

SCHLOSBERG, H. (1934) Conditioned responses in the white rat. *J. genet. Psychol.*, *45*, 303-335.

SCHLOSBERG, H. (1936) Conditioned responses in the white rat: II. Conditioned responses based upon shock to the foreleg. *J. genet Psychol.*, *49*, 107-138.

SCHLOSBERG, H. (1937) The relationship between success and the laws of conditioning. *Psychol. Rev.*, *44*, 379-394.

SCHLOSBERG, H. *See also* Blackwell and Schlosberg (1943), Hughes and Schlosberg (1938), Kappauf and Schlosberg (1937) Pfaffman and Schlosberg (1936), White and Schlosberg (1952).

SCHLOSBERG, H., and SOLOMON, R. L. (1943) Latency of response in a choice of discrimination. *J. exp. Psychol.*, *33*, 22-39.

SCHLOSBERG, H., and PRATT, Cornelia, H. (1956) The secondary reward value of inaccessible food for hungry and satiated rats. *J. comp. physiol. Psychol.*, *49*, 149-152.

SCHNEIDER, D. E. *See* Grant and Schneider (1948) (1949).

SCHNEIRLA, T. C. (1929) Learning and orientation in ants. *Comp. Psychol. Monogr.*, *6*, No. 30.

SCHNEIRLA, T. C. *See also* Maier and Schneirla (1935).

SCHOENFELD, W. N. *See* Bersh, Notterman, and Schoenfeld (1956), Bersh, Schoenfeld, and Notterman (1953), Notterman, Schoenfeld, and Bersh (1952), Estes and others (1954), Keller and Schoenfeld (1950).

SCHOENFELD, W. N., ANTONITIS, J. J., and BERSH, P. J. (1950) A preliminary study of training conditions necessary for secondary reinforcement. *J. exp. Psychol.*, *40*, 40-45.

SCHRODER, H. M. *See* Wickens, Schroder, and Snide (1954).

SCHULMAN, A. *See* Sidman and others (1955).

SCOTT, E. D., and WIKE, E. L. (1956) The effect of partially delayed reinforcement and trial-distribution on the extinction of an instrumental response. *Amer. J. Psychol.*, *69*, 264-268.

SCOTT, V. B. *See* Kellogg and others (1940).

SEARS, R. R. (1934) Effect of optic lobe ablation on the visuo-motor behavior of goldfish. *J. comp. Psychol.*, *17*, 233-265.

SEARS, R. R. *See also* Dollard and others (1938), Hovland and Sears (1938).

SEARS, R. R., and COHEN, L. H. (1933) Hysterical anesthesia, analgesia, and astereognosis. *Arch. Neurol. Psychiat., Chicago*, *29*, 260-271.

SEARS, W. N. *See* Hilgard, Campbell, and Sears (1938).

SECHENOV, I. (1935) *Selected works.* Moscow: State Publishing House.

SEEMAN, W., and WILLIAMS, H. (1952) An experimental note on a Hull-Leeper difference. *J. exp. Psychol.*, *44*, 40-43.

SEGALL, M. *See* Montgomery and Segall (1955).

SEIDEL, R. J. (1958) An investigation of the mediation process in preconditioning. *J. exp. Psychol., 56,* 220-225.

SEIDEL, R. J. (1959) A review of sensory preconditioning. *Psychol. Bull., 56,* 58-73.

SENDEN, M. von (1932) *Raum-und Gestaltauffasung bie operierten Blindgeborenen vor und nach der Operation.* Leipzig: Barth.

SETTLAGE, P. H. *See* Harlow and others (1952), Harlow and Settlage (1939).

SETTLAGE, P. H., and HARLOW, H. F. (1936) Concerning the sensory pathway in the conditioned reflex. *J. comp. Psychol., 22,* 279-282.

SEWARD, J. P. (1942) An experimental test of Guthrie's theory of reinforcement. *J. exp. Psychol., 30,* 247-256.

SEWARD, J. P. (1949) An experimental analysis of latent learning. *J. exp. Psychol., 39,* 177-186.

SEWARD, J. P. (1950) Secondary reinforcement as tertiary motivation: A revision of Hull's revision. *Psychol. Rev., 57,* 362-374.

SEWARD, J. P. (1951) Experimental evidence for the motivating function of reward. *Psychol. Bull., 48,* 130-149.

SEWARD, J. P. (1952) Introduction to a theory of motivation in learning. *Psychol. Rev., 59,* 405-413.

SEWARD, J. P. (1956a) Reinforcement and expectancy: two theories in search of a controversy. *Psychol. Rev., 63,* 105-113.

SEWARD, J. P. (1956b) Drive, incentive, and reinforcement. *Psychol. Rev. 63,* 195-203.

SEWARD, J. P., DATEL, W. E., and LEVY, N. (1952) Tests of two hypotheses of latent learning. *J. exp. Psychol., 43,* 274-280.

SEWARD, J. P., and HANDLON, J. H. (1952) The effect of satiation on the use of habit. *J. genet. Psychol., 81,* 259-272.

SEWARD, J. P., and LEVY, N. (1949) Sign learning as a factor in extinction. *J. comp. physiol. Psychol., 39,* 660-668.

SEWARD, J. P., and LEVY, N. (1953) Choice-point behavior as a function of secondary reinforcement with relevant drives satiated. *J. comp. physiol. Psychol., 46,* 334-338.

SEWARD, J. P., LEVY, N., and HANDLON, J. H., Jr. (1950) Incidental learning in the rat. *J. comp. physiol. Psychol., 43,* 240-251.

SEWARD, J. P., LEVY, N., and HANDLON, J. H., Jr. (1953) Choice behavior in satiated rats as a function of drive during training. *J. genet. Psychol., 83,* 3-18.

SEWARD, J. P., PEREBROOM, A. C., BUTLER, B., and JONES, R. B. (1957) The role of prefeeding in an apparent frustration effect. *J. exp. Psychol., 54,* 445-450.

SEWARD, J. P., and WELDON, R. J. (1953) Response latency as a function of change in delay of reward. *J. comp. physiol. Psychol., 46,* 184-189.

SHAGASS, C. *See* Jasper and Shagass (1941a) (1941b).

SHAGASS, C., and JOHNSON, E. P. (1943) The course of acquisition of a conditioned response of the occipital alpha rhythm. *J. exp. Psychol.*, *33*, 201-209.

SHAW, M. E., and WATERS, R. H. (1950) An experimental test of latent learning in a relatively free-choice situation. *J. genet Psychol.*, *77*, 283-292.

SHEATZ, G. *See* Galambos, Sheatz, and Vernier (1956).

SHEFFIELD, F. D. (1948) Avoidance training and the contiguity principle. *J. comp. physiol. Psychol.*, *41*, 165-177.

SHEFFIELD, F. D. (1949) Hilgard's critique of Guthrie. *Psychol. Rev.*, *56*, 284-291.

SHEFFIELD, F. D. *See also* Campbell and Sheffield (1953).

SHEFFIELD, F. D., and CAMPBELL, B. A. (1954) The role of experience in the "spontaneous" activity of hungry rats. *J. comp. physiol. Psychol.*, *47*, 97-100.

SHEFFIELD, F. D., and ROBY, T. B. (1950) Reward value of a nonnutritive sweet taste. *J. comp. physiol. Psychol.*, *43*, 471-481.

SHEFFIELD, F. D., ROBY, T. B., and CAMPBELL, B. A. (1954) Drive reduction versus consummatory behavior as determinants of reinforcement. *J. comp. physiol. Psychol.*, *47*, 349-354.

SHEFFIELD, F. D., and TEMMER, Helena W. (1950) Relative resistance to extinction of escape training and avoidance training. *J. exp. Psychol.*, *40*, 287-298.

SHEFFIELD, F. D., WULFF, J. J., and BACKER, R. (1951) Reward value of copulation without sex drive reduction. *J. comp. physiol. Psychol.*, *44*, 3-8.

SHEFFIELD, Virginia F. (1949) Extinction as a function of partial reinforcement and distribution of practice. *J. exp. Psychol.*, *39*, 511-526.

SHEFFIELD, Virginia F. (1950) Resistance to extinction as a function of the distribution of extinction trials. *J. exp. Psychol.*, *40*, 305-313.

SHEPARD, R. N. (1957) Stimulus and response generalization: a stochastic model relating generalization to distance in psychological space. *Psychometrika*, *22*, 325-345.

SHEPARD, R. N. (1958) Stimulus and response generalization: Tests of a model relating generalization to distance in psychological space. *J. exp. Psychol.*, *55*, 509-523.

SHERRINGTON, C. S. (1906) *The integrative action of the nervous system.* New Haven: Yale Univ. Press.

SHIPLEY, W. C. (1933) An apparent transfer of conditioning. *J. gen. Psychol.*, *8*, 382-391.

SHIPLEY, W. C. (1935) Indirect conditioning. *J. gen. Psychol.*, *12*, 337-357.

SHOBEN, E. J. (1949) Psychotherapy as a problem in learning theory. *Psychol. Bull.*, *46*, 366-392.

SHUFORD, E. H. Jr. *See* Young and Shuford (1954) (1955).

SHURRAGER, H. C. *See* Shurrager and Shurrager (1941) (1946) (1950).

SHURRAGER, P. S. *See* Dykman and Shurrager (1956).

SHURRAGER, P. S., and CULLER, E. A. (1938) Phenomena allied to conditioning in the spinal dog. *Amer. J. Physiol., 123,* 186-187.

SHURRAGER, P. S., and CULLER, E. (1940) Conditioning in the spinal dog. *J. exp. Psychol., 26,* 133-159.

SHURRAGER, P. S., and CULLER, E. (1941) Conditioned extinction of a reflex in the spinal dog. *J. exp. Psychol., 28,* 287-303.

SHURRAGER, P. S., and SHURRAGER, H. C. (1941) Converting a spinal CR into a reflex. *J. exp. Psychol., 29,* 217-224.

SHURRAGER, P. S., and SHURRAGER, H. C. (1946) The rate of learning measured at a single synapse. *J. exp. Psychol., 36,* 347-354.

SHURRAGER, P. S., and DYKMAN, R. A. (1951) Walking spinal carnivores. *J. comp. physiol. Psychol., 44,* 252-262.

SHURRAGER, P. S., and SHURRAGER, H. C. (1950) Comment on "a search for 'spinal conditioning' and for evidence that it can become a reflex." *J. exp. Psychol., 40,* 135-137.

SIDMAN, M. (1950) A note on functional relations obtained from group data. *Psychol. Bull., 49,* 263-269.

SIDMAN, M. (1953a) Avoidance conditioning with brief shock and no exteroceptive warning signal. *Science, 118,* 157-158.

SIDMAN, M. (1953b) Two temporal parameters of the maintenance of avoidance behavior by the white rat. *J. comp. physiol. Psychol., 46,* 253-261.

SIDMAN, M. (1954) The temporal distribution of avoidance responses. *J. comp. physiol. Psychol., 47,* 399-402.

SIDMAN, M. (1955a) On the persistance of avoidance behavior. *J. abnorm. soc. Psychol., 50,* 217-220.

SIDMAN, M. (1955b) Technique for assessing the effects of drugs on timing behavior. *Science, 122,* 925.

SIDMAN, M. *See* also Boren, Sidman, and Herrnstein (1959), Brady, Boren, Conrad, and Sidman (1957), Geller, Sidman, and Brady (1955).

SIDMAN, M., BRADY, J. V., BOREN, J. J., CONRAD, D. G., and SCHULMAN, A. (1955). Reward schedules and behavior maintained by intracranial self-stimulation. *Science, 122,* 830-831.

SIEGEL, Helen S. *See* Siegel and Siegel (1949).

SIEGEL, P. S. (1950) Reactive inhibition as a function of a number of response evocations. *J. exp. Psychol., 40,* 604-608.

SIEGEL, P. S., and BRANTLEY, J. J. (1951) The relationship of emotionality to the consummatory response of eating. *J. exp. Psychol., 42,* 304-306.

SIEGEL, P. S., and SIEGEL, Helen S. (1949) The effect of emotionality on the water intake of the rat. *J. comp. physiol. Psychol., 42,* 12-16.

SILVER, C. A., and MEYER, D. R. (1954) Temporal factors in sensory preconditioning. *J. comp. physiol. Psychol., 47,* 57-59.

SIMMONS, R. (1924) The relative effectiveness of certain incentives in animal learning. *Comp. Psychol. Monogr., 2,* 1-79.

SINGER, E. A. (1911) Mind as an observable object. *J. Phil. Psychol. sci. Meth., 8,* 180-186.

SISKEL, M., Jr. *See* Collier and Siskel (1959).

SJOBERG, W. E. *See* Brown and Sjoberg (1950).

SKINNER, B. F. (1930) On the conditions of elicitation of certain eating reflexes. *Proc. nat. Acad. Sci., 16,* 433-438.

SKINNER, B. F. (1931) The concept of the reflex in the description of behavior. *J. gen. Psychol., 5,* 427-458.

SKINNER, B. F. (1932) On the rate of formation of a conditioned reflex. *J. gen. Psychol., 7,* 274-285.

SKINNER, B. F. (1933) The rate of establishment of a discrimination. *J. gen. Psychol., 9,* 302-350.

SKINNER, B. F. (1934a) The extinction of chained reflexes. *Proc. nat. Acad. Sci., 20,* 234-237.

SKINNER, B. F. (1934b) A discrimination without previous conditioning. *Proc. nat. Acad. Sci., 20,* 532-536.

SKINNER, B. F. (1935a) A discrimination based upon a change in the properties of a stimulus. *J. gen. Psychol., 12,* 313-336.

SKINNER, B. F. (1935b) Two types of conditioned reflex and a pseudo type. *J. gen. Psychol., 12,* 66-77.

SKINNER, B. F. (1936a) A failure to obtain "disinhibition." *J. gen. Psychol., 14,* 127-135.

SKINNER,. B. F. (1936b) Conditioning and extinction and their relation to drive. *J. gen. Psychol., 14,* 296-317.

SKINNER, B. F. (1936c) The effect on the amount of conditioning of an interval of time before reinforcement. *J. gen. Psychol., 14,* 279-295.

SKINNER, B. F. (1936d) The reinforcing effect of a differentiating stimulus. *J. gen. Psychol., 14,* 263-278.

SKINNER, B. F. (1936e) Thirst as an arbitrary drive. *J. gen. Psychol., 15,* 205-210.

SKINNER, B. F. (1937) Two types of conditioned reflex: a reply to Konorski and Miller. *J. gen. Psychol., 16,* 272-279.

SKINNER, B. F. (1938) *The behavior of organisms; an experimental analysis.* New York: Appleton-Century.

SKINNER, B. F. (1948a) *Walden Two.* New York: McMillan.

SKINNER, B. F. (1948b) Superstition in the pigeon. *J. exp. Psychol., 38,* 168-172.

SKINNER, B. F. (1950) Are theories of learning necessary? *Psychol. Rev. 57,* 193-216.

SKINNER, B. F. (1957) *Verbal behavior.* New York: Appleton-Century-Crofts.

SKINNER, B. F. *See also* Estes and Skinner (1941), Ferster and Skinner (1957).

SKOLNICK, A. *See* Wedell, Taylor, and Skolnick (1940).

SLIVINSKE, A. J. *See* Reid and Slivinske (1954).

SMITH, K. (1954) Conditioning as an artifact. *Psychol. Rev., 61,* 217-225.

SMITH, M. H., and DUFFY, M. (1957) Consumption of sucrose and saccharine by hungry and satiated rats. *J. comp. physiol. Psychol., 40,* 65-69.

SMITH, M. H., and HOY, W. J. (1954) Rate of response during operant discrimination. *J. exp. Psychol., 48,* 259-265.

SMITH, M. H., and KINNEY, G. C. (1956) Sugar as a reward for hungry and nonhungry rats. *J. exp. Psychol., 51,* 348-352.

SMITH, M. P. (1951) The stimulus-trace gradient in visual discrimination learning. *J. comp. physiol. Psychol., 44,* 154-161.

SMITH, M. P., and BUCHANAN, G. (1954) Acquisition of secondary reward by cues associated with shock reduction. *J. exp. Psychol., 48,* 123-126.

SMITH, M. P., and CAPRETTA, P. J. (1956) Effects of drive level and experience on the reward value of saccharine solutions. *J. comp. physiol. Psychol., 49,* 553-557.

SMITH, R. L. *See* Lacey and Smith (1954), Lacey, Smith, and Green (1955).

SMITH, S., and GUTHRIE, E. R. (1921) *General psychology in terms of behavior.* New York: Appleton-Century-Crofts.

SMITH, W. C. *See* Bullock and Smith (1953).

SNIDE, J. D. *See* Wickens, Schroder, and Snide (1954), Wickens and Snide (1955).

SOLLENBERGER, R. T. *See* Dollard and others (1939).

SOLOMON, L. N. *See* Mowrer and Solomon (1954).

SOLOMON, R. L. (1948a) The influence of work on behavior. *Psychol. Bull., 45,* 1-40.

SOLOMON, R. L. (1948b) Effort and extinction rate: A confirmation. *J. comp. physiol. Psychol., 41,* 93-101.

SOLOMON, R. L. *See also* Brush, Brush, and Solomon (1955), Church, Brush, and Solomon (1956), Church and Solomon (1956), Lambert and Solomon (1952), Wynne and Solomon (1955).

SOLOMON, R. L., and BRUSH, Elinor S. (1956) Experimentally derived conceptions of anxiety and aversion. In M. R. Jones (Ed.) *Nebraska symposium on motivation.* Lincoln: University of Nebraska Press.

SOLOMON, R. L., KAMIN, L. J., and WYNNE, L. C. (1953) Traumatic avoidance learning: the outcomes of several extinction procedures with dogs. *J. abnorm. soc. Psychol., 48,* 291-302.

SOLOMON, R. L., and WYNNE, L. C. (1953) Traumatic avoidance learning: Acquisition in normal dogs. *Psychol. Monogr. 67,* No. 354, pp. 19.

SOLOMON, R. L., and WYNNE, L. C. (1954) Traumatic avoidance learning: the principles of anxiety conservation and partial irreversibility. *Psychol. Rev., 61,* 353-385.

SPELT, D. K. (1938) Conditioned responses in the human fetus *in utero. Psychol. Bull., 35,* 712-713.

SPELT, D. K. (1948) The conditioning of the human fetus *in utero. J. exp. Psychol., 38,* 338-346.

SPENCE, K. W. (1934) Visual acuity and its relation to brightness in chimpanzee and man. *J. comp. Psychol., 18,* 333-361.

SPENCE, K. W. (1936) The nature of discrimination learning in animals. *Psychol. Rev. 43,* 427-449.

SPENCE, K. W. (1937a) Analysis of the formation of visual discrimination habits in chimpanzee. *J. comp. Psychol., 23,* 77-100.

SPENCE, K. W. (1937b) The differential response in animals to stimuli varying within a single dimension. *Psychol. Rev. 44,* 430-444.

SPENCE, K. W. (1938) Gradual vs. sudden solution of discrimination problems by chimpanzees. *J. comp. Psychol., 25,* 213-224.

SPENCE, K. W. (1939) A reply to Dr. Razran on the transposition of response in discrimination experiments. *Psychol. Rev., 46,* 88-91.

SPENCE, K. W. (1940) Continuous versus non-continuous interpretations of discrimination learning. *Psychol. Rev., 47,* 271-288.

SPENCE, K. W. (1941) Failure of transposition in size-discrimination of chimpanzees. *Amer. J. Psychol., 54,* 223-229.

SPENCE, K. W. (1942a) The basis of solution by chimpanzees of the intermediate size problem. *J. exp. Psychol., 31,* 257-271.

SPENCE, K. W. (1942b) Theoretical interpretations of learning. In F. A. Moss, (Ed.), *Comparative psychology.* New York: Prentice-Hall.

SPENCE, K. W. (1944) The nature of theory construction in contemporary psychology. *Psychol. Rev., 51,* 47-68.

SPENCE, K. W. (1945) An experimental test of the continuity and non-continuity theories of discrimination learning. *J. exp. Psychol., 35,* 253-266.

SPENCE, K. W. (1947) The role of secondary reinforcement in delayed-reward learning. *Psychol. Rev., 54,* 1-8.

SPENCE, K. W. (1948) The postulates and methods of behaviorism. *Psychol Rev., 55,* 67-68.

SPENCE, K. W. (1950) Cognitive vs. stimulus-response theories of learning. *Psychol. Rev., 57,* 159-172.

SPENCE, K. W. (1951a) Theoretical interpretations of learning. In C. P. Stone (Ed.) *Comparative psychology.* (3rd ed.) New York: Prentice-Hall.

SPENCE, K. W. (1951b) Theoretical interpretations of learning. S. S. Stevens (Ed.), *Handbook of experimental psychology.* New York: Wiley, 690-729.

SPENCE, K. W. (1952) The nature of the response in discrimination learning. *Psychol. Rev., 59,* 89-93.

SPENCE, K. W. (1953) Learning and Performance in eyelid conditioning as a function of the intensity of the UCS. *J. exp. Psychol., 45,* 57-63.

SPENCE, K. W. (1956) *Behavior theory and conditioning.* New Haven: Yale University Press.

SPENCE, K. W. (1958a) A theory of emotionally based drive (D) and its relation to performance in simple learning situations. *Amer. Psychol., 13,* 131-141.

SPENCE, K. W. (1958b) Behavior theory and selective learning. In M. R. Jones (Ed.) *Nebraska symposium on motivation.* Lincoln: University of Nebraska Press.

SPENCE, K. W. *See also* Bergmann and Spence (1941) and (1944), Diesenroth and Spence (1941), Hull and Spence (1938), Farber and Spence (1953), Taylor and Spence (1952).

SPENCE, K. W., and BEECROFT, R. S. (1954) Differential conditioning and level of anxiety. *J. exp. Psychol., 48,* 399-403.

SPENCE, K. W., BERGMANN, G., and LIPPITT, R. A. (1950) A study of simple learning under irrelevant motivational-reward conditions. *J. exp. Psychol., 40,* 539-551.

SPENCE, K. W., and FARBER, I. E. (1953) Conditioning and extinction as a function of anxiety. *J. exp. Psychol., 45,* 116-119.

SPENCE, K. W., and FARBER, I. E. (1954) The relation of anxiety to differential eyelid conditioning. *J. exp. Psychol., 47,* 127-134.

SPENCE, K. W., FARBER, I. E., and TAYLOR, Elaine (1954) The relation of electric shock and anxiety to level of performance in eyelid conditioning. *J. exp. Psychol., 48,* 404-408.

SPENCE, K. W., GOODRICH, K. P., and ROSS, L. E. (1959) Performance in differential conditioning and discrimination learning as a function of hunger and relative response frequency. *J. exp. Psychol., 58,* 8-16.

SPENCE, K. W., HAGGARD, D. F., and ROSS, L. E. (1958a) UCS intensity and the associative (habit) strength of the eyelid CR. *J. exp. Psychol., 55,* 404-411.

SPENCE, K. W., HAGGARD, D. F., and ROSS, L. E. (1958b) Intrasubject conditioning as a function of the intensity of the unconditioned stimulus. *Science, 128,* 774-775.

SPENCE, K. W., and LIPPITT, R. (1940) "Latent" learning of a simple maze problem with relevant needs satiated. *Psychol. Bull. 37,* 429 (Abstract).

SPENCE, K. W., and LIPPITT, R. (1946) An experimental test of the sign-gestalt theory of trial-and-error learning. *J. exp. Psychol., 36,* 491-502.

SPENCE, K. W., and NORRIS, Eugenia B. (1950) Eyelid conditioning as a function of the inter-trial interval. *J. exp. Psychol., 40,* 716-720.

SPENCE, K. W., and ROSS, L. E. (1957) Experimental evidence on the relation between performance level in evelid conditioning and anxiety (drive) level. Technical report 5. Studies of influence of motivation on performance in learning. pp. 21.

SPENCE, K. W., and ROSS, L. E. (1959) A methodological study of the form and latency of eyelid responses in conditioning. *J. exp. Psychol., 58,* 376-385.

SPENCE, K. W., and TAYLOR, Janet (1951) Anxiety and strength of the UCS as determiners of the amount of eyelid conditioning. *J. exp. Psychol., 42,* 183-188.

SPERLING, D. S. *See* Calvin, Bicknell, and Sperling (1953a) and (1953b).

SPIEGEL, J. P. *See* Grinker and Spiegel (1945).

SPIELBERGER, C. D., and KATZENMEYER, W. G. (1959) Manifest anxiety, intelligence, and college grades. *J. cons. Psychol., 23,* 278.

SPIKER, C. C. *See* Cantor and Spiker (1954).

SPOONER, A., and KELLOGG, W. N. (1947) The backward-conditioning curve. *Amer. J. Psychol., 60,* 321-334.

SPROW, A. J. (1947) Reactively homogeneous compound trial-and-error learning with distributed trials and terminal reinforcement. *J. exp. Psychol., 37,* 197-213.

STAGNER, R. *See* Harlow and Stagner (1933).

STANLEY, J. C., Jr. *See* Jenkins and Stanley (1950).

STANLEY, W. C. (1952) Extinction as a function of the spacing of extinction trials. *J. exp. Psychol., 43,* 249-260.

STANLEY, W. C., and AAMODT, Marjorie S. (1954) Force of responding during extinction as a function of force requirement during conditioning. *J. comp. physiol. Psychol., 47,* 462-464.

STEBBINS, W. C. *See* Brady, Stebbins, and Galambos (1953), Brady, Stebbins and Hunt (1953).

STECKLE, L. C. (1936) Two additional attempts to condition the pupillary reflex. *J. gen. Psychol., 15,* 369-377.

STECKLE, L. C., and RENSHAW, S. (1934) An investigation of the conditioned iridic reflex. *J. gen. Psychol., 11,* 3-23.

STEIN, L. *See* Brown, Clarke, and Stein (1958).

STELLAR, E., and HILL, J. H. (1952) The rat's rate of drinking as a function of water deprivation. *J. comp. physiol. Psychol., 45,* 96-102.

STEVENSON, H. W., and BITTERMAN, M. E. (1955) The distance-effect in the transposition of intermediate size by children. *Amer. J. Psychol., 68,* 274-279.

STEVENSON, H. W., and ISCOE, I. (1954) Overtraining and transposition in children. *J. exp. Psychol., 47,* 251-255.

STEVENSON, H. W., and ISCOE, I. (1955) Transposition in the feebleminded. *J. exp. Psychol., 49,* 11-15.

STEVENSON, H. W., ISCOE, I., and McCONNELL, Claudia (1955) A developmental study of transposition. *J. exp. Psychol., 49,* 278-280.

STEVENSON, H. W., and WEISS, E. S. (1955) Time as a variable in transposition. *Amer. J. Psychol., 68,* 285-288.

STEVENSON, J. A. *See* Miller, Bailey, and Stevenson (1950).

STEVENSON, S. S. *See* Miller and Stevenson (1936),

STRAIN, E. R. (1953) Establishment of an avoidance gradient under latent learning conditions. *J. exp. Psychol., 46,* 391-399.

STRANGE, J. R. (1950) Latent learning under conditions of high motivation. *J. comp. physiol. Psychol., 43,* 194-197.

STRASSBURGER, R. C. (1950) Resistance to extinction of a conditioned operant as related to drive level at reinforcement. *J. exp. Psychol., 40,* 473-487.

STRAUGHAN, J. H. *See* Estes and Straughan (1954).

STRONG, P. N., Jr. (1957) Activity in the white rat as a function of apparatus and hunger. *J. comp. physiol. Psychol., 50,* 596-600.

STRZELECKI, Joanna. *See* Bindra, Paterson, and Strzelecki (1955).

STUBBS, D. W. *See* Runquist, Spence, and Stubbs (1958).

SWITZER, S. A. (1930) Backward conditioning of the lid reflex. *J. exp. Psychol., 13,* 76-97.

SWITZER, S. A. (1933) Disinhibition of the conditioned galvanic skin response. *J. gen. Psychol., 9,* 77-100.

SWITZER, S. A. (1935) The effect of caffeine on experimental extinction of conditioned reactions. *J. gen. Psychol., 12,* 78-94.

SYMONDS, P. M. (1927) Laws of learning. *J. educ. Psychol., 18,* 405-413.

SZYMANSKI, J. S. (1918) Versuche uber die wirkung der Factoren, die als Antrieb zum Erlernen einer Handlung dienen, Konnen. *Pflug. Arch. ges. Physiol., 171,* 374-385.

TAFFEL, C. (1955) Anxiety and the conditioning of verbal behavior. *J. abnorm. soc. Psychol., 51,* 496-501.

TAYLOR, Elaine. *See* Spence, Farber, and Taylor (1954).

TAYLOR, F. V. *See* Wedell, Taylor, and Skolnick (1940).

TAYLOR, Janet A. (1951) The relationship of anxiety to the conditioned eyelid response. *J. exp. Psychol., 41,* 81-92.

TAYLOR, Janet A. (1953) A personality scale of manifest anxiety. *J. abnorm, soc. Psychol., 48,* 285-290.

TAYLOR, Janet A. (1956a) Drive theory and manifest anxiety. *Psychol. Bull. 53,* 303-320.

TAYLOR, Janet A. (1956a) Level of conditioning and intensity of the adapting stimulus. *J. exp. Psychol., 51,* 127-130.

TAYLOR, Janet A., and CHAPMAN, J. P. (1955) Paired-associate learning as related to anxiety. *Amer. J. Psychol., 68,* 671.

TAYLOR, Janet A., and SPENCE, K. W. (1952) The relationship of anxiety to performance in serial learning. *J. exp. Psychol., 44,* 61-64.

TAYLOR, Janet A. *See also* Spence and Taylor (1951).

TEAS, D. C., and BITTERMAN, M. E. (1952) Perceptual organization in the rat. *Psychol. Rev., 59*, 130-140.

TEEL, K. S. (1952) Habit strength as a function of motivation during learning. *J. comp. physiol. Psychol., 45*, 188-191.

TEEL, K., and WEBB, W. B. (1951) Response evocation on satiated trials in the T-maze. *J. exp. Psychol., 41*, 148-152.

TEICHNER, W. H. (1952) Experimental extinction as a function of the intertrial intervals during conditioning and extinction. *J. exp. Psychol., 44*, 170-178.

TEMMER, Helena W. *See* Sheffield and Temmer (1950).

TEN CATE, J. (1934b) Die Pupillenverengerung, als bedingter Reflex auf akustische Reize und ihre Beziehung zu der Grosshirnrinde. *Arch. neerl. Physiol., 19*, 417-425.

TEN CATE, J. (1934c) Konnen die bedingten Reaktionen sich auch ausserhalb der Grosshirnrinde bilden? *Arch. Neerl. Physiol., 19*, 469-481.

THISTLETHWAITE, D. (1951a) A critical review of latent learning and related experiments. *Psychol. Bull., 48*, 97-129.

THISTLETHWAITE, D. (1951b) An experimental test of reinforcement interpretation of latent learning. *J. comp. physiol. Psychol., 44*, 431-441.

THISTLETHWAITE, D. (1952) Conditions of irrelevant-incentive learning. *J. comp. physiol. Psychol., 45*, 517-525.

THOMAS, D. R. *See* Butter and Thomas (1958).

THOMPSON, M. E. (1944) Learning as a function of absolute and relative amounts of work. *J. exp. Psychol., 34*, 506-515.

THOMPSON, R. *See* Hayes, Thompson, and Hayes (1953a) (1953b).

THOMPSON, R., and DEAN, W. (1955) A further study on the retroactive effect of ECS. *J. comp. physiol. Psychol., 48*, 488-491.

THOMPSON, R., and McCONNELL, J. (1955) Classical conditioning in the planarian, *dugesia dorotocephala. J. comp. physiol. Psychol., 48*, 65-68.

THOMPSON, R. F. *See* Hoffeld, Thompson, and Brogden (1958).

THOMSON, C. W., and PORTER, P. B. (1953) Need reduction and primary reinforcement: Maze learning by sodium-deprived rats for a subthreshold saline reward. *J. comp. physiol. Psychol., 46*, 281-287.

THORNDIKE, E. L., (1898) Animal intelligence. An experimental study of the associative processes in animals. *Psychol. Monogr., 2*, No. 8.

THORNDIKE, E. L. (1909) Darwin's contribution to psychology. *University of California Chronicle, XII*, 65-80.

THORNDIKE, E. L. (1911) *Animal intelligence.* New York: The Macmillan Co.

THORPE, W. H. (1954) Some concepts of ethology. *Nature, 174*, 101-105.

THORPE, W. H. (1956) *Learning and instinct in animals.* London: Methuen.

THRUSH, R. S. *See* Fitzwater and Thrush (1956).

THUNE, L. E. (1950) The effect of different types of preliminary activities on subsequent learning of paired-associate material. *J. exp. Psychol., 40*, 423-438.

THURSTON, J. R. *See* Cohen, Kalish, Thurston, and Cohen (1954).

TIGHE, T. J. *See* Gibson and others (1958), Walk and others (1958), Walk, Gibson, and Tighe (1957).

TINBERGEN, N. (1951) *The study of instinct.* London: Oxford.

TITCHENER, E. B. (1909) *A textbook of psychology.* New York: Macmillan.

TOLMAN, E. C. (1922a) A new formula for behaviorism. *Psychol. Rev., 29,* 44-53.

TOLMAN, E. C. (1923) The nature of instinct. *Psychol. Bull. 20,* 200-216.

TOLMAN, E. C. (1926) A behavioristic theory of ideas. *Psychol. Rev. 33,* 352-369.

TOLMAN, E. C. (1927) A behaviorist's definition of consciousness. *Psychol. Rev., 34,* 433-439.

TOLMAN, E. C. (1932) *Purposive behavior in animals and men.* New York: Appleton-Century.

TOLMAN, E. C. (1934a) Theories of learning. In F. A. Moss, *Comparative psychology.* New York: Prentice-Hall.

TOLMAN, E. C. (1934b) Backward elimination of errors in two successive discrimination habits. *Univ. Calif. Public. Psychol., 6,* 145-152.

TOLMAN, E. C. (1936a) Sign-gestalt or conditioned reflex? *Psychol. Rev., 43,* 258-281.

TOLMAN, E. C. (1936b) Operational behaviorism and current trends in psychology. *Proc. 25th Anniv. Inauguration Graduate Studies.* Los Angeles: University of Southern California Press.

TOLMAN, E. C. (1938) The determiners of behavior at a choice point. *Psychol. Rev. 45,* 1-41.

TOLMAN, E. C. (1939) Prediction of vicarious trial and error by means of the schematic sowbug. *Psychol. Rev., 46,* 318-336.

TOLMAN, E. C. (1942) *Drives toward war.* New York: Appleton-Century-Crofts.

TOLMAN, E. C. (1943) A drive-conversion diagram. *Psychol. Rev., 50,* 503-513.

TOLMAN, E. C. (1948) Cognitive maps in rats and men. *Psychol. Rev., 55,* 189-208.

TOLMAN, E. C. (1949) There is more than one kind of learning. *Psychol. Rev. 56,* 144-155.

TOLMAN, E. C. (1955) Principles of performance. *Psychol. Rev., 62,* 315-325.

TOLMAN, E. C., and GLEITMAN, H. (1949a) Studies in spatial learning: VII. Place and response learning under different degrees of motivation. *J. exp. Psychol., 39,* 653-659.

TOLMAN, E. C., and GLEITMAN, H. (1949b) Studies in learning and motivation: I. Equal reinforcements in both end-boxes, followed by shock in one end-box. *J. exp. Psychol., 39,* 810-819.

TOLMAN, E. C., and HONZIK, C. H. (1930) Introduction and removal of reward, and maze performance in rats. *Univ. Calif. Publ. Psychol., 4,* 257-275.

TOLMAN, E. C., and POSTMAN, L. (1954) Learning. *Ann. Rev. Psychol., 5,* 27-56.

TOLMAN, E. C., and RITCHIE, B. F. (1943) Correlation between VTE's on a maze and on a visual discrimination apparatus. *J. comp. Psychol., 36,* 91-98.

TOLMAN, E. C., RITCHIE, B.F., and KALISH, D. (1946a) Studies in spatial learning. I. Orientation and the short-cut. *J. exp. Psychol., 36,* 13-24.

TOLMAN, E. C., RITCHIE, B. F., and KALISH, D. (1946b) Studies in spatial learning: II. Place learning versus response learning. *J. exp. Psychol., 36,* 221-229.

TOLMAN, E. C., RITCHIE, B. F., and KALISH, D. (1947a) Studies in spatial learning. IV. The transfer of place learning to other starting paths. *J. exp. Psychol., 37,* 39-47.

TOLMAN, E. C., RITCHIE, B. F., and KALISH, D. (1947b) Studies in spatial learning. V. Response learning vs. place learning by the non-correction method. *J. exp. Psychol., 37,* 385-392.

TOLTZIEN, F. *See* Harlow and Toltzien (1940).

TRACY, F. W. (1927) Experiments on the establishment of conditioned motor responses. M. A. thesis., Ohio State University.

TROLAND, L. T. (1928) *The fundamentals of human motivation.* New York: Van Nostrand.

TURBEVILLE, J. R., CALVIN, A. D., and BITTERMAN, M. E. (1952) Relational and configurational learning in the rat. *Amer. J. Psychol., 65,* 424-433.

TYLER, D. W. *See* Bitterman, Fedderson, and Tyler (1953), Bitterman, Tyler, and Elam (1955), Elam, Tyler, and Bitterman (1954).

TYLER, D. W., MARX, M. H., and COLLIER, G. (1959) Frustration stimuli in discrimination. *J. exp. Psychol., 58,* 295-301.

TYLER, D. W., WORTZ, E. C., and BITTERMAN, M. E. (1953) The effect of random and alternating partial reinforcement on resistance to extinction in the rat. *Amer. J. Psychol., 66,* 57-65.

v. UEXKÜLL, J. *See* Beer, Bethe, and v. Uexküll (1899).

UKHTOMSKI, A. A. (1926) Concerning the condition of excitation in dominance. *Nov. Refl. Fiziol. Nerv. Sist., 2,* 3-15. (*Psychol. Abstr.,* 1927, *I.* No. 2388).

UNDERWOOD, B. J. *See* Kendler and Underwood (1948).

UPTON, M. (1929) The auditory sensitivity of guinea pigs. *Amer. J. Psychol., 41,* 412-421.

VALENTINE, C. W. (1930) The innate bases of fear. *J. genet. Psychol., 37,* 394-419.

VANDERMEER, S., and AMSEL, A. (1952) Work and rest factors in eyelid conditioning. *J. exp. Psychol., 43,* 261-266.

VERNIER, V. G. *See* Galambos, Sheatz, and Vernier (1956).

VERPLANCK, W. S. (1942) The development of discrimination in a simple locomotor habit. *J. exp. Psychol., 31,* 441-464.

VERPLANCK, W. S. (1955a) The control of the content of conversation: reinforcement of statements of opinion. *J. abnorm. soc. Psychol., 51,* 668-676.

VERPLANCK, W. S. (1955b) The operant, from rat to man: an introduction to some recent experiments on human behavior. *Trans. N. Y. Acad. Sci., 17,* 594-601.

VERPLANCK, W. S. (1956) The operant conditioning of human operant behavior. *Psychol. Bull., 53,* 70-83.

VERPLANCK, W. S. *See also* Estes and others (1954).

VERPLANCK, W. S., and HAYES, J. R. (1953) Eating and drinking as a function of maintenance schedule. *J. comp. physiol. Psychol., 46,* 327-333.

VINCENT, S. B. (1912) The function of the vibrissae in the behavior of the white rat. *Behav. Monogr., 1,* No. 5, pp. 81.

VIEK, P. *See* Mowrer and Viek (1948).

VINEBERG, R. (1953) The relation of irrelevant incentive learning to motivation and reward during exploratory experiences and training. *J. exp. Psychol., 46,* 237-242.

VINEY, W. *See* Capehart, Viney, and Hulicka (1958).

VOEKS, Virginia W. (1950) Formalization and clarification of a theory of learning. *J. Psychol., 30,* 341-362.

VOEKS, Virginia W. (1954) Acquisition of S-R connections: A test of Hull's and Guthrie's theories. *J. exp. Psychol., 47,* 137-147.

VOEKS, Virginia W. (1955) Gradual strengthening of S-R connections or increasing number of S-R connections. *J. Psychol., 39,* 289-299.

WADE, M. *See* Lashley and Wade (1946).

WAGNER, A. R. (1959) The role of reinforcement and non-reinforcement in an "apparant frustration effect." *J. exp. Psychol., 57,* 130-136.

WAGNER, A. R. *See also* Goodrich, Ross, and Wagner (1957).

WALK, R. D. (1958) "Visual" and "visual-motor" experience: A replication. *J. comp. physiol. Psychol., 51,* 785-787.

WALK, R. D. *See also* Gibson and Walk (1956), Gibson and others (1958).

WALK, R. D., GIBSON, E. J., PICK, H. L., and TIGHE, T. J. (1958) Further experiments on prolonged exposure to visual forms: The effect of single stimuli and prior reinforcement. *J. comp. physiol. Psychol., 51,* 483-487.

WALK, R. D., GIBSON, E. J., and TIGHE, T. J. (1957) Behavior of light-and dark-reared rats on a visual cliff. *Science, 126,* 80-81.

WALKER, E. L. (1948) Drive specificity and learning. *J. exp. Psychol., 38,* 39-49.

WALKER, E. L. (1951) Drive specificity and learning: Demonstration of a response tendency acquired under a strong irrelevant drive. *J. comp. physiol. Psychol., 44,* 596-603.

WALKER, E. L. (1957) Learning. *Ann. Rev. Psychol., 8,* 113-138.

WALKER, E. L. *See also* Kellogg and Walker (1938a) and (1938b).

WALKER, E. L., KNOTTER, Margaret C., and DEVALOIS, R. L. (1950) Drive specificity and learning: The acquisition of a spatial response to food under conditions of water deprivation and food satiation. *J. exp. Psychol., 40,* 161-168.

WALKER, K. C. (1942) Effect of a discriminative stimulus transferred to a previously unassociated response. *J. exp. Psychol., 31,* 312-321.

WALKER, R. W., Jr. *See* Jenkins, Pascal, and Walker (1958).

WALLACE, S. R., Jr., BLACKWELL, M. G., Jr., and JENKINS, G. (1941) Pre-reward and post-reward performance in the "latent learning" of an elevated maze. *Psychol. Bull., 38,* 694.

WALTON, C. *See* Fleure and Walton (1907).

WARD, J. S. *See* Amsel and Ward (1954).

WARDEN, C. J. (1931) *Animal motivation studies. The Albino Rat.* New York: Columbia University Press.

WARDEN, C. J., and DYMOND, S. (1931) A preliminary study of the effect of delayed punishment on learning in the white rat. *J. genet. Psychol., 39,* 455-461.

WARDEN, C. J., JENKINS, T. N., and WARNER, L. H. (1940) *Comparative psychology.* New York: Ronald.

WARNER, L. H. (1932) The association span of the white rat. *J. genet. Psychol., 41,* 57-90.

WARNER, L. H. *See also* Warden, Jenkins, and Warner (1940).

WARREN, J. M. *See* Harlow and Warren (1952).

WARREN, J. M., and BARON, A. (1956) The formation of learning sets by cats. *J. comp. physiol. Psychol., 49,* 227-231.

WATERS, R. H. *See* Shaw and Waters (1950).

WATSON, J. B. (1913) Psychology as the behaviorist views it. *Psychol. Rev., 20,* 158-177.

WATSON, J. B. (1916a) The place of the conditioned-reflex in psychology. *Psychol. Rev., 23,* 89-116.

WATSON, J. B. (1916b) Behavior and the concept of mental disease. *J. Philos. Psychol. sci. Meth., 13,* 589-597.

WATSON, J. B. (1917) The effect of delayed feeding upon learning. *Psychobiology I,* 51-60.

WATSON, J. B. (1919) *Psychology from the standpoint of a behaviorist.* Philadelphia: Lippincott.

WATSON, J. B. (1925) *Behaviorism.* New York: Norton.

WATSON, J. B., and MORGAN, J. J. B. (1917) Emotional reactions and psychological experimentation. *Amer. J. Psychol., 28,* 163-174.

WATSON, J. B., and RAYNER, R. (1920) Conditioned emotional reactions. *J. exp. Psychol., 3,* 1-14.

WEBB, W. B. (1949) The motivational aspect of an irrelevant drive in the behavior of the white rat. *J. exp. Psychol., 39,* 1-14.

WEBB, W. B. (1952) Response in absence of the acquisition drive. *Psychol. Rev., 59,* 54-61.

WEBB, W. B. (1955) Drive stimuli as cues. *Psychol. Rep., 1,* 287-298.

WEBB, W. B. *See* Bloomberg and Webb (1949), Teel and Webb (1951).

WEBB, W. B., and NOLAN, C. Y. (1953) Cues for discrimination as secondary reinforcing agents. *J. comp. physiol. Psychol., 46,* 180-181.

WEBER, H., and WENDT, G. R. (1942) Conditioning of eyelid closures with various conditions of reinforcement. *J. exp. Psychol., 30,* 114-124.

WEDELL, C. H., TAYLOR, F. V., and SKOLNICK, A. (1940) An attempt to condition the pupillary response. *J. exp. Psychol., 27,* 517-531.

WEGNER, Norma. *See* Zeaman and Wegner (1954) (1957).

WEGNER, Norma, and ZEAMAN, D. (1958) Strength of cardiac CR's with varying unconditioned stimulus durations. *Psychol. Rev., 65,* 238-241.

WEINSTOCK, S. (1954) Resistance to extinction of a running response following partial reinforcement under widely spaced trials. *J. comp. physiol. Psychol., 47,* 318-323.

WEINSTOCK, S. (1958) Acquisition and extinction of a partially reinforced running response at a 24-hour intertrial interval. *J. exp. Psychol., 56,* 151-158.

WEISE, P., and BITTERMAN, M. E. (1951) Response selection in discriminative learning. *Psychol. Rev., 58,* 185-195.

WEISS, E. J. *See* Wilson, Weiss, and Amsel (1955).

WEISS, E. S. *See* Stevenson and Weiss (1955).

WELCH, L. (1955) The relationship between conditioning and higher learning. *J. gen. Psychol., 53,* 221-229.

WELCH, L. *See* also Goodwin, Long, and Welch (1945).

WELDON, R. J. *See* Seward and Weldon (1953).

WELLS, F. L. (1916) Von Bechterev and Ubertragung. *J. Phil. Psychol. sci. Meth., 13,* 354-356.

WENDT, G. R. (1930) An analytical study of the conditioned kneejerk. *Arch. Psychol., N. Y. 19,* No. 123.

WENDT, G. R. (1934) Auditory acuity of monkeys. *Comp. Psychol. Monogr. 10,* No. 49.

WENDT, G. R. *See also* Cohen, Hilgard, and Wendt (1933).

WENGER, M. A. (1936b) An investigation of conditioned responses in human infants. *Univ. Ia. Stud. Child Welf., 12,* No. 318, 7-90.

WENGER, M. A., JONES, F. N., and JONES, H. J. (1956) *Physiological psychology.* New York: Henry Holt.

WERTHEIMER, M. (1959) On discrimination experiments: I. Two logical structures. *Psychol. Rev., 66,* 252-266.

WESLEY, E. L. (1953) Perseverative behavior in a concept-formation task as a function of anxiety and rigidity. *J. abnorm. soc. Psychol., 48,* 129-134.

WEYANT, R. G. *See* Perkins and Weyant (1958).

WHATMORE, G. B., and KLEITMAN, N. (1946) The role of sensory and motor cortical projections in escape and avoidance conditioning in dogs. *Amer. J. Physiol., 146,* 282-292.

WHATMORE, G. B., MORGAN, E. A., and KLEITMAN, N. (1946) The influence of avoidance conditioning on the course of non-avoidance conditioning in dogs. *Amer. J. Physiol., 145,* 432-435.

WHITE, S. H. (1958) Generalization of an instrumental response with variation in two attributes of the CS. *J. exp. Psychol., 56,* 339-343.

WHITE, C. T., and SCHLOSBERG, H. (1952) Degree of conditioning of the GSR as a function of the period of delay. *J. exp. Psychol., 43,* 357-362.

WHITING, J. M. W., and CHILD, I. L. (1953) *Child training and personality: A cross-cultural study.* New Haven: Yale University Press.

WHITING, J. W. M., and MOWRER, O. H. (1943) Habit progression and regression —a laboratory study of some factors relevant to human socialization. *J. comp. Psychol., 36,* 229-253.

WICKENS, Carol D. *See* Wickens and Wickens (1940) (1942).

WICKENS, D. D. (1938) The transference of conditioned excitation and conditioned inhibition from one muscle group to the antagonistic muscle group. *J. exp. Psychol., 22,* 101-123.

WICKENS, D. D. (1939a) A study of voluntary and involuntary finger conditioning. *J. exp. Psychol., 25,* 127-140.

WICKENS, D. D. (1939b) The simultaneous transfer of conditioned excitation and conditioned inhibition. *J. exp. Psychol., 24,* 332-338.

WICKENS, D. D. (1943) Studies of response generalization in conditioning. I. Stimulus generalization during response generalization. *J. exp. Psychol., 33,* 221-227.

WICKENS, D. D. (1948) Stimulus identity as related to response specificity and response generalization. *J. exp. Psychol., 38,* 389-394.

WICKENS, D. D. *See also* Cotterman, Meyer, and Wickens (1956), Maher and Wickens (1954), Miles and Wickens (1953).

WICKENS, D. D., and BRIGGS, G. E. (1951) Mediated stimulus generalization as a factor in sensory preconditioning. *J. exp. Psychol., 42,* 197-200.

WICKENS, D. D., and PLATTE, C. E. (1954) Response termination of the cue stimulus in classical and instrumental conditioning. *J. exp. Psychol., 47,* 183-186.

WICKENS, D. D., SCHRODER, H. M., and SNIDE, J. D. (1954) Primary stimulus generalization of the GSR under two conditions. *J. exp. Psychol., 47,* 52-56.

WICKENS, D. D. ,and SNIDE, J. D. (1955) The influence of non-reinforcement of a complex stimulus on resistance to extinction of the complex itself. *J. exp. Psychol., 49,* 257-259.

WICKENS, D. D., and WICKENS, Carol D. (1940) A study of conditioning in the neonate. *J. exp. Psychol., 26,* 94-102.

WICKENS, D. D., and WICKENS, Carol D. (1942) Some factors related to pseudo-conditioning. *J. exp. Psychol., 31,* 518-526.

WIKE, E. L. (1953) Extinction of a partially and continuously reinforced response with and without a rewarded alternative. *J. exp. Psychol., 46,* 255-260.

WIKE, E. L. *See also* McNamara, Long, and Wike (1956), McNamara and Wike (1958), Scott and Wike (1956).

WIKE, E. L., and CASEY, A. (1954a) The secondary reinforcing value of food for thirsty animals. *J. comp. physiol. Psychol., 47,* 240-243.

WIKE, E. L., and CASEY, A. (1954b) The secondary reward value of food for satiated animals. *J. comp. physiol. Psychol., 47,* 441-443.

WILCOXON, H. C. (1952) "Abnormal fixation" and learning. *J. exp. Psychol., 44,* 324-333.

WILDER, D. H. *See* Woodbury and Wilder (1954).

WILLIAMS, H. *See* Seeman and Williams (1952).

WILLIAMS, K. A. (1929) The reward value of a conditioned stimulus. *Univ. Calif. Publ. Psychol., 4,* 31-55.

WILLIAMS, S. B. (1938) Resistance to extinction as a function of the number of reinforcements. *J. exp. Psychol., 23,* 506-522.

WILLIAMS, S. B. (1941) Transfer of reinforcement in the rat as a function of habit strength. *J. comp. Psychol., 31,* 281-296.

WILSON, M. P., and KELLER, F. S. (1953) On the selective reinforcement of spaced responses. *J. comp. physiol. Psychol., 46,* 190-193.

WILSON, W., WEISS, E. J., and AMSEL, A. (1955) Two tests of the Sheffield hypothesis concerning resistance to extinction, partial reinforcement, and distribution of practice. *J. exp. Psychol., 50,* 51-60.

WINNICK, Wilma A. (1950) The discriminative function of drive-stimuli independent of the action of the drive as motivation. *Amer. J. Psychol., 63,* 196-205.

WINNICK, Wilma A., and HUNT, J. McV. (1951) The effect of an extra stimulus upon strength of response during acquisition and extinction. *J. exp. Psychol., 41,* 205-215.

WINTERBOTTOM, M. R. (1958) The relation of need for achievement to learning experiences in independence and mastery. In J. W. Atkinson (Ed.), *Motives in fantasy, action and society.* New York: D. Van Nostrand.

WODINSKY, J. *See* Bitterman and Wodinsky (1953).

WODINSKY, J., and BITTERMAN, M. E. (1952) Compound and configuration in successive discrimination. *Amer. J. Psychol., 65,* 563-572.

WOLF, I. S. *See* Kellogg and others (1940), Kellogg and Wolf (1939).

WOLFE, J. B. (1934) The effect of delayed reward upon learning in the white rat. *J. comp. Psychol., 17,* 1-21.

WOLFE, J. B. (1936) Effectiveness of token-rewards for chimpanzees. *Comp. Psychol. Monogr., 12,* No. 60.

WOLFE, J. B. *See also* Crawford, Fulton, Jacobson, and Wolfe (1948), Jacobsen, Wolfe, and Jackson (1935).

WOLFLE, D. L. See Gulliksen and Wolfle (1938a) (1938b).

WOLFLE, Helen M. (1930) Time factors in conditioning finger-withdrawal. *J. gen. Psychol., 4,* 372-378.

WOLFLE, Helen M. (1932) Conditioning as a function of the interval between the conditioned and the original stimulus. *J. gen. Psychol.*, *7*, 80-103.

WOODBURY, C. B. (1943) The learning of stimulus patterns by dogs. *J. comp. Psychol.*, *35*, 29-40.

WOODBURY, C. B., and WILDER, D. H. (1954) The principle of selective association of drive stimuli. *J. exp. Psychol.*, *47*, 301-302.

WOODGER, J. H. (1938) The formalization of a psychological theory. *Erkenntnis*, *7*, 195-198.

WOODROW, P. *See* Miller, Sampliner, and Woodrow (1957).

WOODWORTH, R. S. (1918) *Dynamic psychology*. New York: University Press.

WULFF, J. J. *See* Sheffield, Wulff, and Backer (1951).

WYCKOFF, L. B., Jr. (1952) The role of observing responses in discrimination learning. Part I. *Psychol. Rev.*, *59*, 431-442.

WYCKOFF, L. B., Jr. (1954) A mathematical model and an electronic model for learning. *Psychol. Rev.*, *61*, 89-97.

WYNNE, L. C. *See* Solomon, Kamin, and Wynne (1953), Solomon and Wynne (1953) (1954).

WYNNE, L. C., and SOLOMON, R. L. (1955) Traumatic avoidance learning: Acquisition and extinction in dogs deprived of normal peripheral autonomic function. *Genet. Psychol. Monogr.*, *52*, 241-284.

YACORZYNSKI, G. K., and GUTHRIE, E. R. (1937) A comparative study of involuntary and voluntary conditioned responses. *J. gen. Psychol.*, *16*, 235-257.

YAMAGUCHI, H. G. (1951) Drive (D) as a function of hours of hunger (h). *J. exp. Psychol.*, *42*, 108-117.

YAMAGUCHI, H. G. (1952) Gradients of drive stimulus (S_D) intensity generalization. *J. exp. Psychol.*, *43*, 298-304.

YAMAGUCHI, H. G. *See also* Buchwald and Yamaguchi (1955), Felsinger and others (1947), Gladstone and others (1947), Hull and others (1947).

YERKES, R. M., and DODSON, J. D. (1908) The relation of strength of stimulus to rapidity of habit-formation. *J. comp. Neurol. Psychol.*, *18*, 458-482.

YERKES, R. M., and MORGULIS, S. (1909) The method of Pavlov in animal psychology. *Psychol. Bull.*, *6*, 257-273.

YOSHIOKA, J. G. (1929) Weber's law in the discrimination of maze distance by the white rat. *Univ. Calif. Publ. Psychol.*, *4*, 155-184.

YOUNG, F. A. (1954) An attempt to obtain pupillary conditioning with infrared photography. *J. exp. Psychol.*, *48*, 62-68.

YOUNG, F. A. (1958) Studies of pupillary conditioning. *J. exp. Psychol.*, *55*, 97-110.

YOUNG, P. T. (1936) *Motivation of behavior*. New York: Wiley.

YOUNG, P. T. (1945) Studies of food preference, appetite, and dietary habit. V. Techniques for testing food preference and the significance of results obtained with different methods. *Comp. Psychol. Monogr.*, *19*, No. 1.

YOUNG, P. T. (1947) Studies of food preference, appetite, and dietary habit. VII. Palatability in relation to learning and performance. *J. comp. physiol. Psychol.*, *40*, 37-72.

YOUNG, P. T. (1952) The role of hedonic processes in the organization of behavior. *Psychol. Rev.*, *59*, 263-267.

YOUNG, P. T. (1959) The role of the affective processes in learning and motivation. *Psychol. Rev. 66*, 104-125.

YOUNG, P. T., and SHUFORD, E. H., Jr. (1954) Intensity, duration, and repetition of hedonic processes as related to acquisition of motives. *J. comp. physiol. Psychol.*, *47*, 298-305.

YOUNG, P. T., and SHUFORD, E. H., Jr. (1955) Quantitative control of motivation through sucrose solutions of different concentrations. *J. comp. physiol. Psychol.*, *48*, 114-118.

YOUTZ, R. E. P. (1938a) Reinforcement, extinction, and spontaneous recovery in a non-Pavlovian reaction. *J. exp. Psychol.*, *22*, 305-310.

YOUTZ, R. E. P. (1938b) The change in time of a Thorndikean response in the rat. *J. exp. Psychol.*, *23*, 128-140.

YOUTZ, R. E. P. (1939) The weakening of one Thorndikean response following the extinction of another. *J. exp. Psychol.*, *24*, 294-304.

YUSHCHENKA, A., ROLLE, S. D., and PUPKO, L. K. (1934) The conditioned reflex with a temporary disorder of conduction in the ascending part of the unconditioned reflex arc. *Arkh. biol. Nauk, 34*, 559-568. (*Psychol. Abstr.*, 1935, *9*, No. 1711.)

ZEAMAN, D. (1949a) Response latency as a function of the amount of reinforcement. *J. exp. Psychol.*, *39*, 466-483.

ZEAMAN, D. (1949b) An application of $_sE_R$ quantification procedure. *Pychol. Rev.*, *56*, 341-350.

ZEAMAN, D. *See also* House and Zeaman (1958) (1959), Wegner and Zeaman (1958).

ZEAMAN, D., and HOUSE, Betty J. (1951) The growth and decay of reactive inhibition as measured by alternation behavior. *J. exp. Psychol.*, *41*, 177-186.

ZEAMAN, D., and WEGNER, Norma (1954) The role of drive reduction in the classical conditioning of an autonomically mediated response. *J. exp. Psychol.*, *48*, 349-354.

ZEAMAN, D., and WEGNER, Norma (1957) A further test of the role of drive reduction in human cardiac conditioning. *J. Psychol.*, *43*, 125-133.

ZEIGLER, H. P. (1957) Electrical stimulation of the brain and the psychophysiology of learning and motivation. *Psychol. Bull.*, *54*, 363-382.

ZELIONY, G. P. (1929) Effets de l'ablation des hemispheres cerebraux. *Rev. med., Paris, 46*, 191-214.

ZELIONY, G. P. *See also* Poltyrev and Zeliony (1930), Prokofiev and Zeliony (1926).

ZELIONY, G. P., and KADYKOV, B. I. (1938) Contribution to the study of conditioned reflexes in the dog after cortical extirpation. *Eksp. Med., Kharkov,* 31-34. (*Psychol. Abstr.,* 1938, *12,* No. 5829.)

ZENER, K. (1937) The significance of behavior accompanying conditioned salivary secretion for theories of the conditioned response. *Amer. J. Psychol., 50,* 384-403.

ZIMMERMAN, D. W. (1957) *Durable secondary reinforcement. Method and theory. Psychol. Rev., 64,* 373-383.

ZIMMERMAN, D. W. (1959) Sustained performance in rats based on secondary reinforcement. *J. comp. physiol. Psychol., 52,* 353-358.

ZININA, N. V. *See* Gakkel and Zinina (1953).

INDEXES

AUTHOR INDEX

SUBJECT INDEX